Fifth Edition

The Enduring Democracy

Kenneth Dautrich

Associate Professor of Public Policy
University of Connecticut

David A. Yalof

Department Head and
Professor of Political Science
University of Connecticut

Christina E. Bejarano

Associate Professor of Political Science
University of Kansas

CENGAGE
Learning·

Australia • Brazil • Mexico • Singapore • United Kingdom • United States

The Enduring Democracy,
Fifth Edition
Kenneth Dautrich, David A. Yalof,
Christina E. Bejarano

Product Director: Paul R. Banks

Senior Product Manager: Bradley J. Potthoff

Product Team Manager: Carolyn Merrill

Senior Content Developer: Laura Hildebrand

Content Development Manager: Megan Garvey

Product Assistant: Staci Eckenroth

Senior Marketing Manager: Valerie Hartman

Senior Content Project Manager: Corinna Dibble

Digital Content Designer: Milica Golubovic

Art Director: Sarah Cole

Manufacturing Planner: Fola Orekoya

IP Analyst: Alexandra Ricciardi

IP Project Manager: Betsy Hathaway

Production Service and Compositor:
    Phil Scott/SPi Global

Text Designer: Delgado and Company

Cover Designer: Sarah Cole

For product information and technology assistance, contact us at
Cengage Learning Customer & Sales Support, 1-800-354-9706
For permission to use material from this text or product, submit all requests
online at **www.cengage.com/permissions.**
Further permissions questions can be emailed to
permissionrequest@cengage.com.

Library of Congress Control Number: 2016953710

Student Edition:
ISBN: 978-1-337-09298-2

Loose-leaf Edition:
ISBN: 978-1-337-09321-7

Cengage Learning
20 Channel Center Street
Boston, MA 02210
USA

Cengage Learning is a leading provider of customized learning solutions with employees residing in nearly 40 different countries and sales in more than 125 countries around the world. Find your local representative at **www.cengage.com.**

Cengage Learning products are represented in Canada by Nelson Education, Ltd.

To learn more about Cengage Learning Solutions, visit **www.cengage.com.**
Purchase any of our products at your local college store or at our preferred online store **www.cengagebrain.com.**

Printed in the United States of America
Print Number: 01   Print Year: 2016

Brief Contents

Detailed Contents

PART II Institutions

Appendix

Glossary 516

Notes 528

Index 541

Letter to Instructors

This is a textbook about American government, the success of which depends upon a responsible citizenry willing to ask tough questions of its leaders and demand reasonable answers in return. This book encourages student readers to hone their critical thinking skills, ask the tough questions, and become responsible citizens. We encourage students to become educated citizens through two paths: (1) by learning how the problems and controversies characterizing American government today have been successfully tackled in America's past; and (2) by examining how the changing demographics of America have affected its political landscape.

The first path to understanding focuses on history. Certainly history tends to repeat itself, and we can learn much of importance from the lessons of history to better address the problems we face today. American government and politics have changed dramatically in the more than two centuries of the nation's existence, yet certain issues persist. The challenge facing instructors of American government is how to take adequate account of all these changes while never losing sight of the issues and events from the nation's past and their significance today. We thus offer in this fifth edition of *The Enduring Democracy* all the nuts and bolts of the U.S. government and how it works, but we also seek to educate students about American politics in ways that go beyond the essentials by placing current political issues and debates in historical perspective. This theme runs throughout the book's narrative and is reflected in its organization. The book begins with a discussion of how the roadmap of history provides a guide to the future, how the use of a historical perspective on American politics can add to and help shape our understanding of contemporary problems and the creation and evolution of its institutions and processes, before diving into the foundations of U.S. government, the institutions of government formed under the Constitution, and then later to political behavior and public policy.

The second path examines diversity by considering the changing demographic of our polity, and the various ways in which those changes have an impact on our politics. Over and over during the 2016 presidential campaign, America's diverse character became a focal point for discussion, as both major parties' candidates faced an electorate more diverse than ever before. These changing demographics also have a sizeable impact on governing political institutions, their public policy formulation, and nearly all types of informal political behavior as well, including media coverage and interest group dynamics. Accordingly, this textbook considers American politics in ways that are informed by these fundamental changes in the political landscape. Throughout the book's narrative, we take note of the ways in which traditional institutions and entities have successfully (or in some cases, not so successfully) taken account of this changing political reality.

Many of the book's past features support these themes, and they return in the fifth edition. For example, Then and Now boxes continue to give ample attention to the premise that American political history has a habit of repeating itself through examples of contemporary problems and controversies that have been identified, tackled, and in some cases resolved in earlier years. Supreme Court feature boxes in nearly every chapter provide an account of how important Supreme Court decisions in recent history affect the political landscape today, as well as how our political institutions and behavior influence Supreme Court decision making. Cases such as *Brown v. Board of Education* (1954) and *Obergefell v. Hodges* (2015) remind us that the high Court often accelerates the very change that some political entities may be resisting; yet just as often the high Court stubbornly relies on principles that no longer apply to ever-changing multiracial and multicultural landscape. Finally, the end-of-chapter sections continue to tie the Chapter Summary and Test Yourself quizzes to clearly defined Learning Objectives, creating an in-text study guide for students to review and assess their comprehension of each chapter's key concepts.

New to This Edition

- *The Enduring Democracy* has been updated to include complete coverage of the 2016 election results and a brief consideration of the challenges facing the new administration; a reflection and analysis of the policy agenda for the final two years of the Obama administration;

a primer on how the polls, parties, and other elements of the political environment shaped (and were shaped by) the 2016 election campaigns of Hillary Clinton and Donald Trump, as well as important down ballot races; new perspectives on President Obama's executive orders; the most current domestic and foreign policy events, including incidents of gun violence in Orlando and elsewhere, as well as the more general growth of ISIS; and much more.

- A completely revised civil rights, equality, and social movements chapter more comprehensively considers racial/ethnic politics, especially Latino politics, and the evolution of discrimination against disadvantaged groups in the political arena as well as in the courts.

- All new "Who Are You?" exercises at the outset of every chapter encourage students to consider how their own views and assumptions (and in some cases, biases) shape their positions on contemporary issues in American politics; students then have the opportunity to discover how their views compare with other subgroups, or with the population as a whole.

- "Diversity Dilemma" boxes found within every chapter offer examples and illustrations of how America's changing demographics and increased diversity have altered the political landscape. This feature touches on many contemporary political debates, such as voting rights and immigration policy, across the broad range of American politics. Our ever-changing population poses significant challenges that must be addressed by local institutions such as schools, and by national institutions including Congress, executive agencies, and the U.S. Supreme Court. Students will consider these dilemmas, and then address questions that seek students' reflections on how we as a society should most effectively address the challenges and opportunities presented with our diversity.

MindTap: Your Course Stimulus Package

As an instructor, MindTap is here to simplify your workload, organize and immediately grade your students' assignments, and allow you to customize your course as you see fit. Through deep-seated integration with your Learning Management System, grades are easily exported and analytics are pulled with just the click of a button. MindTap provides you with a platform to easily add in current events videos and RSS feeds from national or local news sources. Looking to include more currency in the course? Add in our KnowNow American Government Blog link for weekly updated news coverage and pedagogy.

By examining the current state of American politics through the lens of American history and the nation's changing demographics, we hope to encourage students to think critically about the significance of certain persons, places, and events in American politics and consider all the different ways in which they might be viewed and interpreted. The historical perspective and the materials that address American politics from students' own perspectives—do not interfere with the description of essential foundations. Rather, they spark student interest in revisiting what they learned in high school, from the media, and elsewhere about American politics with a more discerning and critical eye. Perhaps many students will take this critical approach beyond the course itself and become actual participants in the process. If they do so with a more critical and skeptical eye, our democratic system can only benefit.

Sincerely,

Kenneth J. Dautrich
k.dautrich@uconn.edu

David A. Yalof
david.yalof@uconn.edu

Christina E. Bejarano
cbejaran@ku.edu

Letter to Students

The idea that "history repeats itself" is not merely a piece of conventional wisdom. Looking back provides important lessons applicable to today's challenges. In examining the past we find that some of our new and "unprecedented" political controversies are neither new nor unprecedented. By the same token, changes in the demographics of our population should force a reconsideration of many aspects of American political behavior, past and present. The faces may have changed and the policies may have been modernized, but the challenges the nation faces today are often newer versions of past dilemmas and problems.

In *The Enduring Democracy*, you will learn the essentials of American government with a dual focus on placing current issues and controversies into historical perspective, as well as on considering how the changing face of the American public influences those issues and controversies. By adopting these perspectives, you'll gain a greater appreciation for American government—both its flaws and its successes – as well as its challenges. At the conclusion of each chapter we frame contemporary problems from the perspective of what they mean to college students like you, so that you can see the relevance of American government in your life.

Special Features

- Learning Objectives open each chapter and serve as a road map to the key concepts and major sections you'll find within, helping you focus on the most important points and assess your comprehension as you read. We conclude each chapter with a review of those objectives and a Test Yourself quiz that you can use to gauge your mastery of the chapter's material. Additionally, within each chapter key terms are highlighted in boldface type and defined in the margins of the pages. These key terms are also listed at the end of the chapter, and the terms and definitions are repeated in a glossary at the end of the book.

- Who Are You? exercises at the outset of every chapter force you to consider how your own views and assumptions shape your views on contemporary issues in American politics; After answering the questions at the end of each exercise, you will have the opportunity to discover how your views actually compare with other political or demographic subgroups, or with the population as a whole.

- Diversity Dilemma boxes found within every chapter offer examples and illustrations of how America's changing demographics and increased diversity change the American political landscape. The feature touches on many contemporary political debates, such as voting rights and immigration policy, across the broad range of American politics. Our ever-changing population poses significant challenges that must be addressed by local institutions such as schools, and by national institutions including Congress, executive agencies, and the U.S. Supreme Court itself. You will have the opportunity to consider these dilemmas, and then address questions that seek your reflections on how we as a society should most effectively address the challenges and opportunities presented by our diversity.

- Then and Now boxes show that although the specific names and details change, most contemporary problems and controversies have been identified, tackled, and in some cases outright resolved over and over at different points in the past. It is thus no wonder that "those who cannot remember the past are condemned to repeat it."

- From Your Perspective features consider contemporary political issues from the unique perspective of college students like yourself, tapping into the experiences you bring to the table when studying American government. They'll help you consider your own views and find opportunities to get involved in your community and American politics.

- Supreme Court boxes provide a deeper look at a variety of important Supreme Court cases, what influenced their outcomes, and how they affect your life today.

- Critical Thinking questions at the end of every thematic box help you think about the material in new and interesting ways and may spark discussions with your classmates.

The Benefits of Using MindTap as a Student

As a student, the benefits of using MindTap with this book are endless. With automatically graded practice quizzes and activities, an easily navigated learning path, and an interactive eBook, you will be able to test yourself inside and outside of the classroom with ease. The accessibility of current events coupled with interactive media makes the content fun and engaging. On your computer, phone, or tablet, MindTap is there when you need it, giving you easy access to flashcards, quizzes, readings, and assignments.

A thorough examination of past problems, issues, and conflicts does not negate the uniqueness of the current American condition, but it does offer a better understanding of contemporary issues. In some cases, studying the past assures us that the political process does work in a positive way; in other cases, it reminds us that we are not the first to face certain difficulties, and it suggests that we may want to seek more direction from the past about what works and what does not. We hope that this exploration encourages you not only to succeed in your intro class, but also to join the conversation on a larger scale and become an active participant in your community and *your* American government.

Sincerely,

Kenneth J. Dautrich
k.dautrich@uconn.edu

David A. Yalof
david.yalof@uconn.edu

Christina E. Bejarano
cbejaran@ku.edu

Resources

Students

Access *The Enduring Democracy, 5e*, resources by visiting
www.cengagebrain.com/shop/isbn/9781337093132

If you purchased MindTap access with your book, click on "Register a Product" and then, enter your access code.

Instructors

Access *The Enduring Democracy, 5e*, resources via
www.cengage.com/login.

Log in using your Cengage Learning single sign-on user name and password, or create a new instructor account by clicking on "**New Faculty User**" and following the instructions.

The Enduring Democracy, 5e — *Text Only Edition*

ISBN: 9781337092982

This copy of the book does not come bundled with MindTap.

MindTap for
The Enduring Democracy, 5e

ISBN for Instant Access Code: 9781337093132
ISBN for Printed Access Card: 9781337093125

MindTap for *The Enduring Democracy, 5e*, is a highly personalized, fully online learning experience built upon Cengage Learning content and correlating to a core set of learning outcomes. MindTap guides students through the course curriculum via an innovative Learning Path Navigator where they will complete reading assignments, challenge themselves with focus activities, and engage with interactive quizzes. Through a variety of gradable activities, MindTap provides students with opportunities to check themselves for where they need extra help, as well as allowing faculty to measure and assess student progress. Integration with programs like YouTube and Google Drive allows instructors to add and remove content of their choosing with ease, keeping their course current while tracking local and global events through RSS feeds. The product can be used fully online with its interactive eBook for **The Enduring Democracy, 5e**, or in conjunction with the printed text.

CourseReader for MindTap, is now available for every Political Science MindTap through the MindTap Instructor's Resource Center. This new feature provides access to Gale's authoritative library reference content to aid in the development of important supplemental readers for political science courses. Gale, a part of Cengage Learning, has been providing research and education resources for libraries for more than 60 years. This new feature capitalizes on Cengage Learning's unique ability to bring Gale's authoritative library content into the classroom. Instructors have the option to choose from thousands of primary and secondary sources, images, and videos to enhance their course. This capability can replace a separate reader and conveniently keeps all course materials in one place within a single MindTap. The selections within CourseReader are curated by experts and designed specifically for introductory courses.

Instructor Companion Website for
The Enduring Democracy, 5e

ISBN: 9781337093118

This Instructor Companion Website is an all-in-one multimedia online resource for class preparation, presentation, and testing. Accessible through Cengage.com/login with your faculty account, you will find available for download: book-specific Microsoft® PowerPoint® presentations; a Test Bank compatible with multiple learning management systems (LMSs); an Instructor Manual; Microsoft® PowerPoint® Image Slides; and a JPEG Image Library.

The Test Bank, offered in Blackboard, Moodle, Desire2Learn, Canvas, and Angel formats, contains learning objective–specific multiple-choice and essay questions for each chapter. Import the Test Bank into your LMS to edit and manage questions, and to create tests.

The Instructor's Manual contains chapter-specific learning objectives, an outline, key terms with definitions, and a chapter summary. Additionally the Instructor's Manual features a critical-thinking question, a lecture-launching suggestion, and an in-class activity for each learning objective.

The Microsoft® PowerPoint® presentations are ready-to-use, visual outlines of each chapter. These presentations are easily customized for your lectures and offered along with chapter-specific Microsoft® PowerPoint® Image Slides and JPEG Image Libraries. Access the Instructor Companion Website at www.cengage.com/login.

Cognero for
The Enduring Democracy, 5e

ISBN: 9781337093163

Cengage Learning Testing Powered by Cognero is a flexible, online system that allows you to author, edit, and manage Test Bank content from multiple Cengage Learning solutions; create multiple test versions in an instant; and deliver tests from your LMS, your classroom, or wherever you want. The Test Bank for *The Enduring Democracy*, 5e, contains learning objective–specific multiple-choice and essay questions for each chapter.

Acknowledgments

The fifth edition of *The Enduring Democracy* is the product of the hard work of many, many people. Though she has moved on to other creative challenges, we owe much to our original product team manager, Carolyn Merrill, for this and all previous editions. At Cengage she was the prime mover of this project, just as she was for each of our earlier editions. It is impossible to imagine pulling off a project like this without the management skills, temperament, and good humor that Carolyn provided.

Thankfully, some extremely talented individuals at Cengage have stepped in to supervise this book's production and marketing, and we have barely missed a beat. The Senior Product Manager, Brad Potthoff, brought his innovative and out-of-the-box thinking to every aspect of this project. Cengage's Product Director and Education Technology Executive, Paul Banks, injected his energy and enthusiasm into the project as well. We also lucked out with the appointment of Laura Hildebrand as our content developer for this edition. Laura has kept us on schedule with her hard work and no-nonsense approach to moving the books through its various stages of production. We are also indebted to Phil Scott, Corinna Dibble, Milica Golubovic, and Emily Hickey for their hard work; as well as to Julie Tesser for her photo research and Sara Cole for the new edition's design. Finally we want to extend our gratitude to the many other members of the Cengage staff we have come to depend upon in writing and producing this book and its supplemental materials: Chief among them is our always awesome marketing manager, Valerie Hartman.

The many sales representatives at Cengage not only do a great job in getting the word out on our book, but they also have collected feedback from instructors and relayed it back to us. In many instances, our reps have provided their own guidance and feedback as well. Thankfully, all their efforts have helped improve the content of the book, and make it more responsive to the perspective of instructors who use it. Our hats are off to this terrific sales force. We are grateful for your many efforts.

Appreciation also goes to our colleagues at the University of Connecticut and the University of Kansas, especially those in the Department of Political Science and the Department of Public Policy, of which there are too many to list by name. Their patience, support, and advice in our writing of this fifth edition have not gone unnoticed, nor has the input we have received from our graduate students and undergraduate users of the text.

The many professionals, colleagues, and students who provide support and advice are not the only ones who influence the writing of a textbook. Our families must live with us through the writing and production cycles. Not only do they tolerate the fact that we often bring our work home, but they also give us strong motivation to get the job done. We cannot thank our families enough, especially two of our better halves Andrea and Mary Beth, and the Bejarano family: Benita, Ray, Chris, and Jessica. Our children are never shy about offering their ideas. As always, the book benefits from their youthful perspectives and advice.

Finally, there are many members of our profession and many practitioners in American politics who put in countless hours and intellectual energy aiding in the writing of this manuscript and the book's supplements. A special thanks goes to Tracy Cook of Central Texas College for creating past editions' Test Banks and to J. Aaron Knight of Houston Community College Northeast for creating earlier versions of the Instructor's Manual. Some participated in focus groups, others in informal conversations with us, and still others spent much time marking up chapters. We are indebted to all those who have generously given time to this effort. A list of these contributors is found in the listing of reviewers. Please note, however, that any errors that remain are entirely our own.

Reviewers

We would also like to thank the instructors who have contributed their valuable feedback through reviews of this text:

Augustine Ayuk, *Clayton State University*
Andrea Aleman, *University of Texas at San Antonio*
Mary Balchunis, *LaSalle University*
Chief Justice Richard Barajas (Ret.), *Cathedral High School / El Paso Community College*
Murray Bessette, *Morehead State University*
Holly Brasher, *University of Alabama at Birmingham*
Robert Bromber, *University of Maryland—University College*
Steven Collins, *Oklahoma State University—Oklahoma City*
Tracy Cook, *Central Texas College*
Thom Costa, *Florida State College at Jacksonville*
McKinzie Craig, *Marietta College*
Nicholas D'Arecca, *Temple University*
Christi Dayley, *Weatherford College*
Lance Denning, *Metropolitan State College of Denver*
Sheng Ding, *Bloomsburg University*
Joseph Engle, *Blinn College, Bryan Campus*
Lon Felker, *East Tennessee State University*
Bernard Fitzpatrick, *Naugatuck Valley Community College*
Donald Gawronski, *Maricopa Campus Community College—Mesa*
Jeff Gulati, *Bentley University*
Lauren Hall, *Rochester Institute of Technology*
M. Ahad Hayaud-Din, *Brookhaven College*
David Head, *John Tyler Community College*
Samuel B. Hoff, *Delaware State University*
Donna Hooper, *North Central Texas College*
Melody Huckaby, *Cameron University*
Juan Carlos Huerta, *Texas A&M Corpus Christi*
Terri Jett, *Butler University*

Joseph Jozwiak, *Texas A&M Corpus Christi*
Gina Keel, *SUNY Oneonta*
Jeffrey Key, *Hardin-Simmons University*
Richard Kiefer, *Waubonsee Community College*
Patricia Knol, *Triton College*
Kyle Kopko, *Elizabethtown College*
Christopher Latimer, *SUNY Cortland*
J. Wesley Leckrone, *Widener University*
Michael Lenaghan, *Miami Dade College*
Randolph Lightfoot, *Saint Petersburg College—Tarpon Springs*
Kara Lindaman, *Winona State University*
Gary Malecha, *University of Portland*
Roger Marietta, *Darton College*
Scott Meinke, *Bucknell College*
Rhonda Miller, *Dallas County Community College*
Jason Mycoff, *University of Delaware*
Chris Newman, *Elgin Community College*
Timothy Oye, *Texas Woman's University*
Richard Pacelle, *Georgia Southern University*
Greg Rabb, *Jamestown Community College*
Lee Rademacher, *Purdue University, Calumet*
Cherry Rain, *Redlands Community College*
Mitzi Ramos, *University of Illinois at Champaign*
Susan Roomberg, *University of Texas at San Antonio*
Sandy Self, *Hardin-Simmons University*
Patrick Shade, *Edison Community College*
Nicole Shoaf, *Lincoln University*
David Ross Stark, *State College of Technology*
Dari Sylvester, *University of the Pacific*
Roy Tate, *Redlands Community College*
Robert Wood, *University of North Dakota*

About the Authors

Kenneth J. Dautrich

(Ph.D., Rutgers, 1995) is an associate professor of public policy at the University of Connecticut. He is also the founder and former director of the Center for Survey Research & Analysis at the University of Connecticut. Previously, Dr. Dautrich was a Research Fellow at the Media Studies Center in New York and has served as a senior faculty fellow at the Heldrich Center at Rutgers. His first book, *How the News Media Fail American Voters* (Columbia University Press, 1997), received scholarly praise in numerous political science circles. He also co-authored *The First Amendment and the Media in the Court of Public Opinion* (Cambridge University Press, 2002) and *The Future of the First Amendment* (Rowman & Littlefield, 2008). Dr. Dautrich's research and teaching focus on public opinion and American elections. For the past four years he has directed a set of national surveys on civic literacy in the American public and the role of higher education in advancing knowledge about American government. He directs an annual national survey on the *State of the First Amendment* for the Freedom Forum's Newseum Institute and a bi-annual survey of the millennial generation on the *Future of the First Amendment* for the Knight Foundation.

David A. Yalof

(Ph.D., Johns Hopkins University, 1997; J.D., University of Virginia, 1991) is department head and professor of political science at the University of Connecticut in Storrs. His first book, *Pursuit of Justices: Presidential Politics and the Selection of Supreme Court Nominees* (University of Chicago Press, 1999), was awarded the American Political Science Association's Richard E. Neustadt Award as the best book published on presidential studies in 1999. His most recent book is *Prosecution Among Friends: Presidents, Attorneys General and Executive Branch Wrongdoing* (Texas A & M University Press, 2012). He is also the co-author of *The First Amendment and the Media in the Court of Public Opinion* (Cambridge University Press, 2002), *The Future of the First Amendment* (Rowman & Littlefield, 2008), and another textbook, *Constitutional Law: Civil Liberty and Individual Rights* (Foundation Press, 2007). Dr. Yalof has written extensively on issues in constitutional law and Supreme Court appointment politics—his work has been published in *Political Research Quarterly, Judicature, Constitutional Commentary,* and various other journals.

Christina E. Bejarano

(Ph.D. and M.A., University of Iowa; B.A., University of North Texas) is an associate professor of political science at the University of Kansas. Her research and teaching interests are in American politics, in particular the areas of gender, race/ethnicity, and political behavior. She is particularly interested in studying the conditions under which racial/ethnic minorities and women successfully compete for U.S. electoral office, which is reflected in her book, *The Latina Advantage: Gender, Race, and Political Success* (University of Texas Press, 2013). Her work also focuses on how racial/ethnic minorities and women can shape or influence the current electoral environment, which is reflected in her book, *The Latino Gender Gap in U.S. Politics* (Routledge Press, 2014). Professor Bejarano has also written journal articles for publication in *Political Research Quarterly* and *Politics & Gender.*

Career Opportunities: Political Science

Introduction

It is no secret that college graduates are facing one of the toughest job markets in the past fifty years. Despite this challenge, those with a college degree have done much better than those without since the 2008 recession. One of the most important decisions a student has to make is the choice of a major; many consider future job possibilities when making that call. A political science degree is incredibly useful for a successful career in many different fields, from lawyer to policy advocate, pollster to humanitarian worker. Employer surveys reveal that the skills that most employers value in successful employees—critical thinking, analytical reasoning, and clarity of verbal and written communication—are precisely the tools that political science courses should be helping you develop. This brief guide is intended to help spark ideas for what kinds of careers you might pursue with a political science degree and the types of activities you can engage in now to help you secure one of those positions after graduation.

Careers in Political Science

LAW AND CRIMINAL JUSTICE

Do you find that your favorite parts of your political science classes are those that deal with the Constitution, the legal system, and the courts? Then a career in law and criminal justice might be right for you. Traditional jobs in the field range from lawyer or judge to police or parole officer. Since 9/11, there has also been tremendous growth in the area of homeland security, which includes jobs in mission support, immigration, travel security, as well as prevention and response.

PUBLIC ADMINISTRATION

The many offices of the federal government combined represent one of the largest employers in the United States. Flip to the bureaucracy chapter of this textbook and consider that each federal department, agency, and bureau you see looks to political science majors for future employees. A partial list of such agencies would include the Department of Education, the Department of Health and Human Services, and the Federal Trade Commission. There are also thousands of staffers who work for members of Congress or the Congressional Budget Office, many of whom were political science majors in college. This does not even begin to account for the multitude of similar jobs in state and local governments that you might consider as well.

CAMPAIGNS, ELECTIONS, AND POLLING

Are campaigns and elections the most exciting part of political science for you? Then you might consider a career in the growing industry based around political campaigns. From volunteering and interning to consulting, marketing and fundraising, there are many opportunities for those who enjoy the competitive and high-stakes electoral arena. For those looking for careers that combine political knowledge with statistical skills, there are careers in public opinion polling. Pollsters work for independent national organizations such as Gallup and YouGov, or as part of news operations and campaigns. For those who are interested in survey methodology there are also a wide variety of nonpolitical career opportunities in marketing and survey design.

INTEREST GROUPS, INTERNATIONAL AND NONGOVERNMENTAL ORGANIZATIONS

Is there a cause that you are especially passionate about? If so, there is a good chance that there are interest groups out there that are working hard to see some progress made on similar issues. Many of the positions that one might find in for-profit companies also exist in their non-profit interest group and nongovernmental organization counterparts, including lobbying and high-level strategizing. Do not forget that there are also quite a few major international organizations—such as the United Nations, the World Health Organization, and the International Monetary Fund—where a degree in political science could be put to good use. While competition for those jobs tends to be fierce, your interest and knowledge about politics and policy will give you an advantage.

FOREIGN SERVICE

Does a career in diplomacy and foreign affairs, complete with the opportunity to live and work abroad, sound exciting for you? Tens of thousands of people work for the State Department, both in Washington, D.C. and in consulates throughout the world. They represent the diplomatic interests of the United States abroad. Entrance into the Foreign Service follows a very specific process, starting with the Foreign Service Officers Test (FSOT)—an exam given three times a year that includes sections on American government, history, economics, and world affairs. Being a political science major is a significant help in taking the FSOT.

GRADUATE SCHOOL

While not a career, graduate school may be the appropriate next step for you after completing your undergraduate degree. Following the academic route, being awarded a Ph.D. or Master's degree in political science could open additional doors to a career in academia, as well as many of the professions mentioned earlier. If a career as a researcher in political science interests you, you should speak with your advisors about continuing your education.

Preparing While Still on Campus

INTERNSHIPS

One of the most useful steps you can take while still on campus is to visit your college's career center in regards to an internship in your field of interest. Not only does it give you a chance to experience life in the political science realm, it can lead to job opportunities later and add experience to your resume.

SKILLS

In addition to your political science classes, there are a few skills any number of which will prove useful as a complement to your degree:

Writing: Like anything else, writing improves with practice. Writing is one of those skills that is applicable regardless of where your career might take you. Virtually every occupation relies on an ability to write cleanly, concisely, and persuasively.

Public Speaking: An oft-quoted 1977 survey showed that public speaking was the most commonly cited fear among respondents. And yet oral communication is a vital tool in the modern economy. You can practice this skill in a formal class setting or through extracurricular activities that get you in front of a group.

Quantitative Analysis: As the Internet aids in the collection of massive amounts of information, the nation is facing a drastic shortage of people with basic statistical skills to interpret and use this data. A political science degree can go hand-in-hand with courses in introductory statistics.

Foreign Language: One skill that often helps a student or future employee stand out in a crowded job market is the ability to communicate in a language other than English. Solidify or set the foundation for your verbal and written foreign language communication skills while in school.

One attribute that many employers look for is "leadership potential" which can be quite tricky to indicate on a resume or cover letter. What can help is a demonstrated record of involvement in clubs and organizations, preferably in a leadership role. While many people think immediately of student government, most student clubs allow you the opportunity to demonstrate your leadership skills.

Conclusion

Hopefully reading this has sparked some ideas on potential future careers. As a next step, visit your college's career placement office, which is a great place to further explore what you have read here. You might also visit your college's alumni office to connect with graduates who are working in your field of interest. Political science opens the door to a lot of exciting careers, have fun exploring the possibilities!

Spencer Platt/Getty Images

LEARNING OBJECTIVES

1-1 Millennials, History, Diversity, and American Politics
- The influence of millennials on American politics
- Analyzing current problems and issues in American government by applying historical perspectives
- The "diversity dilemma" in American politics

1-2 Forms and Functions of Government
- Explain the philosophical underpinnings of the American political system through the exploration of important theories such as the "social contract" theory and the concept of the "natural law"
- Compare and contrast democracy with other forms of government

1-3 American Government and Politics
- Assess the importance of the value of popular sovereignty, and how that value is realized through "representative democracy" in the United States

1-4 American Political Culture
- Define *political culture* and describe the unique combination of political beliefs and values that form the American political culture, including majority rule, liberty, limited government, diversity, individualism, and equality of economic opportunity

1-5 Is American Democracy in Decline?
- Assess the health of American democracy and evaluate whether the American system is in decline by applying a historical perspective on contemporary politics
- Evaluate contemporary problems by placing them in historical context

1

Introduction to the Enduring Democracy

The final outcome of the 2016 elections surprised many journalists, pollsters, politicians, political scientists and citizens. Donald Trump, who had never before run for political office of any kind, defeated 16 other Republican candidates earlier in the year to win the GOP nomination. Despite lagging behind Democratic candidate Hillary Clinton in the polls for much of the general election campaign, Trump managed a clear electoral college victory on Election Day, even as he narrowly lost the popular vote to his Democratic rival in one of the most negative presidential contests in history.

The 2016 elections also provided the Republican Party with continued majorities in both the House of Representatives and the Senate. Thus, for the first time in more than a decade, the GOP achieved "united" Republican government. The last time either party controlled the two political branches was during the first two years of Barack Obama's presidency (2009–2010). By controlling the White House and the Congress at the outset, the Democrats were able to pass landmark legislation such as the Affordable Care Act, to overhaul the U.S. healthcare system, the Dodd-Frank Act, which reformed the financial industry, and a trillion-dollar stimulus spending bill to jump–start an economy in recession.

Since the beginning of 2017, the new President and a united Republican Congress have had ample opportunities to make their own legislative mark on the country; with a vacancy on the high court, the Republicans also were able to make an immediate appointment to the United States Supreme Court. In this book we present the actors, institutions and rules governing how this new government is able to operate.

3

Do You Think Like the "Typical" Millennial?

While authors and social scientists often like to characterize the values, opinions, and beliefs of various generations (such as millennials, baby boomers, and Gen Xers), those characterizations tend to describe general tendencies and stereotypical behavior. The truth is that while millennials as a group exhibit patterns unique from other generations, there is tremendous diversity of thought and behavior among this group. For example, millennials (age 18-33) are much more likely to identify with the Democratic Party than the Republican Party, while their older counterparts are about equally divided between the two parties.[1] Still, while a majority of millennials prefer the Democratic Party, many side with the GOP.

How do you compare to the "typical" millennial when it comes to your own political attitudes? How would you answer the following questions?

- Which candidate did you support in the 2016 presidential election?
- For you personally, is the idea of the American dream dead or alive?
- Do you consider yourself to be a liberal, conservative or moderate?
- How confident are you in the U.S. judicial system's ability to fairly judge people without bias for race and ethnicity?

To see how your answers compare to others, take the **Who Are You?** poll in MindTap!

1-1 | Millennials, History, Diversity, and American Politics

The Millennial Generation and American Politics

The millennial generation, normally defined as those born between the early 1980s and early 2000s, has already made its mark on American politics. It is a generation that was school-age during the September 11, 2001, terrorist attacks, and so the terrible events of that day play an important role in the formation of their political attitudes. In addition, the great recession of 2007–2009 soured the economic prospects for this generation as it entered the workforce for the first time, presenting unique financial pressures on this cohort. On social issues, millennials tend to be more socially liberal on issues such as same-sex marriage, abortion rights, and the legalization of marijuana.

Moreover, this generation has had a profound impact on presidential politics, as it contributed significantly to the victories of Barack Obama in 2008 and 2012, and

TABLE 1-1	Presidential Vote in 2016 by Age	
	Hillary Clinton	**Donald Trump**
18–29	55%	37%
30–44	50%	42%
45–64	44%	53%
65 and older	45%	53%
Source: www.cnn.com/election/results/exit-polls/national/president		

also to the support that Hillary Clinton received in the 2016 presidential election, as seen in Table 1-1. In addition, Millennials were the key driving force behind Senator Bernie Sanders' bid to win the Democratic nomination in 2016. Given the significance of the millennial generation, this book emphasizes the critical role that it plays in the American political system.

Then & Now

When the Popular Vote and the Electoral Vote Diverge

The Electoral College offers a unique, if sometimes controversial system for selecting America's chief executive every four years. Occasionally, the Electoral College and the popular vote even produce different results in the same contest.

Then

In 1888, the presidential race featured a contentious face-off between the Republican challenger, Benjamin Harrison, and the Democratic incumbent, President Grover Cleveland. On November 6th, voters cast their ballots and the national vote tally provided nearly 100,000 more votes to Cleveland. However, the result in the Electoral College, which decides presidential elections, gave Harrison nearly 60 more electoral votes, and thus a resounding victory. This electoral vote/popular vote divergence came only 12 years after the same event occurred in the course of Rutherford B. Hayes' victory over Samuel Tilden in 1876. That time too, the Republican rode to victory, courtesy of the Electoral College.

Now

In 2016, at the conclusion of the most recent presidential contest, voters cast their ballots for Democrat Hillary Clinton, Republican Donald Trump, or one of two third-party candidates. After the election, the popular vote favored Clinton by about 700,000. Still, Donald Trump managed to muster about 60 more electoral votes than Clinton to put him over the top in the Electoral College count. This electoral vote/popular vote divergence came only 16 years after the same anomaly resulted in George W. Bush's victory over Al Gore.

History Repeats Itself

The patterns of history provide a powerful tool for understanding American government today. In recent years, for example, the Internet and social media have revolutionized American politics. In 2008, presidential candidate Barack Obama used Facebook to build extensive volunteer networks and campaign donations to the tune of a half billion dollars. Obama captured the attention of young people and those affected by the Great Recession of 2008, offering a message of hope and change. His campaign actively encouraged social networking to mobilize voters to his cause. The result: voter turnout and interest spiked, and helped to pave the way to victory. Other politicians have tried to duplicate Obama's model; by 2016, social media began to dominate the campaign process. Voters of all political persuasions use social media to connect with their favorite campaigns. Consider the possibilities: in 2014 Facebook subscribed 134 million voting-age users in

Many college students report that they get most of their information about campaigns and politics from social media.

antoniodiaz/Shutterstock.com

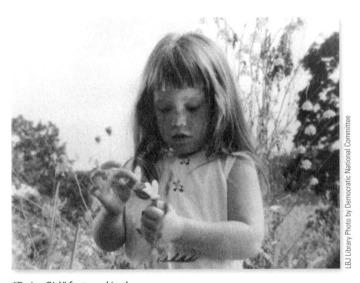

"Daisy Girl," featured in the 1964 political commercial of the Lyndon Johnson campaign, is shown above. The ad cut to a mushroom cloud explosion of an atomic bomb as the girl pulled off the last petal of the daisy.

the United States. Not only is this a massive audience, but it is an active audience, as social networks allow users to trade and share information and opinions with their friends and families. In the past, political strategists were forced to rely on the paid TV spot as the primary way to communicate with voters. Today, however, there is a noticeable shift toward using social media to send messages, raise money, and mobilize voters. Why? A message from a friend is considered much more personal, powerful, and effective than an impersonal TV spot.

Of course, social network sites like Facebook are not the only type of breakthrough technology to revolutionize political campaigns. Although Barack Obama was the first candidate to win the presidency by making extensive use of social media, John F. Kennedy pioneered the use of television to win the White House over a half century ago. When he ran for the presidency in 1960, TV was dramatically changing American society, just as social media are changing it today. As a relatively new medium with a mass audience in Kennedy's time, TV provided prospective voters with what no communications platform had offered ever before—the chance to see the candidates' campaign on a daily basis. Television audiences could tune in to watch TV spots, and they could see the candidates actually debate each other live in their own living rooms; voters saw the candidates in action. Kennedy's youth and enthusiasm made effective use of television commercials touting his candidacy. His ability to "out-charisma" Richard Nixon in the 1960 debates led to a surge in turnout, and helped to pave the way for a Kennedy victory. Kennedy's use of this new medium provided a model for how presidents would interact with voters over the next four decades. By 1964, candidates had mastered the art of the 30-second spot, as evidenced by Lyndon Johnson and his now-famous "Daisy Girl" commercial.

Although revolutionary, TV was not the first communications medium to transform political campaigns. Radio, which by 1932 had reached most U.S. households, enabled voters to listen to the candidates' voices, instead of just reading their speeches or statements. Franklin Delano Roosevelt (FDR) and President Herbert Hoover both used radio addresses and advertising extensively during the 1932 campaign. However, whereas Roosevelt's voice on the radio inspired confidence and enthusiasm for tackling the ills of the Great Depression, Hoover's logical and monotone monologue was far less effective. From that point forward, candidates could not just focus on the words that they used; they also had to excel in articulating those words with passion. FDR's use of radio eventually mobilized voters, particularly those who were most negatively affected by the economic doldrums of the Great Depression. After winning the 1932 election, FDR continued to use radio to personally connect with voters and inspire them through his "fireside chats," which he broadcast for the next 12 years.

One hundred years earlier, yet another communications revolution occurred that had a lasting impact on political campaigns. By the 1830s, newspapers were changing in a number of ways. The invention of the "rotary press" in 1815 facilitated the mass production of affordable newspapers, and eventually gave way to the so-called penny press. A decade later, the invention of the telegraph enabled penny-press papers to quickly produce stories on breaking-news events. Further, the laying of railroads to all parts of the country to accommodate rapid westward expansion paved the way for mass distribution of newspapers. Americans gobbled up this new source of information, and Andrew Jackson used this medium to engage voters, bypass the political elite, and communicate his message of rugged individualism and "the rise of the common man" to help him capture the White House in 1832. The newspaper, which became a common person's medium, enabled Jackson to distribute his message widely to an audience that was willing and eager to read what he had to say. Jackson's use of the newspaper was critical to his success, just as Obama's use of social media was critical to his own success. Never again would presidential political campaigns be targeted exclusively at political elites, thanks to Jackson's use of the penny press to effectively appeal to the masses.

This book explores the role of history as a guide to understanding contemporary American politics.

The Diversity Dilemma in American Politics

As part of this book's exploration of our country's history, we also highlight the country's ongoing struggles with our growing diversity. It is critical to highlight and understand the unique role of diversity in our evolving democracy. We take a broad view of diversity to examine how differences in various identity characteristics (such as gender, race, ethnicity, and sexuality) can impact not only our place in society but also our opportunities to have a voice in American government. We hope to challenge you to think broadly not only on "who are you" but also on how your particular identity impacts your understanding and participation in American politics.

Some people worry that growing diversity introduces an essential dilemma in American politics since it requires society and government to evolve and change. Even during the 2016 presidential campaign, for example, Donald Trump stirred up racial and religious tension by speaking negatively about our nation's diversity, especially in terms of the supposed dangers brought by the Latino and Muslim populations in the country. However, throughout this book we will highlight not only how our diversity has always been viewed as a potential challenge, but also how it has been seen as a source of our country's strength. In the first diversity dilemma the country faced, the U.S. government was challenged to define who was a citizen for purposes of the U.S. Census population count. Even though our definition of a citizen was rather limited at our country's founding, we have thankfully evolved our understanding of the American people. We are now challenged to keep working on our country's evolution, which includes a discussion of how far we still need to go.

In this book we examine the major topics and concepts in American government and politics. We attempt to answer sweeping questions about how American government works: How does policy get made? Who are the major players and institutions that make the laws? How do these players achieve their position? How do disputes get resolved? What are the role and power of the people? Throughout these discussions, we pay special attention to the millennial generation, the contributions and challenges of diversity, and how we might better understand American government today by observing the patterns of history.

government The collection of public institutions in a nation that establish and enforce the rules by which the members of that nation must live.

President Barack Obama speaks to a gathering of the National Association for the Advancement of Colored Peoples (NAACP) at the group's 100th anniversary celebration in July 2009.

1-2 | Forms and Functions of Government

Government is the collection of public institutions in a nation that establish and enforce the rules by which the

Saul Loeb/AFP/Getty Images

The Diversity Dilemma

Changing Racial Categories in the U.S. Census

Since 1790, the U.S. government has implemented a nationwide census to count the population in the country every 10 years. This population information is used for a variety of reasons, including distribution of federal spending and planning for the growing population. The U.S. Census questionnaire has evolved since 1790, often as a result of the changing understanding of diversity. The first census collected very rudimentary information on racial makeup of the country, which was restricted to asking if you were white and if you had slaves. The census racial categories have evolved; however, they are still limited to five very basic categories, including White, Black or African American, American Indian or Alaska Native, Asian, and Native Hawaiian or Other Pacific Islander.

It was not until 1970 that the Census began to ask respondents about their ethnicity, which was restricted to asking a subsample of respondents whether they had a Hispanic family origin. In addition, the Census began to allow respondents to choose more than one racial category after 2000. We are now challenged with understanding the

9. **What is Person 1's race?** *Mark* ☒ *one or more boxes.*

☐ White
☐ Black, African Am., or Negro
☐ American Indian or Alaska Native – *Print name of enrolled or principal tribe.*↗

[ ][ ][ ][ ][ ][ ][ ][ ][ ][ ][ ][ ][ ][ ][ ][ ][ ][ ]

☐ Asian Indian   ☐ Japanese   ☐ Native Hawaiian
☐ Chinese   ☐ Korean   ☐ Guamanian or Chamorro
☐ Filipino   ☐ Vietnamese   ☐ Samoan
☐ Other Asian – *Print race. For example, Hmong, Laotian, Thai, Pakistani, Cambodian, and so on.*↗   ☐ Other Pacific Islander – *Print race. For example, Fijian, Tongan, and so on.*↗

[ ][ ][ ][ ][ ][ ][ ][ ][ ][ ][ ][ ][ ][ ][ ][ ][ ][ ]

☐ Some other race – *Print race.*↗

[ ][ ][ ][ ][ ][ ][ ][ ][ ][ ][ ][ ][ ][ ][ ][ ][ ][ ]

The 2000 U.S. Census was the first to allow respondents to self-identify as a member of more than one race.

true diversity of the U.S. population, which may require further Census revisions.

For Critical Thinking and Discussion

1. How would you answer the Census question on race and Hispanic ethnicity?
2. Do you believe the current Census questions are sufficient?

---

anarchy A state of lawlessness and discord in the political system caused by lack of government.

social contract From the philosophy of Jean-Jacques Rousseau, an agreement people make with one another to form a government and abide by its rules and laws, and, in return, the government promises to protect the people's rights and welfare and promote their best interests.

authority The ability of public institutions and the officials within them to make laws, independent of the power to execute them.

members of that nation must live. Even the most primitive of societies have found government to be necessary. Without government, society would be in a state of **anarchy**, a situation characterized by lawlessness and discord in the political system. Thomas Hobbes, a seventeenth-century British political philosopher, wrote that without government, life would be "solitary, poor, nasty, brutish and short."[2] Government is necessary to make the rules by which citizens must abide, promoting order, stability, and protection for the society. It exists in part to resolve conflicts that naturally arise when people live in communities. Elaborating on the role of government, Jean-Jacques Rousseau, an eighteenth-century French philosopher, posited that in fact a "social contract" exists.[3] A **social contract** is an agreement people make with one another to form a government and abide by its rules and laws. In return, the government promises to protect the people's rights and welfare and to promote their best interests.

A government's **authority** over its citizens refers to the ability of public institutions and the officials within them to make laws, independent of the power to execute them. People obey authority out of respect, whereas they obey power out of fear. Numerous different forms of government with governing authority can be found around the nations of the world. One such form—the form that will receive extended attention throughout this book—is **democracy**, defined as a government in which the people, either directly or through elected representatives, hold power and authority. The word *democracy* is derived from the Greek *demos kratos*, meaning "rule by the people."

By contrast, an **oligarchy** is a form of government in which a small exclusive class, which may or may not attempt to rule on behalf of the people as a whole, holds supreme power. In a **theocracy**, a particular religion or faith plays a dominant role in the government; Iran is just one example of a theocratic nation in the world today. A **monarchy** is a form of government in which one person, usually a member of a royal family or a royal designate, exercises supreme authority. The monarch may be a king or queen, such as Queen Elizabeth II of Great Britain. In the past, monarchies were quite common; today they are rarely practiced in the absolute sense. Although the United Kingdom continues to pay homage to its royalty, true political power rests in the Parliament, the members of which are elected by the people.

Many of the nations in the world today have an **authoritarian** form of government in which one political party, group, or person maintains such complete control over the nation that it may refuse to recognize, and may even choose to suppress, all other political parties and interests. The nation of Iraq, before the American military intervention in 2003, was considered by most to be an authoritarian government under the dictatorial rule of Saddam Hussein. North Korea under Kim Jong-un is an authoritarian government in existence today.

An important characteristic of any government, whether democratic or not, is its power to exercise authority over people. **Power** is the capacity to get individuals to do something that they may not otherwise do, such as pay taxes, stop for red lights, or submit to a search before boarding an airplane. Without power, it would be very difficult for a government to enforce rules. The sustained power of any government largely rests on its legitimacy. **Legitimacy** is the extent to which the people (or the "governed") afford the government the authority and right to exercise power. The more that people subscribe to the goals of a government, and the greater the degree to which that government guarantees the people's welfare (for example, by supporting a strong economy or providing protection from foreign enemies), the higher will be the government's level of legitimacy. When the governed grant a high level of legitimacy to their government, the government wields its power to make and enforce rules more successfully.

1-3 | American Government and Politics

Politics is defined as the way in which the institutions of government are organized to make laws, rules, and policies, and how those institutions are influenced. More than 70 years ago, political scientist Harold Lasswell proposed a brief but very useful definition of politics as "who gets what, when and how."[4] In American politics, the "who" includes actors within and outside the formal government, such as citizens, elected officials, interest groups, and state and local governments. The "what" are the decisions the government makes and take the form of what government funds, the way it raises revenue, and the policies it produces and enforces. The "when" relates to setting priorities about what government does. The concerns and issues that government addresses differ in importance, and issues of greater importance tend to be addressed more quickly. Finally, the "how" refers to the way in which the government goes about its work, based on the political institutions that exist and the formal and informal procedures and rules that define the governing process. In describing American politics, this book provides answers to Lasswell's "who gets what, when and how?"[3]

democracy Form of government in which the people, either directly or through elected representatives, hold power and authority. The word *democracy* is derived from the Greek *demos kratos*, meaning "rule by the people."

oligarchy A form of government in which a small exclusive class, which may or may not attempt to rule on behalf of the people as a whole, holds supreme power.

theocracy A form of government in which a particular religion or faith plays a dominant role in the government.

monarchy A form of government in which one person, usually a member of a royal family or a royal designate, exercises supreme authority.

authoritarian A form of government in which one political party, group, or person maintains such complete control over the nation that it may refuse to recognize and may even suppress all other political parties and interests.

power The ability to get individuals to do something that they may not otherwise do, such as pay taxes, stop for red lights, or submit to a search before boarding an airplane.

legitimacy The extent to which the people afford the government the authority and right to exercise power.

politics The way in which the institutions of government are organized to make laws, rules, and policies, and how those institutions are influenced.

Government in the United States is especially complex. It is organized into multiple layers (national, state, and local) and contains many governing units, as shown in Table 1-2. It encompasses a number of political institutions that share power—the executive (the president), the legislature (Congress), and the judiciary (the courts)—and it provides countless methods for individuals and groups to influence the decisions made by those institutions. In this book, we will examine this complex organization of American government, describe the political institutions that exercise power, and explore the varied ways that people and groups exert influence. As we sort through this complexity of American government, we will seek to explain how and why the American political system has been able to endure the conflicts, both internal and external, that it has faced and currently faces. We will attempt to show how the American government is uniquely designed to stand up to its many challenges.

The strength and stability of the U.S. government are grounded in the high level of legitimacy it maintains with the American public. Americans may disagree vehemently with public officials, but rarely do they question their claim to authority. The Framers of the U.S. Constitution were keenly aware of the importance of the legitimacy of the system. They knew that if the government was to withstand the test of time, it must serve the people well. These ideas about legitimacy drew largely on the theories of seventeenth-century British political philosopher John Locke (1632–1704).[5] Locke proposed that people are born with certain *natural rights*, which derive from **natural law**, the rules of conduct inherent in the relationship among human beings and thus more fundamental than any law that a governing authority might make. Government cannot violate these natural rights, which include life, liberty, and property. Therefore, government, or human law, must be based on the "consent of the governed." That is, citizens are responsible for choosing their government and its leaders. This theory loomed large in the mind of Thomas Jefferson as he drafted the Declaration of Independence to

natural law According to John Locke, the most fundamental type of law, which supersedes any law that is made by government. Citizens are born with certain natural rights (including life, liberty, and property) that derive from this law and that government cannot take away.

TABLE 1-2 Governments in the United States

The government of the United States might be more correctly described as a system of governments. In addition to the federal government, there are 50 state governments and thousands of local governments. The 2012 U.S. Census Bureau's *Census of Governments* listed these totals for the number of governments operating throughout the nation.

Government	Number
Federal	1
State	50
County	3,013
Municipal	19,522
School district	13,051
Township/town	16,364
Special district	37,203
Total	**89,004**

Based on data from U.S. Census Bureau's *Census of Governments,* 2012 justify the American colonies' split with the British government: "All men . . . are endowed by their creator with certain unalienable rights . . . [and] whenever any form of government becomes destructive of these ends, it is the right of the people to alter or abolish it." A government maintains legitimacy as long as the governed are served well and as long as government respects the natural rights of individuals.

Drawing on this philosophy, the Framers drafted a Constitution that created a political system able to manage the inevitable conflicts that occur in any society. Mindful of Thomas Hobbes's notion that the essence of government is to manage naturally occurring conflicts, the Framers designed a government that encourages conflict and competition rather than attempting to repress it. As we shall see in the chapters that follow, the U.S. Constitution includes a number of mechanisms that allow naturally occurring conflict to play out in as productive a manner as possible. Mechanisms are also in place to resolve conflicts and arrive at consensus on issues. Those who disagree and come up on the short side of political battles are guaranteed rights and liberties nonetheless. Further, the rules by which conflicts are settled are predicated on fairness and proper procedures.

The significance of what the Framers of the Constitution accomplished cannot be overstated. They not only addressed the short-term problems challenging the new nation; they also drafted a blueprint for how government should go about dealing with problems and conflicts into the future. The U.S. Constitution has served as the cornerstone of an American political system that routinely attempts to tackle some of the thorniest problems imaginable. In Chapter 2 of this book, we examine the enduring principles and processes outlined in the Constitution.

The Constitution provides a way for the American government to navigate through the many problems and conflicts that have faced the nation, including severe economic depressions, two world wars, nuclear confrontations with the former Soviet Union, and persisting questions of equality. Through all these difficulties, the American government has endured. The foresight of the Framers to create a Constitution that possesses the flexibility to adapt to changing times has served as a basis for the enduring democracy of the United States.

The preamble to the U.S. Constitution perhaps best summarizes the broad goals of American government:

> *We the People of the United States, in Order to form a more perfect Union, establish Justice, insure domestic Tranquility, provide for the common defence, promote the general Welfare, and secure the Blessings of Liberty to ourselves and our Posterity, do ordain and establish this Constitution for the United States of America.*

It is no accident that the first three words of the Constitution are "We the People." With this phrase, the Framers acknowledged that the ultimate source of power rests with the people, a concept known as **popular sovereignty**. The U.S. Constitution provided for a form of **representative democracy**,

ARPL/HIP/The Image Works

popular sovereignty The idea that the ultimate source of power in the nation is held by the people.

representative democracy A form of government designed by the U.S. Constitution: Free, open, and regular elections allow voters to choose those who govern on their behalf; it is also referred to as *indirect democracy* or a *republican* form of government.

"I agree to this Constitution, with all of its faults, if they are such: because I think a general government necessary for us, and there is no form of government but what may be a blessing to the people if well administered. I doubt too whether any convention we can obtain may be able to make a better constitution. For when you assemble a number of men to have the advantage of their joint wisdom, you inevitably assemble with those men all their prejudices, their passions, their errors of opinion, their local interests, and their selfish views. From such an assembly can a perfect production be expected? It therefore astonishes me . . . to find this system approaching so near to perfection."
—*Benjamin Franklin (1788)*

ROBYN BECK/AFP/Getty Images

Regular elections are an important feature of America's "republican" form of government. In 2016, 17 GOPers and 5 Democrats ran for president. Pictured here, some of the GOP contenders debate: (from left) Mike Huckabee, Jeb Bush, Marco Rubio, Donald Trump, Ben Carson, and Carly Fiorina.

direct democracy A system of government in which all citizens participate in making policy, rules, and governing decisions.

political culture The values and beliefs about government, its purpose, and its operations and institutions that are widely held among citizens in a society; it defines the essence of how a society thinks politically and is transmitted from one generation to the next.

under which regular elections are held to allow voters to choose those who govern on their behalf. In this sense, individual citizens do not directly make policies, rules, and other governing decisions (that system of government is known as a **direct democracy**). Rather, representative democracy, also referred to as *indirect democracy* or a *republican* form of government, rests on the notion that consent of the governed is achieved through free, open, and regular elections of those who are given the responsibility of governing.

An important source of the legitimacy of the U.S. government is the nation's commitment to representative democracy, which features the notion of majority rule. Majorities (more than 50 percent of the voters) and pluralities (the leading vote getters, whether or not they constitute absolute majorities) choose the winners of election contests, and so officeholders take their positions on the basis of whom most voters prefer. If officeholders fall from public favor, they may be removed in subsequent elections.

Legitimacy is also enhanced by broad public support for the specific purposes of government stated in the preamble to the Constitution: to "insure domestic tranquility" (produce laws that maintain a peaceful and organized approach to living in the nation), to "provide for the common defence" (establish and maintain a military force to protect the nation from outside threats), to "promote the general welfare" (develop domestic policy programs to promote the welfare of the people), and to "secure the blessings of liberty" (guarantee basic freedoms, such as the rights of free expression and the ownership of property, even to those in the minority). Though people may have different opinions on how to achieve these broad goals, few in the United States would disagree with the ideals as stated in the abstract, or with the broad outlines of our republican form of government. Problems arise when public officials stray so far from these goals that their actions are deemed illegitimate by a near, if not absolute, majority. Yet the political system as a whole has been able to maintain its legitimacy, even under such trying circumstances, because it has been flexible enough to eventually rid itself of those ineffective actors, whether through elections, impeachment, or some other means. The relatively high degree of legitimacy that is maintained in the United States has helped the American government persist under the U.S. Constitution through good times and bad since 1789.

1-4 | American Political Culture

Political culture refers to the core values about the role of government and its operations and institutions that are widely held among citizens in a society. Political culture defines the essence of how a society thinks politically. It is transmitted from one generation to the next, and thus has an enduring influence on the politics of a nation. Every nation has a political culture, and the United States is no exception.

Whereas common ancestry characterizes the core of the political culture of many other nations, the United States has no common ancestry. Most other nations around the world, such as France, Britain, China, and Japan, are bound by a common birth lineage that serves to define the cultural uniqueness of the nation. For example, the Russian people share common political values and beliefs as part of their ancestors' historical experiences with czars, and then later with the communist regime. Britain, despite being a democracy, retains a monarchy as a symbolic gesture toward its historical antecedents. In many nations rich with such common ethnic traditions, these routines often serve to underscore the political culture of the nation.

The United States has no such common ancestry to help define its political culture. Its land was first occupied by many different Native American tribes, and then settled by people from many different parts of the world. Most of the immigrants who settled the colonies were seeking a better life from the political or religious persecution they experienced in their native countries, or they were seeking improved economic opportunities for themselves and their families. As America continued to grow through the centuries, it attracted immigrants from around the world, anxious to find a better life. These circumstances had a profound influence on the core values that have become engrained in the American political culture. The ideas generated by democratic political philosophers such as Thomas Hobbes and John Locke also significantly contributed to American political culture. These ideas were used by the Founders to justify the Declaration of Independence and the U.S. Constitution, and they continue to underlie American political culture today.

The circumstances surrounding America's first and current immigrants, as well as the great ideas generated by Enlightenment philosophers, form the core set of values that define the American political culture. One of these core values is **majority rule**. From its earliest times, the American nation has been committed to the notion that the "will of the people" ought to guide public policy, thus underscoring the importance of popular sovereignty in the thinking of the Founders. Majority rule is the way in which popular sovereignty is actually exercised. Rarely will all of the people agree all of the time; and so it is what the majority of people prefer that generally guides decision making. Early local governments, such as town governments in some of the New England colonies, relied on town meetings, where all citizens were invited to attend, discuss, and vote, to make governmental decisions. Elections for most local and state offices, and elections for the U.S. Congress, are all based on the idea that those who make and enforce laws are duly elected by majorities. A more recent aspect of U.S. commitment to majority rule is its heavy reliance on public opinion polling as a gauge for assessing the performance of elected leaders, and to ensure that leaders respect public preferences for certain policy positions.

majority rule The notion that the will of the majority should guide decisions made by American government.

Although the preferences of the majority rule the day, another core value in the American political culture is minority rights. Those in the minority enjoy certain rights and liberties that cannot be taken away by government. The idea of the natural law (e.g., that people are "endowed by their creator with certain unalienable rights" that government cannot deny) is an important corollary to majority rule. The rights to speak freely, to choose a religion, or to decide not to practice religion at all are among the many liberties that are protected by the U.S. Bill of Rights, and are widely endorsed by the American public.

These rights are intended to inspire debate on issues, to guarantee religious

Rep. Keith Ellison (D-MN) takes the oath of office on January 4, 2007. Ellison became the first Muslim elected to the U.S. Congress.

Win McNamee/staff/Getty Images

freedoms, and to afford due process rights to those accused of crimes. The American political culture places a high value on individual liberty. The fact that many immigrants came to this country for the promise of greater freedom adds further credence to this proposition. Certainly there are some terrible black marks in American history that belie this claim. Among them are the perpetuation of slavery in the country up until the Civil War, the internment of Japanese Americans during World War II, and the treatment of early 1960s civil rights protesters in the South. Still, many Americans today view their nation as the world's "garden" of freedom and liberty, even if it has come to this status only slowly and sometimes with reluctance during its more than two centuries of existence.

limited government The value that promotes the idea that government power should be as restricted as possible.

Another core value in American political culture is the idea of **limited government**. Americans have generally supported the idea expressed by Thomas Jefferson that "the government that governs least governs best." From the days of the American Revolution, the colonists believed that the corruptive power of King George III and the British Parliament led to unfair treatment of the colonies. Suspicion of the government and those with power is firmly rooted in the psyche of American political culture. The "watchdog" function of the press, the separation of powers and the system of checks and balances among political institutions, and the rather negative connotation of the word "politics" all reflect an appreciation for limits and checks on those with authority. Corresponding to the value of limited government is the notion that communities and the private sector should take a role in helping fellow citizens. Problems that may be solved without government should be solved that way. The French journalist Alexis de Tocqueville observed this tradition when he visited the United States in the early 1800s and credited the success of the American political system in part to citizens' strong interest in community and helping one another apart from government.[6]

Because the United States has no common ancestral or cultural bloodline, American political culture recognizes the value and strength derived from the diversity of its population—another important core value. At the base of the Statue of Liberty in

---

TABLE 1-3 Daniel Elazar's Typology of American Political Culture

Many observers of American politics have used different approaches and typologies to describe American political culture. The late political scientist Daniel Elazar described three competing political subcultures, which he believed differentiated American political culture from that found in any other country in the world:*

Subculture	Description
Individualistic Subculture	Is skeptical of authority, keeps government's role limited, and celebrates the United States' general reliance on the marketplace
Moralistic Subculture	Has faith in the American government's capacity to advance the public interest and encourages citizens to participate in the noble cause of politics
Traditionalistic Subculture	Maintains a more ambivalent attitude toward both government and the marketplace, believing that politicians must come from society's elite, whereas ordinary citizens are free to stand on the sidelines

According to Elazar, different subcultures can be found in different geographic areas, and sometimes within a single area itself. For example, he described the political subculture in Texas as part traditionalistic (as manifested in the long history of one-party dominance in state politics) and part individualistic (as seen in the state government's commitment to support for private business and its opposition to big government).

* See Daniel J. Elazar, *American Federalism: A View from the States* (New York: Thomas Y. Crowell, 1966).

New York Harbor is inscribed a poem by Emma Lazarus beginning with the phrase "Bring me your huddled masses, yearning to be free." Until the U.S. government adopted a restrictive immigration policy in the early 1920s, those huddled masses arrived in waves from different parts of the world, as the United States became the chosen destination for those seeking a better life. Joining freed African American slaves who were originally brought here against their will were legions of Italians, Irish, Germans, and other immigrants from Europe and elsewhere. This surge in immigration occurred from 1880 through 1920, as immigrants left the economic and political strife of Europe seeking jobs and opportunities in America.

National Public Radio's popular Latino USA *host Maria Hinojosa (right) provides commentary on Latino politics. Here she appears on NBC's* Meet the Press *with Yahoo News columnist Matt Bai.*

One of the most profound population developments in the recent history of the United States has been the skyrocketing growth of the nation's Hispanic population. The Hispanic or Latino/a populations have expanded from what was once a small, regionally concentrated subgroup of fewer than 6 million in 1960 to a now widely dispersed population of more than 50 million (or 16 percent of the nation's population) today. The recent explosion of immigrants from Latin America is largely a product of the difficult economic and social conditions they face in their home countries, as well as the opportunity for a better life they believed was possible in the United States.

As shown in Figure 1-1, the Pew Research Center projects that this modern immigration wave will drive U.S. population growth and change at least through 2065. The projections also include a growing Asian American foreign-born population that will even surpass Hispanics as the country's largest immigrant group by 2055. Such a massive swelling in the ranks of Hispanics and Asian Americans has the potential to create major political change in America.

This population growth has transformed the United States to one of the most racially and ethnically diverse nations in the world. Integrating these many people into a united nation has not been easy; in fact, resistance to the notion of a "melting pot" has been common. The nation has been wracked at times with racial and ethnic strife to a degree that more homogeneous countries can more easily avoid. Government officials occasionally exacerbate these tensions by promoting policies that discriminate against various groups, including Native Americans, African Americans, Asian Americans, and Hispanics. No stranger to ethnic and racial tensions himself, German dictator Adolph Hitler calculated that the diversity of the United States would eventually hamper its resistance against Germany's totalitarian aggression; in fact, American soldiers of different backgrounds, ethnicities, and religions fought in World War II. Much to Hitler's chagrin, U.S. diversity proved to be a source of strength, rather than weakness. Indeed, many Americans today believe that the heterogeneity of our society enhances the quality of our culture and helps guarantee the fairness of the government.

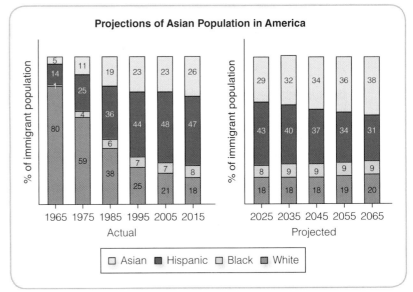

FIGURE 1-1 **Asians Projected to Become the Largest Immigrant Group, Surpassing Hispanics**

Sources: Pew Research Center estimates for 1965–2015 based on adjusted census data; Pew Research Center projections for 2025–2065.

Note: Whites, blacks, and Asians include only single-race non-Hispanics. Asians include Pacific Islanders. Hispanics are of any race. Other races shown but not labeled.

Americans also generally subscribe to the notion that individuals are primarily responsible for their lot in life—a value referred to as **individualism**. The seeds of this value were sown hundreds of years ago with the Puritans and their commitment to a strong work ethic that stressed that "what one sows determines what one reaps." In other words, hard work and intelligence should be rewarded. Although the U.S. government has assumed some responsibility to provide a safety net for citizens who suffer economically, the American political culture, through its primary reliance on a capitalist economic system, free markets, and individual effort, is one that promotes individual initiative and responsibility. Figure 1-2 depicts the heightened importance of the value of individualism in the American political culture, compared to other European democracies.

The value of individualism promotes another core value—equality of opportunity, or the idea that the role of government is to set the stage for individuals to achieve on their own, and that everyone should be given the same opportunity to achieve success. Indeed, America has been an attractive place for highly motivated individuals from around the world to immigrate so that they might have a fair chance of achieving personal success. Many immigrants today, particularly from Asia and Latin America, are attracted to the United States for the opportunities to achieve individual success.

The United States has long set itself apart from those nations whose histories include traditions of a rigid class system of privileged aristocracies and oligarchies and peasants with few or no rights or freedoms. In the United States there is no formal recognition of a class system; nor is there a tradition of royalty, nobility, or monarchy. Indeed, Article I of the Constitution specifically prohibits both the federal government and the state governments from granting any title of nobility upon its citizens. Instead, American political culture values the so-called Horatio Alger myth. Alger was a popular writer in the late 1800s whose characters came from impoverished backgrounds but through pluck, determination, and hard work achieved huge success. Although this idealistic rags-to-riches notion often ignores the many harsh economic disparities that exist in the United States, it remains central to the American political culture. The stories of Benjamin Franklin and Abraham Lincoln exemplified this road to success, as do the more recent examples of Presidents Bill Clinton and Ronald Reagan, both

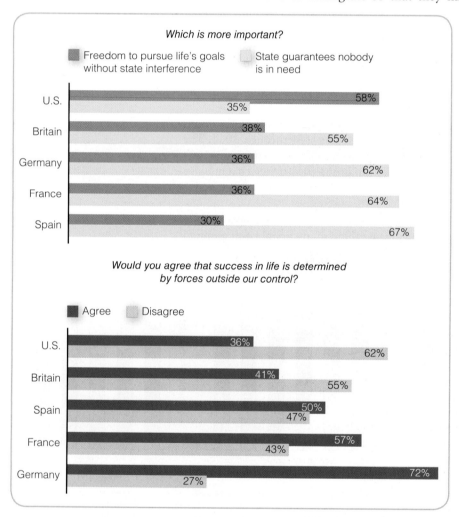

FIGURE 1-2 Individualism as a Value in the United States Compared to Other Democracies

A recent Pew Global Survey shows that Americas are more likely than their European counterparts to believe that "it is more important to pursue life's goals without government interference" and to disagree with the statement "success in life is determined by forces outside our control."

of whom came from less-than-privileged circumstances to win the nation's highest political office and become leaders of the free world. Perhaps it is because of these success stories that so many Americans believe that they have boundless opportunities to better their lot on the basis of diligence and hard work.

These core values provide a window into American political culture. To be sure, there is plenty of room for disagreement as to how these values might be applied to specific situations, which we address in Chapter 10. In addition, these values are often in conflict. At the heart of the debate over affirmative action, for example, lies the value conflict pitting individualism against equality of opportunity. Those who oppose affirmative action in hiring claim that individuals should be evaluated exclusively based on who they are and what they can do rather than on their gender, race, or other demographic characteristic. Those supporting affirmative action claim that historical discrimination has led to a current job market that provides unequal opportunities for certain groups, such as racial minorities and women. Although these values do not always solve problems and policy debates, they do lay the groundwork for how American politics goes about settling problems and debating issues.

1-5 | Is American Democracy in Decline?

The old saying that "those who ignore the problems of the past are destined to repeat them" holds as true in American politics as it does in any other context. Certainly new issues and problems may arise, requiring innovative new thinking to address them. But many other difficulties the United States faces can be effectively addressed by casting an eye on the distant or not-so-distant past. A historical view can help place modern dilemmas in proper perspective.

The Case for Decline

Some recent observers of American politics have suggested that the American political system is in decline. Are we currently witnessing a deterioration of democracy in the United States? Is the American political system in jeopardy? Are the problems that the American system of government faces today beyond repair? To try to answer these questions, let's first look at the factors some cite as contemporary indicators of the decline of American democracy.

1. **The decline of the United States as an economic superpower?** The growth of the national economy from the Industrial Revolution through the post–World War II era established the United States as the preeminent fiscal power in the world for much of the twentieth century. This fiscal strength enabled the United States to establish the dollar as the benchmark unit of currency for the world, to defeat the Soviet Union in the Cold War, to build a military capability vastly superior to that of other nations, and to provide the leadership that brought democracy to many other nations. However, the significant growth of the Chinese economy over the past decade, coupled with the exploding U.S. national debt (and the willingness of China to underwrite much of that debt), has raised serious questions about the future of U.S. dominance over the world's economy. Concerns over the economic rise of China and the decline of the United States are summarized in a recent study by the Congressional Research Service: ". . . the emergence of China as a major economic superpower has raised concern among many U.S. policymakers . . . that China will overtake the United States as the world's largest trade economy in a few years and the world's largest economy within the next two decades. In this context, China's rise is viewed as America's relative decline." This report offers evidence of a decline in economic power citing projections of U.S. and Chinese gross domestic product (GDP), depicted in Table 1-4.

TABLE 1-4 Projections of U.S. and Chinese Gross Domestic Product (GDP), in Billions

	China	United States
2015	22,210	20,169
2020	35,734	27,584
2025	57,145	35,963

Source: Congressional Research Service

2. **The death of capitalism?** The collapse of many of the largest financial institutions in the United States in 2008, and the subsequent "Great Recession," has raised questions about the viability of the free market system in contemporary society. In large part, the financial industry's drive in the 1990s and 2000s to capitalize on rising real estate markets drove financial institutions to rely on increasingly risky lending practices. Risky loans were bundled and sold off to investors in the form of real estate securities. (These practices were depicted in the award-winning movie *The Big Short*). Multibillion-dollar financial institutions, such as Citibank, Morgan Stanley, Lehman Brothers, Countrywide Mortgage, and AIG, among many others, found themselves in the red at the exact same time that the real estate market collapsed, thus freezing credit in the United States. The stock market tumbled, and the U.S. government needed to bail out many of the largest financial institutions just to keep the nation's financial system from collapse. The frantic drive for profits among the largest of these companies was identified as the source of economic ills not only in the United States, but around the world. Greed, inspired by capitalism, seemed to be the culprit of the world's economic woes, thus leading to questions about the viability of the free market system in the modern age.

3. **Policy paralysis caused by partisan gridlock?** Relations between the two major parties tend to ebb and flow with changing political moods and circumstances. Still, cross-party relations between Republicans and Democrats seemed to have reached such a low between 2011 and 2016 that policymaking all but ceased to function. In recent years, whichever party has carried the White House has been forced to brace for a Senate opposition that uses the filibuster freely and with few limitations to impose a supermajority requirement of 60 senators for all legislative enactments. Many other bills can never even get out of committee. Meanwhile, in the House of Representatives, the president's opposition has ruled with an iron hand, rendering matters that had in the past proven perfunctory (such as the routine raising of the nation's debt ceiling) into a knockdown, drag-out fight between the two parties in Congress. The prospect of a government shutdown has loomed over every budget fight, and in October of 2013 partisan tensions did in fact lead to a shutdown of many federal government functions for more than two weeks. Party-line votes in Congress on most major legislative initiatives indicate a lack of any common ground whatsoever.

4. **Has money ruined American politics?** "Big money" now dominates American elections, in the form of contributions from those who seek to influence future officials, personal expenditures from candidates themselves, and general expenditures by political parties. The Supreme Court's landmark decision in *Citizens United v. FEC* (2010) seemed to cement the role that big money plays in determining election outcomes, paving the way for independent-expenditure political action committees

(often called "super-PACs") to accept unlimited contributions from individuals, unions, and corporations for the purpose of making so-called independent expenditures on behalf of candidates; it thus enabled wealthy individuals to dominate the process. In the year following *Citizens United*, just 22 donors provided the money for half of the $67 million funded by super-PACs! In some instances, anonymous outside groups poured millions of dollars into the process. Others were willing to stand up and be counted: Consider that billionaire Sheldon Adelson singlehandedly kept Newt Gingrich's struggling presidential campaign afloat in 2012 with his donation of $10 million to a pro-Gingrich super-PAC. With a handful of individuals responsible for a large percentage of the donations in these campaigns, the corruptive influence of money appears to have reached new, dangerous heights.

The influence of money on politics is never more evident than during presidential election campaigns. Shown here is billionaire investor Warren Buffet, speaking at an event for Hillary Clinton in December 2015.

But Do These Problems Really Signify a Decline?

If we reexamine some of the criticisms of contemporary American politics with the benefit of historical perspective, we may reach far different conclusions about whether American democracy is now in a state of decline.

1. **The United States will remain an economic superpower.** Challenges to U.S. fiscal dominance, such as the current challenge of China, are nothing new. Forty years ago, for example, many policymakers expressed similar concerns about the imminent decline of U.S. economic power. In this era the concern was focused not on China, but on Japan. The Japanese economy flourished in the decades after World War II. A latecomer to modernization, Japan was able to avoid the pitfalls of industrialization experienced by the United States and other advanced democracies prior to World War II. Once converted to a free market system after the war, Japan's economy took off quickly. By the 1970s, Japan had the world's second largest economy and appeared to be closing in on the United States. Gross domestic product (GDP) in Japan grew from $8 billion in 1955, to $32 billion in 1965, to $148 billion in 1975, to $323 billion in 1985. By 1990 Japan's per capita GDP exceeded per capita GDP in the United States. The sharp upward trajectory alarmed many U.S. policymakers, who felt that Japan's rise would ultimately derail the U.S. dominance of world fiscal policy. Yet today Japan offers no significant threat to the economic power of the United States. The rapid rise of Japan's economy left it unable to effectively deal with a recessionary period of any length. Consequently, the dire predictions of the U.S. economic fall to Japan were never realized. Furthermore, by 2016 China's economy had already showed signs of slower growth, leading economists to recognize the likely continued dominance of the United States well into the twenty-first century.[8]

2. **Capitalism is not dead.** The Great Recession of 2008 and the events that led up to it certainly do not mark the first time that speculation in free markets led to economic catastrophe. A panic in 1837 led to stymied economic growth for more than three years, a severe recession in 1873 retracted growth for six years, and an economic panic in 1893 set off a series of bank failures. A stock market crash in 1929 produced a decade-long "Great Depression." These and many other economic downturns in U.S. history, aggravated by speculation and overly exuberant investors, have led to extremely tough economic times. But the ills of

Trading on the floor of the New York Stock Exchange remains an important symbol of American capitalism.

the free market have never limited the ability of capitalism to provide the medicine for recovery, and then some. Panics, recessions, and depressions have always been corrected by bull markets, opportunities, and resurgences. Capitalism has been declared dead many times in U.S. history. The approach of each economic downturn was accompanied by claims that the U.S. experiment with a free market system had finally failed. In fact, the free markets operate in natural cycles of growth and retraction. Just as the free market system was declared dead at earlier times in American history, so too were many claiming that the Great Recession of 2008 was the last nail in the coffin of American capitalism. However, just as the cyclical nature of free market growth calmed the fears of the skeptics before, so too has the recent growth of the U.S. stock market and decline in unemployment quieted the naysayers once again.

3. **The polarization of the two major political parties has not paralyzed the lawmaking process.** The political parties' recent polarization is hardly unprecedented: at various times in history (e.g., during the Civil War, the New Deal) the parties have stood in stark contrast on nearly all the major issues of the time. Some democratic theorists argue that a marked differentiation between the two parties may actually contribute to democracy under a "responsive theory of democracy": the two parties disagree on the issues and then allow the public to express its opinion through elections. For all the talk of polarization, the 111th Congress passed 43 major pieces of legislation in 2009–2010, including the Obama administration's centerpiece, health care reform. Since the 2010 midterm elections, Republicans and Democrats have managed to approve hundreds of bills and resolutions. The parties may be growing more distinct, but government continues to make decisions.

4. **The influence of money does not spell the end of American politics.** American elections have always been dominated by individuals with immense power and influence. For much of this nation's history, political machines all but controlled the nomination process and wielded heavy influence on politicians who benefitted from their respective handouts and other forms of largesse. Whether it was Boss Tweed and Tammany Hall in New York City, the Thomas Prendergast political machine in Missouri, or the Daley machine in Chicago, power has always been wielded by a relatively few, elite individuals. The recent dominance of money in politics

has shifted the source of power from those machines to the extremely wealthy, but that may actually represent a positive development of sorts, as both parties have enjoyed their share of big donors and fund-raising prowess in recent years. Moreover, well-financed campaigns like Governor Jeb Bush's unsuccessful bid for the White House in 2016 proves that money can only go so far without the right messenger and the right message. Those who think money corrupts politics might want to consider these caveats, as well as the far less attractive alternative that used to mark the elections process.

History does not literally repeat itself. The specific people, circumstances, and events certainly change. But history can help us identify patterns, recurring problems, and trends in how the American political system functions and resolves conflicts. The preceding discussion of some of the contemporary arguments for why American democracy may be in a state of decline helps us frame current conditions. In doing so, we may gain a greater understanding of the challenges facing the nation today. Certainly, many contemporary challenges are no less daunting than problems the nation has encountered over the past two centuries. Throughout this book, a historical perspective on contemporary problems offers a sense of how the past might help us understand politics today.

 From Your Perspective

Courting the Youth Vote

Candidates and political parties often try to increase turnout as a means of enhancing their prospects in an election. However, numerous nonpartisan organizations also engage in special efforts to encourage the so-called youth vote in particular. These organizations may target young voters primarily for two reasons: (1) young voters represent the future of American democracy and (2) youth turnout has tended to be lower than turnout among older Americans. Even in 2008 and 2012—when the youth vote increased substantially as compared to past presidential elections—barely more than half of eligible voters aged 18 to 29 voted, leaving that group well behind turnout rates of the electorate as a whole (more than 60 percent or more of eligible Americans voted in 2008 and 2012).

Among the many organizations that run programs to encourage young voters to exercise their voting rights are the following:

1. Rock the Vote, which claims to have registered more than two million new voters in 2008 alone (see rockthevote.com);
2. CIRCLE (Center for Information and Research on Civic Learning and Engagement), which studies the voting behavior of young people (see www.civicyouth.org); and
3. YouthVote.org, a website that provides a plethora of information to help young people learn how to register to vote and why it is important to do so.

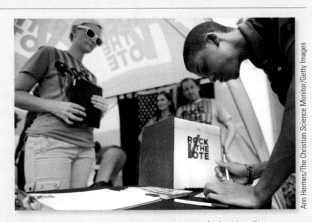

College students participating in the "Rock the Vote" campaign in 2016.

Ann Hermes/The Christian Science Monitor/Getty Images

For Critical Thinking and Discussion

1. Which of the presidential candidates do you think won the vote among college students in 2016? Why did this candidate appeal more to students?
2. Why do you think college-age students turn out in relatively lower numbers, compared to older voters?
3. How effectively did the candidates in 2016 address issues that were important to college students?

Summary

1-1 Millennials, History, Diversity, and American Politics

- The millennial generation now as a group is the youngest cohort of voters in the American electorate. Millennials' political attitudes and voting patterns are distinct from their older generational counterparts.
- The American public may be characterized as being quite diverse in terms of race, ethnicity, gender, and region. This large and growing diversity of the American nations results in great differences in political attitudes in public opinion.
- The patterns of history provide a powerful tool for understanding American politics today.

1-2 Forms and Functions of Government

- The development of the American political system is grounded in the philosophy of John Locke and Jean-Jacques Rousseau, who argued that government is necessary and that it exists for the purpose of protecting the people that it serves. The "social contract" theory states that natural law gives people certain unalienable rights that government cannot take away, and that the people give government authority to rule, but the people can withdraw that authority if government does not serve the people's interests.
- Democracy may be distinguished from other forms of government in that it is a form of government in which the people, either directly or through elected representatives, hold power and authority.

1-3 American Government and Politics

- Democracy includes at its core the idea of popular sovereignty. The United States practices a form of democracy known as "representative democracy," where the people indirectly rule by electing leaders who are responsible for making and carrying out policies and laws.

1-4 American Political Culture

- The political culture in America is reflected in the Constitution and the way in which the political system deals with and decides political debates. Among the core values guiding the American political culture are majority rule, liberty, limited government, diversity, individualism, and equality of economic opportunity.

1-5 Is American Democracy in Decline?

- Although the current American government has been in place for more than 200 years, questions have been raised about whether this political system is in a state of decline. Lower voter turnout, confusing election outcomes, negativity in politics, and the influence of money in policy outcomes have been offered as evidence of a decline. However, a review of historical patterns in American politics suggests that these seemingly contemporary problems are chronic, and the American political system has effectively dealt with these and many other problems in the past.
- Viewing American government from a historical perspective may enrich our understanding of how the political system works. History can help us identify patterns, recurring problems, and trends in how the American political system functions and resolves conflicts. Many contemporary challenges are no more significant than problems the nation has encountered over the past two centuries.

Key Terms

anarchy (p. 8)
authoritarian (p. 9)
authority (p. 8)
democracy (p. 9)
direct democracy (p. 12)
government (p. 7)
individualism (p. 16)

legitimacy (p. 9)
limited government (p. 14)
majority rule (p. 13)
monarchy (p. 9)
natural law (p. 10)
oligarchy (p. 9)
political culture (p. 12)

politics (p. 9)
popular sovereignty (p. 11)
power (p. 9)
representative democracy (p. 11)
social contract (p. 8)
theocracy (p. 9)

Test Yourself

1. The "social contract" theory between the governing and the governed was first developed by
   a. Thomas Jefferson.
   b. Socrates.
   c. Thomas Hobbes.
   d. Jean Jacques Rousseau.

2. A form of government in which one political party, one group, or one person maintains control and suppresses the views of outsiders is
   a. theocracy.
   b. an oligarchy.
   c. authoritarian.
   d. in anarchy.

3. Distinguish between the political concepts of "power" and "legitimacy."

4. The form of government that best describes that in the United States is
   a. direct democracy.
   b. representative democracy.
   c. oligarchy.
   d. monarchy.

5. Which of the following documents establishes the principle of popular sovereignty?
   a. The preamble to the Constitution
   b. The Bill of Rights
   c. The Declaration of Independence
   d. Article I of the Constitution

6. What did John Locke mean by the term *natural law*, and how is that concept reflected in the Declaration of Independence?

7. Which of the following of Elazar's "subcultures" in the United States is characterized by a skeptical view of authority and a desire to limit the role of government?
   a. Individualistic
   b. Moralistic
   c. Traditionalistic
   d. Rationalistic

8. The notion of popular sovereignty is best supported by which of the following values?
   a. Minority rights
   b. Diversity
   c. Individualism
   d. Majority rule

9. Individualism and equality are two values that underlie the American political culture. Define each and describe how these values may come into conflict on a specific policy issue.

10. Today many policymakers are concerned that China will soon overtake the role of the world's leading economic power. In the 1970s and 1980s, which nation was the subject of similar fears?
    a. Germany
    b. Brazil
    c. Japan
    d. Pakistan

11. The U.S. Supreme Court ruling in 2010 that paved the way for the so-called super-PACs was
    a. *Citizens United v. FEC.*
    b. *Miller v. California.*
    c. *Miranda v. Arizona.*
    d. *U.S. v. Davis.*

12. What are the key arguments in support of and in opposition to the notion that partisan gridlock has paralyzed policymaking over the past few years? Which side of the argument do you support? Why?

---

1. d. (LO 1-2); 2. c. (LO 1-2); 4. b. (LO 1-3); 5. a. (LO 1-3); 7. a. (LO 1-4); 8. d. (LO 1-4); 10. c. (LO 1-5); 11. a. (LO 1-5)

LEARNING OBJECTIVES

2

The Founding
and the Constitution

The U.S. Constitution has governed the United States continuously since 1789; it is the longest-lasting governing document in the world today. Thus, the enduring capacity of the U.S. Constitution to govern for better than two centuries represents something of a miracle: by one estimate, the average lifespan of national constitutions over this same period was just 17 years. Other countries' constitutions have been especially vulnerable during crises; by contrast, the U.S. Constitution has survived many such crises, including the Civil War of the 1860s, the Great Depression of the 1930s, two world wars, the Cold War against the Soviet Union, and the 9/11 terrorist attacks. How has the American constitutional experiment succeeded for so long? The secret lies in its capacity to serve two functions at the same time: it provides stability (just 17 amendments passed during the last two centuries), while at the same time offering the flexibility to adapt to changes in America's political culture. Woodrow Wilson addressed this when he wrote: "the Constitution of the United States is not a mere lawyers' document: it is a vehicle of life, and its spirit is always the spirit of the age."

Interpreting the Constitution

When the written constitution that set the terms for our new republic was ratified by the required three-fourths of states in 1788, several critical questions concerning the new document remained unanswered. Most critical among them concerned the proper method of interpreting the Constitution. Was it a "fixed constitution" with its rules and understandings to remain the same as at the time of its creation? Or was this an "organic" or "living constitution" that future judges would interpret according to changing ideals and evolving understandings? This question remains unanswered even today, as many judges and justices (the late Justice Antonin Scalia was prominent among them) advocate "originalism" as a means of interpreting the document according to the Founders' understandings, while more liberal or progressive judges (such as Justice Stephen Breyer) demand that the Constitution evolve with more modern understandings of race relations, privacy and our global economy, among other issues.

- Where do you stand on the spectrum ranging from supporters of a "fixed constitution" to supporters of a living constitution?
- Do you consider yourself an originalist?
- Do you believe that the Framers' understanding of the Constitution can only be ignored by passage of a constitutional amendment?

To see how your answers compare to others, take the **Who Are You?** poll in MindTap!

2-1 | The Beginnings of a New Nation

Throughout the seventeenth and early eighteenth centuries, thousands of people migrated to North America. Many came in search of greater economic opportunities; others fled to escape religious persecution and sought freedom to worship as they pleased. Slowly, a culture dedicated to the protection of social and civil rights began to take shape in the colonies.

The political structures that governed the colonies up through the early 1760s roughly paralleled those of England during the same period: (1) royal governors served as substitutes for the king in each individual colony; (2) a governor's council in each colony served as a mini House of Lords, with the most influential men in the colony serving effectively as a high court; and (3) the general assembly in each colony was elected directly by the qualified voters in each colony and served essentially as a House of Commons, passing ordinances and regulations that would govern the colony. Up until the middle of the eighteenth century, the colonies' diverse histories and economies had provided little incentive for them to join together to meet shared goals. In fact, those in Great Britain feared other European powers attempting to encroach on their American holdings far more than they feared any form of uprising on the part of the colonists.

The French and Indian War that was waged in the colonies from 1754 through 1763 was a significant turning point in British–colonial relations.[1] For nearly a decade, the French, from their base in Canada, fought the British in the colonies for control of the North American empire. Both nations were interested in rights to the territory that extended west of the colonial settlements along the Atlantic seaboard and over the Appalachian Mountains into the Ohio Valley. Britain defeated France, and under the terms of the Treaty of Paris (1763), which settled the war, all territory from the Arctic Ocean to the Gulf of Mexico between the Atlantic Ocean and the Mississippi River (except for New Orleans, which was ceded to Spain, an ally of Britain during the war) was awarded to Britain. But along with the acquisition of all this new territory came a staggering debt of approximately 130 million pounds. Administering its huge new North American empire would be a costly undertaking for Britain.

British Actions

Following the war, Britain imposed upon its colonies a series of regulatory measures intended to make the colonists help pay the war debts and share the costs of governing the empire. To prevent colonists from ruining the prosperous British fur trade, the Proclamation of 1763 restricted them to the eastern side of the Appalachian chain, angering those interested in settling, cultivating, and trading in this new region. The Sugar Act of 1764 was the first law passed by Parliament for the specific purpose of raising money in the colonies for the Crown. (Other regulatory acts passed earlier had been enacted for the purpose of controlling trade.) The Sugar Act (1) increased the duties on sugar; (2) placed new import duties on textiles, coffee, indigo, wines, and other goods; and (3) doubled the duties on foreign goods shipped from England to the colonies. The Stamp Act (1765) required the payment of a tax on the purchase of all newspapers, pamphlets, almanacs, and commercial and legal documents in the colonies. Both acts drew outrage from colonists, who argued that Parliament could not tax those who were not formally represented in its chambers. Throughout late 1765 and early 1766, angry colonists protested the Stamp Act by attacking stamp agents who attempted to collect the tax, destroying the stamps, and boycotting British goods. When English merchants complained bitterly about the loss of revenue they were suffering as a result of these colonial protests, Parliament repealed the Stamp Act in March 1766.[2]

Colonial Responses

As a result of the Stamp Act fiasco, positions on the state of British rule were articulated both in the colonies and in Parliament. Following the lead of the Virginia assembly, which sponsored the Virginia Resolves that had declared the principle of "no taxation without representation," an intercolonial Stamp Act Congress met in New York City in 1765. This first congressional body in America issued a Declaration of Rights and Grievances that acknowledged allegiance to the Crown but reiterated the right to not be taxed without consent. Meanwhile, the British Parliament—on the same day that it repealed the Stamp Act—passed into law the Declaratory Act, asserting that the king and Parliament had "full power and authority" to enact laws binding on the colonies "in all cases whatsoever."

Despite the colonists' protests, Parliament continued to pass legislation designed to raise revenue from the colonies. The Townshend Acts, passed in 1767, imposed duties on various items, including tea, imported into the colonies and created a Board of Customs Commissioners to enforce the acts and collect the duties. When the colonists protested by boycotting British goods, in 1770 Parliament repealed all the duties except that on tea. The Tea Act, enacted in 1773, was passed to help the financially troubled British East India Company by relaxing export duties and allowing the company to sell its tea directly in the colonies. These advantages allowed the company to undersell colonial merchants. Angry colonists saw the act as a trick to lure Americans into buying the cheaper tea and thus ruining American tea sellers. On December 16, 1773, colonists disguised as Mohawk Indians boarded ships in Boston Harbor and threw overboard their cargoes of tea. Outraged by this defiant Boston Tea Party, Parliament in 1774 passed the Intolerable Acts (known in the colonies as the Coercive Acts), designed to punish the rebellious colonists. The acts closed the port of Boston, revised the Massachusetts colonial government, and required the colonists to provide food and housing for British troops stationed in the colonies.

The colonists had had enough. In September 1774, 56 leaders from 12 colonies (there were no delegates from Georgia) met in Philadelphia to plan a united response to Parliament's actions. This First Continental Congress denounced British policy and organized a boycott of British goods. Although the Congress did not advocate outright independence from England, it did encourage the colonial militias to arm themselves

Patrick Henry, a leading revolutionary who coined the phrase "Give me liberty or give me death," speaking before the Virginia House of Burgesses in 1775.

and began to collect and store weapons in an arsenal in Concord, Massachusetts. The British governor general of Massachusetts ordered British troops to seize and destroy the weapons. On their way to Concord, the troops met a small force of colonial militiamen at Lexington. Shots were exchanged, but the militiamen were soon routed and the British troops marched on to Concord. There they encountered a much larger group of colonial militia. Shots again were fired, and this time the British retreated. The American Revolution had begun.

The Decision for Independence

Despite the events of the early 1770s, many leading colonists continued to hold out hope that some settlement could be reached between the colonies and Britain. The tide turned irrevocably in early 1776, when one of the most influential publications of this period, *Common Sense*, first appeared. In it, Thomas Paine attacked King George III as responsible for the provocations against the colonies, and converted many wavering Americans to the cause of independence.[3]

On June 7, 1776, Richard Henry Lee, a delegate to the Second Continental Congress from Virginia, proposed a resolution stating that "these United Colonies are, and of right ought to be, free and independent States." Of course, the Congress needed a formal document both to state the colonies' list of grievances and to articulate their new intention to seek independence. The Congress thus appointed a committee to draft a document that would meet those objectives.

The committee, consisting of Thomas Jefferson, John Adams, Roger Sherman, Robert Livingston, and Benjamin Franklin, appointed Jefferson to compose the document. At first, Jefferson may have seemed an unlikely choice to produce such a declaration. The 33-year-old lawyer and delegate to the Continental Congresses of 1775 and 1776 had played a relatively minor role in those bodies' deliberations. But according to historian David McCullough, Adams initially believed that the document was really just a symbolic "side show," and quickly justified the choice of Jefferson over himself as follows: "Reason first: you are a Virginian and a Virginian ought to appear at the head of this business. Reason second: I am obnoxious, suspected and unpopular. You are very much otherwise. Reason third: You can write ten times better than I can." Later, Adams fumed for decades over the larger-than-life reputation Jefferson gained on the basis of authoring the nation's first great political document.[4]

The committee submitted its draft to Congress on July 2, 1776; after making some changes, Congress formally adopted the document on July 4. The **Declaration of Independence** restated John Locke's theory of natural rights and the social contract between government and the governed.[5] Locke had argued that although citizens sacrifice certain rights when they consent to be governed as part of a social contract, they retain other inalienable rights. In the Declaration, Jefferson reiterated this argument with the riveting sentence: "We hold these truths to be self-evident, that all men are created equal, that they are endowed by their Creator with certain inalienable rights, that among these are life, liberty and the pursuit of happiness." Jefferson went on to state that whenever government fails in its duty to secure such rights, the people have the right to "alter" or "abolish" it and institute a new one. Through the centuries, America's political leaders have consistently invoked the Declaration of Independence as perhaps the truest written embodiment of the American Revolution. Before independence could become a reality, however, the colonists had to fight and win a war with Great Britain.

Declaration of Independence Formal document listing colonists' grievances and articulating the colonists' intention to seek independence; formally adopted by the Second Continental Congress on July 4, 1776.

The First National Government: The Articles of Confederation

The colonies also needed some sort of plan of government to direct the war effort. The Second Continental Congress drew up the **Articles of Confederation**, a written statement of rules and principles to guide the first continent-wide government in the colonies during the war and beyond. Although the document was initially adopted by Congress in 1777, it was not formally ratified by all 13 states until 1781. The Articles of Confederation created a "league of friendship" among the states, but the states remained sovereign and independent, with the power and authority to rule the colonists' daily lives. The sole body of the new national government was the Congress, in which each state had one vote. As shown in Table 2-1, the Congress enjoyed only limited authority to govern the colonies: it could wage war and make peace, coin money, make treaties and alliances with other nations, operate a postal service, and manage relations with the Native Americans.[6] But Congress had no power to raise troops, regulate commerce, or levy taxes, which left it dependent on state legislatures to raise and support armies or provide other services. Congress's inability to raise funds significantly hampered the efforts of George Washington and the Continental Army during the war against Britain. Although Congress employed a "requisition system" in the 1780s, which essentially asked that states voluntarily meet contribution quotas to the federal government, the system proved ineffective. New Jersey, for example, consistently refused to pay such requisitions. Reflecting the colonists' distrust of a strong centralized government, the Articles made no provision for a chief executive who could enforce Congress's laws.

The limited powers of the central government posed many problems, but changing the Articles of Confederation to meet the needs of the new nation was no easy task. The Articles could be amended only by the assent of all 13 state legislatures, a provision that made change of any kind nearly impossible. Wealthy property owners

Articles of Confederation The document creating a "league of friendship" governing the 13 states during and immediately after the war for independence; hampered by the limited power the document vested in the legislature to collect revenue or regulate commerce, the Articles eventually proved unworkable for the new nation.

TABLE 2-1 The Articles of Confederation and the U.S. Constitution: Key Features

Articles of Confederation Provisions	Problems Generated	1787 Federal Constitution
Unicameral (one-house) Congress with each state having one vote, regardless of population	Gave smaller, less populated states disproportionate power in lawmaking	Bicameral (two-house) legislature with one house apportioned by population (House of Representatives) and second house (Senate) apportioned equally among states (two senators from each state)
Approval by 9 of 13 states required for most legislative matters	Restricted lawmaking by simple majorities, halting the legislative process in most cases	Approval of simple majority (one-half plus one) of both houses required for most legislation
No separate executive or judiciary	Legislative abuses went unchecked	Three separate branches of government: legislative, executive, and judicial
Congress did not have the power to regulate foreign or interstate commerce	States negotiated separately among themselves and with foreign powers on commercial matters, to the detriment of the overall economy	Congress given power to regulate interstate and foreign commerce
Congress did not have the power to levy or collect taxes	Suffering from the economic depression and saddled with their own war debts, states furnished only a small portion of the money sought by Congress	Congress given power to levy and collect taxes
Congress did not have the power to raise an army	Once the war with Britain had ended, states were reluctant to provide any support for an army	Congress given power to raise and support armies
Amendments to Articles required unanimous approval of state legislatures	Articles were practically immune from modification, and thus inflexible to meet changing demands of a new nation	Amendments to Constitution require two-thirds vote of both houses of Congress, ratification by three-fourths of states

and colonial merchants were frustrated with the Articles for various reasons. Because Congress lacked the power to regulate interstate and foreign commerce, it was exceedingly difficult to obtain commercial concessions from other nations. Quarrels among states disrupted interstate commerce and travel. Finally, a few state governments (most notably, that of Pennsylvania) had come to be dominated by radical movements that further threatened the property rights of many wealthy, landowning colonists.

These difficulties did not disappear when the war ended with the Americans' victory in 1783. Instead, an economic depression, partially caused by the loss of trade with Great Britain and the West Indies, aggravated the problems facing the new nation. In January 1785, an alarmed Congress appointed a committee to consider amendments to the Articles. Although the committee called for expanded congressional powers to enter commercial treaties with other nations, no action was taken. Further proposals to revise the Articles by creating federal courts and strengthening the system of soliciting contributions from states were never even submitted to the states for approval; congressional leaders apparently despaired of ever winning the unanimous approval of the state legislatures needed to create such changes.

Then in September 1786, nine states accepted invitations to attend a convention in Annapolis, Maryland, to discuss interstate commerce. Yet when the Annapolis Convention opened on September 11, delegates from only five states (New York, New Jersey, Delaware, Pennsylvania, and Virginia) attended. A committee led by Alexander Hamilton, a leading force at the Annapolis meeting, issued a report calling upon all 13 states to attend a convention in Philadelphia the following May to discuss all matters necessary "to render the constitution of the federal government adequate to the exigencies of the Union." At the time, few knew whether this proposal would attract more interest than had previous calls for a new government.

Events in Massachusetts in 1786–1787 proved a turning point in the creation of momentum for a new form of government. A Revolutionary War veteran, Daniel Shays was also one of many debt-ridden farmers in Massachusetts, where creditors controlled the state government. Shays and his men rebelled against the state courts' foreclosing on the farmers' mortgages for failure to pay debts and state taxes.[7] When the state legislature failed to resolve the farmers' grievances, Shays's rebels stormed two courthouses and a federal arsenal.[8] Eventually the state militia put down the insurrection, known as **Shays's Rebellion**, but the message was clear: a weak and unresponsive government carried with it the danger of disorder and violence. In February 1787, Congress endorsed the call for a convention to serve the purpose of drafting amendments to the Articles of Confederation, and by May 11 states had acted to name delegates to the convention to be held in Philadelphia.

North Wind Picture Archives

Daniel Shays leads a rebellion of farmers to a Massachusetts courthouse in 1786 to protest the state legislature's inaction.

Shays's Rebellion Armed uprising by debt-ridden Massachusetts farmers frustrated with the state government.

Constitutional Convention Meeting of delegates from 12 states in Philadelphia during the summer of 1787, at which was drafted an entirely new system to govern the United States.

2-2 | The Constitutional Convention

The **Constitutional Convention** convened on May 25, 1787, with 29 delegates from nine states in attendance. Over the next four months, 55 delegates from 12 states would participate. Fiercely resistant to any centralized power, Rhode Island sent no delegates. Some heroes of the American Revolution like Patrick Henry refused appointments due to their opposition to the feelings of nationalism that had spurred the convention to be held in the first place. Meanwhile, lending authority to the proceedings were such well-known American figures as George Washington, Alexander Hamilton, and Benjamin Franklin. (The 36-year-old James Madison of Virginia was only beginning to establish a reputation for himself when he arrived in Philadelphia; meanwhile, John Adams and Thomas Jefferson were both on diplomatic assignment in Europe.)

The delegates, who unanimously selected Washington to preside over the convention, were united by at least four common concerns: (1) the United States was being

Portrait of George Washington, circa 1775. Washington was elected president of the Constitutional Convention in Philadelphia.

Mansell/Time Life Pictures/Getty Images

treated with contempt by other nations, and foreign trade had suffered as a consequence; (2) the economic radicalism of Shays's Rebellion might spread in the absence of a stronger central government; (3) the Native Americans had responded to encroachment on their lands by threatening frontiersmen and land speculators, and the national government had been ill-equipped to provide citizens with protection; and (4) the postwar economic depression had worsened, and the national government was powerless to take any action to address it.[9] Of course, on many other matters the delegates differed. Those from bigger, more heavily populated states such as Virginia and Pennsylvania wanted a central government that reflected their larger population bases, whereas those from smaller states like Georgia and Delaware hoped to maintain the one-state, one-vote principle of the Articles.

Plans and Compromises

It quickly became evident that a convention originally called to discuss amendments to the Articles of Confederation would be undertaking a more drastic overhaul of the American system of government. Members of the Virginia delegation got the ball rolling when they introduced the **Virginia Plan**, also known as the "large states plan," which proposed a national government consisting of three branches—a legislature, an executive, and a judiciary. The legislature would consist of two houses, with membership in each house proportional to each state's population. The people would elect members of one house, and the members of that house would then choose members of the second house. The legislature would have the power to choose a chief executive and members of the judiciary, as well as the authority to legislate in "all cases to which the states are incompetent" or when the "harmony of the United States" demands it. Finally, the legislature would have power to veto any state law. Under the plan, the only real check on the legislature would be a Council of Revision, consisting of the executive and several members of the judiciary, which could veto the legislature's acts.

To counter the Virginia Plan, delegates from less-populous states proposed the **New Jersey Plan**, which called for a one-house legislature in which each state, regardless of size, would have equal representation. The New Jersey Plan also provided for a national judiciary and an executive committee chosen by the legislature; expanded the powers of Congress to include the power to levy taxes and regulate foreign and interstate commerce; and asserted that the new constitution and national laws would become the "supreme law of the United States." Both the Virginia and New Jersey plans rejected a model of government in which the executive would be given extensive authority.

By July 2, 1787, disagreements over the design of the legislature and the issue of representation had brought the convention to a near dead end. The delegates then agreed to submit the matter to a smaller committee in the hope that it might craft some form of compromise.

The product of that committee's deliberations was a set of compromises, termed the **Great Compromise** by historians. (Formally proposed by delegate Roger Sherman of Connecticut, the agreement is also known as the Connecticut Compromise.) As shown in Table 2-2, its critical features included (1) a bicameral (two-house) legislature with an upper house or "Senate," in which the states would have equal power with two representatives from each state, and a lower House of Representatives, in which membership would be apportioned on the basis of population; and (2) the guarantee that all revenue bills would originate in the lower house. The convention delegates settled as well on granting

TABLE 2-2   The Virginia Plan, the New Jersey Plan, and the Great Compromise

The Virginia Plan	The New Jersey Plan	The Great Compromise
Introduced on May 29, 1787, by Edmund Randolph of Virginia; favored initially by delegates from Virginia, Pennsylvania, and Massachusetts	Introduced on June 15, 1787, by William Paterson of New Jersey; favored initially by delegates from New Jersey, New York, Connecticut, Maryland, and Delaware	Introduced by Roger Sherman of Connecticut; approved at the convention by a narrow 5–4 vote on July 16, 1787
Bicameral legislature with one house elected by the people and second house chosen by the first	Unicameral legislature elected by the people	Bicameral legislature with one house elected by the people and second house chosen by state legislatures
All representatives and senators apportioned by population	Equal representation among states	Members of one house (representatives) apportioned by population (five slaves counted as three free men); members of second house (senators) apportioned equally among states
Singular executive chosen by the legislature	Plural executive chosen by the legislature	Singular executive chosen by the "electoral college" (electors appointed by state legislatures choose president; if no one receives majority, House chooses president)
Congress can legislate wherever "states are incompetent" or to preserve the "harmony of the United States"	Congress has the power to tax and regulate commerce	Congress has power to tax only in proportion to representation in the lower House; all appropriation bills must originate in lower House

Congress the authority to regulate interstate and foreign commerce by a simple majority vote but required that treaties be approved by a two-thirds vote of the upper house. The Great Compromise was eventually approved by a narrow 5–4 margin of the state delegations. Connecticut, New Jersey, Delaware, Maryland, and North Carolina approved; Pennsylvania, Virginia, South Carolina, and Georgia opposed; New York and New Hampshire were absent, and the Massachusetts delegation was deadlocked. Thus a vote margin of just one state paved the way for the creation of a new federal government.

Compromise also resolved disagreement over the nature of the executive. Although rejecting the New Jersey Plan's call for a plural executive—in which officials would have exercised executive power through a multiperson council—the delegates split on whether the executive should be elected by members of Congress or directly by the people. The agreement reached called for the president (and vice president) to be elected by an electoral college. Because the number of electors equaled the number of representatives and senators from each state, this system gave disproportionately greater influence to smaller states. As chief executive, the president would have the power to veto acts of Congress, make treaties and appointments with the consent of the Senate, and serve as commander-in-chief of the nation's armed forces.

The Slavery Issue

The issue of representation collided with another thorny issue looming over the convention proceedings: the issue of slavery. Four Southern states—Maryland, Virginia, North Carolina, and South Carolina—had slave populations of more than a hundred

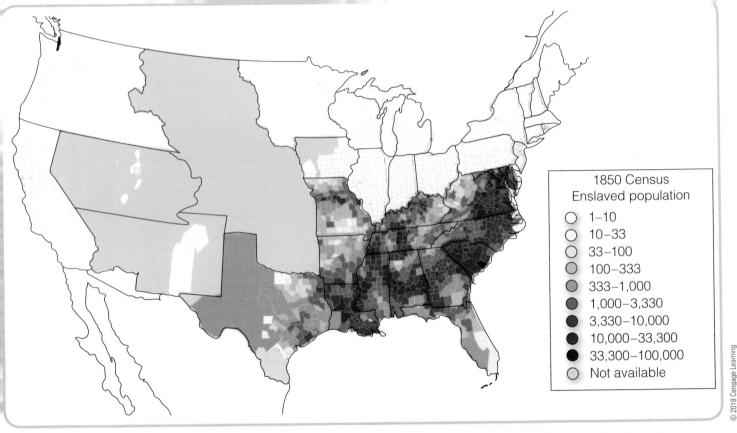

FIGURE 2-1 The Spread of U.S. Slavery, 1790–1850. At the time of the founding, Northern states still featured limited slavery within their borders. Yet over the following half century the concentration of slaves would shift to the point that by 1850, slavery had become an exclusively southern institution. Thus the delicate compromise over slavery that the founding fathers struck at the Constitutional Convention would be put to the test during this later period.

thousand each, two New England states, Maine and Massachusetts, had already banned slavery and another four Northern states—Vermont, New Hampshire, Rhode Island, and Connecticut—maintained extremely low concentrations of slavery within their borders. The steady march of abolition in the North was matched by a Southern slave population that had been doubling every two decades. (And as shown in Figure 2-1, slavery would continue to predominate in the deep South up through the eve of the Civil War). The convention delegates who advocated a new form of government were wary of the role slavery would play in this new nation, but they were even more wary of offending Southern sentiments to the point that consensus at the convention would be endangered.

Some delegates from the Northern states who had already voted in favor of banning slavery sought a similar emancipation of slaves in all the colonies by constitutional edict. Southerners hoping to protect their plantation economy, which depended on slave labor, wanted to prevent future Congresses from interfering with the institution of slavery and the importation of slaves. Moreover, even among Northerners there was disagreement on how emancipation should proceed: some favored outright freedom, whereas others argued for some form of colonization of the slaves, which would in effect ship them back to Africa. Many delegates feared that any extended discussion of slavery at the convention would become so divisive that it might bring the entire gathering to a standstill.

Southern delegates also wanted slaves to be counted equally with free people in determining the apportionment of representatives; Northerners opposed such a scheme for representation because it would give the Southern states more power, but the North did want slaves counted equally for purposes of apportioning taxes among the states. In an effort to forestall the convention's collapse, the delegates crafted a series of compromises that amounted to misdirection, and in some instances outright silence, on the issue of slavery.[10] By the agreement known as the **Three-Fifths Compromise**, five slaves would be counted as the equivalent of three "free persons" for purposes of taxes *and* representation. Delegates from Southern states also feared that a Congress dominated by representatives from more populous Northern states might take action against the slave trade. Most Northerners continued to favor gradual emancipation. Once again, neither side got exactly what it wanted. The new constitution said nothing about either preserving or outlawing slavery. Indeed, the only specific provision about slavery was a time limit on legislation banning slave importation: Congress was forbidden from doing so for at least 20 years. In 1807, however, with the slave population steadily outgrowing demand, many Southerners allied with opponents of the slave trade to ban the importation of slaves. Not until the Civil War decades later would the conflict over slavery be finally resolved.

On September 17, 1787, after four months of compromises and negotiations, the 12 state delegations present approved the final draft of the new constitution. By the terms of Article VII of the document, the new constitution was to become operative once ratified by 9 of the 13 states.

Three-Fifths Compromise A compromise proposal in which five slaves would be counted as the equivalent of three free people for purposes of taxes and representation.

2-3 | The New Constitution

As a consequence of the many compromises in the draft constitution, few of the delegates were pleased with every aspect of the new document. Even James Madison, later heralded as the "Father of the Constitution" for his many contributions as a spokesman at the convention, had furiously opposed the Great Compromise; he hinted at one point that a majority of the states might be willing to form a union outside the convention if the compromise were ever approved, and he convinced the Virginia delegation to vote "no" when it came up for a formal vote.

Nonetheless, the central desire of most of the delegates to craft a new government framework did lead them to consensus on a set of guiding principles evident throughout the document. The following principles continue to guide politicians, lawyers, and scholars today as they study the many ambiguous provisions of the U.S. Constitution:

- Recognizing that calls for fairer representation of colonists' interests lay at the heart of the Declaration of Independence, popular sovereignty was a guiding principle behind the new constitution. The document's preamble beginning with "We the People" signified the coming together of people, not states, for the purposes of creating a new government. Under the proposed constitution, no law could be passed without the approval of the House of Representatives, a "people's house" composed of members apportioned by population and subject to reelection every two years. Of even greater significance, the delegates agreed that all revenue measures must originate in the House, an explicit affirmation of the principle that there would be "no taxation without representation."
- The delegates recognized the need for a **separation of powers**. The Founders drew upon the ideas of the French political philosopher Baron de Montesquieu, who had argued that when legislative, executive, and judicial power are not exercised by the same institution, power cannot be so easily abused. Mindful of the British model in which Parliament combined legislative and executive authority, the drafters of the new constitution assigned specific responsibilities and powers to each branch of the government—Congress (the legislative power), the president (the executive power), and the Supreme Court (the judicial power).

separation of powers The principle that each branch of government enjoys separate and independent powers and areas of responsibility.

checks and balances A system of limits imposed by the Constitution that gives each branch of government the limited right to change or cancel the acts of other branches.

In the new government, individuals were generally prohibited from serving in more than one branch of government at the same time. The vice president's role as president of the Senate was a notable exception to this rule.

- While establishing separate institutions, the drafters of the new constitution also created a system of **checks and balances** to require that the branches of government would have to work together to formulate policies (see Figure 2-2).

CHECKS BY JUDICIARY

Checks on Congress
✓Federal judicial power extends to all cases arising under the laws of the United States (Art. III, § 2, Cl. 1) **(subsequently interpreted to include power to invalidate unconstitutional laws passed by Congress)**

Checks on Executive
✓Federal judicial power extends to all cases or controversies to which the U.S. government is a party (Art. III, § 2, Cl. 1) **(subsequently interpreted to include power to invalidate unconstitutional acts by president)**

✓Chief justice shall preside over Senate impeachment trials of the president (Art. I, § 3, Cl. 6)

CHECKS BY EXECUTIVE

Checks on Congress
✓Presidential power to sign or veto bills (Art I, § 7, Cl. 2)

✓In alternate role as president of Senate, vice president of United States can cast votes to break ties in a divided Senate (Art. I, § 3, Cl. 4)

✓President can bypass Senate temporarily by filling vacancies during Senate recess that expire at end of next Senate session (Art. II, § 2, Cl. 3)

✓President may "on extraordinary occasions" convene or adjourn either or both houses of Congress (Art. II, § 3)

✓President must "take care" that congressional laws are faithfully executed (Art. II, § 3)

Checks on Judiciary
✓President nominates and (with Senate advice and consent) appoints Supreme Court justices (Art. II, § 2, Cl. 2)

CHECKS BY CONGRESS

Checks on Executive
✓Impeachment by House (Art. I, § 2, Cl. 5) and removal by Senate (Art. I, § 3, Cl. 6) of president, vice president, and all civil officers of the United States (Art. II, § 4)

✓Congressional override of presidential vetoes by two-thirds vote of both houses (Art. I, § 7, Cl. 2)

✓Senate must approve all treaties by two-thirds vote (Art. II, § 2, Cl. 2)

✓House selection of president and Senate selection of vice president in event there is no Electoral College majority (Art. II, § 1, Cl. 3, Twelfth Amendment)

✓Senate advice and consent required for appointment of "Officers of the United States" (Art. II, § 2, Cl. 2)

Checks on Judiciary
✓Senate advice and consent required for appointment of Supreme Court Justices (Art. II, § 2, Cl. 2)

✓Impeachment by House (Art. I, § 2, Cl. 5) and removal by Senate (Art. I, § 3, Cl. 6) of Supreme Court justices

✓Congress can make exceptions to appellate jurisdiction of the Supreme Court (Art. III, § 2, Cl. 2)

FIGURE 2-2 Checks and Balances in the U.S. Constitution

This system of "separate institutions sharing power" helped ensure that no one interest or faction could easily dominate the government. Through the exercise of presidential vetoes, Senate advice and consent, and judicial interpretations and other tools, each institution would have an opportunity to contend for influence.

- Dividing sovereign powers between the states and the federal government—a system later termed *federalism*—is also a defining characteristic of the government framework established by the new constitution. Rather than entrusting all powers to a centralized government and essentially reducing the states to mere geographical subdivisions of the nation, the convention delegates divided powers between two levels of government: the states and the federal government. The distinction drawn between local concerns—controlled by state governments—and national concerns—controlled by the federal government—was as confusing then as it is today. But the delegates determined that such a division was necessary if they hoped to achieve any consensus. It would be politically impossible to convince the states to become mere geographic subdivisions of a larger political whole.

- Although united by the belief that the national government needed to be strengthened, the framers of the new constitution were products of a revolutionary generation that had seen governmental power abused. Thus, they were committed to a government of limited or **enumerated powers**. The new constitution spelled out the powers of the new federal government in detail, and it was assumed that the government's authority did not extend beyond those powers. By rejecting a government of unlimited discretionary power, James Madison argued, individual rights, including those "inalienable rights" cited in the Declaration of Independence, would be protected from the arbitrary exercise of authority.

- Finally, some delegates believed that the new constitution should be a "living" document; that is, it should have some measure of flexibility in order to meet the changing demands placed on it over time. Perhaps the most frustrating aspect of the Articles of Confederation was the near impossibility of any sort of modification: because any change to the Articles required the unanimous consent of the states, even the most popular reform proposals stood little chance of being implemented. Thus, the Framers decided that the new constitution would go into effect when it had been ratified by 9 of the 13 states. Furthermore, once ratified, the constitution could be amended by a two-thirds vote of each house of Congress (subject to subsequent ratification by three-fourths of the state legislatures).

enumerated powers Express powers explicitly granted by the Constitution, such as the taxing power specifically granted to Congress.

2-4 | The Ratification Battle

Federalists versus Anti-Federalists

Once Congress submitted the new constitution to the states for approval, battle lines were formed between the **Federalists**, who supported ratification of the new document, and the **Anti-Federalists**, who opposed it. From the outset, the Federalists enjoyed a number of structural and tactical advantages in this conflict:

- **Nonunanimous consent.** The rules of ratification for the new constitution, requiring approval of just 9 of the 13 states, were meant to ease the process of adopting the new document. The delegates understood that once the constitution had been approved, it would be difficult for even the most stubborn of state holdouts to exist as an independent nation surrounded by this formidable new national entity, the United States of America.

- **Special "ratifying conventions."** The delegates realized that whatever form the new constitution might take, state legislatures would have the most to lose from

Federalists Those who supported ratification of the proposed constitution of the United States between 1787 and 1789.

Anti-Federalists Those who opposed ratification of the proposed constitution of the United States between 1787 and 1789.

an abandonment of the Articles. Thus they decided that the constitution would be sent for ratification not to state legislatures, but instead to special state ratifying conventions that would be more likely to approve it.

- **The rule of secrecy.** The Constitutional Convention's agreed-upon rule of secrecy, which forbade publication or discussion of the day-to-day proceedings of the convention, followed the precedent established in colonial assemblies and the First Continental Congress, where it was thought that members might speak more freely and openly if their remarks were not subject to daily scrutiny by the public at large. In the fall of 1787, the rule of secrecy also gave the Federalists on the inside a distinct advantage over outside opponents, who had little knowledge of the new document's provisions until publicized. Because the number of convention delegates who supported the new constitution far exceeded the number of delegates opposed, the rule of secrecy gave the Federalists a distinct advantage. As it turned out, five state ratifying conventions approved the new constitution within four months of the convention's formal conclusion, just as Anti-Federalist forces were collecting their strength for the battle ahead.

- **Conventions held in the winter limited rural participation.** Winter was approaching just as the fight over the new constitution was being launched. This timing gave the Federalists another advantage, especially in the critical ratification battlegrounds of Massachusetts, New Hampshire, and New York. It would be difficult for rural dwellers—mostly poor farmers resistant to a strong central government and thus opposed to the new constitution—to attend the ratification conventions if they were held in the dead of winter. Supporters of the new constitution successfully pressed for the ratifying conventions to be held as soon as possible. And of the six states that held such conventions over the winter, all voted to ratify by substantial margins.

The Federalist Papers

Between the fall of 1787 and the summer of 1788, the Federalists launched an aggressive media campaign that was unusually well organized for its time. James Madison, Alexander Hamilton, and John Jay wrote 77 essays explaining and defending the new constitution and urging its ratification. Signed under the name "Publius," the essays were printed in New York newspapers and magazines. These essays—along with eight others by the same men—were then collected, printed, and published in book form under the title *The Federalist*.[11] The essays allayed fears and extolled the benefits of the new constitution by emphasizing the inadequacy of the Articles of Confederation and the need for a strong government. Today these essays are considered classic works of political philosophy. The following are among the most frequently cited Federalist Papers:

Federalist Papers A series of articles authored by Alexander Hamilton, James Madison, and John Jay that argued in favor of ratifying the proposed constitution of the United States; the Federalist Papers outlined the philosophy and motivation of the document.

- **Federalist No. 10.** In Madison's first offering in the **Federalist Papers**, he analyzes the nature, causes, and effects *of factions*, by which he meant groups of people motivated by a common economic and/or political interest. Noting that such factions are both the product and price of liberty, Madison argued that by extending the sphere in which they can act, "you make it less probable that a majority of the whole will have a common motive to invade the rights of other citizens." Political theorists often cite Federalist No. 10 as justification for pluralist theory—the idea that competition among groups for power produces the best approximation of overall public good.
- **Federalist No. 15.** Hamilton launched his attack on the Articles of Confederation in this essay. Specifically, he pointed to the practical impossibility of engaging in concerted action when each of the 13 states retained virtual power to govern.

- **Federalist No. 46.** In this essay, Madison defended the system of federalism set up by the new constitution. He contended that the system allowed the states sufficient capacity to resist the "ambitious encroachments of the federal government."
- **Federalist No. 51.** In perhaps the most influential of the essays, Madison described how the new constitution would prevent the government from abusing its citizens. His argument is that the "multiplicity of interests" that influences so many different parts of the government would guarantee the security of individual rights. Because the federal system of government divides the government into so many parts (federal versus state; legislative versus executive versus judicial branches; and so on), "the rights of the individual, or of the minority, will be in little danger from interested combinations of the majority."
- **Federalist No. 69.** Hamilton in this essay defined the "real character of the executive," which, unlike the king of Great Britain, is accountable to the other branches of government and to the people.
- **Federalist No. 70.** In this essay, Hamilton presented his views on executive power, which had tempered considerably since the convention, when he advocated an executive for life. Still, Hamilton argued for a unitary, one-person executive to play a critical role as a check on the legislative process (that is, by exercising vetoes), as well as in the process of negotiating treaties and conducting war. According to Hamilton, "energy in the executive is a leading character in the definition of good government"; by contrast, "the species of security" sought for by those who advocate a plural executive is "unattainable."
- **Federalist No. 78.** In this essay—often cited in U.S. Supreme Court opinions— Hamilton argues that the judiciary would be the weakest of the three branches because it has "neither FORCE nor WILL, but merely judgment." Because the Court depends on the other branches to uphold that judgment, Hamilton called it "the least dangerous branch."

In late 1787 and early 1788, Anti-Federalists countered the Federalist Papers with a media campaign of their own.[12] In letters written under the pseudonyms "Brutus" and "The Federal Farmer" and published by newspapers throughout the colonies, the Anti-Federalists claimed that they were invoking a cause more consistent with that of the revolution—the cause of freedom from government tyranny. For them, the new national government's power to impose internal taxes on the states amounted to a revival of the British system of internal taxation. Perhaps the Anti-Federalists' most effective criticism was that the new constitution lacked a bill of rights that explicitly protected citizens' individual rights. They rejected Madison's contention in Federalist No. 51 that limitations on the central government provided those protections.

Ratification ultimately succeeded, but by a somewhat narrow margin (see Table 2-3). Of the first five states to ratify, four (Delaware, New Jersey, Georgia, and Connecticut) did so with little or no opposition, whereas Pennsylvania did so only after a bitter conflict at its ratifying convention. Massachusetts became the sixth state to ratify when proponents of the new constitution swung the convention narrowly in their favor only by promising to push for a bill of rights after ratification. By June, three more states (Maryland, South Carolina, and New Hampshire) had voted to ratify, providing the critical threshold of nine states required under the new constitution. Still, the Federalists worried that without ratification by the major states of New York and Virginia, the new union would not succeed.

Opposition in Virginia was formidable, with Patrick Henry leading the Anti-Federalist forces against James Madison and the Federalists.[13] Eventually Madison gained the upper hand with an assist from George Washington, whose eminent stature helped capture numerous votes for the Federalists. Madison also promised to support adding a bill of rights to the new constitution. Then, Alexander Hamilton and John Jay capitalized on the positive news from Virginia to secure victory at the New York ratifying convention.

TABLE 2-3 Ratifying the Constitution

State	Vote	Date of Ratification
Delaware	30–0	December 7, 1787
Pennsylvania	43–23	December 12, 1787
New Jersey	38–0	December 18, 1787
Georgia	25–0	January 2, 1788
Connecticut	128–40	January 9, 1788
Massachusetts	187–168	February 16, 1788
Maryland	63–11	April 26, 1788
South Carolina	149–73	May 23, 1788
New Hampshire	57–46	June 21, 1788
Virginia	89–79	June 25, 1788
New York	30–27	June 26, 1788
North Carolina*	194–77	November 21, 1789
Rhode Island	34–32	May 29, 1790

* Despite strong Federalist sentiment at the convention, North Carolina withheld its vote in 1788 until a draft bill of rights was formally introduced. The submission by Congress of 12 proposed amendments to the states on September 25, 1789, led North Carolina to hold a second ratifying convention the following November.

With more than the required nine states—including the crucial states of New York and Virginia—the Congress did not wait for the votes from North Carolina or Rhode Island; on July 2, 1788, it appointed a committee to prepare for the new government.

A Bill of Rights

Seven of the state constitutions created during the Revolutionary War featured a statement of individual rights in some form. The Virginia Declaration of Rights of 1776, for example, had borrowed (from John Locke) its grounding of individual rights in a conception of natural law and social contract: "All men are by nature equally free and independent, and have certain inherent rights, of which, when they enter into a state of society, they cannot, by any compact, deprive or divest their posterity." Later, during the battle over ratification, five state ratifying conventions had stressed the need for amendments to the proposed constitution in the form of a bill of rights, which would expressly protect fundamental rights against encroachment by the national government.[14]

Still, not all Federalists saw the need for a federal bill of rights. Madison, for one, believed a bill of rights was unnecessary because the central government held only those powers enumerated in the Constitution. He explained: "The rights in question are reserved by the manner in which the federal powers are granted . . . the limited powers of the federal government and the jealousy of the subordinate governments afford a security which has not existed in the case of the state governments, and exists in no other." Madison was also concerned about the dangers of trying to enumerate all important rights: "There is great reason to fear that a positive declaration of some of the most essential rights could not be obtained," leaving some essential rights omitted

The Continuing Call to the Federalist Papers

The Federalist Papers had a significant impact on the birth of the new nation. The essays argued persuasively that the Articles of Confederation were inadequate. Many scholars today attribute the narrow margin in favor of ratification of the new constitution at New York's ratification convention to the sophisticated media campaign waged by the Federalists, especially through the Federalist Papers.

Then

In 1905, the Supreme Court's controversial decision in *Lochner v. New York*, which invalidated a New York State health regulation restricting the hours that bakers could be exposed to flour dust, set off a furious political debate about the role government should play in a newly industrialized society. Advocates on both sides of the debate repeatedly cited the Federalist Papers to bolster their arguments. Those who supported government regulation argued that it was not the job of courts to disagree with the decisions of legislatures on such public-interest issues; even if factions and interest groups had produced such legislation, they cited Federalist No. 10 to claim that the corrupting spirit of "factions" distinguished democracy from true republics.

Opponents of government regulations countered that Madison's preference for more factions was simply his way of reaching toward an ideal politics in which all of these factions would cancel themselves out—by contrast, they argued that factions remained heavily influential in state legislatures. In support of the Court's ruling, they cited Federalist No. 78, in which Hamilton argued that "the independence of the judges may be an essential safeguard against the effects of occasional ill humors in the society." Only a sudden switch by the Supreme Court to stop interfering with industrial regulations in 1937 saved the nation from a constitutional crisis fueled in part by dramatically contrasting readings of the Federalist Papers.

Now

By 2012, same-sex marriage had become a reality in an increasing number of states. Up through March of that year, eight states in all had passed laws recognizing same-sex marriage; meanwhile, a handful of states were actively considering joining that list, including New Jersey, whose legislature passed a same-sex marriage recognition law in mid-February. Republican New Jersey Governor Chris Christie, who would eventually become a much-touted contender for the White House in 2016, had previously indicated he would veto that bill if given the chance. Christie followed through on that promise on February 17, 2012, but the debate over Christie's actions raged on as the governor defended his action on talk shows and before the public as a whole. Knowing that a direct vote of the population on same-sex marriage was likely to support his view, Christie called for voters to petition for a constitutional amendment that would change the definition of marriage. Critics charged that by asking for a popular vote and ignoring the vote of the people's

representatives, Christie ran up against the purpose of the U.S. Constitution as outlined by Federalist No. 51, in which Madison described the ideals of republican government over a democratic one as the most crucial "political safeguard against tyrannical majorities . . . if a majority be united by a common interest, the rights of the minority will be insecure." Christie's call for a popular vote clearly placed him on the side of democracy; the Federalist Papers offered Christie and others a reminder that many of the Constitution's founders never intended it to promote the interests of a majority over the minority. In October of 2013, a trial court invalidated the state's restriction of marriage to persons of different sexes, which effectively authorized the issuance of marriage licenses to same-sex couples in New Jersey. Two years later, the U.S. Supreme Court declared that same-sex marriage was a constitutionally protected right, effectively taking the New Jersey governor and all other state and local officials out of the debate altogether.

For Critical Thinking and Discussion

1. Are calls to the Federalist Papers still persuasive in the modern age?
2. Given that the Constitution has been amended 27 times since it was ratified, should excerpts from the Federalist Papers (written to defend the new constitution prior to those amendments being ratified) still carry the same degree of authority?

for the future. Hamilton underscored this sentiment in Federalist No. 84, arguing that such a list of rights might invite governmental attempts to exercise power over those rights not included in the list.

Among the most ardent supporters of adding a bill of rights to the Constitution was Thomas Jefferson, who warned about the dangers of abuses of power.[15] From his distant vantage point in France, where he continued to serve as an American minister, Jefferson was in the dark about the new constitution until November 1787. Then, in a December 20, 1787, letter to his friend and political protégé from Virginia, James Madison, Jefferson wrote: "A bill of rights is what the people are entitled to against every government on earth, general or particular, and what no just government should refuse, or rest on inference." Although recognizing Madison's fears of omissions as legitimate, Jefferson continued to argue the point. In a subsequent letter dated March 15, 1789, Jefferson argued that "half a loaf is better than no bread. If we cannot secure all our rights, let us secure what we can."

In the end Jefferson's arguments prevailed, and Madison (by this time a congressman from Virginia) became a principal sponsor of a bill of rights in the first Congress. Introducing the bill in the House of Representatives, he declared: "They will be an impenetrable bulwark against every assumption of power in the legislative or executive." On September 9, 1789, the House of Representatives voted to submit a list of 12 **amendments** to the states; 10 of these were ratified by the required nine states by December 15, 1791, and compose today's **Bill of Rights**.

Among the rights protected by the Bill of Rights are the rights of free religious exercise, free speech, free press, and assembly (First Amendment); rights against search and seizure without a warrant stating "probable cause" (Fourth Amendment); and rights of due process and no self-incrimination (Fifth Amendment). The two amendments not ratified in 1791 did not relate to individual rights at all. They were (1) a prohibition on salary increases for legislators taking effect prior to the next congressional election (in 1992—more than two hundred years later—this became the Twenty-seventh Amendment) and (2) a provision defining the rules for determining the number of members of the House of Representatives.

amendments Modifications or additions to the U.S. Constitution passed in accordance with the amendment procedures laid out in Article V.

Bill of Rights The first 10 amendments to the U.S. Constitution, which protect various rights of the people against the new federal government.

2-5 | Changing the Constitution

The Formal Amendment Process

Although political circumstances dictated that the Bill of Rights be passed in a relatively speedy fashion, future proposed amendments would not have it so easy. In crafting the rules for amending the new constitution, the Framers sought to balance two competing interests: (1) the need to protect the Constitution from short-lived or temporary passions by making amendments exceedingly difficult to pass and (2) sufficient flexibility to allow for amendments to be added when the needs of the nation demanded change. Their determination to strike such a balance was shaped by their experience in dealing with the Articles of Confederation, whose "unanimous consent of states" rule had left the document immune from even the most necessary of reforms.

As shown in Figure 2-3, Article V of the Constitution specifies two ways in which amendments can be proposed and two methods of ratification. Congress may propose an amendment by a two-thirds vote of both houses; alternatively, two-thirds of the state legislatures may apply to Congress to call a special national convention for proposing amendments. Amendments take effect when ratified either by a vote of three-fourths of the state legislatures or by special ratifying conventions held in three-fourths of the states. To date, all 27 amendments (including the Bill of Rights) have been proposed by Congress, and all but one (the Twenty-first Amendment) have been ratified by the state legislatures.

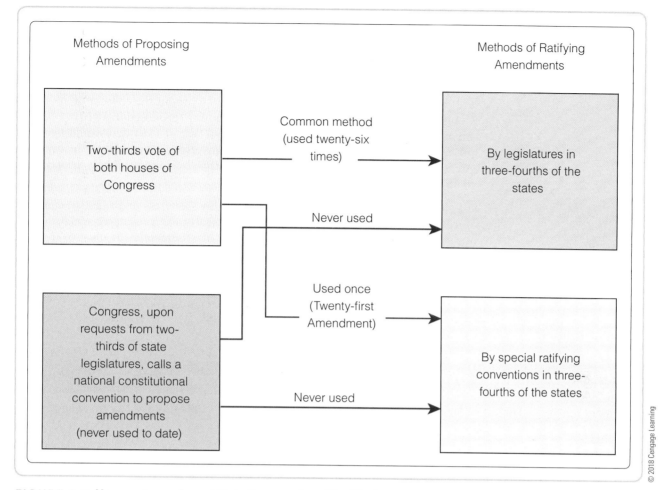

Methods of Proposing Amendments

Methods of Ratifying Amendments

Two-thirds vote of both houses of Congress

Common method (used twenty-six times)

By legislatures in three-fourths of the states

Never used

Used once (Twenty-first Amendment)

Congress, upon requests from two-thirds of state legislatures, calls a national constitutional convention to propose amendments (never used to date)

Never used

By special ratifying conventions in three-fourths of the states

© 2018 Cengage Learning

FIGURE 2-3 How an Amendment Gets Proposed and Ratified

No national convention has ever been called for the purpose of proposing amendments. Indeed, the closest the states have ever come to applying to Congress for such an event occurred in 1967, when 33 states (just one short of the required number) petitioned Congress to call a convention that would propose an amendment reversing the 1964 Supreme Court ruling requiring that both houses of each state legislature be apportioned according to population. Given the ambiguity of Article V, numerous questions have been raised about the form such a convention would take.

How would delegates be chosen? When Congress proposed the Twenty-first Amendment, it left it to each state to determine the manner in which delegates to the ratifying conventions would be chosen. How would the convention be run? Could a convention go beyond the limitations placed on it by Congress? What would happen if a convention went far afield and proposed an entirely new constitution, just as the convention in 1787 did? Congress has to date refused to pass laws dictating the terms of future conventions, in part because it has not wanted to encourage such an event.[16]

Critics of the amendment process charge that it is undemocratic, as today just 13 of the 50 states can block amendments desired by a large majority. Additionally, amendments, especially those ratified by special conventions, may be adopted even if they lack widespread popular support.

Although 27 amendments have been ratified since 1789, only 17 of those were ratified after 1791 (see Table 2-4 on next page). More than 5,000 amendments have been introduced in Congress since that time, but only 33 have been formally proposed by Congress. Today, different amendments sponsored by Congress garner varying levels of support. Among the proposed amendments that failed in the ratification process are the following:

- An amendment that would withdraw citizenship from any person who has accepted a title of nobility or who has received (without the consent of Congress) an office or salary from a foreign power (proposed in 1810)
- An amendment proposed on the eve of the Civil War in 1861 that would have prohibited further interference by the federal government with slavery in any state
- An amendment that would have prohibited labor by young children (proposed in 1924)

The Equal Rights Amendment (ERA) proposed by Congress in 1972 also came up short during the ratification process, after years of effort to secure its passage. Although the courts have consistently held that ratification of an amendment must take place within a "reasonable time," it has been left up to Congress to determine what constitutes a reasonable time. When drafting the proposed Eighteenth Amendment in 1917, Congress placed into the text of the amendment a seven-year limit on ratification and

TABLE 2-4 Amendments, Date of Ratification, and Length of Ratification Process

Amendment	Subject of Amendment	Date Proposed	Date Ratified	Length
Bill of Rights				
First	Free speech, press, religion, assembly	Sept 25, 1789	Dec 15, 1791	2+ years
Second	Right to bear arms			
Third	No quartering of troops in homes			
Fourth	No unreasonable searches/ seizures			
Fifth	Right to due process, grand jury, no double jeopardy, self-incrimination			
Sixth	Right to speedy and public trial, counsel			
Seventh	Right to trial by jury in civil cases			
Eighth	No excessive bail, fines, cruel/ unusual punishment			
Ninth	Rights not enumerated retained by people			
Tenth	Powers not delegated to Congress or prohibited to states belong to states or people			

© 2018 Cengage Learning

(Continued)

Amendment	Subject of Amendment	Date Proposed	Date Ratified	Length
Eleventh	No federal cases between state, citizen of other state	March 5, 1794	Jan 8, 1798	3+ years
Twelfth	Modification of electoral college rules	Dec 12, 1803	Sept 25, 1804	9+ months
Thirteenth	Ban on slavery	Feb 1, 1865	Dec 18, 1865	10+ months
Fourteenth	States can't deprive right to due process, equal protection, privileges and immunities	June 16, 1866	July 28, 1868	2+ years
Fifteenth	Right to vote can't be denied by race	Feb 27, 1869	March 30, 1870	1+ years
Sixteenth	Congress can levy individual income taxes	July 12, 1909	Feb 25, 1913	3+ years
Seventeenth	Direct election of senators	May 16, 1912	May 31, 1913	1+ years
Eighteenth	Prohibition of liquors	Dec 18, 1917	Jan 29, 1919	1+ years
Nineteenth	Women's right to vote	June 4, 1919	Aug 26, 1920	1+ years
Twentieth	Dates for inauguration, Congress's session	March 2, 1932	Feb 6, 1933	1+ months
Twenty-first	Repeal of prohibition	Feb 20, 1933	Dec 5, 1933	9+ months
Twenty-second	Presidential term limits	March 24, 1947	Feb 26, 1951	3+ years
Twenty-third	D.C. residents' vote for president	June 16, 1960	March 29, 1961	9+ months
Twenty-fourth	Ban on poll taxes	Aug 27, 1962	Jan 23, 1964	1+ years
Twenty-fifth	Appointment of new vice president, presidential incompetence	July 6, 1965	Feb 10, 1967	1+ years
Twenty-sixth	Eighteen-year-olds' right to vote	March 23, 1971	July 1, 1971	3+ months
Twenty-seventh	Congressional pay raises effective only after election	Sept 25, 1789	May 7, 1992	202+ years

Based on Paul Murphy, *Background of the Bill of Rights* (New York: Taylor & Francis, 1990)

continued to do so with subsequent amendments it proposed up until 1960. That year, when Congress proposed the Twenty-third Amendment giving residents of the District of Columbia the right to vote in presidential elections, it began the practice of setting time limits in the resolution accompanying submission of the amendment to Congress, rather than in the formal part of the amendment. As a consequence, when it appeared that the ERA would not be ratified, proponents of the amendment managed to get the ratification period extended to June 30, 1982 (an additional three years and three months beyond the original deadline), by a majority vote of both houses. Despite the

Alex Wong/Getty Images

U.S. Representative Carolyn Maloney (D-NY), surrounded by fellow legislators, speaks out in favor of the Equal Rights Amendment in 2011. Although the Amendment has been reintroduced in nearly every session of Congress since 1972, the closest it ever came to passage was in 1979, when it fell three states short of the 38 needed for ratification. Since then some state legislatures have actually rescinded their earlier ratification votes.

extension, however, the proposed amendment still failed to win the approval of more than 35 state legislatures.

The "reasonable time" requirement for ratification of an amendment reached an extreme with the Twenty-seventh Amendment (forbidding congressional pay raises from taking effect until an intervening election in the House of Representatives has occurred). Originally proposed in 1789 as part of the Bill of Rights, it was finally ratified in 1992, just over 202 years later. (See the "From Your Perspective" box on page 48 for more detailed discussion of what occurred.)

Informal Processes of Change

After the Constitution and Bill of Rights were ratified, there remained the difficult task of interpreting those documents for use by the different branches of government. Among the Framers, Alexander Hamilton was perhaps most attuned to the danger that Anti-Federalists and other opponents of the Constitution might attempt to overturn the convention's carefully crafted compromises so many years later by judicial fiat. Certainly most of the Constitution's provisions were vague enough that they allowed discretion for maneuvering by the generation that interprets them—but how much discretion was justified in the process of constitutional interpretation?

As it turned out, the Supreme Court under Chief Justice John Marshall was the first to put its own lasting imprint on the Constitution. Marshall, who hailed from Virginia, served as the chief justice of the United States[17] from 1801 until his death in 1835. Marshall believed in a **loose construction** (or interpretation) of the Constitution, meaning that under his leadership, many of the Constitution's provisions enjoyed broad and quite open-ended meanings. Thus, for example, Article I, Section 8, Clause 18 empowered Congress "to make all laws which shall be necessary and proper for carrying into execution" any of the powers specifically listed in the Constitution. Marshall's loose construction of that provision gave the federal government considerable implied powers (those not explicitly stated) to regulate the economy. For example, in the 1819 case of *McCulloch v. Maryland*,[18] the Marshall Court ruled that Congress had the power to create a national bank, even though the Constitution said nothing explicitly about such a power. The Court determined that a national bank was "necessary and proper" to assist in regulating commerce or raising armies. This philosophy of loose constitutional interpretation underlies the concept of a "living Constitution," one that is adaptable to changing times and conditions.

Thomas Jefferson, James Madison, and many others viewed the powers of the central government more narrowly. They favored a **strict construction**, arguing that the government possessed only those powers explicitly stated in the Constitution. Thus, although Article I, Section 8, Clause 3 gave Congress the power to regulate interstate commerce, it could not do so by creating a national bank or utilizing any other means not specifically mentioned in the Constitution. They supported a "fixed Constitution," one that could be changed only by the formal amendment process, not by congressional action or judicial ruling.

The tension between advocates of strict and loose constructions of the Constitution continues to this day. The late Robert Bork, a former Yale law professor and failed Supreme Court nominee, argued that overly loose interpretations of the Constitution are outside the Court's proper task. In particular, Bork wrote, the Supreme Court has "simply abandoned" the Constitution by refusing to enforce limits on the subjects

loose construction Constitutional interpretation that gives constitutional provisions broad and open-ended meanings.

strict construction Constitutional interpretation that limits the government to only those powers explicitly stated in the Constitution.

The Supreme Court and the Federalist Papers

Nixon v. General Services Administration (1977)

In *Nixon v. General Services Administration*, the U.S. Supreme Court considered whether the Presidential Recordings and Material Preservation Act—which entitled the public to view a president's confidential documents after he leaves office— was constitutional in the face of the ex-president's objections. Richard Nixon had filed the original lawsuit protecting his papers, claiming that the act violated the separation of powers by undermining his own executive privilege.

In authoring the court's 7–2 ruling against the former president, Justice William Brennan drew heavily on the Federalist Papers for guidance on the constitutional structure. Though these papers were published in New York newspapers to lobby in favor of ratification, they themselves provide no legal authority per se. Try telling that to Justice Brennan and his colleagues,

whose final judgment in this case was clearly influenced by their contents. Rejecting Nixon's argument that the separation of powers put up near absolute barriers between Congress and the president, the Court instead chose "the more pragmatic, flexible approach of [James] Madison in the Federalist Papers." Those who seek to determine the original intent of the Founding Fathers must now extend their inquiry to these well-known documents as well.

For Critical Thinking and Discussion

1. Do you think courts in resolving modern disputes should draw on originalist documents such as the Federalist Papers?
2. What are the dangers in using documents more than two centuries old?

---

that come within congressional reach.[19] Another strict constructionist, Justice Antonin Scalia, rejected the notion of constitutional standards evolving over time; in 2008 Scalia told one reporter that while change in a society can be reflected in legislation, "society doesn't change through a Constitution."[20] In accordance with this philosophy, the more conservative Supreme Court of the late 1990s (which included Scalia) struck down federal statutes regulating guns in the schools and domestic violence, on the theory that such regulations were not grounded in any specifically enumerated power of Congress, such as the power to regulate interstate commerce.

This strict-construction approach contrasts markedly with the approach advocated by Professors Lawrence Tribe[21] and John Hart Ely,[22] as well as former Supreme Court Justice William Brennan, who argued for a loose or more flexible interpretation of the Constitution. Advocates of a loose construction view the document as evolving with the times. In the 1960s and 1970s, the Supreme Court (with Brennan presiding) utilized a loose-construction approach to interpret congressional power more broadly to include the power to create civil rights legislation and federal criminal laws.

With so few amendments proposed and ratified during the nation's history, students of American politics may wonder how a Constitution written in 1787 has developed to meet the needs of a changing nation. In truth, an informal constitutional convention occurs on a frequent basis in the American political system. Congress, the president, and the courts engage in constitutional interpretation every day through their respective activities, both official and unofficial. Thus, the Constitution has not been a straitjacket at all—rather, its elegant vagueness has opened it up to a variety of interpretations.

Much of the rise in presidential power during the twentieth century occurred in the absence of any formal amendments conferring new powers on the chief executive; the president of the United States reacted to circumstances facing the executive office by assuming greater authority over foreign and domestic policymaking, and the other branches of government deferred to the president in many such matters. With its ruling in *Marbury v. Madison* (1803),[23] the Supreme Court asserted its right of judicial review; that is, its authority to review acts of Congress for their constitutionality and void those that the Court determines are contrary to the Constitution. As part of its decision in *McCulloch v. Maryland* (1819), the Court ruled that when state and federal powers collide, federal powers take precedence. With some notable exceptions, the

One Student's Term Paper Proves That the Constitution Is Indeed a "Living Document"?

College students may be forgiven for assuming that classroom assignments that invite them to propose constitutional amendments are strictly theoretical exercises. Yet in the case of one University of Texas student, such an assignment on constitutional change became much more than theoretical. Gregory Watson chose as the topic for his research a long-forgotten amendment to forbid congressional pay raises from taking effect until an intervening election in the House of Representatives had occurred. Originally proposed in 1789 as part of the Bill of Rights, the amendment was finally ratified 203 years later, thanks largely to Watson. The sophomore had discovered the amendment while doing research for a paper on American government. Watson's final paper—in which he argued that the amendment was still viable for ratification—garnered a mere "C" from his professor. But Watson continued his quest to secure ratification of the amendment. Tapping into the resentment of citizens over various instances in which members of Congress had quietly passed pay raises for themselves without calling attention to their actions, Watson joined forces with several state lawmakers to get the required number of states to ratify the provision. Their efforts succeeded, and the Twenty-seventh Amendment was eventually ratified in May 1992. Although Watson's grade from a decade earlier remained unchanged, he at least had the satisfaction of knowing that he had made history—literally.

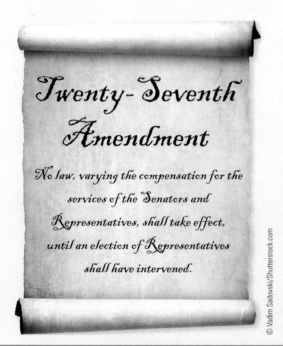

Twenty-Seventh Amendment

No law, varying the compensation for the services of the Senators and Representatives, shall take effect, until an election of Representatives shall have intervened.

© Vadim Sadovski/Shutterstock.com

For Critical Thinking and Discussion

1. What amendments to the Constitution would you like to see implemented?
2. Would you be willing to sacrifice your own time, energy, and resources to organize interest-group activities on an amendment's behalf?

other branches of the federal government and state courts have more or less acquiesced to such exercises of power.

When the states in 1791 ratified the Bill of Rights, citizens must have marveled at the flexibility of the new U.S. Constitution. After all, it had been amended 10 times in just two years! And yet the Constitution has proven remarkably resistant to change since then, incorporating only 17 additional amendments over the following two centuries. How has the federal Constitution survived so long, and in nearly the same form as the original document? The demands of modern government, which manages an advanced welfare state that serves the needs of hundreds of millions of Americans, press the Constitution into service even when traditional rules of constitutional interpretation would seem to offer an insurmountable obstacle. Advocates of the New Deal were undaunted by the strictures of the "non-delegation doctrine," and they stretched the Constitution's language to advance the modern welfare state; supporters of President Obama's individual health care mandate similarly pressed ahead, confident that more traditional constitutional principles would not stand in the way if the measures proved popular. The calculus is straightforward: The so-called higher law found in the Constitution must ultimately defer to the same public that vests it with that supreme authority in the first place.

The Right to Sexual Autonomy, Sexual Expression, and Diverse Notions of Sexuality

The U.S. Constitution as amended does not explicitly spell out all individual rights; accordingly, it is left to politicians, judges, and society as a whole to address these missing links. In particular, throughout our country's history we have been continually challenged with questions over our essential rights to sexual autonomy and privacy. This debate has only intensified in recent times as society's notions of sexuality and sexual expression evolved. Today individuals who favor these new understandings must sometimes go to court to ensure that they are fully realized.

Vin Testa, a gay rights activist, waves a flag in front of the U.S. Supreme Court building in Washington, D. C., in June 2013. The high Court dismissed an appeal request on California's Proposition 8, which allowed for same-sex marriage to be reinstated in the state.

In the landmark Supreme Court case of *Obergefell v. Hodges* (2015),[24] the high Court extended the fundamental right to marry to same-sex couples, even though no constitutional amendment was ratified on this subject. In his majority opinion, Supreme Court Justice Anthony Kennedy wrote that the Framers of the Constitution "did not presume to know the extent of freedom in all of its dimensions, and so they entrusted to future generations a charter protecting the right of all persons to enjoy liberty as we learn its meaning." Of course future challenges remain, as many reformers call for changes to the Constitution itself in hopes of cementing these gains into the law, as well as to force the actual language of the Constitution to reflect our nation's growing diversity on the nature of sexual autonomy, sexual expression, and sexuality more generally.

For Critical Thinking and Discussion

1. What rights of sexual autonomy, sexual expression, and sexuality more generally can be implied from the Constitution? Do these rights fall under the more general "right to privacy" or are they implied elsewhere?
2. What amendments to the Constitution are necessary to ensure our sexuality rights going forward? Would you prefer constitutional interpretation by judges that reflect evolving notions of sexuality over amendments as a method of reflecting these changes?

Summary

2-1 The Beginnings of a New Nation

- The American Revolution arose a decade after Britain's victory in the French and Indian War; to pay off its significant war debts, Britain imposed numerous regulatory measures on the colonies, which generated outrage, protests, and eventually armed resistance from the colonists.
- First established during the American revolutionary war, the Articles of Confederation created a "league of friendship" among the 13 states by vesting them with equal authority in a weak government with only limited powers to raise revenue and regulate commerce. The weakness of the Articles hampered early American foreign policy; its weak Congress proved unable to stamp out political unrest throughout the states.

2-2 The Constitutional Convention

- In 1787 a Constitutional Convention of delegates from 12 states considered both the "Virginia Plan," which favored larger, more populous states, and a "New Jersey Plan" based on the principle of equal representation of the states. The Convention ultimately accepted the "Connecticut Compromise" and its bicameral legislature featuring a House of Representatives apportioned by population and a Senate allotting equal power to each state. The delegates sidestepped the slavery issue by settling on the "Three-Fifths Compromise" (counting five slaves as three people for purposes of taxes and representation) and by deferring a ban on slave importation for at least 20 years.

2-3 The New Constitution

- The new constitution combined features of popular sovereignty, separation of powers, and checks and balances with a commitment to a system of "federalism," which divides sovereignty between state and federal governments.

2-4 The Ratification Battle

- The battle over ratification was waged between the Federalists, who supported the new constitution, and the Anti-Federalists, who opposed it. In advocating the merits of the document, Federalists benefitted from the convention's rule of secrecy and the rule requiring the approval of just 9 of 13 state ratifying conventions for ratifications.

- Additionally, Federalists employed a well-crafted media campaign in support of ratification; this included the anonymous publication of the Federalist Papers in newspapers justifying various provisions of the new constitution. Several state ratifying conventions insisted that the new government add a bill of rights to the Constitution; James Madison, the "father of the Constitution," was initially reluctant to propose such a bill for fear that it might omit important rights, but eventually he sponsored a new Bill of Rights in the first Congress.

2-5 Changing the Constitution

- Article V of the Constitution makes it exceedingly difficult to amend the document. Since the Bill of Rights was ratified in 1791, all but one of the 17 amendments that followed resulted from a two-step process: (1) two-thirds support of both houses of Congress, followed by (2) ratification by three-fourths of the state legislatures. (The Twenty-first Amendment was ratified by three-fourths of special state ratifying conventions). To date, a national constitutional convention (also authorized by Article V) has never been held.

- Informal constitutional change often occurs through U.S. Supreme Court interpretation of the document's text. The Supreme Court under Chief Justice John Marshall favored a loose construction of several provisions, giving the federal government considerable implied powers; Thomas Jefferson and Jeffersonian Republicans favored a stricter construction of the Constitution's provisions.

Key Terms

Test Yourself

1. The first law passed by Parliament for the purpose of raising money from the colonies for the British Crown was the
   a. Sugar Act.
   b. Stamp Act.
   c. Townsend Acts.
   d. Tea Act.

2. Which of the following political philosophers helped inspire ideas found in the Declaration of Independence?
   a. Voltaire
   b. Hobbes
   c. Descartes
   d. Locke

3. What were the main weaknesses of the Articles of Confederation?

4. The compromise plan at the Constitutional Convention that featured a Senate with states equally represented and a House whose members would be apportioned by popular vote was called which of the following?
   a. The New Jersey Plan
   b. The Connecticut Plan
   c. The Virginia Plan
   d. The Georgia Plan

5. Who was selected to be the presiding officer at the Constitutional Convention?
   a. George Washington
   b. Thomas Jefferson
   c. John Adams
   d. Alexander Hamilton

6. What was the "Three-Fifths Compromise," and why was it adopted at the Constitutional Convention?

7. The powers that are expressly granted to Congress in the Constitution are referred to as
   a. implied powers.
   b. enumerated powers.
   c. reserved powers.
   d. shared powers.

8. The sharing of powers between the national government and the state governments is based on a principle known as
   a. checks and balances.
   b. separation of powers.
   c. federalism.
   d. distributed authority.

9. Identify three "checks" that Congress has on the power of the president.

10. The fact that the proposed constitution would be debated by the states during the winter months gave an advantage to
    a. the Federalists.
    b. the Anti-Federalists.
    c. smaller states.
    d. none of the above.

11. In order for the proposed constitution to be adopted, how many of the 13 states had to ratify it?
    a. 7
    b. 9
    c. 11
    d. All 13

12. In order to guarantee that the proposed constitution would be adopted, Federalists promised that which of the following would be incorporated into the new constitution by the first Congress?
    a. The Declaration of Independence
    b. Federalist No. 10
    c. *Common Sense*
    d. A bill of rights

13. Why did the Anti-Federalists oppose the adoption of the new constitution?

14. Which of the following is *not* required for passage of a constitutional amendment?
    a. Two-thirds vote in both houses of Congress
    b. Approval by three-quarters of the state legislatures or ratifying conventions
    c. Presidential approval
    d. All of the above are required.

15. Would those who are concerned about limiting the power of the federal government favor a "loose" or "strict" construction of the Constitution? Why?

1.a. (LO 2-1); 2. d. (LO 2-1); 4. b. (LO 2-2); 5. a. (LO 2-2); 7. b. (LO 2-3); 8. c. (LO 2-3); 10. a. (LO 2-4); 11. b. (LO 2-4); 12. d. (LO 2-4); 14. c. (LO 2-5)

LEARNING OBJECTIVES

3-1 What Is Federalism?

- Define *federalism* and compare it to other forms of government, including confederations and unitary systems of government
- Explain how the Constitution differentiates between federal government powers, state government powers, and concurrent powers
- Describe the powers accorded to Congress under Article I
- Explain the significance of the supremacy clause, the preemption doctrine, and the full faith and credit clause of Article IV in distributing sovereignty

3-2 The History of American Federalism

- Define the five eras of American federalism and assess the role played by the Supreme Court in articulating state–federal relations during each era
- Evaluate different forms of federalism (layer-cake federalism versus marble-cake federalism) in the modern era

3-3 Why Federalism? Advantages and Disadvantages

- Identify the advantages and disadvantages of federalism in terms of fairness and accountability

3

Federalism

The term *federal* comes from the Latin *foedus*, which means a covenant, or an agreement linking different entities. A federal (or federated) system of government is one in which power is divided between a central authority and constituent political subunits. Both types of government are linked in order to provide for the pursuit of common ends; at the same time, each government maintains its own integrity. Federalism, the doctrine underlying such a system, generally requires the existence of a central government tier and at least one major subnational tier of governments (usually referred to as "states" or "provinces"). Each tier is then assigned its own significant government powers. What may sound simple in the abstract has proven quite difficult in practice. How exactly does a political system divide sovereignty between two thriving branches of government without creating animosities among the competing branches that may threaten to undermine the system in the first place?

3-1 | What Is Federalism?

federalism The doctrine underlying a system of government in which power is divided between a central government and constituent political subunits.

sovereignty The supreme political power of a government to regulate its affairs without outside interference.

Federalism is the doctrine underlying a political system in which power is divided between a central authority and constituent political subunits. For a system of federalism to maintain itself, it must sustain this division of powers by whatever means possible, including—but not limited to—a resort to the courts to define the proper bounds of authority. Perhaps the greatest challenge facing any federalist system is the task of determining **sovereignty**, defined as the supreme political power of a government to regulate its affairs without outside interference. In a system based on federalism, sovereignty resides not just in the central government, but also within each of the subunits, which in the case of the United States are the individual 50 states. Yet how can there be two separate sovereign governments sharing power over the exact same territory? The distribution of national and local responsibilities to more than one sovereign power depends on how the terms *national* and *local* are defined. These definitions are important, for a government based on federalism must both achieve national unity for certain overarching purposes and also preserve local governments' autonomy to respond to diverse subsets of citizens.

Related to these issues are complex questions concerning the nature of national citizenship. American federalism rests on the principle that two separate sovereigns—the state government and the federal government—both exert authority over the individual. But can an individual citizen really be subject to two separate sovereign governments at the same time? U.S. citizens have official status as citizens both of the state where they reside and of the nation as a whole. Many take pride in *both* associations. What remains

Hispanic immigrants take the oath to become U.S. citizens.

Jack Kurtz/The Image Works

unclear are the obligations and duties that dual citizenship requires. Is national citizenship every citizen's primary form of identification? To which sovereign government is the citizen obligated when the nation and individual states are in conflict? Although these conceptual difficulties tend to be unique to a federal system, there are other forms of government that involve multiple governments or tiers of government, and these alternative forms have significant problems of their own.

Comparing Federalism to Other Systems of Government

A federal system of government can be thought of as existing on a continuum of different forms of government. At one end of the continuum is a **confederation** (or "confederacy"), defined as a league of two or more independent states that unite to achieve certain specified common aims. Those aims may be quite limited, as is often the case with offensive or defensive military alliances. For example, the Articles of Confederation, which prescribed the rules of government for the newly independent colonies until 1788, featured 13 states entering into "a firm league of friendship with each other, for their common defense, the security of their liberties, and their mutual and general welfare." Recently the European Community, a collection of European nations united in a commercial alliance, has acquired its own status as a type of confederation.[1] Similarly, the United Nations is a league of countries from around the world that work together to enforce various provisions of international law. Although a confederation may be a useful arrangement to achieve some aims, it can result in political chaos, as when separate member countries bound only by limited rules strike out on their own at critical times, often to the detriment of the larger confederation.

> **confederation** A system of government (or "league") in which two or more independent states unite to achieve certain specified common aims.

At the other end of the continuum is a **unitary system of government**, which subordinates the independent aims of constituent states (if any even exist) to the goals of the central whole. Although individual states within such a government may enjoy some form of representation in the central legislature (such as through the election of state senators) and may even assert their own systems of municipal law, sovereignty rests in the central government alone, with states exerting authority over citizens only through the larger government entity. Of the Western industrialized nations, Great Britain and France perhaps come closest to this unitary government ideal, with their provinces and subunits having little or no power independent of the national government. Problems with a unitary system of government often arise from the tendency toward *hypercentralism*, that is, the more or less complete reliance on the central government and the extinguishing of individual state differences. Such a system often hampers local officials from responding to the particular needs of their varying constituencies.

> **unitary system of government** A system of government in which the constituent states are strictly subordinated to the goals of the central government as a whole.

As Figure 3-1 shows, a federal system of government sits in the middle of this continuum, granting its member states significant power but still subordinating them to the national government in critical instances. James Madison believed this federal system was the preferred "middle ground" of government types. At least 20 countries today, including Canada, Germany, Australia, and Switzerland, may be characterized as federal systems. It is the United States' brand of federalism, however—first established with the ratification of the Constitution in 1788—that represents the most significant breakthrough in the evolution of this government type among modern nation-states.

Government Powers in a Federal System

Under the U.S. Constitution, the national government of the United States was formed to serve a community of 13 states, and each state delegated to the new central government significant powers while retaining full powers within its own constitutionally designated sphere of authority. The Framers of this new government relied on no

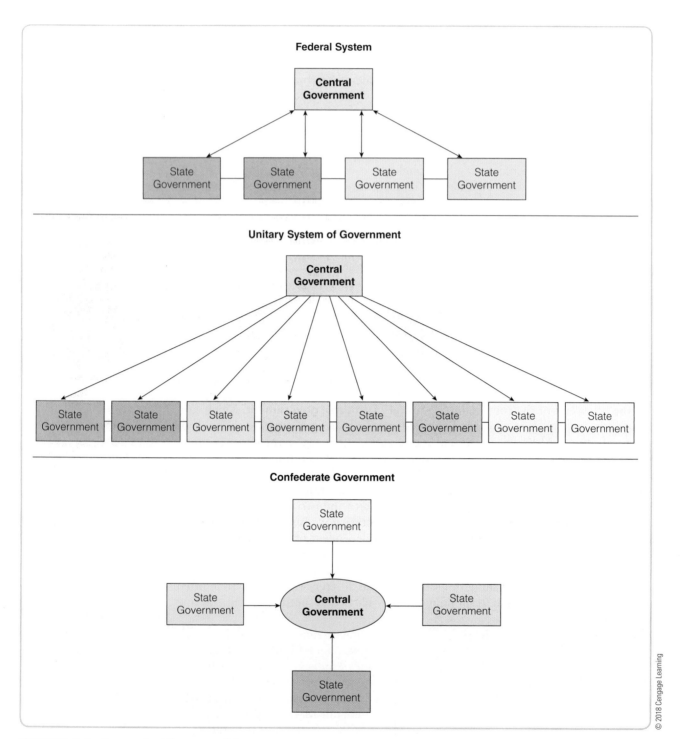

FIGURE 3-1 Comparing Systems of Government

These three figures illustrate the most common configurations for (1) federal systems of government, (2) unitary systems of government, and (3) confederate systems of government. The directions of the arrows indicate the relationship that exists between the different forms of government. Note the two-way arrows found in the federal system.

reserved powers Those powers expressly retained by the state governments under the Constitution.

overarching philosophy or political theory in designing this federalist form of government; federalism was simply a political compromise calculated to build consensus among them. The powers delegated to Congress under Article I of the Constitution are called enumerated powers. The powers retained by the states are **reserved powers**.

And the powers shared by the federal and state governments are generally referred to as **concurrent powers** (see Table 3-1).

Article I, Section 8 enumerates the specific powers held by the national government. Among these are economic powers such as the authority to levy and collect taxes, borrow money, coin money, and regulate interstate commerce and bankruptcies; military powers such as the authority to provide for the common defense, declare war, raise and support armies and navies, and regulate the militia; and legislative powers such as the authority to establish regulations governing immigration and naturalization. Congress also enjoys the prerogative to make laws that are "necessary and proper" to carry out these foregoing powers.[2]

On its face, the Constitution appears to draw clear and explicit lines between the powers afforded the state and national governments: the national government assumes responsibility for great matters of national importance, including the protection of national economic interests, relations with other countries, and the military security of the United States. All local and/or internal matters—including the health, safety, and welfare of citizens—were to be to the province of state governments. Indeed, in a delayed victory for states' rights advocates who had opposed the proposed constitution before its ratification, the Tenth Amendment restates this fundamental division of powers: that any specific power not assigned to the federal government by the Constitution may be exercised by the states, unless the Constitution prohibits the states from exercising that power.

concurrent powers Those powers shared by the federal and state governments under the Constitution.

TABLE 3-1 The Powers of the Federal and State Governments under the Constitution

Federal Government Powers (Enumerated Powers)	State Government Powers (Reserved Powers)	Concurrent Powers (Shared Powers)
Borrow money on U.S. credit	Regulate intrastate commerce	Spend money for general welfare
Regulate foreign commerce	Regulate state militias	Regulate interstate commerce
Regulate commerce with Indian nations	Conduct elections/qualify voters	Establish bankruptcy laws
Conduct foreign affairs	Regulate safety/health/morals	Lay and collect taxes
Coin money/punish counterfeiting	Ratify amendments	Charter/regulate banks
Establish courts inferior to Supreme Court		Establish courts
Establish post offices		Establish highways
Establish patent/copyright laws		Take private property for public purposes (with compensation)
Define/punish high-seas offenses		
Declare war		
Raise and support armies, navies		
Call forth militias		
Govern District of Columbia matters		
Admit new states to the Union		
Establish rules of naturalization		

necessary and proper clause The clause in Article I, Section 8 of the Constitution that affords Congress the power to make laws that serve as a means to achieving its expressly delegated powers.

supremacy clause The provision in Article VI, Clause 2 of the Constitution that provides that the Constitution and federal laws override any conflicting provisions in state constitutions or state laws.

Martin v. Hunter's Lessee **(1816)** The Supreme Court case that established that state governments and state courts must abide by the U.S. Supreme Court's interpretation of the federal Constitution.

preemption The constitutional doctrine that holds that when Congress acts affirmatively in the exercise of its own granted power, federal laws supersede all state laws on the matter.

full faith and credit clause The provision in Article IV, Section 1 of the Constitution that forces states to abide by the official acts and proceedings of all other states.

The Framers of the Constitution believed that Congress should legislate only within its enumerated powers under Article I; in their view, the **necessary and proper clause** (later referred to as the elastic clause) was *not* to be used as an instrument to expand federal legislative authority unnecessarily. Yet within a few years, competing views of the necessary and proper clause arose, giving the national government far more discretion in determining how to carry out its enumerated powers.

The Supremacy Clause

Overlaying this explicit system of enumerated powers for Congress and reserved powers for the states is the **supremacy clause** of Article VI, which provides that the Constitution and the laws passed by Congress shall be "the supreme law of the land," overriding any conflicting provisions in state constitutions or state laws. The supremacy clause gives special weight to the federal Constitution by ensuring that it cannot be interpreted differently from state to state. In the landmark case of *Martin v. Hunter's Lessee (1816)*,[3] the U.S. Supreme Court rejected the Virginia Supreme Court's attempt to interpret the federal Constitution in a way that conflicted with the U.S. Supreme Court's own rulings. Accordingly, each state legislature and state judiciary not only must abide by the terms of the federal Constitution, it must also abide by the interpretation of those terms laid out by the U.S. Supreme Court.

The language of the supremacy clause also gives rise to the doctrine of preemption. When Congress exercises power granted to it under Article I, the federal law it creates may supersede state laws, in effect "preempting" state authority. In practice, when a federal law clearly bars state action, the doctrine of **preemption** is relatively uncontroversial. For example, when the federal government acted to regulate the commercial advertising of tobacco products, it essentially "occupied the field," and all state rules governing tobacco advertising immediately gave way to the new federal standard. But when Congress enacts a law that does not clearly articulate its intentions with regard to state laws, a court may have to decide whether the doctrine of preemption applies, subject to later court review. In addition, Congress's lack of action within its enumerated powers opens the door to limited state regulations. For example, a state government can enact transportation regulations affecting truck drivers in the state so long as Congress has not passed any similar laws and the state law does not burden interstate commerce.

Gay marriage ceremony in Massachusetts.

Elise Amendola/AP Images

Relations between the States

A federalist system must not only manage relations between the state governments and the federal government, but also arbitrate disagreements among member states. A feature of American federalism in this regard is the requirement that individual states must respect the civil laws of all other states, as guaranteed by the **full faith and credit clause** of Article IV, Section 1 of the Constitution. This clause provides that each state must abide by the decisions of other state and local governments, including their judicial proceedings. This clause acts to assure stability in commercial and personal relations that extend beyond one state's borders. For example, contracts duly entered into in California under the laws of that state cannot simply be ignored or invalidated by the courts in Arizona or any other state. Similarly, when an unhappy married couple meets the legal requirements of divorce in one state and ends their marriage, they are not required to meet new divorce requirements in other states, as the divorce decree of one state must be recognized as valid by every other state.

Even though the full faith and credit clause has traditionally required states to respect the public proceedings of every other state, controversies over interstate recognition sometimes arise. Prior to the U.S. Supreme Court's decision in *Obergefell v. Hodges* (2015),[4] which established the right of same-sex marriage in all 50 states, many state legislatures attempted to prevent same-sex couples who married in one state from asserting their newfound status as married couples. At least 31 states at various times passed laws denying recognition to same-sex marriages before the Supreme Court stepped in to end the controversy, at least as a matter of constitutional law. The full faith and credit clause serves as a continued obstacle for states that refuse to recognize legal contracts or other actions duly taken in other states.

Another clause that provides for the equal treatment of out-of-state citizens is the privileges and immunities clause of Article IV. Through this clause, which guarantees that the citizens of each state are "entitled to all Privileges and Immunities of Citizens in the several States," the Constitution protects the rights of every citizen to travel through other states, to reside in any state, and to participate in trade, agriculture, and professional pursuits in any

The Diversity Dilemma

Federalism Debates over Immigration Policy

The enforcement of immigration laws across the country has sparked a fierce debate on the nature of federalism in our modern constitutional system. Immigration is predominately a federal issue, as Article I vests in Congress the power to "establish a uniform rule of Naturalization," and with it, the power to determine how citizenship is conferred. However, many states and localities have taken up the issue of citizenship on their own to address increasing rates of immigration in the country, which (they argue) has not been adequately addressed by Congress.

In fact, many of the nation's border states have at one time or another tried to enact immigration-related laws and resolutions. This immigration-related legislation touches on a multitude of related issues affecting citizens including the budget, education, employment, health, and public benefits. These policies vary drastically from state to state: some have passed severe restrictions on undocumented immigrants, denying them a host of government services. In recent years the most notable state immigration policies impose strict law enforcement over undocumented immigrants. For example, Arizona's controversial SB1070 legislation required police to determine the immigration status of individuals held for "reasonable suspicion" by demanding that they "show me your papers." These state policies eventually came under the scrutiny of the

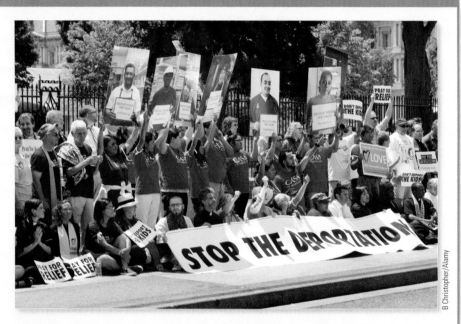

Inter-faith leaders and immigration reform activists gather in front of the White House in July 2014 to urge President Obama to stop deportations of immigrant families.

Supreme Court, which ruled that the law requiring officials to verify the immigration status of all people stopped or detained for any reason were preempted by federal law, and thus invalid.

For Critical Thinking and Discussion

1. Why do you think states have increased their efforts to enact immigration-related legislation, and do you expect that these efforts will increase over time? Why or why not?
2. How do statewide efforts to restrict immigration conflict with the federal government's constitutional authority over immigration?

state.[5] Some states have tried to limit memberships to in-state residents, or to impose hefty commuter taxes on out-of-staters who cross state lines each day for work. Such legislative efforts potentially conflict with the privileges and immunities clause. Article IV also provides that the criminal laws of individual states must be respected across state lines. When a criminal in one state escapes to another state, he or she is normally "extradited" or handed over to the original state either to stand trial or to complete a previously imposed sentence.

Article III, Section 2 of the Constitution gives the U.S. Supreme Court the authority to decide disputes between states. Although such jurisdiction is rarely exercised, the Court has taken its responsibility to arbitrate state conflicts seriously on those occasions when it has been asked to do so. For example, when officials in New York and New Jersey were battling in the late 1990s over which of those two states could claim sovereign authority over Ellis Island, the site where millions of immigrants to the United States were initially processed, the Supreme Court authorized a fact-finding investigation on the issue. Presented with the evidence of that investigation, the Court ruled that Ellis Island was within the state boundaries of New Jersey—news no doubt to the millions of immigrants who thought they had disembarked in New York.[6] The Framers of the Constitution believed it was critically important that the highest federal court enjoy the power to arbitrate disputes between state governments, a key component of American federalism.

3-2 | The History of American Federalism

In the more than two centuries that have passed since the ratification of the Constitution, different conceptions of federalism have prevailed during different eras. Some of these shifting patterns in state–federal relations were inevitable given the changing state of the nation and the increasingly important role it would play in world politics. The dominance of a global economy in the late-twentieth and early-twenty-first centuries, changing patterns in population growth, and technological developments in communication and transportation all spurred wholesale reexamination of the nature of federal and state governmental functions. Various government figures—presidents, Supreme Court justices, and members of Congress—have also played a role in shaping the nature of federalism. The flexibility of the federalist system has allowed it to adapt to changing circumstances.

Although a clear delineation of periods may oversimplify history, scholars have identified at least five eras of American federalism:

1. state-centered federalism, 1789–1819;
2. national supremacy period, 1819–1837;
3. dual federalism, 1837–1937;
4. cooperative federalism, 1937–1990; and
5. the "new federalism," 1990–present.

Each of these periods is defined by some shift in the power relationship between the national and state governments.

State-Centered Federalism, 1789–1819

The Framers' vision of federalism was relatively clear at the time the Constitution was ratified: other than in those policy areas expressly identified in Article I as subject to the national government's control (the military, foreign affairs, creation of currency, and so on), state governments would have full sovereignty over all matters involving the health, safety, and welfare of individuals. Indeed, it is tough to imagine the Constitution being ratified by the requisite number of states had it called for any further subordination of traditional state authority. And with some notable exceptions, the national government's reach was exceedingly limited during the first 30 years of the Constitution's history.[7]

At the urging of Treasury Secretary Alexander Hamilton, the Washington administration cautiously undertook some first steps in nationwide economic planning when it chartered the first National Bank of the United States and the federal government assumed all the debts of the state governments. Nevertheless, during this earliest period of federalism, states remained the principal authority for American citizens. For the most part, each state managed its own affairs, often with little interference from the federal government.

The Nebraska capitol, home to the nation's only unicameral state legislature.

National Supremacy Period, 1819–1837

Just before leaving office in 1801, President John Adams installed as chief justice of the Supreme Court a fellow nationalist, John Marshall of Virginia. That appointment may have been the most significant act of Adams's presidency; although the Federalists would never again occupy the White House or control Congress, the national-government-oriented party would influence American politics through Chief Justice Marshall for the next three decades.

Marshall's **national supremacy doctrine** of federalism is most evident in the Supreme Court decision in ***McCulloch v. Maryland* (1819)**,[8] which concerned the National Bank of the United States. As Secretary of the Treasury during the Washington administration, Alexander Hamilton successfully pushed for Congress to charter the first bank of the United States in 1792, arguing that such an institution would help provide for a sound national currency and a national system of credit. Thomas Jefferson, then Secretary of State, and James Madison opposed the bank, believing that the Constitution gave Congress no authority to charter such a bank. Consequently, when the bank's 20-year charter expired, the Jeffersonian Republican–controlled Congress declined to recharter it. Recognizing that the lack of a national bank had hindered American efforts to obtain needed financial resources throughout the War of 1812, many in the Democratic-Republican Party, including Madison, who was now president, swallowed their pride and supported the chartering of a second national bank in 1816.

Marshall's Court also refuted the power of state courts to interpret and apply the Constitution in ways that conflicted with the Supreme Court's own interpretations. Thus the Constitution assumed its status as the uniform governing law of all the states. To Marshall, the Court's duty was not to preserve state sovereignty, but rather "to protect national power against state encroachments." Consistent with this view, the Marshall Court routinely interpreted Congress's legislative authority quite broadly. In ***Gibbons v. Ogden* (1824)**,[9] for example, the Court invalidated a monopoly granted by the New York legislature covering the operation of steamboats in New York waters because the New York monopoly was in conflict with a federal license.

The national supremacy doctrine articulated by Marshall was not without its critics. State politicians accused the Court of ignoring the sovereign power of the states. Some national politicians were no less sympathetic. As president, Andrew Jackson opposed the National Bank and all internal improvements (such as the building of roads or canals) ordered by Congress as unconstitutional. He even vetoed a rechartering of the bank in 1832. Yet, at the same time, he also applied Marshall's national supremacy doctrine in defending the Tariff of 1828. After Congress passed a highly protectionist tariff over the objections of Southern free-trade adherents, the South Carolina legislature adopted a series of resolutions negating the tariff on the theory that state sovereignty allowed each state to nullify any law passed by Congress that the state deemed unconstitutional. (New Englanders had used that same argument during the War of 1812 when a convention of the region's states met in Hartford, Connecticut, in early 1815 and endorsed the right of states to interpose themselves against "dangerous

national supremacy doctrine Chief Justice John Marshall's interpretation of federalism as holding that states have extremely limited sovereign authority, whereas Congress is supreme within its own sphere of constitutional authority.

McCulloch v. Maryland (1819) The Supreme Court case that established that Congress enjoys broad and extensive authority to make all laws that are "necessary and proper" to carry out its constitutionally delegated powers.

Gibbons v. Ogden (1824) The Supreme Court case that held that under the Constitution, a federal license to operate steamboats overrides a state-granted monopoly of New York water rights.

Then & Now

Compelling the States to Fall in Line

Citizens of the United States are also citizens of one of the 50 states. Policies in the states are by no means uniform. Notwithstanding some of the uniform testing requirements imposed by federal No Child Left Behind legislation, educational policy differs widely from state to state. So too will an individual accused of a crime find one state's criminal justice system far more onerous and difficult than another's. The federal government (which includes federal courts) has occasionally stepped in to smooth out those differences, much to the chagrin of states that prefer to maintain their own unique identity on specific issues. Sometimes uniformity is favored as a matter of good policy; at other times it may be mandated by the Constitution itself. This delicate balancing act between state interests and the need to maintain states' unique political and cultural identities has never been easy to maintain.

Then

In 1963, uniformity in the treatment of criminal defendants was squarely at issue before the U.S. Supreme Court. By late 1962, close to half of the states were automatically providing indigent defendants a right to free counsel whenever jail time was a possibility. In fact, just prior to the landmark Supreme Court case of *Gideon v. Wainwright* (1963),[10] 22 of those states urged the Court to adopt this right as a federal standard. By contrast, many states (including Florida) provided such counsel only on a case-by-case basis—if an indigent defendant seemed competent enough to try his or her own case, judges usually insisted that he or she do so. Could such a patchwork of protections stand under the Sixth Amendment? "No," said the Supreme Court, which in *Gideon* effectively nationalized the requirement that counsel be provided to indigent defendants. Following the landmark decision, the second half of the 1960s witnessed the creation of public defender programs across the country.

Now

In 2010, the U.S. Supreme Court once again inserted itself into a social and cultural debate where individual feelings tended to run high. This time the issue was gun control. In 2008 the Court ruled that the Second Amendment protects an individual's right to possess a firearm for public use. Its ruling was limited, however, to federal restrictions on firearms (in that case it was a D.C. law); the Supreme Court did not address whether the Second Amendment applied to state laws as well under the process known as *incorporation*. (Incorporation is discussed in detail in Chapter 4.) Certainly the possession of firearms has different implications for residents of the South Bronx than it does for residents of rural farmland in Wyoming. Does the Fourteenth Amendment hold all governments accountable to the protections afforded by the Second Amendment? The Supreme Court's answer was "yes." On June 28, 2010, the Court held in *McDonald v. Chicago*[11] that the Second Amendment right to bear arms applies to all 50 states as well as the District of Columbia.

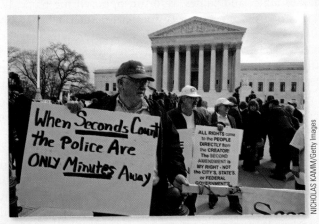

Pro-gun advocates march in front of the United States Supreme Court in 2008.

For Critical Thinking and Discussion

1. If the Bill of Rights was intended to provide certain fundamental rights for all citizens, shouldn't those rights be uniform from state to state?
2. Can you justify, for example, giving criminal defendants in one state less constitutional protection than defendants in another state? If so, on what basis?

infractions" of the Constitution by the federal government.) In response to the action by South Carolina, President Jackson declared that such a nullification was an "impractical absurdity" and rejected the right of individual states to refuse to obey federal laws. A call by South Carolina Senator John Calhoun and others for a "general convention of the states" to reconsider state–federal relations, including possible secession from the Union, elicited enthusiasm from numerous Southern states, but eventually the nullification crisis passed when Congress approved a compromise tariff that progressively lowered rates until they reached the same level they had been at in 1816.[12]

Although slavery was a crucial component of the fight between the Union and the Confederacy, the Civil War was at its core a struggle about the relationship between the states and the federal government. The Union's victory undermined dual federalism's "compact of states" premise by rejecting the authority of states to leave the compact. Then, in a series of cases handed down after the Civil War, a newly constituted Supreme Court acknowledged national power and congressional authority to set the terms for readmitting former Confederate states into the Union. This power was considered an outgrowth of Congress's exclusive and unquestioned authority not only to regulate the territories of the United States, but also to oversee the admission of new states to the Union. With 24 of the 50 states joining the Union between 1836 and 1912 (see Figure 3-2), admission to statehood was an important function of the federal government during this period.

Under **dual federalism**, however, the states did retain considerable authority to regulate economic affairs that were not directly within the "stream of commerce" between two or more states, including matters concerning the manufacturing of products and the health and safety of factory workers. Ignoring *McCulloch v. Maryland*, the Supreme Court refused to give Congress the discretionary authority it enjoyed during the era of the national supremacy doctrine. Regulatory legislation passed by Congress, such as child labor laws and many minimum wage laws, were set aside as unconstitutional. Once again the Court had greatly diminished the scope of the necessary and proper clause. Despite the onset of the Industrial Revolution, Congress was eventually rendered helpless to regulate the abuses of some businesses. Later, in the 1930s, the Court struck down a series of New Deal laws implementing pension and retirement systems for workers and regulating industrial relations.[13] In this way,

dual federalism The doctrine of federalism that holds that state authority acts as a significant limit on congressional power under the Constitution.

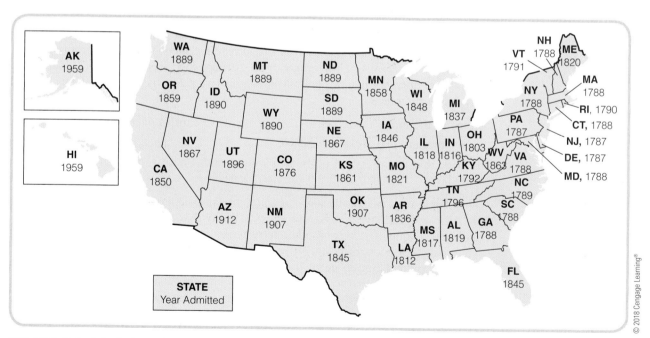

FIGURE 3-2 **Admission of States to the Union**

© 2018 Cengage Learning®

dual federalism prevented Congress from addressing the hardships brought on by the Great Depression.

Cooperative Federalism, 1937–1990

Faced with judicial opposition to New Deal policies regulating the workplace, retirement policies, and other subjects traditionally ceded to the states, President Franklin D. Roosevelt (FDR) and his supporters grew increasingly frustrated. To them, the economic hardships of the Great Depression demanded an activist federal government, and a conservative Supreme Court now stood in the way. FDR and his allies in Congress proposed slowly expanding the size of the Supreme Court from 9 to what would eventually become 15, which would allow Roosevelt to "pack" the Supreme Court with advocates of a broader vision of federal legislative power.[14] The proposed "court-packing plan" became unnecessary, however. As public frustration with the Court was mounting, one member of the Court in 1937 (Justice Owen Roberts) suddenly did an about-face, abandoning dual federalist principles in favor of a more expansive view of congressional authority. A shift in just one vote had a significant impact; a shift in two votes on the Supreme Court meant that nearly all federal legislation would now survive High Court scrutiny. Once Roosevelt was able to add his own judicial appointees to the mix, the Court as a whole was ready to support unprecedented exercises of congressional power.

Social scientists speak of the post–New Deal period as marking a shift from **layer-cake federalism**, in which the authority of state and federal governments is distinct and more easily delineated, to a system of **marble-cake federalism**, in which state and federal authority are intertwined in an inseparable mixture. This new era, later labeled as the period of **cooperative federalism**, in some ways harkened back to the national supremacy doctrine articulated by John Marshall. Congress once again became the judge of its own powers, including those powers implied under the necessary and proper clause. Congress could, for example, restrict the activities of labor unions, criminalize loan sharking, or enact any policy under the theory that it may be "necessary and proper" to exercise enumerated powers such as the power to regulate interstate commerce. The limits on congressional power under so-called cooperative federalism were thus quite small: so long as some link to commerce could be offered, for example, no matter how tenuous such a link might be, Congress remained free to exert its authority over the states. When Congress passed civil rights laws in 1964 under the premise that racial discrimination in restaurants and hotels "burdened" interstate commerce, the Supreme Court barely batted an eye at what was in fact an extremely broad reading of congressional authority.[15]

Cooperative federalism, however, can be distinguished from Marshall's doctrine of national superiority. Whenever concurrent legislative power is exercised, Congress can act in one of three ways:

1. Preempt the states altogether and assert exclusive control over the subject matter.

2. Leave the states to act on their own.

3. Provide that the operation of its own law depends on or is qualified by existing state laws.

This last category provides an opening in state–federal relationships that even Marshall could not have anticipated: the possibility that the federal government might actually enlist state officials and other state actors to implement federal policies.

The positive aspects of cooperative federalism are obvious. The expansion of the central government beginning in the 1930s into the $6.3-trillion-per-year behemoth that it is today means that federal officials now have huge sums of money at their disposal, as shown in Figure 3-3. Individual states can benefit from this pool of funds whenever the federal government passes on some of its revenues directly to the states to initiate and administer programs. **Grants-in-aid** from the federal government to the states have been used to fund state educational initiatives, build roads, and provide

layer-cake federalism Description of federalism as maintaining that the authority of state and federal governments exists in distinct and separate spheres.

marble-cake federalism Description of federalism as intertwining state and federal authority in an inseparable mixture.

cooperative federalism The doctrine of federalism that affords Congress nearly unlimited authority to exercise its powers through means that often coerce states into administering and/or enforcing federal policies.

grants-in-aid Grants from the federal government to states that allow state governments to pursue specific federal policies, such as highway construction.

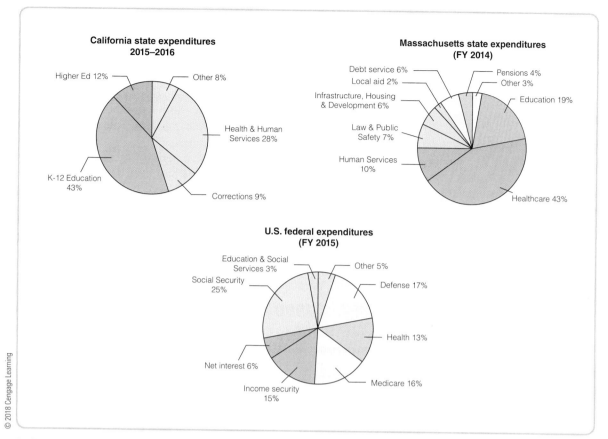

FIGURE 3-3 Comparing Federal Expenditures to State Expenditures

The system of federalism dictates that the federal government, not the states, must provide national defense. By contrast, state expenditures focus on educational expenses, criminal justice, and social services in particular. Although different systems of categorization make budget comparisons among governments difficult, a glimpse of the budgets of the federal government and two state governments provides some interesting insights as to where your tax dollars are going . . . or not going.

Source: ebudget.ca.gov (FY 2015-16); Massachusetts Budget and Policy Center (www.massbudget.org) (FY 2014); and U.S. Office of Management and Budget (FY 2015).

unemployment relief, among other programs that fulfill purposes expressly approved by Congress and/or its federal regulatory agencies. Federal grants also help balance the economic inequities that arise because states have vastly different tax bases. Occasionally the federal government has transformed grants-in-aid, which are allocated only for specific programs or policies, into **block grants**, which state or local governments may use at their discretion for more generalized programs.

The collaboration between state governments and the federal government in the era of cooperative federalism also carried some negative implications for state sovereignty. Federal government officials increasingly insisted that federal appropriations to the states be accompanied by various conditions. Often these consisted of "protective conditions," designed to ensure that the state would administer its program consistent with the objectives of Congress. For example, Congress required that states receiving educational assistance meet federal requirements for educating handicapped children, including the creation of individualized education programs for students with special needs. On occasion, however, Congress has imposed coercive burdens on states that increasingly rely on such federal assistance. In 1984, for example, Congress passed the National Minimum Drinking Age Amendment, which withheld 5 percent of federal highway funds from any state "in which the purchase or public possession of any alcoholic beverage by a person who is less than 21 years of age" is lawful. The purpose of the law was to decrease the number of

block grants Grants from the federal government to the states that may be used at the discretion of states to pursue more generalized aims.

serious automobile accidents among those aged 18 to 20—statistics showed that this group was responsible for a high percentage of accidents on the nation's highways.

Although the conditions imposed by the National Minimum Drinking Age Act essentially coerced state governments to pass laws at the behest of the federal government, the Supreme Court generally approved of such tactics in **South Dakota v. Dole** (1987).[16] Yet when Ronald Reagan was elected president in 1980, he openly trumpeted federal initiatives to return policymaking authority to the states. In his first State of the Union Address in early 1981, Reagan proposed to terminate the federal role in welfare and return to the states 43 other major federal grant programs.

The voluntary transfer of power by the central government to state or local governments is known as "devolution."[17] If Reagan's proposals had been fully implemented, such a large-scale devolution of federal programs would have returned federal–state relations to the version of federalism that existed before the New Deal. As it turned out, however, strong resistance from the Democratic-controlled House led to the defeat of many of Reagan's devolution initiatives. Nonetheless, Reagan administration rhetoric emphasizing federal deregulation and increased state responsibilities set the stage for more sweeping reforms to be implemented in the years ahead.

The "New Federalism," 1990–Present

Scholars assessing the state of federalism since 1990 have failed to reach a consensus on the proper label for characterizing what appears to be a counterthrust favoring states' rights in certain areas. This new era of federal–state relations has been marked by a resuscitation of state authority, helped by a Supreme Court that, since the early 1990s, has been far more attentive to protecting states' rights. The changed composition of the Court accounts for this shift. Between 1991 and 2005, four Reagan appointees to the Court (Chief Justice Rehnquist and Associate Justices Antonin Scalia, Sandra Day O'Connor, and Anthony Kennedy) and one of George H. W. Bush's appointees (Associate Justice Clarence Thomas) generally favored states' rights in federalism disputes.[18] (The death of Justice Scalia in early 2016 offered those who opposed the "new federalism" their first real opportunity to reverse that trend with the appointment of a new justice). The modern Court's decisions on federalism fit into a number of different categories.

Second, since the mid-1990s, Congress's virtually unlimited authority to regulate interstate commerce has been scaled back somewhat. In *United States v. Lopez* (1995), the Supreme Court declared that Congress could not ban guns in school zones.[19] Whereas during the cooperative federalism era Congress regulated all manner of criminal and social activities, the present-day Supreme Court has more strenuously insisted that Congress must show a clear connection with commerce when exercising its power to regulate interstate commerce, for example. Then, in 1997, Congress ran into more obstacles when it enacted a law entitling sexual assault victims to sue their perpetrators in federal court. Once again, the Supreme Court stood firm for state sovereignty, ruling in *United States v. Morrison* (2000) that the law was unconstitutional, on the grounds that domestic abuse had only a slight connection to commerce.[20] Even when the High Court upheld the controversial individual mandate provisions of Obamacare in *NFIB v. Sebelius* (2012), it did so while offering a key concession to states' rights enthusiasts: that while the mandate to purchase insurance may have survived scrutiny as a valid exercise of Congress's power to tax, such a penalty on inactivity was *not* a proper use of Congress's commerce clause powers.[21] In that sense, the Court's decision in the case continued down the path set out by *Lopez* and *Morrison*.

Meanwhile a Supreme Court increasingly intent on protecting states' rights has given new teeth to the Eleventh Amendment, which bars citizens of one state from bringing suit against another state in federal court. As a result of Court decisions, many plaintiffs are now restricted from bringing lawsuits in federal court against public employers; instead, plaintiffs must bring suit in state courts.[22]

South Dakota v. Dole (1987) The Supreme Court case that allowed Congress to coerce state governments to pass state laws by conditioning grants to those states, so long as the requirements are related to the overall spending in question.

Of course, Supreme Court decisions are not solely responsible for the resurrection of state sovereignty that has occurred over the past decade and a half. Political developments have also altered the character of American federalism in important ways. Many of President Reagan's federalism initiatives met with limited success in a Democratic-controlled House of Representatives. For example, his own Republican Party's platform in the 1980s called for the abolition of the Department of Education; yet that controversial proposal proved a nonstarter in the Congress. Still, his administration managed to push through deregulation initiatives in a number of partially preempted programs, and it relaxed federal oversight of state performance to a considerable degree. In addition, six years after Reagan left office, Republicans took control of both the House and the Senate for the first time since the early 1950s. In 1994, Newt Gingrich (R-GA), then House Minority Whip, and 366 other Republican candidates for Congress rallied around the "Contract with America," a series of initiatives they promised to introduce in the first 100 days of the 104th Congress. (Republicans would maintain control of at least one and usually both houses of Congress for more than a decade, up until the Democratic sweep of both houses in 2006.)

In the end, that Congress passed few revolutionary new laws. A standoff between President Bill Clinton, who refused to sign the budget resolutions, and Congress, which threatened to close down the government unless the president gave way, led to government shutdowns in November 1995 and January 1996; eventually, on April 26, 1996, Clinton signed a budget bill that cut federal domestic discretionary spending for the first time in three decades. Yet the bill did not achieve anything close to the revolution that the leaders of the 104th Congress had hoped for. Devolution of programs to the states has instead evolved far more gradually, through legislation like the Personal Responsibility and Work Opportunity Reconciliation Act of 1996, which capped federal block grants to states for welfare aid. States have been encouraged by the law to create their own cost-efficient welfare benefits programs. But the states' rights movement stopped significantly short of the vaunted "devolution revolution" promised by Republican House leaders when they first took control in 1995.

In the wake of the terrorist attacks that occurred on September 11, 2001, Americans rallied around the flag, offering their support for a strong and emboldened federal government, as seen in Figure 3-4. But in the decade and a half since then, support for the federal government has dropped sharply, falling even below pre-9/11 levels. For better or worse, public frustration with the immense size and power of the federal government is a modern reality, and politicians in Washington, D.C., must account for this sentiment when they introduce new programs.

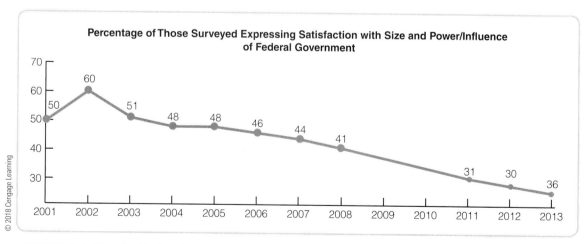

© 2018 Cengage Learning

FIGURE 3-4 Has the Federal Government Gotten Too Big?

Source: Gallup poll, January 17, 2013. www.gallup.com/poll/159875/americans-similarly-dissatisfied-corporations-gov.aspx

The fence separating Texas from Mexico does not run continuously, creating considerable challenges for customs and border officials charged with controlling the borders.

3-3 | Why Federalism? Advantages and Disadvantages

Supporters of federalism point to several advantages offered by this form of government, and opponents of federalism counter with arguments of their own concerning the disadvantages of this form of government.

Advantages of Federalism

Supporters of federalism cite among the specific advantages of this form of government that it is more likely to accommodate the needs of a diverse citizenry, to strengthen liberty by dividing powers between levels of government, to encourage experimentation, and to respond to change.

Accommodation of diversity. If a unitary system of government threatens to treat citizens of different states as interchangeable parts for purposes of quick and easy administration, federalism acts as an important counterbalance to this trend. A citizen of the United States can also take pride in being a citizen of Texas or some other state with a clearly defined culture or character. State and local politicians can perhaps respond to the specific demands or needs of their citizens better than a central government can. The culture of a state may be reflected in that state's handgun control laws, its rules on the distribution of alcohol, or its laws concerning abortion, prostitution, the use of land, and many other issues that tend to receive differing levels of support across America.

Strengthening of liberty through the division of powers. In Federalist No. 51, James Madison argued that "in the compound republic of America" the power surrendered by the people is divided between two distinct governments. This division provides security against a concentration of power in a single, unitary government. Madison also considered the division agreement between these two separate governments to last for long—in the unlikely event that one entire government turns corrupt, the other government would still be available to check that government's abuses. Thus, the existence of two distinct levels of government, combined with the separation of executive, legislative, and judicial powers within each of those governments, offers individuals considerable protection. Accordingly, Madison argued that "a double security arises to the rights of the people."

Encouragement of laboratories of democracy. In 1932, Supreme Court Justice Louis Brandeis made famous a metaphor for creative federalism when he wrote that "a single courageous state may, if its citizens choose, serve as a laboratory, and try social and economic experiments without risk to the rest of the country."[23] This notion of states serving as "laboratories of democracy" is encouraged by a federalist system that gives the states authority to craft policies at the outset, while at the same time affording the central government authority to implement policies that prove successful throughout the nation. During the 1930s, FDR borrowed from the experience of various states in crafting many New Deal policies. In 1993, the Brady Bill passed by Congress drew heavily on successful state gun-control provisions that established waiting periods for handgun purchases. The flip side of such successes is also significant: state policies that proved to be failures discourage broad-based applications by the federal government. For example, given that California's deregulation of utilities helped bring about an energy crisis in that state in early 2001, it seems unlikely that other states or the federal government will seek similar forms of deregulation anytime soon.

Disadvantages of Federalism

Opponents of federalism present arguments of their own concerning the disadvantages of this form of government. Chief among their objections to a federalist system are the unfairness caused by economic disparities among the states, questions about government accountability for many public programs that are inherent with competing sovereigns, and the system's heavy reliance on the courts to define the nature of federalism.

The Supreme Court and Federalism

Gonzales v. Raich (2005)

In 1996 California voters passed Proposition 215, making it the 14th state to legalize the use of marijuana for medicinal purposes. Of course those laws stand in conflict with federal statutes criminalizing all forms of marijuana use, as Angel Raich learned in 2002 when she was arrested under the Federal Controlled Substances Act for using homegrown marijuana. Raich's doctors claimed that without the marijuana her life would be threatened by excruciating pain. So which law applies under those circumstances? In *Gonzales v. Raich*, the Supreme Court held that Congress does indeed have the power to control or ban marijuana for medical and nonmedical uses.[24] Subsequently, the federal government essentially determines the state of the law

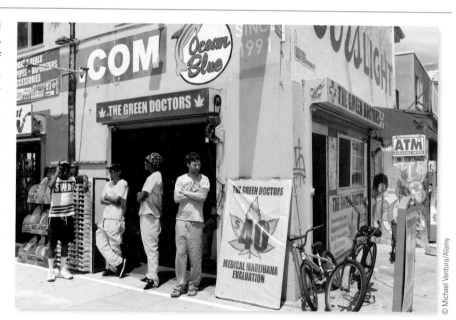

A medical marijuana store on the Ocean Walk in Venice Beach, California.

by its own patterns of enforcement. Between 2006 and 2009 the federal government used criminal raids and other means to thwart California's marijuana users, including those using it for medicinal purposes. The Obama administration, however, consistently adhered to an enforcement policy that countenanced medical marijuana distribution/use in California and elsewhere. Thus, while the federal government enjoys superiority in the world of drug enforcement, federal policy is not tone-deaf to the reality that the use of marijuana for medical purposes enjoys increasing levels of support from the public.

For Critical Thinking and Discussion

1. Should the federal government enforce unpopular drug laws in the face of reluctant state governments?
2. Do competing governments in this context offer more effective checks and balances, or do they simply create a source of confusion for citizens?

Fiscal disparities among the states. States differ markedly in the wealth of their citizens, and thus in the taxable resources available to them for programs. According to the U.S. Census Bureau, Maryland's citizens in 2014 boasted a median household income of $76,165, more than two times higher than that enjoyed by Mississippi households ($35,521).[25] Because of these fiscal differences, the amount that states have available to spend on governmental programs varies widely. Furthermore, when the central government defers to state entities in the governing process, such as when it requires states to fund their own welfare programs, wide fiscal inequalities among states (and localities) may mean disparate—and inequitable—programs for citizens in different states. Advocates of social equity and justice routinely complain about this consequence of federalism. Although federal financing of state developmental projects or other state programs relieves some of these inequities, the current trend toward reducing state dependency on the federal government promises more, not less, equity in the distribution of government benefits across states.

Lack of accountability. Numerous government programs fall under the exclusive authority of neither the state governments nor the federal government; both may act, either may act, or, in some cases, neither may act. At least in the abstract, federalism creates the prospect of multiple levels of government vying for the opportunity to address economic or social problems. In practice, however, the federal and state governments often play a game of "chicken," each hoping the other will act first and assume greater economic responsibility, and perhaps accountability for failures. In an era when public frustration with rising taxes discourages government spending, this "blame game" may go on for years, with both sides accusing the other of shirking its responsibilities to the public. During the 1990s, for example, many state governments eliminated benefits for the needy and imposed stricter requirements on those seeking welfare. State legislatures facing growing budget deficits hoped to "push" the poverty problem onto other states by passing laws that encouraged poor people to move to states with more liberal benefits programs. During this same period Congress passed welfare legislation in 1996 that transferred welfare responsibilities back to states. Critics charge that this arrangement of shared accountability quickly transforms into a lack of accountability, with neither government accepting responsibility for dealing with problems.

Contentious issues often begin as debates over the substance of legislation: Should fugitive slaves who escape to freedom be returned to their masters? Should immigration enforcement extend to local police officers stopping individuals and demanding that they produce evidence of citizenship? Yet when significant questions about resources and enforcement inevitably arise, those issues quickly transform into even larger questions of jurisdiction and sovereignty: Can the federal government order states to accept Medicaid expansion funds? If it cannot, are states entitled to the money when they offer alternatives better suited to their own needs, but that accomplish federal goals? States tend to respond to federal programs and the mandates that flow from those programs based on political factors as well: Do the citizens of the state want to be part of the federal program? Are they willing to pay more taxes to fund their own programs? Sweeping federal programs ensure a measure of uniformity from state to state; sometimes uniformity also helps to avoid confusion and prevent abuse; at other times, however, variations among the states allow for valuable policy experimentation as well as the protection of local concerns and interests. Dividing sovereignty is never easy: As long as federal and state governments keep the public interest in mind, the debate over applications of federalism should continue to serve as a mostly healthy (if a bit uncomfortable) form of political dialogue.

From Your Perspective

The Real-Life Benefits of Attending College Close to Home

Many high school seniors dream of attending colleges or universities in distant and exotic locations, far from the watchful eyes of parents or guardians who may be footing the bill. Did you ever dream of attending the University of Hawaii, or perhaps the Florida Keys Community College?

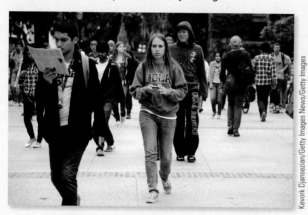

UCLA students walking to class on the school's Westwood campus. In recent years, state universities such as UCLA have increased the number of admissions offers extended to nonresidents as a means of generating more revenue.

Kevork Djansezian/Getty Images News/Getty Images

While admission standards to such schools may or may not pose an obstacle, the bigger issue may be financial. State legislatures try to attract in-state students by offering lower-cost in-state tuition: They know that those students will often stay in the state after graduation and secure good jobs, contributing to the state's economy. For example, if you live in Wisconsin and you want to go to the University of Rhode Island, your college tuition in 2015 would have cost you $28,852. But if you were from Rhode Island, it would only cost you $12,862. UCLA offers perhaps the biggest home-state discount in the country: $37,959 in tuition per year for out-of-staters, as compared to just $13,251 for California residents.

For Critical Thinking and Discussion

1. Did you consider attending (or are you currently attending) a school far from your own home state?
2. As a high school senior, were you aware of the significant disparities in tuition charged by some public universities to students from other states?
3. Should states be allowed to financially discriminate against out-of-state applicants? Why or why not?

Summary

3-1 What Is Federalism?

- Federalism links the central government of the United States to all 50 state governments. Sovereignty resides concurrently in both the central government and state governments, as distinguished from confederations (simple alliances of powerful independent states) or unitary systems of government (in which the subunits are subordinate to the central government).

- The Framers of the Constitution assigned to the federal government matters of great national importance (including foreign and military affairs) and assigned to the states all local and internal matters, including those relating to the health, safety, and welfare of citizens. Concurrent (or "shared") powers include taxation, banking and bankruptcy regulations, spending for highways, and other forms of general welfare.

- In addition to managing foreign and military affairs, Article I also vests Congress with the power to borrow money on U.S. credit, coin money, establish post offices, admit new states, and establish rules of naturalization, among other authorities.

- The supremacy clause of Article VI provides that the Constitution and all federal laws override (or "preempt") conflicting provisions in state constitutions or state laws. The full faith and credit clause of Article IV requires that states respect each other's acts and official proceedings.

3-2 The History of American Federalism

- Beginning in 1819, the Supreme Court under Chief Justice John Marshall substituted the Framers' vision of state-centered federalism with a national supremacy doctrine that deferred to Congress as the supreme authority within the sphere of its own constitutional powers. Beginning in 1837 a system of "dual federalism," in which state authority served as a severe limit on congressional power, reigned for nearly a century. The Great Depression ushered in an era of "cooperative federalism" (1937–1990), which allowed Congress nearly free reign. During the current period of "new federalism" (1990–present), state sovereignty has once again been resuscitated to resist certain forms of congressional coercion.

- In the modern era, relatively clear divisions between state and federal authority (i.e., "layer-cake federalism") have given way to an intertwining of federal and state authority (i.e., "marble-cake federalism"). Through grants-in-aid and block grants, the national government has placed huge sums of federal money at the disposal of states, while still imposing conditions on states and state officials to help administer federal laws.

3-3 Why Federalism? Advantages and Disadvantages

- Supporters of federalism argue that it accommodates diversity, strengthens liberty, and encourages states to serve as "laboratories of democracy." Opponents of federalism object to the unfairness caused by economic disparities among the states. They also complain about the lack of government accountability for programs managed by competing sovereign powers, as well as the system's heavy reliance on the judiciary to define the nature of federalism and enforce its perimeters.

Key Terms

block grants (p. 65)
concurrent powers (p. 57)
confederation (p. 55)
cooperative federalism (p. 64)
dual federalism (p. 63)
federalism (p. 54)
full faith and credit clause (p. 58)

Gibbons v. Ogden (1824) (p. 61)
grants-in-aid (p. 64)
layer-cake federalism (p. 64)
marble-cake federalism (p. 64)
Martin v. Hunter's Lessee (1816) (p. 58)
McCulloch v. Maryland (1819) (p. 61)
national supremacy doctrine (p. 61)

necessary and proper clause (p. 58)
preemption (p. 58)
reserved powers (p. 56)
South Dakota v. Dole (1987) (p. 66)
sovereignty (p. 54)
supremacy clause (p. 58)
unitary system of government (p. 55)

Test Yourself

1. The provision of the Constitution declaring that state constitutions and state laws may not conflict with the Constitution is known as the
   a. elastic clause.
   b. supremacy clause.
   c. necessary and proper clause.
   d. dominance clause.

2. The requirement that all states recognize and abide by the official acts of other states is known as
   a. full faith and credit.
   b. preemption.
   c. privileges and immunities.
   d. extradition.

3. The specific powers delegated to Congress, such as the power to coin money, are referred to as
   a. reserved powers.
   b. concurrent powers.
   c. shared powers.
   d. enumerated powers.

4. What clause in the U.S. Constitution makes it easy for a citizen to change his or her official state of residence? In what other ways do Americans benefit from this clause?

5. Which of the following Supreme Court cases did *not* favor broad federal government power to regulate?
   a. *McCulloch v. Maryland*
   b. *Gibbons v. Ogden*
   c. *South Dakota v. Dole*
   d. *Lopez v. United States*

6. The doctrine of federalism that gives Congress nearly unlimited authority to exercise its powers to coerce states into enforcing federal policies is
   a. dual federalism.
   b. layer-cake federalism.
   c. marble-cake federalism.
   d. cooperative federalism.

7. Funds provided by the federal government to the states that may be used at the discretion of the states for more generalized policy goals are called
   a. grants-in-aid.
   b. block grants.
   c. federal matching funds.
   d. continuing appropriations.

8. In this period of "new federalism," the Supreme Court has issued a number of decisions that have resuscitated state authority. What are some of these decisions, and how did they empower state authority?

9. Which of the following individuals made famous the metaphor that states might serve as "laboratories of democracy"?
   a. Thomas Jefferson
   b. James Madison
   c. Louis Brandeis
   d. Ronald Reagan

10. Differences in per capita income among states
    a. lead states to spend different amounts of money on government programs.
    b. do not matter, thanks to federal financing initiatives.
    c. decrease state dependency on the federal government.
    d. are relatively insignificant.

11. What are the main arguments that have been advanced in favor of the system of federalism in the United States?

12. What are the main arguments against the system of federalism in the United States?

1. b. (LO 3-1); 2. a. (LO 3-1); 3. d. (LO 3-1); 5. d. (LO 3-2); 6. d. (LO 3-2); 7. b. (LO 3-2); 9. c. (LO 3-3); 10. a. (LO 3-3)

LEARNING OBJECTIVES

4-1 The Bill of Rights: Origins and Evolution
- Compare civil rights to civil liberties; discuss the origins of the Bill of Rights and the process of incorporation

4-2 Freedom of Religion and the Establishment Clause
- Describe the free exercise clause; identify the rules governing the separation of church and state and explain the tests for upholding government accommodations of religion

4-3 Free Expression Rights
- Outline the theories that justify giving heightened protection to expression rights
- Assess the scope of free speech rights, free press rights, and symbolic speech; summarize the rules for exempting from protection lesser-value speech, including libel and obscenity

4-4 The Right to Bear Arms
- Identify the scope of the right to bear arms and the constitutional limits on gun control laws

4-5 The Rights of the Criminally Accused
- Assess the scope of Fourth and Fifth Amendment rights aimed at the accused, including the rights against search and seizure, double jeopardy, and the privilege against self-incrimination
- Summarize the rights granted under the Sixth and Eighth Amendments

4-6 The Modern Right to Privacy
- Define the modern privacy rights that apply to government restrictions on abortion, sodomy, and euthanasia

4

Civil Liberties

The concept of **civil liberties**—those specific individual rights that cannot be denied by government—dates all the way back to the original English legal charter, the Magna Carta of 1215. Yet civil liberties remain just as significant and hotly contested today. In the United States, most discussions of civil liberties begin with the Bill of Rights, which amended the Constitution in 1791. The Bill of Rights affords to individuals numerous protections, including the freedom of speech and the right of protection against self-incrimination. All these individual rights are subject to formal interpretation from the courts, and to informal interpretation by those charged with their enforcement. Civil liberties may be distinguished from civil rights (sometimes called *equal rights*), which refer to rights that members of various groups (racial, ethnic, gender, and so on) have to equal treatment by government under the law as well as equal access to society's opportunities. This chapter deals with civil liberties, whereas Chapter 5 deals with civil rights.

National Security versus Individual Rights

The terrorist attacks of September 11, 2001, had a profound impact on American public opinion about national security, at least in the short term. Government must necessarily strike a balance between respecting the individual rights of its citizens on one hand, and doing everything it can to combat terrorism at home and abroad on the other. Yet in the months and years that followed those terrorist attacks, the USA PATRIOT Act, NSA surveillance, and other programs tended to weigh down the scale in favor of the war on terrorism. These programs enjoyed popular support at the time. In recent years, however, classified information leaked to the public by Edward Snowden revealed the existence of numerous global surveillance programs that escaped public scrutiny altogether; those revelations in turn led some to question the motives behind the government's overall national security program.

- Where do you stand on the question of how to most effectively balance national security concerns with individual privacy rights and other civil liberties?
- What concerns you more about the government's anti-terrorism policies: that they have gone too far in restricting the average person's civil liberties or that they have not gone far enough to adequately protect the country?
- How concerned are you about losing some of your privacy as a result of steps taken by the federal government to fight terrorism: are you very concerned, somewhat concerned, not very concerned, or not at all concerned?
- In recent years the National Security Administration has collected and analyzed information on the phone calls of many Americans in order to locate suspected terrorists. Do you think Congress should or should not allow the collection of such telephone data to continue?

To see how your answers compare to others, take the **Who Are You?** poll in MindTap!

4-1 | The Bill of Rights: Origins and Evolution

civil liberties Those specific individual rights that are guaranteed by the Constitution and cannot be denied to citizens by government. Most of these rights are in the first 10 amendments to the Constitution, known as the Bill of Rights.

What are rights? Strictly speaking, they are powers or privileges to which individuals are entitled. The central question is: where do rights come from, and are they absolute? *Natural rights*, which are based on the natural laws of human society, exist even in the absence of a formal government. Because natural rights theoretically transcend government entities, no authority can legitimately take them away. As Thomas Jefferson so eloquently stated in the Declaration of Independence, human beings are endowed with certain rights that are "unalienable," which means they cannot be denied by government.

Positive rights, by comparison, are granted by government authority and can usually be shaped and modified by that authority according to certain rules. An indigent person's right to a lawyer paid by the state in felony cases, for example, is a positive right. The term *liberty* refers to a right received from a higher authority, such as a government. As they articulated the basis for a new government, many of the Framers grappled with these and other terms in the nation's founding documents.

It is sometimes easy to forget that, as U.S. Supreme Court Justice Antonin Scalia once stated, individual rights are only "the fruits, rather than the roots, of the Constitutional tree."[1] The Constitution of the United States was intended to provide individuals with protection by guaranteeing a framework of limited government based on a theory of enumerated powers—the central government was allowed to exercise only those powers delegated to it by the Constitution. As James Madison wrote in Federalist No. 14, "the general government is not to be charged with the whole power of making and administering laws … its jurisdiction is limited to *certain enumerated objects*."[2] Thus, by Madison's logic, separate provisions for the protection of individual rights were unnecessary; protection for those rights was inherent in the nature of limited government with enumerated powers. Because the government possessed no explicit power to infringe on those rights in the first place, they should never be in danger.

Yet Madison's logic ran up against an early American tradition that called for the explicit delineation of individual rights. The Declaration of Independence not only formally recognized that certain "unalienable rights" exist, it also stated that when a government created by "the consent of the governed" fails to protect those rights, the people have the right to "alter or abolish such government." At the time of the founding, individual rights were considered an important element of America's political culture because they embodied the principles that justified the American Revolution. Many of the former colonists wanted those rights clearly spelled out, lest there be any doubt of their significance to the new nation.

When the U.S. Constitution was created in 1787, most state governments already maintained a bill of rights to protect citizens against government encroachment. As the final draft of the proposed constitution was being debated at ratification conventions in the states, it became evident to the new constitution's supporters that its approval was going to require the inclusion of a more formal bill of rights to protect citizens against the federal government. George Mason and Patrick Henry of Virginia cast votes against ratification, in part because the proposed constitution lacked a formal statement of rights. Thomas Jefferson was also an early proponent of a bill of rights. To Madison's fears that such a declaration of rights could never be comprehensive, and thus might leave out something important, Jefferson replied: "Half a loaf is better than no bread."[3]

Eventually it was Madison who framed the list of rights that the first Congress proposed in 1789—10 amendments to the Constitution were ratified by the required three-fourths of state legislatures. These are normally regarded as the "Bill of Rights." Whereas the first eight amendments guarantee specific rights, the Ninth and Tenth Amendments offer more general statements describing divisions of power between the federal and state governments under the Constitution.

The provisions listed in the Bill of Rights enjoyed little influence in late-eighteenth- and early-nineteenth-century America because they were understood to be restrictions on the federal government only. The Supreme Court confirmed as much in the case of *Barron v. Baltimore* (1833),[4] which pitted a wharf owner against the city of Baltimore. City officials had lowered the water level around the wharves, causing him a significant economic loss. The wharf owner thus sued the city under the Fifth Amendment's "taking clause," which stated that no private property could be taken from an individual for public use without just compensation. But the Supreme Court dismissed the suit because at that time only the federal government could be held up to the standards of the Bill of Rights. In light of the dominant role state governments played in regulating individuals' daily lives during most of this period, the *Barron v. Baltimore* decision essentially reduced the Bill of Rights to paper guarantees that only occasionally provided protection for ordinary citizens.

That all changed in the twentieth century, as the Supreme Court grew increasingly willing to protect individuals against intrusive state actions. Its instrument for doing so was the Fourteenth Amendment (ratified in 1868), which provided that no *state* could "deprive any person of life, liberty or property without due process of law." The Fourteenth Amendment had been passed immediately after the Civil War to protect freed slaves from discriminatory state laws. Yet at the beginning of the twentieth century and increasingly throughout the century, the Supreme Court, by a process known as **incorporation** (or "nationalization"), demonstrated a new willingness to hold state governments accountable to the Bill of Rights by utilizing the Fourteenth Amendment's vague requirement that states respect "due process." Specifically, the Court carefully considered individual clauses from the Bill of Rights, and if the right was deemed fundamental enough, the Court held that no state could legitimately ignore the right without depriving an individual of the right to "life, liberty and property, without due process of law." By this incorporation process, states were required to live up to the dictates of the First Amendment free speech clause beginning in 1925, the Fourth Amendment right

incorporation The process by which the U.S. Supreme Court used the due process clause of the Fourteenth Amendment to make most of the individual rights guaranteed by the Bill of Rights also applicable to the states. Incorporation provided that state and local governments, as well as the federal government, could not deny these rights to citizens.

against unreasonable searches and seizures beginning in 1949, and the Sixth Amendment right to a speedy trial beginning in 1967. (See Table 4-1.) Slowly but surely the provisions of the Bill of Rights were incorporated by the Fourteenth Amendment to apply to state governments as well as to the federal government.

At present there remain just a handful of provisions of the Bill of Rights that theoretically provide protection against the federal government only:

- The Third Amendment safeguard against the involuntary quartering of troops
- The Fifth Amendment requirement that defendants be indicted by a grand jury
- The Seventh Amendment guarantee of a trial by jury in civil cases
- The Eighth Amendment prohibition against excessive bail and fines

Virtually all other provisions contained within the first eight amendments of the Constitution are considered applicable to all state governments and to all local governments within the states in exactly the same manner as they are applicable to the federal government.

TABLE 4-1 Incorporating the Bill of Rights to Apply to the States

Provision (Amendment)	Year	Case
Protection from government taking property without just compensation (Fifth)	1897	*Chicago, Burl. & Quincy Ry. v. Chicago*
Freedom of speech (First)	1925	*Gitlow v. New York*
Freedom of the press (First)	1931	*Near v. Minnesota*
Right to assistance of counsel in capital cases (Sixth)	1932	*Powell v. Alabama*
Freedom of assembly (First)	1937	*Delaware v. Van Arsdall*
Free exercise of religion (First)	1940	*Cantwell v. Connecticut*
Protection from establishment of religion (First)	1947	*Everson v. Board of Education*
Right to public trial (Sixth)	1948	*In re Oliver*
Right against unreasonable search and seizure (Fourth)	1949	*Wolf v. Colorado*
Exclusionary rule (Fourth and Fifth)	1961	*Mapp v. Ohio*
Protection against cruel and unusual punishment (Eighth)	1962	*Robinson v. California*
Right to paid counsel for indigents in felony cases (Sixth)	1963	*Gideon v. Wainwright*
Right against self-incrimination (Fifth)	1964	*Malloy v. Hogan*
Right to confront witnesses (Sixth)	1965	*Pointer v. Texas*
Right to an impartial jury (Sixth)	1966	*Parker v. Gladden*
Right to compulsory process to obtain witnesses (Sixth)	1967	*Washington v. Texas*
Right to speedy trial (Sixth)	1967	*Klopfer v. North Carolina*
Right to jury in nonpetty criminal cases (Sixth)	1968	*Duncan v. Louisiana*
Right against double jeopardy (Fifth)	1969	*Benton v. Maryland*
Right to keep and bear arms (Second)	2010	*McDonald v. Chicago*

© 2018 Cengage Learning

4-2 | Freedom of Religion and the Establishment Clause

THE FIRST AMENDMENT: *Congress shall make no law respecting an establishment of religion, or prohibiting the free exercise thereof . . . .*

Although the first words of the Bill of Rights speak to the freedom of religion, the actual rights guaranteeing religious freedom did not become widespread until the latter half of the twentieth century. In early America, Protestantism played a highly influential role in public life, and the First Amendment was intended to provide a limited barrier against its influence. In 1802, Thomas Jefferson described the First Amendment as erecting a "wall of separation" between church and state,[5] but that metaphor captured his hopes more than the reality of the time. Although there existed no official church of the United States, government aid to religion—in particular to certain Protestant sects—stood little chance of being overturned by a court on constitutional grounds. And for much of American history, minority religious groups such as Mormons, Jehovah's Witnesses, and the Amish were forced to change or abandon some of their religious practices whenever public policy conflicted with them. By the 1940s, however, American public life had grown increasingly secular, and application of the First Amendment's guarantees of freedom of religion was transformed. Even today the interest in accommodating religion continues to run up against the desire to create a "wall of separation" emphasizing government neutrality.

The Free Exercise of Religion

The **free exercise clause** of the First Amendment bans government laws that prohibit the free exercise of religion. Debate over the clause has largely focused on whether government laws can force adherents of a certain religion to engage in activities that are prohibited by their religious beliefs or prevent them from performing acts that are compelled by their religious beliefs. During the heart of World War II, the Supreme Court in *West Virginia v. Barnette* (1943)[6] ordered school officials to reinstate the children of Jehovah's Witnesses who had been suspended for refusing to salute the American flag in their public school classrooms. Yet although those children could claim legitimate religious objections to the law (the Jehovah's Witnesses' creed forbids them from saluting any "graven image"), they also could claim more generally the right of free expression—those who disagreed with the U.S. government were free to withhold displays of public support for the nation's symbol. It remained for the Court in subsequent years to sort out what rights of religious freedom might exist under the free exercise clause.

free exercise clause The religious freedom clause in the First Amendment that denies government the ability to prohibit the free exercise of religion. Debate over the clause has largely focused on whether government laws can force adherents of a certain religion to engage in activities that are prohibited by their religious beliefs or prevent them from performing acts that are compelled by their religious beliefs.

Seventh-Day Adventists and the Refusal to Work. In the landmark case of *Sherbert v. Verner* (1963),[7] the Supreme Court ordered the state of South Carolina to pay unemployment benefits to a Seventh-Day Adventist who refused to work on Saturdays. Even though the state's unemployment laws required that she make herself available for work on Saturday, the Court refused to apply that law to this worker because Saturday is the Seventh-Day Adventists' Sabbath. Although the state could provide legitimate reasons for refusing to pay her benefits (guarding the unemployment insurance fund against running low, for example), the Supreme Court declared that only a *compelling state interest* could justify denying her such an exception on the basis of religion. What interest counts as "compelling"? Although no precise definition is available, the Court has held that administrative convenience is not compelling; rather, the Court must be convinced that the government program (whether the draft, Social Security, unemployment benefits, and so on) would be significantly undermined by religious exemptions in order to say that the government's interest is compelling.

Stocktrek/Photodisc/Getty Images

The Amish and Mandatory School Attendance. Continuing to accept exemptions for religious reasons, the Supreme Court in *Wisconsin v. Yoder* (1972)[8] held that members of the Amish religion were not required to send their children to school after the eighth grade. Even though Wisconsin law compelled high school attendance, the Court ruled that the enforcement of that law would undermine Amish religious principles, which include the value of "learning through doing" and support for "community welfare" over all other interests.

Amish children walking to school in Ohio. In 1972 the U.S. Supreme Court declared that members of the Amish religion could not be compelled to send their children to school after the eighth grade.

The Mormons and Polygamy Laws. Up until the late nineteenth century, a central tenet of the Mormon Church, also called the Church of Jesus Christ of Latter-Day Saints, required some of its adherents to practice polygamy—the act of having multiple spouses "when circumstances would permit." During the 1870s, many Mormons were prosecuted under a federal anti-bigamy statute that applied to federal territories, including the new Utah territory where many Mormons had settled. George Reynolds, secretary of one of the founders of the Mormon Church in America as well as the founder of Brigham Young University, brought suit in 1878, challenging the law as destructive to the Mormon Church, and thus a violation of the free exercise clause of the First Amendment.

The Supreme Court, in a unanimous decision, rejected Reynolds's argument that the First Amendment protects plural marriage. According to the Court, religious practices that impair the "public interest" do not receive constitutional protection; such practices were to be distinguished from religious "beliefs," which the government had no power to regulate. *Reynolds v. United States*[9] remains the law today, and polygamy is now banned in all 50 states. Additionally, since 1890 the Mormon Church has formally renounced the practice of polygamy by its members.

Illegal Drug Use and the *Smith* Case. In 1990, the Supreme Court adopted a new approach to the free exercise of religion, one that dramatically diminished the likelihood that future religious exemptions might be granted. Two Native Americans were dismissed from their jobs as drug rehabilitation counselors when it was discovered that they had ingested the illegal drug peyote as part of their tribe's religious rituals. Because their drug use violated the Oregon criminal code, the two men were subsequently denied unemployment compensation. The Supreme Court ruled in *Employment Division v. Smith* (1990)[10] that the state's legitimate interest in maintaining its unemployment insurance fund at a high level outweighed the Native Americans' religious rights and thus that it could deny the two men unemployment benefits. State governments may choose to accommodate otherwise illegal acts done in pursuit of religious beliefs, but they are not *required* to do so.[11]

Today *Smith* remains the rule for judicial interpretation of free exercise cases: instead of being forced to show a *compelling* government interest (which is extremely hard to do), a government interested in applying its neutral laws over religious objections may do so based on any *legitimate state interest* it might claim. What is a legitimate state interest? The bar here is quite low; only an arbitrary or irrational objective by government will fail the test of legitimacy. The Religious Freedom Restoration Act passed by Congress in 1993 attempted to reverse the Court's holding in

Smith and revert to the more liberal rules established in the *Sherbert* and *Yoder* decisions. However, the Supreme Court invalidated the religious freedom law in 1997 (*Yoder* and *Sherbert* remain as valid exceptions to the *Smith* doctrine). The Supreme Court—and not the Congress—holds the lever of power in the debate over religious exemptions. And, at least for the time being, that means the courts generally will not grant such exemptions.

The Establishment Clause

Even more controversial than the debate over religious exemptions from public policies has been the battle over what role religion may play in American public life under the **establishment clause**, which prohibits the government from enacting laws "respecting an establishment of religion." Most Americans take it for granted that during the holiday season they will see Christmas decorations prominently displayed in government buildings, in front of the town hall, and in public squares. But what about nativity scenes? Menorahs? The Ten Commandments? What types of religious activities and symbols are considered acceptable in public places, and which ones run afoul of the First Amendment, whose prohibition of government "respecting an establishment of religion" has been interpreted to mean creating a "wall of separation" between church and state?

Modern debates over the proper role religion may play under the establishment clause generally divide advocates into two camps. Those who advocate a strict dividing line between church and state support a principle of "separation," which holds that

establishment clause The clause in the First Amendment that prohibits government from enacting any law "respecting an establishment of religion." Separationist interpretations of this clause affirm that government should not support any religious activity. Accommodationists say that support for a religion is legal provided that all religions are equally supported.

 The Diversity Dilemma

Religious Divide in Teaching of Evolution

Those holding different religious beliefs often find themselves in conflict with each other, or with the government itself. In the context of public education, several religious beliefs clash over the teaching of evolution to students. Central questions include "how was the universe created?" and "which theory or scientific facts should be used for our public education science standards?" Some religious groups favor the teaching of intelligent design and creationism, as they believe the universe was either intelligently designed by some entity or that the universe was created by god. These beliefs may come into sharp conflict with those who favor the teaching of Charles Darwin's theory of evolution. Many states and school boards have sided with religious groups in challenging the teaching of evolution.

Are school boards required to balance religious or academic freedoms with the more secular focus of education standards? The Supreme Court has responded in various cases. Most notably in *Edwards v. Aguillard* (1987),[12] the high Court outlawed the teaching of creationism in American public school science classes. Still, this battle remains far from settled, as statewide efforts challenging the teaching of evolution have continued in the decades since that landmark decision.

Pictorial Press/Alamy

John Scopes, on trial in 1925, was convicted of teaching human evolution in a Dayton, Tennessee high school.

For Critical Thinking and Discussion

1. What side do you take in this religious divide over the teaching of evolution? Should school boards be allowed to dictate that teachers teach theories of intelligent design or creationism alongside the teaching of evolution theory?
2. Do you recall how your previous schools responded to the debate over evolution? Were you taught one theory or both?

government should have no involvement whatsoever with religious practices, although religion remains free to flourish privately on its own, with its own resources.[13] Opponents of strict separation argue instead for the principle of "accommodation," which holds that government neutrality toward religion requires only that it treat all religions equally. Government should be free to aid and subsidize religious activities as long as it does so fairly across different religions, and aids comparable nonreligious activities as well. In recent decades, the Supreme Court has moved from a position of especially strict separation to one that shifts back and forth between principles of separation and accommodation.

Historically Accepted Practices. Certain religious practices have been a part of political and public life for generations, and the Supreme Court has generally allowed such activities to continue. Congress opens each legislative session with a prayer from a clergy member, chaplains serve in religious capacities with the U.S. armed forces, and U.S. currency proclaims "In God We Trust." Even the Supreme Court opens every court session to a marshal's bellowing pronouncement: "God save this honorable court!" All of these are considered acceptable practices, products of the American historical tradition. Moreover, just recently (in 2014) the high Court ruled that one town's practice of opening its town board meetings with a sectarian prayer did not violate the Establishment Clause because it comported with the town's traditions and it did not coerce nonadherents. Still, not all religious displays on public property will be automatically deemed "historically accepted practices." On occasion, the Court has ordered the removal of nativity scenes and other religious displays during Christmastime.

In Kentucky, versions of the Ten Commandments were posted on the walls of several county courthouses. In Texas, a six-foot-high monolith inscribed with the Ten Commandments sits among numerous other monuments and historical markers outside the state capital building commemorating the "people, ideals, and events that compose Texan identity." Do these public displays of the Ten Commandments, which feature such statements as "Thou shalt have no other gods before me" and "Thou shalt not take the name of the Lord thy God in vain," violate the establishment clause of the First Amendment?

In a set of cases handed down in 2005, the Supreme Court ordered the Kentucky courthouses to remove their displays but allowed the Texas display to remain standing. In explaining its different approach to these cases, the Court ruled that even though the Ten Commandments are inherently religious, their placement in a monument outside the state capital is an essentially "passive" act, whereas their placement within the courthouse had been motivated by a desire on the part of legislators to advance religion. Of course, the members of the U.S. Supreme Court need not be reminded that a frieze in their own courtroom depicts Moses holding tablets exhibiting a portion of the secularly phrased Commandments in the company of 17 other lawgivers. Perhaps the Court believes that there is little risk that such a depiction of Moses would strike an observer as evidence of the federal government violating religious neutrality.

Religious Prayers in Public School Classrooms. The public school classroom has always been viewed as a unique context in which to assess claims that the government has violated the establishment clause. Judges and politicians alike assume that students—particularly elementary school students—have not yet formed firm beliefs about religion and thus may be susceptible to even subtle forms of religious coercion. Public officials interested in promoting religion in society as a whole have focused on the school as a place to encourage religious practices; as a consequence, school policies touching on the subject of religion have undergone serious scrutiny in the courts.

In 1962, the Supreme Court in *Engel v. Vitale*[14] invalidated the New York public schools' policy of having each class recite a specified nondenominational religious prayer each day. That prayer, which proclaimed in nondenominational terms, "Almighty God, we acknowledge our dependence upon thee," was held to be a violation of the First Amendment's prohibition against the establishment of religion. In *Abington School*

District v. Schempp (1963),[15] the Court refused to allow spiritual Bible readings in public school classrooms, and in *Wallace v. Jaffree* (1985)[16] it outlawed "moments of silence" authorized by government officials to encourage religious prayer during those moments. The Court held that in neither of those instances was the government acting with a "secular purpose"—one not grounded in a desire to "advance religion." These decisions are especially difficult to enforce, as the closed nature of most public school classrooms allows prayer to escape the notice of those seeking to enforce these landmark decisions. And it remains unclear whether the general ban on religious prayer in public schools extends to the teaching of the Ten Commandments, among other issues.

Despite these seemingly clear rulings against school prayer, some teachers continue to lead students in prayer in public school classrooms across the country. Defiance has become widespread in some instances, forcing one court in Alabama to forbid prayer in schools throughout the state fully 35 years after *Engel v. Vitale* invalidated the practice. Anecdotal evidence of violations continue to mount as well: in one highly publicized case, officials in DeKalb County, Georgia, helped lead a religious revival at a public high school in admitted disobedience of the Supreme Court. Defiance persists in part because public schools are so rarely challenged in court for their violations. Community sentiment has also played an influential role in squelching potential litigation, as dissenting parents quickly realize that only continued and expensive litigation over many years will bring a defiant school into line.

Financial Aid and the *Lemon* Test. During the last several decades, government officials seeking to promote religion as part of the educational process have expanded the variety and scope of their efforts. Many initiatives have occurred in public schools— provisions for school prayer recitations, released-time programs (allowing students to visit religious schools for instruction during normal school hours), and the teaching of subjects with religious content, such as creationism. Efforts to provide religious private schools that teach students full time with public funds have met with some recent success. In 2000, the Supreme Court approved of a program to provide government-funded computers and other teaching aids to certain parochial schools. Two years later, the Court in *Zelman v. Simmons-Harris* (2002)[17] upheld a system of private school vouchers, whereby parents are given coupons that can be used to pay tuition at private schools, including parochial schools. Such programs continue to be a source of heated policy debate between proponents of separation and accommodation.

Since 1971, issues involving the separation of church and state have often been governed by the **Lemon test** articulated by the Supreme Court in the landmark decision of *Lemon v. Kurtzman* (1971).[18] Under the test, government aid to public or private schools is considered unconstitutional if it fails to meet three separate criteria: "First, the statute must have a secular [that is, not religious] purpose; second, its principal or primary effect must be one that neither advances nor inhibits religion; finally, the statute must not foster 'an excessive government entanglement with religion.'" The test has been criticized by many, including a number of the Supreme Court justices, who assert that its requirements are so stringent that literally all deliberate government accommodation of religion is presumptively invalid. The Court has never renounced the test, and it continues to play a role in the consideration of various types of financial aid.

Lemon **test** The legal test that determines if a government statute aiding public or private schools is an unconstitutional violation of the establishment clause. The statute is unconstitutional if the statute has no secular purpose, if its principal or primary effect advances or inhibits religion, or if it fosters "an excessive government entanglement with religion."

Prayers at Graduation Ceremonies and Football Games. In recent years, some school officials have attempted to facilitate student prayers in school contexts outside of the classroom. Those efforts have met with little success. In *Lee v. Weisman* (1992),[19] the Supreme Court ordered a Providence, Rhode Island, middle school to stop its practice of permitting prayers to be read at the school's graduation ceremony, even though attendance was voluntary. Eight years later, in *Santa Fe v. Doe* (2000),[20] the Court ruled that a student-led prayer before a football game at a Texas public high school violated the separation of church and state. The Court believed that both

Group prayer before a high school football game in Austin, Texas.

Bob Daemmrich/The Image Works

practices forced all of those present to participate in an act of religious worship. In addition, these practices could have been interpreted as state endorsements of prayer, which is unconstitutional.

The debate over the role religion should play in American public life remains a highly charged topic. Public schools especially will continue to be a focus of intense interest, as the proponents of a greater role for religion seek ever more creative ways to combine the educational process with efforts to encourage spirituality and religious participation.

4-3 | Free Expression Rights

THE FIRST AMENDMENT: *Congress shall make no law … abridging the freedom of speech, or of the press.*

Among the many civil liberties guaranteed by the Bill of Rights, the First Amendment rights of free speech and press enjoy especially revered status. That wasn't always the case. The Sedition Act of the late 1790s egregiously restricted speech that negatively reflected on the Federalists who were in power; during the Civil War, the Lincoln administration took harsh action against those who sought to undermine the Union's cause. Today, nearly all politicians openly celebrate rights of free expression, at least in the abstract. For many, these rights of free expression serve as a cornerstone for all other individual rights, facilitating the more effective realization of such freedoms as the right to vote and participate in the democratic process.

What accounts for the lofty status of free expression rights in the American political system? Several theories have been offered to justify this high level of respect:

- **"The marketplace of ideas,"** a phrase coined by Supreme Court Justice Oliver Wendell Holmes in 1919, is a metaphor for the premise that the best test of truth is the free trade of ideas; only through such free exchange and presentation of all arguments, valid and invalid, can the truth prevail. To ensure a robust "marketplace of ideas," government restrictions on speech must be kept to a minimum.

- **Self-governance** is another frequently cited justification for protecting free expression. Speech is considered essential to representative government because it provides the mechanism by which citizens deliberate on important issues of public policy. Free speech also serves as a means for ordinary citizens to check the abuse of power by public officials.
- **Self-fulfillment.** Some philosophers have emphasized the importance of free speech and expression as a means of achieving individual self-fulfillment. The human capacity to create ideas and express oneself is thus considered central to human existence; government restrictions on free speech invariably threaten that human capacity. Such a justification of free speech rights extends as well to the protection of music, pictures, and other forms of artistic expression.
- **A "safety valve."** Free speech also serves a critical role in encouraging adaptability and flexibility according to the changing circumstances in society. If the suppression of free speech forces citizens to adopt more extreme means of enacting change, such as violence, the promotion of free speech provides an essential mechanism for balancing the need for order with cries for reform.

Each of these justifications for free speech protection may be subject to legitimate criticisms as well. But for better or worse, the First Amendment's protection of free expression today enjoys a special status in our constitutional system, even though that was not always the case.

Free Speech During the Early Twentieth Century: The Clear and Present Danger Test

The modern status of free expression rights is a far cry from the low level of protection the First Amendment afforded to free speech nearly a century ago. Many of the early cases pitting dissenting speakers against the government came before the Court when tensions were great—first during wartime, then at the height of the Cold War when fears of communist infiltration in American society gripped many ordinary Americans. In neither instance did free speech fare well.

The Supreme Court gave birth to the "clear and present danger" test in *Schenck v. United States* (1919).[21] In 1917, with the United States readying for active participation in World War I, Charles Schenck, a general secretary for the American Socialist Party, was tried and convicted for distributing leaflets arguing that the military draft was immoral. Although the pamphlet posed little danger of interfering with the draft, the Supreme Court refused to release Schenck from jail. Writing the majority opinion for a unanimous court, Justice Oliver Wendell Holmes stated that there was in fact "a clear and present danger" that the pamphlet could bring about the damage being claimed by the government.

In practice, the clear and present danger test soon became a hammer on speakers' rights rather than a shield against government suppression. Under the doctrine, members of the Socialist and Communist parties were tried and punished for participating in organizational meetings or declaring allegiance to their party's principles. Justice Holmes was clearly alarmed by the legacy his *Schenck* decision had wrought; in subsequent decisions he modified his earlier view by insisting that the present danger must relate to an "immediate evil" and a specific action. But Holmes was now in the minority, and there was little he could do to stop the momentum. During the late 1940s and early 1950s, when the fear of communism in the United States was reaching a fever pitch, members of the Communist Party were convicted for their advocacy of sedition. In *Dennis v. United States* (1951),[22] the Supreme Court gave a measure of credibility to this red scare when it upheld the convictions of numerous communist defendants for "teaching and advocating the overthrow and destruction of the Government of the United States."

The Warren Court and the Rise of the "Preferred Freedoms" Doctrine

By the late 1950s, fears of subversion and communist infiltration in the United States were beginning to subside. However, it was the ascension of former California Governor Earl Warren to the position of chief justice of the United States in 1953 that eventually changed the Court's free speech doctrine from one that offered little protection to dissenting speakers into one that protected even the most unpopular speakers against suppression by the majority. The Warren Court brought about this change by embracing a doctrine first articulated by Justice Harlan Fiske Stone in 1938. In a footnote to the otherwise forgettable case of *United States v. Carolene Products* (1938),[23] Justice Stone declared that various civil liberties guaranteed in the Bill of Rights, including the right of free expression, enjoyed a "preferred position" in constitutional law. Stone's explicit support for this preferred freedoms doctrine did not take immediate hold. Yet in the 1960s, when new social tensions such as the battle over civil rights and resistance to the Vietnam War threatened to wreak havoc on civil liberties, the Warren Court issued several key decisions that shattered any possibility that the government might be able to suppress the exercise of free speech rights under the Constitution, as it had in the earlier part of the century.

In 1969, the Supreme Court in *Brandenburg v. Ohio* (1969)[24] abandoned the clear and present danger test and replaced it with a test that was much more protective of free speech. A Ku Klux Klan rally in Cincinnati, Ohio, featured numerous figures in white hoods uttering phrases that demeaned African Americans and Jews. The principal speaker had argued that some form of vengeance be taken against both groups. The group's leader was convicted under a law criminalizing the advocacy of violence. The Supreme Court overturned his conviction. In the process, it declared a new "imminent danger" test for such speech: first, is the speech "directed to inciting or producing imminent lawless action," and second, is the advocacy *likely* to produce such action? Few of the speakers jailed in the previous half century for seditious speech could have been convicted under this new standard.[25]

The preferred freedoms doctrine also offered protection to those exercising their rights of free expression in other contexts—to writers and publishers, filmmakers, and protesters, for example. Indeed, it provided a foundation for the protection of such modern activities as the dissemination of information on the Internet. Even speakers and publishers of certain categories of speech that have not traditionally enjoyed First Amendment protection—obscenity and libel, for example—soon discovered that the preferred freedoms doctrine provided protection for their activities.

The Freedom of the Press, Libel Laws, and Prior Restraints

Freedom of the press enjoys a long and storied tradition in the United States. Well before the American Revolution or the drafting of the Constitution, the trial of newspaper publisher John Peter Zenger in 1734 on charges of libel laid the foundation for robust press freedoms. **Libel** is the crime of printing or disseminating false statements that harm someone. Zenger was accused of attacking the corrupt administration of New York's colonial governor in his weekly newspaper. When he was acquitted on the basis of his lawyer's argument that he had printed true facts, Zenger's case helped to establish the legal principle that truth would serve as a defense to any libel action. In the late 1790s, after many Republican editors and publishers had been jailed under the highly controversial Sedition Act, public distaste for the act helped to catapult Thomas Jefferson and his Republican Party into power in the election of 1800.

Despite the general recognition of the importance of the press, newspapers traditionally enjoyed few special privileges under the law. Specifically, individuals whose

libel Printing or disseminating false statements that harm someone.

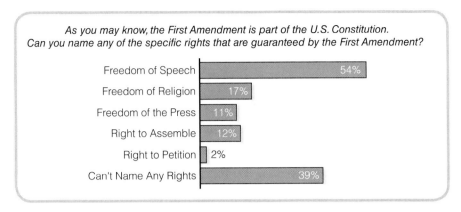

FIGURE 4-1 Do You Know What Rights Are in the First Amendment?
A June 2016 national survey conducted by the Newseum Institute found that few Americans are aware of all five rights in the First Amendment. And fully 39 percent couldn't even name one of those five rights.

reputations were harmed were free to bring libel suits against newspapers and other publications without any implications for the First Amendment. That all changed in 1964 with the landmark decision of *New York Times v. Sullivan*.[26] A Montgomery, Alabama, police commissioner sued *The New York Times* in March 1960 for an advertisement the newspaper had published. The ad—charging the existence of "an unprecedented wave of terror" against blacks in Montgomery—had been signed by several black clergymen. In its description of events that had transpired, the ad also contained some minor inaccuracies. Although the police commissioner was unable to prove that he had suffered any actual economic harm, he still sought a $500,000 judgment against the *Times*. But the Supreme Court refused to allow the official to claim damages, and in the process articulated a much more stringent test to be met by public officials suing for libel: they must prove that the newspapers had published false facts with malice (bad intentions) or reckless disregard for the truth (they ignored clear evidence of contrary facts).[27]

In subsequent years, the *New York Times v. Sullivan* decision has applied to public figures as well as public officials; today a libel lawsuit brought by any famous person—whether it's the president of the United States, LeBron James, or Julia Roberts—must prove that the newspaper or magazine in question not only printed false facts, but did so either with "malicious intent" or in "reckless disregard" for the truth. Of course, an important question remains: Who is a public figure? This was the question raised in the case of Richard Jewell, a security guard suspected of setting off a bomb in Centennial Park in Atlanta, Georgia, during the 1996 Summer Olympics. Two people died in the explosion. Jewell was initially portrayed as a hero for his role in discovering the bomb, alerting authorities, and evacuating bystanders from the immediate vicinity. But when Jewell's status changed from hero to suspect, the resulting media coverage of the criminal investigation caused Jewell and his family considerable anguish. Although the investigation ultimately cleared Jewell of any involvement in the bombing, his reputation had been harmed enough that he decided to sue *The Atlanta Journal-Constitution*, which had rushed to judgment against him.

Jewell's entire lawsuit rested on the premise that he was (and continued to be) a private figure. Unlike public figures who had to prove the libeling newspaper had demonstrated a "reckless disregard for the truth," private figures seeking monetary damages need only show that the newspaper was "negligent." Immediately following the bomb explosion, but before he became a suspect, Jewell granted one photo shoot and 10 interviews to the media, including *Larry King Live* and the *Today* show. During the course of these interviews, Jewell repeatedly stated that he had spotted a suspicious bag after a group of rowdy, college-age men had left the park, and announced that he had matched one of the men to a composite sketch. These interviews proved Jewell's undoing, as both a trial judge and the Georgia Court of Appeals ruled that his media activities meant he had "voluntarily assumed a position of influence in the controversy," and thus was a public figure for purposes of his lawsuit. Jewell never received any monetary relief from *The Atlanta Journal-Constitution*.

Whereas libel laws punish publications after the fact, a **prior restraint** imposes a limit on publication *before* the material has actually been published. Securing a prior restraint is very difficult for government to accomplish. In the *Pentagon Papers Case* (1971),[28] the Supreme Court refused the U.S. government's request to stop *The Washington Post* and *The New York Times* from publishing a classified study of U.S. decision making about the Vietnam War. The courts have made it very difficult for government to implement a prior restraint of expression. In only the rarest of cases, such as the publication of information about troop movements during wartime, has government been able to block the publication of a story.

prior restraint The government's requirement that material be approved by government before it can be published.

Obscenity and Pornography

Despite the exalted status free expression rights enjoy under the Constitution, obscenity has long been recognized as an exception to the rule. Even through the so-called sexual revolution of the 1960s and 1970s, the Supreme Court continued to adhere to the premise that truly obscene speech—words or publications that tend to violate accepted standards of decency by their very lewdness—may, under certain circumstances, be regulated. When asked how he would define obscene pornography, Justice Potter Stewart in 1964 uttered his now celebrated phrase: "I can't define it, but I know it when I see it." Stewart's statement captures the often confusing state of obscenity law in the United States. The First Amendment does not allow governments simply to ban all sexually explicit materials. But what types of materials can be banned? Is all pornography to be considered "obscene"?

In *Miller v. California* (1973),[29] the Supreme Court created the modern legal test for determining what sexually explicit materials may be legitimately subject to regulation under the Constitution. According to the Court, a work is obscene if *all* of these three conditions are met:

SLAPS test A standard that courts established to determine if material is obscene based in part on whether the material has serious literary, artistic, political, or scientific value. If it does, then the material is not obscene.

Poster advertising Lady Chatterley's Lover. *The film was based on a book that was the target of a New York State ban during the 1950s.*

1. The average person applying contemporary community standards would think that the work (taken as a whole) appeals to the "prurient" (that is, lustful) interest.

2. The work depicts sexual conduct in a patently offensive way.

3. The work taken as a whole lacks "serious literary, artistic, political or scientific value."

This third condition has come to be known as the **SLAPS test** (derived from taking the first letter of each word in the quoted phrase). In theory, adherence to the SLAPS test allows a jury to apply its own conception of "contemporary community standards" and thus ban relatively innocent sexual materials. In practice, however, courts have found very few materials able to survive the

NOW YOU CAN SEE IT!

The most whispered about book in the world becomes the MOST TALKED ABOUT PICTURE OF THE YEAR!

THE FILM WITHOUT FALSE MODESTY!

D. H. LAWRENCE'S CONTROVERSIAL MASTERPIECE

"Lady Chatterley's Lover"

DANIELLE DARRIEUX
LEO GENN
and Introducing
ERNO CRISA

A Kingsley International Release

Everett Collection

SLAPS test (after all, who is to say what possesses "artistic value"?). None of the above rules apply to child pornography, which enjoys no First Amendment protection whatsoever under the Constitution.

The rise of the Internet as a medium of communication in recent years has caused even more confusion as to what types of obscenity and/or pornography can be regulated. In *Reno v. ACLU* (1997),[30] the Supreme Court invalidated a federal law passed to protect minors from "indecent" and "patently offensive" communications on the Internet. The Court feared that in denying minors access to potentially harmful speech, the law had suppressed a large amount of speech that adults have a constitutional right to receive. Still, the question of how to restrict sexually explicit speech on the Internet will remain an issue for years to come.

Symbolic Speech and the Flag-Burning Controversy

When school officials in Des Moines, Iowa, suspended two students for wearing black armbands in protest of the Vietnam War in the 1960s, they claimed they were not restricting free speech rights at all—rather, the students were engaging in conduct that could be regulated by authorities.[31] The Supreme Court in 1969 disagreed and the students were vindicated;[32] but the line between speech and conduct remains difficult to draw. Protesters often engage in disruptive activities that make powerful statements about important issues of public policy. They may camp out in public parks overnight to bring attention to the plight of the homeless or burn their draft cards as a statement of opposition to a war. Are such forms of **symbolic speech** protected by the First Amendment?

In 1968, the Supreme Court in *United States v. O'Brien*[33] refused to allow a Vietnam War protester to burn his draft card in violation of federal law. That case introduced three criteria for determining whether the regulation of symbolic speech may be justified:

1. The government interest must be valid and important.
2. The interest must be unrelated to the suppression of free speech.
3. The restriction should be no greater than is essential to the furtherance of that interest.

In *United States v. O'Brien*, the key was motive: the Court believed the government actions were motivated by the need to operate a military registration system during wartime, rather than simply to suppress the ideas and message of this particular protester. Similarly, protesters do not have the right to violate federal park service rules and sleep in parks after closing—those rules were established for one reason: to prevent damage to public property. By contrast, students were granted the constitutional right to wear black armbands in school to protest the Vietnam War—their "conduct" was considered the equivalent of "pure speech" and school officials' arguments about the maintenance of order and discipline were given little credibility.

The constitutionality of flag burning has been a source of considerable debate in recent years. To many, the American flag is a symbol of nationhood and national unity, and thus must be preserved at all costs. For that very reason, protesters seeking to attract publicity for their ideas have burned or desecrated the flag in public places. The Supreme Court ended the legal debate over flag burning

symbolic speech Nonspoken forms of speech that might be protected by the First Amendment, such as flag burning, wearing armbands at school to protest a war, or camping out in public parks to protest the plight of the homeless.

Protesters rally in April 1977 where neo-Nazis planned to march: on the streets of Skokie, a predominantly Jewish suburb of Chicago.

AP Images/Charles Knoblock

Jonathan Butler's seven-day hunger strike in 2015 drew national attention to the issue of institutional racism.

with its decision in *Texas v. Johnson* (1989).[34] In 1984, Gregory Lee Johnson was arrested and convicted for "desecrating a venerated object" at a political demonstration in Dallas, the site of the Republican National Convention. Johnson had been leading a protest against the Reagan administration; he eventually set an American flag on fire, after which he and the other protesters chanted: "America, the red, white and blue, we spit on you." But the Supreme Court threw out Johnson's conviction because the "government may not prohibit the expression of an idea simply because society finds the idea itself offensive or disagreeable."[35]

Despite the Supreme Court's apparent resolution of the matter, heated feelings on both sides of the flag-burning issue have kept it alive. After an initial attempt by Congress to pass flag-burning legislation failed to withstand judicial scrutiny in 1990, some members of Congress proposed passage of an amendment to the Constitution that would make flag burning unconstitutional. Although that proposed amendment has on several occasions achieved the necessary level of support in the House of Representatives, the U.S. Senate has so far failed to approve it, thus preventing it from being promulgated to state legislatures for ratification.

Hate Speech Codes

Since the 1970s, communities have sought to prevent speakers who preach hatred for certain groups—whether racial, religious, or some other classification—from exercising their rights of free speech in certain specified neighborhoods or other places where the perceived harms may be great. Such efforts have not always passed constitutional muster. In one instance during the late 1970s, the courts refused to deny neo-Nazis the right to march in a parade in Skokie, Illinois, home to a large number of Holocaust victims.[36] By contrast, efforts to ban cross burning and other controversial forms of expression have sometimes been upheld. In *Virginia v. Black* (2003),[37] the U.S. Supreme Court ruled that the state of Virginia could prohibit cross burning with the "intent to intimidate any person or group" because the law applied only to intimidation and not to cross burning in general. The law also applied to all groups, not just racial or ethnic groups.

It is a considerable challenge for school officials to restrict hate speech by students at public colleges and universities, even when that speech proves disruptive to the school's mission of providing a constructive environment for learning.[38] In 1988, the University of Michigan passed a regulation subjecting individuals to discipline for "behavior, verbal or physical" that stigmatized or victimized an individual on the basis of race, ethnicity, religion, sex, or a host of other criteria. Stanford University similarly attempted to prohibit "discriminatory harassment," which was defined to include speech intended to stigmatize or insult on the basis of sex, race, and so on. Lower courts invalidated both of these "hate speech codes" on grounds that they violated the First Amendment.

Regulating the Internet

Meanwhile, high school principals and superintendents face their own set of twenty-first-century challenges, thanks to the Internet and popular social networking sites like Facebook and Twitter. Recently, some public school students found themselves the target of "cyberbullying" from classmates who posted nasty comments about them on social media sites. If the harassing posts originated from a school or library computer, the school would obviously have the authority to punish the cyberbullies. But what if a student posted the harassing comment from his or her own computer or a mobile device while at home? What if the student posted the offending comments on a discussion thread open only to his or her closest friends? Does school authority extend to students' behaviors in their own private spheres? Lower courts are still sorting out such issues as they await eventual judgment from the U.S. Supreme Court.

Cyberbullying messages can be posted anonymously and pervasively. Tracing the source, and deleting the messages, can be difficult.

What about congressional attempts to curb the online theft of music, movies, and other popular content? The 112th Congress considered two new bills—the Stop On-Line Piracy Act (SOPA) and the Protect Intellectual Property Act—that would have made the unauthorized streaming of protected content a criminal offense. Fearful that law enforcement might use the laws to block access to entire Internet domains, some Internet companies argued that the bills would harm the "free, secure and open Internet" and encourage censorship. As a means of protest, Wikipedia and over 7,000 other websites led a self-imposed blackout of their own content for a 12-hour period on January 18, 2012. The show of force proved effective, as members of Congress postponed plans to move forward with SOPA until it could create a wider consensus on a solution. In the years to come, Congress is expected to keep searching for a solution that strikes a balance between deterring piracy on one hand and encouraging the open exchange of information on the other hand.

4-4 | The Right to Bear Arms

> **THE SECOND AMENDMENT:** *A well regulated militia, being necessary to the security of a free State, the right of the people to keep and bear Arms, shall not be infringed.*

The Second Amendment "right to keep and bear arms" remains something of a puzzle for Americans. On one hand, the second part of the amendment appears to trumpet the "people's" right to own firearms at their discretion, and has taken its place as a central tenet in the platforms of interest groups such as the National Rifle Association (NRA), which opposes nearly all government attempts to restrict gun ownership. On the other hand, the first part of the amendment speaks directly of a "well-regulated militia," and implies that some relationship must exist between the private gun owner's rights and more formal state activities. The U.S. Supreme Court finally weighed in on the subject in 2008. In *District of Columbia v. Heller* (2008),[39] the Supreme Court by a 5–4 vote held that the Second Amendment forbids the government from banning all forms of handgun possession in the home for purposes of immediate self-defense.

In *McDonald v. Chicago* (2010),[40] the Supreme Court went a step further, ruling that the right to bear arms is incorporated by the due process clause of the Fourteenth Amendment, and thus applies to all 50 states as well. However, this Second Amendment right is not absolute: the Court in *Heller* noted that government can still regulate the commercial sale of handguns; it can also prohibit their possession by felons and the mentally ill, or in sensitive places such as school buildings.

Second Amendment considerations aside, Congress has been reluctant to regulate gun ownership—only rarely are the sponsors of gun control able to overcome fierce lobbying efforts by the NRA and others in opposition. Advocates of gun control scored some success following the attempted assassination of President Ronald Reagan in 1981. Reagan was wounded in the attempt, as was James Brady, his press secretary. Although the president fully recovered from his injuries in a matter of weeks, Brady sustained serious head injuries because a bullet tore into his temple and lodged in the base of his brain. He ultimately experienced a partial recovery, although he permanently lost the use of his left arm and left leg and suffers from slurred speech.

In 1985, Brady and his wife, Sarah, became spokespersons for gun control measures. Their efforts resulted in the Brady Handgun Violence Prevention Act, signed by President Clinton in 1993. The "Brady Law" required a five-day waiting period and a background check on handgun purchases from licensed firearms dealers to ensure that felons, drug users, fugitives, and other specified categories of individuals are not permitted to purchase guns. The NRA avoided any direct court challenges to the law on Second Amendment grounds, hammering instead at more peripheral aspects of the law, such as the requirement that local sheriffs conduct these checks as part of a federal regulatory scheme. In 1997, the Supreme Court struck down this aspect of the Brady Law as a violation of federalism, although leaving the substance of the law in place. Congress has also attempted to restrict the carrying of firearms near schools, even though some of these efforts have been invalidated by the Supreme Court on the grounds that the federal government cannot commandeer the states to enforce federal legislation.

4-5 | The Rights of the Criminally Accused

A few rights for the accused may be found in the language of the original Constitution. Article I prohibits Congress from passing a **bill of attainder**, which is an act of a legislature declaring a person (or group) guilty of some crime and then carrying out punishment without a trial. It also prohibits **ex post facto laws**, which are new criminal laws retroactively applied to those who engaged in activities when they were not yet illegal. But the vast majority of constitutional rights for those accused of crimes are contained in the Fourth, Fifth, Sixth, and Eighth Amendments to the Constitution. Despite the seemingly explicit protections found in those four amendments, accused individuals enjoyed only limited substantive protection from arbitrary violations of criminal due process for better than a century and a half of this nation's history, as they protected defendants primarily only against intrusions by the federal government.

Much of that changed in the 1960s with a number of decisions handed down by the Warren Court. During that period, the Supreme Court applied many of the provisions of the Bill of Rights against state governments by incorporating most of the protections given to accused persons in the federal judicial system. In addition, the Warren Court gave increased substance to these rights, holding government officials accountable under the Bill of Rights for their actions at highway road stops, during the interrogation of witnesses at the police station, and elsewhere.[41] Even the right to counsel was broadened to extend to far more of those accused of committing crimes. During the late 1980s and 1990s under Chief Justice William Rehnquist, the Court scaled back some of these protections. Nevertheless, defendants forced to weave their way through the criminal justice system today still enjoy numerous rights protections that were not guaranteed before the Warren Court era.

bill of attainder An act of a legislature declaring a person (or group) guilty of some crime, and then carrying out punishment without a trial. The Constitution denies Congress the ability to issue a bill of attainder.

ex post facto law A law that punishes someone for an act that took place in the past, at a time when the act was not illegal. The Constitution denies government the ability to write laws ex post facto.

Fourth Amendment Rights

THE FOURTH AMENDMENT: *The right of the people to be secure in their persons, houses, papers and effects, against unreasonable searches and seizures, shall not be violated, and no Warrants shall issue, but upon probable cause. ...*

The right of citizens to be free from unreasonable searches and seizures has a long history in America. Before the American Revolution, colonists loudly protested English abuses of the power to inspect merchants' goods through the use of an unlimited "general warrant." Although the Fourth Amendment had been in place for nearly two centuries, the Warren Court modernized the rules governing police searches with its decision in *Katz v. United States* (1967).[42] The Court's ruling created the **Katz test**, which requires that the government attain a warrant demonstrating "probable cause" for any investigative activity that violates a person's reasonable expectation of privacy, whether or not the person is at home. A **warrant** is a document issued by a judge or magistrate that allows law enforcement to search or seize items at a home, business, or anywhere else that might be specified.

Perhaps the most controversial aspect of the Fourth Amendment is the mechanism by which it is enforced. Although no specific provision for enforcing civil liberties is provided in the amendment, since its 1961 decision in *Mapp v. Ohio*,[43] the Supreme Court has demanded that the states adhere to the **exclusionary rule**, by which all evidence obtained by police in violation of the Bill of Rights must be "excluded" from admission in a court of law, where it might have assisted in convicting those who have been accused of committing crimes. Complaints about the exclusionary rule focus on its most likely beneficiaries: those who are guilty of committing some wrongdoing. They are the ones with the most potential evidence against them and thus have the most to gain from such exclusion. Detractors also complain about the "injustice" of the rule—whenever evidence is thrown out because of a warrantless search by police, "the criminal is to go free because the constable has blundered." Defenders of the rule counter that without a means of excluding such evidence, the government could violate the rights of guilty and innocent individuals alike by conducting the equivalent of fishing expeditions.

Since the 1960s, the Court has modified application of the exclusionary rule somewhat, although it has refused to back down from its central requirements. The most significant of these modifications is the **good faith exception** to the rule, which was first instituted in 1984: if a search warrant is invalid through no fault of the police (for e.g., the judge puts the wrong date on the warrant), evidence obtained under that warrant may still be admitted into court. Police may also, under certain circumstances, conduct warrantless searches of a defendant's premises. The allowable circumstances for a warrantless search include (1) the search is incidental to a lawful arrest; (2) the defendant has given consent to be searched; (3) the police are in "hot pursuit" of the defendant; and (4) the evidence is in "plain view" of police standing in a place where they have the legal right to be. Police may also briefly stop individuals driving in their cars, or conduct a "pat down" of suspicious individuals for weapons—in neither case is a warrant required. Nevertheless, police should conduct such warrantless searches with caution, as the good faith exception may be relied on only when conducting searches under the authority of a warrant.

Advances in technology and new innovations in police work have invited new types of Fourth Amendment civil liberties claims, and a potential reinterpretation of those rights by the U.S. Supreme Court. The testing of defendants for drug or alcohol use through breathalyzer tests and the taking of blood samples may require the police to jump through a series of procedural hoops imposed on them by the state, but no warrant is generally required in either instance when the defendant is in the legitimate custody of the police. Similarly, the DNA testing of defendants has provided a significant breakthrough in the prosecution of difficult cases that lack

Katz **test** The legal standard that requires the government to attain a warrant demonstrating "probable cause" for any "search" that violates a person's actual and reasonable expectation of privacy.

warrant A document issued by a judge or magistrate that allows law enforcement to search or seize items at a home, business, or anywhere else that might be specified.

exclusionary rule The legal rule requiring that all evidence illegally obtained by police in violation of the Bill of Rights must be "excluded" from admission in a court of law, where it might have assisted in convicting those accused of committing crimes.

good faith exception An exception to the exclusionary rule stating that if a search warrant is invalid through no fault of the police, evidence obtained under that warrant may still be admitted into court.

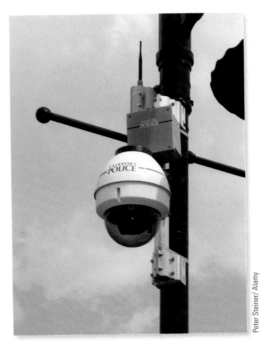

Peter Steiner/ Alamy

The Syracuse Common Council spent $150,000 on police surveillance cameras such as these. Critics complain that this type of comprehensive surveillance by police violates citizens' privacy rights.

eyewitnesses or other "hard" evidence of the crime. The use of thermal imaging scans, which expand police investigative tactics from afar, has also been tested in the courts. A thermal imaging scan detects infrared radiation, which then converts radiation into images based on relative warmth, operating somewhat like a video camera showing heat images. In the mid-1990s, police forces began to employ the device to detect the presence of indoor halide lights used to grow marijuana plants inside large buildings; police are able to conduct these scans from vehicles parked across the street from the buildings in question. Do such scans violate a person's reasonable expectation of privacy? "Yes," said the Supreme Court, in a narrow 5–4 decision handed down in 2001:[44] "Where the Government uses a device that is not in general public use, to explore details of the home that would previously have been unknowable without physical intrusion, the surveillance is a 'search' and is presumptively unreasonable without a warrant."

Recently, some communities have posted cameras at stoplights that produce photographic evidence of traffic violations. Other communities have installed cameras on street corners in busy areas. When used in conjunction with computer databanks of convicted criminals, these cameras can provide surveillance capable of instantly detecting the presence of such figures on the street. Officials in Tampa, Florida, have recently turned to closed-circuit television systems to assist police departments in performing surveillance. Specifically, face-recognition software programmed to identify certain wanted individuals has been employed on the streets of Tampa as well as in certain airports; an extensive network of cameras deployed throughout those areas can theoretically identify the faces of wanted individuals and alert authorities quickly and efficiently of their presence.

Reviews of this technology have so far been mixed: Critics complain that the system often makes false matches in the same way that humans so often are mistaken. Civil libertarians further complain that the use of surveillance cameras in general violates many citizens' privacy rights, which they believe extend beyond the privacy of their own homes. Tampa abandoned the face-recognition system in April 2001, but other cities continue to rely on closed-circuit cameras in general as a means of detecting crime—or, if possible, preventing it from taking place.

To date, none of these modern police tactics has been successfully challenged on Fourth Amendment grounds. But as the use of these techniques is broadened—perhaps to facilitate racial profiling or other controversial forms of police investigation—it is certain that legal challenges will be waged.

Fifth Amendment Rights

THE FIFTH AMENDMENT: *No person shall be held to answer for a capital, or otherwise infamous crime, unless on a presentment or indictment of a grand jury . . . nor shall any person be subject for the same offense to be twice put in jeopardy of life or limb; nor shall be compelled in any criminal case to be a witness against himself.*

Under the Fifth Amendment, the accused enjoy an assortment of rights that may prove crucial to their defense. The requirement that a grand jury, a jury that meets to decide whether the evidence is sufficient to justify a prosecutor's request that a case go to trial, be convened for serious crimes is theoretically significant; it forces prosecutors to convince an initial jury that a defendant should rightfully be forced to go to trial. (Grand juries do not decide on a defendant's guilt or innocence.) In practice, however, the grand jury requirement is rarely much of an obstacle to a skilled prosecutor, who can selectively present evidence to the jury members outside the view of the defendant or the defendant's lawyer. Moreover, because the grand jury requirement was never incorporated, it applies only to federal prosecutors in federal court.[45]

The **double jeopardy clause** is a source of much greater protection for defendants: it provides that no defendant may be tried twice for the same crime. Prosecutors must weigh carefully their probability of success at trial and bring forth all the relevant resources at their disposal. If the jury acquits the defendant, the prosecutor cannot try the defendant again. Still, the double jeopardy clause does not stop an altogether different government from retrying the defendant for violating that government's own laws. This occurred in the high-profile case of several white Los Angeles police officers who were accused in 1991 of beating Rodney King, an African American motorist whom they had stopped for a traffic violation. The acquittal of the police set off a series of race riots in Los Angeles. Later, federal charges were brought against the police for violating King's civil rights. At the federal trial, the officers were convicted.

Another provision of the Fifth Amendment is the so-called self-incrimination clause, which prevents individuals from being compelled to testify against themselves. Although originally interpreted to provide protection for defendants only in the courtroom, the self-incrimination clause today offers substantial protection to defendants being questioned by police at the station house or elsewhere. Certainly the clause protects defendants from being coerced or tortured into confessing to crimes. (That form of protection is valuable enough: as shown in Figure 4-1, the right against self-incrimination ranks high in public support.) But the Warren Court truly changed this area of the law in the now famous case of *Miranda v. Arizona* (1966).[46] In that ruling, the Supreme Court announced the requirement that **Miranda warnings** be read to all defendants in custody before they are questioned by police.

Ernesto Miranda was convicted of the March 1963 kidnapping and rape of an 18-year-old girl in Phoenix, Arizona. Soon after the crime, the police picked up Miranda, who fit the description of the girl's attacker. Officers immediately took him into an interrogation room and told him (falsely) that he had been positively identified by his victim. After two hours of questioning, Miranda confessed. At trial, the defense counsel prodded one of the detectives into admitting that Miranda had never been given the opportunity to seek advice from an attorney prior to his interrogation. Miranda was nevertheless convicted and sentenced to 40 to 60 years in prison. On appeal, the U.S. Supreme Court in 1966 set aside Miranda's conviction. Chief Justice Warren wrote: "Prior to any questioning, the person must be warned that he has a right to remain silent, that any statement he does make may be used as evidence against him, and that he has a right to the presence of an attorney, either retained or appointed. …"

Miranda was retried, this time without his confession being introduced into evidence at the trial, and again convicted. Although his original confession could not be used, a former girlfriend testified that Miranda had told her about the kidnapping and rape. After Miranda was paroled in 1972, he spent time in and out of prison before being stabbed fatally in a bar at the age of 34. Thanks to police drama shows and movies, the *Miranda* warnings are better known to citizens today than are any other constitutional protections: police must routinely tell suspects being questioned that they have the right to remain silent and the right to a court-appointed attorney, and confirm that

double jeopardy clause The constitutional protection that those accused of a crime cannot be tried twice for the same crime.

Miranda **warning** The U.S. Supreme Court's requirement that an individual who is arrested must be read a statement that explains the person's right to remain silent and the right to an attorney.

Balancing Police Surveillance Techniques with the Need for Individual Privacy

Americans have long accepted that even in a free society they must consent to some degree of police surveillance of their activities. When an individual takes a walk in a public park or drives a car along a public thoroughfare, he or she can expect those activities will be observed by complete strangers, including members of law enforcement. Under Fourth Amendment precedents, the government must have a warrant to search someone—even in a public place—if the person maintains a "reasonable expectation of privacy" in his or her actions. Of course, law enforcement officers' increasing use of technology for surveillance purposes complicates this area of the law, forcing the Court to weigh the interests of society against those of the individual in this context.

Then

In 1967, the Supreme Court for the first time ruled that nonphysical government intrusion may require a warrant. In *Katz v. United States*, the court considered the case of Charles Katz, who made illegal gambling wagers by using a public pay phone booth—the Federal Bureau of Investigation (FBI) had secretly attached an electronic bugging device (without a warrant or probable cause) to the outside of the booth to record all conversations. The government defended its actions by asserting that the phone booth was in the public, and the bugging device was on the outside of the booth, where others could legally go. The Supreme Court rejected this argument: By a 7–1 vote, it held that the recording of Katz's conversation violated the privacy "upon which he justifiably relied." *Katz* established that the Fourth Amendment protects not just "things," but the reasonable expectations of people as well.

In 1986, the Court ruled that this new Fourth Amendment doctrine was not unlimited. In *California v. Ciraolo*,[47] Dante Ciraolo was charged with growing marijuana in his backyard. Ciraolo put up two large fences to keep the activity private; meanwhile, the Santa Clara police photographed the marijuana plants from a private airplane 400 feet above the ground. This time, by a 5–4 vote, the Supreme Court held that so long as the plants were visible to the "naked eye" from above, the government did not require a search warrant, and Ciraolo's reasonable expectation of privacy was not violated.

Now

In 2012, the police learned that they could not over-rely on technology to conduct surveillance. In *U.S. v. Jones*,[48] the Supreme Court ruled that the police decision to attach a global positioning system (GPS) device to a vehicle without a warrant, thus allowing them to monitor its movements on a nearly continuous basis, was unconstitutional. The Court held that because the police had physically intruded onto the defendant's private property to attach the device, the information discovered from the device could not be admitted in court. Unfortunately, the Court's opinion left many significant questions unanswered: Could the government monitor movements from a distance if no physical intrusion was necessary? What about the acquisition of text messages and e-mails retained by the individuals' cell phone providers? As technology grows more sophisticated, the police will enjoy a significant advantage over targets, so long as privacy expectations do not raise even more red flags with the Court.

In 2012 the Supreme Court ruled that the police cannot attach GPS tracking devices such as this one to cars without a warrant.

For Critical Thinking and Discussion

1. Have advances in modern technology expanded or contracted citizens' conceptions of what privacy they actually enjoy? Is it still reasonable to assume that conversations on cell phones remain private? What about e-mail messages and texts? Is anything that you do or write on a social networking site such as Facebook actually private?

2. What steps must an individual take to keep his or her activities private from government?

the suspects understand these rights. Perhaps that's why a more conservative Supreme Court conceded in the case of *Dickerson v. United States* (2000)[49] that *Miranda* has become so "embedded in routine police practice" that the warnings have become "part of our national culture." Thus a failure to read the list of *Miranda* rights to witnesses may still result in any subsequent confession to the police being thrown out of court by virtue of the exclusionary rule.[50]

Sixth Amendment Rights

THE SIXTH AMENDMENT: *In all criminal prosecutions, the accused shall … have the Assistance of Counsel for his defense.*

Images of beleaguered and confused defendants trying desperately to defend themselves against experienced and well-seasoned prosecutors are now mostly a thing of the past. In 1963, the Supreme Court in *Gideon v. Wainwright*[51] ordered a new trial for an indigent defendant who had been ordered by the state of Florida to defend himself in a criminal trial, even though he possessed no legal training. Under prevailing Sixth Amendment standards today, no indigent criminal defendant can be sentenced to jail unless the defendant has been provided with a lawyer at no cost. This constitutional right to the assistance of counsel even extends beyond the trial: a court-appointed lawyer must assist the defendant in preparing the case and in all other hearings and meetings before trial. Some critics of the criminal justice system cite the disparity that often exists between the quality of court-appointed counsel and of paid counsel for well-off defendants. Nevertheless, public defenders' offices have been established all over the country in response to the requirement that indigent defendants be provided with lawyers.

Eighth Amendment Rights

THE EIGHTH AMENDMENT: *Excessive bail shall not be required, nor excessive fines imposed, nor cruel and unusual punishments inflicted.*

The Eighth Amendment deals in a limited way with defendants being held for trial: according to its language, **bail**, which is an amount of money paid to the court as security against a defendant's illegal flight before trial, may not be excessive. In practice, that provision applies only when bail is proper in the first place; many high-risk defendants are held either to prevent flight or to ensure that they do not cause more harm while on release. In those instances, bail may be denied altogether without any violation of the Constitution.

Far more significant are the concluding words of the Eighth Amendment with respect to "cruel and unusual punishment." No government may impose a cruel and unusual punishment on an individual, but there remains heated debate over what is "cruel and unusual." Traditionally, the clause prohibited only those punishments that even the drafters of the Bill of Rights would have disapproved of—drawing and quartering, beheading, and other forms of extreme torture. In recent times, the Court has added to the mix the requirement of "proportionality," in which serious punishments may not be imposed for relatively minor offenses. Thus, for instance, the Court struck down imprisonment for the controversial offense of "being addicted to the use of narcotics" on the ground that the state was punishing someone for an illness.

The Supreme Court currently rejects the premise that all applications of the death penalty are inherently "cruel and unusual." Most modern lawsuits by prisoners on "death row" focus on the manner by which the death sentence has been imposed. Any judge or jury that imposes capital punishment must have the opportunity to consider

bail An amount of money determined by a judge that the accused must pay to a court as security against his or her freedom before trial.

Whole Woman's Health v. Hellerstedt (2016)

In *Whole Woman's Health v. Hellerstedt* (2016),[52] the U.S. Supreme Court considered two Texas laws that, once they took effect, would decrease the number of clinics performing abortions in that state from 41 (in 2013) to less than 10. The first of the two provisions at issue required each abortion clinic to be outfitted with the physical and professional facilities equal to a surgical center, even if the clinic mainly performs abortions by the use of drugs rather than surgery. The second provision would require any doctor who performed abortions in a clinic to have the professional privilege of admitting patients to a full-scale hospital within 30 miles of the clinic in case of medical emergencies. Do such laws cause an "undue burden" on a woman's right to abortion (the two-decades-old standard in abortion cases) if they have the effect of decreasing so dramatically the number of abortion clinics in the state? On June 27, 2016, the Supreme Court said "Yes" and struck both laws down as unconstitutional by votes of 5-3. The high Court found that both laws placed a substantial obstacle in the path of women seeking a pre-viability abortion, and thus were unconstitutional.

A Planned Parenthood medical clinic in St. Paul, Minnesota.

For Critical Thinking and Discussion

1. When the Court is considering a civil liberties claim, should it weigh heavily the degree to which the law in question chills or reduces the likelihood that a constitutional right can be exercised?

2. Would you prefer constitutional rules that are more cut and dry; i.e., that any burden on the right is unconstitutional … not just undue burdens? Does the determination of whether a burden is "undue" give too much discretionary power to judges?

3. Are you confident that courts are more qualified than legislatures to determine the actual real-life effect of such restrictions?

mitigating circumstances that might generate some sympathy for the accused. Nor can a jury impose a death sentence at the same time that it finds the defendant guilty; the defendant's lawyers must be given a chance to argue against imposition of the death penalty without also having to prove the defendant is innocent. Finally, certain defendants may not receive the death penalty. In 2002, the Court in *Atkins v. Virginia* ruled executions impermissible in the case of defendants with an intellectual disability.[53] Then in 2005, the Court also ruled executions impermissible for defendants who committed their crimes while under the age of 18.

Critics of the system claim that so many death penalty cases are held up on appeal that bad luck and misfortune are inevitable in the process.[54] Furthermore, advances in DNA testing technology have revealed that some prisoners on death row were innocent of the crime for which they had been sentenced to death. Even in the face of unrelenting popular support for the death penalty, governors in Illinois and Maryland recently announced a "moratorium" on executions in their respective states, to be continued as long as the process by which death sentences are determined remains so riddled with errors.

4-6 | The Modern Right to Privacy

Perhaps no single constitutional right garnered more controversial attention during the second half of the twentieth century than the right to have an abortion. Unlike all the other rights mentioned so far in this chapter, however, neither the specific right to abortion nor the more general right to privacy is explicitly referred to in the Constitution or in the amendments to the Constitution. The right to privacy is thus often referred to as an unwritten or "unenumerated" right. The Ninth Amendment counsels against dismissing such rights offhand. It reads: "The enumeration in the Constitution of certain rights, shall not be construed to deny or disparage others retained by the people." In other words, the fact that other rights such as freedom of speech are written down in the Bill of Rights does not mean that the Constitution doesn't also recognize certain unwritten rights.

The recognition of unstated rights in the Constitution raises difficult questions, such as how to justify recognizing certain unenumerated rights but not others. In 1965, the Supreme Court stepped into this controversy with its decision in *Griswold v. Connecticut*,[55] when it invalidated an 1879 Connecticut law prohibiting the dissemination of information about and the sale of contraceptives. Seven of the nine justices ruled that although the right to birth control is not explicitly mentioned in the Constitution, several provisions of the Bill of Rights (the First, Third, Fourth, and Fifth) and the Fourteenth Amendment, taken together, suggest that these provisions create a "zone of privacy" that includes within it the right to decide whether or not to bear a child. Although the Supreme Court's methods were considered highly speculative, widespread acceptance of birth control devices allowed the Supreme Court to avoid controversy in the years following the decision.[56]

No such sidestepping of heated controversy was possible in 1973, when the Supreme Court formally recognized the constitutional right to abortion in *Roe v. Wade*.[57] By the early 1970s, nearly 15 states had passed liberal abortion laws, but lawyers for Norma McCorvey (she used the pseudonym of "Jane Roe" for purposes of her lawsuit) argued that the decision to end a pregnancy was a constitutional right that *all 50 states* must adhere to. McCorvey herself had been unable to secure a legal abortion in Texas and so eventually gave birth and put her baby up for adoption. The Supreme Court agreed to take her case and rule on the general constitutionality of abortion restrictions.

In ruling in McCorvey's favor, the Supreme Court affirmed that the Constitution recognizes a right to privacy in general—and thus a right to abortion more specifically—even though neither of those rights is ever spelled out explicitly. Such a right is not absolute throughout the term of the pregnancy, however. The author of the opinion, Justice Harry Blackmun, divided the pregnancy into three stages as part of a highly controversial *trimester framework*. During the first trimester, a woman's right to end her pregnancy is absolute. During the second trimester, the right is nearly absolute, although the government has the right to restrict abortions that might pose threats to a woman's health. Finally, in the third trimester (when the fetus is potentially viable), the state government is allowed to impose any abortion restrictions on the mother, so long as they do not limit efforts to protect the life or health of the mother.[58]

The number of legal abortions that occurred in the United States rose dramatically in the years immediately following *Roe v. Wade*. The decision also unleashed a fury of controversy from antiabortion interest groups and conservative lawmakers. The election of Ronald Reagan to the presidency in 1980 and his reelection in 1984 set the stage for *Roe v. Wade*'s weakening; as a candidate for high office, Reagan had specifically targeted *Roe v. Wade* as a case of illegitimate judicial activism and had promised to nominate Supreme Court justices who would overturn the controversial decision. Reagan's more conservative Supreme Court appointments began to make their presence known during the late 1980s, when increasingly severe restrictions on abortion were upheld by the Court.

In 1992, the Supreme Court overhauled *Roe v. Wade*'s controversial trimester framework in *Planned Parenthood v. Casey*.[59] Although the Court did not specifically overturn *Roe*, the justices replaced the trimester framework with a less-stringent *undue burden test*: does the restriction at issue—regardless of what trimester it affects—*unduly burden* a woman's right to privacy under the Constitution? One example of this new constitutional test at work can be found in the Court's approach to state-mandated 24-hour waiting periods for abortions. Under *Roe v. Wade*, the requirement that a woman wait for an abortion in either of the first two trimesters would have been unconstitutional. Yet in *Casey*, the Court held that such a waiting period does not unduly burden the woman's right to privacy. Other regulations that have been upheld under the *Casey* framework include the requirement that minors seek permission from a parent or a court before having an abortion and the requirement that women seeking abortions be provided information about the specific medical effects an abortion will have on the fetus.

Not all abortion restrictions are allowed under this new framework. In *Casey*, the Supreme Court invalidated a requirement that women notify their spouses of their intention to have abortions. Yet many more provisions restricting abortion have been upheld since 1992 under the less restrictive *Casey* doctrine. In *Gonzales v. Carhart* (2007),[60] the Supreme Court upheld the Partial Birth Abortion Act of 2003, which effectively banned the use of the "intact dilation and extraction" abortion procedure, most often performed during the second trimester of pregnancy. By contrast, the Court more recently held that laws which place substantial obstacles in the path of women seeking abortions may be unconstitutional if those obstacles cannot be defended on clear medical or other legitimate grounds.

Once the unwritten right to privacy became a reality in constitutional law, it seemed inevitable that citizens might try to claim other unwritten rights implicating privacy in the same fashion. Although most efforts to expand the right to privacy beyond abortion and birth control have met with limited success, the Court has not always shut the door on these claims. In 1986, the Court held that a Georgia law that criminalized acts of sodomy by homosexuals was constitutional. Seventeen years later in the case of *Lawrence v. Texas*,[61] the Court reversed itself, holding that a Texas law making it a crime for two people of the same sex to engage in certain types of intimate sexual conduct did in fact violate the individual's right to due process.

The highly visible prosecutions of Dr. Jack Kevorkian for helping terminally ill patients end their lives has brought added attention to the issue of physician-assisted suicide in recent years. On April 13, 1999, Kevorkian, a retired pathologist, was sentenced to jail in Michigan for helping a terminally ill man die by direct injection, a form of voluntary euthanasia. Kevorkian, labeled by many of his opponents as "Dr. Death," had already acknowledged publicly that he had helped at least 90 other people to die by assisted suicide in Michigan between 1990 and 1997. Indeed, when enforcement authorities in Michigan initially refused to charge Kevorkian with killing his most recent patient, he took a tape of the incident to CBS television and aired it on the widely watched news program *60 Minutes*. On the program, Kevorkian challenged the state to act; three days later, he got his wish.

Questions remain about Kevorkian's tactics—do terminally ill patients have the right to end their lives, and if so, can a licensed physician assist them in doing so? Although the Court has been willing to recognize a right of terminally ill patients to end their medical treatment, it has steadfastly refused to extend that privilege to the active termination of one's life. In 1997, the Supreme Court held that no such constitutional right exists, although the justices were significantly divided as to the specific reasons why that is so. But the Court also indicated that states are free to legalize physician-assisted suicide. Since then, only one state (Oregon) has enacted an assisted-suicide law. As for Kevorkian, after serving eight years of his prison sentence for second-degree murder, he was granted parole on June 1, 2007, and died four years later at the age of 83.

From Your Perspective

Arming Teachers Behind the Schoolhouse Door

In response to incidents of gun violence on college campuses, the Texas legislature in 2015 passed a law allowing licensed gun owners to carry concealed handguns in classrooms, libraries, and other campus buildings. Apparently there is also growing support for teachers to carry licensed weapons in high schools, middle schools, and even some elementary schools. Does the constitutionally guaranteed right to possess a firearm extend to teachers seeking to protect themselves and their students in the classroom? In more than half of the 50 states, adults who legally own guns are not prohibited from carrying them in public schools—and in seven of those states, teachers and staff are explicitly empowered to do so. In most cases, they do not have to inform principals, other teachers, or parents that they have done so. School administrations, of course, can decide to gather the information from their employees, but they may decide not to disclose the information to anyone else. Consider that since the Utah legislature in 2004 specifically authorized teachers to carry guns in classrooms, no fatal K–12 school shootings have occurred in that state. Still, some parent groups argue that guns in classrooms present more risk than the potential for reward.

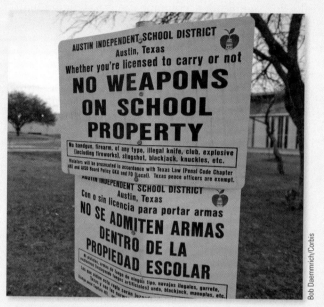

A sign in English and Spanish on the grounds of Lyndon Baines Johnson High School in Austin, Texas, warns of a prohibition against weapons on school grounds.

For Critical Thinking and Discussion

1. Do you think the Second Amendment right to bear arms extends to teachers who teach in K–12 public schools? Why or why not?

2. If arming teachers reduces the number of violent incidents that take place in schools, does the reward justify the potential risks?

3. Does the government have a compelling reason to prohibit teachers from bringing lawfully owned firearms into schools? What reason could they offer?

Summary

4-1 The Bill of Rights: Origins and Evolution

- Civil liberties are rights that government cannot deny to citizens, whereas civil rights are owed to members of certain groups that afford them equal treatment under the law. The Framers guaranteed ratification of the proposed constitution by promising that Congress would propose a "bill of rights" protected from intrusion by the federal government; not until the mid-twentieth century did the U.S. Supreme Court, through a process known as incorporation, use the Fourteenth Amendment's due process clause to require that state governments uphold most of these protections as well.

4-2 Freedom of Religion and the Establishment Clause

- The free exercise clause arguably bans the government from forcing adherents of a certain religion to engage in activities that would otherwise violate their religious beliefs, except through neutral, generally applicable laws. The establishment clause prohibits the government from enacting any law "respecting an establishment of religion"; in recent decades this has led to a strict separation between church and state on some issues, while allowing significant accommodations to religion in other cases.

4-3 Free Expression Rights

- The First Amendment rights of free speech and press are "preferred freedoms" that enjoy heightened protection under the Constitution because free expression promotes the marketplace of ideas, acts as a watchdog on government, and advances the capacity for individuals to create ideas and improve society.
- Speech includes such activities as flag burning (referred to as symbolic speech) and other forms of expressive conduct, all of which enjoy a high level of protection from the courts. By contrast, the Supreme Court has exempted obscenity, libel, fighting words, and other lesser-value speech from this heightened level of protection. Meanwhile, the press is afforded significant protection from libel suits (which are exceedingly difficult to prosecute) and from prior restraints, granted only under extremely rare conditions.

4-4 The Right to Bear Arms

- The Constitution protects the right of individuals to possess a firearm, although government retains the power to enact a broad range of firearms laws, including reasonable restrictions on possession by felons, or in sensitive places such as schools or government buildings.

4-5 The Rights of the Criminally Accused

- The Fourth Amendment protects the right of citizens to be free from unreasonable searches and seizures; with some exceptions, a warrant (issued only based on probable cause) is necessary for a valid search. Additional rights of the accused are articulated in the Fifth Amendment, including the double jeopardy clause, the grand jury requirement, and the self-incrimination clause. The Supreme Court has ruled that police must read the *Miranda* warnings to anyone who is arrested, which indicates not only the right to remain silent, but also the right to an attorney. (A failure to read *Miranda* rights to a suspect in custody may lead to a confession being excluded as evidence at trial.)
- A more comprehensive right to counsel is protected by the Sixth Amendment, and the Eighth Amendment protects against the government imposing excessive bail requirements or cruel and unusual punishment.

4-6 The Modern Right to Privacy

- The Supreme Court has recognized a general right to privacy under the due process clause, which includes a qualified right to abortion and a limited right to die. *Roe v. Wade* was the 1973 case that first established abortion rights under the Constitution; however, a more conservative Supreme Court in recent years has allowed the states to place more restrictions on abortion rights, so long as those restrictions are justified on some medical or other ground beyond simply the desire to reduce the number of abortions. And although the Court has recognized the right of terminally ill patients to end their medical treatment, it has refused to extend that privilege to the active termination of one's life. By contrast, the Court has recognized greater rights of sexual privacy in recent years, including a right to sodomy.

Key Terms

bail (p. 97)
bill of attainder (p. 92)
civil liberties (p. 76)
double jeopardy clause (p. 95)
establishment clause (p. 81)
ex post facto law (p. 92)

exclusionary rule (p. 93)
free exercise clause (p. 79)
good faith exception (p. 93)
incorporation (p. 77)
Katz test (p. 93)
Lemon test (p. 83)

libel (p. 86)
Miranda warning (p. 95)
prior restraint (p. 88)
SLAPS test (p. 88)
symbolic speech (p. 89)
warrant (p. 93)

Test Yourself

1. Who framed the original Bill of Rights in the First Congress, prior to its formal ratification in 1791?
   a. Alexander Hamilton
   b. John Jay
   c. Thomas Jefferson
   d. James Madison

2. What provision of the Constitution was used by the Supreme Court to "incorporate" most of the Bill of Rights against the states as well as the federal government?
   a. The Fourteenth Amendment's due process clause
   b. Article I's elastic clause
   c. Article I's enumerated powers
   d. The Fourteenth Amendment's equal protection clause

3. The "unalienable rights" that Jefferson talked about in the Declaration of Independence constitute what kind of rights?
   a. Positive rights
   b. Natural rights
   c. Equal rights
   d. Fundamental rights

4. Distinguish between "civil liberties" and "civil rights." Give an example of each.

5. Which of the following practices by government have been upheld as constitutional by the Supreme Court?
   a. Providing private school vouchers to parents
   b. Offering a religious prayer for students during the school day

   c. Reading a religious prayer at a high school graduation ceremony
   d. Having a religious prayer read at the start of a high school football game

6. Which Supreme Court decision articulated a controversial three-part test to determine if a law or practice violates the establishment clause?
   a. *Barron v. Baltimore*
   b. *Lemon v. Kurtzman*
   c. *Engel v. Vitale*
   d. *Lee v. Weisman*

7. What are the different schools of thought when it comes to interpreting the establishment clause?

8. Which Supreme Court ruling effectively ended the legal debate over flag burning by declaring it a form of constitutionally protected speech?
   a. *Miller v. California*
   b. *Texas v. Johnson*
   c. *Tinker v. Des Moines*
   d. *United States v. O'Brien*

9. The "SLAPS" test was articulated by the Supreme Court in *Miller v. California* to provide a framework for determining speech that
   a. is libelous.
   b. is slanderous.
   c. promotes riotous behavior.
   d. is obscene.

10. The current test that is used to determine whether political speech that advocates unlawful action is protected is the
    a. clear and present danger test.
    b. imminent danger test.
    c. compelling state interest test.
    d. legitimate state interest test.

11. What is "symbolic speech"? What forms of symbolic speech has the Supreme Court ruled are protected by the Constitution?

12. What was the Supreme Court case that ruled that the Second Amendment forbids the government from banning all forms of handgun possession in the home for the immediate purpose of self-defense?
    a. *McDonald v. Chicago*
    b. *Virginia v. Black*
    c. *Reno v. ACLU*
    d. *District of Columbia v. Heller*

13. What is it about the language of the Second Amendment that has caused differences in interpretations about the right to own a gun?

14. An act of a legislature that declares a person to be guilty of a crime without a trial is called a(n)
    a. ex post facto law.
    b. habeas corpus law.
    c. bill of attainder.
    d. letter of marquee.

15. Which of the following is *not* a valid exception to the Fourth Amendment requirement that the police obtain a proper warrant?
    a. At a traffic stop, a police officer seizes a gun that he sees in the back seat of a car.
    b. A police officer searches an apartment for a weapon based on a reliable tip from an informant.
    c. A police officer searches a suspect running from the scene of a crime.
    d. A warrant unintentionally lists the wrong address to be searched and the search (conducted in good faith) produces valuable evidence.

16. The legal standard that a judge uses to determine whether or not a warrant should be issued is
    a. reasonable cause.
    b. imminent danger.
    c. clear and present danger.
    d. probable cause.

17. How did the Supreme Court's decision in *Gideon v. Wainwright* alter the Sixth Amendment's mandate for a "right to an attorney"?

18. Which was the first Supreme Court case that recognized a right that was not explicitly mentioned in the Constitution?
    a. *Roe v. Wade*
    b. *Planned Parenthood v. Casey*
    c. *Griswold v. Connecticut*
    d. *Lawrence v. Texas*

19. *Roe v. Wade* guaranteed a women's right to an abortion
    a. unconditionally during the first three months of pregnancy.
    b. only when the mother's life is in danger.
    c. only in cases of rape or incest.
    d. with consent of the fetus's father.

Chip Somodevilla/Getty Images News/Getty Images

LEARNING OBJECTIVES

5-1 Types of Equality
- Define civil rights and the three types of equality: political, social, and economic.

5-2 The Struggle for Equality: Approaches and Tactics
- List the means groups employ to pursue equality within and outside the system.

5-3 The Struggle for Equality: Race, Ethnicity, and Civil Rights
- Assess the history of discrimination against racial and ethnic groups in America, including the role courts played in initially denying minorities full equality.
- Describe the court-created framework of equality, the voting rights legislation, and the challenges they have presented in recent times.

5-4 The Women's Movement and Gender Equality
- Summarize the history of women's rights, including the role of the courts in recognizing

such rights, from women's suffrage up through the present.
- Explain Title IX's effect on women's rights.

5-5 Other Group Struggles for Equality
- Trace the struggles for equality waged by other minority groups, including older Americans, Americans with disabilities, and gays and lesbians.

5-6 Continuing Struggles Over Equality in the Modern Era
- Assess the impact the war on terrorism has had on Muslim Americans.
- Evaluate the more recent battles waged over affirmative action, racial profiling, and the targeted policing of neighborhoods.

5

Civil Rights, Equality, and Social Movements

In the abstract, the word *equality* sits alongside lofty terms such as *liberty*, *freedom*, and *justice* as values that underlie American political culture. Unfortunately, when it comes to settling on a formal definition of equality, no consensus exists. "All men are created equal" was the phrase Thomas Jefferson penned in the Declaration of Independence of 1776. But Jefferson never intended that document to extend to African American slaves, at least not in the short run. When Abraham Lincoln warned in 1859 that "those who deny freedom to others, deserve it not for themselves," the future president of the United States did not consider the lot of women in American society, who at that time were not yet guaranteed the freedom to vote or own property, among other rights. As with any other abstract ideal, we must fully define *equality* and appreciate its implications in order to understand all that it encompasses.

Views on Racial and Ethnic Profiling

Many Americans have at one time or another experienced that uncomfortable sensation in their stomach upon seeing the blinking red and blue lights of a police car suddenly appear in the rear view mirror. Will the officer give me a ticket? Have I done something else wrong? Of course, this routine level of anxiety may increase significantly if the driver believes he or she has been singled out by law enforcement for extra scrutiny as a member of a racial or ethnic minority group. As a general matter, racial profiling violates the constitutional requirement that all persons be accorded equal protection of the law. Yet such practices persist. In Ferguson, Missouri—site of the controversial shooting of an 18-year-old African American (Michael Brown) by a white police officer in 2014—blacks accounted for 93 percent of all traffic stops during that calendar year. Meanwhile, FBI arrest data reveal that 1,581 other U.S. police departments (including those in Chicago and San Francisco) arrest African Americans at rates even higher than that in Ferguson.[1] If anything, the use of racial profiling has actually surged in the years since the 9/11 terrorist attacks, as the public seems increasingly willing to sacrifice principles of fair treatment in the name of national safety. Where do you stand in this conflict?

- Do you think it is ever justified for police to use racial or ethnic profiling when stopping motorists on roads and highways? What about at airport checkpoints or in shopping malls?
- Do you think views on racial profiling vary widely among the different racial and ethnic groups? If so, why do you think so?

To see how your answers compare to others, take the **Who Are You?** poll in MindTap!

5-1 | Types of Equality

References to different types of equality tend to appear again and again in discussions of American politics; political equality, social equality, and economic equality are among those most often referred to.

Political equality generally refers to a condition in which members of different groups possess substantially the same rights to participate actively in the political system. These rights include voting, running for office, and formally petitioning the government for redress of grievances. In a democracy, the rights to free speech, to free press, and to a quality education may also be considered necessary elements of political equality, as those who are denied such rights often are less able to exercise influence over the political process in any meaningful way. In the years immediately following the Civil War, some moderates in Congress argued that if freed slaves were simply given formal political equality, other benefits and privileges would inevitably follow. Reality quickly proved otherwise, as even African Americans in the North who were able to exercise their right to vote were generally unable to influence the political process.

Social equality extends beyond the granting of political rights; it refers additionally to equality and fair treatment within the various institutions in society, both public and private, that serve the public at large. Social equality calls for a sameness of treatment in stores, theaters, restaurants, hotels, and public transportation facilities, among many other operations open to the public. Jim Crow laws passed in the South during the late nineteenth century segregated many of these institutions, thus denying social equality to racial and ethnic minorities.

Economic equality remains the most controversial form of equality—indeed, its very mention often touches off heated debate among political officials. To some, society's responsibility to promote economic equality requires only that it provide equality of economic "opportunity," by which different groups enjoy substantially the same rights to

political equality A condition in which members of different groups possess substantially the same rights to participate actively in the political system. In the United States, these rights include voting, running for office, petitioning the government for redress of grievances, free speech, free press, and the access to an education.

social equality Equality and fair treatment of all groups within the various institutions in society, both public and private, that serve the public at large, including in stores, theaters, restaurants, hotels, and public transportation facilities, among many other operations open to the public.

economic equality May be defined as providing all groups the equality of opportunity for economic success, or as the equality of results. In the United States, the latter has been the more common understanding of economic equality.

108 **CHAPTER 5** CIVIL RIGHTS, EQUALITY, AND SOCIAL MOVEMENTS enter contracts, marry, purchase and sell property, and otherwise compete for resources in society. To others, economic equality extends beyond equality of economic opportunity to something approaching an "equality of results." Whichever meaning one gives to the term, economic equality has been exceedingly difficult to achieve. Although the government has introduced a graduated income tax and other resource-leveling measures during the past century to improve economic opportunities for the poor, large variances in the quality of education afforded to different groups continue to render economic equality an elusive ideal.

The term **civil rights** refers to those positive rights, whether political, social, or economic, conferred by the government on individuals or groups that had previously been denied them. What type of equality does the guarantee of civil rights promote? Immediately after the Civil War, civil rights legislation that provided for greater social equality (equal accommodations in hotels, restaurants, trains, and other public facilities) was struck down as unconstitutional by the U.S. Supreme Court. As a result, the package of civil rights granted to freed slaves included only limited political rights, including the right to vote. In the late 1950s and 1960s, renewed efforts to guarantee equality in all areas of American life led to the civil rights movement.

Many civil rights battles in American history have been waged by members of racial and ethnic minority groups, women, the physically disabled, the aged, and homosexuals who have also sought the political, social, and economic equality denied them. The Constitution of the United States and the amendments to it have provided a framework for these groups to use to win equality. As a result, the meaning of civil rights has been significantly expanded both in the scope of its protection and in the variety of groups who seek its guarantees.

civil rights Those positive rights, whether political, social, or economic, conferred by the government on individuals or groups.

5-2 | The Struggle for Equality: Approaches and Tactics

The methods and tactics various groups use to achieve equality have evolved since the end of the Civil War. Initially, the battle over what constituted the most effective means of fostering change—at least in the context of challenging racial discrimination—pitted two competing philosophies against each other. Booker T. Washington, who founded Tuskegee Normal and Industrial Institute (today Tuskegee University) in Alabama in 1881, advocated a philosophy of *accommodation*, which promoted vocational education for African Americans and opposed confrontation with the mostly white power structure in place in post–Civil War America. Washington urged his fellow African Americans to accept existing conditions, even to the point of tolerating racial segregation and all but surrendering the newly won right to vote. According to his philosophy, engaging in law-abiding practices and standing by former white oppressors would best prepare African Americans for the exercise of the franchise. Washington's philosophy of accommodation fit comfortably within the dominant conservative political and economic structure of his time. Although some critics charged him with accepting second-class citizenship for his race, Washington was perhaps the most powerful and influential figure in African American affairs until his death in 1915.[2]

Rep. G.K. Butterfield, Jr. (D-NC), Chairman of the Congressional Black Caucus since 2015.

Earl Gibson III/Getty Images

Washington's passive approach contrasted with the philosophy of *agitation*, which challenged racial discrimination and injustice through various forms of political activity. Among Washington's contemporaries, the most widely recognized proponent of this alternative approach was W. E. B. Du Bois. At the beginning of the twentieth century, Du Bois and his associates proposed a specific platform of legal, political, and social reforms to achieve social, economic, and political equality for African Americans.[3] Their demands included the unfettered right to vote and an immediate end to all segregation. Agitation eventually replaced accommodation as the dominant mode by which African Americans and other groups sought equality in twentieth-century America. New debates emerged, however, over what would be the most effective means and methods for achieving these reforms. Tactics that various groups have used to seek their civil rights are discussed next.

Working Within the Political System. Some groups have used the political process to implement reforms to end discrimination. In recent decades, for example, African Americans have used their substantial power as a voting bloc to influence the outcome of some elections. Various groups have expanded their influence more directly over public policies and programs by lobbying and petitioning government officials; in some cases members of these groups have been elected to high public office, giving them a place at the table of political power.

Litigation. When the political arena fails to provide adequate remedies to discrimination, a lawsuit brought before a court may afford a better opportunity for success. Founded in 1909 for the purpose of ensuring the political, educational, social, and economic equality of rights of all Americans, the National Association for the Advancement of Colored People (NAACP) focused its efforts on legal challenges to discrimination and segregation because the political arena had offered inadequate remedies. Civil rights legislation in particular had proven ineffective, with Southern state legislatures either ignoring or circumventing the laws. The NAACP and the Mexican-American Legal Defense and Education Fund, among other groups, won numerous legal battles that gradually broke down racial and ethnic barriers in education and elsewhere. These efforts culminated with high court decisions such as ***Brown v. Board of Education* (1954)**,[4] which ordered desegregation of public schools. In subsequent years women's groups, disabled people, and other victims of discrimination have similarly turned to the courts for remedies to discriminatory practices.

Legal Boycott. The organized refusal to buy, sell, or use certain goods or to perform certain services has long been a tool in economic battles waged between employers and unions. Adopting this tactic for use in the war on racial discrimination, African American citizens of Montgomery, Alabama, refused to ride the city's buses for more than a year in the mid-1950s; their efforts drained the city's public transportation budget and ultimately forced city officials to desegregate the bus system. In 2003, women's rights organizations discouraged some companies from sponsoring the Masters Golf Tournament held at the all-male Augusta National Golf Club in Augusta, Georgia.

Civil Disobedience. Sometimes citizens resort to passive resistance to what they see as an unjust government policy or law by openly refusing to obey it. Such a tactic may result in arrests, fines, or even jail time for those who practice it. Still, civil disobedience may also call attention to a group's plight in an especially effective way. The Reverend Martin Luther King Jr., who had studied the methods used by Mohandas Gandhi of India and other nonviolent protestors, applied these methods to the civil rights movement in the American South.

Brown v. Board of Education (1954) The 1954 U.S. Supreme Court decision that declared school segregation to be unconstitutional.

5-3 | The Struggle for Equality: Race, Ethnicity, and Civil Rights

The metaphor of the "melting pot" evokes an image of cultural assimilation in America achieved by the fusion of different nationalities, ethnicities, and cultures into a greater whole. In recent decades, increasing numbers of social scientists have rejected the melting pot image in favor of *multiculturalism*, a theory that views ethnic and racial groups as maintaining their own cultural distinctions and integrity within American society. Of course, the reality of the immigrant experience in America probably resides somewhere in between these two competing theories. Regardless, prejudice, stereotyping, and other discriminatory practices targeting racial and ethnic minorities have been a persistent theme throughout American history, and any rendering of how American society has evolved must take careful account of that reality.

Colonists who supported the American Revolution trumpeted the notion of equality as a means of justifying their war with England. Yet when the U.S. Constitution was drafted in 1787, the document said nothing about such a call to equality, nor did the Bill of Rights (ratified in 1791) guarantee to all citizens "equal protection of the law." The period following the Revolution offered equality primarily to property-owning white men. Nowhere did Jefferson's call for equality, as stated in the Declaration of Independence, seem more hollow than in the area of racial and ethnic group discrimination. Throughout the North, African Americans were denied the right to vote and numerous other economic and social privileges enjoyed by white citizens. In the South, the institution of slavery thrived for more than a half century after the Constitution was ratified.

Meanwhile, immigrants from a multitude of Spanish-speaking nations, Far East Asia, and elsewhere were treated as second-class citizens as well, suffering especially intense forms of discrimination both in economic relations as well as in society as a whole.

Racial Discrimination: From Slavery to Reconstruction

The organized antislavery movement in the United States began in the late eighteenth century as an effort to eradicate slavery through progressive elimination. Advocates of gradual emancipation believed that by preventing the extension of slavery to new areas and relocating emancipated slaves to areas outside the United States, slavery would eventually die out. Opposed to gradual emancipation were the abolitionists, who sought the immediate emancipation of all slaves. A leader of the abolitionist movement was William Lloyd Garrison, who founded the antislavery periodical *The Liberator* in 1831. It is noteworthy, however, that even extreme abolitionists such as Garrison believed that the "fatal characteristic" of slavery was that it denied African Americans the basic legal rights to own property, enter into contracts, and testify in court. Many abolitionists at the time did *not* believe that emancipation automatically entitled freed slaves to the right to vote or serve on juries. Even among some of the most ardent advocates of equality before the Civil War, a sharp distinction was often drawn between economic rights— which they felt African Americans were entitled to—and basic political rights including suffrage, which were somehow not viewed as natural entitlements.

Neither conception of civil rights for slaves gained much favor in the South, where the economy of the plantation system depended on slave labor. The southerners' approach to racial equality was perhaps best summed up by Chief Justice Roger Taney of Maryland, who in the landmark Supreme Court case of *Dred Scott v. Sandford* (1857)[5] wrote that blacks were "so far inferior that they had no rights which the white man was bound to respect." The initial rhetoric surrounding the outbreak of the Civil War in 1861 focused on issues such as states' rights and territorial expansion in addition to slavery. The Emancipation Proclamation issued by President Lincoln in 1863 declared the freedom of all slaves in states fighting the Union and allowed blacks to enlist in the Union Army. By the end of the struggle in 1865, the war was essentially transformed into a battle over the end of the institution of slavery.

With the Union victory in the Civil War, the complete emancipation of African Americans after the war was a foregone conclusion. Former slaves were able to legally marry, worship as they wished, and migrate to different parts of the country. But the years following the Civil War—normally referred to as the Reconstruction era (1865–1877) in American history—proved a mixed blessing for the newly freed slaves.[6] The **Civil War Amendments** to the Constitution did grant African Americans the rights of citizenship. The Thirteenth Amendment (ratified in 1865) banished slavery from all states and U.S. territories. The Fourteenth Amendment (ratified in 1868) granted full U.S. and state citizenship to all people born or naturalized in the United States and guaranteed to each person "the equal protection of the laws." Finally, the Fifteenth Amendment (1870) forbade the denial or abridgement of the right to vote by any government on account of race. The Republican-controlled Congress hoped that these three amendments would institutionalize freedom for the former slaves and protect their rights from being undermined by future generations.

During the Reconstruction era, many freed slaves were successful in getting on ballots in the former Confederate states—in all, 22 African Americans were elected to the House and 1 (Hiram Revels of Mississippi) was elected to the Senate during the latter part of the nineteenth century. African American participation in Congress trailed off at the beginning of the twentieth century, however, because restrictions on the franchise curtailed the political viability of most black candidates. No African American served in either house of Congress for most of the first three decades of the twentieth century, and just four served in the House up to 1954. After George Henry White (R-NC) left Congress in 1901, no African American was elected from a Southern state again until 1973, when Barbara Jordan (D-TX) and Andrew Young (D-GA) were elected to serve in the 93rd Congress.

Although African Americans achieved some gains during Reconstruction, the Reconstruction-era generation posed the greatest threat to those civil rights victories. The Fourteenth Amendment had been proposed in part to negate the infamous *Black Codes* passed by the southern states, which denied African Americans numerous economic and social rights. However, in *The Slaughterhouse Cases* (1873),[7] a conservative U.S. Supreme Court narrowly defined the scope of rights protected by the Fourteenth Amendment, holding that the great body of civil rights still lay under the protection of state governments, not the U.S. Constitution. The Civil Rights Act of 1875 attempted to ensure the social and political rights of freed slaves by, among other provisions, prohibiting discrimination in public accommodations. The Supreme Court invalidated the act in *The Civil Rights Cases* (1883),[8] ruling that whereas the Constitution prohibits the states from discriminating by race against certain civil rights, it does not protect the invasion of such civil rights by private individuals unaided by state authority. Therefore, privately owned restaurants and hotels could freely discriminate on the basis of race without violating the Constitution.

This judicial gutting of federal civil rights guarantees opened the way for numerous abuses of freed slaves once the federal government's military occupation of the South ended in 1877. Although the Fifteenth Amendment had given African American men the right to vote, the southern states imposed new barriers to disenfranchise the former slaves. They levied *poll taxes*, which a voter had to pay before being allowed to vote; they required potential voters to pass *literacy tests*; they demanded some form of property-owning and residency documentation; they issued a grandfather clause requirement, which stated that to be eligible to vote one's grandfather had to have voted; and they restricted blacks from participating in crucial party primaries. Discrimination against African Americans in all areas of public life soon became the norm. Terrorist groups like the Ku Klux Klan intimidated or threatened African Americans to keep them

Civil War Amendments The Thirteenth Amendment (ratified in 1865) banished slavery from all states and U.S. territories. The Fourteenth Amendment (ratified in 1868) granted full U.S. and state citizenship to all people born or naturalized in the United States and guaranteed to each person "the equal protection of the laws." The Fifteenth Amendment (1870) forbade the denial or abridgement of the right to vote by any government on account of race.

under control, sometimes backing up their threats with beatings, arson, or murder. White vigilante groups resorted to lynching in an effort to restore white supremacy and deny blacks their rights. Thus, while post–Civil War blacks were no longer slaves, they could hardly be considered equal citizens under the laws in place during the latter parts of the nineteenth century.

Other Forms of Discrimination in Nineteenth and Early Twentieth-Century America

Other racial and ethnic minority groups also struggled during this post-bellum period, suffering terrible hardships at the hands of the government and private groups. Hispanics—many of whom were descended from Mexicans living in the Southwest when it became part of the United States in the 1840s—were among the earliest victims of governmental discrimination as well. Even after immigration laws were tightened in the 1890s, hundreds of thousands of Mexicans continued to enter the United States both legally and illegally, drawn by opportunities in farming, mining, and other industries. Unfortunately, beginning in 1885, California and other states formally segregated Mexican students from white students in schools; this pattern continued up through the 1950s.

While white Americans migrated west during this period, millions of Native Americans were herded onto reservations according to a removal policy backed by the federal government. By a federal law passed in 1871, the government no longer agreed to recognize Native American tribes or nations as independent powers capable of entering treaties with the United States—all future tribal affairs were to be managed by the federal government without tribal consent. With passage of the Dawes Severalty Act in 1887, the U.S. government divided tribal lands still in existence among individual Indians who renounced their tribal holdings, further undermining tribal cultures and structures.

Although certain Native American tribes received piecemeal U.S. citizenship beginning in the 1850s and the Dawes Act granted citizenship to those who ceded their tribal holdings, the class of Native Americans as a whole was not admitted to full citizenship until 1924, nearly 60 years after freed slaves had been afforded that same privilege. The federal government's attempt to undo the tribal structure did not produce widespread assimilation of Indians into American society as proponents of the Dawes Act intended; many chose to remain on reservations in an attempt to protect their culture from outside influences.

Asian Americans were also victims of prejudice and mistreatment during the latter part of the nineteenth century. While immigrants from Japan and China in particular supplied much of the labor for building U.S. railroads in the nineteenth century, most were excluded from labor unions and denied other civil rights in the process. In the years that followed, the government enacted several immigration acts specifically designed to limit or prevent Asian immigration. For example, the Chinese Exclusion Act, passed in 1882, prohibited Chinese laborers from immigrating and denied U.S. citizenship to Chinese living in the United States. (Later the 1907 Gentleman's Agreement with Japan prohibited the immigration of Japanese laborers; the National Origins Act of 1924 then banned *all* Asians from further immigration to the United States.) In many West coast cities, Asian children were segregated into separate public schools in San Francisco, and the state of California restricted Japanese immigrants' rights to own farmland.

Racial and Ethnic Segregation and Governmental Barriers to Equality

Following the Civil War, some racial and ethnic minorities were able to use public accommodations as long as they could afford to pay for them. By the turn of the twentieth century, however, growing racial tensions, exacerbated by urbanization and industrialization, led to racial segregation throughout America. The Southern states

Jim Crow laws Laws used by some southern states that required segregation of non-whites and whites in public schools, railroads, buses, restaurants, hotels, theaters, and other public facilities. The laws excluded nonwhites from militias and denied them certain education and welfare services.

Plessy v. Ferguson (1896) The Supreme Court case that upheld a Louisiana segregation law on the theory that as long as the accommodations between the racially segregated facilities were equal, the equal protection clause was not violated. The Court's ruling effectively established the constitutionality of racial segregation and the notion of "separate but equal."

Mendez v. Westminster (1947) The federal court decision that ended the segregation of Mexican Americans in California primary schools.

enacted **Jim Crow laws**, which required segregation of whites and nonwhites in public schools, railroads, buses, restaurants, hotels, theaters, and other public facilities. The laws excluded nonwhites from militias and denied them certain education and welfare services. When Homer Plessy (described in court filings as being "seven-eighths Caucasian and one-eight African blood") was arrested on a Louisiana train for refusing to leave a seat in a coach section designated for whites, he challenged the Louisiana law requiring segregated railroad cars, arguing that the law violated the equal protection clause of the Fourteenth Amendment. In *Plessy v. Ferguson* **(1896)**,[9] the Supreme Court upheld the Louisiana law on the theory that as long as the accommodations between the racially segregated cars were equal, the equal protection clause was not violated. The Court's ruling established the constitutionality of racial segregation according to the *separate but equal* doctrine. To the argument that such an enforced separation of the two races stamps the colored race with a "badge of inferiority," the Supreme Court replied matter-of-factly: "If this be so, it is not by reason of anything found in the act, but solely because the colored race *chooses* to put that construction upon it."

Civil rights leaders responded to the spread of racial segregation throughout the United States in markedly different ways. Initially, Booker T. Washington's accommodationist philosophy prevailed. W. E. B. Du Bois, by contrast, advocated direct and militant challenges to segregation. Perhaps the greatest breakthrough against segregation occurred through the legal arm of the organization that Du Bois helped found: the NAACP. Beginning in the late 1930s, NAACP lawyers Charles Houston and Thurgood Marshall began attacking the legal basis for segregation in the courts.[10] As detailed in Table 5.1, they won their first battles against state-mandated segregation in institutions of higher education, as the Supreme Court eventually recognized that separate accommodations in law schools and colleges had failed to meet the essential requirements of equality mandated by the Fourteenth Amendment.

World War II eventually proved to be a rallying point for many in the ongoing battle against racial and ethnic discrimination. Perhaps the most notorious incident of state-sponsored discrimination occurred in 1942, when the U.S. government—in response to the Japanese bombing of Pearl Harbor—forcibly relocated 110,000 Japanese Americans to inland internment camps and seized their property. The Supreme Court upheld the internment policy in 1944, perpetuating an especially egregious brand of racial discrimination committed against legal residents of the country, including more than 60,000 legal U.S. citizens. National security concerns used to justify the policy at that time were later exposed as essentially baseless. Other racial and ethnic minorities returned from the fighting in Europe to find their home country of the United States far less enlightened on race issues. Nor did they fail to see the irony that Adolph Hitler's defeated Third Reich had been built on a theory of racist superiority that still held sway in large portions of America.

Some federal courts led the way in ending ethnic segregation within the public schools soon after the war had concluded. In *Mendez v. Westminster* **(1947)**,[11] the U.S. Court of Appeals for the Ninth Circuit upheld a lower court order striking down the policy of Orange County, California, to segregate Mexican and Mexican American children into separate schools in what was the first ruling by a U.S. court in favor of desegregation. Though the lower court found the policy to be an unconstitutional denial of equal protection, the Court of Appeals did not go that far—rather, it held that the segregationist policy was invalid because it had not been specifically authorized by state law. Still, the case offered hope that courts might be willing to take on legislatures and school boards that proved equally determined to protect the "separate but equal" doctrine for as long as possible.

Following in those footsteps, the NAACP utilized its own incremental approach to eliminate racial segregation in education. Its efforts eventually reached their climax in 1954 with the Supreme Court's landmark decision in *Brown v. Board of Education*.

TABLE 5.1 Tracking the Legal Assault on Racially Segregated Education

U.S. Supreme Court Case	Description
Missouri ex. rel. Gaines v. Canada (1938)	Invalidated the exclusion of black students from the University of Missouri's School of Law absent some other provision for their legal training.
Mendez et al v. Westminster School District of Orange County (1947)	Ruled the school segregation of Mexicans students into separate schools was unconstitutional.
Sipuel v. Board of Regents of University of Oklahoma (1948)	Rejected Oklahoma's attempt to create a separate law school for blacks by roping off a section of the state capitol for black law students and assigning three law teachers to them; such a form of separation failed to comply with the constitutional requirement of "equality."
Sweatt v. Painter (1950)	Invalidated Texas's attempt to create an alternative to the University of Texas law school for blacks because any such alternative would be inherently different in the reputation of its faculty, the experience of its administration, the position and influence of its alumni, its standing in the community, and so on.
McLaurin v. Oklahoma State Regents (1950)	Rejected as "unequal" Oklahoma's attempt to provide graduate education to a black student by making him sit in a classroom surrounded by a railing marked "reserved for colored," assigning him a segregated desk in the library, and requiring him to sit separately from whites in the cafeteria.
Brown v. Board of Education (1954)	Rejected the "separate but equal" doctrine altogether, declaring that in the field of public education, "separate educational facilities are inherently unequal."
Hernandez v. Texas (1954)	Held that Mexican Americans and all other racial or national groups in the United States enjoyed the right to equal protection under the Fourteenth Amendment of the U.S. Constitution.
Cooper v. Aaron (1958)	Condemned the attempts of the Little Rock, Arkansas, school board to postpone desegregation efforts, ruling that no scheme of racial discrimination against black schoolchildren can stand if "there is state participation through any arrangement, management, funds, or property."

© 2018 Cengage Learning®

Chief Justice Earl Warren, writing for a unanimous Court, held that racial segregation in any facet of public education constituted a denial of equal protection by the laws. Recognizing the psychological harms of segregation on racial and ethnic minority children, the Court declared that segregated schools were "inherently unequal."

The *Brown* decision also confirmed that in all future cases related to racial and ethnic discrimination, the Court would apply a standard of **strict scrutiny**, a level of judicial review that requires the government to prove that the racial classification of the law or practice in question is "narrowly tailored" to meet a "compelling state interest." What precisely does this mean? At a minimum, there should be no less-restrictive alternative means available for achieving the government's objectives, and those objectives should stand among the most necessary that may be pursued by any government. Many legal scholars and judges say the strict scrutiny standard tends to invalidate nearly all government laws and programs. In the years following *Brown*, the courts would apply the standard of strict scrutiny in decisions on segregated public swimming pools, police forces, and laws banning interracial marriages.

strict scrutiny A legal standard set in *Brown v. Board of Education* for cases related to racial discrimination that tends to invalidate almost all state laws that segregate racial groups.

A year after handing down the *Brown* decision, the Supreme Court declared that its implementation should proceed "with all deliberate speed." Despite that decree, many local school boards resisted desegregation. The school board of Little Rock, Arkansas, adopted a plan for "phased integration" over a 10-year period, spurring more lawsuits to speed up the process. Undeterred, Arkansas Governor Orval Faubus declared that no "*Brown* decisions" enjoyed "the force of law" in his state. In one famous instance, he placed soldiers of the Arkansas National Guard at Little Rock's Central High School to stop African American students from entering the school. Governor Ross Barnett of Mississippi refused to comply with court desegregation orders on so many occasions that a federal court held him in contempt and committed him "to the custody of the Attorney General of the United States." Alabama Governor George Wallace blocked a University of Alabama doorway, refusing to allow black students to pass through, in 1963. One hundred members of Congress signed a "Southern Manifesto" declaring their intention to use "all lawful means" to reverse the *Brown* decision. On several occasions, the Supreme Court was forced to reassert its authority over state governments. In *Cooper v. Aaron* (1958),[12] for example, the Court held that the rights of African American students could "neither be nullified openly and directly by state legislatures or state executive officials . . . by evasive schemes for segregation."

Other racial and ethnic groups also made significant civil rights gains beginning in the 1950s. The ban on Asian immigration was officially lifted in 1952, and provisions of federal law encouraging the immigration of professionals helped attract to the United States large numbers of educated and highly skilled Asian professionals.

Yet despite the Supreme Court's increasingly clear edicts against segregation, many school districts in the South and North continued to drag their feet.[13] Significant and widespread change would not occur until after passage of civil rights legislation in the mid-1960s, which gave the executive branch of the government increased power to enforce school desegregation in local districts. Additionally, a sudden influx of federal money into local schools gave extra bite to court desegregation decrees. As scholar Gerald Rosenberg remarked: "Put simply, courts could hold up federal funds." Many school districts in the Deep South where less than half of all blacks were being educated alongside whites as late as 1967 were almost fully integrated by 1971.

In urban areas where whites and racial/ethnic minorities lived largely apart, strict adherence to a neighborhood school system meant indefinitely perpetuating a racially unmixed setting; thus, massive court-ordered "busing" in the late 1960s and 1970s became a controversial feature of efforts to integrate these schools. Many such court orders were issued in both Northern and Southern cities, as the Supreme Court required communities to cease both *de jure discrimination* (segregation sanctioned by the law), which was found mostly in the South, and *de facto discrimination* (segregation in reality, such as that which occurs when different racial groups voluntarily choose to live in different neighborhoods or attend different schools), which was found in both the North and the South. Yet busing was a remedy limited to a single metropolitan area, and comprehensive efforts to integrate schools were further hindered by white flight to suburbia, which left inner-city school districts in many large northern cities predominantly black and Hispanic. Today, fully 70 percent of the nation's African American students attend schools that are predominantly black. Thus, more than 50 years after the *Brown* decision, de facto discrimination in public education remains a reality in many parts of America.

The Beginnings of the Civil Rights Movement

Although *Mendez* and *Brown* signaled the end of state-sponsored segregation, the Supreme Court took pains to note that its holding applied only to discriminatory acts by the government. The extension of civil rights protections to all public accommodations did not occur until the civil rights movement began to gather momentum in the late 1950s and early 1960s. In December 1955, Rosa Parks, an African American seamstress in Montgomery, Alabama, was arrested for refusing to give up her seat at the front of a city bus. Her arrest sparked a racial boycott of the city's bus system. Leading the boycott was Martin Luther King Jr., pastor of the Dexter Avenue Baptist Church. King's eloquent speeches and his methods of nonviolent civil disobedience brought national attention to the boycott. King had been introduced to these tactics of nonviolent protest when he was a student at Crozer Theological Seminary in Chester, Pennsylvania, and studied the pacifist philosophy of Mohandas Gandhi of India, whose unshakable belief in nonviolent protest and religious tolerance helped secure independence for his country from Great Britain.

In 1957, King and other African American ministers in the South formed the Southern Christian Leadership Conference (SCLC), which encouraged Ghandian practices of nonviolent civil disobedience as a way to gain equal rights for blacks and spur white politicians into action. African American and white college students in numerous cities across the South eventually became the engine for pressing such change. One early tactic the students used was the sit-in. On February 1, 1960, four freshmen from the black North Carolina A&T College in Greensboro sat down at a whites-only lunch counter and refused to move after being denied service. The next day more students—black and white—joined them. Angry mobs harassed the students verbally and physically. Committed to nonviolence, the students endured the abuse. The episode brought considerable publicity to the civil rights movement. In 1961, interracial groups of students sponsored "Freedom Rides," traveling together from Washington, DC, to the South to test court decisions prohibiting segregation on interstate buses and in bus terminals; many within the groups of interstate travelers of mixed races were beaten when their buses arrived in Alabama. Eventually President John F. Kennedy was forced to nationalize the Alabama police to help assure the freedom riders safe passage.

Hispanics also charged ahead in the battle for civil rights. Though its origins dated back to the middle of the nineteenth century, the "Chicano movement" (one example of Latino civil rights movements) reached its peak as a symbol of self-determination and ethnic pride in the 1960s. Spurred on by the Supreme Court's holding in *Hernandez v. Texas* (1954)[14] that Mexican Americans and other subordinated groups were entitled to equal protection under the Fourteenth Amendment, the movement addressed private and public discrimination in the courts and elsewhere. Cesar Chavez, Dolores Huerta, and the National Farm Workers' Association fought to make the struggle of migrant workers in particular and Hispanic empowerment more generally a moral cause through the use of hunger strikes and other nonviolent tactics. Meanwhile, the American GI Forum and the Mexican-American Legal Defense and Education Fund continued its battle in the courts.

Birmingham 1963: The Turning Point of the Civil Rights Movement

The civil rights movement's strategy of nonviolent civil disobedience reached a climax between 1963 and 1965.[15] The year 1963 will long be remembered as the "Year of Birmingham." Tension was growing between King's SCLC and new civil rights groups

Michael Evans/Hulton Archive/Contributor/Getty Images

A 19-year-old student named Martin Luther King Jr. was first introduced to the pacifist philosophy of Mohandas Gandhi. By seeking a nonviolent confrontation with the segregation laws, King's followers practiced Gandhi's philosophy in a way that sent shock waves throughout the South and eventually the entire nation. King would continue to preach Gandhi's call for nonviolent protest up until his assassination in 1968.

In 1963, firefighters in Birmingham, Alabama, sprayed civil rights demonstrators with fire hoses.

that favored more radical and militant action, including the use of violence. Looking for a site where nonviolent demonstrations might succeed and draw national attention to the civil rights movement, King and his followers settled on Birmingham, Alabama. Birmingham was an obvious target, for several reasons. First, as an industrial city (unlike most southern cities), it had a sizable concentration of workers. Also, during the 1930s and 1940s, the labor movement had introduced to the city a tradition of organized protest unusual throughout most of the South. And finally, the city was a stronghold of segregation; city leaders included the notoriously racist Public Safety Commissioner Eugene "Bull" Connor, who ruthlessly enforced segregation laws throughout the city.

In Birmingham, King led other demonstrators in a nonviolent march downtown, where he was arrested and placed in solitary confinement. While confined, he wrote his famous "Letter from Birmingham City Jail," addressed to the white Alabama clergymen who had criticized King's campaign. In the letter, King explained his philosophy and defended his strategy of nonviolent protest. Despite King's arrest, the demonstration in Birmingham continued. The marchers, including more than a thousand black schoolchildren, were met by attack dogs, cattle prods, and fire hoses. Pictures of children being attacked flashed across the nation's television sets and the violence was covered by newspapers and magazines across the world. The nation would be forever aroused by these events; the civil rights movement had finally been transformed into a truly national cause.

Birmingham businessmen, fearing damage to their downtown stores, hastened negotiations with King and his fellow civil rights leaders. An accord was eventually reached on May 10, 1963, with merchants agreeing to desegregate lunch counters and hire more black workers for clerical and sales positions. Yet the agreement did not bring peace to Birmingham: On the night of May 11, a Ku Klux Klan rally outside the city was followed by the explosion of bombs at the motel where King was staying. Riots erupted and some stores were set ablaze. This time, however, the federal government got involved; President Kennedy dispatched soldiers to Fort McClellan, 30 miles outside of Birmingham. Nevertheless, in September a bombing at the city's Sixteenth Street Baptist Church killed four African American schoolgirls.

The events in Birmingham were not the last of the civil rights demonstrations, nor did they mark the end of violence in response to those activities. In August 1963, more than 250,000 people participated in the March on Washington, where King delivered his memorable "I Have a Dream" speech from the steps of the Lincoln Memorial. In 1964, the murder of three civil rights workers and a local NAACP leader in Mississippi revealed the depth of continuing opposition to racial equality. In 1965, King and other civil rights leaders organized a march from Selma, Alabama, to the state capital in Montgomery to bring attention to harsh political realities in the South, where African Americans had been denied the right to vote by illegitimate tests and in some instances outright intimidation.

President Lyndon Johnson and the U.S. Congress were eventually prodded into action. Johnson signed into law the **Civil Rights Act of 1964**, which banned racial discrimination in all public accommodations, including those that were privately owned; it also prohibited discrimination by employers and created the Equal Employment Opportunity Commission to investigate complaints of discrimination; and it denied public funds to schools that continued to discriminate on the basis of race.[16]

Civil Rights Act of 1964 The federal law that banned racial discrimination in all public accommodations, including those that were privately owned; prohibited discrimination by employers and created the Equal Employment Opportunity Commission to investigate complaints of discrimination; and denied public funds to schools that continued to discriminate on the basis of race.

The **Voting Rights Act of 1965**, enacted the following year, invalidated literacy tests and property requirements and required that certain states and cities with a history of voting discrimination obtain pre-approval from the Justice Department for all future changes to their voting laws. As shown in Table 5.2, the act proved largely successful, as millions of African Americans were effectively reenfranchised in the South in subsequent decades. The 1965 Voting Rights Act (VRA) was further updated to extend the protections to other racial/ethnic groups, starting in 1970.

Notable extensions of the VRA included the following:

- 1970: Congress extended the threshold for coverage
- 1975: Congress extended VRA protection to all language minorities
- 1982: Congress eliminated at-large districts and replaced them with single-member districts that increased opportunities for minority groups' representation
- 1992: Congress extended bilingual voting assistance

The **Civil Rights Act of 1968** banned race discrimination in housing and made interference with a citizen's civil rights a federal crime. Even the state legislatures played a role in this civil rights transformation by ratifying the **Twenty-fourth Amendment** in 1964, which banned poll taxes in federal elections.

The focus of the civil rights movement began to shift in the mid-to-late 1960s with the rise of "black and brown nationalism," which was grounded in the belief that African Americans and Latinos/Chicanos could not effectively work within the confines of a racist political system to produce effective change. Malcolm X, a leading advocate of Black Nationalism, sought to turn the characteristic of being black-skinned into a source of strength, and he urged African Americans to shun white culture and the values promoted by white society. He and other black nationalists criticized the civil rights leaders who advocated integration into white society rather than building separate black institutions. The influence of Black Nationalism in the civil rights movement reached its peak during the late 1960s and early 1970s

Voting Rights Act of 1965 The federal law that invalidated literacy tests and property requirements and required select states and cities to apply for permission to the Justice Department to change their voting laws. As a consequence, millions of African Americans were effectively reenfranchised in the South.

Civil Rights Act of 1968 The federal law that banned race discrimination in housing and made interference with a citizen's civil rights a federal crime.

Twenty-fourth Amendment A 1964 constitutional amendment that banned poll taxes in federal elections.

TABLE 5.2   The Effect of the Voting Rights Act on Registration Rates in the South

The following table compares black voter registration rates with white voter registration rates in seven Southern states in 1965 and 1988. All numbers are percentage rates.

State	March 1965			November 1988		
	Black	**White**	**Gap**	**Black**	**White**	**Gap**
Alabama	19.3	69.2	49.9	68.4	75.0	6.6
Georgia	27.4	62.6	35.2	56.8	63.9	7.1
Louisiana	31.6	80.5	48.9	77.1	75.1	−2.0
Mississippi	6.7	69.9	63.2	74.2	80.5	6.3
North Carolina	46.8	96.8	50.0	58.2	65.6	7.4
South Carolina	37.3	75.7	38.4	56.7	61.8	5.1
Virginia	38.3	61.1	22.8	63.8	68.5	4.7

Sources: The U.S. Commission on Civil Rights; Chandler Davidson and Bernard Grofman, *Quiet Revolution in the South* (Princeton, NJ: Princeton University Press, 1994).

The Diversity Dilemma

Contemporary Challenge to Voting Rights

Today we take for granted that all citizens may effectively exercise the right to vote. Unfortunately, some political actors continue to place obstacles in the way of voters, and their efforts could well influence elections in some cases. The recent controversy over strict voter identification laws exemplifies this problem. As of early 2016, a total of 36 states had already passed laws requiring voters to show some form of identification at the polls. This included strict photo ID requirements instituted by Georgia, Indiana, Kansas, Mississippi, North Dakota, Tennessee, Texas, Virginia, and Wisconsin.[17] Supporters of such voter restrictions argue that they are necessary to curb voter fraud. However, the laws' opponents argue that they place undue discriminatory restrictions on an individual's ability to vote, especially among certain groups (including racial/ethnic minorities, women, low-income persons, seniors, and college-age citizens). These groups are disproportionately less likely to own the required government-issued photo identification, and they normally have fewer opportunities to obtain the needed documents. So far, this battle remains unsettled, as civil

Voter ID laws in Texas and elsewhere that require driver's licenses (or similar forms of validation) to vote have been challenged in court by civil rights groups.

rights groups continue to challenge many of the stricter state voter ID laws in the courts, enjoying only mixed success to date.

For Critical Thinking and Discussion

1. Do you think photo identification should be required to vote? If so, why? Should it be more difficult to vote than it is to purchase gas for one's car?
2. What are the ramifications of government efforts to place obstacles in the way of greater voter turnout? Do you think strict voter ID restrictions significantly influenced voter turnout in the 2016 election?

following the assassination of Martin Luther King Jr. in 1968. Epitomizing a revolutionary vision of society that replaced the strategy of nonviolence with confrontational tactics, the Black Panther Party became a controversial militant presence in some cities.

Although the Black Panther Party had all but faded as a significant entity by 1972, black separatist organizations continue to maintain a strong presence. For example, the Nation of Islam (Black Muslims), led by Louis Farrakhan, preaches class consciousness and the concept of black self-rule. In 1995, Farrakhan's Nation of Islam led the Million Man March in Washington, D.C., which far outdrew the 1963 March on Washington. This Million Man March garnered international attention for Farrakhan's movement. Four years later, African American women held their own million women march.

Beginning in the latter part of the twentieth century, some Native Americans also embraced activism to protest their mistreatment by government authorities. From November 1969 until June 1971, 78 members of one tribe occupied Alcatraz Island in San Francisco Bay, demanding that it be made available as a cultural center to the tribes. Members of the American Indian Movement (AIM), an organization founded in 1968 to promote civil rights for Native Americans, occupied the Washington, D.C., offices of the Bureau of Indian Affairs in 1972, demanding that they receive the rights and privileges that had been promised them under the original treaties entered into by the federal government. This activism drew public attention to Native American causes and spurred action by Congress, which formally terminated its policy of assimilation and began to recognize the autonomy of Native American tribes to administer federal programs on their own lands. In the past quarter century, the U.S. government has settled millions of dollars in legal claims pressed by Native American tribes and has returned nearly half a million acres of land to the Navajo and Hopi tribes alone.

The end of the Vietnam War in 1975 also brought a great influx of immigrants from Vietnam, Laos, and Cambodia to the United States. With increasing numbers of immigrants from South Korea and the Philippines, the Asian American population today stands at approximately 4 percent of the American population as a whole.

Barack Obama's historic election as the first African American president may have fundamentally changed how African Americans as well as other racial and ethnic minorities perceive their national government. Still, members of those groups continue to face immense challenges in making their voices heard in other institutions on the national political scene. Consider that Obama left a Senate chamber in November 2008 in which he had been the only African American then serving, and where he was just the third popularly elected African American senator to serve since Reconstruction. (During Obama's two terms as president, just two African Americans were elected as U.S. senators in their own right: Sen. Tim Scott (R-SC) and Sen. Corey Booker (D-NJ).) African Americans have enjoyed a bit more success in the other house of Congress, as a record 48 African American members (8.9 percent of the total membership) held seats in the 114th Congress.

Meanwhile, Hispanics form the nation's largest language minority today, as more than 35 million people of Hispanic descent currently live in the United States. In recent years, Mexico in particular has been the source of 29 percent of the overall growth in foreign-born persons living in the United States. Latin America as a whole has accounted for 58 percent of the growth in the immigrant population since 2000. Thus, Mexicans, Cubans, Puerto Ricans, and numerous immigrants and refugees from other Central American countries all contribute to the ranks of this rapidly growing minority group.

Some of the Cubans who left their native land hailed from privileged socioeconomic conditions. Their goal was to flee Fidel Castro's communistic agenda, but they also immigrated to the United States as part of an effort to preserve their standard of living. Barack Obama's historic visit to Havana during the spring of 2016 received only a mix of support from this politically active community. By contrast, most immigrants from Latin American countries such as Mexico and Cuba sought to escape some severely adverse economic circumstances in those nations.

Of course, discrimination against Hispanics also contributes to the overall disproportionate levels of poverty and unemployment in this group. In New Mexico and California they have been a large and influential minority for several decades. And yet despite the large number of Hispanics, the group's political power has yet to receive its due influence on public policy in those southwestern states, perhaps because many Hispanics are not yet citizens and thus do not have the right to vote. Certainly, the appointment of Judge Sonia Sotomayor as the first Latina (and more specifically, Puerto Rican) to the U.S. Supreme Court in 2009 was a source of pride among the Hispanic community, and officials in both major parties made appeals to the Hispanic community a top priority going into the 2016 presidential election. Given that hopeful backdrop, leaders of the Hispanic community were particularly dismayed by comments from then 2016 Republican presidential nominee Donald Trump that compared Mexican immigrants

TABLE 5.3 Countries Sending the Most Immigrants to the United States, 1990, 2000, and 2010

Country	2010	2000	1990
1 Mexico	11,711,103	9,177,487	4,298,014
2 China, Hong Kong, and Taiwan	2,166,526	1,518,652	921,070
3 India	1,780,322	1,022,552	450,406
4 Philippines	1,777,588	1,369,070	912,674
5 Vietnam	1,240,542	988,174	543,262
6 El Salvador	1,214,049	817,336	465,433
7 Cuba	1,104,679	872,716	736,971
8 Korea	1,100,422	864,125	568,397
9 Dominican Republic	879,187	687,677	347,858
10 Guatemala	830,824	480,665	225,739
11 Canada	798,649	820,771	744,830
12 United Kingdom	669,794	677,751	640,145
13 Jamaica	659,771	553,827	334,140
14 Colombia	636,555	509,872	286,124
15 Germany	604,616	706,704	711,929
16 Haiti	587,149	419,317	225,393
17 Honduras	522,581	282,852	108,923
18 Poland	475,503	466,742	388,328
19 Ecuador	443,173	298,626	143,314
20 Peru	428,547	278,186	144,199
All Immigrants	39,955,854	31,107,889	19,767,316
All of Latin America	**21,224,087**	**16,086,974**	**8,407,837**

Source: Center for Immigration Studies. cis.org/sites/cis.org/files/articles/2011/record-setting-decade.pdf.

(and all Latinos) to rapists and drug dealers. The quest to reward this exploding Latino population with political clout reflective of its numbers is certain to remain a continuing challenge in the years to come.

5-4 | The Women's Movement and Gender Equality

The process by which women achieved their own degree of equality during the course of the twentieth century took a circuitous route. In the early part of the twentieth century, women's rights leaders linked their calls for equality to other social movements of the same period, including those calling for child labor laws and increased literacy for immigrants. Initially, the women's rights movement pressed for protective laws, arguing that such legislation was necessary because of women's otherwise inferior legal status. For example, in *Muller v. Oregon* (1908),[18] the Supreme Court upheld an Oregon law that prohibited women laundry workers from being required to work more than 10 hours a day; similar laws applied to male workers had been invalidated as beyond the government's authority. Yet the reason for the holding could hardly have cheered advocates of women's equality: according to the Court, "a woman's physical structure and the performance of maternal functions place her at a disadvantage in the struggle for subsistence."

Judicial Scrutiny of Gender Discrimination and the Equal Rights Amendment

After ratification of the Nineteenth Amendment in 1920 guaranteed women the right to vote, women's rights groups began to alter their strategy for pursuing gender equality through the courts. In attempting to expand women's legal rights, these groups now argued that men and women should be treated equally. Their efforts met with only limited success at first. Although the NAACP achieved a string of successful challenges to racial discrimination in the 1940s and 1950s, the Supreme Court refused to view gender discrimination as similarly deserving of suspect scrutiny. In *Goesaert v. Cleary* (1948),[19] the Court upheld a Michigan law that banned women from tending bar unless they were the daughter or wife of the bar owner. Thirteen years later, the Court accepted as legitimate a Florida law that gave only women the right to excuse themselves from jury duty. In both cases, the Court continued to accept sex-role stereotypes of women as weak, and as dedicated above all else to taking care of the children at home. As the Court pointed out in *Hoyt v. Florida* (1961), "despite the enlightened emancipation of women from the restrictions and protections of bygone years . . . woman is still regarded as the center of home and family life."[20]

The women's rights movement did not achieve any significant breakthroughs in this regard until the early 1970s. Although the National Women's Party had first proposed an equal rights amendment to the Constitution in 1923 and in nearly every session of Congress since then, the amendment never got very far. In 1966, the newly formed National Organization for Women (NOW) became a new and forceful advocate for the Equal Rights Amendment (ERA) and other equal rights in education, employment, and political opportunities for women. NOW and other women's groups vigorously pressed for passage of the ERA, which stated simply that "equality of rights under the law shall not be denied or abridged by the United States or any state on account of sex." In 1972, Congress passed the amendment and sent it to the state legislatures for ratification. Even after the deadline for ratification was extended to June 1982, the amendment failed to achieve the approval of the three-fourths of state legislatures necessary for passage, falling just three states shy. Members of Congress reintroduce the ERA in nearly every session of Congress.

Although the ERA initially failed, women have recently achieved some noteworthy victories in politics. For example, women made political history in 2003 when Democrat Nancy Pelosi of California was elected minority leader in the House, the first woman ever to hold that high of a position in either branch of Congress. When Democrats won control of Congress after the 2006 midterm elections, Pelosi was elected Speaker of the House, again the first woman to hold that exalted position. (Between 2011 and 2016, she served as House minority leader in the Republican-controlled Congress.) Pelosi's ascension to such high congressional leadership positions contrasts with the way women in Congress were often relegated to lesser committees and noninfluential positions in the past. When the 115th Congress began in 2017, 83 women were serving in the U.S. House of Representatives and 21 in the U.S. Senate.

When Hillary Clinton became the first female to serve as a major party's presidential nominee, her campaign hoped the women's vote would provide her with the electoral edge she needed to win the White House. Yet as it turned out, while women voters overall preferred Clinton by 13 percentage points (54%–41%) to Donald Trump, white women preferred Trump by 10 points (53%–43%) and white women without a college degree preferred Trump by an overwhelming 28 percentage points (62%–34%). In that sense, Hillary Clinton performed about the same among women voters as Barack Obama did in 2012. Clearly, the first woman president may have to wait for a time when she can inspire women across the board to support her in realizing that history-making moment.

Legal Challenges to Gender Discrimination

Ironically, some attributed the failure of the Equal Rights Amendment to other legal developments that may have rendered it unnecessary. The American Civil Liberties Union (ACLU), an organization traditionally dedicated to protecting the First Amendment rights of political dissidents and labor unions, turned its attention to women's rights in the late 1960s. Led in court by board member Ruth Bader Ginsburg (who was later appointed by President Clinton to the U.S. Supreme Court), the ACLU brought suit on behalf of women who charged that they had been victims of gender discrimination. Although the Court refused to accord gender discrimination the strict scrutiny normally reserved for racial discrimination, the ACLU achieved several victories in cases brought before the Supreme Court. In *Reed v. Reed* (1971),[21] the Court invalidated an Idaho law that gave males preference over females as administrators of estates. In *Frontiero v. Richardson* (1973),[22] the Court struck down a federal law requiring only female members of the armed forces to show proof that they contributed more than 50 percent to the income of their household in order to receive certain fringe benefits. And in the landmark case of *Craig v. Boren* (1976),[23] the Court invalidated an Oklahoma law that prohibited the sale of 3.2 percent beer to males under the age of 21 and to women under the age of 18.

Since *Craig*, the Supreme Court has applied *intermediate scrutiny* in all gender discrimination cases, a standard requiring the government to show that the gender classification is "substantially related to an important state interest." This level of scrutiny is less than that of strict scrutiny, which tends to invalidate all racial classifications. But under intermediate scrutiny, *nearly* all laws that discriminate against women will be invalidated. That fact alone distinguishes intermediate scrutiny from *rational basis* (or *minimum*) *scrutiny*, which asks only whether the law is "rationally related to a legitimate state interest"—a question to which courts can readily answer "yes" in nearly every instance.

In fact, in the modern era the Court has upheld only a handful of gender classifications as constitutional. For example, in 1981 the Court upheld a challenge to federal laws that required selective military service registration for males, but not for females. That same year the Court upheld a statutory rape law in California that punished men for having sex with underage females, although not vice versa. In each of those two instances, perceptions of real and relevant differences between men and women persuaded the Court to allow the discrimination to stand.

The highest-profile lawsuits charging gender discrimination targeted two all-male southern military academies, The Citadel in Charleston, South Carolina, and the Virginia Military Institute (VMI) in Lexington, Virginia. Both were classified as state institutions because they accepted significant funds from their respective states' budgets; thus, each was hard-pressed to continue excluding women in violation of the Fourteenth Amendment's equal protection clause. Shannon Faulkner's frustrating experience as the first female cadet at The Citadel paved the way for future women to apply and be accepted to the institution in subsequent years. In an attempt to fend off gender integration of its own student body, VMI contracted with nearby Mary Baldwin College to create a parallel military program for women called the Virginia Women's Institute for Leadership (VWIL). But in 1996, the Supreme Court ruled that VWIL did not approximate VMI in terms of student body, faculty, course offerings, facilities, or opportunities for its alumni and ordered VMI to accept women. The issue of "separate but equal" that was resolved by the Supreme Court for racial classifications in 1954 was still being litigated for gender classifications well into the 1990s.

The Supreme Court and Affirmative Action

Fisher v. University of Texas (2016)

During the past 20 years, the federal courts have invalidated many state-sponsored affirmative action programs in such contexts as education, government contracting, and the hiring and firing of public workers. Even those programs that remain are controversial: Just ask officials at the University of Texas in Austin. The University's current admissions program utilizes a two-step process: (1) it accepts all students who finish in the top 10 percent of their high school class, regardless of race: and (2) additional students can be admitted by scoring highly in an individualized review process that evaluates the applicants' talents, leadership qualities, family circumstances, and race. In response to the university's rejection of her application in 2008, Abby Fisher sued the University of Texas, charging that the current program, which explicitly takes race into account, violates the Equal Protection Clause.

On June 23, 2016, the U.S. Supreme Court upheld the University of Texas admissions policy by a narrow 4-3 vote. According to the Court, the university had justified its plan as achieving diversity-associated goals without resorting to a quota.

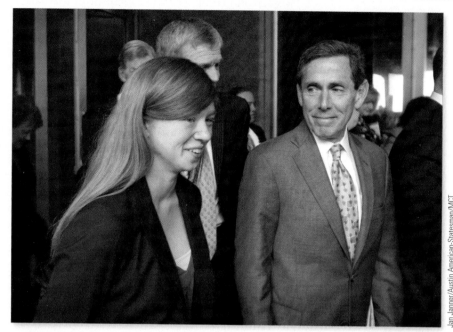

Abigail Fisher, left, and her attorney leave the courthouse in Austin, Texas, in November 2013. Fisher's lawsuit claimed the University of Texas had unconstitutionally denied her admission due to her race.

For Critical Thinking and Discussion

1. Do you believe it is possible to encourage racial diversity in college admissions *without* resorting to race-conscious policies?

2. Who should define what "critical mass" of racial minority students is actually necessary to achieve the desired measure of diversity? Should the measure be adjusted over time?

As with race discrimination, discrimination against women has been mostly eliminated in the formal sense. **Title IX** of the Federal Educational Amendments of 1972 prohibited the exclusion of women from an educational program or activity receiving financial assistance from the federal government. Courts have interpreted those provisions to force colleges and universities to provide as many athletic teams for women as they do for men. Title VII of the Civil Rights Act of 1964 extended to women protection against discrimination in private and public businesses alike. Armed with equal rights to education and to entry in the workforce, women made considerable occupational gains during the twentieth century.

Women have also benefited from affirmative action programs, especially in the workplace and in admission to professional and trade schools. **Affirmative action** programs are generally laws or practices designed to remedy past discriminatory hiring practices, government contracting, and school admissions. To rectify long traditions of excluding women from certain occupations, scores of businesses and firms have aggressively recruited women. The period of most striking change occurred over the two decades

Title IX The section of the Federal Educational Amendments Law of 1972 that prohibits the exclusion of women from an educational program or activity receiving financial assistance from the federal government. Courts have interpreted those provisions to force colleges and universities to provide as many athletic teams for women as they do for men.

affirmative action Programs, laws, or practices designed to remedy past discriminatory hiring practices, government contracting, and school admissions.

between 1970 and 1990, when the proportion of women physicians doubled from 7.6 percent to 16.9 percent, and the percentage of women lawyers and judges nearly quadrupled from 5.8 percent to 22.7 percent. The percentage of women who are engineers rose over that same period from 1.3 percent to 8.6 percent. Still, complaints remain that in some occupations women continue to be clustered in low-paying positions. Thus, women still compose only 3 percent of the nation's firefighters, 8 percent of state and local police officers, 1.9 percent of construction workers, 11.8 percent of college presidents, and 3 to 5 percent of senior-level positions in major companies. Some observers contend that a "glass ceiling" exists in many businesses, whereby women are prevented from receiving raises and promotions due them because of the subjective biases of their male bosses.

The securing of formal equality under the law and the proliferation of affirmative action programs have not always translated into actual equal opportunities to succeed. Women today continue to earn less than men in comparable positions—calls for "equal pay for equal work" have not always generated substantive changes in the pay structures of private companies or even the government. When women's salaries are compared with those of equally qualified men, the differences remain dramatic. Although Congress passed the Equal Pay Act in 1963 to ensure that women would be paid the same as men for work that is "substantially equal" (that is, almost identical unless the pay difference is based on seniority, experience, or other legitimate factors), in the year 2013 a woman on average still earned less than 80 cents for every dollar a man received.[24] During the 2008 presidential campaign, Barack Obama highlighted the issue of equal pay and he followed through by signing the Lilly Ledbetter Fair Pay Act of 2009 as his first official act after he became president. This act provided some important revisions to the Civil Rights Act of 1964 by instituting more flexibility in the statute of limitations for filing an equal-pay lawsuit.

In April of 2014 President Barack Obama also issued two executive orders meant to pressure federal contractors on pay equity, a move that drew praise from advocates and criticism from conservatives who accused the administration of pandering to female voters. Even the president's own Office of Personnel Management conceded that factors other than discrimination could contribute to the differences in pay between men and women, including differences in prior work experience, care-giving responsibilities, motivation, and work performance. Given the growing political power of women in the electorate, officials from both political parties can expect to answer even more questions about pay equity in the years to come.

Sexual harassment, normally in the form of unwelcome sexual advances by superiors, continues to pose a threat to working women in America. Since the mid-1980s the Supreme Court has considered such harassment—which includes any and all actions that create a hostile working environment, such as putting up provocative posters, making lewd comments, and so forth—to be a form of sexual discrimination actionable under Title VII of the 1964 Civil Rights Act. Still, many such sexual advances in the workplace continue despite the law, either because women remain unclear about the bounds of permissible conduct or because they fear reprisals for reporting the legal violations of superiors. Indeed, more than 4 in 10 women employed in federal agencies say they have experienced some form of harassment.[25] For all the legal equality that is now afforded to women, discrimination continues on a level that falls under the radar screen of the legal and judicial process.

5-5 | Other Group Struggles for Equality

American history is replete with accounts of discrimination against other underrepresented groups as well. In recent years these other groups have begun to see their own claims to fairness and equal treatment recognized and vindicated within the American political system.

Older Americans

Today approximately 13 percent of Americans are over the age of 65, compared with just 4 percent of Americans who were at that age at the beginning of the twentieth century. With their increased numbers has come increased political power; older Americans are among the most politically active of all citizens, and groups such as AARP (formerly the American Association of Retired Persons), with more than 40 million members on its rolls, have become especially influential players on the political scene. This increased influence has been used to counteract incidents of age discrimination in the workplace and elsewhere. The Age Discrimination in Employment Act, passed in 1967 and broadened in 1986, makes it unlawful to hire or fire a person on the basis of age. Older Americans have also been at the forefront of lobbying efforts to protect Social Security trust funds and to ensure the continuation of cost-of-living adjustments to their payments. Ironically, older Americans' success at wielding influence within the political system has given credence to the suggestion that age classifications do not require suspect scrutiny by courts; at least in this instance, the political system appears to protect the civil rights of this particular subset of Americans.

Activists for the rights of individuals with disabilities at a rally advocating broader enforcement of the Americans with Disabilities Act of 1990.

Individuals with Disabilities

As with age classifications, discrimination against Americans with physical and mental disabilities has never received heightened scrutiny from the courts. Misperceptions about the nature of certain disabilities have on occasion led to discriminatory treatment of individuals with disabilities. In the 1920s, some states passed laws authorizing the sterilization of institutionalized "mental defectives"—Justice Oliver Wendell Holmes callously dismissed all legal challenges to such laws with the statement that "three generations of imbeciles are enough."

Today, thanks to significant technological and medical advances, a more enlightened social understanding, and a more sophisticated approach to educating citizens about the nature of these limitations, millions of Americans with disabilities have been mainstreamed into society, attending school, going to work, and living otherwise normal lives. The Americans with Disabilities Act of 1990 established a national commitment to such mainstreaming efforts and extended to those with disabilities protection from discrimination in employment and public accommodations comparable to that afforded women and racial minorities under the 1964 Civil Rights Act.

LGBTQ

Of the many groups that have legitimate claims as victims of discrimination in the United States, LGBTQ (Lesbian, Gay, Bisexual, Transgender, and Queer) once stood among the least successful in seeing those claims vindicated. Up through the end of the twentieth century, LGBTQ members suffered significant discrimination in society, whether from those whose religions frowned on homosexuality in general or from those who were simply uncomfortable with this lifestyle. In the period immediately following World War II, a movement for gay rights emerged with generally integrationist goals, encouraging gays and lesbians to conform to most existing social standards. Homosexuals then assumed a more activist quest for equality beginning in the late 1960s, marching for "gay power," urging reluctant gays to "out" themselves by openly admitting their sexual orientation, and interrupting government meetings to draw attention to their cause of equal treatment and nondiscrimination.

Although LGBTQ activists made some limited advances, no significant antidiscrimination legislation followed. Some communities reacted by passing laws that prohibited the granting of "any special rights or privileges" to homosexuals. The Supreme Court in *Romer v. Evans* (1996)[26] struck down such a provision of the Colorado Constitution in 1996. Yet perhaps the biggest court victory of all for gays and lesbians occurred in 2003, when the Supreme Court in *Lawrence v. Texas* (2003)[27] struck down a Texas law that forbade same-sex partners from engaging in certain types of intimate relations. Despite these victories, the Supreme Court has still never recognized homosexuals as a protected class on a par with women or African Americans. Battles over the right to same-sex marriage were initially waged state by state during the first decade of the twenty-first century. All those legislative gains were rendered irrelevant, however, when the Court in *Obergefell v. Hodges* (2015) held that a fundamental right to marry was guaranteed to same-sex couples by the Fourteenth Amendment to the U.S Constitution.

Of course, anti-LGBTQ discrimination remains. The issue of homosexuals in the military first drew intense national attention when U.S. Army Colonel Margarethe Cammermeyer was discharged from the armed forces in June 1992; during a routine security clearance interview, she acknowledged that she was a lesbian. Cammermeyer hinged her hopes for reinstatement on a promise made to her by candidate Bill Clinton during his successful presidential campaign that fall. Yet soon after taking office, President Clinton began to backtrack on his promise: at his first televised news conference two weeks into his presidency, he indicated he might go along with a supposed compromise that would segregate gays within the military. The ultimate compromise reached was a "don't ask, don't tell" policy that would allow gays still in the closet to stay in the military, so long as they never publicized their status. Later, after a federal court ruled in July 2011 that a ban on openly gay troops was unconstitutional, President Obama and the Chairman of the Joint Chiefs of Staff certified to Congress that ending the "don't ask, don't tell" policy would not harm the nation's "military readiness." With the support of Congress, the federal government then formally ended the controversial policy on September 20, 2011.

Despite suffering countless setbacks, gays and lesbians continue to enjoy a significant presence in the political system, forging alliances with more liberal administrations and even electing some openly gay politicians. Clearly, LGBTQ represent a political force in America today that can no longer be ignored by officials of both major political parties.

5-6 | Continuing Struggles over Equality in the Modern Era

There are several contemporary and hotly debated topics related to equality, including those related to the war on terrorism, affirmative action initiatives, and racial profiling.

The War on Terrorism and Its Impact on Muslim Americans

The events of September 11, 2001, had a profound impact on America's foreign policy priorities and its approach to international terrorism. Those events have also taken a toll on citizens' perceptions of Muslim Americans, a group already set apart by its members' distinct religious practices and forms of dress. When plans for an Islamic community center and mosque to be built near the site of "Ground Zero" were revealed in early 2010, anger directed at Muslim Americans suddenly found a new cause. Polls showed a clear majority of Americans opposed to the project, even though most of those surveyed also recognized that the Muslim group had a legal right to build there. Politicians of all stripes, including Sarah Palin and Senate Majority Leader Harry Reid (D-NV), were quick to oppose the proposal, knowing that such opposition would offer them immediate political benefits.

The Shifting Battle Lines of Equality

Then

Beginning in the 1860s and continuing through World War I, demands for women's suffrage stood front and center in the battle lines of equality. Activists at the outset were mostly older women of English or German descent; frustrated that Congress had placed the African American male's right to vote as a higher priority, several women's groups began working to achieve the right to vote, including the New England Woman Suffrage Association and the American Woman Suffrage Association. By the 1890s, these voices had merged into a movement, led at first by Susan B. Anthony. Opposition was widespread: upper-class women worried that their behind-the-scenes influence would be diluted once all women could vote, southern white males feared that African American women would vote, and liquor interests worried that women voters would favor prohibition. Pro-suffrage groups managed some limited victories, particularly in the newly settled western states of Utah, Colorado, Idaho, and Wyoming, which all granted women suffrage before the turn of the century. Still, they experienced continued setbacks at the federal level during the first decade of the new century. The tide may have finally turned with President Woodrow Wilson's call for American entry into World War I. When Wilson termed the battle ahead as a "war for democracy," his point rang hollow among disenfranchised women. Reluctantly, Wilson shifted his position in favor of women suffrage. Finally, in 1919, the Nineteenth Amendment passed, guaranteeing women the right to vote nationwide.

Rep. Jeannette Rankin (R-MT), speaking from a balcony at the National American Woman Suffrage Association in Washington, DC, in May 1912.

Now

By the 1970s, gay and lesbian advocacy groups had begun organizing to achieve equality on a number of fronts. The going was tough at first. In 1973, just three years after Jack Baker and Michael McConnell applied unsuccessfully for a marriage license in Minnesota, Maryland became the first state to statutorily ban same-sex marriage. During the remainder of the twentieth century, 44 more states followed Maryland's lead, undermining gay advocacy groups' efforts to secure equal access to marriage at every turn. Even the Democratic Party, which strategically embraced gay rights as a general matter, refused support for same-sex marriage in its party platform. Then in 1996 President Bill Clinton signed into law the Defense of Marriage Act (DOMA), which banned federal recognition of same-sex unions. During the first decade of the twenty-first century, however, the tide began to turn in the opposite direction. First, gay and lesbian groups achieved some limited success in Vermont, which established a law providing for same-sex civil unions. The movement for same-sex marriage then earned its first major breakthrough in 2004 when Massachusetts became the first state to formally authorize marriages for gay and lesbian couples. In the decade that followed, at least 17 states and the District of Columbia followed suit. By 2014, a Gallup poll registered 54 percent of Americans supporting gay marriage, and the Supreme Court eventually validated this progress, holding that same-sex marriage was a constitutional right in *Obergefell v. Hodges* (2015).[28]

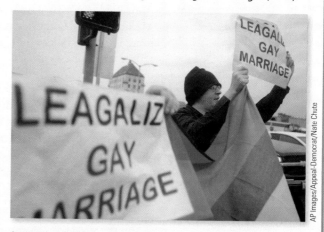

A protestor holding up a rainbow flag in support of same-sex marriage in Marysville, California.

For Critical Thinking and Discussion

1. How was the modern battle over same-sex marriage similar to the century-old battle over a woman's right to vote? How were they different?
2. The suffragettes did not rest until the right to vote had been established as a permanent part of the Constitution in the form of the Nineteenth Amendment. Should gay rights activists pursue a same-sex marriage amendment as well? Would pursuing such a goal require a shift in strategy or tactics?

The stereotype that associates the Islamic religion with terrorism is hardly applicable to the vast majority who practice the faith, but post–September 11 initiatives sanctioned by Congress under the USA PATRIOT Act targeted many Muslim Americans for questioning, and in some cases temporary detention. Of course, African Americans, Hispanics, and other racial and ethnic minorities have long suffered from racial profiling in criminal law enforcement; still, the level and degree to which Muslim Americans have been singled out has been a special source of worry for civil rights groups. Their fears only escalated when, during the 2016 primary season, Republican presidential frontrunner Donald Trump supported a temporary ban on all Muslims entering the United States. Clearly Muslim Americans have a long way to go in their quest to debunk negative stereotypes, especially those that unfairly label all members of the religious minority as perpetrators of terrorism.

Affirmative Action

Some observers have called the civil rights movement a "Second Reconstruction" because it eliminated most of the vestiges of racial discrimination and segregation from the books. But would this successful legal revolution translate into real change? Various civil rights leaders in the 1970s and 1980s shifted their focus to affirmative action as a means of promoting racial and ethnic minority gains in education and the workplace. The women's movement also has benefited from affirmative action programs in the workplace and elsewhere. Although "quotas" (specifically defined numerical goals for hiring or admitting members of certain groups) have been used in the past, more often such programs involve giving some form of preferential treatment, whether by adding points to a mathematical score due to a person's status as a member of a particular racial group, or by creating economic or other incentives for administrative bodies to increase the diversity of their incoming workforce and/or educational institutions.

Proponents of affirmative action argue that past discriminatory practices have deprived certain racial groups and women of opportunities to get the skills or experiences they need to compete for jobs or college admissions on an equal footing with those who have not experienced such discrimination. The issue of affirmative action reached the U.S. Supreme Court in the case of *Regents of the University of California v. Bakke* (1978).[29] In 1973, Alan Bakke, one of 2,664 applicants for 100 seats at the University of California–Davis Medical School, interviewed with one of the school's officials, Dr. Theodore West. At that time, West told Bakke that he was a "very desirable applicant to the medical school." Thus Bakke was quite surprised when he was denied admission. Bakke in fact was rejected not once but twice for admission: in 1973 and again in 1974. In both instances, 16 applicants with lower grade point averages and MCAT (Medical College Admission Test) scores than Bakke's were admitted to the school under a special minority admissions program. Bakke challenged the program as a violation of the Fourteenth Amendment's equal protection clause. In previous years, the courts had dismissed most lawsuits because they were quickly rendered "moot," a legal term that indicates that circumstances have removed the practical significance of deciding the case. (By attending some other school, those unsuccessful applicants had essentially prevented their cases from ever being decided.) But Bakke was determined to go to University of California–Davis Medical School and thus his case eventually reached the U.S. Supreme Court.

In deciding the case, the Supreme Court ruled that a university could take into account race and ethnicity when making decisions about the admission of students, as long as it did not utilize specifically assigned numerical goals. To the Court, no constitutional infirmity exists where "race or ethnic background is simply one element—to be weighed fairly against other elements—in the selection process." In his majority opinion, Justice Lewis Powell also heralded the benefits of a diverse student body, noting that students with particular racial backgrounds may bring to a school "experiences, outlooks and ideas that enrich the training of its student body."[30]

Students at the University of Michigan rally in support of affirmative action. In 2003 the U.S. Supreme Court upheld the use of affirmative action by the University of Michigan's Law School, but struck down the affirmative action program utilized in that university's undergraduate admissions.

Five years after he was first denied admission, Bakke got what he wanted: on June 28, 1978, the U.S. Supreme Court directed that he be admitted to the university's medical school. Opponents of affirmative action thought they had received the victory they were looking for; after all, the Court held that the university could not use fixed racial quotas in this instance. But schools and universities took refuge in the Court's statements favoring the consideration of racial criteria more generally, and in the quarter century that followed, countless schools of higher education utilized race-conscious admissions programs. Thus, although Alan Bakke won his personal battle for admission, the war over affirmative action would continue to be waged in the years that followed.

Opponents of affirmative action complain that such programs punish white applicants who played no role at all in the original discriminatory practices. They also claim that a racial divide that currently exists in this country may be exacerbated by affirmative action because members of racial groups who benefit from such programs may be stigmatized by the perception that they are not fully deserving. Finally, affirmative action programs are explicit racial classifications, and thus may be thought to violate the principle of a "color-blind Constitution" that was celebrated by the Supreme Court's decision in *Brown v. Board of Education*.

A string of Supreme Court decisions in the late 1980s and 1990s effectively ended explicit affirmative action programs in public employment and contracting. The final nail in the coffin for affirmative action in contracting may have been the Court's decision in *Adarand v. Peña* (1995),[31] which held that any racial classification may be considered unconstitutional unless it meets the test of strict scrutiny: It must be "narrowly tailored" to further a "compelling governmental interest," a standard that has proved nearly impossible for the government to meet. In fact, no affirmative action employment plan has been upheld as constitutional by the Supreme Court since the early 1990s.

By contrast, affirmative action in education remains steeped in controversy; the confusion over what is legal in this context was only partially resolved by two University of Michigan cases in 2003 that essentially reaffirmed *Bakke*'s finding that diversity constitutes a "compelling state interest" under certain circumstances. In *Grutter v. Bollinger* (2003),[32] the Court upheld the university's law school admission program because it only considered race as a positive factor in a review process where all individual applications were carefully reviewed and analyzed on their own merits. Yet that same day in *Gratz v. Bollinger* (2003),[33] the Supreme Court struck down the same university's undergraduate admissions program because instead of providing such careful, individualized review, it automatically awarded 20 points to all students from underrepresented groups, greatly enhancing their chances of being admitted. The Court declared that such a blanket award of benefits was not "narrowly tailored" enough to promote diversity.

In an attempt to balance the interests of having a diverse student body with frequently heard criticisms of affirmative action, state governments in Texas, Florida, and California have enacted alternative programs that would guarantee a place at the state's top universities for every student who finishes in the upper tier (normally the top 5 or 10 percent) of his or her high school class. Given that racial minorities tend to predominate at high schools both in the inner city and in especially poor rural neighborhoods in the South, these percentage plans tend to guarantee seats at major state universities to minority students who would otherwise have been denied admission. Critics of the plans charge that they capitalize on patterns of segregation in housing and geography. Regardless, the Supreme Court upheld this type of program in *Fisher v. Texas* (2016). By a 4-3 vote, the Court affirmed a University of Texas admission policy that featured both a "top 10 percent plan" as well as a secondary plan by which race was considered, along with other factors, as part of an individualized review.

Racial Profiling

Statistics pertaining to the criminal justice system also testify to continuing racial inequality and racial tensions. For instance, although African American youth at the end of the twentieth century represented just 15 percent of the nation's total youth population, they made up 26 percent of the youth arrested, 31 percent of the youth referred to juvenile court, and 44 percent of the youth detained by the police.[34] African American males in particular compose a disproportionate number of those imprisoned. Critics of the system charge that it is racially biased, especially in how it metes out capital punishment. A study conducted by social scientist David Baldus in the early 1990s concluded that the victim's race was a significant factor in predicting which convicted murderers receive the death penalty. Specifically, killers of whites were 4.3 times more likely to be sentenced to death than killers of African Americans.

Racial discrimination may also characterize the initial phases of gathering information about a crime. For example, some law enforcement officials admit to using **racial profiling**—the practice of taking race into account when investigating crimes. Racial/ethnic minorities may be stopped, questioned, and even held in custody not because there is specific evidence that links them to a particular crime, but because they fit a "profile" of the perpetrator that includes the characteristic of race.

Even in the wake of the civil rights revolution of the 1960s, little objection was raised against the practice, provided that it

racial profiling The law enforcement practice of taking race into account when identifying possible suspects of crimes.

A policeman interviews several teenagers that he suspects of being undocumented on a street corner in Tucson, Arizona.

Protesting Injustice on College Campuses

In 2012, George M. Zimmerman, a neighborhood watch coordinator for a gated community in Sanford, Florida, shot and killed 17-year-old African American high school student Trayvon Martin. At the time, Martin was temporarily staying in the community where the shooting took place. After Zimmerman was acquitted in 2013, the internationalist activist movement titled Black Lives Matter (BLM) began to campaign on social media and elsewhere against violence committed by law enforcement officials against African Americans, as well as against police brutality and racial equality more generally. The movement received national acclaim after it successfully organized street demonstrations around the country; later it began to lobby for politicians to state their positions on BLM issues. In 2015 the BLM movement and related groups such as the Black Justice League took their battle to college campuses following the failure of several college administrations to adequately respond to racist incidents on campus. At least two university presidents and numerous deans and administrators resigned over allegations of racial insensitivity. At the time this book went to press, many colleges were considering the removal of statues and the renaming of buildings that celebrate racist founders or donors. In pressing for such actions, the BLM

Protesters in Washington, D.C., march against police brutality and the killing of unarmed black men by police on December 13, 2014.

movement on campuses made it clear that colleges and universities matter in the continuing quest for social equality.

For Critical Thinking and Discussion

1. Have you ever participated in protests for equal treatment on your college campus or elsewhere?
2. Do you think campus buildings should be renamed due to the racist political stances and policies associated with the names on those buildings?

was done for purposes of "bona fide law enforcement" and not racial harassment, and so long as race was one of several factors that police officers considered when investigating crimes. But racial profiling became a source of considerable controversy in the 1990s. During the spring of 1999, victims of the New Jersey State Police force's allegedly overaggressive racial profiling testified at hearings held by the Black and Latino Caucus of the state's legislature. President Bill Clinton publicly condemned racial profiling as a "morally indefensible, deeply corrosive practice." Finally, in March 2003, New Jersey became the first state in the nation to enact an antiprofiling law, which made any profiling by police punishable by five years in prison and a $15,000 fine. Yet by the end of that decade, a majority of states still had not banned racial profiling as a law enforcement practice. In June 2003, President George W. Bush issued a directive that banned racial profiling by federal law enforcement agencies, although critics complained about both the law's exception for the use of racial profiling in "national security" investigations and the lack of enforcement mechanisms provided. Accordingly, claims of profiling in the past decade have focused on

Naturalization, Customs, and Border Patrol agents accused of improperly restricting Muslims' entry or reentry into the United States.

More recently, Arizona law enforcement officials were accused of racial profiling under the auspices of the Arizona Law Enforcement and Safe Neighborhoods Act, better known as SB 1070. Passed in 2010, the act authorized the police to arrest individuals if there was a mere "suspicion" that the persons were undocumented immigrants. Critics were quick to complain that the law was directed at those who merely "looked" like they were from foreign countries, a clear form of racial profiling. In 2012, the Supreme Court struck down most provisions of the Arizona law, including the power of police to arrest a person on the mere suspicion that he or she is an undocumented immigrant.

Are criticisms of racial profiling exaggerated? Statistics overwhelmingly confirm that African American young men commit a disproportionate share of street crime in the United States. Thus, not all racial profiling may be driven by prejudice against African Americans—civil rights leader Jesse Jackson admitted in 1993 that he was less fearful of white strangers than black strangers on dark streets, if only because, statistically speaking, he stands a greater risk of being robbed by a black person than a white person. At the same time, defenders of racial profiling (as one of many factors in the investigative process) tend to minimize the extent to which the practice adds to the sense of resentment of law enforcement felt by rich and poor minorities alike. No court has ever banned the practice outright. Moreover, even if a court did take such a bold action, it would be difficult to disprove an officer's claim that nonracial factors were in fact the primary consideration in his or her decision-making process.

The controversy over racial profiling entered the national conversation once again in 2012 with the fatal shooting of an unarmed 17-year-old African American, Trayvon Martin, by a multiracial neighborhood watch coordinator in a Sanford, Florida, gated community. Although there was no indication that Martin was involved in any criminal activity, the coordinator, George Zimmerman, initially reported Martin to the police and then shot him in an altercation that took place before the police arrived. The local police chose not to charge Zimmerman; nearly six weeks passed before Zimmerman was charged by a specially appointed prosecutor with second-degree murder. In the meantime, allegations of racist motivations by both the shooter and the police dominated media coverage of the incident. Critics also charged that laws like Florida's "Stand Your Ground Law"—which allows the use of force in self-defense without a duty to retreat—encourages racial profiling by citizens. Thus, few were surprised when Zimmerman was acquitted on charges of second-degree murder and manslaughter in June of 2013. The riots in Ferguson, Missouri, over the killing of Michael Brown by a white police officer added even more fuel to the fire of resentment that this issue continues.

Controversies surrounding the war on terrorism, affirmative action, and racial profiling highlight a vexing challenge in modern society. Even if all vestiges of formal racial classifications under the law are eliminated, calculations of racial differences inevitably enter into the subjective judgments of those in positions of authority. Thus, for all the successful challenges launched against the racist legal and political structures that prevailed in American society during much of the twentieth century, the greater challenge of winning over the "hearts and minds" of individuals still remains.

Summary

5-1 Types of Equality

- Civil rights are those political rights (focusing on the right to participate in the political system), social rights (focusing on equality within institutions that serve the public), or economic rights (focusing on competition over resources) conferred by the government on members of groups that had previously been denied those rights. The battle for civil rights in America has focused primarily on African Americans and other ethnic groups (Hispanics, Asian Americans, Native Americans, Muslim Americans), women, older Americans, individuals with physical disabilities, and gays and lesbians.

5-2 The Struggle for Equality: Approaches and Tactics

- The tactics used by groups seeking to achieve civil rights include working within the existing rules and political process, litigation, boycotts, and civil disobedience

5-3 The Struggle for Equality: Race, Ethnicity and Civil Rights

- The hard-fought struggle by racial/ethnic minorities for equality dates back to the Constitutional Convention, which controversially left the institution of slavery intact in the South. The Civil War Amendments ended slavery, granted citizenship to former slaves, guaranteed all Americans "equal protection under the laws," and denied states the ability to prevent voting rights on the basis of race.

- The states used many means to prevent racial/ethnic minorities from obtaining equality, including *Black Codes*, literacy tests, poll taxes, and Jim Crow laws; by distinguishing state action from private discrimination and upholding the controversial "separate but equal doctrine" in public accommodations, the courts up through the middle of the twentieth century allowed such discrimination to continue. Native Americans (as well as Far East Asians and Hispanics) have also struggled to receive all the rights and privileges of U.S. citizenship since the federal government herded them onto reservations in the eighteenth and nineteenth centuries.

- The movement toward civil rights for racial and ethnic minorities in all public accommodations began in the late 1950s and emerged as a major force under the leadership of Martin Luther King Jr., Cesar Chavez, and others. A number of court decisions, including *Mendez v. Westminster* (1947) and *Brown v. Board of Education* (1954), eventually eliminated the "separate but equal" doctrine. By offering heightened scrutiny to laws that discriminated on the basis of race, the courts eventually ended "de jure" racial discrimination. The Civil Rights Act of 1964 and the Voting Rights Act of 1965 brought America closer to the goal of equality for racial/ethnic minorities.

- Additionally, the Civil Rights Act of 1968 prohibited discrimination in housing and made it a federal crime to deny individuals their civil rights. Still, so-called "de facto" discrimination remains a challenge, as racial housing patterns often undermine efforts to erect equitable school districts and legislative districts on a nonracial basis.

5-4 The Women's Movement and Gender Equality

- The seeds were sown for the movement toward gender equality in the early twentieth century with the ratification of the Nineteenth Amendment, guaranteeing women the right to vote. However, not until the formation of the National Organization for Women (NOW) and its emergence as a significant political force did women's equality start to capture national attention. Beginning in the 1970s, the Supreme Court gave intermediate scrutiny to gender classifications as well, invalidating all but a handful of laws that discriminated on the basis of gender.

- Congress passed Title IX in 1972, prohibiting the exclusion of women from any educational programs receiving financial assistance from the federal government. Courts have interpreted Title IX as requiring colleges to provide as many opportunities for female athletes as male athletes.

5-5 Other Group Struggles for Equality

- More recent debates over racial and ethnic equality have focused on discrimination against older Americans, disabled Americans, and LGBTQ.

- Courts have vindicated some of the rights of LGBTQ, upholding the constitutional right of same-sex marriage. Considerable discrimination in other contexts remains. Additionally, Congress has passed laws protecting the rights of older Americans and disabled Americans from discrimination, especially in the workplace.

5-6 Continuing Struggles Over Equality in the Modern Era

- Racial and ethnic differences are not the only type of discrimination practiced by governments. Recent battles have focused on discrimination against Muslim Americans (and how to protect their civil rights in the post-9/11 era).

- Two contemporary issues relating to civil rights are affirmative action and racial profiling. The courts have struck down affirmative action programs that feature quotas and other fixed advantages for racial minorities; still, many states continue to try to find ways for government to level the playing field in college admissions in particular, including the establishment of "top-10 percent plans" and more individualized forms of review. Racial profiling remains a controversial practice, especially as practiced by state officials against immigrant populations and others.

Key Terms

affirmative action (p. 125)

Brown v. Board of Education (1954) (p. 110)

civil rights (p. 109)

Civil Rights Act of 1964 (p. 118)

Civil Rights Act of 1968 (p. 119)

Civil War Amendments (p. 112)

economic equality (p. 108)

Jim Crow laws (p. 114)

Mendez v. Westminster (1947) (p. 114)

Plessy v. Ferguson (1896) (p. 114)

political equality (p. 108)

racial profiling (p. 132)

social equality (p. 108)

strict scrutiny (p. 115)

Title IX (p. 125)

Twenty-fourth Amendment (p. 119)

Voting Rights Act of 1965 (p. 119)

Test Yourself

1. The Civil Rights Act of 1968 was aimed primarily at advancing
   a. political equality.
   b. social equality.
   c. economic equality.
   d. cultural equality.

2. The notion of "equality" as a value defining American political culture was articulated specifically in which of the following documents?
   a. Declaration of Independence
   b. Bill of Rights
   c. Articles of Confederation
   d. Article I of the Constitution

3. Distinguish between political and social equality. Give an example of each.

4. Which of the following Supreme Court decisions declared that racial segregation in public schools was unconstitutional?
   a. *Dred Scott v. Sanford*
   b. *Plessy v. Ferguson*
   c. *Marbury v. Madison*
   d. *Brown v. Board of Education*

5. The civil rights leader who first advocated pursuing equality for African Americans using "agitation" techniques rather than accommodation was
   a. Booker T. Washington.
   b. W. E. B. Du Bois.
   c. Al Sharpton.
   d. Martin Luther King Jr.

6. What is "civil disobedience," and how does its use advance the goals of the civil rights movement?

7. Which of the following most directly played a role in bringing about the Civil War?
   a. *Plessy v. Ferguson*
   b. The *Dred Scott* decision
   c. The ratification of the Bill of Rights
   d. *Brown v. Board of Education*

8. Which of the following banished slavery from all states and U.S. territories?
   a. Thirteenth Amendment
   b. Fourteenth Amendment
   c. Fifteenth Amendment
   d. Sixteenth Amendment

9. The legal standard advanced in *Brown v. Board of Education* and other cases that tends to invalidate most state laws that discriminate on the basis of race is
   a. reasonable intent.
   b. probable cause.
   c. eminent domain.
   d. strict scrutiny.

10. In the *Bakke* decision, the Supreme Court ruled that
   a. the use of racial quotas violates the equal protection clause.
   b. quotas may be used to achieve equality.
   c. affirmative action of any kind is unconstitutional.
   d. quotas may be used in medical school admissions but not in law school admissions.

11. What is "affirmative action," and how has the court squared its application with the constitutional promise of "equal protection under law"?

12. Which U.S. Supreme Court justice led the ACLU in its legal fight during the 1960s and 1970s to achieve protection against gender discrimination?
   a. Sandra Day O'Connor
   b. Ruth Bader Ginsburg
   c. Elana Kagan
   d. Sonia Sotomayor

13. Which of the following statements is true?
   a. Women have achieved parity with men in salaries.
   b. The Equal Rights Amendment was passed in 1972.

c. Title IX substantially increased women's opportunities to participate in college sports.

d. About half of all college presidents are now women.

14. What is meant by the legal standard of "intermediate scrutiny," and how does this concept apply to gender discrimination?

15. The law passed by Congress in 1887 that attempted to divide tribal lands and undermine Native American cultures was the

a. Indian Limitation Act.

b. Jim Crow Act.

c. Dawes Act.

d. Native American Assimilation Act.

16. The fastest-growing minority group in the United States is

a. African Americans.

b. Asian Americans.

c. Native Americans.

d. Hispanics.

17. The first state to pass a law formally authorizing the granting of licenses for same-sex marriages was

a. Vermont.

b. California.

c. Massachusetts.

d. Florida.

18. Why is the USA Patriot Act the subject of controversy among those who are concerned about equal rights for Muslim Americans?

---

1. b (LO 5-1); 2. a (LO 5-1); 4. d (LO 5-2); 5. b (LO 5-2); 7. b (LO 5-3); 8. a (LO 5-3); 9. d (LO 5-3); 10. a (LO 5-3); 12. b (LO 5-4); 13. c (LO 5-4); 15. c (LO 5-5); 16. d (LO 5-5); 17. c (LO 5-5)

Tupungato/Shutterstock.com

LEARNING OBJECTIVES

6-1 Article I and the Creation of Congress
- Define the role the U.S. Congress plays as the legislative branch of government.

6-2 The Structure and Organization of Congress
- Identify the structure and powers of Congress, explain bicameralism, and distinguish between the roles of the House and Senate.
- Assess the role that political parties play in the leadership of Congress.
- Identify key leadership positions and their functions in Congress.
- Explain reapportionment and redistricting.

6-3 The Committee System
- Compare and contrast the different types of committees found in Congress.

6-4 How a Bill Becomes a Law
- Describe the various steps necessary for a bill to become a law.

6-5 Oversight and Personnel Functions of Congress
- Explain why Congress often delegates its lawmaking authority to regulatory agencies.
- Describe the role of the Senate in confirming presidential appointments, and the congressional procedures for impeachment and removal of executive and judicial officers.

6-6 Constituent Service: Helping People Back Home
- Assess the "casework" functions of members of Congress in assisting constituents, educating them on policy issues, and performing other services on their behalf.

6

Congress

Congress is a large and complex institution. It is the branch of government that is primarily responsible for creating new laws, but it largely takes its cues from the White House. Although the Constitution makes no mention of the role that political parties might play in making laws, partisanship has become the primary factor that organizes Congress and its daily operations. Nonetheless, the nuances of the legislative process provide ample opportunities for the minority party, or even a small set of members, to thwart new laws from passage, contributing to the so-called gridlock in Washington, D.C. Among the three branches of government, intense partisan divisiveness is most likely found in the halls of Congress. In this chapter, we explore the organization of the Congress and its leadership structure. We trace the steps of the complex lawmaking process, the checks that Congress has on the other branches of government, and the important role the members of Congress play back in their home districts.

WHO ARE YOU?

How Much Confidence Do You Have in Congress?

The partisan gridlock and divisiveness that has characterized the U.S. Congress over the past decade has taken its toll on public confidence in the national legislature. Frustrated with the progress of the Iraqi war in 2006, voters handed the Democrats a new House majority in the 2006 midterm elections. Then in 2008, an economic collapse and the "great recession" led voters to give control of both houses of Congress (and the presidency) to the Democratic Party. Of course, many voters grew frustrated with the Democrats over the passage of Obamacare and a fledgling economy, and so returned GOP majorities to the House in 2010 and then to the Senate in 2014. As voters shifted partisan control of Congress, Congress featured more partisan bickering, divisiveness, and legislative gridlock. There were even instances when such bickering resulted in temporary government shutdowns. All this has led to a sharp decrease of public confidence in Congress.

In the Gallup Poll's annual measurement of public confidence in a variety of institutions, only 8 percent in 2015 said they have either "a great deal" or "a lot" of confidence in Congress.

- How do you rate the job that Congress is doing? And how do you compare Congress's job performance to other institutions, such as big business, religion, the presidency, the Supreme Court, and the U.S. military?

To see how your answers compare to others, take the **Who Are You?** poll in MindTap!

6-1 | Article I and the Creation of Congress

Article I of the U.S. Constitution created Congress; and the fact that it came first was no accident. James Madison, the Father of the Constitution, referred to Congress as the "first branch of government," and as a graduate student, Woodrow Wilson (later the 28th president of the United States) wrote in his book *Congressional Government* (1885) that "anyone who is unfamiliar with what Congress actually does and how it does it . . . is very far from a knowledge of the constitutional system under which we live."[1] As the legislative branch of the federal government, Congress has ultimate authority for enacting new laws. Because this authority is central to any system of government, the Founders engaged in considerable debate and took great care in building this first branch.

There was little question that a congress of some type would be the central institution in the new political system—a congress had been a central feature in all attempts to organize the states up through and including the Constitutional Convention of 1787. The Albany Congress of 1754 was the first attempt to unite the colonies—at the time for common defense against the French in the pending French and Indian War. The Albany Plan of Union called for the colonies to organize through the vehicle of a "congress." In addition, colonial efforts to deal with emerging conflicts with the British led to the formation of two congresses: the First Continental Congress in 1774 and then the Second Continental Congress in 1775. After the revolutionary war was won, the first official government of the United States, created under the Articles of Confederation, again used a congress as its organizing principle. It is not surprising, then, that Article I, Section 1 of the U.S. Constitution states: "All legislative Powers herein granted shall be vested in a Congress of the United States."

Joseph Rainey of South Carolina was the first African American elected to the House of Representatives. He took office in 1870 and was reelected four times.

The Founders engaged in plenty of debate, negotiation, and compromise in defining the powers, functions, and structure of the U.S. Congress. The complexity of this institution continues today. Congress is filled with paradoxes. On one hand, it is a highly democratic institution in which senators and representatives are selected in free and open elections; on the other hand, Congress often is responsive to an exceedingly narrow set of specialized interests. Citizens and journalists frequently criticize the institution as being too slow to act responsively; yet voters return more than 9 in 10 of their elected members to office. At times, such as in the weeks following the terrorist attacks of September 11, 2001, Congress can show enthusiasm for tackling large issues expeditiously: within days of the attacks, it passed the USA PATRIOT Act, which featured numerous antiterrorism measures. At other times, it seems to avoid taking positions on important issues, such as campaign finance reform and abortion rights. Many of these factors have led to very low confidence ratings in Congress from the American public. Figure 6-1 shows the results of the Gallup Poll's survey on confidence levels in a variety of institutions. As the chart shows, confidence in Congress ranks the lowest.

Most significantly, Congress is the branch of the U.S. government that ensures representation of the people through the direct election of members of the House and, in more recent times, of members of the Senate as well. Through its 535 members, Congress provides representation of many groups throughout the country, such as women, African Americans, Native Americans, gays and lesbians, the physically disabled, and Hispanics.

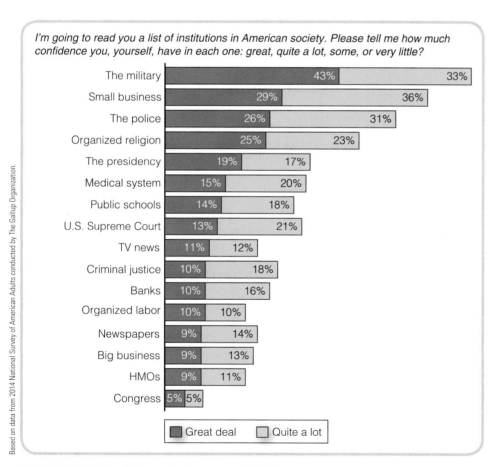

I'm going to read you a list of institutions in American society. Please tell me how much confidence you, yourself, have in each one: great, quite a lot, some, or very little?

Institution	Great deal	Quite a lot
The military	43%	33%
Small business	29%	36%
The police	26%	31%
Organized religion	25%	23%
The presidency	19%	17%
Medical system	15%	20%
Public schools	14%	18%
U.S. Supreme Court	13%	21%
TV news	11%	12%
Criminal justice	10%	18%
Banks	10%	16%
Organized labor	10%	10%
Newspapers	9%	14%
Big business	9%	13%
HMOs	9%	11%
Congress	5%	5%

Based on data from 2014 National Survey of American Adults conducted by The Gallup Organization.

FIGURE 6-1 **Confidence in Congress (2014)**

Does Congress Look Diverse?

Does the racial, ethnic, and gender diversity of Congress reflect the reality of the America that it purports to represent? One way to evaluate congressional representation is to examine descriptive representation, or the descriptive characteristics of members of Congress as compared to the corresponding makeup of the U.S. population. Such an exercise depicts a congressional delegation far from reflective of the American population.

The Reflective Democracy Campaign project calls attention to this lack of diversity in the national legislature. The project created a National Representation Index, which measures political representation by race and gender, then weighted to account for geographic population differences across the country (www.wholeads.us). Their stark figures show that white men are 31 percent of the population but hold 65 percent of elected positions. In other words, they have four times more political representation than other gender/racial groups.[2] Women represent 51 percent of the U.S. population but only hold 19 percent of congressional seats. Racial/ethnic minorities represent 38 percent of the U.S. population but only occupy

Members of the Congressional Black Caucus hold a press conference to discuss their plans for the 2016 congressional campaigns.

11 percent of the seats in Congress (7 percent minority males and 4 percent minority females).

For Critical Thinking and Discussion

1. Are you surprised or concerned about the lack of racial, ethnic, and gender diversity in Congress?
2. What are the important implications of this lack of congressional diversity?

6-2 | The Structure and Organization of Congress

bicameral legislature
A legislature composed of two separate chambers.

Congress is organized into two separate chambers, the Senate and the House of Representatives, and is thus termed a **bicameral legislature**. Creating a bicameral legislature enabled the Founders to reach a compromise between two factions at the Constitutional Convention—those who represented large states and wanted congressional representation according to population and those from small states who favored the model of the Articles of Confederation: that each state, regardless of population, would be equally represented in Congress. The "Great Compromise" reached by the convention delegates allowed for equal state representation in the Senate and representation based on population in the House. These two chambers have shared lawmaking responsibilities since 1789.[3]

This nearly equal sharing of legislative power between the two chambers is significant. Many other nations in the world have bicameral legislatures, but the two legislative houses are rarely equal in power and usually do not share power. In the British Parliament, for example, the House of Lords has little power and serves a mostly symbolic function in that nation's politics, whereas the House of Commons wields the most authoritative power. Legislatures in other nations, such as Canada, France,

Germany, Israel, and Japan, are also heavily dominated by one house. By contrast, in the U.S. Congress, the Senate and House are coequal chambers, with each enjoying about as much power as the other. Similar to the United States, the national legislatures in Italy and Mexico include two houses with nearly equal power. Many nations have *unicameral* legislatures that consist of only one body, such as the 275-member legislature elected to govern in Iraq in 2005.

Bicameralism has important implications for the legislative process in American politics—passing new laws is difficult because the two chambers, constructed so differently, must come to absolute agreement before a new law is enacted. The slowness that often characterizes lawmaking in Congress is, in part, a product of this reality. The sharing of power and the "checks" that each chamber has on the other are no mistake. Indeed, the Founders intentionally built a Congress that would move slowly and carefully in the adoption of new laws, a process that, although often characterized as gridlock, ensures that change is well contemplated before it is adopted.

The House of Representatives: The "People's House"

The Founders intended the House of Representatives to be the "people's house," or the institution through which ordinary people would be represented in government. At the time the Constitution was adopted, the only federal officials directly elected by the people were members of the House of Representatives. Senators were chosen by state legislatures; the president and vice president were selected by electors in the electoral college; and judges, ambassadors, and high-ranking officials in the executive branch were nominated by the president and approved by the Senate. In Federalist No. 51, James Madison admonished, "As it is essential to liberty that the government in general should have a common interest with the people, so it is particularly essential that the branch of it under consideration [the House] should have an immediate dependence on, and an intimate sympathy with, the people."[4] The House of Representatives thus directly connects voter sentiment with popular representation.

So that members of the House would be held accountable, Article I, Section 2 sets the term of a House member at two years, keeping members constantly attentive to public opinion. Indeed, because of their relatively brief term of office, members of the House are typically consumed with concerns about winning reelection. This preoccupation has been well documented by scholars such as Thomas Mann, who argues that incumbent House members are in campaign mode most of the time, feeling "unsafe at any margin" of victory.[5]

Article I also ensures that the House of Representatives reflects the popular will by requiring that the number of representatives from each state be proportional to each state's population. States are not equally represented in the House of Representatives; rather, the population of each state is proportionately represented, at least to a large degree. This means that a more populous state has greater representation than a less populous one. The state of California, for example, now has 53 seats in the House of Representatives, compared to Wyoming, which has only one.

The first Congress in 1789 included 65 members, consistent with the Article I requirement that the number of House members should not exceed one for every 30,000 people in a state. As the nation grew in both the number of states and number of people, the number of members of the House of Representatives also grew. If the ratio of 30,000 people to one representative applied today, there would be about 10,000 members of the House of Representatives! By the mid-1800s, Congress began enlarging the population size of a congressional district to keep the membership of the House from getting too large. Public Law 62-5, passed in 1911 to take effect in 1913, capped the total number of House seats at 435.[6]

Today there are still 435 **congressional districts**, each represented by one House member. The number of people who are represented in a congressional district is tied to

congressional district
A geographic region (either a state itself or a region located entirely within one state) whose residents select one member to represent it in the House of Representatives.

RICHARD MICHAEL PRUITT/KRT/Newscom

U.S. Rep. Linda Sánchez (D), a labor lawyer and first generation American, entered politics after the 2000 Census led to the creation of a new 39th congressional district in California.

a number that changes after every census. Since fixing the number of seats at 435, Congress has struggled to find an equitable way to allocate House seats to the states—a process known as **reapportionment**.

Several U.S. Supreme Court decisions in the early 1960s[7] established the basic principle that guides the process of reapportionment after every census—the "one person, one vote" principle. According to this principle, the population size of congressional districts must be as equal as possible. Currently, that amounts to roughly 650,000 people per district. The requirement that each state maintain at least one House district causes some variance among the population sizes of each district. The single congressional district for Wyoming, for example, has a population of about 570,000 because that is the number of people who live in that state. Consequently, Wyoming's population is proportionately "overrepresented," compared to most other congressional districts. Because congressional districts cannot cross state boundaries, the population size of congressional districts across states also varies. Yet once congressional districts are officially allocated to states based on the U.S. Census, the size of each district within a state must be as close to equal as possible.

The Constitution requires that a new census of the population be taken every 10 years, which is used to reapportion seats in the House of Representatives to each state. The states are then responsible for **redistricting** congressional boundary lines to achieve equal representation in each of the congressional districts; that is, redrawing congressional district lines to achieve the "one person, one vote" principle within the borders of the state.

In addition to equalizing the size of congressional districts, parties in each state try to optimize the partisan characteristics of each district to their advantage. This drawing of district boundaries to favor one party over the other is referred to as **gerrymandering**, a term named for Elbridge Gerry, who was a signer of the Declaration of Independence, a Massachusetts delegate to the Constitutional Convention, a U.S. congressman, governor of Massachusetts, and vice president under James Madison. While governor, he endorsed legislation that redrew districts in Massachusetts, resulting in huge advantages for his political party, the Democratic-Republicans. The map of one of the new districts took on an odd shape, that of a salamander. Gerry's political opponents, the Federalists, dubbed the plan the "gerrymander plan." The political fallout for Gerry was significant—he lost his next bid for governor. But the legacy of gerrymandering continues. Every decade or so, parties in states with more than one House member must ultimately negotiate a redistricting plan based on gerrymandered district boundaries that each party hopes will optimize its electoral successes.

Amendments to the Voting Rights Act in 1982 have required that some states apply the gerrymandering concept to create "**majority-minority districts**." That is, the boundaries of some congressional districts are drawn to ensure that the majority of voters are member of minority groups, thus enhancing the chances that a minority group member will win the congressional seat. Such "racial gerrymandering" is intended to prevent the dilution of minority representation in Congress. The creating of majority-minority districts has substantially increased racial/ethnic minority representation in the House.

Article I requires that all members of the House of Representatives be at least 25 years of age, have been a U.S. citizen for a minimum of seven years, and live in the

reapportionment The allocation of a fixed number of House seats to the states.

redistricting The act of redrawing congressional boundaries to achieve equal representation in each of the congressional districts.

gerrymandering The drawing of House district boundaries to the benefit of one political party over another. The term is named for Elbridge Gerry, a Massachusetts delegate to the Constitutional Convention, who (as governor) redrew districts in this fashion to favor the Democratic-Republicans.

majority-minority district A congressional district drawn with geographic boundaries that promote the chances of electing a minority member to represent that district.

state (though not necessarily the congressional district) from which they are elected. These requirements are somewhat less restrictive than those for the Senate—another indication of the Founders' intention to give the people a greater role in deciding on who members of the House should be.

The Senate: A Stabilizing Factor

Whereas the Founders wanted to make the House of Representatives highly responsive to the people, their idea for the Senate was quite different. The Senate was to represent the states—with each state having two senators, or equal representation. As adopted, the Constitution specified that senators were to be elected not by the people of the state, but by the state legislatures, another way to recognize states' importance. Not until passage of the Seventeenth Amendment to the Constitution in 1913 were senators elected directly by the people of the state they represented.

The Founders were also concerned that the "people's house" might be too prone to radical changes in membership resulting from swift changes in popular opinion. James Madison in particular regarded the U.S. Senate as "a necessary fence against this danger,"[8] able to resist fast changes in federal legislation because it was less accessible to the people. In fact, during the first five years of our constitutional government, the U.S. Senate met in closed session. By sharing legislative power with the House of Representatives, the Senate, a slower, more deliberative body, would be the mechanism for protecting against the potential tyranny of the masses. Thus, the creation of new laws would be forced to proceed at a more thoughtful pace.

The Constitution sets the term of a U.S. senator at six years, three times the length of that for a House member. The Founders staggered the terms of senators. Every two years, only one-third of the seats in the Senate are up for reelection, as compared to all of the seats in the House. So although in theory all of the seats in the House can change every other year, the Senate may change only by a maximum of 34 seats every two years and is thus less prone to drastic changes in membership.

The qualifications for becoming a U.S. senator are also tighter. The minimum age is 30, five years older than in the House. The Founders based this provision on the theory that older people would be less likely to endorse radical change. Also, a U.S. senator must have been a citizen for at least nine years (rather than seven for the House) and be a resident of the state that he or she represents.

Article I requires that there be two senators from each state. The total number of senators grew from 26 in 1789 to 100 in 1959, the year Alaska and Hawaii became the 49th and 50th states, respectively. Although the size of the Senate has grown, it still remains small, at least relative to the size of the House of Representatives. The smaller size of the Senate is often cited as the primary reason why debate in the Senate tends to be more civil and camaraderie between individuals more important.

Leadership in Congress

Unlike the executive branch, which is headed by the president, no one person or office leads Congress as a whole. Leadership is distinct in the Senate and the House of Representatives. Though both chambers must work together to pass new laws, each chamber maintains its own leadership structure to work on bills, pass laws, and conduct its other business. Cooperation between the House and Senate is necessary to accomplish legislation.

The principal factor driving leadership in each chamber is the political party system, which, interestingly, is not mentioned in the U.S. Constitution.[9] The two-party system in America generates a majority of members from one of the two major parties, in both the Senate and House of Representatives. Since 1851, the majority party in each house has been either the Democratic Party or the Republican Party. Members of the party

majority caucus The
members of the party that has
the majority of seats in a
particular chamber.

minority caucus The
members of the party that has a
minority of seats in a particular
chamber.

that has the majority of seats constitute the **majority caucus**, whereas those who are members of the party with a minority of seats constitute the **minority caucus**. The majority caucus in the House and the majority caucus in the Senate use their respective majorities to elect leaders and maintain control of their chamber. The larger the party's majority, and the more discipline and unity among party members, the stronger the power of the majority party's leadership ability.

From 1954 through 1980, the Democrats held the majority caucus in the Senate. Since then partisan control of the Senate has shifted five times. More recently, the Democrats won back a narrow majority in 2007, and then widened its margin to 60–40 as a result of the 2008 elections. While the Republican margin narrowed in each of the 4 subsequent elections (2010 through 2016), the GOP remains the majority party.

By contrast, the House of Representatives has enjoyed a bit more stability, undergoing fewer changes in party control of the majority caucus since 1954. Up through 1994, the Democratic Party had maintained a seemingly iron grip of control over the House. Finally, after 40 years, the 1994 elections transformed a Democratic majority to a Republican majority. The Republicans continued to dominate the House until the 2006 midterm elections, at which point the Democrats regained leadership of the people's chamber. Democratic control of the House, however, proved short lived. In 2010, the GOP won back more than 60 House seats from the Democrats and reestablished a Republican majority, which it has since retained.

Leadership in the House of Representatives

The only guidance the Constitution offers regarding House leadership is contained in Article I, Section 2: "The House of Representatives shall choose their Speaker and other Officers." The **Speaker of the House** is the title given to the leader of this chamber. Every two years, when a new Congress takes office, the full House of Representatives votes to determine who the Speaker will be from among its 435 members. In practice, the selection of Speaker is made by the majority caucus, which meets prior to the vote for Speaker and agrees on their leader, who receives virtually all the votes from the majority party members, thus guaranteeing that the majority party will occupy the Speaker of the House post.

As presiding officer, the Speaker of the House is the most powerful member of the House of Representatives, although the position was not always so powerful. Through the 1800s, the Speaker acted mostly as procedural leader, or presiding officer, of the House. However, with the accession of Joe Cannon to Speaker in 1903, this post became much more powerful. Cannon, a Republican from Illinois, served in the House for more than 50 years and was Speaker from 1903 to 1911. As Speaker, Cannon used the House Rules Committee to amass a tremendous amount of power.[10] Known as "Uncle Joe," he arbitrarily recognized who could speak in the House chamber and required that any measure passing the Rules Committee would have to be personally approved by him. Cannon also made a practice of filling important committee posts with those who were loyal to him. A coalition of Democrats and insurgent Republicans eventually unseated Cannon, but Uncle Joe permanently changed the visibility and power of the Speaker position.

The Speaker remains powerful today for a variety of reasons. First, as the person responsible for assigning new bills to committees, the Speaker can delay the assignment of a bill or assign it to a committee that is either friendly or hostile to its contents, a power that gives the Speaker control over much of the House agenda. Second, the Speaker has the ability to recognize members to speak in the House chamber. Because an important part of the legislative process involves members debating bills on the House floor, the Speaker's authority over this process is significant.

Speaker of the House The leader of the House of Representatives, responsible for assigning new bills to committees, recognizing members to speak in the House chamber, and assigning chairs of committees.

Third, the Speaker is the ultimate arbiter and interpreter of House rules. The ability to cast final judgment on a rule of order can make or break a piece of legislation. Fourth, the Speaker appoints members to serve on special committees, including conference committees, which iron out differences between similar bills passed in the House and Senate. The Speaker's influence is thus felt in the final changes made to a bill before Congress completes work on it. Fifth, the Speaker plays an influential role in assigning members to particular permanent committees. Some committees, as we will see later in this chapter, are more important than others. Being on the Speaker's "good side" can help in getting a good committee assignment. In addition, the Speaker hand-picks the nine members of the all-important Rules Committee.

Speaker of the House Paul Ryan (R-WI) was elected by the GOP members in 2015 after the former Speaker, John Boehner (R-OH), resigned from Congress.

Finally, the Speaker has ultimate authority to schedule votes in the full House on a bill, an authority that allows the Speaker to speed the process or delay it, using timing to either improve or subvert a bill's chances of being passed.

Partisan control of the House is the key factor regarding how that body is organized to do its work. Because the party that holds a majority of seats selects the Speaker, the majority party controls the legislative agenda through members serving in other leadership posts, including chairs of committees.

To promote partisan leadership, the majority caucus in the House votes for a House **majority leader**, and the minority caucus for a House **minority leader**. These leaders oversee the development of their party platforms and are responsible for achieving party coherence in voting. Other important party leadership positions in the House are the House minority and majority **whips**. Whips report to their respective party leaders in the House and are primarily responsible for counting up the partisan votes on bills—that is, they contact members of their party caucus and try to convince them to vote the way their party leadership wants them to vote. The whips spend much of their time on the floor of the House, on the phone, or in the offices of their party colleagues, counting votes and urging their members to vote the party line on bills.

Leadership in the Senate

The Constitution prescribes that the presiding officer of the Senate is the vice president of the United States. In this capacity, the vice president also holds the title of president of the Senate. Unlike the Speaker of the House, who is necessarily a member of the House of Representatives, the president of the Senate is not a member of the Senate. The president of the Senate cannot engage in debate on the floor of the Senate and has no legislative duties in the Senate, with one notable exception: to cast a vote in the Senate in the event of a tie. John Adams, the first vice president of the United States, was the most frequent tiebreaker in U.S. history, casting a vote 21 times in the Senate.

In practice, the vice president rarely shows up on the Senate floor to preside over its session. The presiding officer, in the absence of the vice president, is the **president pro tempore** (*pro tempore* is Latin, meaning "for the time being"). By custom, the official president pro tempore is the senator in the majority caucus who has served the longest number of consecutive years in the Senate. Again, however, in practice the president pro tempore rarely exercises the authority to preside over the Senate. With fewer rules and a greater culture of respect to fellow members than in the House, the presiding officer of the Senate serves what is largely a ceremonial role.

majority leader In the Senate, the controlling party's main spokesperson who leads his or her party in proposing new laws and crafting the party's platform. The Senate majority leader also enjoys the power to make committee assignments. In the House, the majority leader is the controlling party's second in command, who helps the Speaker to oversee the development of the party platform.

minority leader The leader of the minority party in each chamber.

whips (majority and minority) Member of Congress elected by his or her party to count potential votes and promote party unity in voting.

president pro tempore In the absence of the vice president, the senator who presides over the Senate session. By tradition, this is usually the senator from the majority caucus who has served the longest number of consecutive years in the Senate.

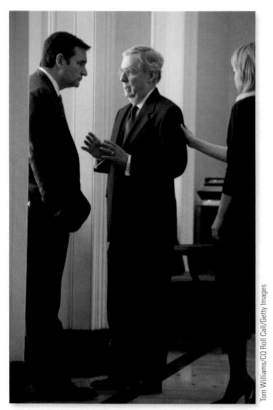

Leadership in the Senate is principally a function of partisanship, with the majority and minority caucuses organizing through leadership posts similar to those of the House of Representatives. As in the House, the majority party exercises tremendous power by controlling the agenda and mobilizing majority votes on important issues for the party. The majority caucus elects a Senate majority leader, and the minority caucus a Senate minority leader. These leaders are the main party spokespersons in the Senate, lead their party caucuses in proposing new laws, and are the chief architects of their party's platform. As leader of the majority, the Senate majority leader enjoys special power in making assignments to leadership of committees.

As in the House, the Senate majority and minority leaders are supported by whips, majority and minority. The whips in the Senate serve the same function as those in the House—they keep track of how caucus members are planning to vote on upcoming bills and they communicate the positions of party leaders on upcoming legislative votes.

Leaders in the Senate generally have far less power than their counterparts in the House. The smaller number of senators requires less discipline in membership, and the culture of the Senate includes a greater amount of deference from one senator to another. Because there are fewer rules and formal procedures in the Senate, leaders and rule-making members have less power to control debate in that body.

Senator Ted Cruz (R-TX), left, a leader in the Tea Party wing of the GOP, confers with Senate Majority Leader Mitch McConnell (R-KY).

6-3 | The Committee System

The work of a member of Congress can be classified into four categories: (1) running for reelection, (2) serving constituents, (3) working on legislation, and (4) providing oversight of federal agencies. Working on legislation involves two activities: working on bills in committees and voting on proposed bills.[11] The bulk of work on legislation consists of what members do in committees, which includes generating ideas for new laws, debating the merits of those ideas, holding hearings, conducting investigations, listening to the testimony of experts, offering modifications and additions to proposed bills, and giving important advice to all House and Senate members regarding how they should vote on a new bill. Committee work also is the means through which members fulfill their role of oversight of federal agencies. Voting, on the other hand, is a rather simple and straightforward process. Members show up on the House or Senate floor and cast a vote of either "aye," "nay," or "present," indicating their support for, opposition to, or abstention from voting on a proposed piece of legislation.

bill A proposed law presented for consideration to a legislative body.

Every year about 10 thousand bills are introduced into Congress. A **bill** is a formally proposed piece of legislation, and many bills are long, complex documents with much legal and technical information. It is not practical to assume that each senator and House member reads and digests every bill that is introduced. As a way to manage the workload, both chambers of Congress rely heavily on a committee system. In both the House and Senate, each member is assigned to a few committees and becomes an expert in the subject area of the committee. Most of members' legislative work revolves around the committees to which they are assigned.

Congressional committees also include subcommittees, providing for even more specialization and division of labor. Currently there are more than 100 subcommittees in the House alone. Each of the subcommittees is also assigned a chair, so many members in the majority party of the House are chairs of either a committee or subcommittee.

In the Senate, with fewer members, all members of the majority are usually the chair of at least one committee or subcommittee. A House member sits on an average of five different committees, whereas a senator sits on an average of seven committees.

What makes the committee system so powerful a force in legislation? It is the deference that most members give to the work of their colleagues in committees. Recognizing specialized knowledge, respecting the need for division of labor, and protecting one's own authority in the committees in which one serves all lead senators and House members to vote on the basis of a committee's recommendation on a bill.

Types of Committees in Congress

There are four general types of congressional committees: standing committees, select committees, conference committees, and joint committees.

Standing committees are permanent committees that exist in both the House and Senate. Most standing committees focus on a particular substantive area of public policy, such as transportation, labor, foreign affairs, and the federal budget. A few focus on procedural matters of the House and Senate, such as the House Rules Committee and the Senate Rules and Administration Committee. The most significant power of the standing committee is that of **reporting legislation**—which means that the full House or Senate cannot vote on a bill unless the committee votes to approve it first. No other type of congressional committee has the power to report legislation. Table 6.1 lists the standing committees of the House and Senate.

Standing committees have been the heart and soul of congressional legislative work since the very early 1800s. Just like today, standing committees then were divided into substantive policy areas and had plenty of authority to determine the future of a bill within their jurisdiction. For example, in 1802 the House of Representatives established the Ways and Means Committee to set policies for America's federal tax system. Any bill dealing with changes in the tax system had to pass through this committee, as it still does today. The House Ways and Means Committee remains the primary author of tax bills.

Though most standing committees focus on a substantive area of public policy, such areas of focus are often broad and complex. In order to further divide labor and provide for even greater levels of specialization, most standing committees include subcommittees. For example, the House Transportation and Infrastructure Committee includes the following subcommittees: Aviation; Coast Guard and Marine Transportation; Economic Development, Public Buildings, Hazardous Materials, and Pipeline Transportation; Ground Transportation; Oversight, Investigations, and Emergency Management; and Water Resources and Environment.

Before the House of Representatives or the Senate can vote on any bill, it must first be approved by a majority of members on the committee. A number of factors can affect a committee's consideration of a bill, which can seriously slow down the process of a bill becoming law and create a sense of "legislative gridlock." When a committee gets a new bill, the chair usually directs the bill to a subcommittee. The subcommittee discusses the bill, holds hearings, and makes changes, additions, or deletions to the bill. Usually, after a successful subcommittee vote, the bill moves back to the full committee, where additional debate and hearings might occur. Only after a successful committee vote is the bill ready to be considered by the full House and/or Senate. This process occurs in both the House and the Senate. There are, therefore, many opportunities for standing committees to slow the policymaking process, or bring it to a grinding halt.

A second general type of committee in Congress is the **select committee**, a special committee established to examine a particular issue of concern. Select committees do not have the power to report legislation, and they are not permanent. Once their work on a particular issue of the day is complete, the select committee is dissolved. Select

standing committee A permanent committee that exists in both the House and Senate; most standing committees focus on a particular substantive area of public policy, such as transportation, labor, foreign affairs, and the federal budget.

reporting legislation The exclusive power of standing committees to forward legislation to the full House or Senate. Neither chamber can vote on a bill unless the committee votes to approve it first.

select committee A committee established by a resolution in either the House or the Senate for a specific purpose and, usually, for a limited time.

TABLE 6.1 The Standing Committees in Congress

Committees in the House	Committees in the Senate
Agriculture	Agriculture, Nutrition, and Forestry
Appropriations	Appropriations
Armed Services	Armed Services
Budgets	Banking, Housing, and Urban Affairs
Education and Labor	Budget
Energy and Commerce	Commerce, Science, and Transportation
Financial Services	Energy and Natural Resources
Homeland Security	Environment and Public Works
House Administration	Finance
Intelligence*	Foreign Relations
Judiciary	Health, Education, Labor, and Pensions
Natural Resources	Homeland Security and Governmental Affairs
Oversight and Government Reform	Judiciary
Rules	Rules and Administration
Science and Technology	Small Business and Entrepreneurship
Small Business	Veterans Affairs
Standards of Official Conduct	
Transportation and Infrastructure	
Veterans Affairs	
Ways and Means	

*Technically a "permanent select committee."

committees are often formed to deal with a particularly serious national problem—a problem for which legislation may not be considered but rather a recommendation might be made. In 2009, for example, the Democratic leadership in both houses established the Select Committee on Energy Independence and Global Warming. When the GOP won back the House, its new leaders indicated they no longer wanted this committee to continue its work, and so it was disbanded.

A third type of committee found in Congress is the **conference committee**. As described earlier in this chapter, the House and Senate are equal players in the legislative process. This means that both chambers debate, hold hearings on, comment on, and vote on individual pieces of legislation. A bill, then, is considered, modified, and voted on by both the House and the Senate. Assuming that a bill survives both chambers and passes, it is likely that the changes made to the bill during the standing committee process will differ between the House and Senate. Conference committees consist of both House members and senators, who work together to iron out differences in the House and Senate versions of a bill.

conference committee
A joint committee of Congress appointed by the House of Representatives and the Senate to resolve differences on a particular bill.

A fourth type of committee is the **joint committee**, which consists of members from both chambers. Joint committees do not propose legislation and have no reporting power, but rather are investigative in nature, focusing on issues of general concern, such as oversight of programs that are administered by the executive branch of the federal government. Unlike select committees, which are temporary and focus on a narrower topic, joint committees are typically permanent and focus on broader policy areas. An example is Congress's Joint Economic Committee. This committee keeps tabs on the performance of the nation's economy and provides oversight to the Federal Reserve Board, the unit that, among other things, has authority to adjust the federal prime interest rate.

joint committee A committee composed of members of both the House and the Senate that is investigative in nature.

Leadership of Congressional Committees

Although there are a handful of broad leadership positions such a presiding officers and "party leaders" in the House and Senate, the vast majority of leaders are the chairs of the many committees and subcommittees in the two chambers. The power of the majority caucus is fully felt in the committee and subcommittee chairs, as all chairs are members of the majority caucus. Committees are where Congress gets most of its work done, and the chairs of committees have a great deal of power in determining what gets done and when it gets done.[12]

For example, the chairs decide how much time, if any, to spend on a new bill; they choose the people who will testify before the committee; and they allot the time to be spent on testimony and committee discussion. House and Senate leaders choose committee chairs from members of the majority caucus, a selection generally based on seniority and party allegiance. For each committee, the majority party's ranking, or senior, member is typically the person who becomes the committee chair, although the Speaker of the House ultimately determines the chairs for House committees and the Senate majority leader does the same for Senate committees.[13] Though still important, congressional reforms in 1974 and 1994 have somewhat reduced the power of seniority in the determination of committee chairs. More recently, the selection of chairs and the chairs' adherence to party leadership have provided a strong basis for party influence in congressional leadership.

Partisan Nature of the Committee System

The large number of standing committees and subcommittees, along with the significant power of the committee given its expertise in the policy area, disperses legislative power. It is in the interest of the majority party, however, to control what bills are given priority, how bills are written, and what bills get passed. Thus, the primary organizational characteristic of most committees in Congress is partisanship. To control the committee agenda and the committee votes, the majority caucus ensures that all committees have a majority of members of their party.[14] Furthermore, the chair of each committee is from the majority caucus. In addition, the majority caucus typically reserves a "supermajority" of seats on the most powerful committees, such as the Rules and Appropriations Committees.

Congressional Staffing

The 435 House members and 100 senators are supported by a large professional staff, many of whom are young, recent college graduates. Staffers perform a variety of support functions related to the roles of members of Congress. They conduct background research on bills, help generate new ideas for bills, provide services to constituents, and aid in the oversight of executive agencies. There are three categories of congressional staff.

First is the member's **congressional personal staff**. Members of Congress are given a budget to support a group of staffers to assist them. They typically have a staff in their

congressional personal staff A group of workers who assist an individual member of Congress in performing his or her responsibilities.

Washington, D.C., office and one in their home district office. The personal staffers serve a number of legislative support functions, including tracking bills that the member has introduced and conducting research on ideas for new bills. They also work with the local media in the member's home district, answering journalists' questions and providing information on the member's legislative activities. Perhaps the personal staffers' most important responsibility is responding to constituents in the district. House and Senate members receive many kinds of communications from constituents, ranging from requests for information about bills and explanations of why they voted a particular way, to letters expressing opinions on various issues and requests for speaking engagements. The personal staffers are responsible for dealing with these myriad constituent inquiries.

A second type of staffing resource at Congress's disposal is the **congressional committee staff**. Each standing committee of Congress employs a professional staff, many of whom are policy or legal experts in the policy area of the committee.

The third form of support for members of Congress is **congressional agencies**. The volume of legislative work has grown substantially over the years, as has the complexity of the federal budget and the policy issues with which Congress deals. One way that Congress has dealt with problems of growth and complexity has been to delegate authority to executive agencies. Consequently, Congress began to lose control of the ability to keep tabs on what those agencies were doing. The explosion of budget deficits in the 1970s and suspicions about the administration that were inspired by the Watergate scandal also left Congress feeling that it lacked necessary information for effective executive oversight. Through the 1970s, Congress relied on budget data from the Office of Management and Budget (OMB), which reports to the president. Congress suspected that the budget figures produced by the OMB were compiled with an eye toward supporting the president's point of view. In response, in 1974 Congress created a new congressional agency, the Congressional Budget Office (CBO), to monitor the nation's economic situation and provide objective projections of the national budget. It reports directly to Congress. With the CBO, Congress no longer relies exclusively on the executive branch to gather economic data and produce information to help Congress oversee the budget process.

At the same time, Congress also substantially expanded the size and funding of the Government Accountability Office (GAO; formerly called the General Accounting Office) and the Congressional Research Service (CRS). Congress uses the GAO to monitor executive agency expenditures. Essentially, the GAO audits the spending of federal organizations to find and remove any abuses. The CRS is Congress's information and statistical data archive. It provides members with information they might need in preparation for writing a bill, conducting a hearing or investigation, or making a speech. Other important agencies of Congress include the Library of Congress, which acts both as the de facto national library of the United States as well as a research arm for congressional members, and the Government Printing Office, which prints and provides access to documents produced by and for all three branches of the federal government.

6-4 | How a Bill Becomes a Law

It is not easy for a bill to become a law. Though most work on bills occurs in committees, there are numerous other points at which a bill might be "killed." The Speaker of the House, the Senate majority leader, and the president all have means at their disposal to kill a bill. There are other points, as well, when bills might be stopped dead in their tracks. Not surprisingly, of the 10,000 or so bills introduced annually in Congress, only about 500 to 1,000 end up becoming law. The more recent political divisiveness and partisan differences have produced even less legislation. For example, the 112th Congress (which sat from 2011 through 2012) passed only about 280 laws annually.[15]

congressional committee staff A group of workers assigned to congressional committees to support each committee's legislative work.

congressional agencies Government bodies formed by and relied on by Congress to support members of Congress in performing their functions.

Partisan Divisiveness in the Halls of Congress

Partisan divisiveness often prevails in the Congress; still, during certain periods of our nation's history, the level of partisan nastiness and incivility has been especially high, all but paralyzing the legislative branch.

Then

In the 1850s, just before the Civil War, the Congress was frequently stymied by especially hostile relations between the two major parties in Congress. On one occasion actual physical violence erupted in the halls of Congress. Most notably, in 1856 House member Preston Brooks of South Carolina actually walked over to the Senate floor and clubbed Senator Charles Sumner of Massachusetts nearly to death because of their disagreements over slavery. Indeed, Congress was bitterly divided in all its feeble attempts at passing legislation. The issues that divided the parties were not limited to slavery, though the Kansas-Nebraska Act of 1854 proved so controversial that it actually gave birth to the Republican Party in opposition to it. The party divisions also reflected a commercial-versus-agricultural conflict. The term *filibuster*—from a Dutch word meaning "pirate"—first became popular during the 1850s, when it was applied to efforts by the Senate minority to hold the Senate floor in order to prevent a vote on a bill. The heightened divisiveness of the 1850s led to extreme dysfunction, driven by congressional party-based factions that could not work together to solve America's problems.

Senator Preston Brooks shown clubbing Senator Charles Sumner on the floor of the U.S. Senate during an antislavery debate in 1856.

Now

In the 2010s, congressional approval ratings fell to all-time lows, according to many polls. Certainly, these ratings were a product of the vitriol and partisanship that began in 2009 with the 111th Congress. That year, the Senate witnessed a record number of filibusters, as not one simple majority vote on a substantive bill prevailed throughout this period. The legislative battle over health care reform the following year epitomized this bitter partisan reality, as Senate Republicans voted over and over along party lines to reject any and all bills proposed by the Democrats. Consider this telling statistic: for the first time ever, the *National Journal*'s vote ratings showed that the most conservative Democratic senator was now more liberal than the most liberal Republican, an indication that there was no longer any ideological overlap among the two parties. In the House there were contentious, drawn-out partisan battles as well. During a speech that President Obama delivered at the Capitol to promote health care reform, Representative Joe Wilson (R-SC) shouted, "You lie!" in response to an Obama claim about coverage of illegal immigrants under the proposal. In 2013 a squabble over the normally perfunctory matter of raising the statutory debt ceiling ensued, and led to the shutting down of many government functions for weeks. Moreover, Congress

Rep. Joe Wilson shouts to President Barack Obama, "You lie!," during a 2009 Obama address to Congress discussing the health care reform debate.

could not even manage a full-fledged substantive debate on pressing issues such as climate change, unemployment benefits, and immigration reform. The extreme partisan divisiveness in Congress that began in 2009 had led to congressional dysfunction once again.

For Critical Thinking and Discussion

1. Why has partisan divisiveness and gridlock in Congress become so prevalent over the past decade? What issues and events contribute to the intense partisan bickering we have witnessed in the modern era?

2. Do you think that the results of the 2016 congressional elections are likely to improve the cooperation of the parties in Congress, or do you believe they will only contribute to even more partisan divisiveness?

Rarely does a bill, as originally introduced, become law without significant revision on its way to becoming law. An important book on the process of a bill becoming law by is *The Dance of Legislation*, by Eric Redman.[16] As the title suggests, the lawmaking process involves many people and much politicking; the process is difficult and often follows no regular or consistent path. The steps to a bill becoming law (highlighted in Figure 6.2) are also highly influenced by partisan politics, lobbyists and special interest groups, public opinion, and powerful voices in and out of government. Even though the actual dance of legislation typically follows no neat pattern or order, we describe here the general steps in which a bill becomes a law.

Step 1: A Bill Is Introduced

With the exception of tax or revenue proposals, which must originate in the House of Representatives, a bill can be first introduced into either the Senate or the House. The revenue exception, as stipulated in the Constitution, is a product of the American colonial experience with England, and the famous cry "no taxation without representation." Because the House provides popular representation, and representation is the philosophical basis undergirding taxation, the Founders gave the House sole authority to originate tax and revenue bills.

Whereas the Constitution requires that only a House member or a senator can introduce a bill, the ideas for new bills come from a variety of sources. Many come from the president of the United States or someone in the president's office or executive branch of government. Others come from lobbyists. Because House members and senators depend on lobbyists for information, and lobbyists represent groups who support candidates for congressional office, those with access to members are an

FIGURE 6-2 The Steps in a Bill Becoming a Law

important source of ideas for new legislation. Business leaders, educators, journalists, and regular constituents may also generate ideas for new bills. The next step for those with a suggestion for a new law is to find a sponsor in the House or Senate to introduce the idea in the form of a bill.

Whether the idea for a law comes directly from a member of Congress or from some other source, the first official step in the process is for the sponsoring member to submit the bill to the House or Senate clerk, who issues a unique number to the bill. The clerk in the House sends the bill to the Speaker of the House; the Senate clerk forwards the bill to the Senate majority leader.

Step 2: The Bill Is Sent to a Standing Committee for Action

Next, the bill is assigned to the standing committee that has policy jurisdiction over the topic the bill addresses. Sometimes a bill never makes it to this step. For example, the GOP majority in the House introduced dozens of bills from 2011 through 2013 aimed at contracting or eliminating Obamacare. None of these bills was even sent to a Senate committee by Democratic Majority Leader Harry Reid.

More times than not, however, the Speaker and majority leader do assign a bill for committee work. A bill introduced in the Senate to raise the minimum wage, for example, would likely be sent to the Senate Labor and Human Resources Committee; a bill proposing increased criminal penalties for mail fraud introduced into the House might be assigned to the House Judiciary Committee.

Most bills die during their initial consideration by the committee. In some cases, the committee chair simply ignores it. In other cases, the full committee, without deliberation, votes to kill the bill. If the committee decides to give the bill serious consideration, the committee chair usually assigns it to a subcommittee. The subcommittee may hold hearings, conduct investigations, and deliberate on the merits of the bill. Often the subcommittee will make amendments to the bill before sending it back to the full committee.

When a bill is back in full committee, the recommendations of the subcommittee may be accepted, rejected, or further revised. The full committee may conduct additional hearings, call more witnesses and experts to testify, and debate the bill. At the end of this process, a "markup," or final version of the bill, is prepared. The markup is the proposed legislation on which the full committee will vote. If a majority of committee members vote against the bill, the bill goes no further, so here is another point in the process where a bill might be stopped. If a majority of committee members vote in favor of the bill, it moves forward in the process.

Rules Committee A committee in the House of Representatives that determines the rules by which bills will come to the floor, be debated, and so on.

Step 3: The Bill Goes to the Full House and Senate for Consideration

At this next stage, the full House or Senate debates the bill and proposes amendments. The start of this process differs in the House and Senate. In the House, a bill that makes it through the committee is immediately assigned to the House **Rules Committee**. The Rules Committee decides when the bill will be debated, the amount of time that will be allotted for debate, and the extent to which amendments may be added from the floor of the House. The ability to control the timing and amount of time for debate is significant, thus making this committee one of the most

Representative Kevin Brady (R-TX) is chair of the powerful Ways and Means Committee, which is responsible for most modifications to the U.S. tax code.

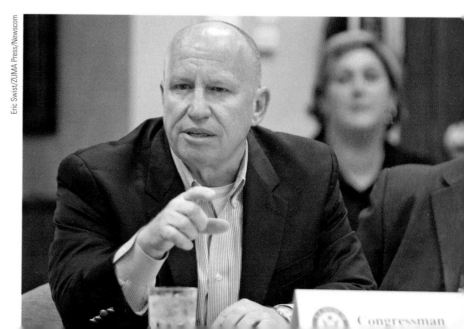

Eric Swist/ZUMA Press/Newscom

closed rule A rule of procedure adopted by the House Rules Committee that severely limits the ability of members of Congress to amend a bill.

open rule A rule of procedure adopted by the House Rules Committee that permits amendments to a bill.

filibuster The action by a single senator or a minority of senators to block a bill from passage by refusing to end discussion.

cloture A Senate debate procedure that permits that body to end debate and force a vote on a bill by a vote of 60 senators.

important ones in the House. The ability to control the amendment process is even more powerful. If the Rules Committee issues a **closed rule**, House members are severely limited in their ability to amend the bill. An **open rule** order, on the other hand, permits amendments to the bill.

In the Senate, there are no rules set up ahead of time for debate. The Senate majority leader decides when to bring a bill to the floor. But, in theory, there are no limits on the amount of time the bill will be debated, and all senators are given the courtesy of speaking on any bill, if they so wish. The fact that the Senate includes far fewer members than the House allows for less structured debate. With no rules about how long a senator might speak, there is a possibility that a minority of senators—or even one senator—might try to block a bill from passage by refusing to end discussion, a process known as a **filibuster**.[17]

In 1917, a group of senators successfully filibustered to thwart a bill that would have armed American ships in anticipation of the nation's entry into World War I. In response to this event, the Senate adopted a **cloture** rule, which permitted the Senate to end debate and force a vote on a bill by approval of a two-thirds vote. The Senate left a loophole in place, however: if any senator, once properly recognized, refuses to concede the floor, he or she can exercise the equivalent of a one-person filibuster for as long as his or her voice will hold out. Accordingly, in 1957 South Carolina Senator Strom Thurmond spoke for more than 24 hours in an attempt to block the Senate from passing civil rights legislation. For many years, Senate filibusters successfully blocked legislation supported by a majority of senators. Then in 1975, the Senate modified the cloture requirement, so that currently a less stringent three-fifths vote of the Senate (60 out of 100 senators) is required to end debate.

Between 2009 and 2015 (when party control shifted once again), Senate Republicans increasingly resorted to the use of filibusters in their attempts to block the Democratic

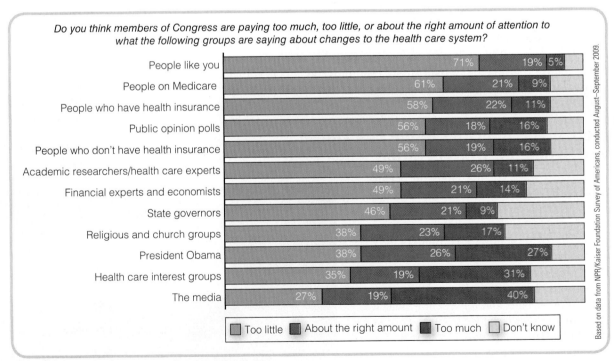

FIGURE 6-3 Whom Does Congress Listen to?

majority from passing legislation endorsed by the Obama administration. At the end of 2009, the House and Senate each passed a version of the Obama administration's health care reform legislation. Yet final passage was initially thwarted by a threatened filibuster in the Senate after the election of Senator Scott Brown (R-MA) in February 2010 gave the Republicans the necessary 41 votes to defeat cloture on a party-line vote. (Ultimately the Obama administration pressed successfully for House passage of the original Senate version, which did not require a revote by the Senate, in 2010.) In all, Senate Republicans made use of the filibuster more than a hundred times during the 111th Congress.

Frustrated by GOP filibuster threats for presidential nominees to the judiciary and senior executive positions, the Democratic majority in the Senate modified its rules in 2013 by eliminating the possibility of a filibuster for such nominees. (The new rule did not apply to Supreme Court nominees.) Some Democrats feared that this move might come back to threaten their own party's senators, should the GOP regain a majority in the future. The filibuster does, however, remain a thorn in the side of the Senate majority for legislative processes outside of these presidential appointments.

At the end of the debate and amendment process, the House and Senate take a vote on the proposed bill. Passage of a bill must achieve a majority of votes (half of all present for voting, plus one) from members on the floor. A majority of votes must be achieved in both the Senate and House for the bill to survive to the next step in the legislative process.

How any one member of the House or Senate makes the decision to vote "aye" or "nay" on a given proposed bill differs from one bill to another, and from one member to another. But there are six common explanations, which vary in importance, depending on the situation:

1. **Personal opinion and judgment.** Many members of Congress have strong personal opinions and convictions on issues, and cast their votes on bills on the basis of those opinions. Rep. Henry Waxman (D-CA), for example, is an ardent environmentalist and consistently votes this position on environmental bills. Similarly, Rep. Chris Smith's (R-NJ) pro-life stance on abortion leads him to vote that position on bills. When members use their own personal judgment, they are said to be exercising their role as a "trustee."

2. **Constituent opinion.** Members of Congress want to be liked by their constituents, and most want to be reelected. In voting on particular bills, members often use results from polls, editorial commentary in local media, and letters written to them by their constituents to help them make up their minds in voting on a particular bill. When members use constituent opinion as a cue to casting a vote, they are said to be exercising their role as a "delegate" of the people they represent.

3. **Interest groups and lobbying.** As a way of achieving their goals, interest groups exert influence on congressional voting in a number of ways, including making contributions to congressional campaigns and hiring lobbyists to provide arguments to members regarding why they should vote a particular way on a bill. So members use both information provided by lobbyists to aid in their voting and the campaign support from interest groups to prompt how they will vote.

4. **Political parties.** The party of a member often conveys quite a bit about his or her political positions and ideology, with Democrats tending to be more liberal on social and economic issues and Republicans tending to be more conservative on these issues. So party membership is an important cue. In addition, the leadership of each party is organized to influence party members to vote the "party line" on bills. Members voting with their party tend to be rewarded with better committee assignments and greater campaign funding, thus making party a very important factor in voting on legislation.

5. **The president.** Presidents are the focus of national attention and have, as President Teddy Roosevelt once said, a "bully pulpit" to make their case and influence others, including members of Congress. Presidents are quite influential in directing congressional members of their own party how to vote, but often exert influence on members of the opposition party as well. Particularly in times of international crisis, presidents can effectively make appeals to put partisanship aside and convince members to vote in the interests of the country.

6. **Logrolling.** Members often enter into an agreement with other members to vote a certain way on one bill in exchange for a favorable vote on another bill. This process is known as **logrolling**. Members vote on thousands of bills every term. Giving up a vote on less important bills in exchange for favorable votes on more important bills is a common practice, and one that often guides congressional voting behavior.

Many Americans have expressed frustration over how Congress makes decisions on important bills before it. During the highly charged debate over the health care reform legislation in 2009 and 2010, for example, most Americans felt that Congress paid too little attention to the public and people who would be affected by the changes to heath care, and too much attention to the media and interest groups, as shown in Figure 6.3.

logrolling The trading of influence or votes among legislators to achieve passage of projects that are of interest to one another.

Step 4: Conference Committee Action

Often, the version of a bill that passes the Senate differs from that passed by the House. To iron out any differences between Senate and House bills, Congress has two options. The first and most common route is to work out the differences informally. Of course, the ability to do this depends on the extent of differences in the two versions of the bill and the closeness of the votes in committee and in the full chambers. When the versions are not far apart in content and when the margins of approval are large, informal discussions between House and Senate leaders and committee chairs are usually sufficient to strike a deal. When the prospects for informal agreement are less likely, then House and Senate leaders select a conference committee to work out the kinks. The conference committee consists of House and Senate members—usually drawn from the standing committees that worked on the bills.

Step 5: Presidential Action

The president plays both an informal and a formal role in the passage of new laws. The president's informal role is to develop new ideas for laws and urge members of Congress to introduce them. The president also lobbies Congress, attempting to persuade members to support or oppose certain bills. The president's strong presence in the American political system, along with attention from the national media, offers the president a unique platform from which to lobby on behalf of or against certain legislation.

The formal constitutional role that the president plays in legislation is the fifth step in the process by which a bill becomes law. Once both chambers of Congress have agreed to a bill, the bill is sent to the president for action. The president has three options for dealing with the congressionally approved bill. First, the president can sign the bill, which officially makes it new law. Second, the president can **veto** (or refuse assent to) the bill, which stops the bill from becoming law. If the bill is vetoed, Congress has one more opportunity to pass the bill, by **overriding** the presidential veto. This requires a two-thirds vote in favor of passage in both the Senate and the House, a margin substantially more difficult to achieve than the simple majority vote required prior to a presidential veto. Third, the president can decide not to act on a bill (that is, neither sign it nor veto it), in which case the bill automatically becomes law after it has sat on the

veto The constitutional procedure by which the president refuses to approve a bill or joint resolution and thus prevents its enactment into law.

overriding (a veto) The power of the Congress to enact legislation despite a president's veto of that legislation; requires a two-thirds vote of both houses of Congress.

President Obama signs the health care reform bill into law at the White House in March 2010.

president's desk for 10 days. If Congress passes a bill and sends it to the president within 10 days of the end of a congressional session and the president does not act on the bill, then the bill does not become law, a process known as a **pocket veto**.

6-5 | Oversight and Personnel Functions of Congress

In addition to creating new laws, Congress performs a number of oversight functions: oversight of federal agencies, confirmation of top federal executives and judges, approval of treaties, and impeachment of top federal executives and judges.

Congressional Oversight

Congress's principal responsibility is to enact new laws to deal with national problems and concerns. But given the complexity of many issues (disposing of nuclear and toxic wastes, creating new sources of energy, promoting the role of high technology, and enhancing the performance of a multitrillion-dollar economy that has become highly integrated in the global economy, to name just a few), Congress often lacks the scientific and technological expertise needed to enact laws. In addition, for political reasons, sometimes Congress prefers not to deal with issues on its own, but rather to "pass the buck" to a bureaucratic agency. Defining the limits of genetic cloning is one such political hot potato. Whether the reason is technical capability or politics, Congress often delegates more specific legislative authority to the executive branch, which has the resources and expertise to make more highly technical policy decisions. The delegation of congressional power to the executive branch has become more frequent as our society has become more complex.

This delegation of authority, however, is not carried out blindly or without accountability. When Congress delegates its authority, it generally monitors the activities of agencies and administrators who are given this power through congressional oversight. One agency to which Congress has delegated considerable authority is the Federal Reserve Board (known as "the Fed"). Established by the Federal Reserve Act of 1913, the Fed has authority over credit rates and lending activities of the nation's banks. Congress created the agency because it recognized that specialized monitoring of the economy and the technical expertise of economists were necessary to make decisions about credit rates and lending activities in order to maintain a viable economy. The act gave the Fed the authority to adjust the supply of money to banks and to shift money from where there is too much to where there is too little. The Fed also has the power to take means to ensure that banks do not overextend themselves in lending so that a sudden economic scare will not cause a sudden run on banks for money. For nearly 100 years, Congress has given this agency the power to set important monetary policy for the nation. But Congress retains its authority to exercise oversight of the Fed. The Joint Economic Committee in Congress carefully monitors the Fed's performance and regularly holds hearings to inquire about its policies and decisions. In addition, newly appointed members of the Federal Reserve Board must be approved by Congress.

In his book on Congress titled *Congress: Keystone of the Washington Establishment*,[18] political scientist Morris Fiorina notes other important reasons for congressional delegation of power to executive agencies, including garnering political rewards while shifting blame to the executive branch, enabling Congress to blame federal agencies for failing to fulfill legislative intent, and taking credit for problem solving by holding oversight and investigative hearings.

Confirmation of Presidential Nominations and Approval of Treaties

The U.S. Senate plays a pivotal role in the selection of cabinet officers, other agency and executive branch heads, federal judges, and foreign ambassadors. The president nominates individuals for these posts, but the Senate must consent to the nomination with a majority vote in favor of the candidate. This function is one performed solely by the U.S. Senate, and not the House of Representatives.

At the beginning of a new presidential administration, the U.S. Senate is typically quite busy reviewing the president's nominations for high executive office positions.[19] Although the Senate usually endorses most nominees, there have been a number of high-profile instances when the Senate has been unwilling to confirm the nominee, typically occurring during eras of divided government when the political party of the president is different from the majority party in the Senate. The threat of a denial has become somewhat less likely since the Senate modified its rules in 2013 to eliminate the possibility of a filibuster for presidential appointments to the judicial and executive branches.

When there is a vacancy on the U.S. Supreme Court, a situation that often draws considerable interest from both the press and the public, the president nominates a new justice, whom the Senate also must confirm with a majority vote. Conflict between the Senate and the president over Supreme Court nominees goes all the way back to the first U.S. president, George Washington, and his choice of John Rutledge for chief justice of the United States. Although Rutledge appeared eminently qualified for the post (he was associate justice on the Supreme Court from 1789 to 1791 and chief justice of the South Carolina Court of Common Pleas from 1791 to 1795), he had openly criticized the highly controversial Jay Treaty with Britain (backed by Washington and the Federalists), which reneged on the terms of America's 1778 treaty with France. Rutledge's criticism was directed as much at its chief negotiator, John Jay, as at the treaty itself, which reassured Britain of American neutrality. Apparently, Rutledge still harbored a grudge against Jay, who had edged him out to become the nation's first chief justice in 1789. Although Washington stood behind his nominee and gave him a temporary recess appointment as chief justice, Federalist senators argued that confirmation of Rutledge would be an extreme embarrassment to their party and denounced him publicly. One called him a character "not very far above mediocrity." On December 15, 1795, the Senate rejected Rutledge's nomination by a 14–10 vote.

A more recent example of Senate opposition to a Supreme Court nominee occurred in the case of Clarence Thomas, nominated for the Court by President George H. W. Bush in 1991. The Democrat-controlled Senate opposed Thomas, an African American who held conservative views on numerous issues. Thomas's problems mounted further when one of his former employees at the Equal Employment Opportunity Commission, Anita Hill, testified that he had sexually harassed her while he was her boss. Thomas ultimately won confirmation by a close 52–48 vote and currently sits on the Supreme Court. The two major party roles were reversed in 2016, when Democratic president Barack Obama submitted the Supreme Court nomination of Merrick Garland to a Senate controlled by the Republicans. Partisan opposition to Garland was fierce from

The Supreme Court And Congressional Lawmaking

Immigration and Naturalization Service v. Chadha (1983)

The rapid growth of the welfare state and the proliferation of federal workers charged with its implementation posed serious challenges for those concerned with the specter of a federal bureaucracy out of control. Searching for a more efficient means to reign in these bureaucratic agencies, Congress in the mid-twentieth century began to increasingly rely on the so-called legislative veto, a device by which just one house of Congress (or, in some cases, a mere committee of Congress) can exercise the power to veto individual agency decisions.

After the Immigration and Naturalization Service (INS) initiated deportation proceedings against Jagdish Rai Chadha, a Kenyan-born holder of a British passport residing in America, the agency reversed itself and sought to accommodate Chadha's request to stay in the United States permanently. Disagreeing with the agency's decision, the House of Representatives exercised its right to veto the INS suspension, and thus reinstitute the deportation of Chadha. Was an act of Congress necessary in this instance? Yes, said the Supreme Court, by a 7–2 decision. Any law that modifies the rights and duties of individuals must conform to the constitutional process for passing laws: (1) bicameralism (both the House and the Senate must approve the law) and (2) presentment (the president must have the power to veto that law as a means of resisting legislative

encroachment). The legislative veto of the INS abided by neither of those two principles, so Chadha's deportation remained suspended. Three years later, Chadha became a citizen of the United States. Meanwhile, legislative vetoes quickly fell out of favor, giving way to other devices intended to speed up the legislative process such as so-called fast-track legislation (providing the president with authority to negotiate international agreements, for example, that Congress can approve or disapprove but cannot amend or filibuster). In *INS v. Chadha*,[20] we learned that the lessons of "how to make a law" first learned in civics class are not just theoretical, even in a welfare state that often begs for ways to quickly and efficiently check executive agencies.

For Critical Thinking and Discussion

1. If Congress has the exclusive power to enable executive agencies in the first place, shouldn't it also have the power to attach "strings" to the authority it grants, such as the requirement that agencies be subject to a one-house veto?
2. If legislative vetoes are no longer available, won't that make Congress more reluctant to grant executive agencies power in the first place?
3. Do you think Congress or government agencies should have the ultimate power to modify your legal rights?

the outset, as the Senate leadership announced its plans to stall all such nominations until a new president assumed office in 2017.

Under certain circumstances, Congress may also become involved in the selection of president and vice president of the United States. When no candidate receives a majority of electoral votes, the House of Representatives chooses the president and the Senate chooses the vice president. This has happened three times in the history of the nation: in 1801 when the House chose Thomas Jefferson as president, in 1825 when the House chose John Quincy Adams, and in 1877 when the House appointed a commission to resolve the controversial 1876 election (it chose Rutherford B. Hayes).

In the event of a vacancy in the vice presidency, the Twenty-fifth Amendment to the Constitution stipulates that the president's nomination of an individual to fill that position is subject to the approval of both the House and Senate by majority vote. This has happened twice since adoption of that amendment: in 1973 when Vice President Spiro Agnew resigned and Nixon's nomination of Gerald Ford was quickly approved and in 1974 when Ford became president due to Nixon's resignation and Congress approved Ford's nomination of Nelson Rockefeller as vice president.

Finally, the Senate has the power to approve treaties that the president negotiates with foreign countries. The Constitution stipulates that approval of a treaty requires the consent of two-thirds of the Senate. Even though the standard for treaty approval is much higher than a simple majority, most treaties do obtain the necessary two-thirds approval. Perhaps the most important rejection concerned the Treaty of Versailles following World War I. The relatively low number of rejected treaties may be due to presidents' reluctance to negotiate treaties that they are not reasonably certain will pass. President Woodrow Wilson's failure to consult with the Senate and consider its objections to the Treaty of Versailles led to the treaty's twice being rejected by the Senate, once in 1919 and again in 1920. More recently, the House has also played an important role in approving treaties because most of them involve financial issues that require the approval of that chamber.

Impeachment and Removal of Federal Judges and High Executives

Congress also has the authority to impeach and remove federal judges, cabinet officers, the president, the vice president, and other civil officers. The removal process requires an impeachment action from the House and a trial in the Senate. Only two presidents (Andrew Johnson in 1867 and Bill Clinton in 1998) have been impeached, and neither was actually removed from office.

Impeachment is the formal process by which the House brings charges against federal officials. A judge, president, or executive official who is "impeached" by the House is not removed; he or she is charged with an offense. In this sense, the House acts as an initial forum that makes the decision about whether a trial is warranted. An impeachment occurs by a majority vote in the House of Representatives. An official may be impeached by the House on more than one charge, each of which is referred to as an article of impeachment.

Assuming the House passes at least one article of impeachment, the official must then stand trial in the Senate. The prosecutors in the trial are members of the House of Representatives and are referred to as House "managers." Selected by the House leadership, the House managers present the case for removal to the full Senate. If the defendant is the president, the chief justice of the U.S. Supreme Court presides over the trial; otherwise the vice president of the United States (who is president of the Senate) or the president pro tempore of the Senate presides. Other than in the impeachment of a president or vice president, the Senate in recent times has usually designated a committee to receive evidence and question the witnesses. The impeached official provides lawyers in his or her own defense. A two-thirds vote of the full Senate is required for removal of an official.

6-6 | Constituent Service: Helping People Back Home

Much of what has been discussed thus far in this chapter pertains to what members of Congress do in Washington. As the people's representatives, members are sent to Washington to develop new laws and deliberate on important issues. They are expected to safeguard the nation's security, act as watchdogs against fraud, and ensure that judges and high-ranking executive officers are qualified for office. An integral part of the way members serve their constituents is by reflecting the opinions and input of those whom they represent while carrying out these legislative functions.

However, the service of members of Congress does not stop with the work they do in Washington. Often constituents will call upon a House member or senator to provide information about federal programs, to render assistance in getting benefits from federal programs, or to prepare a talk or visit with a community group to educate its members about the political system or on a specific legislative or policy topic. Members are often asked by officials in state or local government to facilitate federal help for a local or state issue. The direct assistance that a member provides to a constituent, community group, or local or state official is referred to as **casework**. A now classic book by Richard F. Fenno Jr., titled *Home Style: House Members in Their Districts*, provides a rich description of this role played by members of Congress.[21]

casework The direct assistance that a member of Congress provides to a constituent, community group, or local or state official.

Casework is important for a number of reasons. First is its electoral importance to members of Congress. Casework raises the visibility of members in their home state or district, which reflects positively on how well the member is regarded and gives members an advantage over their opponents in elections. More than 9 in 10 House and Senate members who run for reelection are returned to office, and effectively managing casework is an important reason for this high return rate.

It has also become an implicit responsibility of members to help their constituents navigate the complex federal bureaucracy. Federal programs are varied and complex, and constituents are often overwhelmed in their efforts to obtain the benefits for which they are eligible. For example, under the Workforce Development Act, the federal government has programs that provide assistance to "displaced workers," defined as those who have lost their jobs due to technological or broad trends in the workplace. Many workers in the manufacturing industry in the United States have lost their jobs over the past decade as the national economy has shifted away from manufacturing and toward technology and information services. Various programs are available for these displaced workers to help them obtain training in new skills necessary to adapt to the new workforce. Finding these programs is often difficult, and members provide information to connect constituents with available programs.

Third, casework provides a direct connection between members and their constituents. Casework requires members to keep in touch with those whom they represent. Giving a speech to a local Rotary club or League of Women Voters meeting, showing up to cut the ribbon at an opening of a new local school building or park, and coming to speak to a group of students or employees all provide face time between the members and their constituents. The experiences that members have and the type of work they do in Washington can shelter them from the real-life concerns of their constituents back home. Casework provides a constant reminder of the needs and interests of those whom members represent.

Sen. Charles Grassley (R-IA), March 28, 2016, holding a town meeting in the northern Iowa community of Ocheyedan, population 490.

Bill Clark/CQ Roll Call/Getty Images

An Internship as a Steppingstone

Many college students interested in politics and public policy seek internships with Congress during the summer. Such an experience allows them to see firsthand how Congress works, gain valuable experience, and prepare for a possible job with the federal government. Recently, the job-search website Monster.com estimated that job opportunities in the federal government would grow from 2.1 million to 2.5 million. Building one's résumé with an internship in Congress can help to jump-start a successful career in public service.

The dozens of committees in Congress all have spots for college interns, as do large congressional agencies such as the Government Accountability Office, the Congressional Budget Office, and the Library of Congress. In addition, all 535 members of Congress maintain offices in Washington, D.C., as well as in their home state or district. Interns are commonly found helping with casework in many of these offices. Moreover, the partisan leadership offices, such as the majority and minority leaders and whips, frequently staff college interns to help them do their work, as do the Democratic and GOP House and Senate campaign committees. Many senators and representatives first got introduced to Congress through an internship that they themselves had. At a minimum, an internship with Congress provides a great résumé item when applying for a full-time position in some part of the federal government.

If you are interested in a congressional internship, there are a number of ways to get one. You can contact the office of a member of the House or Senate directly and inquire about future openings. You can visit the internship coordinator at your college or in your university's political science department and ask what might be available and how to apply. Or you can visit the following websites for information about ongoing internship opportunities:

1. dc.about.com/od/jobs/a/Internships.htm
2. www.twc.edu
3. www.cbo.gov/about/careers/internships

A recent group of interns who work with the Congressional Hispanic Caucus.

For Critical Thinking and Discussion

1. An internship in Congress provides a wonderful experience for interested students to learn firsthand how our government works. However, there are only a handful of these internships, and so getting them is not easy. Should students who are interested in spending a semester in Washington have more opportunities to do so?

---

pork-barrel legislation A government project or appropriation that yields jobs or other benefits to a specific locale and patronage opportunities to its political representative.

Another aspect of constituent service involves what is known as "pork-barrel" politics. The federal budget includes a great deal of money for local projects, such as parks, dams, and road improvements. Members secure federal funds to support these projects in their states and districts through what is often referred to as **pork-barrel legislation**. The pork-barrel reference is based on the idea that members are "bringing home the bacon." Members use their influence on congressional committees and leadership positions to add amendments to bills that authorize pork-barrel spending on projects back home. Though many observers of the political system decry the unfairness of pork-barrel legislation, it has been an important aspect of constituent service since the beginning of our political system and promises to remain so in the future.

When Congress is dealing with major problems or issues of the day, the process of creating new laws, approving new treaties, and approving presidential appointments can be very slow indeed—many observers use the word "gridlock" to describe congressional inaction. Congress's actions are slow and deliberate; there are many points at which the process may be halted, and many actors with the capacity to hinder progress. Further, the compromises necessary to achieve success in Congress rarely prove entirely satisfactory to everyone involved. The slow and grinding legislative process can even lead to bad behavior on the part of members of Congress, such as with Senator Preston Brooks's clubbing of Senator Charles Sumner in a debate on slavery in 1856, and Representative Joe Wilson's "You lie!" shout at President Obama in 2009 during Obama's health care address. The power and significance of individual actors in the legislative process are also significant to understanding how Congress works. Strong individuals such as Senate Majority Leader Harry Reid and House Speaker John Boehner dominated the debate in recent years. Congress is not simply two houses of 535 individuals who vote, with a majority obtaining victory. Those in leadership positions can exert a disproportionate influence on the process. Those with special communication skills enjoy more power, as do those who are highly informed on a particular issue.

Summary

6-1 Article I and the Creation of Congress

- Congress, the legislative branch of the government, was the central institution in America's new political system at the beginning of the republic. It is the branch of government that represents the people, and its primary function is to create laws.

6-2 The Structure and Organization of Congress

- Congress consists of two houses: a "people's house" apportioned by population (the House of Representatives) and a Senate in which the states, regardless of population, have equal representation. States are equally represented in the Senate while the House represents the population.

- Although not mentioned in the Constitution, leadership in Congress is primarily determined based on political parties. The majority party controls the legislative process.

- The Constitution designates that the leader of the House carry the title Speaker of the House. The Speaker is responsible for assigning new bills to committees and recognizing members to speak in the House chamber. The Constitution also prescribes that the vice president is to be the presiding officer of the Senate. Unlike the Speaker, the president of the Senate can vote only to break ties. When the vice president is absent from the Senate chamber, as is quite often the case, the presiding officer is the president pro tempore ("for the time being").

- To ensure the principle of "one person, one vote" in the House, the size of congressional districts must be "reapportioned" so that they are as even as possible, based on the results of the decennial census. Political parties try to maximize their advantage in the redistricting process that occurs after each census by "gerrymandering," which means that the party in control in each state draws district boundaries to favor the dominant party in elections.

6-3 The Committee System

- There are four types of congressional committees: standing committees (permanent), select committees (established to look at a particular issue for a limited time), conference committees (reconcile differences between House and Senate versions of a bill), and joint committees (includes members from both houses, investigative in nature). Most members defer to committee recommendations on a bill.

6-4 How A Bill Becomes A Law

- The lawmaking process is often slow, and bills that survive frequently receive significant revisions along the way. After a bill is introduced by a member of Congress, it is usually sent to a committee for consideration (often in the form of hearings) and possible action. If the bill is endorsed by a majority of the committee, it then goes to the full House and Senate for consideration. Finally, if it is endorsed by a majority of each chamber, a conference committee reconciles differences in versions between the chambers, and then after a vote on the bill's final version, it goes to the president for signature. If the president vetoes the final bill, Congress can override the presidential veto by a two-thirds vote of both houses of Congress.

6-5 Oversight and Personnel Functions of Congress

- Congress delegates considerable legislative authority to the executive branch, whether because it lacks the expertise of bureaucrats or because it wishes to shift blame for policies to the executive branch. Still, Congress may exercise oversight to ensure that the implementation of laws and regulations is consistent with national problems and concerns.

- The U.S. Senate plays an important role in consenting to the president's selection of cabinet officers, other executive branch officials, and judges. Senate confirmation of Supreme Court nominees in particular has been the subject of considerable controversy. If a majority in the House of Representative impeaches a president, federal judge, or other executive official, the official must stand trial in the Senate. A two-thirds vote of the full Senate is required for the removal of an official from office.

6-6 Constituent Service: Helping People Back Home

- Members of Congress play an important role doing casework for local constituents, whether by assisting them in getting federal benefits, educating them on policy issues, or performing some other service on their behalf. Casework provides a direct connection between members and their constituents.

Key Terms

bicameral legislature (p. 144)
bill (p. 150)
casework (p. 165)
closed rule (p. 158)
cloture (p. 158)
conference committee (p. 152)
congressional agencies (p. 154)
congressional committee staff (p. 154)
congressional district (p. 145)
congressional personal staff (p. 153)
filibuster (p. 158)

gerrymandering (p. 146)
joint committee (p. 153)
logrolling (p. 160)
majority caucus (p. 148)
majority leader (p. 149)
majority-minority district (p. 146)
minority caucus (p. 148)
minority leader (p. 149)
open rule (p. 158)
overriding a veto (p. 160)
pocket veto (p. 161)

pork-barrel legislation (p. 166)
president pro tempore (p. 149)
reapportionment (p. 146)
redistricting (p. 146)
reporting legislation (p. 151)
Rules Committee (p. 157)
select committee (p. 151)
Speaker of the House (p. 148)
standing committee (p. 151)
veto (p. 160)
whip (majority and minority) (p. 149)

Test Yourself

1. The first attempt to unite the colonies under a single "congress" was the
   a. Seneca Falls congress.
   b. First Continental Congress.
   c. Albany Congress.
   d. Congress of the States.

2. The primary power given to Congress by Article I of the Constitution is to
   a. create laws.
   b. implement laws.
   c. adjudicate disputes.
   d. execute laws.

3. Which of the following presidents was a congressional scholar and author of "Congressional Government"?
   a. Thomas Jefferson
   b. Theodore Roosevelt
   c. Woodrow Wilson
   d. Harry Truman

4. To qualify for membership in the House of Representatives, an individual must
   a. be 30 years old.
   b. reside in the congressional district he or she represents.
   c. be a natural-born citizen.
   d. be a citizen of the United States for at least seven years.

5. Under the Constitution as it was adopted, which of the following was directly elected by voters?
   a. House members
   b. Senate members
   c. Speaker of the House
   d. Senate majority leader

6. The power structure in Congress is primarily organized around
   a. seniority.
   b. partisan control.
   c. the most powerful committees.
   d. strong personalities.

7. What makes the position of Speaker of the House such a powerful one?

8. The type of committee that irons out differences between House and Senate versions of a bill is a
   a. standing committee.
   b. joint committee.
   c. conference committee.
   d. select committee.

9. The congressional office that provides objective analyses of the budget, separate from the White House analyses, is the
   a. CBO.
   b. OMB.
   c. GAO.
   d. CRS.

10. What is the significance of a standing committee's power of "reporting legislation"?

11. What type of bill may *not* be introduced first into the Senate?
    a. appropriations of money
    b. defense bills
    c. revenue bills
    d. proposed constitutional amendments

12. Which of the following would *not* be found in the House of Representatives?
    a. Rules Committee
    b. a filibuster
    c. a majority leader
    d. a minority caucus

13. The trading of influence or votes among legislators is known as
    a. lobbying.
    b. pocket vetoing.
    c. reporting legislation.
    d. logrolling.

14. What options does the president have when a bill passed by Congress arrives on his desk?

15. Which of the following is responsible for confirming presidential appointments?
    a. the Senate
    b. the House
    c. both the Senate and the House
    d. the Senate Judiciary Committee

16. When no presidential candidate receives a majority of electoral votes, which of the following selects the president?
    a. the Senate
    b. the House
    c. both the Senate and the House
    d. the Supreme Court

17. Under what circumstances is Congress likely to delegate its authority to a bureaucratic agency?

18. A government project that yields jobs or other benefits to a specific locale and patronage opportunities to its political representative is known as
    a. casework.
    b. pork-barrel legislation.
    c. a sausage-casing law.
    d. a continuing resolution.

19. What is meant by congressional "casework," and why is casework an important role of a member of Congress?

1. c. (LO 6-1); 2. a. (LO 6-1); 3. c. (LO 6-1); 4. d. (LO 6-2); 5. a. (LO 6-2); 6. b. (LO 6-2); 8. c. (LO 6-3); 9. a. (LO 6-3); 11. c. (LO 6-4); 12. b. (LO 6-4); 13. d. (LO 6-4); 15. a. (LO 6-5); 16. b. (LO 6-5); 18. b. (LO 6-6)]

MANDEL NGAN/AFP/Getty Images

LEARNING OBJECTIVES

7-1 Where Do Presidents Come From? Presidential Comings and Goings
- Identify the past traits of presidents; assess the requirements for holding the position.
- Describe the process by which presidents may be impeached and removed from office.

7-2 The Evolution of the American Presidency
- Trace the evolution of the presidency from "chief clerk" in the late eighteenth and nineteenth centuries to near dominance over the political system.
- Explain how the modern presidency has persevered in the recent era of divisiveness.

7-3 Express Powers and Responsibilities of the President
- Define the formal powers vested in the president under Article II of the Constitution, including

the veto, appointments, the pardon power, and commander-in-chief of the armed forces.

7-4 Implied Powers and Responsibilities of the President
- Discuss those implied powers of the presidency not spelled out in the Constitution, including the issuing of executive orders and agreements.

7-5 Presidential Resources
- Describe the other individuals and offices in the executive branch that contribute to the modern presidency.

7-6 Important Presidential Relationships
- Assess how the power of the presidency is enhanced by communications with the public, the Congress, and the media.

7

The Presidency

The world's oldest continuous republican chief executive office remains the U.S. presidency. Whereas most other countries divide political and symbolic functions among different officials, the Constitution combines both sets of functions into just one office: the president of the United States is both head of state and chief executive of the federal government. Unfortunately, the Constitution is deliberately vague on the meaning of the chief executive's primary responsibility under Article II: To "take Care that the Laws be faithfully executed." For more than a century it was the U.S. Congress—disciplined by the two major political parties—that served as the dominant institution of government. It was not until the twentieth century that the presidency became the central institution of American political life, with its executive powers expanded to include vast legislative, judicial, economic, administrative, and foreign policy responsibilities. Of course, with that immense power comes an unprecedented level of accountability as well, especially in the modern era when the public watches the president's every move in real time thanks to wall-to-wall television coverage and the power of the Internet. Is presidential government in the early twenty-first century compatible with the Constitution and traditional notions of representative government? This much we know: the individual who occupies the White House will stand at the apex of international attention and power for as long as he or she remains president.

Coming to Grips with Executive Orders

Beginning with the administration of George Washington and continuing up through the modern era, presidents frequently have issued executive orders to guide executive branch agencies. These orders enjoy the full force of law, though they remain subject to judicial review and thus may be invalidated if the courts determine that they violate federal law or the Constitution. In 2014 President Obama's executive orders on immigration, which granted quasi-legal status to millions of otherwise illegal immigrants, were challenged by state authorities as exceeding his Article II authority—two years later the Supreme Court left in place a lower court order blocking the program from being implemented. Even more recently, President Obama issued executive orders on gun control to crack down on Internet gun sales. In all, Obama issued more than 250 such orders during his presidency. And while the president's critics charge Obama with having abused that power, consider that Calvin Coolidge issued 1,203 executive orders and Franklin Roosevelt issued 3,522 in his 12-plus years as chief executive.

Children studying the Constitution for the first time are normally introduced to the document's basic division of government responsibilities: That Congress makes the laws, while the president enforces them. Yet presidential executive orders offer clear evidence that such a depiction of constitutional authority is naïve at best, and quite misleading in practice. Where do you stand on the question of whether presidents should be able to make laws through executive orders, when Congress is either unwilling or unable to act on major issues facing the nation today?

- Do you approve or disapprove of presidents issuing executive orders in general? Are there ever circumstances that justify the issuance of executive orders? If so, what are they?
- Do you believe President Obama abused his authority when he chose to issue executive orders on gun control? Does it matter that Congress was unwilling or unable to pass any gun control laws in recent years?
- Should the president have more authority to issue executive orders in foreign policy than in domestic policy? Why, if at all, are the two contexts different?

To see how your answers compare to others, take the **Who Are You?** poll in MindTap!

7-1 | Where Do Presidents Come From? Presidential Comings and Goings

What career experiences have provided the most effective launching pads for the 44 separate individuals who have attained the presidency? Many vice presidents have gone on to immediate election as president, including most recently George H. W. Bush, vice president under Ronald Reagan, who in 1988 won the White House in his own right. Yet that form of promotion is actually quite rare. Although 5 of the last 14 vice presidents (up through Joseph Biden) eventually became president, among them only Bush won election as a sitting vice president. In fact, in the 132-year period between Vice President Martin Van Buren's presidential victory in 1836 and former Vice President Richard Nixon's election in 1968, every vice president who rose to the presidency did so (at least initially) only as a consequence of the president's untimely death in office.

Although the U.S. Senate has been aptly described as a body of 100 individuals who all think they should be president, only 16 senators have eventually gone on to the White House. (And only three of those individuals—Warren Harding, John F. Kennedy, and Barack Obama—moved *directly* from the Senate to the presidency.) By comparison, 19 governors and 19 members of the House of Representatives eventually served as president. Three presidents—William Henry Harrison, John Tyler, and Andrew Johnson—actually served in all three of those jobs. Another nine presidents formerly served in another president's cabinet. The military has also been something of a breeding ground for presidents: 29 had some military experience, and 12 served as generals. Fully 27 of the 45 chief executives have been lawyers, but the cohort of presidents also includes among its ranks a mining engineer (Hoover), a peanut farmer (Carter), a baseball team executive (George W. Bush), and even a hat salesman (Truman). The current president, Donald Trump, was previously a businessman and real estate magnate who built office towers, hotels, casinos, and golf courses, among other properties. And unlike these other businessmen, he held no public office before assuming the presidency.

As a formal matter, the adage that "anyone can grow up to be president" is not literally true. Article II of the Constitution imposes three prerequisites on those who aspire to the Oval Office. Every president must be (1) a "natural-born" citizen, (2) 35 years of age or older, and (3) a resident within the United States for at least 14 years. Although the Constitution poses no other formal obstacles to the presidency, as a practical matter the first 45 individual holders of the office have tended to fall into several clearly identifiable categories. All but one of these chief executives have been white males (Barack Obama is the lone African American president) between the ages of 42 and 77. All were born Christians, and nearly all identified themselves as Protestants at one point or another in their lifetimes. (John Kennedy was Catholic; Lyndon Johnson was mostly nonobservant in his adulthood.) Twenty-four were firstborn children in their families, and all but nine attended college (since 1897, every president except Harry Truman received some type of higher education degree). Some states have served as birthplaces for a disproportionate share of presidents, including Virginia (eight), Ohio

The Diversity Dilemma

Public Support for Diverse Presidential Candidates

The 2016 presidential campaign was unique in various ways, including its historically diverse pool of candidates, spanning both genders and a variety of racial, ethnic, and other categories. Doubts still arise as to whether or not a majority of Americans are ready to support such a diverse set of political candidates. The Gallup poll, among other well-known survey research companies, continues to ask questions that seek to gauge the public's receptivity to such candidates.[1]

The public's willingness to support diverse candidates has gradually risen since Gallup began asking about these issues in 1937. Gallup started polling the public about its willingness to support a black presidential candidate in 1958: At that time only 37 percent expressed support for such a candidate. Of course, this type of questioning became much more than just a hypothetical exercise with the election of President Obama in 2008 and the subsequent campaigns of frontrunner Hillary Clinton in both 2008 and 2016. In June 2015, this same Gallup question invited a markedly different response: Now a clear majority of the American public expressed a willingness to support a variety of diverse presidential candidates, including the categories listed in the table to the right.

Table of Gallup Poll Results

Catholic (93%)
A woman (92%)
Black (92%)
Hispanic (91%)
Jewish (91%)
Mormon (81%)
Gay or lesbian (74%)
An evangelical Christian (73%)
Muslim (60%)
An atheist (58%)
A socialist (47%)

Source: Gallup

different demographic categories? In short, do you believe the polling results referenced above will translate into real political results now that President Obama has paved the way?

2. What did you learn from the 2016 presidential election on this score? Did the election results serve to confirm or deny these earlier poll results?

For Critical Thinking and Discussion

1. In the wake of Barack Obama's presidency, are Americans ready to vote for presidential candidates in an array of

(seven), New York (five), and Massachusetts (four). Although presidents are not royalty and none is entitled to serve for life, on several occasions birthright has played a role in helping an individual reach the Oval Office. Twenty-six presidents have been related to other presidents by blood; these relationships encompass two father–son combinations (John and John Quincy Adams; George H. W. and George W. Bush), a grandfather–grandson combination (William Henry Harrison and Benjamin Harrison), and cousins (James Madison and Zachary Taylor were second cousins; Theodore Roosevelt and Franklin Roosevelt were fifth cousins).

When George Washington, after serving two terms as the nation's first president, declined to run again, he established an unwritten two-term precedent. No president challenged that precedent until Franklin Delano Roosevelt (FDR) sought a third term in 1940. FDR's successful election to four consecutive terms (he won in 1932, 1936, 1940, and then again in 1944) led to passage of the **Twenty-second Amendment** in 1951, which restricts any one person from being elected to the presidency "more than twice," or from acting as president for longer than two and a half terms. Four chief executives were assassinated while in office, and four others died of natural causes while still serving as president, including FDR, who died in 1945, only a few months into his unprecedented fourth term.

The constitutional means of removing a president from office is by **impeachment** and subsequent conviction. Article II, Section 4, of the U.S. Constitution provides that the president may be removed from office upon impeachment by a majority vote of the House and conviction by two-thirds of the Senate of "Treason, Bribery, or other high Crimes and Misdemeanors." Just what type of offense qualifies as a "high crime and misdemeanor"? It's difficult to say. Just two presidents, Andrew Johnson and Bill Clinton, have ever been impeached under these provisions, and both were impeached for primarily political reasons: Johnson was charged with illegally firing a cabinet member, pardoning traitors, and impeding ratification of the Fourteenth Amendment; Clinton was accused of lying to a grand jury about his sexual relationship with an intern and of obstructing justice. Both men were acquitted on all charges by the U.S. Senate and served out their respective terms.

The only president to resign was Richard Nixon, who was accused of obstructing justice in the now infamous Watergate scandal. Nixon left office less than halfway through his second term in 1974 under the looming threat of impeachment. In practice, unpopular presidents are usually turned out of office not by removal, but by a failed reelection. In recent times, three sitting presidents (Gerald Ford, Jimmy Carter, and George H. W. Bush) lost reelection bids; Lyndon Johnson chose not to run for reelection in 1968 when frustration with his unpopular Vietnam War policy undermined his prospects for victory in the November election.

When President John Adams was defeated for reelection in 1800 and turned over the White House to archrival Thomas Jefferson, he helped establish a precedent of peaceful transition between chief executives that has held firm to this day, despite the hostile feelings that sometimes exist between successive presidents. In the case of the president's removal by death, resignation, or inability to serve, the Constitution requires that the powers and duties of the president "devolve" on the vice president. When William Henry Harrison died barely a month after becoming president in 1841, Vice President John Tyler took over all

Twenty-second Amendment Passed in 1951, this constitutional amendment restricts any one person from being elected to the presidency "more than twice," or from acting as president for longer than two and a half terms.

impeachment The first step in a two-step process outlined in Article II, Section 4, of the U.S. Constitution to remove a president or other high official from office. The House of Representatives, by majority vote, may impeach if the official has committed "Treason, Bribery, or other high Crimes and Misdemeanors." The second step requires a conviction in the Senate by a two-thirds vote.

Bill and Hillary Clinton thanking Democratic members of the House of Representatives who voted against impeachment on December 19, 1998.

AP Images/Greg Gibson

the powers, duties, and responsibilities of the presidency, rejecting any notion that he was simply there to serve as a more limited "acting president" until the next election. Since Tyler, seven vice presidents have become chief executive in this manner, including most recently Lyndon Johnson, who assumed office after John F. Kennedy was assassinated in November 1963. Of the last six vice presidents thrust unexpectedly into office, four—Theodore Roosevelt, Calvin Coolidge, Harry Truman, and Lyndon Johnson—eventually secured election as presidents in their own right.

7-2 | The Evolution of the American Presidency

The U.S. Constitution places as many limitations on the office of the presidency as it grants the president specific powers and duties. Wary of the excessive authority wielded by the king of England, most of the Founders rejected Alexander Hamilton's radical suggestion that the president should be elected for life; instead, they designed a chief executive who would be powerful enough to respond quickly when necessary, but also would be limited by lack of lawmaking power and the need to gain congressional approval for most long-term commitments, whether foreign or domestic.

The presidency has evolved over the past two centuries not so much because of any constitutional expansion of the chief executive's powers, but rather through practice, tradition, and the personal energy of some presidents. The changing dynamics of policymaking in the United States from a mostly local focus to a national phenomenon has given presidents the opportunity to exert unprecedented influence over the process, and many have done exactly that. In many ways, the growth of the power of the presidency has paralleled the growth of the United States.

The President as "Chief Clerk" of the United States, 1789–1836

The earliest presidents established the office as a forceful power in the national government. Still, even the most popular presidents of the period were careful to avoid interfering with the clear legislative prerogatives of Congress. Several played a major role in helping steer America away from or toward war, despite the inclinations of Congress. But the truly dominant chief executive would not emerge until many years later.

When George Washington, the immensely popular former general of the Continental Army, agreed to be nominated as the nation's first president, widespread public confidence in his abilities helped secure immediate respect for this new office. Serving as the first chief executive from 1789 to 1797, Washington established various precedents that helped preserve a republican form of government in the nation's infancy. Washington rejected entrapments of royalty such as being referred to as "Your Majesty," preferring instead to be called "Mr. President." As a practical matter, Washington consulted constantly with the other branches—at one point he even asked the Supreme Court for an advisory opinion about his own interpretations of a foreign treaty. (The Court declined his invitation for comment.) Washington also established the executive's influential role in crafting public policy, siding with his Secretary of Treasury Alexander Hamilton's plans for industrialization and the creation of a national bank, and striving to maintain an isolationist foreign policy. Often serving as a mediator between differing positions in his administration, Washington rejected the less interventionist, farmer-friendly policies favored by his secretary of state, Thomas Jefferson.[2] For better or worse, most subsequent presidents

North Wind/North Wind Picture Archives

Military hero William Henry Harrison won election to the presidency in 1840. Yet fr all of his strengths as a war hero, he was ultimately a victim of his own stubbornness. Inauguration Day, March 4, 1841, was one of the coldest and most blustery days of the year in Washington, D.C. Harrison refused to wear a hat and coat, and his nearly two-hour inaugural address was one of the longest in history. One month later Harrison died of pneumonia, probably contracted during his inaugural speech. He was the first president to die in office, but perhaps the last not to bundle up warmly for his inauguration day celebration.

would be forced to work within the framework of a divided party system that originated as an intramural fight within the Washington administration.

During the four decades after Washington's retirement, most presidents served more as chief "clerks" than as chief "executives," doing Congress's bidding and performing mostly administrative duties on behalf of the federal government. Upon winning the presidency in 1800, Thomas Jefferson (1801–1809)[3] put into practice his own theory "that government is best which governs least." Accordingly, the Jefferson administration abolished many judgeships, trimmed government economic planning efforts, and scaled back the armed forces. The one crucial exception to such downsizing occurred in the area of land acquisition: Jefferson arranged for the purchase of the vast Louisiana territory from France, more than doubling the physical size of the country.

A presidency characterized by limited executive powers soon confronted unexpected challenges. When tensions between Great Britain and the United States erupted into the War of 1812, President James Madison (1809–1817) found himself hampered both by the small size of the federal army and by the lack of a powerful national bank capable of funding the government's prosecution of the war. This war with Britain revealed the limited powers of the president to influence national matters without strong institutional resources at his disposal. Madison's successor, James Monroe (1817–1825), exercised most of his influence in foreign affairs. Monroe's Secretary of State John Quincy Adams, who himself was president from 1825 to 1829, helped craft the "Monroe Doctrine," which declared that the United States would thereafter regard as an "unfriendly act" any attempt by a European nation to increase its possession or otherwise intervene on the American continent. Meanwhile, Congress led the way in domestic matters, crafting key compromises over slavery and paying off much of the public debt incurred during the War of 1812.

Andrew Jackson, who served as president from 1829 to 1837, remade the presidency into an office of tremendous political power. The military hero of the Battle of New Orleans in 1815, Jackson came to the White House as a political outsider but with overwhelming popular support. Capitalizing on this resource, Jackson wielded presidential power in a way that few of his predecessors had, dismissing hundreds of officeholders, forcing out cabinet members who angered him, using his constitutionally authorized power to veto Congress's bill to recharter the Second National Bank of the United States, and introducing the so-called spoils system of doling out federal offices to individuals as rewards for political service.[4]

The Weakened Presidency in the Wilderness Years, 1837–1900

Andrew Jackson raised the profile and authority of the presidency to unprecedented heights, but its ascendancy was largely a product of his own popularity and energetic personality. The pre–Civil War presidents who followed Jackson also proved to be much weaker. The model of president as chief clerk seemed once again alive and well.

Perhaps the only effective president during this antebellum period was James K. Polk (1845–1849), who presided over a period of incredible westward expansion. Polk exercised his powers as commander-in-chief to instigate a successful war with Mexico over the Texas territory; his foreign relations successes included the acquisitions of the California and Arizona territories after the Mexican-American War, and the Oregon territory (including the current-day states of Oregon and Washington) from the British.[5] More typical were Presidents Franklin Pierce and James Buchanan during the 1850s; the failures of both to address growing sectional tensions over slavery left pro-slavery and abolitionist interests alike bitterly frustrated.

The presidency of Abraham Lincoln (1861–1865) thrived due to a rare combination of factors. Frequently underestimated as a great political mind, Lincoln was confronted with the single greatest threat in the history of the republic—the secession of 11 Southern states and the great battle between North and South to restore the Union.

President Abraham Lincoln delivering the Gettysburg Address in 1863.

Although Lincoln proceeded carefully in his prosecution of the war against the South for fear of alienating crucial border states, those acts he did undertake were bold and unprecedented. At the outset of the war in April 1861, with Congress not even in session, Lincoln proclaimed a blockade of Southern ports and called on the Northern states to provide 75,000 soldiers for battle. He (at least in one court's opinion[6]) unconstitutionally suspended the writ of habeas corpus, by which anyone arrested is to be brought before a judge or court to determine if there is sufficient reason to hold the person for trial. Suspending the writ allowed Lincoln to hold some criminal defendants indefinitely. The president also spent freely from the U.S. Treasury without congressional approval. Although Congress ultimately ratified all his actions after the fact, Lincoln's bold exercise of authority essentially reinterpreted Article II into a source of executive authority during emergencies.

Following Lincoln's assassination in April 1865, Congress, dominated at that time by radical Republicans determined to punish the former Confederate states, quickly reasserted its control over the nation's agenda. For the remainder of the century, Congress would determine domestic policy. Indeed, after the former Civil War hero Ulysses Grant left office in 1877, no sitting president won election to a second term until William McKinley accomplished the feat in 1900.

The Birth of the Modern Presidency and Its Rise to Dominance, 1901–1945

The beginning of the twentieth century marked the onset of a new era for the American presidency. In an increasingly global and interconnected world, the power of the presidency grew disproportionately. By the time two world wars had concluded, the presidency had emerged as the premier institution in American politics.

In the fall of 1901, William McKinley was assassinated during the first year of his second term, thrusting his young and ebullient vice-president, 42-year-old Theodore Roosevelt, into office. Roosevelt's presidency (1901–1909) ushered in a new era of presidential authority. He injected a forceful energy and enthusiasm into the White House, using his position as "a bully pulpit" (Roosevelt's own words). As one observer noted, "He wanted to be the bride at every wedding; the corpse at every funeral." Unlike many of his predecessors, Roosevelt was willing to gamble political capital on bold assertions of presidential power. Most notably, the Supreme Court narrowly upheld his efforts to break up corporate monopolies. Through the creative use of executive orders, he also increased the acreage of national parks fivefold. When Roosevelt became president, foreign affairs were assuming an ever more significant place in the nation's list of priorities. In less than two full terms in office, Roosevelt encouraged a Panamanian revolution, initiated the building of the Panama Canal, won a Nobel Peace Prize for mediating war settlements between Japan and Russia, and sent the nation's naval fleet around the world as a demonstration of American military authority.[7] The first president to travel to foreign lands, Roosevelt expanded the Monroe Doctrine by advancing the "Roosevelt Corollary," which declared that the United States would serve as a police power to maintain stability in the Western Hemisphere by opposing any European interference in the affairs of Latin American nations. In foreign affairs, where force of personality is so important, Congress proved little match for this charismatic young president.

As president from 1913 to 1921, Woodrow Wilson achieved some significant successes and suffered some great failures: his aggressive industrial reform agenda marked a successful first term in office; during his second term he eventually led the United States into World War I and received accolades at the Paris Peace Conference following the war. But Wilson's hopes for a stable international order based on a system of collective security ultimately confronted political reality, as Senate leaders whom Wilson had excluded from the peace talks rejected U.S. membership in the League of Nations. Still, Wilson's presidency illustrated just how much more powerful the presidency had become since the mid-nineteenth century. In the early part of the twentieth century, the president came to dominate the political landscape.

The onset of the Great Depression during Herbert Hoover's presidency (1929–1933) and the looming threat of a second world war in the late 1930s demanded a new and innovative approach to the office. Franklin Delano Roosevelt placed his own indelible stamp on the nation by transforming the presidency into an institution marked by permanent bureaucracies and well-established repositories of power. FDR tackled the Great Depression with **New Deal** policies that tied the economic fate of millions of Americans to the fate of the American government: a Social Security program of old-age insurance and unemployment insurance would provide income for the elderly and the jobless; the government would guarantee deposit accounts in commercial banks through the Federal Deposit Insurance Corporation (FDIC); and the government would provide federal jobs to the unemployed to perform various public works. Roosevelt communicated extensively with the American people through the media—millions listened to his "fireside chats" on the radio. By restoring public confidence with his energetic support for New Deal programs, FDR redefined the presidency as a source of national leadership. Future presidents would enjoy significant resources of power simply by taking the helms of the formidable institution FDR established. As indicated in Table 7-1, FDR would go down in history as one of the greatest U.S. presidents, largely because of these domestic accomplishments.

Still, like Theodore Roosevelt and Woodrow Wilson, FDR felt especially at home in foreign affairs. Although adhering to popular sentiment that the United States should maintain strict neutrality in foreign wars, in the early days of World War II, Roosevelt met with British royalty and the British prime minister as a show of support, initiated a "lend-lease" policy by which Britain could purchase war supplies from the United States as long as it paid cash and transported the supplies in its own ships, and traded Britain 50 destroyers in exchange for rights to build military bases on British possessions in the

New Deal A set of aggressive federal domestic policies proposed by President Franklin Delano Roosevelt in the 1930s and passed by Congress as a response to the Great Depression; it ultimately transformed the presidency into an institution marked by permanent bureaucracies and well-established repositories of power.

TABLE 7-1 The 10 Greatest Presidents of All Time

More than half a century ago, historian Arthur M. Schlesinger Jr. began the process of polling historians to rank the presidents of the United States. Recent surveys continue to borrow heavily from Schlesinger's original methodology. In 2009, the C-SPAN Survey of Presidential Leadership ranked the opinions of presidential historians and "professional observers of the presidency." Another poll of presidential scholars was conducted by the *Wall Street Journal* in 2005, with support from the Federalist Society. Interestingly, the results vary. Thus, while Washington, Lincoln, and Franklin D. Roosevelt usually top most lists, presidential scholars substantially disagree on how to complete the list of greatest presidents.

C-SPAN Survey—2009 Top 10	*Wall Street Journal* Poll—2005 Top 10
1. Lincoln	1. Washington
2. Washington	2. Lincoln
3. Roosevelt, F.	3. Roosevelt, F.
4. Roosevelt, T.	4. Jefferson
5. Truman	5. Roosevelt, T.
6. Kennedy	6. Reagan
7. Jefferson	7. Truman
8. Eisenhower	8. Eisenhower
9. Wilson	9. Polk
10. Reagan	10. Jackson

Source: Presidential Leadership; The Rankings," The Wall Street Journal Online, September 12, 2005; C-SPAN,

"2009 Historians Presidential Leadership Survey," www.houmatoday.com/assets/pdf/HC15074217.PDF.

Western Hemisphere—all without the consent of Congress. When America did enter the war in 1941 after the attack on Pearl Harbor, presidential power was put on full display. FDR met personally with British and Soviet leaders to craft military plans; then, near the end of the war, the Allied leaders carved Europe and the Middle East into "spheres of influence" that would establish an American presence across the Atlantic Ocean for decades. With the president playing a dominant role in both national and world affairs, the imperial presidency that took root at the beginning of the twentieth century came to fruition by the mid 1940s.

The Imperial Presidency Comes Under Attack, 1945–1980

By the end of World War II, the presidency had emerged as a very powerful office. FDR's fireside chats on the radio linked average Americans to the occupier of the White House in a fashion that was unimagined by the Founders. In the late 1940s, television became a central influence in American life, and presidents honed their skills with this new medium to further nurture their relationship with the public.

Now recognized as powerful chief executives, those who followed in the footsteps of FDR confronted a new and unprecedented threat to American national security: the presence of a second world military superpower—the Soviet Union. With presidential authority greatest in the area of national security, waging the Cold War that began in the late 1940s consumed much of these presidents' energies. Harry Truman, FDR's immediate successor, proclaimed the "Truman Doctrine" in foreign policy, by which the United States pledged military and economic aid to any nation threatened by communism or the Soviet Union. Like Truman, Presidents Eisenhower and Kennedy also focused their administrations' energies on containing the Soviet communist threat. As long as the Soviet Union challenged American interests, the presidency would remain the focus of attention in the American political system.

Not until the presidency of Lyndon Johnson (1963–1969) was a president able to enact a sweeping domestic agenda similar to FDR's New Deal. Johnson's **Great Society** program featured more than 60 reform measures, including increases in federal aid to education, the enactment of Medicare and Medicaid, and a voting rights act for racial/ethnic minorities. But Johnson's domestic policy success was offset by his failures in foreign policy. Exercising his authority as commander-in-chief, Johnson sent more than half a million troops to Vietnam to fight an increasingly unpopular war. The failure to stop the communists from taking over South Vietnam was laid squarely at the feet of Johnson, just as earlier foreign policy successes had been credited to his predecessors.

The presidents who followed Johnson came under increasing attack in the 1970s. Richard Nixon achieved foreign policy success by improving America's relationship with the Soviet Union and China, but in 1974 he became the first president in history to resign from office before the end of his term when the Watergate scandal enveloped his presidency. Jimmy Carter's presidency (1977–1981) was beset with hardships, as the nation's economy faltered in the 1970s. Carter's failure to resolve an Iranian revolution that included the taking of 50 American hostages further cemented his image as an inept commander-in-chief. Carter thus became the first elected president since 1932 to lose a reelection bid. By the end of the 1970s, the modern presidency created by Theodore Roosevelt and brought to new heights by Franklin Delano Roosevelt found itself increasingly under attack from an emboldened Congress and a frustrated public.

Redefining the Presidency in an Era of Divisiveness, 1981-Present

The election of Ronald Reagan to the White House in 1980 marked the return of the chief executive as an unmatched force over American politics. No president in the twentieth century (save perhaps FDR) could match Reagan's prowess as a "great communicator"; by speaking directly to the American people in terms they could understand, Reagan bypassed Congress and enjoyed early victories with passage of an economic program marked by tax cuts, decreased social spending, and a marked increase in defense spending. Reagan's legislative success was all the more remarkable given that he was working with a divided-party government. The Democrats controlled the House of Representatives in every year of Reagan's presidency; his legislative success thus contrasted favorably with that of previous presidents who had struggled to get legislation passed by a Congress controlled by the opposite party. In foreign policy, Reagan's aggressive program of military buildup combined with his own hardline position against the Soviet Union is credited with helping bring about the fall of communist regimes in Eastern Europe, the breakup of the USSR, and thus victory in the Cold War. In addition, Reagan's immense popularity allowed him to weather numerous crises and scandals in a way that few of his predecessors had.

Reagan's successors also faced the reality of divided-party government at different points in their respective presidencies. George H. W. Bush took the lead in foreign policy, overseeing the dismantling of the Soviet Union and forging international alliances prior to mounting a successful war against Iraqi aggression in Kuwait. However, by compromising with the opposition Democrats on tax legislation, he frustrated some of his more conservative constituencies and undermined his efforts at reelection. Bill Clinton became the first Democratic president in a half century to serve two full terms. Clinton

Great Society A set of aggressive federal domestic policies proposed by President Lyndon Johnson and passed by Congress in the 1960s that further enhanced the role of the presidency.

appealed to moderates largely by borrowing central elements of the opposition party's domestic program: His three main legislative successes (free-trade agreements, budget cutting, and welfare reform) were all programs that had been more closely associated with Republicans than Democrats at the time Clinton took office in the early 1990s.

In the aftermath of the terrorist attacks of September 11, 2001, President George W. Bush moved quickly to position his administration as the eminent world leader in an emerging "war on terrorism." His early efforts to fight terrorism at home and abroad enjoyed congressional support from both parties: His aggressive military intervention against the Taliban-controlled government in Afghanistan in late 2001 proved extremely popular and helped cement his administration's image of toughness and resolve. Yet when the Bush administration expanded the war on terrorism to include military intervention in Iraq, justified on the basis of inaccurate reports that Iraq possessed weapons of mass destruction, these same policies became much more divisive. Though victorious in his 2004 reelection bid, George W. Bush's second term proved even more difficult than the first, with more Americans questioning the war in Iraq as U.S. casualties mounted. By the end of his second term, Bush's ratings had dropped to below 30 percent—in part the consequence of significant problems in the economy, exacerbated further by the Wall Street crisis of September 2008.

Barack Obama's presidency began—as most presidential terms do—buoyed by feelings of goodwill and optimism. A clear majority of the public hoped he would successfully tackle the economic crisis that befell the nation in 2008. Many citizens hoped the young president was serious about his promises to bring "change" to Washington.

Obama's "honeymoon period" ended quickly, however, as the details of his administration's proposals for reform were laid bare for debate. President Obama benefitted from strong Democratic majorities in Congress; he muscled through his legislative agenda almost entirely on the strength of those majorities, and with little support from Republicans. The $787 billion fiscal stimulus bill (the American Recovery and Reinvestment Act of 2009) passed with the help of just three Republican senators and no Republican House members; the landmark health care reform bill of 2010 was even more partisan, garnering not a single Republican vote from either branch of Congress. Facing an emboldened Republican majority following the 2010 midterm elections, Obama soon found himself at loggerheads with the GOP House leadership—this led to a series of threatened government shutdowns prior to the 2012 election and a near paralysis of government following President Obama's successful reelection bid in 2012. Indeed, throughout President Obama's second term, he proved unable to make headway on passing legislation addressing gun violence or immigration reform, two subjects that he had trumpeted as his administration's top priorities. Near the end of his second term, President Obama resorted to executive orders addressing those two policy areas, and he even enjoyed a modest uptick of popularity in the period leading up to the 2016 election. But in the end, a stubborn Republican majority in the Congress limited the 44th President from extending executive power even further. Obama thus learned an important political lesson: The rhetoric of bipartisanship does not easily translate into bipartisan votes and results.

7-3 | Express Powers and Responsibilities of the President

Article II of the Constitution provides that the president of the United States holds executive power, but it is not very detailed about what constitutes executive power. In fact, the Constitution lists only four specific powers of the president: (1) commander-in-chief of the armed forces, (2) power to grant reprieves or pardons, (3) power to make treaties (subject to Senate approval), and (4) power to make certain appointments, including those of ambassadors and justices of the Supreme Court (again subject to Senate approval). Despite this limited number of constitutionally expressed powers, presidents today serve many important functions in the American political system. Noting these varied roles, political scientist Clinton Rossiter referred to the many different hats that the president must wear during the course of a week, or even during just one day.[8] Some of these are specified in the Constitution and laws of the United States, which conceive of a limited executive, but one who possesses the authority to react quickly and energetically to unexpected crises.

Head of State

The office of the presidency combines the political and symbolic functions that are often divided in other countries. As the nation's head of state, the president fulfills numerous formal duties and obligations on behalf of the country. Most visiting foreign heads of state meet directly with the president; sometimes those visits include an official state dinner at the White House hosted by the president and attended by key political leaders from throughout Washington. Article II of the Constitution also carves out a more formal role for the president in foreign affairs; the president's role in receiving ambassadors and other public ministers has often been interpreted as granting the president the discretion to give or deny official recognition to foreign governments. Although such a power may seem mostly honorary, it can have a real political impact in some circumstances. President Woodrow Wilson's refusal to recognize the new government of Mexico in 1913 caused considerable consternation among American supporters of the Mexican revolution and led to growing tensions between the two neighbors. More recently, American presidents during the 1970s and 1980s refused to recognize the Palestine Liberation Organization as the legitimate representative of the Palestinian people, buttressing Israel's own hardline stance against that organization.

Chief Executive and Head of Government

In his *Second Treatise of Government*, political theorist John Locke argued that executive power was so fundamental that it predated civil society.[9] According to Locke, legislatures were ill-equipped to enforce their own laws because they need "perpetual execution," and legislatures sit only infrequently. Moreover, if the same entity both

Donald Trump on stage in St. Louis, Missouri, during the second of three 2016 presidential debates.

made and enforced the laws, it might be tempted to "suit the law to their own particular advantage," regardless of the law's language. Another political theorist, Baron de Montesquieu, also advocated the separation of legislative and executive powers—specifically, he decried the tendency of legislatures to exert too much influence over the executive, increasing the opportunity for abuse.[10]

Influenced in part by these arguments, the Framers of the Constitution vested all executive power in the president alone. Unfortunately, they failed to define that power with any specificity. At a minimum, the Constitution grants presidents alone the responsibility to execute the laws of the United States, which encompasses the implementation and enforcement of measures passed by Congress—in other words, to see that Americans actually abide by those laws in practice. A president's failure to "take Care that the Laws be faithfully executed"—whether intentionally or due to negligent administration of his subordinates—can have obvious implications for the effectiveness of such laws. Actual levels of execution sometimes lie squarely within the discretion of the chief executive. Presidents Reagan and Clinton, for example, defined antitrust laws in markedly different ways simply by offering contrasting approaches to the execution of those laws. During the 1980s, Reagan's lack of enthusiasm for government intervention in the marketplace translated into the prosecution of far fewer antitrust actions than had been brought by previous administrations. By contrast, under President Clinton the Justice Department applied the antitrust laws enthusiastically, such as when it brought suit against the Microsoft Corporation in 1997 for monopolistic practices that stifled competition in the software industry. More recently, Republican President George W. Bush and the Democrats in Congress sparred over the Bush administration's aggressive enforcement of the USA PATRIOT Act against some individuals, which gave the laws far more teeth than was originally anticipated.

The president's power to see that laws are faithfully executed also implies some power to hire and fire those charged with administrative authority to help execute federal laws. The **power of appointment** thus stands among the president's most important executive powers.[11] The Constitution specifically authorizes the president to appoint ambassadors and other public ministers, judges of the Supreme Court, and all other federal officers under his charge. Additionally, the president appoints all federal judges. Most of these appointments require the consent of the Senate. In recent years, senators have subjected the president's nominees to intense scrutiny, occasionally even rejecting the president's choices. President George W. Bush withdrew his second choice for the Supreme Court, White House Counsel Harriet Miers, amid mounting opposition from his own party. And President Obama faced stubborn opposition from Senate Republicans when he nominated Judge Merrick Garland to a vacant Supreme Court seat in 2016. Led by Majority leader Mitch McConnell, the Senate refused to even hold hearings for Garland before Election day, asserting that body's power to withhold consent for the president's nominee during a presidential election year.

Although Supreme Court nominees often receive the most intense investigation, the Senate may occasionally question other executive appointments. In 1989, the U.S. Senate rejected President George H. W. Bush's choice for defense secretary, John Tower, due to allegations that Tower had a drinking problem. Barack Obama's first choice as secretary of health and human services, former Senate Majority Leader Tom Daschle, withdrew his name from consideration in February 2009 amid a growing controversy over his failure to accurately report and pay income taxes.

The president's removal power has been a source of controversy as well. The Supreme Court's decision in *Myers v. United States* (1926)[12] established that chief executives have the power to remove "purely executive officers" without congressional consent. Although independent agency heads can be removed only by congressional action, cabinet heads and military officials can be terminated by the president alone. In one famous instance during the Korean War, President Truman decided in 1951 to fire the extremely popular General Douglas MacArthur, commander of the United Nations forces in Korea.

power of appointment The president's constitutional power to hire and fire those charged with administrative authority to help execute federal laws, such as ambassadors; federal judges, including those on the Supreme Court; and all other federal officers under the president's charge. Most of these appointments require the consent of the Senate.

President Richard Nixon and Vice President Gerald Ford conferring on August 9, 1974, the day Nixon resigned from office.

reprieve The president's constitutional authority to reduce the severity of a punishment without removing the guilt for those who have violated the law.

pardon The president's constitutional authority to relieve an individual of both the punishment and the guilt of violating the law.

Not only is the president responsible for the enforcement of all federal laws, he is also authorized by the Constitution to grant reprieves and pardons to individuals who violate those laws. The Founders vested this power in the chief executive because they believed that the prerogative of mercy, on which the pardon power is based, is most efficiently and equitably exercised by a single individual, as opposed to a body of legislators or judges. A **reprieve** reduces the severity of a punishment without removing the guilt; a full **pardon** relieves an individual of both the punishment and the guilt. A president's decision to exercise the pardon power can invite considerable negative comment and political backlash. Not surprisingly, then, most presidents wait until the end of their presidential terms to grant pardons. Less than two months after being denied his bid for reelection in 1992, President George H. W. Bush pardoned six officials for their involvement in the Iran-Contra scandal from 1987, including former Defense Secretary Casper Weinberger. President Clinton issued 140 pardons on his last day in office in 2001, including one to Marc Rich, who had previously fled the country for tax evasion and whose wife was a major contributor to Clinton's political campaigns. No president received more criticism for granting a pardon than Gerald Ford, who as vice president succeeded to the presidency when Richard Nixon resigned in 1974. Ford's pardon of his former boss for involvement in the Watergate scandal helped undermine his prospects for election to the White House in his own right two years later.

Chief Diplomat

As chief diplomat of the United States, the president has the power to negotiate treaties and appoint diplomatic representatives to other countries, including ambassadors, ministers, and consuls. The president's power over treaties is limited to negotiation and execution—enactment of any treaties requires approval by two-thirds of the Senate. Still, the power to negotiate and execute the terms of treaties affords the president immense authority in the field of foreign affairs. John F. Kennedy used this power to negotiate an end to the Cuban missile crisis in 1962;[13] Jimmy Carter personally presided over the negotiation of the Panama Canal Treaty of 1977–1978, which relinquished U.S. control over the canal by the year 2000. Every president during the latter stages of the Cold War conducted arms control negotiations with the Soviet Union, working to check the spread of nuclear weapons to other nations. Bill Clinton surprised many in his own party when he completed negotiations on the North American Free Trade Agreement, an economic treaty with Canada and Mexico that was favored primarily by Republican presidents who came before him.

Chief Legislator

Although Congress is the branch of government authorized to make laws, modern presidents are involved in nearly every stage of federal lawmaking.[14] The Constitution's express provision that the president recommend for the consideration of Congress "such Measures as he shall judge necessary and expedient" barely hints

Then & Now

Making History on the Road to the White House … Yet Again

When President Obama was inaugurated on January 20, 2009, nearly 2 million people crowded onto the Washington, D.C., mall to be part of history, as the first African American president took the formal oath of office. Little did they know that voters would again make history just eight years later: By early summer of 2016, the three leading candidates for president all offered unusual presidential profiles, at least by historical standards. The Republican nominee, Donald J. Trump was battling to become the first U.S. president who sported no government experience (military or civilian) whatsoever. Meanwhile on the Democratic side, Bernie Sanders continued his uphill fight to become the first Jewish president and—at 75 years of age—the oldest individual elected president. And then, of course, there was Hillary Clinton, who hoped to become the first woman president, a landmark that would more than match Obama's milestone for its historic meaning and importance.

In a nation where Caucasian, male Protestants with government experience have dominated the presidential scene, 2016 was certain to buck this trend in some fashion. Consider some other presidential election firsts as well:

Then

In 1836, Martin Van Buren became the first man elected president who was born in the United States of America (he was born a U.S. citizen in Kinderhook, New York, in 1782—the previous seven presidents were born as British subjects). Van Buren would also become the first president born after the Declaration of Independence.

In 1960, America elected the first Catholic president in Senator John F. Kennedy (D-MA). At 43, Kennedy was also the youngest man ever elected president, the first president born in the twentieth century, and the first president to have previously served in the U.S. Navy.

In 1980, Ronald Reagan became the first divorced individual and the first professional actor to be elected president. The 69-year-old former governor of California was also the oldest man to be elected president for the first time; he was also the first president to be born and raised in Illinois.

In 2008, Barack Obama became the first African American (and the first multiracial American) to be elected president. Born in Hawaii, he was also the first president to be born outside of the contiguous 48 states.

Inauguration day, January 20, 1961.

Now

In 2016, America elected its first true "outsider"—someone with absolutely no military or government experience—as president. After earning his Bachelor's Degree from the Wharton School of Business, Donald Trump rose to prominence by building a real estate and construction firm that was eventually valued in the billions. Trump effectively used television to become a national celebrity—first, by appearing at Miss USA pageants (which he owned from 1996 to 2015) and then later as the host and co-producer of *The Apprentice*, a successful reality television show which ran from 2004 to 2015. Trump toyed with politics often during his career: He had first sought the Reform Party presidential nomination in 2000, but withdrew before voting began. He was also considered as a possible vice presidential running mate by George H.W. Bush in 1988. Still, when Trump declared that he was running for President in June of 2015, few pundits or long-time political observers gave his campaign any real chance of success. And yet 17 months later Trump had overcome exceedingly long odds to win the White House. In doing so, he rewrote the rulebook for what qualifications are necessary to hold the highest office in the government.

Donald Trump was the first American elected president without having ever held any civilian or military government office.

For Critical Thinking and Discussion

1. Why do you think Americans take so much pride (at least initially) in historical breakthroughs when electing a new president?
2. Rather than serving as a source of pride, should the election of an individual with an unusual racial or ethnic background (as compared to past chief executives) serve instead as a sober reminder to the public that the White House has not been a source of access for many such groups in the past?

State of the Union address An annual speech that the president delivers to Congress laying out the status of the nation and offering suggestions for new legislation.

White House Office of Legislative Affairs A presidential office that serves as a liaison between the president and Congress. This office helps the president develop the strategy used to promote passage of the president's legislative agenda.

at the president's real role in this context: major legislation is often the product of a give-and-take process between the president and congressional leaders. Indeed, the president plays a critically important role in helping to set the lawmaking agenda for Congress, especially when the president's party is also in control of the legislative branch of government. While campaigning for the White House, the future president will lay out a policy agenda; once elected, he will claim a legislative mandate to follow through on those campaign proposals. In the **State of the Union address**, an annual speech made to Congress laying out the status of the nation, the president typically proposes suggestions for legislation. The legislative programs of FDR's New Deal and Lyndon Johnson's Great Society were both influenced heavily by the executive branch. Similarly, Congress's reorganization of various executive branch agencies into a unified Department of Homeland Security in 2002 was based on a plan drafted by officials within the Bush administration. According to social scientist Paul Light, recent presidents have tended to offer fewer legislative proposals than presidents of the mid-twentieth century, consistent with the modern administrations' increased emphasis on reducing the size of the federal government.[15] Still, when a national crisis demands legislative solutions, Congress often looks to the president for leadership. House and Senate leaders made few significant modifications to their respective health care bills in 2009 without first huddling with President Obama and his top White House aides; and it was the president's willingness to meet frequently with moderate Democratic members of Congress that kept many in the fold for the final passage of health care reform in 2010.

The **White House Office of Legislative Affairs** serves as a liaison between the president and Congress and helps develop the strategy used to promote passage of the president's legislative agenda. Administration officials often testify before congressional subcommittees on behalf of legislation, and presidents meet with congressional leaders frequently throughout the lawmaking process to negotiate details and discuss strategy. Many bills have the president's imprint squarely upon them, even though the power of lawmaking rests formally with Congress. The president's legislative authority also includes the constitutional power to veto, or reject, legislation that he opposes. Although Congress can technically override a veto by a two-thirds vote of both houses, barely 4 percent of presidential vetoes have been overridden in history.

During the twentieth century, vetoes became a routine form of political exercise for presidents, especially those confronting Congresses controlled by the opposite political party (see Table 7-2). That power includes so-called pocket vetoes, by which presidents may refuse to sign a bill within 10 days of the adjournment of Congress, thus rendering it void. For Richard Nixon, Gerald Ford, and George H. W. Bush, the only three presidents during this span who were never the beneficiaries of unified party rule, the veto became something of an art form. Nixon and Bush vetoed 43 and 44 bills, respectively. (Only eight of those vetoes were overridden.) Gerald Ford vetoed 66 bills in just two and a half years, but more than one in five were overridden, a clear sign of the limited power Ford held during his brief term as president. With Republicans controlling the House during George W. Bush's first six years in office, he did not need to veto any bill until July 19, 2006, when he vetoed the Stem Cell Research Enhancement Bill, legislation that would have eased restrictions on federal funding for embryonic stem cell research. However, after the Democrats' takeover of Congress in 2007, Bush vetoed 11 more bills sent to him by the Democratic Congress. Through October 1, 2016, President Obama had vetoed just 12 bills during his presidency, including the controversial Keystone Pipeline Approval Act and several other environmental bills that highlighted the Republican Congress's disapproval of standards issued by the EPA. In this highly partisan era, congressional Democrats consistently sided with President Obama in all but one case: Obama suffered his first veto override on September 27, 2016, as Congress pressed into law a bill allowing the families of 9/11 victims to sue Saudi Arabia for its alleged role in the terrorist plot.

TABLE 7-2 Vetoes Issued by Modern Presidents (Through October 1, 2016)

President	Congresses	Regular Vetoes	Pocket Vetoes	Total Vetoes	Vetoes Overridden
Theodore Roosevelt	57th–60th	42	40	82	1
William Taft	61st–62nd	30	9	39	1
Woodrow Wilson	63rd–66th	33	11	44	6
Warren Harding	67th	5	1	6	0
Calvin Coolidge	68th–70th	20	30	50	4
Herbert Hoover	71st–72nd	21	16	37	3
Franklin D. Roosevelt	73rd–79th	372	263	635	9
Harry Truman	79th–82nd	180	70	250	12
Dwight Eisenhower	83rd–86th	73	108	181	2
John F. Kennedy	87th–88th	12	9	21	0
Lyndon B. Johnson	88th–90th	16	14	30	0
Richard M. Nixon	91st–93rd	26	17	43	7
Gerald Ford	93rd–94th	48	18	66	12
Jimmy Carter	95th–96th	13	18	31	2
Ronald Reagan	97th–100th	39	39	78	9
George H. W. Bush	101st–102nd	29	15	44	1
William Clinton	103rd–106th	37	1	38	2
George W. Bush	107th–110th	11	1	12	4
Barack Obama	111th–114th	12	0	12	1

U.S. Senate, "Summary of Bills Vetoed, 1789–Present," www.senate.gov/reference/Legislation/Vetoes/vetoCounts.htm.

In recent times, presidents have resorted to other means to undermine laws that stop short of an actual veto. For example, the president's distaste for a law may be so strong that even while signing the bill into law (perhaps for political reasons), the president will still express his intent to thereafter ignore the law in the form of a "signing statement." The past three decades have seen a notable surge in such signing statements (see Figure 7-1). President George W. Bush in particular heavily relied on such signing statements (over 800 times during his eight years in office); thus, for example, in signing the Detainee Treatment Act of 2005, which prohibited cruel, inhumane, and degrading treatment of detainees in U.S. custody, Bush warned that the executive branch would construe the act in a manner consistent with his own views on a president's constitutional authority. To mark a shift in this practice, on March 9, 2009, President Barack Obama announced that he only planned to use signing statements in the case of legislation that contained unconstitutional provisions. Straying a bit from that self-imposed limit, President Obama still issued more than 30 signing statements during his presidency.

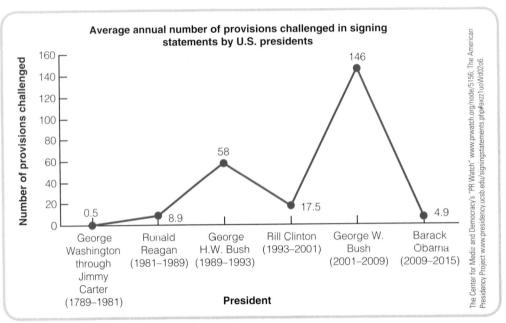

The Center for Media and Democracy's "PR Watch" www.prwatch.org/node/5156; The American Presidency Project www.presidency.ucsb.edu/signingstatements.php#axzz1uoWd02o6.

FIGURE 7-1 Signing Statements Past and Present

Commander-in-Chief

One of the defining features of the American political system is its commitment to civil control of the military, embodied in the president's status as head of the nation's armed forces. As commander-in-chief, the president is the nation's principal military leader, responsible for formulating and directing all military strategy and policy. Although the Constitution awards to Congress the formal power to "declare war," the balance of war-making power has shifted overwhelmingly from Congress to the president during the past century, as modern executives have assumed the nearly unlimited power to send troops into combat.[16] Terming it a "police action," President Harry Truman sent troops to Korea in June 1950 without even asking Congress for a formal declaration of war. In 1973, over President Nixon's veto, Congress passed the War Powers Resolution, which theoretically limits the power of the president to unilaterally commit troops to battle. Ignoring its provisions, Presidents Reagan, George H. W. Bush, and Clinton have deployed U.S. troops to invade Grenada (1983), Panama (1989), and Haiti (1994), respectively. Similarly, in February 2009 President Obama announced his plans to bolster the U.S. military presence in Afghanistan by committing over 17,000 new troops to the region. No presidents are entirely immune from public pressures in this context. After initially threatening to use military action in response to Syria's use of chemical weapons against some of its own citizens in 2013, President Obama eventually backtracked from that position in the face of a conflict-weary American public.

7-4 | Implied Powers and Responsibilities of the President

Article II of the Constitution does not specifically spell out all the powers that a president may exercise; during the past two centuries, presidents have assumed the right to exercise some "implied" or "inherent" powers not listed in the Constitution, and the Supreme Court for the most part has acceded in their right do so. These implied powers allow the president to act quickly in crisis situations, to serve as leader of his political party, and to issue executive orders and make executive agreements that do not require congressional approval.

Crisis Manager

More than any other official in government, the president is in a unique position to respond quickly and effectively to unexpected crises. Consequently, Americans look immediately to the president under such circumstances to provide assurances, comfort, and, where appropriate, a plan to address the difficulties. When a natural disaster strikes, the president will often visit the scene, meet with family members, and in many cases provide aid from the Federal Emergency Management Agency (FEMA). In the days following the September 11 attacks, George W. Bush redefined his presidency as a fight against terrorism—his visits to "Ground Zero," the site of the attacks on the World Trade Center, and his address to a joint session of Congress created indelible images in the media and won him widespread public support. President Obama continually expressed his personal resolve to tackle the nation's economic crisis up to and after his inauguration as president in 2009: Within weeks he pressed forward with a proactive economic stimulus plan in hopes that it might reassure the public that his administration was not taking a passive approach to the problem.

Party Leader

Once elected, the president of the United States assumes the position of de facto leader of his own political party. Not surprisingly, presidents are normally well attuned to how their political decisions will reflect on the party as a whole. A popular president is often expected to campaign for the party's congressional candidates and, if possible, help secure control of Congress for the party. Any assistance the president provides to congressional candidates seeking election may have an important side effect: The president may now have the leverage to demand support from those members of Congress for his own legislative programs. Similarly, the "coattail effect," by which congressional candidates and state and local officials benefit at the polls from the votes of the president's supporters, may strengthen the president's position with party members during the upcoming term.

Executive Orders and Agreements

On their own, presidents can issue **executive orders**, which are rules or regulations issued by the chief executive that have the force of law. Once thought to be an unconstitutional exercise of Congress's lawmaking power, executive orders have now become a routine feature of American government.[17] Since the beginning of the twentieth century, presidents have issued more than 13,000 executive orders regulating all manner of topics, including affirmative action, civil service, federal holidays, the classification of government documents, public land designations, and federal disaster relief. President George W. Bush issued more than 150 executive orders during his first term in office alone. On his first full day in office, Obama issued an executive order mandating that the interrogation of terrorism suspects not include torture. Since then he has issued nearly 200 executive orders, establishing federal rules on such controversial subjects as immigration, gun control, and gender discrimination by federal contractors.

Though executive orders carry the force of federal law, they are subject to judicial review and can be partially or even fully revoked by an act of Congress. FDR strategically issued executive orders to create agencies that Congress refused to establish; eventually, however, he was frustrated by the legislature's refusal to fund those agencies near the end of his presidency. Similarly, Richard Nixon's efforts to dismantle by executive order certain agencies created by his Democratic predecessors, such as the Office of Economic Opportunity, were often stymied because the courts refused to allow the elimination of an agency established with the approval of Congress.

An **executive agreement** is a pact, written or oral, reached between the president and a foreign government. As with executive orders, these agreements do not require the

executive orders Rules or regulations issued by the chief executive that have the force of law and do not require the consent of Congress.

executive agreement A pact reached between the president and a foreign government that does not require the consent of Congress.

The Supreme Court and Executive Orders

United States v. Texas (2016)

The ongoing debate over immigration reform reared its ugly head in 2014 even as the Republican-led Congress refused to take any action on the issue. As noted in the chapter's opening section, in November of 2014, President Barack Obama unilaterally issued an executive order requiring the Department of Homeland Security (DHS) to expand current immigration rules to grant quasi-legal status and work permits to up to five million people either who had entered the United States illegally as children or who themselves have children who are American citizens. Though President Obama defended the order as consistent with his executive authority, Texas and 25 other states brought suit to stop implementation of the controversial order. A Brownsville, Texas–based federal judge agreed with the state authorities, granting an injunction that the Obama administration appealed all the way up to the U.S. Supreme Court. What authority does the president have to act unilaterally on such issues?

In *United States v. Texas* (2016),[18] the U.S. Supreme Court issued a one-line opinion leaving the lower court injunction in place. The ruling offered a major setback to President Obama. Major immigration reform would have to await a future ruling on the merits of the policy, assuming a future administration would continue to stand by this shift in DHS policy.

For Critical Thinking and Discussion

1. When Congress and the president are at loggerheads over an important issue like immigration, should the U.S. Supreme Court intercede to decide the case? Or should such separation-of-powers issues be determined by the political branches themselves in the political arena?
2. Does the growth of the modern welfare state and the creation of large executive agencies like DHS give the president too much power to implement policy rules and regulations?

---

consent of Congress, although Congress does have the power to revoke them. Executive agreements have become important tools by which presidents conduct foreign affairs. FDR agreed to trade U.S. destroyers for British military bases in 1940, more than a year before the United States formally declared war on Germany, thus implicitly supporting the British military cause against Germany. In recent years, the U.S. government's military alliances with Great Britain and other countries in response to Iraqi aggression have not been spelled out in any treaties that required the advice and consent of the Senate; rather, those alliances came in the form of executive agreements between President Bush and the British government.

7-5 | Presidential Resources

More than half a century ago, Professor Richard Neustadt in his landmark book *Presidential Power and the Modern Presidents: The Politics of Leadership* (1960) defined the central problem that all presidents face from the moment they are sworn into office: How do presidents mobilize the powers of the office to work for them? The federal bureaucracy has grown so vast that presidents cannot simply "command" the bureaucracy to do their will. So what exactly can presidents do to make their will felt within the executive branch, and to carry out their choices through that "maze of personalities and institutions called the government of the United States"?

Neustadt argued that the president's most fundamental power is the "power to persuade."[19] Presidents use this power most effectively by keeping themselves informed, employing a system of information that allows them to be at the center of the decision-making apparatus, and carefully cultivating the image of a powerful president. Modern presidents have tended to emphasize certain individuals and offices under their control that play critical roles in the success of their administrations.

The Vice President

After Vice President Martin Van Buren's successful election to the White House in 1836, few vice presidents rose to the presidency by running and winning on their own accord. In fact, after Van Buren, no sitting vice president even emerged as a serious contender for the presidency until the Republicans nominated Richard Nixon, who lost to John Kennedy in 1960. And the next sitting vice president after Van Buren to be elected president was George H. W. Bush in 1988.

Next in line for succession and thus "only a heartbeat away" from the presidency, vice presidents have often been relegated to the very fringes of presidential power.[20] FDR barely communicated with John Nance Garner, who was vice president during FDR's first two terms in office. Of course, Garner did not have a very high opinion of the vice presidency either, referring to the position (in a sanitized version of his remarks) as not worth "a bucket of warm spit." When asked toward the end of his presidency what ideas Vice President Richard Nixon had offered within his own administration, President Dwight D. Eisenhower quipped: "If you give me a week, I might think of one." In fact, up through the 1950s, vice presidents maintained their principal offices on Capitol Hill near the Senate Chamber, where they occasionally performed their one clearly defined constitutional responsibility: to preside over the Senate and to cast a vote in the event of a tie.

Keiko Hiromi/Newscom

Donald Trump's selection for running mate was Republican Governor Mike Pence of Indiana.

The vice presidency, however, has undergone a transformation in recent decades. Modern-day vice presidents have assumed roles as key advisers and executive branch officials working on behalf of the president. Walter Mondale developed U.S. policy on South Africa and was one of President Jimmy Carter's most trusted advisers. Al Gore headed the National Performance Review for the Clinton administration, leading to reforms to increase the federal government's efficiency and reduce its costs. Perhaps no federal official was more influential with President George W. Bush than Vice President Dick Cheney, the driving force behind Bush's controversial decision to invade Iraq in March 2003.[21] Barack Obama's vice president, Joe Biden, was famous for his salty language and verbal gaffes; notably, Biden's declaration on one news show that he was absolutely "comfortable" with granting same-sex couples full marital rights may have been the final factor that forced President Obama to declare his own support for same-sex marriage a few days later. Biden is also credited with helping to press the administration's legislative agenda forward by personally lobbying his former Senate colleagues for votes.

Constitutionally, the vice president is first in line to succeed the president in the event of death or incapacitation. By statute, if the vice president is not available to serve, succession falls in turn to the Speaker of the House, the president pro tempore of the Senate, and then to cabinet-level officials.

The Cabinet

The Constitution specifically affords presidents the power to solicit the advice of the principal officers in each of the executive departments. Thus, in addition to running their own executive departments within the large federal bureaucracy, principal officers also serve as key advisers. Together, they form the president's **cabinet**. Today's cabinet consists of 15 heads of departments and 6 other important officials considered of "cabinet

cabinet The collection of the principal officers in each of the executive departments of the federal government who serve as key advisers to the president.

rank." In reality, such a large body of individuals with different areas of expertise can serve only limited functions for a president, and recent chief executives have convened their full cabinets to serve more as a sounding board and a communications device than as a significant instrument of policymaking. Nevertheless, in individual meetings cabinet-level officials may still provide critical input to the president on issues related to their own departments.

The Executive Office of the President and the White House Staff

Created in 1939 to bring executive branch activities under tighter control, the Executive Office of the President (EOP) and its two thousand federal employees consists of numerous agencies that assist with the management and administration of executive branch departments. Some of these agencies, such as the Office of Management and Budget, the President's Council of Economic Advisors, the National Security Council, and the Office of the U.S. Trade Representative, have near-permanent status. Other EOP agencies come and go, depending on the policy priorities of the current administration. Thus, during the height of the Cold War, the EOP included agencies that focused on preparedness and civil defense in the event of a nuclear attack.

The EOP also includes an expanded White House staff. Until 1939, this staff consisted mostly of assistant secretaries and clerks who helped the president with correspondence; the White House staff today consists of nearly six hundred employees and runs on an annual budget of almost $730 million. In charge of this bureaucracy is the **White House chief of staff**, who manages and organizes the staff to serve the president. Some modern presidents, including Ronald Reagan and George H. W. Bush, have adopted management styles that rely heavily on the chief of staff to control access to the president. Others, such as President Clinton, have utilized a "spokes-of-a-wheel" arrangement in which five or six different advisers have direct access to the president.[22] Regardless of the arrangement chosen, the White House chief of staff will have a significant hand in the success of the modern presidency. The principal duties of the White House staff include, but are not limited to, speechwriting, advance work for presidential appearances, scheduling, congressional relations, public relations, and communications.

White House chief of staff The manager of the White House staff, which serves the president's organizational needs, including speechwriting, advance work for presidential appearances, scheduling, congressional relations, public relations, and communications.

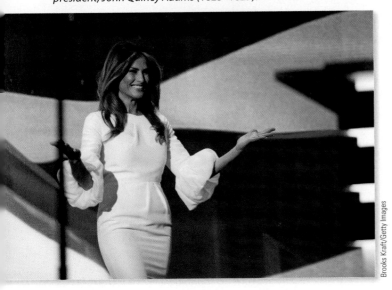

Slovenian-born, Melania Trump is the first First Lady born outside the United States since Louisa Adams, the British-born wife of the sixth president, John Quincy Adams (1825–1829).

Brooks Kraft/Getty Images

The First Lady

All but one president (James Buchanan) have been married at some point in their lifetimes, and the spouses of sitting presidents, now referred to as first ladies, have come to assume an important role in the affairs of the nation. Until recently, presidents mainly relied on their spouses to help them perform social obligations, such as hosting state dinners. Woodrow Wilson's two wives broke somewhat with this mold: his first wife, Ellen, took public positions on bills being considered for Congress and his second wife, Edith, served as an intermediary between the president and other government leaders while Wilson was recovering from a massive stroke in the fall of 1919. Eleanor Roosevelt, wife to Franklin Delano Roosevelt, charted a course for first ladies as aggressive public advocates. Mrs. Roosevelt launched one of the earliest civil rights organizations, the Southern Conference on Human Welfare; she actively supported the building of model communities; and she lobbied for refugees fleeing Nazi persecution. Occasionally, Mrs. Roosevelt even disagreed publicly with some of FDR's policies in foreign affairs.

Although no first lady after Eleanor Roosevelt was willing to so boldly challenge her husband's policies in the media, many did stake out policy areas where they could contribute, and some became active members of their husbands' administrations.[23] They have been assisted in this regard by a formal Office of the First Lady, now staffed by more than 20 aides. Rosalynn Carter lobbied Congress for mental health initiatives; Nancy Reagan became the public voice of the "Just Say No" to drugs campaign; and Barbara Bush (wife of George H. W. Bush) campaigned widely against the problem of illiteracy. A distinguished lawyer, Hillary Rodham Clinton led a task force in 1994 charged with reforming the nation's health care system; Mrs. Clinton's complex plan ultimately proved too ambitious, and it was rebuffed by Congress. In another series of unprecedented moves, Hillary Clinton ran for and won a seat in the U.S. Senate in 2000 and was reelected to the Senate in 2006; she was the front-running Democratic candidate for president in 2008, and became Secretary of State in 2009. Finally, in 2016 she rose to even greater political heights, carrying her party's mantle as the Democratic nominee for president. Unfortunately for Clinton, her quest to become the first female president in U.S. history came up just short, when she was defeated at the polls by Donald Trump on Election Day.

Although an accomplished lawyer in her own right, Michelle Obama returned the Office of the First Lady to its more common role as lobbyist for a cause, expounding on the dangers of childhood obesity. Regardless of what roles first ladies may assume, modern presidents have increasingly come to rely on their spouses as advisers on a range of issues.

7-6 | Important Presidential Relationships

The power of the president is influenced by the relationships that a president develops and cultivates with three important constituencies: the public, Congress, and the news media.

The President and the Public

Catering to the needs and demands of the public mattered little to presidents prior to 1824, when presidential nominees were chosen by congressional leaders in secret caucuses. By contrast, the presidency today is a truly public institution that depends heavily on its public popularity for political effectiveness. Modern presidential nominations and elections are won on an arduous campaign trail in which aspiring chief executives must reach out to, communicate with, and ultimately gain acceptance from large segments of the public. Once in office, presidents must remain constantly attentive to the sentiments of the public at large. FDR was the first president to rely on public opinion polls, and his administration utilized them to monitor support for his New Deal policies. Through his fireside chats, he reached into the living rooms of millions of Americans, winning their support for and confidence in his domestic and foreign policies.

Most modern presidents continuously engage the public to support administration policies, whether through the annual State of the Union address to Congress and other special televised messages, staged events, or interviews and press conferences with the media where they attempt to promote the benefits of their programs. Presidents Richard Nixon and Ronald Reagan preferred the "set piece" speech presented from the Oval Office during prime time; Presidents Jimmy Carter and Bill Clinton occasionally held "town meetings" to discuss issues in open forums with concerned citizens. In bypassing legislators and appealing directly to their constituents, modern presidents have perfected the art of what social scientist Samuel Kernell calls "going public."[24]

Some recent presidents have come under criticism for being too dependent on public opinion polls. President Clinton's critics charged that he too quickly withdrew support for some of his more controversial appointments when public opinion swung against them. Notably, President Obama's decision in May 2012 to declare his own personal support for same-sex marriage coincided with recent polls showing a bare majority's support for that right for the first time in American history. On the other hand, presidents may find themselves in even greater political trouble when they refuse to heed public opinion. President Johnson's escalation of troops in Vietnam during the late 1960s ignored growing public opposition against that war and undermined his hopes for reelection. Just as the Watergate scandal began to engulf Richard Nixon's presidency, his decision to hold press conferences less frequently only fed the impression that he was hiding from the public and fueled even more calls for his resignation. Whereas high levels of public support increase a president's chances to get legislation passed, precipitous drops in public support may stop a president's program in its tracks.

The President and Congress

The history of the American political system is marked by the ebb and flow of power between the president and Congress. For much of the nineteenth century, a form of "congressional government" prevailed, with most presidents acting as dutiful administrators of the laws passed by Congress. Buoyed by advances in communications technology that placed modern presidents at the center of American politics, presidents today play far more influential roles in the legislative process, at times even prodding Congress forward to meet their administrations' goals. Since the 1970s, the frequency of divided-party government, with the executive and the legislature controlled by opposing political parties, has placed the two branches in a near continuous battle over the nation's domestic policy agenda. Because credit for a program's success is rarely spread evenly among the two branches, tensions are inevitable and compromises often difficult to come by. President Reagan managed to get the Democrat-controlled House of Representatives to pass his program of tax decreases and spending cuts in 1981; when the economy rebounded a few years later, Reagan and the Republican Party benefited politically far more than did the Democrats. President Clinton's willingness to sign a welfare reform bill in 1996 aided him in that year's election, when he claimed to have lived up to his earlier promise to "end welfare as we know it." The Republican Congress that actually drafted and passed the welfare bill received far less credit for its accomplishments. In foreign policy, presidents continue to act nearly independent of Congress.

Presidents have many tools at their disposal to influence Congress. As party leader, the president can campaign for congressional candidates, and then leverage that assistance into support. Personal contacts by the president with members of Congress can be effective as well. The White House Office of Congressional Relations (OCR) serves as a liaison to Congress, rounding up support and monitoring events on Capitol Hill. Still, the most effective lobbying for a president's policies comes from members of Congress friendly to the administration, who persuade other members of Congress to vote in favor of the policies. The rewards for such service often come in the form of future appointments, pork-barrel projects for home districts or states, or financial support from the political party for future election bids. FDR rewarded Hugo Black, a key Senate supporter of the president's controversial 1937 plan to increase the size of the Supreme Court, with an appointment to the Court; Bill Clinton was prepared to reward Senate Majority Leader George Mitchell with the same prize in 1994 but held back because he needed Mitchell's support in Congress for a pending health care bill. (Despite Mitchell's efforts, Clinton's health care bill went down to defeat.)[25]

The President and the Media

The relationship between presidents and the media that cover their administrations is important. The media provide perhaps the most effective channel through which presidents can communicate information about their policies to the public. At the same time, the media's desire for interesting headlines to attract greater numbers of readers, listeners, viewers, and online observers leaves them to rely heavily on the executive branch for information. Effective media management has been a hallmark of the most successful modern presidents. Much of the responsibility rests with the **White House press secretary**, who plays an especially important role in briefing the press, organizing news conferences, and briefing the president on questions he may be forced to address.

President John Kennedy in June 1963, taking questions at one of his many press conferences.

White House press secretary The person on the White House staff who plays an especially important role in briefing the press, organizing news conferences, and even briefing the president on questions that may be asked.

The administration that ignores media management does so at its own peril. Social scientists Kathleen Hall Jamieson and Paul Waldman revealed how the mainstream media today do not so much report the news about presidents as create it, transforming "the raw stuff of experience into presumed fact" and "arranging facts into coherent stories" that can prove crucial to presidential success.[26] President Obama enjoyed considerable positive media coverage during his initial months in office; by contrast, after Islamic militants attacked the American diplomatic mission at Bhengazi in Libya in September of 2012, CBS and other media outlets noted possible contradictions in the Obama administration's description of the attack (i.e., was it terrorism or a spontaneous protest?), driving negative media coverage in the months that followed.

Today the president relies heavily on the White House director of communications to articulate a consistent and effective message to the public.[27] But even before that office came into being, chief executives felt the need to craft a message and hone their public images. Although known best for his fireside chats and effective public speeches, Franklin Delano Roosevelt worked hard to cultivate good relations with the media, allowing his administration to set the news agenda and influence the content of the news. Many of his press conferences included off-the-record commentary that fed the media's appetite for information, yet allowed the president to change his position as circumstances changed. John F. Kennedy perfected the modern press conference in the East Room of the White House; his colorful banter with reporters played well as sound bites on the evening television news. Ronald Reagan's reputation as the "great communicator" was enhanced by positive media coverage. His administration perfected the use of "staged" or "pseudo" events, which presented the president in a positive light—perhaps visiting flag factories or reading Shakespeare to children at elementary schools—all packaged in time for the evening newscasts. Even when scandals rocked Reagan's second term in office, his mostly friendly relations with the press paid off when they painted him as the unwitting victim of his own administration's follies.

Borrowing from Reagan's playbook, Presidents George W. Bush and Barack Obama avoided live press conferences wherever possible, preferring controlled situations that could be molded to fit their respective messages. The Bush administration attempted to cultivate the image of a president working hard for the American people—even while vacationing at his ranch in Crawford, Texas, the president was often pictured clearing brush and performing various chores, rather than simply relaxing. President Obama in particular relished hitting the road to drum up support for his policies at large pep rallies. Thus, his aides urged him to travel widely while key legislation was being debated to capitalize on those particular strengths. He was also the first president to use social

Another "Tweet" from the Commander-in-Chief: The Interactive Presidency of Barack Obama

Twitter, an online social networking service, allows every college student to follow friends, experts, celebrities, and breaking news in posts of up to 140 characters, known as "tweets." Enter the president of the United States into this modern world of communication by tweeting. The George W. Bush administration's White House website featured extensive videos and links to speeches and addresses by the 43rd president. By contrast, the Obama administration and its brand-new, state-of-the-art website at www.whitehouse.gov offers visitors the chance to stay connected to presidential events by Facebook, Flickr, and, of course, Twitter. As of April 1, 2016, the president's daily (and sometimes hourly) "tweets" were followed by more than 70 million people around the world. In fact, that same day twitaholic.com's statistical algorithm ranked President Obama as the fourth most popular Twitter user in the United States, trailing only behind entertainers Katy Perry, Justin Bieber, and Taylor Swift.

On July 6, 2011, President Obama responded live to "tweets" on health care, the economy, and other issues at the White House's first ever "Twitter Townhall."

Kevin Dietsch/UPI/Newscom

For Critical Thinking and Discussion

1. What advantages does a modern president have in his ability to communicate with a younger generation of citizens through Twitter?
2. Do you think the political views of a Twitter user affect his or her willingness to visit the White House website? Why or why not?

---

media sites like Twitter to promote legislation and support for his policies. (See the "From Your Perspective" box later in this chapter.)

Although presidents and their staff members take great care to present a positive public image through the media, the glare of the spotlight can sometimes catch off-the-cuff commentary or statements from chief executives that would have best been left unsaid. Some of the more notable gaffes spoken by recent presidents include these remarks:

- "I am not worried about the deficit. It is big enough to take care of itself."
  —President Ronald Reagan
- "My friends, we live in the greatest nation in the history of the world. I hope you'll join with me as we try to change it."
  —President Barack Obama
- "We see nothing but increasingly brighter clouds every month"
  —President Gerald Ford, describing an improving economy
- "I don't see what's wrong with giving Bobby a little experience [as attorney general] before he starts to practice law."
  —President John Kennedy, reacting to critics who argued that his brother Robert was too young to serve as attorney general

- "When I need a little free advice about Saddam Hussein, I turn to country music."
  —President George H. W. Bush, at a country music awards ceremony
- "I would have made a good pope."
  —President Richard Nixon[28]

The Constitution does not spell out all of the roles and responsibilities that have become central to the modern presidency. The office has evolved over the course of the nation's history, and much of that evolution has occurred in response to crisis situations, economic or otherwise. Unlike the Congress, the president is just one person and so can act quickly and decisively. Additionally, the president and the vice president are the only two officials elected by the entire nation—thus, the president alone can claim a mandate to act on behalf of the American people as a whole, rather than on behalf of a state, a district, or one political party. In times of crisis, citizens look to presidents for strength because they alone are in a position to provide it. For that reason more than any other, presidents only rarely have to demonstrate their continued relevance in the modern political system.

Summary

7-1 Where do Presidents Come From? Presidential Comings and Goings

- Although theoretically any American who is at least 35 years old, is a "natural-born" citizen, and has lived in the United States for 14 years is eligible to be president, the vast majority of individuals who have held the office have been older, well-educated, Caucasian Protestant men who have had prior experience in government.
- Although the House of Representatives can impeach the president for committing "High Crimes and Misdemeanors," the Senate alone has the power to actually remove the impeached president by a two-thirds vote. Only two presidents in history have ever been impeached by the House, and none was removed by the Senate.

7-2 The Evolution of the American Presidency

- The office of the president has evolved from what was principally a "chief clerk" in a federal government dominated by Congress, to a modern presidency in which a "chief executive" has come to dominate the political system. This more modern presidency began with the ascension of Theodore Roosevelt, whose strong positions in foreign and domestic policy promoted power in the executive office; it then gained unprecedented strength when FDR's New Deal policies cemented a large role for the president in the American constitutional system.
- Despite an increasingly polarized political system in which divided government and extreme partisanship are the norm, the emergence of the United States as a superpower after World War II helped to cement the role of the U.S. president as a dominant player in world and national politics. Thus, even weak contemporary presidents find themselves as the focal points of policymaking, setting the political and legislative agenda and leading American foreign and domestic policy.

7-3 Express Powers and Responsibilities of the President

• The powers of the president, as expressly stated in the Constitution, are (1) to be commander-in-chief of the armed forces, (2) to grant reprieves or pardons, (3) to "make" treaties (subject to Senate approval), and (4) to make certain appointments, including those of ambassadors and justices of the Supreme Court (again subject to Senate approval).

7-4 Implied Powers and Responsibilities of the President

• Beyond the express powers granted to the president in the Constitution, presidents today also play a key role in setting the legislative agenda, managing national and international crises, and serving as leader of their political party. The singularity of leadership in the executive branch gives presidents the power to command the attention of the nation's people, Congress, and the media, thus enhancing his ability to persuade others concerning what to do.

7-5 Presidential Resources

• The cabinet, the Executive Office of the President, and the White House staff provide large organizational support for the president to administer federal programs and agencies and lead the national government.

7-6 Important Presidential Relationships

• The president enhances his power by continually communicating with the public, maintaining a strong working relationship with congressional leaders from both parties, and cultivating a good relationship with the media through strategic management of the White House's activities.

Key Terms

cabinet (p. 193)
executive agreement (p. 191)
executive orders (p. 191)
Great Society (p. 182)
impeachment (p.176)

New Deal (p. 180)
pardon (p. 186)
power of appointment (p. 185)
reprieve (p. 186)
State of the Union address (p. 188)

Twenty-second Amendment (p. 176)
White House chief of staff (p. 194)
White House Office of Legislative Affairs (p. 188)
White House press secretary (p. 197)

Test Yourself

1. How many U.S. presidents came to the White House directly after serving in the U.S. Senate?
   a. 2
   b. 3
   c. 6
   d. 13

2. The unwritten "two-term precedent" established by George Washington was first violated by
   a. Thomas Jefferson.
   b. Theodore Roosevelt.
   c. Franklin Roosevelt.
   d. Lyndon Johnson.

3. What are the constitutional requirements that must be met to serve as president?

4. Prior to the twentieth century, most American presidents functioned as
   a. strong national leaders.
   b. agents of the federal judiciary.
   c. "chief clerks" who served Congress.
   d. military leaders.

5. Which of the following factors most influenced the development of presidential powers in the twentieth century?
   a. The increased importance of foreign policy
   b. The Twenty-second Amendment
   c. The War Powers Resolution
   d. The emergence of Congress as a major power in the federal system

6. What factors helped produce the recent "era of divisiveness" between the president and Congress?

7. The president's constitutional responsibilities regarding the military reflect the principle of
   a. the chain of command.
   b. civilian control of the military.
   c. the imperial presidency.
   d. congressional subordination to the president.

8. Which of the following presidents vetoed the most bills?
   a. Franklin Roosevelt
   c. Richard Nixon
   b. Harry Truman
   d. George W. Bush

9. Discuss the nature of the relationship between the chief executive and Congress under the Constitution.

10. The president's party is an important resource to him because the party's members in Congress are needed to
    a. work on the president's campaign.
    b. fund the president's reelection effort.
    c. help him to pressure the judiciary.
    d. support the president's legislative agenda.

11. Which of the following presidents is *not* credited with skillfully exercising executive leadership during a time of crisis?
    a. George W. Bush
    c. James Buchanan
    b. Lyndon Johnson
    d. Abraham Lincoln

12. Discuss the informal powers that modern presidents currently exercise.

13. Which of the following presidents involved the vice president in high-level decision making on a regular basis?
    a. Franklin Roosevelt
    c. Gerald Ford
    b. John F. Kennedy
    d. Jimmy Carter

14. Historically speaking, the first lady who originally charted the course for presidential spouses to serve as aggressive public advocates was
    a. Hillary Clinton.
    c. Eleanor Roosevelt.
    b. Jacqueline Kennedy.
    d. Michelle Obama.

15. How has the Executive Office of the President served the White House in modern times?

16. Which of the following is *not* a formal source of presidential power?
    a. Patronage
    c. The media
    b. The cabinet
    d. The White House staff

17. Which of the following sets of two presidents preferred the "set piece" speech as a means of communicating to the public?
    a. Carter and Clinton
    c. Bush and Obama
    b. Roosevelt and Truman
    d. Nixon and Reagan

18. Have modern presidents become too dependent on public opinion polls? Explain.

1. b. (LO 7-1); 2. c. (LO 7-1); 4. c. (LO 7-2); 5. a. (LO 7-2); 7. b. (LO 7-3); 8. a. (LO 7-3); 10. d. (LO 7-4); 11. c. (LO 7-4); 13. d. (LO 7-5); 14. c. (LO 7-5); 16. c. (LO 7-6); 17. d. (LO 7-6)

iStockphoto.com/Skyhobo

LEARNING OBJECTIVES

8-1 What Is Bureaucracy?
- Describe the bureaucracy as part of the executive branch of government organized hierarchically with standard operating procedures for doing business.
- Assess the critical role that the bureaucracy plays in the implementation of federal policy.

8-2 What Does the Federal Bureaucracy Do?
- Define *delegated authority* and apply the conditions under which such authority is granted.
- Distinguish the oversight function of Congress over the bureaucracy.
- Evaluate why Congress has provided some bureaucratic units with administrative judicatory authority.

8-3 The Development of the Federal Bureaucracy
- Describe how the federal bureaucracy has evolved over time, including substantial growth spurts as a result of the New Deal and Great Society programs and the Cold War.

8-4 Getting Control of the Growing Bureaucracy
- Explain methods for attempting to control or reduce the size and scope of the federal bureaucracy through privatization, devolution, deregulation, and accountability.

8-5 The Organization of the Federal Bureaucracy
- Distinguish between the different types of agencies in the federal bureaucracy.

8-6 The Federal Workforce
- Describe the large scope of the federal workforce and the civil service rules governing federal employment.

8

The Federal Bureaucracy

Bureaucracy is a term that usually conjures up negative images. It often refers to overgrown government, excessive rules and paperwork, or a burdensome process for getting something done. Political candidates often extol the vices of "the unresponsive, fat bureaucracy" to strike a sympathetic chord with voters.[1] Despite the negative connotations of the term, bureaucracy is necessary for any government to function. Laws must be enforced, programs must be administered, and regulations must be implemented. Without a federal bureaucracy, the government could not function. To be sure, there are many problems with bureaucracy. It is often hard to get things done in an efficient manner, or to fire workers who do not perform well, or to reward deserving workers. The buck often passes from one desk to another, and silly or irrelevant rules sometimes dictate the actions of the bureaucrats. Despite its problems and the "bad rep" that the term often conjures up, bureaucracy is absolutely essential for any government to implement and carry out its laws and public policies.[2] New presidents quickly learn that to accomplish their policy goals, they must rely on the federal bureaucracy. They frequently are elected to office and claim a mandate to get things done. Getting things done not only requires the passage of laws, but also needs a bureaucracy to carry out those new laws.

A Career Working for the Federal Government

More than two million Americans work for the civilian (nonmilitary) federal bureaucracy. It is the single largest employer in the country. When most people think of federal workers, they think about those who work for an agency in the Washington, D.C., area. Yet while many do hold federal jobs in that area, the vast majority (about 85 percent) are spread throughout the 50 states.

You might be considering a career for yourself in the federal government after you graduate from college. About half of all jobs in the federal bureaucracy require a college degree; by contrast, most jobs outside of the federal government do not require such a degree. Many of those students interested in public service take college courses in political science, public administration, and public policy as they prepare for a potential career working for a federal department or agency.

The average federal employee earns about $80,000 annually, and 91 percent of federal positions are white-collar jobs. Federal workers tend to come from diverse backgrounds (18 percent are African American, 8 percent Hispanic, 6 percent Asian, and 2 percent Native American). The tenure of an employee in the bureaucracy is almost 15 years, which makes those jobs much more secure than most jobs in the private sector.

- What about you? Have you considered the federal government as a potential employer?
- What do you think are the advantages and disadvantages of working for Uncle Sam?
- Do you think your American Government class is helping you prepare for a job in the federal government?

To see how your answers compare to others, take the **Who Are You?** poll in MindTap!

8-1 | What Is Bureaucracy?

bureaucracy An organization set up in a logical and rational manner for the purpose of accomplishing specific functions.

A **bureaucracy** is an organization set up in a logical and rational manner for the purpose of accomplishing specific functions. Sociologist Max Weber (pronounced VAY-ber), an early student of bureaucratic organizations, identified six characteristics of effective bureaucracies[3]:

1. **Bureaucracies are organized on the basis of specialization, expertise, and division of labor.** The organization is divided into subunits based on function, and subunits are staffed by employees who are qualified to administer those tasks.

2. **They are organized in a hierarchical manner with an identifiable "chain of command" from top to bottom.**

3. **A common set of rules for carrying out functions characterizes the operation.** These rules are often referred to as standard operating procedures (SOPs). Employees are trained to know and use these SOPs so that functions are performed smoothly and consistently.

4. **Bureaucracies maintain good records, or a "paper trail," of actions taken and decisions made.** Good record maintenance enables periodic review, efficiency of operation, and proof of action.

5. **Bureaucracies are characterized by an air of professionalism on the part of employees.**

6. **The hiring and promotion process within effective bureaucracies is characterized by merit-based criteria and is insulated from "politics."**

Bureaucracies are created within many types of organizations. Organizations typically exist to carry out a function, or set of functions. Bureaucracies are what actually carry out these functions. Large private companies typically have bureaucracies that divide labor functions into categories or departments such as sales, accounting, human resources (HR), management information systems (MISs), and other divisions. Colleges

204 **CHAPTER 8** THE FEDERAL BUREAUCRACY

and universities have bureaucracies that usually include an admissions department, a registrar's office, an academic counseling center, an athletics department, and so on. Even small organizations such as physicians' offices feature a bureaucracy that includes medical support staff (e.g., nurses), a front-office staff (receptionist and secretary), and business offices (accountant and medical insurance specialist).

Governments maintain bureaucracies to carry out specific functions, and the federal government is no exception. As with political parties, there is no reference to the bureaucracy in the U.S. Constitution. But like parties, the federal bureaucracy is arguably one of the most important features of the American political system because Americans have come to depend on it for many important things, such as the defense of U.S. interests around the world, protection against terrorist attacks, cleaning up of the destruction caused by natural disasters, a financial safety net for those who are unemployed or retired, the maintenance and expansion of the nation's roads and airways, and research for cures to such health problems as heart disease, cancer, and AIDS. In American government, the federal bureaucracy has traditionally come under the authority and jurisdiction of the president and the executive branch. As we will see, however, the modern federal bureaucracy is a complex set of agencies and organizations, parts of which are accountable to the legislative and judicial branches as well.

Citizens are more likely to come into direct contact with the bureaucracy than any other part of government, and so for many Americans the bureaucracy comes to symbolize what government is. A visit to an unemployment office to register for unemployment benefits, a check in the mail from the Social Security Administration, a trip to the Department of Motor Vehicles to renew a driver's license, or a visit to the website of the Consumer Protection Agency to inquire about the safety of a child's car seat—these are just a few of the many ways citizens interact with the bureaucracy.

The federal bureaucracy, in fact, is a huge set of organizations that is expected to serve many different functions. As shown in Figure 8-1, it includes numerous departments, offices, agencies, bureaus, councils, foundations, commissions, boards, services, and authorities. Each of these units, as Weber's analysis of bureaucracies suggests, specializes in an area of public policy, is hierarchically organized to carry out its particular duties, conducts its operation on the basis of a set of standard operating procedures, maintains records of its actions and decisions, is trained to carry out functions in a professional manner, and engages in hiring practices that are based on merit. The vast size and level of responsibility that these units have make the federal bureaucracy a complex and often confusing system to study.

8-2 | What Does the Federal Bureaucracy Do?

Most of the federal bureaucracy is contained within the executive branch of government, and ultimately reports to the president of the United States.[4] Article II of the Constitution states that "the executive Power shall be vested in a President of the United States of America." The executive power, or the power to carry out, administer, and enforce specific laws, then, falls mainly under the purview of presidential responsibility. The president uses the federal bureaucracy to exercise executive authority.

Policy Implementation

The full range of activities in which the federal bureaucracy engages is known as **policy implementation**. Policy implementation is the process of carrying out a law. Laws that are passed by Congress often include the development of new or modification of existing federal programs or services. In order to carry out the specific programs or services outlined in a law, the federal bureaucracy is assigned the task of implementation. For example, in 1935 Congress passed the Social Security Act to provide older Americans

policy implementation The process of carrying out laws, and the specific programs or services outlined in those laws.

Branches

1. LEGISLATIVE BRANCH	2. EXECUTIVE BRANCH	3. JUDICIAL BRANCH

Legislative Branch

Architect of the Capitol
Congressional Budget Office (CBO)
Congressional Research Service
General Accounting Office (GAO)
Government Printing Office (GPO)
Library of Congress
Stennis Center for Public Service

Executive Office of the President
The First Lady
The President
The Vice President
The White House Home Page
Offices within the Executive Office of the President

Judicial Branch

Administrative Office of the United States Courts
Federal Judicial Center
U.S. Sentencing Commission

Cabinet Departments

Department of Agriculture (USDA)
Department of Commerce (DOC)
Department of Defense (DOD)
Department of Education (ED)
Department of Energy (DOE)
Department of Health and Human Services (HHS)

Department of Homeland Security (DHS)
Department of Housing and Urban Development (HUD)
Department of the Interior (DOI)
Department of Justice (DOJ)
Department of Labor (DOL)

Department of the State (DOS)
Department of Transportation (DOT)
Department of the Treasury
Department of Veterans Affairs (VA)

Independent Agencies, Regulatory Agencies, and Government Corporations

Advisory Council on Historic Preservation
African Development Foundation
Bureau of Consumer Financial Protection
Central Intelligence Agency (CIA)
Commission on Civil Rights
Commodity Futures Trading Commission
Consumer Financial Protection Bureau (CFPB)
Consumer Product Safety Commission (CPSC)
Corporation for National and Community Service
Defense Nuclear Facilities Safety Board
Election Assistance Commission
Environmental Protection Agency (EPA)
Equal Employment Opportunity Commission (EEOC)
Export-Import Bank of the United States
Farm Credit Administration
Federal Communications Commission (FCC)
Federal Deposit Insurance Corporation (FDIC)
Federal Election Commission (FEC)
Federal Housing Finance Board
Federal Labor Relations Authority
Federal Maritime Commission
Federal Mediation and Conciliation Service
Federal Mine Safety and Health Review Commission
Federal Reserve System
Federal Retirement Thrift Investment Board
Federal Trade Commission (FTC)
General Services Administration (GSA)
Institute of Museum and Library Services
Inter-American Foundation
International Broadcasting Bureau (IBB)
Merit Systems Protection Board
National Aeronautics and Space Administration (NASA)
National Archives and Records Administration (NARA)

National Capitol Planning Commission
National Council on Disability
National Credit Union Administration (NCUA)
National Endowment for the Arts
National Endowment for the Humanities
National Labor Relations Board (NLRB)
National Mediation Board
National Railroad Passenger Corporation (AMTRAK)
National Science Foundation (NSF)
National Transportation Safety Board
Nuclear Regulatory Commission (NRC)
Occupational Safety and Health Review Commission
Office of Compliance
Office of Government Ethics
Office of National Counterintelligence Executive
Office of Personnel Management
Office of Special Counsel
Overseas Private Investment Corporation
Panama Canal Commission
Peace Corps
Pension Benefit Guaranty Corporation
Postal Rate Commission
Railroad Retirement Board
Securities and Exchange Commission (SEC)
Selective Service System
Small Business Administration (SBA)
Social Security Administration (SSA)
Tennessee Valley Authority
Trade and Development Agency
United States Agency for International Development
United States International Trade Commission
United States Postal Service (USPS)

FIGURE 8-1 The Organization of the Federal Bureaucracy

with a stable source of income during their retirement years and to offer support for the children of deceased workers. The act created the Social Security Administration as the agency in the federal government that had the authority to carry out the provisions of the act. Today, the Social Security Administration remains the unit in the federal bureaucracy responsible for maintaining records and authorizing benefits to those eligible for Social Security payments.

Implementation of a law requires translating the congressional legislation into action. Bureaucratic units begin the process of implementation by developing **regulations**, or sets of rules that guide employees of the agency in carrying out its programs or services. These rules are supported by the force of law. The Social Security Administration, for example, has written a detailed set of regulations defining who is and who is not eligible for Social Security retirement benefits. The rules include a schedule for the amount of monthly payment benefit based on a person's age, the number of years he or she contributed to the Social Security system while working, and other criteria. Regulations are useful not only because they translate laws into actions, but, because they are written down and are usually very specific, they also provide a basis for employees in the bureaucracy to consistently apply them from one case to the next.

> **regulations** Rules or other directives issued by government agencies.

Once an agency drafts a set of regulations to implement a program, the regulations are published in the *Federal Register*. This federal government publication is widely accessible to elected leaders, interest groups, corporations, the media, and regular citizens. The agencies authoring the regulations have an open period where they accept comments on the proposed rules and decide whether to redraft based on the commentary they receive. If the agency refuses to redraft based on an objection, the objector can ask Congress to require the agency to modify the regulations; or the objector might take the matter to court on the basis that the agency was acting outside of Congress's intentions in the law.

> *Federal Register* The journal that publishes regulations that implement federal programs.

Bureaucratic Legislation

The types of laws passed by Congress are many and varied, and thus policy implementation encompasses many different bureaucratic activities. Some laws are very vague and offer agencies very little guidance about implementation. Other laws can be very specific in directing the agency on how to implement them. When laws are vague, agencies are said to have **administrative discretion**, which gives them considerable freedom in deciding how to implement the laws. Vague laws require an agency to spend more time and effort in developing regulations.

Two policy areas where congressional legislation tends to be vague and where agencies have much latitude in making rules and regulations are environmental quality and workplace safety. Important pieces of legislation, such as the Clean Air Act and the Occupational Safety and Health Act, have given agencies such as the Environmental Protection Agency (EPA) and Occupational Safety and Health Administration (OSHA) much discretion in setting specific standards for car emissions, pollution, and workplace safety standards. This discretion usually is the product of at least one of two conditions. First, Congress often does not have the technical expertise to define how to achieve clean air or workplace safety, and so it gives agencies that have such technical capabilities the discretion to set standards. Second, Congress sometimes chooses not to deal with politically difficult issues such as how to clean up toxic-waste dumps, and so it shifts the responsibility to the bureaucracy, forcing an agency to resolve the problem. When an agency makes an unpopular decision as a result of Congress's "passing the buck," the agency's action contributes further to the negative image of bureaucracies.

> **administrative discretion** The freedom of agencies to decide how to implement a vague or ambiguous law passed by Congress.

When Congress writes vague legislation and thus transfers legislative authority to an agency, it gives that agency the effective power to make laws, a constitutional power that is supposed to rest with the Congress alone. When Congress does this, it is said to have **delegated congressional power**. Laws that relate to the authority of administrative

> **delegated congressional power** Congress's transferring of its lawmaking authority to the executive branch of government.

administrative law A law that relates to the authority of administrative agencies and the rules promulgated by those agencies.

agencies and the rules promulgated by those agencies are referred to as **administrative law**. Congress has delegated considerable legislative authority to the EPA and OSHA to craft both environmental and workplace safety laws. Similarly, Congress has delegated a substantial amount of authority to the Federal Reserve to manage the nation's economy. The "Fed" has the power to adjust the prime interest rate in response to economic conditions to encourage investments and ward off inflation.

Delegation of power from Congress to bureaucratic agencies is not, however, typically open-ended. Congress may cede lawmaking authority to the bureaucracy, but it does not relinquish all power. **Congressional oversight** is the term used to describe Congress's regular monitoring of bureaucratic agency performance for the purpose of achieving accountability. Although the vast bulk of bureaucratic agencies ultimately report to the president as chief executive, Congress, through its oversight function, commands a significant amount of accountability from executive agencies.[5]

congressional oversight Congress's exercise of its authority to monitor the activities of agencies and administrators.

If Congress is not satisfied with an agency's performance, it has a variety of means to coerce change: it can reduce or eliminate an agency's budget; it can refuse to confirm presidential appointments to that agency; it can eliminate the agency; it can conduct investigations into the activities and performance of the agency; or it can establish a new agency and shift resources and powers to it. This strong system of checks often renders the federal bureaucracy just as (if not more) responsive to Congress as to the president.

Specific congressional oversight functions may be carried out in a number of ways. Particular committees (or subcommittees) in Congress hold hearings, on either a regularly scheduled or an ad hoc basis, to review agency performance. For example, the House Armed Services Committee meets with the secretary of defense and Joint Chiefs of Staff to review Pentagon programs. The Senate Environment and Public Works Committee holds regular meetings with the administrator of the EPA to review that agency's activities. The House Science and Technology Committee reviews the activities of the National Aeronautics and Space Administration (NASA). In addition, the House Appropriations Committee is divided into a number of subcommittees, each of which regularly reviews pending authorizations for funding individual agencies. These subcommittees often scrutinize agency spending.

Two bureaucratic agencies under the direct control of Congress (rather than the president) that support the oversight function of congressional committees are the Congressional Budget Office (CBO) and the Government Accountability Office (GAO). These offices compile data on federal programs and are staffed with program review and accounting professionals who comply with members' and committees' requests for information on agency performance and cost. Congress uses the GAO to investigate the actions or inactions of an agency, and it uses the CBO to conduct research, such as program effectiveness studies.

Bureaucratic Adjudication

bureaucratic adjudicating Determining the rights and duties of particular parties within the scope of an agency's rules or regulations.

Just as policy implementation sometimes includes the writing of legislation, it also may involve **bureaucratic adjudicating**, or determining the rights and duties of particular parties within the scope of an agency's rules or regulations. Such adjudication might include ruling on whether an individual is eligible to receive Social Security payments or whether a company has violated an air pollution rule. Most adjudication takes place in the court system. However Congress, which has the authority to create federal adjudicating agencies, has placed judicial power in some bureaucratic agencies as well. For example, the Equal Employment Opportunity Commission (EEOC) has the authority to adjudicate cases where an individual or group of individuals charges that a company has violated federal laws preventing discrimination in hiring or promotion practices in the workplace. The EEOC can try a case against a company, and if the finding is that the company violated federal law, the EEOC is authorized to prescribe a punishment or corrective action.

The EEOC and other agencies such as the EPA, the National Labor Relations Board, and the Federal Communications Commission (FCC) employ the personnel, procedures, and case law more typically seen in the judicial branch. Bureaucratic judicial personnel and powers include administrative judges, appellate courts within the agency, and administrative hearings that resemble a trial. Ultimately, any administrative court decision may be appealed to the federal court system because the power of adjudication ultimately rests in the hands of the judicial branch. In reality, however, federal courts routinely uphold cases appealed from administrative courts.

8-3 | The Development of the Federal Bureaucracy

The executive branch of government during the first four years of George Washington's presidency was very limited. Congress created just three departments to aid the first president in executing the law: the Department of State to oversee foreign affairs, the Department of Treasury to oversee fiscal affairs, and the Department of War to oversee military affairs. Washington selected and the Senate confirmed Thomas Jefferson, Alexander Hamilton, and Henry Knox to lead these departments, respectively. Shortly after these departments were created, the president was authorized to hire an attorney general and a postmaster general. During the first year of the Washington administration, the federal bureaucracy employed only about 50 individuals.

As the role of government expanded, and as the United States added new territories, there was a need to expand the size of the federal bureaucracy. Military operations, such as those conducted during the War of 1812, required increased support services and agencies to support military operations. Westward expansion brought with it the need for federal services to settle the new areas. A centralized national bank required federal agencies to centralize the economic and monetary system. By the mid-1800s, Congress saw the need to create a new cabinet department, the Department of the Interior, to manage federally owned lands and to aid in the westward expansion of the nation. The important role of farming in the nation's growth and development led to the establishment of the Department of Agriculture in 1862 to support and promote farming and farm-product commercialization. The Department of Justice was established in 1870 to aid the attorney general in the post–Civil War era in prosecuting violators of federal law and representing the federal government in the courts.

In 1884, a Bureau of Labor was created to address the concerns of the labor force that arose with the growth of the industrial economy. Large-scale industrialization and economic development led to the development of a Commerce Agency in 1888 to help regulate interstate and foreign trade. These agencies were elevated to cabinet status in the early 1900s to reflect the growing role they played in the federal government. The Great Depression set the stage for the election of Franklin Delano Roosevelt (FDR) in 1932. The FDR administration advocated an activist role for the federal government in responding to the economic crisis. Consequently, FDR's New Deal created a myriad of new federal agencies to deal with the nation's fiscal woes, including the Social Security Administration, the Securities and Exchange Commission, the Civilian Conservation Corps, and a host of public works programs to provide jobs for the large number of unemployed. In 1936, Roosevelt established the Brownlow Committee (named for its chair Louis Brownlow) to investigate how to make the growing bureaucracy more efficient and more responsive to the president.[6] The committee unanimously agreed that the president's power should be enhanced to give the president greater authority as manager of the bureaucracy. The Brownlow Committee's recommendations led to the consolidation of presidential authority over the bureaucracy.

By 1940, the federal government accounted for 10 percent of the nation's gross domestic product (GDP), with $9.5 billion spent on federal programs, including the employment of about 700,000 Americans in the federal bureaucracy. The increased role of government led to greater demands for federal services, which in turn necessitated growth in the federal bureaucracy. Between 1940 and 1975, the federal bureaucracy experienced

Many of the federal bureaucracy's "alphabet soup" agencies were created as New Deal programs during the administration of President Franklin Delano Roosevelt. Pictured above are workers at one such agency, the Tennessee Valley Authority, assembling a new power generator at the Cherokee Dam on the Holston River in east Tennessee.

an unprecedented growth spurt. During this period, the number of federal employees more than tripled to 2.2 million, the federal budget increased to $332 billion, and the federal budget as a percentage of GDP reached 22 percent.[7]

Two factors accounted for this massive growth in the bureaucracy. First was President Lyndon B. Johnson's Great Society program of the 1960s. The Great Society encompassed numerous new laws aimed at social and economic improvements to American society through a highly activist role of the federal government. The post–World War II prosperity of the American economy allowed Johnson to convince a Democratic Congress that programs promoting social justice, a safety net for the impoverished, improvements to urban life, health care for the elderly, and greater access to educational opportunities should be guaranteed to all Americans and funded by the great wealth of the American economy. These programs had a large influence on growth of the bureaucracy through the 1970s.

A second factor contributing to the massive growth in the bureaucracy was the Cold War. World War II resulted in two superpowers, the United States and the Soviet Union, vying against each other for global influence. From 1945 to 1991, these superpowers developed expensive nuclear and other war technologies in search of military superiority. The federal budget for defense programs grew dramatically, as did the programs to support intelligence operations and aid to foreign nations for diplomatic purposes.

8-4 | Getting Control of the Growing Bureaucracy

During the mid- to late 1970s, the American economy began to slump. Whereas the prosperity of the 1960s facilitated the creation of a larger-size government to accomplish a number of policy goals, the sluggish economy of the late 1970s was unable to support the by now very large federal bureaucracy. Federal budget deficits began to accumulate, and the United States could no longer afford the huge federal bureaucracy that it had created. During this period critics of the massive federal bureaucracy pointed to many programs that, at least on the surface, appeared to represent wasteful spending (see Table 8.1).

Ronald Reagan was elected president in 1980 with an agenda to scale back the federal bureaucracy. The Reagan administration targeted domestic programs to achieve the reduction in government. Since the 1980s, various administrations have attempted to reduce the size of the federal bureaucracy. The methods they have used include the following:

privatization The process of replacing government-provided services with services provided by the private sector.

Privatization. **Privatization** means replacing government-provided services with services provided by the private sector. The theory of privatization is that if private companies compete to provide services, the cost of those services will be less than if government provides

TABLE 8.1 The "Golden Fleece" Awards

Stories of waste in bureaucratic spending always become fodder for calls to cut federal spending and eliminate unnecessary federal programs. Much of this "wasteful" spending is rooted in congressional pork-barrel spending, that is, spending on projects that benefit individual members' home districts. Perhaps no one took better aim at wasteful pork-barrel spending in the federal bureaucracy than U.S. Senator William Proxmire (D-WI). In 1975, Proxmire began what he called the "Golden Fleece Awards" to target bureaucratic agencies that spent money on wasteful programs. Proxmire announced 150 awards in all. Asked to identify the top 10 most egregious spending wastes, Proxmire provided the following list:

- **Tequila fish.** The National Institute on Alcohol Abuse and Alcoholism for spending millions of dollars to find out if drunken fish are more aggressive than sober fish, if young rats are more likely than old rats to consume alcohol in order to reduce anxiety, and if rats can be turned into alcoholics.

- **The Great Wall of Bedford.** The U.S. Department of Commerce for spending $20,000 to build an eight-hundred-foot limestone replica of the Great Wall of China in Bedford, Indiana.

- **Buying Worcestershire sauce.** The Department of the Army for spending $6,000 to prepare a 17-page document that told the federal government how to buy a bottle of Worcestershire sauce.

- **The New Jersey Sewer Museum.** The Environmental Protection Agency for spending $1 million to preserve a Trenton, New Jersey, sewer as a historical monument.

- **Lessons in watching TV.** The Office of Education for spending $220,000 to develop a curriculum to teach college students how to watch television.

- **Tennis cheating.** The National Endowment for the Humanities for a $25,000 grant to study why people cheat and act rudely on tennis courts in Virginia.

- **Tailhook.** The Department of the Navy for using 64 planes to fly 1,334 officers to the Hilton Hotel in Las Vegas for a reunion of the Tailhook Association.

- **$2 million patrol car.** The Law Enforcement Assistance Administration for spending $2 million on a prototype police car that was never completed.

- **Basketball therapy.** The Health Care Financing Administration for Medicaid payments to psychiatrists for unscheduled meetings with patients who were attending basketball games, which cost the federal government between $40 million and $80 million.

- **Surfing subsidy.** The Department of Commerce for giving the Honolulu city government $28,000 to study how to spend $250,000 for a good surfing beach.

Based on data from Taxpayers for Common Sense, found at www.taxpayer.net

those services directly. Additionally, some contend that private corporations can more flexibly adapt to changing circumstances because they are not weighed down by civil service restrictions and government red tape. Accordingly, a number of federal programs were privatized during the 1980s. For example, the U.S. Department of Labor frequently provided job-training services to the unemployed during the 1960s and 1970s. Federal laws passed in the 1980s eliminated much of the federal management of job training and contracted out these services to private companies. More recently, the federal government has used a number of private contractors, including Halliburton (the company once run by former Vice President Dick Cheney) to help rebuild Iraq after the second Persian Gulf War, under the idea that the costs would be even greater if the federal government played a more direct role.

Deregulation. The development of rules and regulations to achieve a policy goal requires units in the bureaucracy to ensure that such rules and regulations are followed. **Deregulation**, that is, eliminating government oversight and regulation of certain activities,

deregulation The elimination of government oversight and government regulation of certain activities.

results in less government to do the regulating. Prior to the mid-1970s, the trucking and railroad industries, long-distance telephone service, prices for air flights, and the activities of savings and loan institutions were regulated by the federal government. Deregulation of these and other activities resulted in the abolition of a number of federal agencies, including the Civil Aeronautics Board and eventually the Interstate Commerce Commission.

Devolution. A central question in our federal system of government is which level of government—national or state—should have the authority to provide programs and services to citizens. The New Deal and Great Society programs gave the national government increased responsibility and authority for such services. In response to extensive growth of the national government, the 1980s witnessed a **devolution** of power and responsibility back to the states, mainly to shrink the size of the national government. For example, welfare reform in the mid-1990s shifted much responsibility for welfare from the federal to the state governments.

devolution The transfer of power and responsibilities for certain regulatory programs from the federal government back to the states.

"Reinventing government." When Bill Clinton was elected president in 1992, he promised to "reinvent government." This promise translated into an eight-year effort to promote bureaucratic accountability. The Clinton administration instituted mechanisms such as customer satisfaction research with those who received federal services and freedom-of-information policies that gave the public and the news media access to government documents to help promote accountability. In addition, the Government Performance and Results Act, passed in 1997, required that agencies establish goals and set out a plan for achieving those goals. In the book *Reinventing Government*, David Osborne and Ted Gaebler describe how bureaucracy and other aspects of the public sector in the United States have undergone a transformation.[8] They contend that the "entrepreneurial spirit" brought to bear on government performance, which includes market-driven and business-oriented planning, has improved the effectiveness and efficiency of bureaucracy at all levels of government.

In addition to implementing these strategies for reducing the size of the federal bureaucracy, the Cold War, which concluded in 1991 with the collapse of the Soviet Union, put an end to escalating defense budgets to support the arms race with the Soviets.

The end of the Cold War and the implementation of strategies that contain, if not reduce, the size of the federal bureaucracy do appear to have reversed the decades-long trend toward increasing the size of government. Between 1990 and 2000, the number of civilian employees in the federal government declined by about 500,000,[9] and the percentage of the GDP accounted for by federal spending dropped from 21.9 percent to 18.2 percent. Despite these efforts, however, federal spending on the bureaucracy continues to increase annually at a pace that exceeds inflation. In particular, defense spending to fight the war on terrorism and the war in Iraq in recent years has increased federal spending. Also, the Department of Homeland Security, created in response to the terrorist attacks of September 11, 2001, required increased federal dollars to protect the nation within its own borders.

More recently, the administration of President Barack Obama (with the support of congressional Democrats) ushered in a new growth spurt for the federal bureaucracy. A $787 billion federal spending plan to provide an economic stimulus along with a health care reform package and increased regulations on the financial services industry all significantly increased the scope and size of the bureaucracy. Most notably, the Obama administration championed the creation of a new Consumer Financial Protection Bureau designed to provide stricter regulations on the mortgage financing industry in particular.

8-5 | The Organization of the Federal Bureaucracy

The federal bureaucracy is made up of a variety of different types of agencies that are empowered to carry out laws and federal programs. Some of these organizations have broad authority over a public policy area, whereas others have a narrow focus;

some are empowered to implement laws and programs established by Congress, whereas others have the added responsibility of creating rules and policies, and adjudicating. Some report directly to the president, whereas others answer to both the president and Congress. Also, although most organizations in the federal bureaucracy are part of the executive branch, some are part of the legislative and judicial branches. Units of the federal bureaucracy include cabinet departments, independent agencies, regulatory agencies, government corporations, and the Executive Office of the President.

Cabinet Departments

Amid the complex web of bureaucratic units is a select set of 15 organizations called **cabinet departments**, which are the major administrative organizations of the executive branch. These departments, described in Table 8.2, vary in terms of both size and importance. The Department of Defense, for example, employs nearly 1 million civilian workers and another 1.5 million military personnel. By contrast, the Department of Education has only about 5,000 employees.

At the head of each cabinet department is a secretary (with the exception of the Justice Department, which is headed by the attorney general) who reports directly to the president. Along with a few other high-level presidential advisers and the vice president, these secretaries compose the president's cabinet, a set of high-level administrators who report directly to the president. Cabinet heads and their deputies are nominated by the president and must be confirmed by the Senate. Typically, a secretary shares the same views as the president on policy matters and often is a loyal political supporter (if not close friend) of the chief executive. The *inner cabinet* is a term used to describe the secretaries of the most important departments in the cabinet—State, Defense, Treasury, and Justice. Whereas the cabinet once served as the president's primary advisory panel, the growth in the Executive Office of the President, discussed later in this chapter, has shifted primary advisory responsibilities to that office.

Cabinet departments (sometimes referred to as executive departments) generally have a broad scope of authority over a particular policy area, such as the nation's military (the Department of Defense), federal law enforcement (the Department of Justice), the federal road and highway system (the Department of Transportation), and protection of the nation from terrorism and response to emergency situations (Department of Homeland Security). The scope of activities in any one department tends to be so broad that most departments are best viewed as a collection of many different agencies and sub agencies, each with a narrower policy focus.

The U.S. Department of Labor, for example, is charged with promoting the American labor force and the interests of labor. It is organized into a large array of agencies and offices, each of which focuses on a particular aspect of labor issues. The Occupational Safety and Health Administration (OSHA) develops standards to promote safe workplace environments, and implements regulations to ensure that employers live up to these standards. The Bureau of Labor Statistics is responsible for compiling data on the labor force on a regular basis. The Office of Labor-Management Standards sets policies for the conduct of negotiations between employers and employees.

Likewise, the U.S. Department of Defense manages the armed forces and is organized into a number of subunits, including the U.S. Army, Navy, Air Force, and National Guard. The hierarchical organization of departments facilitates the bureaucratic goals of area specialization, division of labor, and chain of command.

Although the head of a cabinet department advises and reports directly to the president, only Congress has the authority to create a new department or eliminate an existing one. The power to define the scope, authority, and, indeed, the very existence of a specific major department in the federal bureaucracy is an important "check" that Congress exercises over the president.

cabinet departments Those federal agencies that qualify as the major administrative organizations of the executive branch.

TABLE 8.2 The Cabinet Departments

Department of State

The Department of State has been the leading U.S. foreign affairs agency since 1789, and the Secretary of State is the president's principal foreign policy adviser. The State Department engages in the following activities: it leads in the coordination and development of U.S. foreign policy; it manages the foreign affairs budget and other foreign affairs resources; it represents the United States abroad, conveying U.S. foreign policy to foreign governments and international organizations through U.S. embassies and consulates in foreign countries and diplomatic missions to international organizations; and it negotiates agreements and treaties on issues ranging from trade to nuclear weapons.

Department of Treasury

The Treasury Department, also established in 1789, is entrusted with a broad range of duties and functions. It is responsible for paying all the bills of the federal government, collecting federal taxes, borrowing money for the federal government, printing money, and overseeing the operations of national banks. In addition to these monetary functions, the Department of the Treasury also oversees critical functions in enforcement and economic policy development. The Internal Revenue Service and the U.S. Mint are part of the Treasury Department.

Department of Defense

Called the Department of War when it was established in 1789, the Department of Defense currently employs nearly one million civilians, far more than any other agency in the federal bureaucracy. Most of these employees work at military bases around the United States. In 1947, the separate Departments of the Army, Navy, Air Force, Marines, and Coast Guard were reorganized into the new Department of Defense to achieve greater efficiency and coordination. In addition to its large civilian workforce, the Department of Defense is responsible for 1.5 million active-duty military personnel and another 1.2 million in the National Guard and Reserve.

Department of Justice

The Office of Attorney General was created in 1789 as an adviser to the president, and in 1870 was elevated to cabinet-department status as the Department of Justice (DOJ). The role of the DOJ is to prevent and control crime, to punish those who are guilty of unlawful behavior, to enforce the nation's immigration laws, and to administer the justice system. The DOJ employs U.S. attorneys who prosecute offenders and represent the U.S. government in court. It also oversees the Federal Bureau of Investigation, the Drug Enforcement Administration, the Bureau of Prisons, and the United States Marshals Service, which protects the federal judiciary, apprehends fugitives, and detains people in federal custody.

Department of the Interior

The Department of the Interior (DOI), created in 1849, is responsible for maintaining and managing federally owned land, which includes about 20 percent of the nation's landmass. It maintains 900 dams and reservoirs that provide water to more than 30 million Americans. The department also handles federal relations with Native American tribes. Located within the department, the Bureau of Indian Affairs manages nearly 60 million acres of land held in trust by the United States. Finally, the DOI manages the national park system, which includes 388 parks and 540 wildlife refuges.

Department of Agriculture

The U.S. Department of Agriculture (USDA) was created in 1862 by Congress at the request of President Abraham Lincoln. At the time, nearly half of all U.S. workers were employed in farming. The USDA originally was created to provide farmers with seeds and information for improving farm production and services. Today, the USDA runs the school lunch, school breakfast, and food stamp programs; brings housing, telecommunications, and safe drinking water to rural farmland areas; is responsible for the safety of meat, poultry, and egg products; and provides research on farm technologies and safe food-handling practices.

Department of Commerce

The U.S. Department of Commerce and Labor was created in 1903 and was renamed the Department of Commerce (DOC) in 1913. Today, the DOC provides comprehensive statistical analysis of economic conditions in the United States, manages patent and trademark protection programs, and is responsible for conducting the U.S. Census. The department also provides grants to economically distressed areas for business and job development, promotes exports of U.S. manufactured goods, promotes the growth of minority-owned businesses, and runs the National Oceanic and Atmospheric Administration, which forecasts weather and environmental conditions.

TABLE 8.2 *(Continued)*

Department of Labor

The Department of Labor was a bureau within the U.S. Department of Commerce and Labor and became a cabinet-level department in 1913. Its mission is to promote the welfare of the job seekers, wage earners, and retirees of the United States by improving their working conditions, advancing their opportunities for profitable employment, protecting their retirement and health care benefits, helping employers find workers, strengthening free collective bargaining, and tracking changes in employment, prices, and other national economic measurements. The department administers a variety of federal labor laws, including those that guarantee workers' rights to safe and healthful working conditions; a minimum hourly wage and overtime pay; freedom from employment discrimination; unemployment insurance; and other income support.

Department of Housing and Urban Development

The Department of Housing and Urban Development (HUD), created in 1965, is the federal department primarily responsible for dealing with the nation's housing needs. It administers programs that help cities and communities develop and rehabilitate. Many of HUD's activities focus on the nation's urban areas, providing housing assistance and public housing projects in many cities.

Department of Transportation

The Department of Transportation (DOT), established in 1966, sets federal transportation policy and works with state and local governments along with private-sector partners to promote a safe, secure, efficient, and interconnected national transportation system of roads, railways, pipelines, airways, and seaways. The DOT is responsible for managing more than a dozen agencies, including the Federal Aviation Administration, the Federal Highway Administration, the National Highway Traffic Safety Administration, and the Federal Railroad Administration.

Department of Energy

The Department of Energy (DOE) was created in 1978 in response to an energy crisis spawned by a reduction in Middle East oil production. Today the DOE helps protect national security by applying advanced science and nuclear technology to the nation's defense, manages programs to promote diverse energy sources, and is responsible for disposal of the nation's high-level radioactive waste.

Department of Education

The U.S. Department of Education, created in 1978, was originally one part of the Department of Health, Education, and Welfare. The department is responsible for administering a variety of federal programs supporting aid to local public schools and college tuition loan programs. The Office of Civil Rights within this department is responsible for administering Title IX of the Education Amendments of 1972 to the Civil Rights Act of 1964, which requires that educational institutions receiving federal funds maintain policies, practices, and programs that do not discriminate on the basis of sex. In accordance with Title IX, colleges must provide the same opportunities for sports-team participation by women as they do for men.

Department of Health and Human Services

Created in 1978, the Department of Health and Human Services (HHS) administers more than three hundred federal programs, covering a wide range of health and human services topics. These programs focus on medical and social science research, prevention of infectious disease outbreaks, immunization services, food and drug safety, financial assistance and services for low-income families, maternal and infant health, prevention of child abuse and domestic violence, substance abuse treatment and prevention, services for older Americans such as home-delivered meals, and comprehensive health services for Native Americans. HHS has the largest of the cabinet department budgets, over $1 trillion for 2017.

Department of Veterans Affairs

This department, created in 1988, is charged with overseeing programs that promote the interest and general welfare of veterans of the U.S. military. The department operates the Veterans Health Administration and the Veterans Benefits Administration.

Department of Homeland Security

Created in 2002, the Department of Homeland Security (DHS) is the newest of the cabinet departments. It was created in response to the terrorist attacks of September 11, 2001. The department's main role is to protect the nation against further terrorist attacks within the nation's borders.

Special situations, and particularly crises, have led the U.S. government to create cabinet-level departments to deal with large-scale national problems. The creation of the Department of Defense in 1947, for example, was in response to large and costly inefficiencies in military operations during World War II. The Department of Energy was established in 1977 in response to the severe energy crisis and gasoline shortage that plagued the country during the 1970s. President Reagan successfully pressed for the creation of a Veterans Affairs Department in 1988 in order to promote his administration's appreciation of those who served in the U.S. military. The newest cabinet department is the Department of Homeland Security (DHS), established in 2002.

The Department of Homeland Security

The terrorist attacks of September 11, 2001, led to President George W. Bush's request to Congress to create the new department. At first, Bush resisted calls for another large unit in the federal bureaucracy. But given strong support in Congress and in the public for a unit to be in charge of the nation's security, he soon became an advocate of its creation. The DHS represents a reorganization of 22 existing federal agencies into one cabinet department. The reorganization was intended to improve the coordination and operations of these agencies in protecting the nation against threats to the homeland.

The primary areas of the DHS are the following:

- **Border and transportation security.** This includes the U.S. Customs Service (previously part of the U.S. Department of Treasury) and the former Immigration and Naturalization Service (previously part of the U.S. Department of Justice).
- **Emergency preparedness and response.** This includes the Federal Emergency Management Agency, formerly an independent agency, and the National Domestic Preparedness Office (previously in the Federal Bureau of Investigation).
- **Science and technology.** This includes a variety of scientific research offices formerly part of the U.S. Departments of Energy, Defense, and Agriculture.
- **Information analysis and infrastructure protection.** This includes the Federal Incident Computer Response Center, which was previously part of the General Services Administration, and the National Incident Protection Center (formerly in the Federal Bureau of Investigation).
- **The Secret Service**, which was previously in the Treasury Department.
- **The U.S. Coast Guard.**

In addition to maintaining the authority to carry out many of the nation's laws, the cabinet also plays a symbolic role in the political system. Many interest groups provide input to the president through leaders in the cabinet, and the voices of community and business leaders are often heard first by cabinet-department officials. As the highest-level units in the bureaucracy, cabinet departments theoretically represent the most important policy areas. Increasingly, presidents have used their cabinet secretary appointments to demonstrate diversity in government. For nearly two centuries, cabinet secretaries were almost exclusively white men, but over the last 25 years presidents have used race and gender as factors influencing their appointments. President Clinton made history by naming women to the inner cabinet for the first time: Janet Reno as attorney general in 1993 and Madeleine Albright as secretary of state in 1997. President George W. Bush then made history by appointing the first African American to the inner cabinet—Colin Powell as secretary of state in 2001,

President Obama appointed a number of Hispanics to leadership positions in the federal bureaucracy. In 2014, he appointed San Antonio Mayor Julian Castro (pictured below) as Secretary of Housing and Urban Development. That same year, Thomas Perez was appointed as Labor Secretary, Maria Contreras-Sweet as head of the Small Business Administration, and Katherine Archuleta as the director of the Office of Personnel Management. This marked the first time that four Latinos/Latinas occupied cabinet-rank positions in a single administration.

Creating New Agencies to Tackle Chronic Problems

Although public skepticism of big government is an ongoing reality, officials charged with tackling big problems invariably turn to new bureaucracies for answers.

Then

Consider the economic crisis that emerged at the end of the "roaring 1920s." American industry flourished in the six years prior to the 1929 stock market crash. The Dow Jones Industrial index grew by a factor of five over that period, luring Americans to the stock market with unprecedented returns on their investments. And invest they did. Few considered what they were actually risking in buying shares in companies that could just as easily fail as succeed. All of this blind risk taking came to a halt on October 24, 1929, when the six-year-old stock bubble burst. On that day alone, the Dow Jones Industrial index suffered an 11 percent decline; through July 1932 the market suffered an 89 percent slide, gutting the savings of hundreds of thousands of Americans. Although a handful of elite investors avoided that fate by capitalizing on insider information, many thousands of less fortunate investors were left to wonder what happened to their money. In response, Congress passed the Securities Act of 1933 and empowered it a year later when it established the Securities and Exchange Commission (SEC). Movie mogul and steel industry executive Joseph P. Kennedy was one of few Americans who escaped the stock market crash unscathed thanks to insider information and friends in high places. Who better than him to prevent other "insiders" like himself from manipulating the future market? Under the leadership of Kennedy, future father of the 35th president, the SEC promulgated new rules governing the disclosure of information affecting the sale and trade of stocks. Thereafter, issuers of securities would be forced to fully disclose all the information that a potential shareholder might need to help make up his or her mind about the investment, thus protecting consumers from deceptive corporate practices. A new bureaucratic agency, the SEC, now stood front and center in implementing this new way of life on Wall Street.

Joseph P. Kennedy, the first chairman of the Securities and Exchange Commission.

Now

As the dark cloud of recession cast a shadow over the American economy in 2007 and 2008, millions of homeowners suddenly found themselves unable to afford their mortgage payments. The housing market had experienced high growth in the decade leading up to this recession as low interest rates, high levels of employment, and federal policies supporting the issuance of subprime loans lured Americans eager to take part in the American dream of homeownership. With the high demand for housing, property values skyrocketed and homeowners took pride in their suddenly lucrative investments. Financial institutions also cashed in on the booming real estate market by closing on new loans and selling those loans off in the form of market-based securities. Unfortunately, the race for profits led some financial institutions to engage in lending practices that caused unwitting consumers to sign up for risky loans they could not afford over the long run. These so-called predatory lending practices included forgoing proper background checks on loan applicants and "qualifying" homebuyers at artificially low initial interest rates, which over time ballooned to much higher rates. When the economy slowed, millions of new homeowners found themselves out of work and holding mortgage payments far higher than what they initially paid. By 2010, a record 2.87 million homes in the United States were in foreclosure. In response, Congress passed the Dodd-Frank Financial Reform Act, which, among other measures, created the Bureau of Consumer Financial Protection (BCFP). The BCFP was charged with establishing new rules for loan-making practices and enforcing those rules to ensure that consumers didn't fall prey to predatory lending practices. Eighty years after the stock market crash kicked off the Great Depression, a new administration had once again retooled the federal bureaucracy to safeguard consumers. For better or worse, new ideas and programs often demand new bureaucracies to put those laws into practice.

Richard Cordray, the first chairman of the Consumer Financial Protection Board.

For Critical Thinking and Discussion

1. Do you think that the BCFP and the SEC "solved" the problems of the Great Recession and Great Depression, or were they an overreach of government's authority?
2. The BCFP remains a controversial agency today. Should Congress reconsider its existence or should it reaffirm its authority?

NASA/Getty Images

NASA is an independent agency with a highly trained technical and scientific staff. Pictured above is the NASA control room in Houston, Texas.

and then an African American woman, Condoleezza Rice, as Powell's replacement in 2005; he also appointed the first Hispanic to the inner cabinet when he named Alberto Gonzales as the nation's attorney general during his second term in office. President Obama's cabinet was also diverse: it featured prominent positions for nine women (Secretary of State Hillary Clinton, Secretaries of Health and Human Services Kathleen Sebelius and Sylvia Burwell, Secretary of Homeland Security Janet Napolitano, Secretary of Labor Hilda Solis, Secretary of Commerce Penny Pritzker, Secretary of the Interior Sally Jewell, and Attorney General Loretta Lynch). The Obama cabinet also included several Latinos and two African Americans.

Independent Agencies

independent agency A department that focuses on a narrower set of issues than do higher-status cabinet departments.

A number of units in the federal bureaucracy do not have the high status of a cabinet department but do report directly to the president. Whereas cabinet departments tend to concentrate on broad areas, such as labor, energy, defense, or education, these **independent agencies**, which are not part of any executive cabinet department, tend to focus on a narrower scope of issues. NASA, for example, focuses on the U.S. space program, while the Small Business Administration concentrates on low-cost loans and support to encourage the development of small businesses. Independent agencies tend to be smaller than cabinet departments. The heads of these agencies are appointed by and report to the president.

Regulatory Agencies

regulatory agency A government body responsible for the control and supervision of a specified activity or area of public interest.

Regulatory agencies are responsible for implementing rules and regulations with respect to individual or corporate conduct related to some aspect of the economy. Such agencies are supposed to be staffed by nonpartisan individuals who are entrusted to make sound decisions that promote fairness and weed out corrupt practices on fiscal matters. To accomplish this, regulatory agencies (unlike cabinet departments and independent agencies) are not under the direct control of the president. They are created by Congress and are run by independent boards or commissions that are not supposed to exert partisan influence.

The first regulatory agency was the Interstate Commerce Commission (ICC), created by Congress in 1887.[10] As with the creation of most regulatory agencies, the ICC was the federal government's response to widespread corruption. In the case of the ICC, the target was corruption in the railroad industry, which led to the high cost of railroad transportation. The ICC's scope of responsibility extended to regulation of commerce via not only railroad, but also pipeline, barge, automobile, and aircraft. The ICC established a complex set of rates for both passenger and freight transportation via the various modes of transport. ICC rules were intended to guarantee that transportation companies pay a fair fee on the value of property they used in carrying out their services. Congress abolished the ICC in 1995 because it determined that the agency was overregulating and thus stymieing growth in certain business sectors.

Today's federal bureaucracy includes a number of important regulatory agencies:

- **The Federal Trade Commission (FTC).** The FTC was established in 1914 and has the authority to develop and implement rules and regulations to encourage competition in industry. Over the years, the FTC has played an instrumental role in preventing price-fixing policies of corporations.

The Diversity Dilemma

Diversity in the Bureaucracy

Every president has the opportunity to increase the diversity of executive branch personnel, including his or her own presidential cabinet. The demographic diversity of these high-level appointees has slowly increased over time; during his two terms in office, President Obama made the most headway of all on this issue. Specifically, Barack Obama's cabinet featured increased representation from women (35.3 percent), African Americans (14.4 percent), Latinos (8.5 percent), and Asian Americans (4.6 percent).[11] The Obama administration "established specific programs to boost diversity among all executive branch appointees," which included utilizing campus recruitment programs to target candidates at minority-serving universities, as well as seeking out referrals from community leaders, including those working with LGBT and those with disabilities.[12] The leading national diversity organizations worked with their communities to supply each recent administration with the résumés of the best and brightest in their ranks, such as the National Hispanic Leadership Agenda and its Latino Appointments Program (see nationalhispanicleadership.org/latino-appointment-program to find out more).

President Obama leading a meeting with his cabinet in the White House.

For Critical Thinking and Discussion

1. What impact will an increasingly diverse federal bureaucracy have on government policies? How will an increasingly diverse cabinet affect policymaking? Is a more diverse workforce likely to engage in more open and inclusive decision making?
2. Do you have any interest in serving in the bureaucracy, and, if so, why? What experience or particular viewpoint would you bring to the federal government?

- **The Federal Communications Commission (FCC).** The FCC was established in 1934 with the authority to regulate radio, television, and interstate telephone companies. Unlike newspapers, which are not regulated, radio and TV stations use public airwaves, making them subject to regulations developed and administered by the FCC.

The Federal Reserve, chaired by Janet Yellen (above) since February 2014, is a regulatory agency that sets monetary policy.

J. M. Eddins, Jr./A.CT/Alamy

- **The Securities and Exchange Commission (SEC).** The SEC is responsible for rule making with respect to the stock market and corporate bookkeeping practices. It was created in 1934 in response to the stock market crash of 1929.
- **The Equal Employment Opportunity Commission (EEOC).** Created by Congress to help administer the Civil Rights Acts of 1964, the EEOC is charged with investigating violations of the act.
- **The Environmental Protection Agency (EPA).** The EPA was created in response to the environmental protection movement of the 1960s and 1970s. Concerns about air and water quality, as well as hazardous-waste materials, led Congress to pass a number of important laws that addressed antipollution measures and empowered the EPA (in 1970) to implement environmental regulations. The EPA is the largest of the regulatory agencies.
- **The Consumer Product Safety Commission (CPSC).** Consumer advocacy was another movement that gained steam in the 1960s and 1970s. Efforts to make manufacturers produce products that were safer for consumers were an important feature of that movement. The CPSC was created in 1972 to protect the public against risks associated with consumer products.

Government Corporations

government corporations Units in the federal bureaucracy set up to run like private companies that depend on revenue from citizens to provide their services.

A small number of units in the federal bureaucracy are set up to run like private companies even though they serve an important public purpose. These are called **government corporations**. The idea behind a government corporation is that there is a market of customers who are willing to pay individually for the services provided by the corporation. The revenue on which the government corporation relies comes primarily from citizens paying for the service provided by the corporation. Unlike private corporations, government has a special interest in the solvency of government corporations because they serve an important public purpose. Consequently, when the revenue of a government corporation falls short of meeting expenses, government often will intervene to keep the unit in business.

The most widely known and used government corporation is the U.S. Postal Service (USPS), which employs nearly one million workers. The primary source of funds for the USPS comes from the sale of U.S. postage stamps. Similar to a private business, the USPS has a product to offer (mail delivery) and charges a fee (the cost of postage) for use of that service.

Another government corporation is the Tennessee Valley Authority (TVA), which serves the power needs of seven states in the Tennessee Valley and operates the system for navigation and flood control of the Tennessee River. Users of TVA's generated power pay for service, as do those who navigate on the Tennessee River. Another well-known government corporation is Amtrak, a railroad service operated by the National Railroad Passenger Corporation. Amtrak maintains more than 20,000 miles of track and operates 500 stations across the nation. Its revenue is largely derived from the sale of passenger tickets; however, in recent years low ridership has forced Congress to subsidize Amtrak from the general revenue fund.

The Executive Office of the President

Executive Office of the President The staffers who help the president of the United States manage the rest of the federal bureaucracy.

The president of the United States has an office staff that reports directly to the president, provides advice and counsel, and helps the president manage the rest of the federal bureaucracy. The **Executive Office of the President** is managed by the White House Chief of Staff and includes a Communications Office, a press secretary, a Council of

Economic Advisors (to provide advice and management of the bureaucratic agencies responsible to the economy), a National Security Council (to provide advice on foreign and military affairs), an Office of Management and Budget (to coordinate and provide data on the national budget), a White House Counsel (to provide legal advice to the president), an Office of Science and Technology, an Office of the U.S. Trade Representative, and an Office of National Drug Control Policy, among others.

8-6 | The Federal Workforce

The federal bureaucracy encompasses an immense workforce. Currently it employs nearly three million civilian personnel, 85 percent of whom work outside of Washington, D.C.[13] In addition, there are about 1.3 million active-duty U.S. military personnel. Although the federal government remains the single largest employer in the United States, Figure 8-2 shows that the total number of federal employees has actually declined over the past half-decade, despite the fact that the total population has nearly doubled (from 179 million to 320 million).

Political Appointees and Career Professionals

About 8,000 members of the federal workforce are presidential appointees, some of whom must be confirmed by the Senate. Those requiring Senate confirmation include cabinet secretaries and the attorney general, heads of independent agencies, ambassadors, U.S. attorneys, and other high-level officers who have administrative responsibility. When a president's term of office expires, the new president generally fills these positions with new appointees. Presidential appointees are frequently referred to as "political" appointees because the job often represents a political reward for past service to the president or the president's political party.

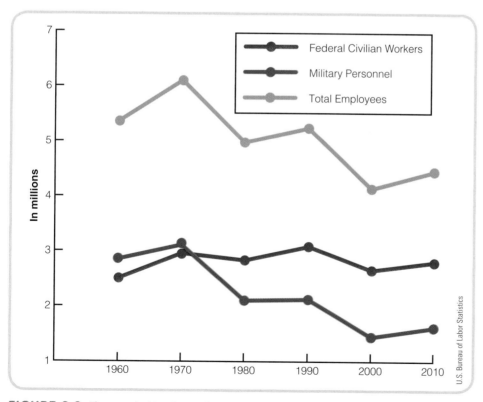

FIGURE 8-2 Changes in Numbers of Federal Workers, Civilian and Military 1960–2010

Senior Executive Service (SES) Since the late 1970s, a defined group of approximately 7,500 career professionals in the federal bureaucracy who provide continuity in the operations of the bureaucracy from one presidential administration to the next.

Another 7,500 civilian federal employees are part of what is called the **Senior Executive Service (SES)**. These are senior officers in the federal bureaucracy who are career professionals. Those in the SES do not leave their positions when a new president takes office but work closely with presidential appointees and provide continuity in the operations of the federal bureaucracy from one presidential administration to the next. Congress established the SES in the late 1970s as a means of providing this continuity in leadership. Congress also spelled out a nonpartisan process for hiring SES officers based on educational background, work experience, and other qualifications.

Presidential appointees are largely selected to reflect the political orientation of the president, and senior executives are selected primarily to find highly qualified career professionals who will maintain stability in the operations of the bureaucracy. Together, these groups of employees provide leadership and senior management of the units in the federal bureaucracy.

The Civil Service

civil service The system whereby workers in the federal bureaucracy are supposed to be immune from partisan political maneuvering.

The vast majority of the federal bureaucracy workforce is known as the **civil service**. Today's civil service includes approximately three million federal workers. This workforce is highly diverse, with 43 percent women and 28 percent racial/ethnic minority employees. Although many of these workers are located in Washington, D.C., the vast majority (90 percent) work outside of the federal Capitol.[14] Similar to the SES, civil service workers in the federal bureaucracy are theoretically hired for their position based on their qualifications and remain employees beyond the term of a particular president. Thus, they are supposed to be immune from partisan political maneuvering. Civil service jobs were not always insulated from partisan politics, as they are today. To understand the rules and processes for employment in the federal bureaucracy, it is useful to examine how employment in the federal workforce has changed over the years.

During the early years of the American republic, continuous recruitment of well-educated, upper-middle-class men characterized the development of the federal bureaucracy. Presidents Washington, Adams, and Jefferson hired political, business, and social elites to carry out the activities of the federal bureaucracy. With the exception of top posts in government such as cabinet secretaries, those in federal jobs usually remained from one presidential administration to the next. This tradition ensured an able and effective federal workforce, albeit a nondiverse one.

President Andrew Jackson, elected to office in 1828, undertook a massive restructuring of the federal workforce. Jackson ran for the presidency as a populist advocating for the interests of the "common man." Upon taking office, he chose to remove individuals in the bureaucracy who were not at all "common" and who found themselves politically at odds with the new president. Resistance among many in the bureaucracy to follow Jackson's orders, along with the president's own desire to see that the bureaucracy more closely reflected the demographics of American society, led Jackson to undertake a major overhaul of the bureaucratic workforce.

spoils system The postelection practice of rewarding loyal supporters of the winning candidates and party with appointive public offices.

patronage The act of appointing people to government positions in return for their partisan and/or political support.

Jackson replaced the long-term, upper-middle-class bureaucrats with political supporters and friends who came from many walks of life. This **spoils system** of hiring federal workers quickly became a steadfast American tradition. To the victors of presidential elections went the spoils of jobs in the federal government. Under this system of **patronage**, campaigning, political party activities, and governing became intertwined. Political parties enticed people to work on political campaigns by promising the payoff of a good federal job with an electoral victory. Often, those who were given a job were expected to return a percentage of their salary to the political party—a very clever fund-raising strategy. Strength of partisan support became the key criterion for landing and maintaining a good job.

Needless to say, this system of hiring workers produced a number of problems. Because qualifications to do the job were not important in the hiring decision, the bureaucracy became inefficient. Bureaucrats were more concerned about campaigning and supporting the political party than they were about doing their job. Further, the bureaucracy lacked any sort of continuity—for when the partisan control of the presidency changed hands, federal workers were fired en masse and replaced by a new set of underqualified political appointees.

By the time of the Civil War, the spoils system was entrenched and the bureaucracy was thoroughly corrupt. A civil service reform movement arose in the post-Civil War era, advocating an end to the spoils system and the development of a "professionalized" bureaucracy. Strong resistance from the political party bosses stalled the reform movement's agenda. But the 1881 assassination of President James Garfield by a disgruntled party worker who did not receive the federal job he thought he deserved gave strength to the movement. In 1883, Congress passed the **Pendleton Civil Service Reform Act**, which did the following:[15]

- It created a **merit system** for hiring many federal workers based on qualifications for the job, including educational background, related job experience, and performance on civil service tests.
- It prevented employees from losing their federal jobs when the presidency changed hands.
- It set up a Civil Service Commission to oversee federal hiring and firing practices.

Pendleton Civil Service Reform Act The 1883 law that created a merit system for hiring many federal workers, protected them from being fired for partisan reasons, and set up a Civil Service Commission to oversee the hiring and firing process.

merit system A system of appointing and promoting civil service personnel based on merit rather than political affiliation or loyalty.

Initially, the Pendleton Act applied only to a limited portion of the federal workforce, but it provided the basis for Progressive Era reformers of the early 1900s to develop a more professional bureaucracy through additional reform legislation. Today job qualifications in federal hiring and federal worker immunity from patronage are firmly rooted in the federal bureaucracy's employment practices. These principles now apply to more than 90 percent of federal workers.

The Hatch Act of 1939 further insulated the civil service from partisan politics by (1) prohibiting the dismissal of an employee for partisan reasons (with the exception of certain high-level political appointments) and (2) prohibiting federal workers from running for office or actively campaigning for a political candidate. In the early 1990s, revisions to the Hatch Act relaxed some of the more stringent requirements of the law and allowed federal workers more flexibility in engaging in political activities. Those in the civil service can now participate in campaigns outside of their work hours, contribute money to a candidate or party, express partisan opinions, and wear campaign buttons, among other activities. However, under the current law, federal workers still cannot be candidates in a partisan election or use their official position to raise money or influence votes.

The **Civil Service Reform Act of 1978** replaced the Civil Service Commission with the Office of Personnel Management (OPM) and the Merit Systems Protection Board (MSPB). The OPM and MSPB, bureaucratic agencies themselves, manage the civil service system today. Their functions include administering the system of federal hiring, protecting the rights of federal employees, conducting hearings and deciding cases where there are charges of wrongdoing in hiring and firing of employees, evaluating the effectiveness of federal hiring and retention practices, and regulating the ways in which federal workers can participate in politics.

Civil Service Reform Act of 1978 The federal act that replaced the Civil Service Commission (the agency that oversaw federal hiring and firing practices) with the Office of Personnel Management (OPM) and the Merit Systems Protection Board (MSPB).

The federal bureaucracy has grown dramatically, particularly since the New Deal era of the 1930s. As new presidents seek to advance new policy goals, federal departments and agencies have been created and expanded. These agencies have aided presidents in accomplishing new feats and bringing the United States to world "superpower" status. These include Lincoln's efforts to withstand the secession of the Southern states and preserve the Union, Theodore Roosevelt's drive to tame the corporate monopolies, Franklin Delano Roosevelt's priming of the federal workforce to tackle the Great Depression, and Barack Obama's attempt to jumpstart the economy through a major

From Your Perspective

You, Your Parents, and the Dreaded FAFSA Form

You have probably seen it. Your parents or legal guardians have seen it. Most of your college friends have seen it too. It is the dreaded "FAFSA" (Free Application for Student Aid) form. The joy and satisfaction of getting accepted into college are often met with the red tape and complexity of applying for student financial aid. The FAFSA form must be filled out by all students applying for federal support to offset the increasingly high costs of college tuition. Most states and colleges also require the FAFSA to help make their own decisions about a student's financial need and thus the aid that may be required. The U.S. Department of Education begins accepting FAFSA applications on January 1 for eligibility during the school year that begins the following fall. FAFSA requires documentation for a myriad of financial information about college students and their legal guardians. If you have never seen the form, either because your parents have done the legwork for you or because you haven't applied for financial aid, take a look at it at on the web at www.fafsa.ed.gov.

Financial planners and other consultants have built an industry out of aiding college students and their families in their efforts to navigate the cumbersome FAFSA form.

The detailed financial information that FAFSA requires is not always handy—gathering that information can be an especially time-consuming and aggravating task. However, the goal of FAFSA remains a laudable one: to fairly and equitably distribute aid to college students based on documented financial need. Still, the challenge of filling out FAFSA and meeting all its requirements can offer a rude awakening indeed to prospective and returning students who have never before confronted the federal bureaucracy in all its glory.

For Critical Thinking and Discussion

1. What do you think about the FAFSA form? Is it too cumbersome or tedious?
2. Is the federal government transforming a simple process into one that is too complex to be effective? Or do you believe this form of red tape is necessary to ensure that colleges and universities can make fair decisions about financial aid for the nation's college students?

FAFSA — U.S. DEPARTMENT OF EDUCATION FEDERAL STUDENT AID

FREE APPLICATION FOR FEDERAL STUDENT AID
July 1, 2011 – June 30, 2012

START HERE GO FURTHER FEDERAL STUDENT AID

Use this form to apply free for federal and state student grants, work-study and loans.

Or apply free online at
www.fafsa.gov.

Applying by the Deadlines

For federal aid, submit your application as early as possible, but no earlier than January 1, 2011. We must receive your application no later than June 30, 2012. Your college must have your correct, complete information by your last day of enrollment in the 2011-2012 school year.

For state or college aid, the deadline may be as early as January 2011. See the table to the right for state deadlines. You may also need to complete additional forms.

Check with your high school guidance counselor or a financial aid administrator at your college about state and college sources of student aid and deadlines.

If you are filing close to one of these deadlines, we recommend you file online at **www.fafsa.gov**. This is the fastest and easiest way to apply for aid.

Using Your Tax Return

If you are supposed to file a 2010 federal income tax return, we recommend that you complete it before filling out this form. If you have not yet completed your 2010 tax return, you can still submit your FAFSA using best estimates. After you submit your tax return, correct any income or tax information that is different from what you initially submitted on your FAFSA.

Filling Out the FAFSA

If you or your family has unusual circumstances that might affect your financial situation (such as loss of employment), complete this form to the extent you can, then submit it as instructed and consult with the financial aid office at the college you plan to attend.

APPLICATION DEADLINES
Federal Deadline - June 30, 2012
State Aid Deadlines - See below.

Check with your financial aid administrator for these states and territories:

AL, AS *, AZ, CO, FM *, GA, GU *, HI *, MH *, MP *, NC, NE, NM, NV *, PR, PW *, SD *, TX, UT, VA *, VI *, VT *, WA, WI and WY *.

Pay attention to the symbols that may be listed after your state deadline.

AK	AK Education Grant - April 15, 2011 (date received)
	AK Performance Scholarship - June 30, 2011 (date received)
AR	Academic Challenge - June 1, 2011 (date received)
	Workforce Grant - Contact the financial aid office.
	Higher Education Opportunity Grant - June 1, 2011 (date received)
CA	Initial awards - March 2, 2011 + *
	Additional community college awards - September 2, 2011 (date postmarked) + *
CT	February 15, 2011 (date received) # *
DC	June 30, 2011 (date received by state) # *
DE	April 15, 2011 (date received)
FL	May 15, 2011 (date processed)
IA	July 1, 2011 (date received); earlier priority deadlines may exist for certain programs.
ID	Opportunity Grant - March 1, 2011 (date received) # *
IL	As soon as possible after January 1, 2011. Awards made until funds are depleted.
IN	March 10, 2011 (date received)
KS	April 1, 2011 (date received) # *
KY	As soon as possible after January 1, 2011. Awards made until funds are depleted.
LA	June 30, 2012 (July 1, 2011 recommended)
MA	May 1, 2011 (date received) #
MD	March 1, 2011 (date received)
ME	May 1, 2011
MI	March 1, 2011 (date received)
MN	30 days after term starts (date received)

STATE AID D

FAFSA form

stimulus spending plan. Over the centuries, presidents, with the support of the American people, have used the bureaucracy to accomplish important policy goals. The bureaucracy has also served as the "whipping boy" in rhetorical campaigns for political office. In many instances, the bureaucracy has earned its reputation as wasteful, inefficient, and bloated. But without the federal bureaucracy, the most important national initiatives could not have been realized. Even those presidents who campaigned on a platform to cut the bureaucracy ended up using it to advance important initiatives. The federal bureaucracy is an easy target of criticism, yet there is no denying the fact that it has contributed as much to the development of the American political system as any other part of the political system.

Summary

8-1 What is Bureaucracy?

- Although the term *bureaucracy* often conjures up negative images, the government could not function effectively without bureaucratic organizations.
- Most units in the vast federal bureaucracy are located within the executive branch of government, and most engage primarily in policy implementation. Such implementation begins with the development of regulations that guide employees of the agency in carrying out particular programs or services.

8-2 What Does the Federal Bureaucracy Do?

- Because Congress lacks technical expertise, it often gives agencies wide administrative discretion to decide how to implement laws. Sometimes Congress also delegates important programs to agencies because it wants to avoid thorny political issues.
- Congressional oversight of executive agencies may occur through legislative hearings or through the use of congressional agencies such as the CBO and GAO. Congress may threaten poorly performing agencies with reduced funding, a refusal to confirm appointments to the agency, or (in some extreme cases) the elimination of the agency altogether.
- Congress has placed judicial power in some bureaucratic agencies to help determine the rights and duties of parties within the scope of an agency's authority.

8-3 The Development of the Federal Bureaucracy

- The size of the federal bureaucracy exploded as the federal government played an increasingly active role in regulating the U.S. economy, overseeing new territories, and conducting overseas military operations. After FDR's New Deal was enacted during the 1930s, the federal government accounted for a sizeable portion of the nation's economy as a whole. The bureaucracy continued to expand in the 1960s and beyond to meet the needs of President Lyndon Johnson's Great Society program and to compete with the Soviet Union in the Cold War.

8-4 Getting Control of the Growing Bureaucracy

- Beginning in the 1980s, some administrations attempted to reduce the size of the federal bureaucracy through (1) the privatization of certain government-provided services, (2) the deregulation of some federal activities, (3) the devolution of various powers and responsibilities back to the states, and (4) efforts to promote greater bureaucratic accountability through initiatives such as the Government Performance and Results Act.

8-5 The Organization of the Federal Bureaucracy

- The federal bureaucracy is organized into 15 cabinet departments, including the recently created Department of Homeland Security; numerous independent agencies that focus on a narrower scope of issues; regulatory agencies that implement rules and regulations of private conduct; government corporations; and the Executive Office of the President.

8-6 The Federal Workforce

- The federal workforce includes 8,000 presidential employees who received their positions through political patronage, a Senior Executive Service consisting of approximately 7,500 senior career professionals, and a vast number of civil service workers whose jobs are immune from partisan politics. Today, most lower-level federal workers are hired through a merit system, rather than through the spoils systems that prevailed throughout much of the nineteenth and early twentieth centuries.

Key Terms

administrative discretion (p. 207)
administrative law (p. 208)
bureaucracy (p. 204)
bureaucratic adjudicating (p. 208)
cabinet departments (p. 213)
civil service (p. 222)
Civil Service Reform Act of 1978 (p. 223)
congressional oversight (p. 208)

delegation of congressional power (p. 207)
deregulation (p. 211)
devolution (p. 212)
Executive Office of the President (p. 220)
Federal Register (p. 207)
government corporations (p. 220)
independent agency (p. 218)
merit system (p. 223)

patronage (p. 222)
Pendleton Civil Service Reform Act (p. 223)
policy implementation (p. 205)
privatization (p. 210)
regulations (p. 207)
regulatory agency (p. 218)
Senior Executive Service (SES) (p. 222)
spoils system (p. 222)

Test Yourself

1. Which of the following is *not* one of the characteristics of successful bureaucracies that were identified by Max Weber?
   a. Power is distributed across all levels of the organization.
   b. They are organized on the basis of specialization, expertise, and division of labor.
   c. They maintain good records of actions taken.
   d. There is a common set of rules for carrying out functions.

2. The vast majority of federal bureaucratic organizations may be found in which branch of government?
   a. Legislative
   b. Executive
   c. Judicial
   d. Parliament

3. Despite the negative connotations of the term *bureaucracy*, why is the federal bureaucracy essential?

4. Bureaucracies are primarily responsible for
   a. adjudication.
   b. legislation.
   c. implementation.
   d. evaluation.

5. Which of the following is the journal that publishes all of the rules and regulations promulgated by the bureaucracy?
   a. *Congressional Record*
   b. *Book of Rules*
   c. *Federal Register*
   d. *U.S. Reports*

6. The freedom of agencies to decide how to implement a vague law is known as
   a. administrative law.
   b. delegated power.
   c. bureaucratic adjudicating.
   d. administrative discretion.

7. How does Congress go about exercising its "oversight" function?

8. The first three departments in the federal bureaucracy created in George Washington's administration included the
   a. Department of Education.
   b. Department of the Treasury.
   c. Environmental Protection Agency.
   d. Department of Veterans Affairs.

9. How did FDR's New Deal contribute to the rapid growth of the federal bureaucracy?

10. The elimination of government oversight of certain activities is known as
    a. privatization.
    b. deregulation.
    c. devolution.
    d. reinventing government.

11. The transfer of power for certain programs from the federal government to state governments is known as
    a. privatization.
    b. deregulation.
    c. devolution.
    d. reinventing government.

12. What did the Government Performance and Results Act of 1997 require of bureaucratic agencies?

13. Which of the following type of units do not report directly to the president but are run by independent boards or commissions?
    a. Independent agencies
    b. Cabinet departments
    c. Regulatory agencies
    d. Government corporations

14. Which of the following is an independent agency?
    a. Justice Department
    b. Federal Trade Commission
    c. Small Business Administration
    d. Interstate Commerce Commission

15. "Secretary" is the title given to the head of what type of bureaucratic unit?
    a. Regulatory agency
    b. Independent agency
    c. Government corporation
    d. Cabinet department

16. What distinguishes a government corporation from other types of bureaucratic units?

17. Which of the following laws instituted a merit system for hiring federal employees?
    a. Pendleton Act
    c. Hatch Act
    b. Civil Service Reform Act
    d. Glidden Act

18. The spoils system is the product of which U.S. president?
    a. Thomas Jefferson
    b. Andrew Jackson
    c. George Washington
    d. John Adams

19. Why was the Senior Executive Service established?

1. a. (LO 8-1); 2. b. (LO 8-1); 4. c. (LO 8-2); 5. c. (LO 8-2); 6. d. (LO 8-2); 8. b. (LO 8-3); 10. b. (LO 8-4); 11. c. (LO 8-4); 13. c. (LO 8-5); 14. c. (LO 8-5); 15. d. (LO 8-5); 17. a. (LO 8-6); 18. b. (LO 8-6)

LEARNING OBJECTIVES

9

The Judiciary

Article III of the U.S. Constitution vests in the Supreme Court the power to decide legal cases or controversies that come before it. As one of the three primary branches of the federal government, the judiciary enjoys a special status in our constitutional system. Many scholars have suggested that courts enjoy heightened prestige over other actors in government as a result of their own conscious efforts to foster the perception that they somehow stand above the political fray. The solemn formalities that pervade so many judicial proceedings conducted by "high priests of the law"—the black robes, the prohibition of cameras in the U.S. Supreme Court, and the general reluctance of judges to seek out publicity—contribute to a mythology about courts in general and to a "cult of the robe" that carries credence with many Americans.[1] This chapter explores the nature of the federal judiciary and the specific role it plays in the U.S. political system by examining types of law and the manner in which the legal system in the United States is organized. It also explores the role state courts play in the political system and then focuses on the U.S. Supreme Court more closely, with an eye toward understanding how that court is confronting some of the great issues of the day.

Confirming the Next Supreme Court Justice

WHO ARE YOU?

By nominating Judge Merrick Garland to the Supreme Court in March of 2016, President Barack Obama inserted the high Court once again into the storm center of American politics. The president and his allies touted Garland as a supremely qualified judge whose moderate views placed him well within the mainstream of judicial decision making. Senate Republicans countered that if Garland were confirmed, the judge's views on such hot-button issues as abortion and affirmative action would alter the court's balance for years to come. In truth, both sides were right: Supreme Court justices influence the polity over the long term with their decisions. And, of course, senators have the right to carefully weigh the positives and the negatives of any nominee, even when the president's choice is not considered a so-called "extremist." If you were a U.S. senator, what factors would you consider in casting a confirmation vote for or against a Supreme Court nominee? Consider three hypothetical nominees:

NOMINEE A:

- Currently the governor of a Midwestern state
- Female, Caucasian, 62 years old
- No judicial experience whatsoever
- Born in Canada, immigrated to the United States as a child
- Attended University of Chicago Law School
- Practiced law in a private firm for 20 years
- Views on abortion and other social issues: unknown

NOMINEE B:

- Currently chief judge of the U.S. Court of Appeals in D.C.
- African American, male, 42 years old
- Over 15 years of experience as a federal judge
- Attended Yale Law School; outstanding academic record
- Grew up in a high-income, privileged suburb of Maryland

- Holds extreme views on abortion and other social issues that are ideologically consistent with the president who nominated him

NOMINEE C:

- Currently Attorney General of the United States; served for five years as a Texas trial court judge before his appointment as AG
- Hispanic male, 55 years old
- Close personal friend of the president dating back to when they were college roommates at Georgetown University
- Grew up in a lower-class neighborhood outside of Dallas
- Earned average grades at the University of Texas School of Law
- Has articulated inconsistent views on social issues; admitted publicly that he is "still formulating his views on those issues"

For Critical Thinking and Discussion

- Of the three nominees described above, which ones, if any, would you support with a confirmation vote?
- Do you think Supreme Court nominees should possess prior judicial experience? Why or why not? Does a nominee's political experience (such as service as a governor or an attorney general) make you more or less likely to cast a vote in favor of confirmation?
- How important is a candidate's academic pedigree and/or his academic record?
- Do you believe diversity should be a primary factor in the confirmation vote, or is that factor irrelevant?

Merrick Garland, the president's nominee to replace the late Supreme Court Justice Antonin Scalia, delivers remarks in the Rose Garden of the White House, March 16, 2016.

Chip Somodevilla/Getty Images

To see how your answers compare to others, take the **Who Are You?** poll in MindTap!

9-1 | Types of Law

The concept of law defies simple understanding. Although law is normally defined simply as "authoritative rules made by government," the philosopher John Locke argued that certain laws precede society and government. These natural laws are god-given, exist within human beings from the time they are born, and are intrinsic to the nature of individuals. Locke's notions of natural law (as distinguished from human-made or government-issued law) have influenced the legal systems of many nations, including the United States. Prior to the Civil War, opponents of slavery challenged its legitimacy with the claim that it ran counter to natural law. During the 1960s, civil rights advocates seeking to overhaul discriminatory practices presented similar arguments.

Still, even the foremost advocates of natural law concede that the rules imposed by sovereign governments enjoy some measure of legitimacy in most instances. Those rules and laws may be created and passed down in different ways. **Civil law** (also called "statutory law") refers to legislative codes, laws, or sets of rules that are enacted by authorized lawmaking bodies such as Congress, state and local legislatures, or any executive authority entrusted with the power to make laws.[2] **Common law** refers to judge-made laws handed down through judicial opinions, which establish slowly evolving precedents over time. Many European legal systems, such as those in France, Germany, and Italy, are characterized as primarily "civil law systems" due to their extensive reliance on detailed legislative codes. The legal system in Britain, by contrast, is recognized as mainly a common law system. The modern U.S. legal system features a combination of these two approaches: although the common law held sway for most of the nation's history, legislatures in all 50 states and Congress during the past century have replaced many traditional common law rules with detailed legislative codes on a number of important topics, including commercial law, probate law, and various aspects of criminal law. Other categories of law include the following:

civil law This term has two meanings: (1) legislative codes, laws, or sets of rules enacted by duly authorized lawmaking bodies such as Congress, state and local legislatures, or any executive authority entrusted with the power to make laws; (2) the body of noncriminal laws of a nation or state that deal with the rights of private citizens.

common law Judge-made law handed down through judicial opinions, which over time establish precedents.

- *Criminal law* is the body of rules and regulations that declare what types of conduct constitute an "offense against society" and prescribe the punishment to be imposed for those offenses. Criminal laws against murder, rape, and burglary can be found in almost any legal system. The body of noncriminal law—which includes the law of property, contracts, and other issues dealing with the private rights of citizens—is sometimes referred to as "civil law." (Be careful not to confuse references to "civil law" in this context with the "civil law" referenced earlier, which primarily concerns the enactment of statutes and codes.) Serious criminal offenses may lead to jail time; by contrast, those who violate non-criminal laws can be fined but not imprisoned. Of course, criminal law and civil law may touch on the same events—for example, a person alleged to have killed someone may be criminally prosecuted for murder and also separately sued in a "wrongful death action" for the same incident. The two sets of proceedings are distinct and separate: The former football star and television personality O. J. Simpson was acquitted of criminal murder charges brought against him by the Los Angeles County district attorney, but subsequent civil suits were successfully brought against him by the victims' families.
- *Constitutional law* is the body of rules and judicial interpretations of rules found in the fundamental law of the nation or state, such as the Constitution of the United States. Normally constitutional law is considered "supreme" and overrides any statutes or executive decisions with which it comes into conflict.
- *Administrative law* is the body of rules, regulations, orders, and decisions issued by administrative agencies of a government, such as the Federal Trade Commission, the Environmental Protection Agency, or a state department of health.

- *Public law*, a term used more by academics than practitioners, refers to the laws and rules that govern disputes and issues involving the government directly acting in its official capacity. Constitutional, administrative, and criminal laws are all subcategories of the general rubric of public law.
- *Private law* refers to all parts of the law concerned with the definition, regulation, and enforcement of rights in cases where either (1) all the parties directly implicated are private individuals (such as a divorce settlement) or (2) the government is acting like any other private citizen when it sues or is being sued. For example, when a private person crashes his car into a government mail truck, the government's lawsuit against that person is usually a matter of private law rather than public law.

Significant overlap exists among all these categories of law. Knowing something about the different types of law is useful in helping to understand courts and the functions they serve in the American political system.

9-2 | The Structure of the U.S. Legal System

Every court occupies a unique position within the larger hierarchy of state and federal courts. As a result, each court performs a variety of specific roles dictated by where it happens to be situated within the larger court structure.

State Legal Systems and State Courts

Most criminal and civil law matters in the United States first find their way into one of the 50 states' legal systems. Together, the state governments process nearly 35 million cases per year, more than 95 percent of the nation's litigation. About a third of the cases in state legal systems involve criminal matters. Each state system features its own unique characteristics and different nuances, an outgrowth of the states' different historical origins and significant population differences. Still, as shown in Figure 9-1, some common elements exist across the vast majority of, if not all, states.

FIGURE 9-1 Common Features of a State Court System

Every state maintains trial courts, which do the bulk of the work processing cases at the lower levels of the state legal system. These trial courts (often called *district courts* or *circuit courts* depending on the state or locality) may hear appeals from subordinate courts such as traffic courts; they also serve as sites for trials of more significant crimes. Thirty-nine of the 50 states have intermediate appellate courts, to which all appeals from trial courts must first be directed. All 50 states maintain at least one supreme court. (Texas and Oklahoma have separate supreme courts for criminal and civil cases.) State supreme courts (or their equivalent of a different name) generally provide the final source of appeal for each state legal system.[3] To appeal beyond the state supreme court directly to the U.S. Supreme Court, a losing party must first exhaust all the remedies available at the state level, including losing his or her case at the state system's court of final appeal. He or she must also demonstrate there is a federal question at issue, whether based on the interpretation of a federal statute or of the U.S. Constitution.

In theory, state courts must comply with pronouncements from the U.S. Supreme Court over the meaning of the federal Constitution. The reality is much more complicated.

During various periods of American history, rebellious state courts tried to evade certain Supreme Court pronouncements by distinguishing or limiting the Supreme Court ruling, and on occasion even by denying the Supreme Court's jurisdiction over the matter. The Virginia Supreme Court resisted various pronouncements of the U.S. Supreme Court in the early part of the nineteenth century; more than a century later, state courts sometimes ignored U.S. Supreme Court decisions protecting the accused. Although the Supreme Court can usually exert its will over defiant state courts, it must be willing to expend key institutional resources and prestige to do so.

Development of the Federal Court System

Article III of the Constitution establishes a Supreme Court and any "inferior courts" that Congress may wish to create. Accordingly, Congress provided at the nation's outset for the creation of district and circuit courts, the latter of which bear little resemblance to modern circuit courts. Specifically, these early federal circuit courts were staffed by Supreme Court justices and district court judges, and they performed both trial and appellate functions. Thus, in addition to their formal duties on the High Court, Supreme Court justices in the early days of the Republic were also required to "ride circuit," traveling to their assigned circuits on a regular basis. (This practice formally ended when Congress reestablished the U.S. Courts of Appeals in 1891.)

During the nation's early history, the Supreme Court was seen as a weak third branch of government, with limited enforcement powers. With his ruling in *Marbury v. Madison* (1803),[4] Chief Justice John Marshall established the Court's power to review all acts of Congress for their constitutionality; even so, during Marshall's 34-year reign as chief justice, the Court struck down just one act of Congress as unconstitutional.

The Constitution makes no reference to the specific size of the Supreme Court. Thus, Congress during the eighteenth and nineteenth centuries altered the size of the Court to consist of one chief justice and anywhere from five to nine associate justices serving on the Court at one time. Occasionally the issue of Court size comes up as a matter of strategic politics: In 1937 President Franklin Delano Roosevelt's ill-fated plan to expand the size of the Court (to up to 15 members depending on the age of the sitting justices) was driven by the president's desire to appoint new justices who would support his New Deal program. Yet even some of President Roosevelt's own Democratic supporters opposed the plan. Since 1869 the Court's composition of nine members (one chief justice and eight associate justices) has remained essentially unchanged. Meanwhile, Congress has been active in creating, disbanding, and modifying the number of other judges who serve throughout the federal court system.

Cases today begin in the federal court system, rather than the state court system, only when they fit into one of three categories: (1) the lawsuit requires interpretation of the U.S. Constitution, a federal law, or a treaty of the United States; (2) the federal government is suing or prosecuting someone, or is itself being sued; or (3) the lawsuit is between two citizens of different states suing for an amount of more than $75,000. Many of the highest-profile legal cases in recent years became federal cases because they featured defendants accused of committing federal crimes. Included on this list are the trial of Oklahoma City bomber Timothy McVeigh and the prosecution of some of the terrorists involved (directly or indirectly) in the attacks of September 11, 2001. In recent decades Congress has become increasingly active in passing legislation to declare new federal crimes. Thus, carjacking, the sale or possession of many types of illegal drugs, money laundering, and various other offenses are now considered federal crimes, and defendants who commit such offenses may face prosecution in federal courts.

Breaking Through Barriers on the Nation's Highest Court

Then

To millions of Americans, the Supreme Court is not just another branch of government: it serves as a symbol of justice, able to rise above the political squabbles that plague the other branches. Of course, to serve that symbolic role, the high Court must appear to represent more than just a narrow slice of the polity. That logic did not escape the 36th president of the United States, Lyndon Baines Johnson. As a product of the rough-and-tumble, often racist world of Texas politics, few would have predicted that Johnson would one day secure a legacy as the president responsible for shepherding major civil rights and voting rights legislation through a resistant Congress. Yet even with that legacy secure, President Johnson went a step further **in 1967**, appointing the first African American justice, Thurgood Marshall, to what had been an all-white U.S. Supreme Court. Marshall's credentials seemed impeccable: a former federal appeals judge, he first made his name as chief Supreme Court advocate on behalf of the National Association for the Advancement of Colored People (NAACP), successfully arguing the landmark case of *Brown v. Board of Education*, among other cases. Eleven Southern senators opposed Marshall's appointment, but those detractors were vastly outnumbered, and he coasted to confirmation by

Solicitor General Thurgood Marshall, preparing to testify at his Supreme Court confirmation hearings in 1967.

a 69–11 vote. Was Marshall's voting record as a Supreme Court justice in the years that followed influenced by his race and background? On this one point, Marshall's enemies and supporters would both answer in the affirmative.

Now

President Barack Obama's ascension to the Oval Office broke perhaps the most visible racial barrier in American politics: the election of an African American to the presidency. Building on themes from his election campaign, Obama did not downplay the potential significance his own victory offered for race relations in America. And yet other racial barriers remained: consider that every session of the U.S. Supreme Court between 1967 and 2008 featured a bench made up of eight Caucasians and just one African American. President Obama altered that landscape when he nominated Judge Sonia Sotomayor, a woman of Puerto Rican descent, to the Supreme Court **on May 26, 2009.** Once confirmed, her appointment promised to diversify the High Court; not incidentally, it also gave Obama instant credibility with a large and powerful ethnic group. The road to Sotomayor's confirmation was rocky at times: Senate Republicans complained of comments she made about how the experiences of a "wise Latina woman" might help her reach better conclusions than a "white male who hasn't lived that life." But Sotomayor's strong academic pedigree, her extensive prosecutorial experience, and her significant judicial experience won her the votes of every Senate Democrat and over

Judge Sonia Sotomayor, nominated to the U.S. Supreme Court, testifying at her Senate confirmation hearings in July 2009.

20 Senate Republicans. Would Sotomayor's ethnic background give her a different perspective on the hardest cases? Debates over that question would be waged in the years to come.

For Critical Thinking and Discussion

1. Do you think it matters whether the Supreme Court is demographically representative of the larger society it serves? Beyond the potential symbolic importance of a diverse court, do you think justices may rule, in some cases, based on their ethnic- or race-oriented experiences in our society?

2. If you were a Senator would you vote to confirm a Supreme Court nominee whose views you disagree with, simply because the nominee would help diversify the court? Why or why not?

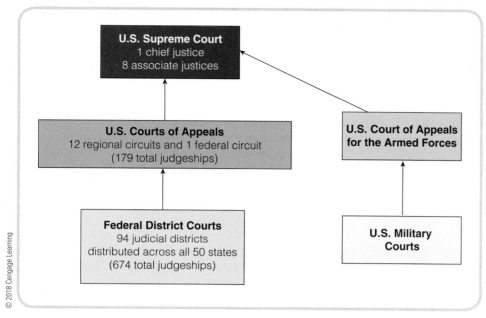

FIGURE 9-2 **The Federal Court System***

*Chart does not include specialized courts, including courts of international trade, tax courts, claims courts, etc.

The federal judicial system today also features a number of specialized courts, including tax courts, bankruptcy courts, and military courts. Most parties to a federal case start out in one of the 94 federal district courts located throughout the country. Federal district court judges have original jurisdiction (the power to rule in the first instance) over criminal and civil trials, and, along with federal magistrates, they provide the initial sources of potential legal relief available in the federal judicial system.

Figure 9-2 depicts the flow of cases in the federal system. After the federal district court has rendered its judgment, appeal is available to one of the 13 federal appeals courts (also referred to as *circuit courts of appeals*) across the country. With some exceptions, federal appeals are normally decided by a panel of three judges selected at random from the pool of 10 or more judges authorized to serve on that court. In some cases, litigants can appeal from the three-judge panel to the full circuit court— this type of hearing is called *en banc*. Because the San Francisco–based Ninth Circuit maintains a roster of 47 judges (spread out from Hawaii and California in the west, to Arizona, Nevada, Montana, and Idaho in the east), the phrase *en banc* on that court refers to 11-judge panels that perform essentially the same function as en banc panels in other circuits.[5]

Litigants who receive an adverse judgment in the federal appeals court and wish to be heard in the U.S. Supreme Court may petition for a *writ of certiorari* (discussed in detail later in this chapter), which is the pleading of a losing party's files with the Supreme Court asking it to review the decision of a lower court. Currently the Supreme Court enjoys near absolute discretion over its docket, and so it remains a long shot (less than 3 percent) that it will even grant the writ of certiorari in the first place.

Petitioning the U.S. Supreme Court for review is the final option available to state court litigants who suffer adverse decisions in the highest state court, and to federal court litigants who suffer adverse decisions after exhausting all forms of appeal in the federal court system. In a normal year, approximately half of the cases heard by the Supreme Court come from federal appellate courts and the other half from the 50 state court systems.

9-3 | The Adversarial System of Justice

Some European legal systems are based on an *inquisitorial system* of justice, in which judges, working on behalf of the government, are responsible for gathering information relevant to the disposition of a particular case. For example, in France—which adheres to the inquisitorial model—judges may initiate a criminal investigation against an individual, commission experts to investigate and report on special aspects of the crime, and even call witnesses and question them intensely. By contrast, the American legal system is primarily an *adversarial system* of justice, in which opposing parties contend against each other for a result favorable to themselves. In jury trials, judges act merely as independent referees overseeing the contest; in so-called bench trials where no jury is present, judges must still remain objective arbiters as they prepare to make final decisions on the merits.[6] In an adversarial system, the judge is entrusted only with ensuring that the litigants achieve procedural fairness and plays no active role in evidence gathering or in the advocacy of one side over the other. Supporters of this system contend that adversarial proceedings pitting zealous representatives of parties against one another offer the best prospect of allowing the judge or jury to determine the truth. Critics counter that inquisitorial systems tend to be free of the many strategic "maneuvers" parties so frequently practice in U.S. courtrooms, such as the withholding of crucial evidence or the presentation of evidence that bears only a minimal relationship to the actual facts at issue.

Elements of Civil Litigation

Countless disputes among individuals or entities are resolved quietly, long before the threat to litigate is even invoked. Still, whenever one private party contests another over the definition or enforcement of certain legal rights or the legal relationship that may exist between them, the disagreement may wind up in the form of a lawsuit brought before a judge in a court of law. Any such judicial contest, including all the events that lead up to a possible court event, is referred to as **litigation**. Although the procedural rules governing such private disputes vary widely from state to state and system to system, some elements of civil litigation are common among all systems. Normally the complaining party who chooses to initiate formal legal proceedings (usually called the **plaintiff**) does so by filing a **complaint**, which is a written document justifying why the court is empowered to hear the case and explaining why the plaintiff is entitled to some form of relief (usually an amount of money) under the current law. The target of the complaint, the **defendant**, normally must respond to the complaint with a formal written defense, in which he or she either admits to or denies what the plaintiff has said.

If the defendant convinces the judge either that the court has no power to hear the case (perhaps it was filed in the wrong court) or that there is no law that provides a remedy to the plaintiff, the case may be dismissed. If the defendant's argument is unsuccessful, the case then moves forward to the stage of pretrial litigation normally referred to as **discovery**. During discovery, each side has the right to find out what information the other side has about the case by requesting documents or materials, access to property, and/or examinations, or by offering answers to questions about the litigation either in written form or verbally at a deposition. Although the judge may play some role in supervising discovery at pretrial conferences, almost all such discovery occurs outside of the courtroom. Following the discovery stage of the proceedings, each side may file new written documents to the court contending that it now has overwhelming evidence in its favor or that the other side has discovered no evidence to prove its own contentions.

The vast majority of civil disputes never make it to trial. In some cases, one party may succeed in convincing the judge that no trial is necessary and that the judge

litigation Any judicial contest, including all the events that lead up to a possible court event.

plaintiff The party that chooses to initiate formal legal proceedings in a civil case.

complaint A document written by the plaintiff arguing why the court is empowered to hear the case and explaining why the plaintiff is entitled to some form of relief under the current law.

defendant The target of a plaintiff's complaint.

discovery A stage of pretrial litigation in which the plaintiff and defendant have the right to learn what information the other side has about the case by requesting documents or materials, access to property, and/or examinations, or by offering answers to questions about the litigation either in written form or verbally at a deposition.

should rule in that party's favor immediately. Far more often, the sides agree to a legally binding "settlement" of claims made against each other, in which one side pays money to the other side, or agrees to cease and desist a certain practice in order to avoid the costs and uncertainties of trial. In civil litigation, judges often play an active role in encouraging the two parties to settle their differences out of court, saving resources for them and the judicial branch that would have been wasted in a long, drawn-out trial.

In some instances, the parties are not able to reach an out-of-court settlement, and a formal trial becomes necessary. In a *bench trial*, the parties present evidence to a judge, rather than a jury of citizens. A jury trial usually takes far longer than a bench trial because of the many procedures required to prevent undue prejudice of the jury. Even if a jury trial is necessary, the judge still plays a role in the courtroom by ensuring that the jury is properly selected and that fair procedures are adhered to during the trial. One of the most crucial roles played by a judge in either type of trial is to rule on the admissibility of evidence that may be used to reach a decision. Only relevant evidence, which logically tends to prove or disprove a disputed fact, may be admitted into the trial proceedings. In civil cases, the complaining party is obligated to prove its allegations by a "preponderance of the evidence," which is generally thought to be anything greater than 50 percent. Although there is widespread disagreement on what this standard exactly means, it is clearly well below the high standard imposed on prosecutors in criminal cases to prove guilt "beyond a reasonable doubt."

Once the judge or jury has reached a final decision on the case, normally called the *verdict* in the case of a jury trial or the *judgment* in a bench trial, and the judge or jury has settled on a monetary amount to be awarded, the trial stage of the process comes to an end. Some post-trial motions may be available, and a dissatisfied party is also free to appeal the decision to a higher court.

The Criminal Justice System at Work

Although the rules of criminal procedure also vary widely, most criminal prosecutions begin with the arrest of a suspect by some law enforcement official at the federal, state, or local level. Once the suspect is formally accused, he or she is also referred to as the *defendant*. Because some criminal charges may be later revealed as groundless or unsubstantiated, the government must quickly demonstrate in one of two ways that the charges against the defendant are valid. Some prosecutors elect to present initial evidence at a preliminary hearing held before a magistrate or trial judge, where they must demonstrate that there is probable cause to proceed to trial against the suspect. Far more often, the prosecutor convenes a **grand jury**, whose duty it is to receive complaints, hear the evidence offered by the prosecutor, and determine whether a trial is justified. Grand juries comprise a greater number of jurors than an ordinary trial jury. Unlike regular juries, which hear only one case, grand juries may be asked to hear evidence on numerous cases over a period of several weeks or even months. Because the grand jury process is supervised entirely by the prosecutor, he or she maintains a distinct advantage—some say a prosecutor could get the grand jury to "indict a bologna sandwich." In the overwhelming majority of cases, the grand jury does indeed return a bill of **indictment** authorizing the government to proceed to trial against the defendant.

Whereas discovery is far-ranging and extensive in civil litigation, it is far more limited in criminal trials. Defense attorneys are usually under little or

grand jury A jury whose duty it is to hear the evidence offered by a prosecutor and determine whether a trial is justified.

indictment A decision by a grand jury authorizing the government to proceed to trial against the defendant.

A jury listens to an attorney present her case.

Jeff Cadge/Getty Images

no obligation to provide any evidence at all to prosecutors; as a general matter, prosecutors are under an obligation to provide defense attorneys only with evidence that tends to "clear" the accused from alleged fault or guilt, although some states and localities provide additional discovery rights to the accused.

Most criminal prosecutions in the United States are resolved through a negotiated **plea bargain** between the defendant and the prosecutor.[7] Indeed, over 90 percent of convictions are the direct product of negotiated plea bargains. Many defendants seek to reduce their jail sentences by entering plea agreements that lead to lesser punishments. Much of the negotiation that occurs between prosecutors and defense attorneys is over the appropriate charges that will be formally filed, as most courts have adopted the equivalent of "going rates" for particular crimes.[8] Prosecutors willingly trade down penalties for crimes either because they are seeking that defendant's cooperation at another trial or because they wish to avoid the uncertainty and huge expenditure of resources that come with a trial.

In criminal cases that do go to trial, the burden rests squarely on the prosecutor to prove that the defendant committed the crime "beyond a reasonable doubt." Defendants, by contrast, do not have to prove their innocence. Unless a defendant waives the right to a jury trial, she or he must be tried by a jury of peers. State courts require anywhere between 6 and 12 jurors, whereas the federal court system requires 12 jurors in all cases where a jury is present. Defendants, shielded by the Fifth Amendment privilege against self-incrimination, are under no obligation to testify. Numerous other constitutional safeguards are available to the defendant, including the right to a public and speedy trial and the right to directly confront witnesses. If the jury renders a "not guilty" verdict, the double jeopardy clause of the Fifth Amendment generally forbids the government from trying the defendant again for the same crime. A defendant who is convicted has a constitutional right to appeal the conviction or the resulting sentence to a higher court.

Although the burdens at trial appear to favor the accused, prosecutors generally have the benefit of experience in prosecuting many other defendants in the same court and can draw on a relatively large pool of resources (such as government investigators or medical examiners) to aid them in securing a conviction.

The Sixth Amendment has been interpreted to guarantee each indigent defendant the right to a government-provided lawyer in any instance where he or she faces the possibility of jail time. Unfortunately, many public defenders' offices are overworked and underfunded, placing defendants at a relative disadvantage. By comparison, wealthy or well-connected defendants who do enjoy access to top legal talent and other resources at trial often fare much better. For example, in 2005 the late recording star Michael Jackson was acquitted on charges of child abduction, molestation, and attempted molestation of several minor boys at his Neverland Ranch in Southern California. That result was due in no small part to the efforts of some of the nation's most well-known lawyers, including celebrity advocates Susan Yu, Mark Geragos, and Benjamin Brafman. Clearly, the American legal system does not always offer the same types of outcomes to those who are not similarly situated or well connected. For the vast majority of defendants, "justice" in the courtroom is meted out at lightning speed, with judges and prosecutors running through multiple criminal trials in a matter of hours with little opportunity to understand all the facts of a particular case. Public defenders only rarely have the chance to contest these trials with witnesses and evidence, lest they ignore all the

plea bargain A pretrial negotiated resolution in a criminal case in which the defendants seek to reduce their jail sentences by pleading guilty and in return prosecutors are willing to trade down the severity of the punishment.

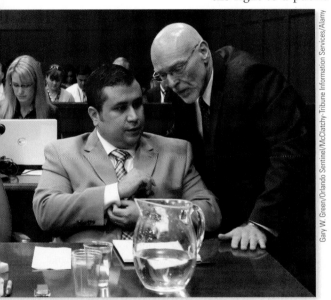

High-profile defendant George Zimmerman, consulting with his lawyer at trial. Zimmerman fatally shot Trayvon Martin, an unarmed African American teen, in Sanford, Florida, in 2012. The events surrounding the murder, Zimmerman's arrest, and his subsequent trial invited charges of racism from Martin's family and others. In 2013, Zimmerman was acquitted.

other defendants under their charge. In sum, the picture of drama-filled trials seen so often on television or in the movies hardly depicts the reality of what goes on in this nation's criminal courtrooms.

9-4 | Judicial Review and Its Implications

Courts in general, and judges in particular, serve in a variety of capacities: supervising the disposition of legal controversies between private parties, overseeing preliminary hearings or trials of criminal defendants, and ruling on important issues concerning the procedures to be followed or the evidence to be introduced at trial. Indeed, the role many judges play as "independent magistrates" is fundamental to the effective functioning of the American legal system. But courts and judges also play a significant and far-reaching role in overseeing the operations of the other branches of government, both by supervising conflicts between those branches and by protecting citizens against government action that may violate the Constitution.

This judicial authority has been magnified by the general recognition that American courts enjoy the added power of **judicial review**, by which they may declare acts of the other branches of the federal or state governments unconstitutional and thus invalid. This dimension of judicial authority is not mentioned anywhere in the U.S. Constitution. Although Article VI of the Constitution declares the Constitution of the United States to be the "supreme Law of the Land . . . any Thing in the Constitution or Laws of any State to the Contrary notwithstanding," nowhere does the document explicitly vest any specific court (including the U.S. Supreme Court) with the authority to determine whether state laws are unconstitutional. Nor does the Constitution authorize the Supreme Court to serve as the authoritative interpreter of the document over the president, Congress, and other federal officials, all of whom are equally sworn to uphold the Constitution. In fact, scholars of the early constitutional period believe the drafters of the Constitution were unable to reach any consensus at all on this issue. How, then, did the power of judicial review arise?

The power of the Supreme Court to exercise judicial review was first established by the fourth chief justice of the United States, John Marshall, in the highly controversial case of *Marbury v. Madison* (1803).[9] With Thomas Jefferson's victory in the presidential election of 1800 and the Jeffersonian Republicans' rise to power in both houses of Congress the following year, nearly all of the nation's most powerful Federalists, including John Adams, Alexander Hamilton, and John Jay, were soon to be relegated to outsider status in the federal government. In his final hours as president, however, Adams appointed 16 circuit court judges and 42 new justices of the peace for the District of Columbia (all loyal Federalists); these positions were fully authorized by Congress, and each of the individuals chosen for the posts was confirmed by the lame-duck Federalist Congress that remained loyal to Adams. President Adams also named John Marshall as chief justice of the United States. Although surrounded by partisan opposition in Washington, Marshall made the Supreme Court into the Federalist Party's beachhead, from which that party's judicial holdovers, enjoying the benefit of life tenure, could continue to espouse their vision of a powerful central government. Immediately after Thomas Jefferson and his Secretary of State James Madison formally took office in March 1801, they learned that several of the commissions for the new justices of the peace appointed by Adams had never been delivered—including one for William Marbury. When Jefferson ordered Madison to withhold the commissions, Marbury asked the Supreme Court to issue a *writ of mandamus*, a judicial order commanding an official (in this case, Madison) to perform a ministerial duty over which his or her discretion is limited (namely, the formal delivery of a duly signed and sealed commission). As authority for the Supreme Court's power to issue such a writ, Marbury cited

judicial review The power of a court to declare acts of the other branches of government or of a subordinate government to be unconstitutional and thus invalid.

the Judiciary Act of 1789, which appeared to give the U.S. Supreme Court exactly that authority.

Marbury was seeking to have the Supreme Court decide the case immediately, without first having to suffer a loss in a lower court. Because Chief Justice Marshall was an ardent Federalist, Marbury further assumed the Court would be sympathetic to his plight. In truth, it was Marshall who was really at fault in the case—as Adams's Secretary of State, he had failed to properly mail the commission. Indeed, given his intimate knowledge of the facts, Marshall should have recused himself from the case, refusing to participate as a judge in the first place. Yet Marshall's Supreme Court rejected Marbury's request. Recognizing the tense political situation that surrounded the case—and all too aware that Jefferson might not abide by court order—Marshall lambasted the Jefferson administration for its refusal to perform its statutorily mandated duty but denied that the Supreme Court possessed the power to issue the writ as requested.

Why the refusal to help his fellow Federalist? Marshall acknowledged that the 1789 law did in fact authorize the Court to issue such a writ in "original jurisdiction." But, Marshall ruled, that law was in explicit violation of Article III, Section 2, Clause 2, which did not specifically list "writs of mandamus" among the types of cases over which the Supreme Court had original jurisdiction. Nor could Congress extend the Court's original jurisdiction by mere statute. Thus, Marshall decided, the 1789 law was repugnant to the Constitution and was therefore null and void. With this decision, Marshall seized for the Court a power of judicial review over congressional laws that is unmentioned in the Constitution. The Supreme Court exercised this power only once more before the Civil War, although it has struck down well over 150 acts of Congress since then.

Two rulings more than a decade later further established the Supreme Court's authority in interpreting the Constitution. In *McCulloch v. Maryland* (1819),[10] the Court upheld the constitutionality of the Bank of the United States, thereby establishing the precedent that congressional power extends beyond those powers specifically listed in Article I of the Constitution. In *Martin v. Hunter's Lessee* (1816),[11] the Supreme Court ruled that the power of federal courts to review government actions for their constitutionality was not just applicable to other federal institutions; the supremacy clause ("The Constitution . . . shall be the Supreme Law of the Land") meant that the Supreme Court could also invalidate any actions of state governments that it believed to be in conflict with the U.S. Constitution. During his 34 years as chief justice, Marshall wrote 519 opinions, many of which remain influential commentary on constitutional power and authority. Under Marshall's leadership, the Court consistently rejected claims of state sovereignty that conflicted with federal interests. It was the special duty of the Supreme Court, Marshall believed, to make difficult judgments on the Constitution that either limited or affirmed the exercise of federal authority. In doing so, Marshall's court defined a strong role for the federal government, which was more clearly realized beginning in the twentieth century.

In the two centuries since Marshall served as chief justice, the Supreme Court has invalidated more than 1,200 state laws. In 1958, it once again reaffirmed the principle of judicial supremacy in *Cooper v. Aaron*[12] in response to official defiance of a lower court's desegregation rulings: governors and state legislatures were bound to uphold decisions of the Supreme Court just as they were bound by oath to uphold the Constitution. At times the exercise of judicial review has been extremely controversial. For example, the Supreme Court in *Dred Scott v. Sandford* (1857)[13] ruled that slaves were forever the property of their owners, even when they were brought temporarily into free states. The decision overturned a congressional law regulating the extension of slavery in the territories and may have helped to precipitate the Civil War four years later. During the Great Depression, the Supreme Court's rulings that many of FDR's New Deal proposals were unconstitutional instigated another constitutional crisis. More recently,

NFIB v. Sebelius (2012)

The date of March 23, 2010, marks perhaps the most significant moment of Barack Obama's presidency. On that day President Obama signed into law the Patient Protection and Affordable Care Act (aka "ACA" or "Obamacare"). The long and complicated piece of legislation required that insurance companies cover all applicants within new minimum standards and offer the same rates regardless of preexisting conditions or sex. It also featured the controversial "individual mandate," fining individuals who failed to sign up for health care insurance by 2014. Passed along strict partisan lines without a single Republican vote, the law was immediately challenged in court, as opponents hoped to short-circuit the law before it could be implemented nation-

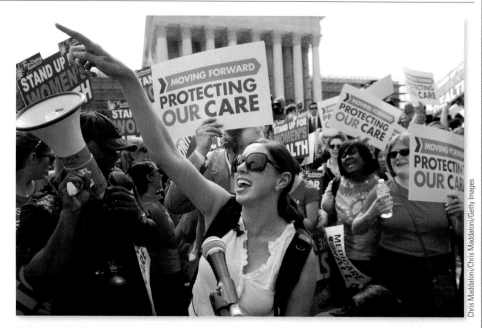

Supporters of the Affordable Care Act celebrate in front of the U.S. Supreme Court building on June 28, 2012, after learning that the Court had affirmed the constitutionality of the controversial law by a 5–4 margin.

wide. Thus, in the spring of 2012, the Supreme Court justices reviewed the case of *NFIB v. Sebelius*, which placed the constitutionality of President Obama's signature accomplishment squarely in its sights. The presidential election campaign provided a key backdrop to these proceedings as well: Would the Court's invalidation of Obamacare hurt the president's chances for reelection that November?

Finally, the Court handed down its decision in the Obamacare case on June 28, 2012. By a narrow 5–4 decision, the Supreme Court upheld most provisions of the ACA as constitutional. Writing for an unusual alliance linking the conservative High Court leader with his four more liberal colleagues, Chief Justice John Roberts declared that while the individual mandate went beyond Congress's power to regulate interstate commerce, it was nevertheless a valid exercise of Congress's Article I power to tax and spend. (Only the part of the law that expanded Medicaid failed to pass constitutional muster.) How ironic that in an increasingly polarized political system, the conservative chief justice appointed by Republican President

George W. Bush had cast the key swing vote to rescue the most significant domestic initiative passed by Bush's Democratic successor.

For Critical Thinking and Discussion

1. The Supreme Court's decision in the Obamacare case clearly influenced the political landscape leading up to the 2012 election. Should the Supreme Court have deferred or delayed its decision until after the 2012 election? Why or why not?

2. At least two of the justices who cast votes to uphold Obamacare (Justices Elana Kagan and Sonya Sotomayor) were appointed by President Obama. Should they have recused themselves from making a decision with such political overtones? Do you trust Supreme Court justices (or any judges) appointed through an overtly partisan political process to set aside their partisan views in such a case?

President Obama suggested that if the Court invalidated his administration's signature health care reform legislation, it would be engaging in improper "judicial activism." As it turned out, the Supreme Court in June 2012 modified just one aspect of the legislation (the Medicare funding provision), leaving the rest of the Patient Protection and Affordable Care Act of 2010 intact. Despite the uncertain beginnings that led to this practice and the tense moments in the nation's history that it has given rise to, judicial review of federal and state laws has become an unchallenged dimension of judicial power within the U.S. political system.

9-5 | Limitations on Courts

In Federalist No. 78, Alexander Hamilton deemed the judiciary "the least dangerous" branch because it had "no influence over either the sword or the purse . . . and can take no active resolution whatsoever." Despite Hamilton's opinion, courts have played a critically influential role in the American political system. When the Supreme Court aggressively interposes itself between aggrieved citizens and the government, as it did when it ordered desegregation of public schools in *Brown v. Board of Education* (1954),[14] or when it helps resolve some great political crisis, as it did when it ordered President Richard Nixon to hand over controversial tapes of White House conversations in *United States v. Nixon* (1974),[15] the judiciary appears more like an all-powerful branch than one that is weak and inconsequential.

The power of American courts is great, but the method by which courts participate in the political system is far more circumscribed than that of the other two branches. The limitations that courts must adhere to include the following:

1. **Courts cannot initiate or maintain lawsuits.** Unlike legislatures, which can propose and pass bills on their own initiative, judges in the United States cannot decide issues that are not currently before them in a legitimately filed lawsuit. If none of the actors in a controversy elects to involve the courts directly, the court has no role whatsoever in resolution of the conflict.

2. **Courts can hear only those lawsuits that constitute true "cases" or "controversies."** Article III imposes on the Supreme Court and all federal courts the same type of limitation that applies to nearly all other courts: judges may hear and resolve only those lawsuits that amount to legitimate "cases" or "controversies" and must ignore mere "hypothetical" or "theoretical" conflicts. Although most of these terms are fuzzy enough to give courts room to maneuver, in practice courts tend to refuse to decide lawsuits that are moot (that is, it is too late to provide any effective remedy), including lawsuits involving affirmative action programs and policies brought against educational institutions by applicants who have since enrolled in (and, in many cases, graduated from) another institution. Courts are equally reluctant to decide cases that are not yet ripe (that is, the actual conflict is still sometime in the future). Accordingly, courts normally refuse to provide executives with what amounts to "legal advice" about future controversies that have not yet occurred. Courts similarly refuse to hear cases that were contrived by the parties in the form of collusion, or cases in which jurisdiction has not been properly invoked.

    The courts have also maintained a long-standing tradition of refusing to decide cases where the Constitution has explicitly entrusted the issue to be decided by one of the other branches of government; such issues are generally referred to as *political questions*. Of course, when attempting to justify its refusal to take on a political question, the Supreme Court often engages in such extensive analysis of the underlying issues that it is hard to distinguish those opinions from analysis of the merits of the case itself. For example, in *Nixon v. United States* (1993),[16] the Supreme Court explained its refusal to reconsider the Senate's process of trying the impeachment of a federal judge, Walter Nixon, by issuing a lengthy opinion that reviewed in considerable detail the constitutional provisions entrusting the Senate with the "sole power" of trying impeachments. Related to the "case or controversy" rule is a requirement that courts impose on the parties themselves: Courts will hear lawsuits only from parties that have proper **standing**, meaning that they are "uniquely" and "singularly" affected" by the controversy. For example, courts usually reject lawsuits brought by individuals who are frustrated with the allotment of their tax dollars because those individuals are not "singularly affected." Nor are individuals with a mere academic or political concern in a conflict allowed in court as parties to a case unless they have suffered some unique economic or physical burden related to the issue being decided. In the mid-twentieth century, Congress and many state legislatures loosened these harsh standing requirements by authorizing lawsuits brought by large numbers of people with clearly defined common interests. Such **class action lawsuits** can proceed through the legal system even when not every member of the class has formally signed on. High-visibility class action lawsuits in recent years include those brought by tobacco users across the country and those by people who have suffered from the effects of asbestos.

standing The requirement that a party must be uniquely or singularly affected by a controversy in order to be eligible to file a lawsuit.

class action lawsuit A lawsuit filed by a large group of people with clearly defined common interests.

3. **Courts must rely on other branches for enforcement.** Unlike the other branches of government, courts rely on other political institutions to put their opinions or orders into direct effect—police officers, marshals, and executive branch officers, among others, must carry out the courts' mandates. Whereas Congress can cut off funding to executive agencies that ignore its dictates, no similar tool is available to the judiciary. In the vast majority of instances, disobedience of the court is not in question. Yet when a court makes a controversial pronouncement, officials may be reluctant to adhere to the court's decision. In some rare cases, a court's decisions may be met with outright disobedience. Sometimes courts even may react negatively to another court's rulings: In July 2001, Chief Justice Roy Moore of the Alabama Supreme Court authorized the installation of a monument to the Ten Commandments in the Alabama state judicial building. Even after a federal district court ruled that the monument violated the separation of church and state, Moore refused to remove it; more than two years after installation of the monument, Moore was removed from office for defying the federal court's order.

In 1832, President Andrew Jackson declined to enforce the Supreme Court's decision in *Worcester v. Georgia*,[17] which ordered that a white Christian missionary be freed from a Georgia prison. Chief Justice Marshall had ruled that the Georgia law imprisoning the missionary for residing on Cherokee Indian property without permission violated a U.S.–Cherokee treaty; yet President Jackson declared—perhaps apocryphally—that "John Marshall has made his decision . . . now let him enforce it." (The missionary served his entire four-year mission in jail.) Sometimes even popular Supreme Court decisions face the threat of resistance. President Richard Nixon considered refusing to comply with the Supreme Court's 1974 decision in *United States v. Nixon* ordering him to hand over the secret tapes he made of conversations in the Oval Office.[18]

Controversial Supreme Court decisions in the 1950s and 1960s occasionally led to significant resistance on the part of ordinary citizens as well.[19] The landmark decisions in *Brown v. Board of Education*,[20] which first held that segregated public schools violated the equal protection clause and then commanded that public schools be desegregated "with all deliberate speed," met with violent reaction in the South. Ultimately, President Dwight Eisenhower sent U.S. marshals to the South to enforce the desegregation decrees; otherwise, there might have been even greater resistance to the Court's controversial decision. The Supreme Court's 1962 decision invalidating school-sponsored religious prayer in public schools (*Engel v. Vitale*[21]) goes ignored in many parts of this country even today—in one instance, a federal district court in Alabama was forced to prohibit prayer in public schools throughout the state in response to reports of widespread defiance.

In addition to these limitations, courts must also adhere to limitations that arise from constitutional or statutory law. For example, Congress can by statute alter the Supreme Court's **appellate jurisdiction**, which is the power to review prior decisions handed down by state and lower federal courts. Thus Congress could in theory declare that federal courts as a whole are not empowered to hear abortion cases. In fact, foes of the Supreme Court's abortion decisions proposed just such a bill in the 1980s, but it was never passed. However, Congress cannot alter the Court's **original jurisdiction**, which is the power to hear a lawsuit at the outset. Article III authorizes the Court's original jurisdiction in cases involving ambassadors and cases in which states are the only parties.

One final limitation on courts is harder to see, but is no less significant. Because judges and justices are normally appointed by politically accountable entities such as executives and legislatures, or in some states elected by the public itself, courts in general rarely stray too far from the reigning political majority. Social scientist Robert Dahl affirmed this hypothesis in his landmark 1957 article, "Decision-Making in a Democracy."[22] Dahl's study of Supreme Court opinions revealed that although the Supreme Court often defies public opinion in the short run, its opinions usually fall in line with the dominant national majority coalition in the long run. The Court's eventual adaptability to shifts in the national mood, although much more subtle and slow-moving than the more political branches of government, has helped sustain it as a vital force in the American political system.

9-6 | Electing and Appointing Judges

The state and federal court systems differ dramatically in the way judges are selected. State court judges tend to be selected in one of five ways. Partisan elections are utilized in some states, with prospective and sitting justices required to campaign for their party's nomination and then to run in a general election. Nonpartisan elections, held in many other states, eliminate party designations from the election process. The "Missouri Plan," or merit plan, selection process features a three-step process by which a judicial nominating commission initially screens candidates and then submits a list of three potential nominees to the governor, who then selects the judge from the list. Shortly thereafter, the new judge must then secure voter approval in a nonpartisan retention election.[23] Several other states authorize gubernatorial appointment of judges, in which the governor appoints judges, subject to approval of the state senate. Finally, a handful of states require that the state legislature appoint judges.

The selection of federal judges follows a more universal formula: All federal district court judges, federal appeals court judges, and Supreme Court justices are appointed by the president, subject to confirmation by a majority vote in the U.S. Senate. Whereas the Constitution dictates this formula for appointment of Supreme Court justices, Congress in its discretion authorized the appointment of lower federal court judges to require the Senate's advice and consent as well. Because all federal judges and Supreme Court justices hold their offices during "good behavior"—the functional equivalent of life tenure—they are thought of as more independent than those state judges who must run for reelection. In fact, the retention rate for state judges is often so high (due to low voter turnout and other factors) that even elected state judges tend to enjoy a large degree of independence in rendering decisions.

appellate jurisdiction The authority of a court to review decisions handed down by another court.

original jurisdiction The authority of a court to be the initial court in which a legal decision is rendered.

The Nomination Process

During a single term in office, a president can expect to make hundreds of federal judicial appointments. The Constitution does not impose any requirements or limits on those who aspire to membership on a federal court or even on the U.S. Supreme Court; it left the question of qualifications—whether education, experience, or anything else—to the political actors who control the process. In practice, a tradition of deference to home-state senators (often called *senatorial courtesy*) provides legislators in the upper chamber—especially those hailing from the president's party—with considerable influence over the selection of district court judges in their own states. (Senatorial courtesy also has a more limited impact on the selection of appeals court judges, as circuits cross individual state boundaries.) In recent decades, presidents have not only relied on senators' recommendations to generate nominees for judgeships; they also consider ideological factors and the personal characteristics of potential nominees.

Some modern presidents have sought to place their own ideological stamp on the lower courts (whether liberal or conservative) by utilizing a committee of White House and Justice Department attorneys to screen and suggest candidates.[24] The Reagan and George W. Bush administrations were especially active in seeking to use the appointment of lower court judges as a means of moving the constitutional landscape in a conservative ideological direction. When the presidency and the Senate are held by different parties, battles over judicial nominees may become especially fierce. In 2002 and 2007–2008, the Democrat-controlled Senate Judiciary Committee gave heightened scrutiny to President George W. Bush's more conservative nominees. Although in the minority, Senate Republicans sought to return the favor to President Obama, delaying many of his court nominees in 2009 and 2010.

Given its place atop the U.S. legal system, vacancies on the U.S. Supreme Court tend to draw far more political attention than do other judicial vacancies. Because the president, the U.S. Senate, and the media follow personnel changes on the Supreme Court more closely, the process by which justices are nominated and confirmed is a major news event. A president may have the opportunity to appoint several Supreme Court justices—Presidents George H. W. Bush and Bill Clinton appointed two justices each, whereas President Ronald Reagan appointed three associate justices and promoted one associate to chief justice (the justice responsible for administering the Court's affairs and heading the federal justice system as a whole) during his eight years in office. President George W. Bush appointed no justices during his first term but filled two vacancies

President Barack Obama introduces his second nominee to the U.S. Supreme Court, Elena Kagan, in 2010.

(including the chief justiceship) during the latter half of 2005. Bush's reelection helped him escape the fate suffered by President Carter, whose lone term in office witnessed no Supreme Court vacancies at all.

If a vacancy occurs in the position of chief justice, the president may choose to promote one of the eight associate Supreme Court justices to this prestigious position, as President Reagan did when he promoted William Rehnquist to the Court's center seat in 1986. More often, presidents reach outside the confines of the current Supreme Court for someone to take the position of chief justice. Chief Justice Earl Warren, for example, served as governor of California immediately prior to becoming chief justice in 1953. President George W. Bush also named an outsider, Judge John Roberts of the U.S. Court of Appeals for the D.C. Circuit, to succeed Rehnquist.

The court's membership as of October 1, 2016, is listed in Table 9-1. In choosing nominees to the High Court, presidents in recent decades have considered several factors:

The nominee's ideological and policy preferences. This factor has enjoyed a place of special importance in presidential calculations. A nominee's views on abortion, school prayer, and other hot-button issues may well tip the balance of the Court in favor of the president's stated views. Certainly there exists little evidence that presidents employ "litmus tests" on nominees, by which they might refuse to appoint individuals unless they explicitly state their views on such issues to the president in advance. President Dwight Eisenhower allegedly referred to his appointments of Chief Justice Earl Warren and Justice William Brennan as the "two biggest mistakes" of his presidency because both men decided cases in a far more liberal direction than Eisenhower would have preferred.

TABLE 9-1	Membership of the U.S. Supreme Court prior to the 2016 Presidential Election*						
Member	**Gender**	**Position**	**Date Born**	**Year Appointed (President)**	**Law School**	**Party**	**Religion**
John Roberts	M	Chief Justice	1/27/55	2005 (Bush II)	Harvard	Republican	Roman Catholic
Anthony Kennedy	M	Associate Justice	7/23/36	1988 (Reagan)	Harvard	Republican	Roman Catholic
Clarence Thomas	M	Associate Justice	6/23/48	1991 (Bush I)	Yale	Republican	Roman Catholic[†]
Ruth Bader Ginsburg	F	Associate Justice	3/15/33	1993 (Clinton)	Harvard/ Columbia	Democrat	Jewish
Stephen Breyer	M	Associate Justice	8/15/38	1994 (Clinton)	Harvard	Democrat	Jewish
Samuel Alito	M	Associate Justice	4/1/50	2006 (Bush II)	Yale	Republican	Roman Catholic
Sonia Sotomayor	F	Associate Justice	6/25/54	2009 (Obama)	Yale	Democrat	Roman Catholic
Elena Kagan	F	Associate Justice	4/28/60	2010 (Obama)	Harvard	Democrat	Jewish

* At the time this book went to press, the Supreme Court seat formerly held by Justice Antonin Scalia remained vacant, pending the nomination and confirmation of his successor.
† At the time of his 1991 appointment, Clarence Thomas regularly attended an Episcopal church, but he later returned to Roman Catholicism, the faith in which he had been raised.

© 2018 Cengage Learning

More recently, the elder George Bush may have been frustrated by the pro-abortion rights opinions of Justice David Souter, his first appointment to the Supreme Court. Still, most modern presidents have mobilized White House and Justice Department resources to conduct extensive research on each candidate's past writings and opinions in hopes of eliminating any surprises.

Judicial competence. Most presidents have an interest in appointing especially qualified candidates for the High Court, if only because it assists in speeding along the confirmation process. The American Bar Association (ABA), an interest group of lawyers, rates candidates for every federal judicial vacancy on a scale from "highly qualified" to "not qualified" on the basis of their legal background and accomplishments. Ethical considerations may also be considered because the ABA may be reluctant to approve candidates who have previously been convicted of crimes, for example. Although a negative rating from the ABA does not always eliminate a candidacy, it may present significant obstacles in the Senate confirmation process. Early in his first term, President George W. Bush announced that he would no longer vet judicial candidates through the ABA prior to their formal nomination. Still, the ABA continued to rate those candidates after their nominations were submitted to the Senate. Two of President Bush's first three nominees for the High Court, John Roberts and Samuel Alito, received the highest rating of "well qualified" just prior to their appearance before the Senate Judiciary Committee. (Bush's other nominee, Harriet Miers, withdrew her name from consideration before the ABA released its rating of her candidacy.)

Political loyalty. Although loyalty has diminished somewhat as a priority in recent years, presidents still occasionally practice old-fashioned politics in the selection of Supreme Court nominees, choosing a justice based on a background of service to the president's party or to the president. During the twentieth century, well over 90 percent of all Supreme Court nominees were members of the president's political party. Of these, many emerged from the president's cabinet, from the members of Congress loyal to the president's legislative program, or from other positions close to the chief executive or his subordinates at the time the appointment was made. Certainly one former president of the United States, William Howard Taft, was well positioned to tout his own appointment as chief justice of the United States; President Warren Harding placed Taft on the High Court just seven years after Taft had left the White House.

Demographic factors. A president may choose a candidate for the diversity the nominee adds to the demographics of the current Supreme Court.[25] As was noted at the outset of this chapter, Lyndon Johnson appointed Thurgood Marshall as the first African American to the Court in 1967; Ronald Reagan appointed Sandra Day O'Connor as the first female justice in 1981; and President Obama appointed Sonia Sotomayor as the first Latina justice in 2009. Obama also appointed a second female, Elena Kagan, to the Court the following year, bringing the number of women on the Court up to three for the time being. The selection of nominees who can diversify the Court may pay political dividends for the White House as well: The president may be counting on such nominations to build support among certain groups.

The current political environment. Supreme Court vacancies do not occur in a vacuum; presidents are well aware of the political conditions that surround a particular court vacancy, and more often than not they respond to it through their nomination choices. Such factors as low presidential approval ratings, a Senate controlled by the political opposition, or the need to achieve other legislative proposals may convince the president to select a more moderate or less controversial nominee. Thus, President Bill Clinton—facing

The U.S. Supreme Court justices, as pictured at the start of the Court's fall 2015 term. Standing, from left to right: Justice Sonia Sotomayor, Justice Stephen Breyer, Justice Samuel Alito, Justice Elena Kagan; Seated, from left to right: Justice Clarence Thomas, Justice Antonin Scalia (now deceased); Chief Justice John Roberts, Justice Anthony Kennedy, Justice Ruth Bader Ginsburg.

The Diversity Dilemma

Diversity in the Judiciary

The increasingly diverse U.S. population is now reflected in the demographic composition of law school classes at leading law schools, and even within the membership of state bar associations across the country. Unfortunately, this diversity is not yet fully reflected in many of our nation's courts. The American Bar Association (ABA) has articulated that part of its mission is to "promote the full and equal participation in the legal profession by minorities, women, persons with disabilities and persons of differing sexual orientation and gender identity."[26] As you can see from the image of the ABA diversity homepage (below), this clearly expressed goal has led this prestigious organization to carefully monitor diversity on the nation's courts, as well as to promote efforts that might increase their diversity. In 2010, the state judiciaries featured 24 percent African American jurists, 4 percent Asian/Pacific Islanders, 11 percent Hispanics, and 2 percent who were classified as Native American/Other. A closer examination finds that while some state supreme courts are still all white, other states are making agonizingly slow progress at diversifying. In Arizona, for example, a state with a large nonwhite population, no racial/ethnic minority justices were sitting on its supreme court in 2016. Scholars at the Brennan Center for Justice at NYU Law School believe the method of selecting judges (whether it is through judicial elections or judicial nominations) does not significantly affect the level of diversity. Instead, they recommend that state judicial nominating commissions implement systematic recruitment efforts, which can in turn expand the pool of diverse applicants and bring about real progress in diversifying state courts.[27]

For Critical Thinking and Discussion

1. What are the ramifications of a lack of diversity in the lower federal courts or in the state judiciaries? Are the ramifications different, depending on what level of the court system is under consideration?
2. What reforms would you favor to promote a more diverse judiciary? Do you agree with the Brennan Center's recommendations?

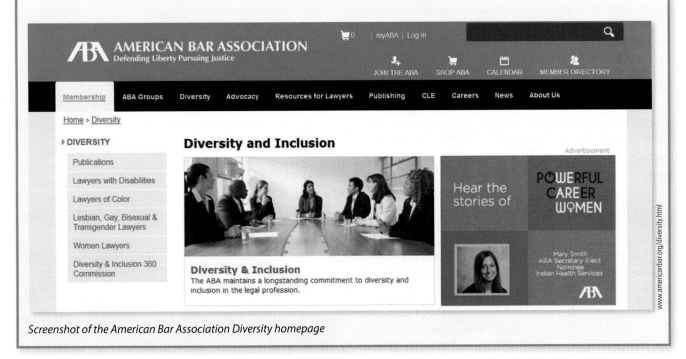

Screenshot of the American Bar Association Diversity homepage

a challenging political environment during his first two years in office—chose two Supreme Court nominees during that period (Ruth Bader Ginsburg and Stephen Breyer) who were deemed acceptable by the ranking Republican member of the Senate Judiciary Committee, Senator Orrin Hatch (R-UT). President Obama hoped that his 2016 nomination of Merrick Garland, a judge who several Republican senators had openly praised, might garner bipartisan support during a presidential election year (Senate Republicans dashed those hopes up through Election Day 2016). On the other hand, a president who enjoys a strong political position may decide to name a more controversial Supreme Court nominee, regardless of the political circumstances.

The Confirmation Process

Until the late 1960s, most confirmation processes tended to be little-noticed events, drawing scarce public attention or press coverage. Beginning at that time, however, with the growth of federal regulatory schemes placing more and more cases in the federal courts, presidents began to routinely utilize judicial appointments as a means of shaping public policy. The confirmation process for those nominees was simultaneously opened up to unprecedented high levels of public scrutiny. All hearings for Supreme Court nominees have been televised live on C-SPAN since 1981. Interest groups have become increasingly active in confirmation proceedings, lobbying senators directly and testifying in favor of or against particular nominees. With the ideological stakes raised, presidents and their aides have become increasingly active in lobbying for their nominees.[28]

The Senate confirms the vast majority of Supreme Court nominees; between 1900 and 2010, 59 of the 63 Supreme Court candidates who came up for a formal Senate vote on their respective nominations were confirmed. Nevertheless, as shown in Table 9-2, controversial nominees in recent decades have experienced their share of public scrutiny—and, in some cases, outright rejection by the Senate—when subjected to the glare of the confirmation process. One of Richard Nixon's nominees to the Supreme Court in 1970, Court of Appeals Judge G. Harrold Carswell of Florida, was rejected by the Senate in part because of his alleged links to white supremacist groups. Carswell was also dogged by charges that he was not competent to serve on the bench; to that came the deadly retort of one Senate supporter that even the mediocre judges "are entitled to a little" representation on the Supreme Court too.[29] Despite all these obstacles, Carswell nearly survived Senate confirmation anyway—he was rejected by a six-vote margin. Frustrated by his defeat, Carswell resigned from the bench a few months later and ran unsuccessfully for the U.S. Senate in 1972.

TABLE 9-2	Failed Supreme Court Nominees Since 1900		
Nominee	**Year Nominated**	**Nominating President**	**Result**
John J. Parker	1930	Hoover	Rejected, 39–41
Abe Fortas	1968	L.B. Johnson	Withdrawn*
Homer Thornberry	1968	L.B. Johnson	Nullified**
Clement Haynsworth	1969	Nixon	Rejected, 45–55
G. Harrold Carswell	1970	Nixon	Rejected, 45–51
Robert H. Bork	1987	Reagan	Rejected, 42–58
Douglas H. Ginsburg	1987	Reagan	Withdrawn
Harriet Miers	2005	G.W. Bush	Withdrawn

* Nomination for chief justice withdrawn
** Nomination for associate justice voided by withdrawal of Fortas nomination

Ronald Reagan's nomination of Judge Robert Bork to the Supreme Court in 1987 was defeated in the Senate amid a cloud of interest-group cries that Bork would reverse liberal precedents on free speech and abortion.[30] Bork, a former Yale law professor, sported a record of opposition to many Supreme Court doctrines supported by political liberals, including the doctrine of constitutionally protected abortion rights that the Court articulated in *Roe v. Wade* (1973).[31] In his award-winning book *The Selling of Supreme Court Nominees* (1994), University of Georgia Professor John Maltese notes that liberal interest groups that were determined to defeat Bork employed "a wide variety of tactics, including advertising, grass roots events, focus groups and polling" to increase public awareness of Bork's controversial positions.

The Reagan White House was caught off guard by the groundswell of opposition to Bork's nomination generated by the intense interest group–driven media campaign. By the time Senate confirmation hearings were held at the end of the summer, the campaign had taken its toll on Bork's candidacy: Several senators, including Joseph Biden (D-DE), chairman of the Senate Judiciary Committee, had already been persuaded to oppose the appointment. The Senate eventually defeated Bork's nomination by a 58–42 vote. Presidents since then have come to understand the new politics of judicial confirmations, working closely with interest groups to mount their own campaigns in favor of judicial nominees. The Bork nomination gave rise to a new term in Washington's political lexicon—"to Bork," which defines the act of challenging a president's nominee through well-financed and well-organized interest-group opposition.

The Bork confirmation fiasco also encouraged subsequent presidents to favor nominees who either possess no paper trail at all or would be far more circumspect than Bork in their willingness to engage the Senate on constitutional issues. Accordingly, in 1990 the first Supreme Court vacancy of George H. W. Bush's presidency went to David Souter, a little-known federal appeals judge who had logged most of his judicial career on the New Hampshire Supreme Court deciding technical issues of state law. Souter's position on issues such as abortion and the establishment clause were never really tested in the state court system, and senators on both ends of the political spectrum thus had little to work with when interrogating Souter. (He was confirmed easily by a 90–9 Senate vote.)

In recent years, the confirmation process for lower court nominees has been politicized as well, with battles being waged with extra ferocity over appointments to the U.S. courts of appeals. During the Clinton administration, Senate Republicans in control of that chamber often delayed nominees they felt were too liberal; Senate Democrats did the same to President George W. Bush's nominees in 2001. Before the Democrats regained control of Congress in the 2006 midterm elections, Senate Democrats opposed to some of George W. Bush's nominees on ideological grounds began to take advantage of Senate rules to stop votes on contested nominees. Specifically, they utilized the filibuster to block 10 of President Bush's appellate court nominees during his first term in office. Bush renominated nine of those blocked nominees at the start of his second term, and a frustrated Republican Senate leadership began to consider rule changes to foreclose the use

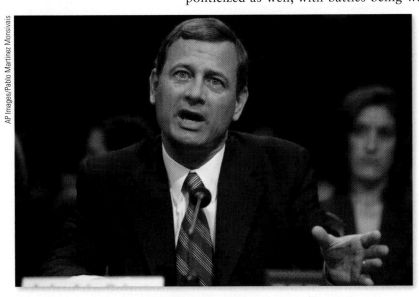

John Roberts, nominee for chief justice of the United States, testifying before the Senate Judiciary Committee in September 2005.

of filibusters against future nominees. Senate Democrats referred to any such rule change as the "nuclear option" because they were prepared to respond by shutting down Senate business through use of the filibuster rule in all other instances. On May 24, 2005, this growing crisis was averted, as a group of 14 moderate senators (seven Republicans and seven Democrats) settled on a plan to allow several of Bush's most controversial nominees to be confirmed, in return for the promise that the filibuster would be reserved for use against judicial appointments when there are "extraordinary circumstances."

9-7 | How a Case Proceeds within the U.S. Supreme Court

The vast majority of cases that come before the U.S. Supreme Court arrive by a **writ of certiorari**, the formal term for an order by which the Court acts in its discretion to hear a case on appeal. Losing parties in the highest state court, a federal circuit court, or (in extremely rare cases) a federal district court can properly file a "cert petition" with the Supreme Court, asking the Court to hear its case. Decisions to grant a writ of certiorari generally follow the *Rule of Four*—if four of the nine justices vote to hear the case, it is placed on the Court's official docket of cases that it will hear during the coming year. Of the many thousands of cert petitions that arrive at the Court during a given year, barely more than 1 percent (fewer than 90 overall) are normally granted.

In theory, the justices decide to hear only those cases that are considered so important that they justify intervention at such a high level. Two other factors may also increase the likelihood that the Supreme Court will grant a writ of certiorari: (1) when the federal government intervenes in the case or (2) when there is a split among two or more of the U.S. circuit courts of appeals on a similar issue. Additionally, some justices as a matter of strategy may vote to deny the petition for cert, even when they think the lower court case was wrongly decided, because they do not want their colleagues to transform the lower court precedent into a Supreme Court edict applicable throughout the land. Regardless of the justices' many motives, denial of a cert petition theoretically casts no aspersions whatsoever on whether a case has been wrongly or rightly decided, although it does allow the lower court decision to stand as the controlling legal decision for the parties in that case. For example, the Supreme Court's 1997 denial of a cert petition in a case concerning affirmative action at the University of Texas did not necessarily imply High Court dissatisfaction with affirmative action; rather, it simply left intact a U.S. Court of Appeals decision that applied only to the three states in that circuit: Texas, Mississippi, and Louisiana. The U.S. Supreme Court waited until six years later to articulate new rules for affirmative action that would become applicable in all 50 states.

As shown in Figure 9-3, if the Court elects to issue a writ of certiorari and hear a case, both the losing and winning parties in the lower court file written documents called **briefs** arguing why constitutional or federal statutory law weighs in favor of their respective positions. Outside parties with an interest in the litigation may also elect to file briefs, known formally as **amicus curiae briefs** (*amicus curiae* is Latin for "friend of the court"), expressing their own views on how the Court should decide a particular case. Interest groups frequently file amicus briefs in Supreme Court cases that affect their members; in doing so, they offer a version of "expert testimony" on the law, albeit with their own strategic bent on the issue in question. The American Medical Association, for example, routinely files amicus briefs in abortion cases; the American Trial Lawyers Association may express its opinion in cases interpreting rules of trial procedure through amicus briefs as well. In some of the more high-profile cases, literally hundreds of such briefs may be filed, offering the Court an admittedly informal tally of the state of public opinion on the issue.

writ of certiorari The formal term for an order by which the Supreme Court acts in its discretion to review a case from a lower court.

briefs Written documents filed by parties in an appealed case arguing why constitutional or statutory law weighs in favor of their respective positions.

amicus curiae briefs Written documents filed by outside parties in the case with an interest in the outcome of the litigation expressing their own views on how the Court should decide a particular case.

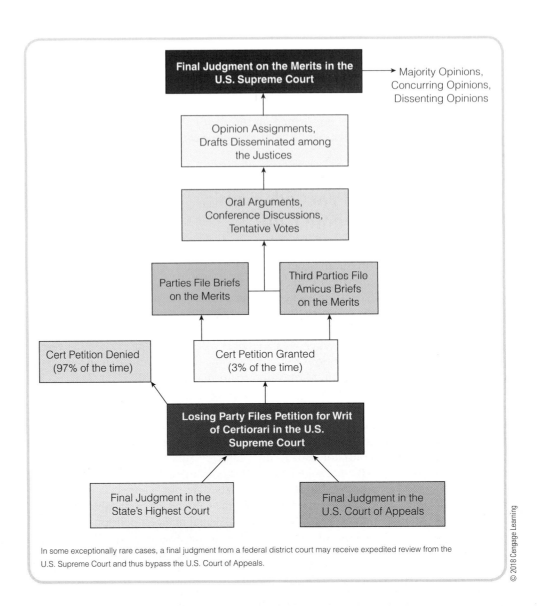

Final Judgment on the Merits in the U.S. Supreme Court → Majority Opinions, Concurring Opinions, Dissenting Opinions

Opinion Assignments, Drafts Disseminated among the Justices

Oral Arguments, Conference Discussions, Tentative Votes

Parties File Briefs on the Merits

Third Parties File Amicus Briefs on the Merits

Cert Petition Denied (97% of the time)

Cert Petition Granted (3% of the time)

Losing Party Files Petition for Writ of Certiorari in the U.S. Supreme Court

Final Judgment in the State's Highest Court

Final Judgment in the U.S. Court of Appeals

In some exceptionally rare cases, a final judgment from a federal district court may receive expedited review from the U.S. Supreme Court and thus bypass the U.S. Court of Appeals.

© 2018 Cengage Learning

FIGURE 9-3 From Cert Petition to Final Judgment in the U.S. Supreme Court

solicitor general The lawyer representing the U.S. government before the U.S. Supreme Court.

The **solicitor general** argues on behalf of the U.S. government in most cases where the federal government is a party. That office also stands among the most influential "friends of the court," filing amicus briefs on behalf of the federal government in approximately a quarter of all cases heard by the Supreme Court each year. Acting through the solicitor general, the U.S. government has enjoyed a disproportionate share of success in affecting Supreme Court case discretionary grants of review and case outcomes.[32]

After all party and amicus briefs have been filed, the Supreme Court justices normally hear oral arguments from opposing counsel in the Supreme Court's chamber. Attorneys licensed to practice before the Supreme Court present their clients' view of the law and facts within an allotted period of time (normally 30 minutes); most of that time is actually spent answering questions and inquiries from the justices. If a justice is truly undecided, he or she may be affected in the margins by the positions of advocates at oral arguments; the give-and-take with the lawyers may also suggest ways to more effectively draft the final opinion. Still, there remains little evidence that the oral arguments actually shift the votes of most justices. Regardless, the hearings in the Supreme Court chamber can still offer moments of high drama, such as when Richard Nixon's attorneys argued for an especially broad interpretation of executive privilege in the 1974 Watergate tapes case. Their argument was ultimately rejected, and Nixon resigned just days after the Court's decision was handed down.

Shortly after the oral arguments are completed and the case has been formally submitted, the justices meet in conference to discuss the case, offer initial votes, and assign opinions. The chief justice presides over all conferences, which culminate in the assignment of opinions to be researched and written by individual justices in accordance with the conference discussions. Each justice employs four clerks—selected from a pool of the top law school graduates from across the country—who work behind the scenes researching the law and creating initial drafts of written opinions according to the justice's specific wishes. In some cases, clerks enjoy even more influence over the justices they work for, assisting them as they sort through competing legal arguments.

A **majority opinion** requires agreement of at least five of the Court's nine members; only a majority opinion carries the force of law. The chief justice has just one vote like his colleagues, but if he is in the majority, the chief justice also has the crucial power to choose who will write the Court's main opinion. (If the chief justice is not in the majority, the senior-most associate justice in the majority retains that power of assignment.) Individual justices may choose to write other opinions either on their own or on behalf of a minority of justices. A **concurring opinion** agrees with the end result reached by the majority but disagrees with the reasons offered for the decision. A **dissenting opinion**, on the other hand, disagrees with the result reached by the majority. Justices write concurring and dissenting opinions both to register their differences with the majority and to lay the groundwork for the future, when those alternate grounds may one day secure the support of a Court majority.

The dissents written by Oliver Wendell Holmes Jr., who served on the U.S. Supreme Court from 1902 to 1932, established him as one of the most important legal thinkers in American history. When President Theodore Roosevelt appointed Holmes to the U.S. Supreme Court in 1902, the Court majority at the time appeared to be favorably disposed to protect the rights of big business. Armed with his own "realist" view of law that emphasized the "necessities of the time," Holmes dissented vigorously from the Court's majority opinions invalidating industrial reform laws and other progressive legislation. With speech restrictions on the rise in America during and immediately after World War I, Holmes eventually adjusted his own philosophy to promote a broader conception of free speech under the Constitution. Along with fellow justice Louis Brandeis, Holmes dissented from the majority's opinions allowing the government to punish minority views. (Holmes also made famous the metaphor of a "marketplace of ideas" and cautioned that even liberal protections of free speech would not protect a man from "falsely shouting 'fire!' in a crowded theater.") For Holmes, "the life of law" was never logic; rather, it was "experience." Justices after Holmes came to embrace his practical, real-world approach to the law. For instance, in *New York Times v. Sullivan* (1964),[33] the Supreme Court built on Holmes's theories about the First Amendment to apply a more protective approach to libel law, making it harder for public officials to sue newspapers that criticized their actions.

Once drafts of the justices' opinions in a case have been circulated and finalized, the decision can be announced. Occasionally the justices can shift their votes near the end of the process. For example, in 1986 Justice Lewis Powell seemingly resolved his own inner struggles over the scope of privacy rights when he chose to join Justice Byron White's four-person opinion in *Bowers*

majority opinion The opinion of a majority of members of the U.S. Supreme Court, which carries the force of law.

concurring opinion The opinion of one or more justices that agrees with the end result reached by the majority but disagrees with the reasons offered for the decision.

dissenting opinion The opinion of one or more justices who disagree with the result reached by the majority.

The Great Dissenter, Justice Oliver Wendell Holmes Jr., was appointed to the Supreme Court by President Theodore Roosevelt in 1902. Holmes's dissenting opinions on behalf of the freedom of expression would garner the support of Supreme Court majorities several decades later.

MPI/Getty Images

v. Hardwick.[34] Powell's vote gave White the slim majority and determined that the right to homosexual sodomy would not receive constitutional protection. That decision was finally reversed in 2003, when the Court overturned *Bowers* in *Lawrence v. Texas*.[35] Powell later publicly recanted his support of *Bowers*, proving that his inner struggle had actually continued. Normally the justices issue written opinions only, but on special occasions, the justices may even decide to read from key passages of the opinions they authored.

9-8 | Why the Justices Vote the Way They Do

Although it is difficult to determine what causes Supreme Court justices to vote as they do on certain issues, social scientists and legal scholars have identified a number of factors that may play a role in a judge's decision making:

- **Legal rules and precedents.** The law itself—including constitutional law, statutes, rules and regulations, and past court decisions interpreting those sources—may be unambiguous enough to counsel one particular application to the case at hand. Previous court decisions are especially hard to avoid—when judges follow the decisions of past judges' rulings in similar cases, they are adhering to the long-standing doctrine of *stare decisis*, which is Latin for "stand by the decision" that has already been settled. For example, although Justice Byron White dissented from the original decision in *Miranda v. Arizona* (1966)[36] providing unprecedented rights to the accused, in later decisions he actively applied the *Miranda* holding to other cases, deferring to a High Court precedent that he personally opposed. Although the language of Supreme Court opinions suggests that stare decisis is always at work, often more than one reasonable interpretation of a law or legal opinion exists. In recent years, some judges have turned to international law and judicial opinions handed down in foreign courts as well. Most notably, Justice Anthony Kennedy in *Lawrence v. Texas* (2003) cited the European Court of Human Rights in support of the Court's protection of homosexual privacy rights. Defenders of this practice claim that because Americans share some values with the wider civilization, judges should be able to cite any and all sources of law in rendering their decisions; critics respond that there is no basis for U.S. judges to impose foreign "moods or fads" on Americans.
- **Changes in circumstances.** Sometimes changes in real-life conditions and circumstances may influence how laws are interpreted. In the school desegregation cases of the 1950s, the Supreme Court openly considered the newly discovered harmful effects of segregation on African American children. Similarly, in 1973, the Supreme Court took into account changes in modern medicine when it formulated the definition of constitutionally protected abortion rights in *Roe v. Wade*. Some jurists and scholars believe such changes in circumstances are irrelevant—rather, they view the Constitution as fixed in time and thus limited in scope to what the Framers envisioned. The search for the Framers' original intent about the Constitution is often referred to as "originalism." By contrast, other judges and scholars advocate the more flexible view of the Constitution as a "living, breathing document," which must adapt to changing circumstances and conditions.
- **Ideological "attitudes."** Many political scientists argue that Supreme Court justices' personal attitudes (liberal or conservative on law enforcement issues, free speech, and so forth) influence their judicial decision making. This model of understanding how justices decide cases has been labeled "the attitudinal model." Defenders of the model cite numerous statistics that support their understanding of the way judges decide cases. For example, William O. Douglas was a New Deal liberal who voted in the liberal direction in criminal procedure cases nearly 90 percent of the time and in civil rights cases 93 percent of the time.[37]

- **Personal traits and characteristics.** Males and females may approach political events differently; accordingly, the gender of a Supreme Court justice affects his or her reaction to legal issues and cases to some degree. Just as some demographic groups tend to be more conservative, justices who fit into those groups may be expected to vote accordingly. A justice's personal experiences may also play a role in how he or she judges. Biographers of Justice Oliver Wendell Holmes, for example, contend that Holmes's near-death experiences as a soldier in the Civil War colored his approach to judging.[38]
- **Intra-court politics.** A justice's interest in maintaining good relations with fellow justices may push him or her to vote in a certain way; behind-the-scenes bargaining and negotiating have also been features of Supreme Court politics throughout its history. In the late 1950s and early 1960s, Chief Justice Earl Warren and Justice William Brennan were famed for their ability to sway undecided justices in their favor; by contrast, Justice Felix Frankfurter's condescending attitude toward his fellow justices persuaded few and alienated many.
- **External political pressures.** Although Supreme Court justices enjoy life tenure and are thus theoretically immune to outside political pressures, the reality is much more complicated. Aware that the Court's prestige often rests on its ability to persuade the other branches, as well as the public, to comply with the Court's decisions, justices often react to the political environment that surrounds the Court when issuing legal opinions. *Roe v. Wade* survived its widely predicted demise in 1992 because at least two conservative justices feared its reversal would deal a blow to the Supreme Court's prestige. Chief Justice Roberts's concern with threats to the Court's prestige may have led him to defer to the political branches in the health care case of *NFIB v. Sebelius* (2012).[39] Public opinion may thus play a role in determining the language of opinions and even the outcome of some cases.

9-9 | Current Debates Over the Exercise of Judicial Power

American courts often find themselves the subject of controversy. Many of the recurring debates over the proper role of courts include the following:

- **Judicial restraint versus judicial activism.** The Supreme Court struck down several New Deal statutes in the 1930s; a few decades later, it invalidated state laws banning the use of contraceptive devices (in 1965) and state laws restricting the right to abortion (in 1973). Critics of those decisions protested the exercise of judicial activism by the High Court. Specifically, they charged that rather than deferring to the elected branches of government as a general matter, the justices responsible for those controversial decisions had effectively turned the Court into a "super legislature" that makes social policy. More recent cases such as *Citizens United v. FEC* (2010),[40] in which the Court struck down a federal law banning corporations from most forms of participation in election campaigns, have revived those charges once again. Critics of judicial activism argue in favor of a philosophy of judicial restraint by which judges act more slowly and incrementally, affording the democratically elected branches considerable discretion to enact whatever laws they choose, so long as there is no clear and unambiguous prohibition against those laws in the Constitution itself. (Given the so-called elegant vagueness of the Constitution's language, advocates of judicial restraint believe those instances are rare indeed.)
- **Electing judges versus appointing judges.** Federal judges are appointed by the president with the advice and consent of the Senate and then serve for life. Many state judges are appointed as well, for either fixed or indefinite terms; others must run for election and then must seek reelection to stay on the bench. These varying

methods of judicial selection may have significant implications on judicial decision making. Appointed judges no longer accountable to the public or to any political processes enjoy increased independence in their decision making. Although many judicial elections pose little or no challenge to the incumbents, these election contests have become dramatically more contested in recent decades. For instance, in 1986 conservative groups disgruntled with liberal decisions rendered by the highest state court in California campaigned successfully to defeat three of its more liberal justices in recall elections, including Chief Justice Rose Bird. What elected judges may lack in independence they make up for in accountability; unlike judges appointed for life, elected judges should be more responsive to the public as a whole. The debate over judicial selection mechanisms often boils down to a question of how to strike the proper balance between the competing interests of judicial independence and accountability to the public.

- **Law versus politics.** Do judges sit on a court of law, or is their institution simply another political body exercising its political will? Certainly the judicial process is fashioned to trumpet the court's role as a legal body that transcends ordinary politics. The judicial robes, magisterial courtrooms, and reliance on formality give rise to this "cult of the robe" as the "apolitical" branch. Canons of judicial ethics require that judges avoid even the appearance of impropriety by not participating in political debates and lobbying other branches on various matters. At the same time, the U.S. Supreme Court in particular often finds itself at the storm center of American politics. In some instances the other branches actually come to the Court in search of legal answers to what are essentially political problems. The Court's 5–4 decision in *Bush v. Gore* (2000),[41] which ended the manual recounts for the 2000 presidential election in Florida and made George W. Bush the president-elect, illustrates just one way that law and politics can become intertwined. Over a decade later, the Supreme Court's decision to uphold President Obama's health care reform legislation offered political fodder for both sides of the political spectrum in the months leading up to the 2012 presidential election. In extremely rare cases, the elected branches essentially abdicate their responsibility to act altogether, forcing the courts to step in by enforcing judicial decrees. For example, federal courts have on rare occasions supervised the construction of prisons and the implementation of busing programs. The highly political manner in which judges are chosen and the ambiguous nature of so many legal provisions mean that the tension between law and politics is perhaps inevitable in the U.S. political system.

- **Cameras in the courtroom.** The Constitution guarantees to every criminal defendant a public trial; courts can satisfy that requirement by allowing the media and some members of the public access to the trial. Many states go a step further, allowing television cameras in state courtrooms, but the federal judicial system has so far resisted any such development. Do lawyers play up to the television cameras, undermining the interests of justice? It's hard to say. When Casey Anthony was tried for the murder of her two-year-old daughter in a Florida courtroom in 2011, the trial received gavel-to-gavel television coverage. In April 2005, Senator Charles Grassley (R-IA) introduced in Congress the so-called Sunshine in the Courtroom Act, which would allow cameras into federal courtrooms. Specifically, the bill would give the presiding federal judge in every case the authority to determine whether cameras would be permitted and, if so, for how long. Even if such legislation one day passes, it is unlikely that

The late Justice Antonin Scalia, being interviewed here by Chris Wallace on Fox News Sunday in 2013. Justice Scalia was consistently opposed to televising the Supreme Court's oral arguments during his nearly 30 years of service on the High Court.

Paul Morigi/Stringer/Getty Images

cameras will appear any time soon in the U.S. Supreme Court, where Chief Justice John Roberts continues to defer to a handful of older justices who remain adamantly opposed to television coverage. (See the timeline in Figure 9-4.) The late Justice Antonin Scalia noted his objection in especially stark terms during a 2005 interview when he was still serving on the High Court: "I think there's something sick about making entertainment out of other people's legal problems . . . I don't like it in the lower courts, and I don't particularly like it in the Supreme Court."[42] Until the makeup of the current Court changes significantly, Supreme Court observers unable to observe oral arguments in person will have to settle for audiotapes of the oral arguments made available a short time later.

Since the outset of the republic, U.S. presidents have appointed justices to the Court who have gone on to make decisions that transform the constitutional landscape for decades after their presidents have already passed from the scene. That explains much of the controversy surrounding President Obama's nomination of Judge Merrick Garland to replace Justice Antonin Scalia on the Supreme Court in March of 2016: Both political sides realized that the next nominee would hold the balance of power in many close Supreme Court decisions, and neither side was willing to concede that power without a fight with the 2016 presidential election looming in the background.

Of course, Obama and his political opponents should be forewarned: the justices themselves are not always predictable. Life appointments to the Court allow justices to rule without regard for their own political futures, and sometimes the justices' decisions do not fit into a well-understood political or legal framework. Thus, consider that it was Justice Anthony Kennedy, an appointment of Republican President Ronald Reagan, who defied conservative hopes with his key votes to save *Roe v. Wade* and to constitutionalize same-sex marriage. Recent presidents have made it a top priority to choose predictable nominees with sound ideological credentials on one end or the other of the political spectrum. Unfortunately for them, the political circumstances and the legal issues that face the Court may change as well, rendering those predictions useless for future times. The least dangerous branch has never been more powerful, and ambitious presidents will always be limited in their capacity to tame the highest court in the land.

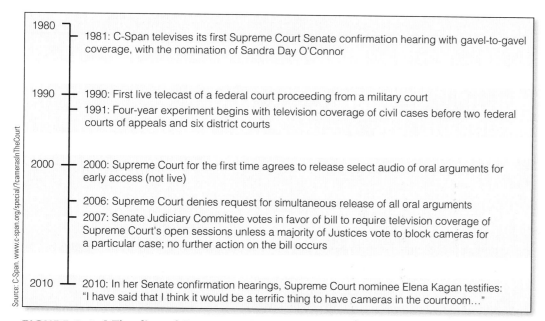

Source: C-Span. www.c-span.org/special/?camerasInTheCourt

1980

1981: C-Span televises its first Supreme Court Senate confirmation hearing with gavel-to-gavel coverage, with the nomination of Sandra Day O'Connor

1990

1990: First live telecast of a federal court proceeding from a military court

1991: Four-year experiment begins with television coverage of civil cases before two federal courts of appeals and six district courts

2000

2000: Supreme Court for the first time agrees to release select audio of oral arguments for early access (not live)

2006: Supreme Court denies request for simultaneous release of all oral arguments

2007: Senate Judiciary Committee votes in favor of bill to require television coverage of Supreme Court's open sessions unless a majority of Justices vote to block cameras for a particular case; no further action on the bill occurs

2010

2010: In her Senate confirmation hearings, Supreme Court nominee Elena Kagan testifies: "I have said that I think it would be a terrific thing to have cameras in the courtroom..."

FIGURE 9-4 A Timeline of Cameras in the Federal Courts

Is Law School the Right Choice for You and, If So, When Should You Apply?

Currently there are almost two hundred law schools in the United States accredited by the American Bar Association (ABA) that award juris doctor degrees to students upon completion of three years or more of legal education. You are no doubt familiar with the names of many of these schools: Harvard, Yale, Columbia, the University of Chicago, and several others that enjoy sterling reputations and are well known around the world. Many graduates of these schools work in prestigious short-term clerkships for judges and then go on to enjoy their pick of legal jobs at extremely high starting salaries. Other law school graduates are not so fortunate, however. According to lawjobs.com, graduates of law schools ranked below the top 25 have a less-than-one-in-five chance of beginning their careers at a large law firm with relatively high starting salaries; and nearly 15 percent of all students at ABA-accredited schools either flunk out or are unemployed for at least nine months after graduation. Moreover, at 44 ABA-accredited schools, fully 20 percent of students have flunked out or remain unemployed. Considering the high price of law school today (many students graduate with debts of $100,000 or more), these are daunting figures indeed.

Of course, for many college graduates who attend the right law school at the right moment in their young careers, legal education offers significant benefits, including the prospect of an exciting and lucrative career. Because the average age of entering law students across the nation is 25 years old (the average age is higher at some top-ranked schools), most college graduates will consider other post-graduation opportunities before law school, both to prepare them for the rigors of law school and to enhance their chances of admission at top schools.

A law professor lectures to a large class of first-year law students.

For Critical Thinking and Discussion

1. Can you think of any benefits that accrue to law students who take time off after college?
2. Many college graduates apply to law school not so much because they dream of a legal career, but because they are unaware of any other promising options. What other types of graduate schools might be of interest to students who enjoy crafting arguments and debating public policy?
3. Law school applications tend to rise during difficult economic times. Why do you think that is true?

Summary

9-1 Types of Law

- *Civil law* refers to statutes enacted most often by legislative bodies; common law consists of the rulings handed down by judges that establish precedents. Other types of law include criminal, civil, constitutional, and administrative law.

9-2 The Structure of the U.S. Legal System

- Article III of the U.S. Constitution established the judicial branch, including the U.S. Supreme Court. Federal district courts are the trial courts, whose decisions may be appealed to the U.S. courts of appeals, and then in turn to the U.S. Supreme Court. The decisions of the 50 state supreme courts that raise federal issues may also be brought directly to the U.S. Supreme Court.

9-3 The Adversarial System of Justice

- The U.S. legal system is an adversarial system of justice in which opposing parties contend against each other for a result favorable to themselves; disputes between parties may be settled through civil litigation, whereas those accused of crimes are prosecuted through a criminal justice system that primarily produces plea bargains between defendants and the government.

9-4 Judicial Review and Its Implications

- Chief Justice John Marshall's opinion in *Marbury v. Madison* (1803) established the Supreme Court's authority to review the constitutionality of any act passed by Congress, as well as any order of the U.S. president.

9-5 Limitations on Courts

- Courts in the United States cannot initiate lawsuits. They can only hear true controversies, their decisions affect only those parties that are part of a case, and they have no ability to enforce their decisions.

9-6 Electing and Appointing Judges

- State judges are selected in various ways: Some are appointed by governors or legislatures; others must run in an election; still others are chosen by a merit plan system. By comparison, all federal court judges are nominated by the president and must be confirmed by the U.S. Senate.

9-7 How a Case Proceeds within the U.S. Supreme Court

- In order to grant a writ of certiorari to review a case, four of the nine justices must approve. After briefs are filed and oral arguments are heard, the justices vote on the merits and issue their majority opinion accordingly; concurring and dissenting opinions may also be issued.

9-8 Why the Justices Vote the Way They Do

- Various factors influence a judge's decision making, including legal precedents, new circumstances, ideological attitudes, personal traits, intracourt politics, and external pressures.

9-9 Current Debates Over the Exercise of Judicial Power

- The courts are not free from their own controversy. Justices who frequently overturn state and federal laws may be accused of judicial activism; state judges who must run for election occasionally face some opposition, which in turn forces them to be more responsive to the public. A majority of justices continue to oppose allowing television cameras to cover oral arguments.

Key Terms

amicus curiae briefs (p. 251)
appellate jurisdiction (p. 244)
briefs (p. 251)
civil law (p. 231)
class action lawsuit (p. 243)
common law (p. 231)
complaint (p. 236)
concurring opinion (p. 253)

defendant (p. 236)
discovery (p. 236)
dissenting opinion (p. 253)
grand jury (p. 237)
indictment (p. 237)
judicial review (p. 239)
litigation (p. 236)
majority opinion (p. 253)

original jurisdiction (p. 244)
plaintiff (p. 236)
plea bargain (p. 238)
solicitor general (p. 252)
standing (p. 243)
writ of certiorari (p. 251)

Test Yourself

1. A rule or regulation issued by the Federal Trade Commission is an example of which type of law?
   a. Civil law
   b. Common law
   c. Constitutional law
   d. Administrative law

2. Judge-made law handed down through judicial opinions that over time establish precedents is
   a. civil law.
   b. common law.
   c. constitutional law.
   d. administrative law.

3. Do generalist courts that handle criminal, civil, and constitutional cases still make sense in the modern era? Or should more courts specialize in different areas of the law?

4. The U.S. Constitution specifically establishes which of the following?
   a. Federal district courts
   b. U.S. courts of appeals
   c. The U.S. Supreme Court
   d. All of the above

5. Frustrated by a Supreme Court that struck down a number of his policies as unconstitutional, which president unsuccessfully attempted to add new justices?
   a. Abraham Lincoln
   b. Franklin Roosevelt
   c. John Kennedy
   d. Ronald Reagan

6. Under what circumstances would a party in a legal case file a writ of certiorari?

7. A party that initiates a formal legal proceeding in a civil case is referred to as a
   a. defendant.   c. defense attorney.
   b. plaintiff.   d. prosecutor.

8. An indictment is authorized by which of the following?
   a. Grand jury   c. Judge
   b. Trial jury   d. Prosecutor

9. The vast majority of criminal cases are resolved by which of the following methods?
   a. Jury conviction   c. Hung jury
   b. Jury acquittal   d. Plea bargain

10. One stage of the pretrial process is known as *discovery*. What occurs at this stage?

11. The power of the Court to review a law passed by Congress as unconstitutional was established in which of the following decisions?
    a. *Marbury v. Madison*
    b. *McCulloch v. Maryland*
    c. *Martin v. Hunter's Lessee*
    d. *Dred Scott v. Sandford*

12. The authority of the Supreme Court to determine the scope of congressional power under the "necessary and proper clause" was established in
    a. *Marbury v. Madison*.
    b. *McCulloch v. Maryland*.
    c. *Martin v. Hunter's Lessee*.
    d. *Dred Scott v. Sandford*.

13. The power of the Supreme Court to exercise judicial review over coordinate branches is not found in the Constitution itself. How, then, did it become so firmly established?

14. The authority of a court to review decisions handed down by another court is called
    a. standing.
    b. appellate jurisdiction.
    c. original jurisdiction.
    d. judicial review.

15. What are the limitations of judicial power that do not present such limitations for the other branches of government?

16. Who nominates federal district judges?
    a. The president
    b. Senators
    c. The Supreme Court justices
    d. The Speaker of the House

17. The current chief justice of the U.S. Supreme Court is
    a. Sonia Sotomayor.
    b. Elena Kagan.
    c. John Roberts.
    d. Ruth Bader Ginsburg.

18. What are the various factors that presidents consider when nominating an individual to serve on the Supreme Court?

19. A minimum of how many Supreme Court justices is required for a case to be added to the docket?
    a. Two
    b. Four
    c. Five
    d. Six

20. Who normally represents the U.S. government when arguing a case before the Supreme Court?
    a. The attorney general
    b. The president's chief counsel
    c. The solicitor general
    d. Any member of the Washington, D.C., bar

21. The judicial principle of adhering to long-standing doctrinal decisions is known as
    a. amicus curiae.
    b. stare decisis.
    c. nolo contendere.
    d. cogito ergo sum.

22. Distinguish between a *concurring* opinion and a *dissenting* opinion.

23. Which justice was particularly effective at swaying his judicial colleagues to vote with him in landmark cases such as *Brown v. Board of Education*?
    a. Oliver Wendell Holmes
    b. Felix Frankfurter
    c. Anthony Kennedy
    d. Earl Warren

24. What kind of external political pressures led two conservative justices to uphold *Roe v. Wade* in 1992?

25. What kind of judges may be elected?
    a. Federal district court judges
    b. State superior court judges
    c. Judges on the U.S. Court of Appeals
    d. U.S. Supreme Court justices

26. Distinguish between judicial activism and judicial restraint. Did the Court's 2003 *Lawrence v. Texas* decision represent activism or restraint?

1. d. (LO 9-1); 2. b. (LO 9-1); 4. c. (LO 9-2); 5. b. (LO 9-2); 7. b. (LO 9-3); 8. a. (LO 9-3); 9. d. (LO 9-3); 11. a. (LO 9-4); 12. b. (LO 9-4); 14. b. (LO 9-5); 16. a. (LO 9-6); 17. c. (LO 9-6); 19. b. (LO 9-7); 20. c. (LO 9-7); 21. b. (LO 9-7); 23. d. (LO 9-8); 25. b. (LO 9-9)

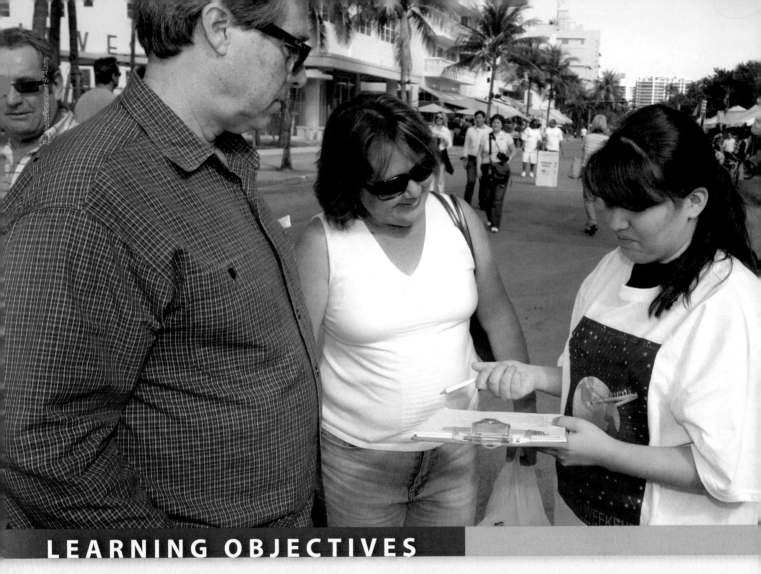

LEARNING OBJECTIVES

10-1 Public Opinion in American Politics
- Appraise the role that public opinion plays in American democracy and the policymaking process

10-2 How Is Public Opinion Expressed?
- Compare and contrast the different ways in which public opinion may be expressed.

10-3 The Levels of Public Opinion
- Distinguish between the different levels of public opinion, from broad values and beliefs, to partisan and ideological orientations, to attitudes and opinions on specific items

10-4 How Informed Is Public Opinion?
- Assess the mass public's level of knowledge about American politics and the capacity of the public to contribute to the political process

10-5 How Does Public Opinion Form?
- Assess the political socialization process and identify the important factors (such as the family, schools, friends, religion) that contribute to the development of political opinions

10-6 How Is Public Opinion Measured?
- Differentiate between a scientific poll and an unscientific poll
- Apply the criteria for asking unbiased poll questions

10-7 Interpreting Public Opinion Data
- Analyze the findings from a poll along the dimensions of direction, intensity, and stability of public opinion

10

Public Opinion

For political leaders and citizens alike, the appetite for information on what the public thinks has always been hearty. Today, this appetite is fed through the large number of opinion polls whose results are disseminated through newspapers, magazines, television, radio, and the Internet. The methods of gauging public opinion have advanced quite dramatically over the nation's history, and this advancement has been driven in no small part by the obsession to know what Americans think. The nation's democratic roots, featuring a commitment to majoritarian rule and the "consent of the governed," raise public opinion to a lofty status in the workings of American politics. Indeed, the willingness of officials to heed the people's voice has become firmly entrenched in American political culture. Scientific measurement of public opinion is a relatively recent phenomenon in American politics, but the significant role that public opinion plays in the formulation of policy is as old as American democracy itself. Understanding what public opinion is, how it is expressed, how it forms, and how it is measured in contemporary politics is critical to understanding how American government works.

WHO ARE YOU?

What Is Your Political Ideology?

Are you a liberal? A moderate? A conservative? If conservative, are you a social and/or economic conservative? Or maybe you consider yourself to be a progressive? Or a democratic socialist? Perhaps a libertarian? Public opinion pollsters use a number of labels in an attempt to describe the political ideology of Americans. One of the more straightforward approaches to measuring political ideology

is to ask a national sample of Americans the question: "How would you describe your political views: conservative, moderate, or liberal?" The Gallup Organization has been measuring the political ideology of Americans this way for many years. The following graphic shows how Americans place themselves on this question from 1992 through 2015. While more than one-third think of themselves as either "conservative" or "moderate" over this time period, an increasing, yet lower, percentage describe themselves as "liberal."

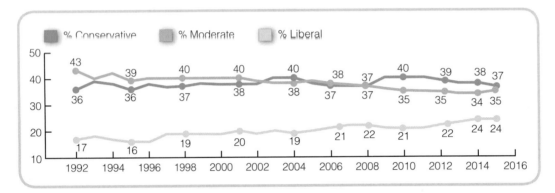

Source: www.gallup.com/poll/188129/conservatives-hang-ideology-lead-thread.aspx

While the Gallup Poll question allows respondents to choose the label that describes them, terms such as liberal and conservative may be interpreted very differently by different people. Someone who says he or she is "conservative" may do so either because he or she supports social conservative policies (such as opposition to abortion or same-sex marriage) or supports economic conservative

policies (such as cutting taxes and government spending). Since 1987 the Pew Research Center has been surveying Americans and classifying them into a more nuanced set of eight different political ideology categories, such as "business conservatives," "next generation left," "faith and family left," and "young outsiders." Here are the results of the most recent Pew poll on the ideology of Americans:

Polarized Wings, a Diverse Middle	General public %	Registered voters %	Politically engaged %
The Partisan Anchors	**36**	**43**	**57**
• **Steadfast Conservatives** *Socially conservative populists*	12	15	19
• **Business Conservatives** *Pro-Wall Street, pro-immigrant*	10	12	17
• **Solid Liberals** *Liberal across-the-board*	15	17	21
Less Partisan, Less Predictable	**54**	**57**	**43**
• **Young Outsiders** *Conservative views on government, not social issues*	14	15	11
• **Hard-Pressed Skeptics** *Financially stressed and pessimistic*	13	13	9
• **Next Generation Left** *Young, liberal on social issues, less so on social safety net*	12	13	11
• **Faith and Family Left** *Racially diverse and religious*	15	16	12
• **Bystanders** *Young, diverse, on the sidelines of politics*	<u>10</u>	<u>0</u>	<u>0</u>
	100	100	100

Source: Pew Research Center www.people-press.org/2014/06/26/the-political-typology-beyond-red-vs-blue/

• Who are you, and what is your own political ideology in this Pew political typology? To find out, take the 23-question test developed by Pew and see which label fits you, at: www.people-press.org/quiz/political-typology.

To see how your answers compare to others, take the **Who Are You?** poll in MindTap!

10-1 | Public Opinion in American Politics

The concept of public opinion is central to the American system of government. But the way in which public opinion is gauged and its relevance and uses in American politics has changed over the nation's history. The U.S. Constitution begins with the words "We the People," highlighting the important role of the *public* in the creation of the government. Nonetheless, there is no mention of the term *public opinion* in the Constitution. The word *democracy* literally translated (from its Greek roots *demos* and *kratos*) means "rule by the people," and thus the opinions of the public take on a particularly important role in governing. The American system of government was founded on a set of democratic principles, first articulated by Plato and Aristotle and later popularized by political philosophers of the eighteenth-century Enlightenment, such as Montesquieu.[1] These principles herald the role of the public in governing and in consenting to what government does.

From the time of the Founders up through the present day, the virtues of public opinion and its role in American democracy have been continually extolled. James Madison argued that the "public voice" and its formal role in voting provided primary justification for adopting the proposed Constitution. Borrowing from the political theories of John Locke, Madison acknowledged that government must serve the "will of the people." Andrew Jackson's presidency encouraged and empowered the rise of the "common man" to express his opinion for the purpose of influencing government.

Political leaders recognize that public opinion plays not only a theoretically important role in our democratic form of government, but an important tactical role as well. Political scientist E. E. Schattschneider, in an influential book titled *The Semisovereign People*, argued that "public opinion can emerge as a key factor in any political context" and that public opinion often is responsible for determining the outcome of important political battles. Long before Schattschneider, President Abraham Lincoln expressed this idea based on his own experiences, saying: "Public sentiment is everything. With public sentiment, nothing can fail; without it, nothing can succeed."[2]

Although most scholars, elected leaders, and everyday citizens would agree that **public opinion** is and should be very important in our system of government, the concept remains hard to define and measure. Many scholars regard public opinion as simply the summation of individual opinions on any particular issue or topic. Political scientist V. O. Key Jr., however, defined public opinion more specifically as "those opinions held by private persons which government finds it prudent to heed." As an input in the American political system, public opinion must not only exist, Key argued, but it must also be "heeded" or at least heard by those making policy decisions.[3]

Public opinion is a vague, although important, concept. It is regularly used by presidents to justify their policies, by political candidates to mount campaigns, by interest groups to promote their causes, by journalists to describe public preferences, and by scholars to understand the American government. Today opinion polls—for better or worse—have become the yardstick through which public opinion is understood and evaluated. The barrage of polls released daily by major media organizations provides a plethora of data describing the American psyche. There are, however, numerous practices in addition to polling through which public opinion in America may be expressed.

public opinion The summation of individual opinions on any particular issue or topic.

Screenshot of Andrew Sullivan's blog, "The Daily Dish."

dish.andrewsullivan.com/

10-2 | How Is Public Opinion Expressed?

The formal constitutional mechanism by which public opinion influences the federal government is the free, open, and regular election of House members. Since ratification of the Seventeenth Amendment in 1913, the direct election of U.S. senators has served as yet another constitutional means for the expression of public opinion. Chapter 14 covers this form of expressing public opinion in detail. Voting is one important expression of public opinion and provides guarantees that officials are responsive to voters. In many state and local elections, voters are asked to respond to referendum questions, which empower the public to directly resolve policy issues. But there are a number of additional ways beyond voting in which public opinion has an influence on government. The First Amendment's guarantees that the people have the right to free speech, to peaceably assemble, and to petition their government pave the way for political rallies and protest rallies, which are important manifestations of public opinion.

Supporting a candidate and engaging in attempts to elect an individual or political party to office through a monetary contribution or a contribution of time and effort is another way that public opinion is expressed. Likewise, contributing time or money to an interest group or political action committee enables individuals to express their opinion indirectly and may have a significant impact on what government does.

Public opinion is also expressed through the news media. Journalists often provide commentary on politics and public issues through talk radio shows, websites, editorial pages, and television news talk shows that provide perspectives on public opinion. Individual citizens may also use the media to express their opinion, by writing letters to the editor. In addition, members of the public often choose to express their opinion directly to elected officials by contacting them, via either a letter or e-mail, a phone call, or the Internet, for their views on a particular issue. Although many politically aware Americans still express their opinions on politics in these *traditional* ways, millions of others now take advantage of their laptops, smartphones, and tablets to post comments on blogs. One of the first political blogs was Andrew Sullivan's "The Daily Dish," founded in 2000. Since then the number of blogs has exploded. Today, blogs vary widely in form, but most feature some type of personal commentary, references to data, and links to other sources on the Internet related to a topic of political discussion. Most bloggers don't aspire to the goal of providing *objective* commentary. Rather, they aim to provide up-to-date, personal, and often partisan perspectives on current political topics. Many liberals tend to flock to more left-leaning blogs such as *The Daily Kos* and *Talking Points Memo*, whereas conservatives frequent conservative blog sites, such as *Powerline* or the blog of conservative author Michelle Makin. Social networks, such as Facebook, Twitter, and Tumblr, also provide a means for people to express opinions to their "friends" or others in their social network.

In addition, a highly visible and widely used expression of public opinion in contemporary politics is the public opinion poll. Most major and many smaller media organizations today regularly conduct polls on politics and policy issues, and publish the results of those polls in the form of news stories. The *USA Today*/Gallup Poll, the CBS/*New York Times* poll, the Fox News/Opinion Dynamics poll, and the NBC/*Wall Street Journal* poll are only a few examples of media-based polls that, on a regular basis, provide data on American public opinion.

10-3 | The Levels of Public Opinion

Public opinion exists at three basic levels: the broad level of values and beliefs, an intermediate level of political orientations, and the specific level of preferences about particular topics.

Values and Beliefs

values and beliefs The broad principles underlying the American political culture that citizens support and adhere to.

At the highest, most abstract level are the **values and beliefs** of the American people. Values are the broad principles underlying the American political culture that most citizens support and adhere to; they represent that which people find most important in life. Beliefs are the facts derived from values that people take for granted about the world. Although there are a number of values that Americans hold dear, political scientist Samuel Huntington[4] has identified four politically relevant values that are widely accepted in the American political culture and serve as the basis for defining political beliefs on which there is great consensus in America: liberty, equality, individualism, and the rule of law.

The vast majority of Americans support the idea of basic freedoms and liberties, such as freedom of religion and freedom of speech. These liberties are embedded in our political culture and serve as the basis for many government policies. Because Americans value liberty, for example, they believe that people should have the right to choose a religion or not to choose a religion, the right to publicly disagree with the president or the party in power, and the right to publish articles or news stories without government retribution.

Likewise, a majority of Americans firmly value the concept stated in the Declaration of Independence that "all men are created equal." Regardless of economic status, race, or gender, the American public on the whole subscribes to the belief that all people should be treated equally under the law and that all people should have equal opportunities for economic success.

Americans also show a strong propensity to support the value of individualism. Over the years, Americans have consistently shown a preference for rewarding individual hard work and for limiting the role of government.[5] Jefferson's maxim "that government is best which governs the least" presumes that society will advance by encouraging individuals to succeed and leads to a belief in capitalism and free enterprise as the optimal economic system. Also, the Puritan work ethic that served as an important value in early American society continues to be reflected in Americans' affinity for the value of individualism.

Finally, the value of the "rule of law" encourages a strong belief in the legitimacy of the U.S. Constitution, in the importance of elections as a way to configure government, and in the beliefs that the opinion of the majority should prevail, that those in the minority should have the right to challenge the majority, and that those accused of a crime should be entitled to fair procedures.

Unlike other levels of public opinion, values and beliefs are unique in that they generally receive a high level of support and consensus. Whether individuals are Democrats or Republicans, from the far right or the far left, elites or more representative of the masses—the vast majority generally subscribes to these broad values. Accordingly, values are the level of public opinion that define our political culture; widespread agreement and support for them is thus critical to the maintenance of the American political system.

Political Orientations

Values and beliefs are very broad and abstract notions held by Americans that provide general guidance to people in thinking about politics. **Political orientations** are the translation of these values and beliefs into a systematic way of assessing the political environment. Although there may be broad consensus about values and beliefs among Americans, the translation of these values into an organized way of thinking about politics and issues is considerably more varied.

The two primary ways in which Americans orient themselves toward political topics and issues are partisanship (see Figure 10-1) and political ideology. Partisanship, which is discussed in a later chapter, features a psychological attachment to one of the main political parties, generally either the Democrats or the Republicans.[6] A partisan identification provides an orientational mechanism for understanding how to apply one's values and beliefs to the political world. Consider, for example, the political debate over affirmative action policies. A Democratic orientation largely applies the value of equality and the belief that people of all races and creeds should enjoy equal opportunities, therefore suggesting support for affirmative action programs, which attempt to level the playing field and make corrections for policies that have historically benefited white males. A Republican orientation, on the other hand, generally places a higher priority on the value of individualism and the belief that government should not interfere

political orientations The translation of values and beliefs into a systematic way of assessing the political environment.

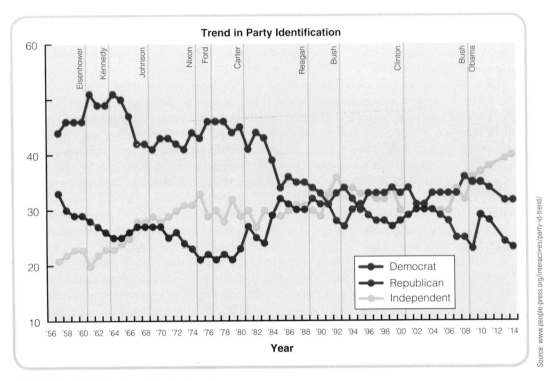

FIGURE 10-1 Partisanship in America

Source: www.people-press.org/interactives/party-id-trend/

with individual initiatives to succeed, thus suggesting opposition to affirmative action programs. Partisan orientation often helps people translate values into specific opinions.

Likewise, political ideology provides an orientation for translating values into specific opinions. **Political ideology** is a philosophical guide that people use to help translate their values and beliefs into specific political preferences. The dominant ideologies in America are liberalism and conservatism. The contemporary **liberal ideology**, which is more closely associated with the modern Democratic Party, prefers that government take a more assertive role in the redistribution of economic resources but that government advocate positions that emphasize individual freedom on a range of social issues. Today's **conservative ideology**, which is more closely identified with the Republican Party, favors government activism in defense of more traditional values on social issues but prefers government restraint in economic redistribution.

The liberal and conservative camps largely agree on the basic values and beliefs of the American political culture—in the rule of law and majority rule and minority rights and in the idea that the free enterprise system will generally guarantee the most robust economy. But liberals and conservatives often differ when seeking to translate these values and beliefs into actual policies.

Partisanship and political ideology are two very important topics in the study of American public opinion. They provide a framework for individuals to translate broad values and beliefs into preferences for issue positions and political candidates. These orientations help people to efficiently form opinions and express those opinions. Partisanship and political ideology also enable both political leaders and scholars to better understand why Americans think what they think about particular issues and vote the way they vote in elections.

The political orientations of Americans tend to be quite stable and lasting[7]—more so than the specific preferences that people have toward policies and political actors. The stability in American political orientations provides an order and consistency to American public opinion, which ultimately promotes stability in the political system as a whole.

Political Preferences

The most discussed level of public opinion is the particular **political preferences** that Americans have on policy issues, their attitudes regarding the performance of political leaders and institutions, and their candidate preferences in elections. Support for the minimum wage, gun control proposals, the use of U.S. troops in fighting terrorism, abortion policy, campaign finance reform proposals, tax increases, and tax cuts are all specific policy issues on which the American public expresses opinions. In addition to policies, Americans also hold specific opinions about the performance of their elected leaders such as the president, as well as their confidence in institutions such as Congress, the U.S. Supreme Court, and the military.

What Americans think about the minimum wage, the performance of the president, or the candidates in a political campaign is highly influenced by their political orientations. For example, an individual who identifies as a Republican and considers herself ideologically conservative is much less likely to say she approves of President Obama's performance than would a Democrat who considers himself to be liberal.

Figure 10-2 depicts public opinion on two preference questions that have experienced considerable change in the recent past: attitudes about gay marriage (for which public support has increased) and the percentage saying that the most important problem in America relates to economic conditions (which spiked in 2008 at the outset of the economic recession, and then dropped significantly in 2013 as the economy rebounded).

political preferences The attitudes people maintain regarding the performance of political leaders and institutions, their candidate preferences in elections, and specific policy issues.

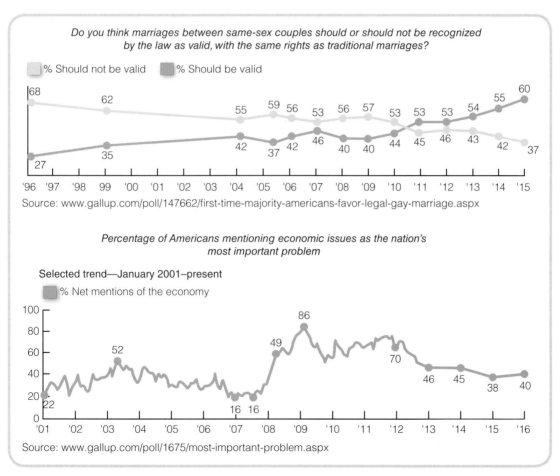

FIGURE 10-2 **Preferences of Americans**

10-4 | How Informed Is Public Opinion?

As discussed earlier in this chapter, American democracy relies on public opinion to choose leaders and inform public policy. This reliance is based on an important assumption about democracy—that citizens have the necessary information and skills to be able to understand political issues and provide informed input. Since the time of Plato and Aristotle, political philosophers have dealt with questions about this important assumption: is the public capable of democracy?

In the Federalist Papers, Alexander Hamilton and James Madison expressed concerns about the fickleness of public opinion and the potential "tyranny of the masses," which could lead to instability in governance.[8] Hamilton's solution for this problem was a republican form of government, in which the public chooses leaders who run the government, rather than a direct democracy, in which the public rules directly.

Suspicions about the capacity of the public for meaningful contributions to governance were also articulated quite well by Walter Lippmann in the early twentieth century.[9] Lippmann, a well-known public opinion scholar, delivered withering attacks on ordinary citizens' lack of knowledge regarding politics. He argued that citizens invest very little energy and effort in acquiring information about politics, and, as a consequence, the public lacks the necessary knowledge for their opinions to provide value. Subsequent research in the 1960s and 1970s, most notably by Philip Converse and his colleagues in *The American Voter*, used scientific surveys to support the argument that ordinary citizens tend to be ill-informed about political issues, ill-equipped to understand politics, and quite fickle in how they stand on issues.[10]

More contemporary studies indicate that the American public today is uninformed about politics. For example, Figure 10-3 depicts how many Americans lack knowledge on some important aspects of the American political system.[11]

Some political scientists have come to the defense of the American public in this regard. V. O. Key Jr., in his work *The Responsible Electorate*,[12] stated that although "many voters act in odd ways indeed," if one studies the electorate more carefully, one would find that "voters are not fools." Key observed that "in the large, the electorate behaves about as rationally and responsibly as we should expect, given the clarity of the alternatives presented to it and the character of the information available to it." If political leaders don't rationally discuss issues and provide a framework for voters to use to understand politics, it is not the voters who should be blamed, but rather the leaders. Considering this caveat, Key extolled the capacity of the public to form stable, responsible opinions and to contribute to the governing process.

Benjamin Page and Robert Shapiro extended Key's ideas in their book *The Rational Public*.[13] They used decades of public opinion poll data to show that over the long haul, public opinion on many issues does remain fairly stable, and when it does change, it moves in logical directions. The aggregate responses of the public in polls, Page and

FIGURE 10-3 American Lack of Political Knowledge

Shapiro found, make sense and demonstrate rationality. They also found that the public makes distinctions between important policy areas and that public opinion tends to form meaningful patterns, consistent with a set of underlying beliefs and values.

The link between public opinion on an issue and public policy is a difficult one to establish. Page and Shapiro report that over the long haul, there does seem to be a relationship between public attitudes on policy issues and the public policies that emerge from government. These researchers also argue that when public opinion shifts, a corresponding shift in public policy is likely to follow.

Political scientist Samuel Kernell has noted a more indirect link between public opinion and public policy: Political actors (most notably the president) who have high levels of public support are generally better able to get legislation passed.[14] President Bush, for example, in 2003 was able to get Congress to pass a new tax cut package in part because of the high job performance ratings Americans gave him at that time. High levels of public support may be translated into an officeholder's greater political power to influence the legislative process.

10-5 | How Does Public Opinion Form?

Through voting, opinion polls, protest rallies, communications with leaders, and newspaper editorials, public opinion is expressed and provides an important input for public policymaking. But how do individuals develop their particular political orientations, and how do they come to hold their specific political preferences? How do the more deep-seated values and beliefs form? What influences the values that people hold, their partisan and ideological orientations, and their opinions on specific issues?

Political socialization is the process by which an individual acquires values, beliefs, and opinions about politics. Political socialization is a lifelong process, beginning in early childhood and continuing throughout an individual's life. The learning process that leads to the acquisition of values and opinions not only applies to politics—it also applies to other orientations of people, including their beliefs about religion and culture.

Just as there are a number of factors and influences that lead individuals to consider themselves Democrats or Republicans or supporters of gun control or gun rights, there are also numerous factors and influences that lead people to choose a particular religion, such as Protestant or Catholic, or to choose no religion at all. Socialization is important not only in the development of political learning for individuals, but also in the transmission of the fundamental beliefs and values of the American political culture from one generation to the next.

Although political socialization is a lifelong process, there are certain times in life when political learning is greater. For example, the political socialization that occurs early in life has a more profound impact on political orientations than learning that occurs in adulthood. The impressions and information that are acquired while the individual is younger tend to be most influential and the longest lasting. Psychologists refer to this as the **primacy tendency**.

Early political learning tends to be most profound, but socialization to politics remains at work through a number of influences over the course of a person's life. Numerous factors and institutions, known as **agents of political socialization**,[15] have been identified as having a particularly relevant impact on one's socialization to politics.

Certainly demographic factors such as race, ethnicity, gender, age, and economic status go a long way toward defining individuals' identities and can influence their political values. But a list of the most important agents of political socialization also includes such influences as family, friends and peer groups, schools, the media, and religion. Collectively, these agents promote the acquisition of the political values, beliefs, and opinions that an individual comes to hold.

political socialization The process by which an individual acquires values, beliefs, and opinions about politics.

primacy tendency The theory that impressions acquired while an individual is younger are likely to be more influential and longer lasting.

agents of political socialization Factors that have a significant impact on an individual's socialization to politics.

Parents provide an important influence in socializing their children to appreciate American political values. Above, a father teaches his son to appreciate the values associated with Independence Day.

Family

Because much of the early years in a person's life is dominated by experiences with the family, the primacy tendency leads many to develop values and beliefs consistent with parents' values and beliefs. Parents begin to teach their children about the political world early in the child's life. They transfer feelings about such concepts as authority, freedom, democracy, and racial prejudice to their children in both formal and informal ways. By standing at attention during the playing of the national anthem or attending a Memorial Day service, parents are informally communicating important values about politics. Telling children that skin color should not affect how to think about a particular person or explaining why it is important to vote in an election are formal ways political information is communicated.

These early formal and informal cues from parents have a long-term and lasting impact on a child's political socialization. Over the years, researchers have found that children whose parents are more involved in politics tend to be more involved in politics themselves. The transference of party identification from parent to child is also significant. Children who grew up in homes where parents regard politics as important also tend to regard politics as important throughout their lives. Because children generally want to be like their parents, the

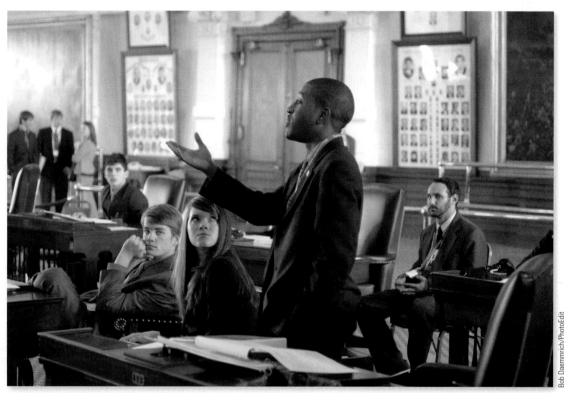

High schools, such as this one in Austin, Texas, help to teach the values of the democratic process by providing mock trials in which students learn how our legal system works.

many cues, both formal and informal, that they receive from their parents are a strong influence on the formation of political orientation.

Friends and Peer Groups

As children grow older, they begin to interact with people outside of their immediate family. They seek friendships with others and show a desire to get along in social groups. Children acquire a great deal of new political learning through their friends and associates, as well as from the social groups that they seek to join. Often, the values, beliefs, and opinions of social peers are the same as or similar to those of the family, so friends and peers reinforce what was learned from parents. For example, wealthy people tend to live together in particular neighborhoods, and so as children from wealthy families find friends and peers, they are likely to find people who have been socialized by their parents in ways similar to themselves.

By the fifth or sixth grade, children become cognitively equipped to better understand the world of politics. Whereas previous learning tends to be based on unquestioned acceptance of what is being communicated, young adults have the ability to critically analyze new information. This cognitive skill development comes at a time in life (young adolescence) when friends and peer groups are particularly influential. Thus the desire to get along and to form social relationships has an important influence on political learning at this point in life.

The Schools

Part of the curriculum in many school systems across the United States focuses on the development of political values, such as respect for authority, the legitimacy of our political institutions, patriotism, and capitalism. Classes in civic education and American government, the daily morning pledge of allegiance to the flag, and pictures of American presidents are just some of the mechanisms by which schools act as an agent of socialization.

Schools serve as an important mechanism for the positive development of attitudes about basic American democratic values, thus promoting general positive attitudes about the legitimacy of the democratic system. Research conducted by David Easton and his colleagues in the 1950s and 1960s demonstrated that schools promoted a positive affective attachment to the concept of "democracy" by the third grade.[16] During the early grades, children acquire beliefs regarding a citizen's role in politics—obeying laws, voting, and paying attention to political events.

Reciting the "Pledge of Allegiance" in elementary school helps to socialize the young to their government.

Political socialization from the school is not limited to elementary and high school. The college experience also has an important socializing effect on citizens' political development. College graduates tend to be more likely to vote and participate in politics, are more likely to follow news and political campaigns, and are better able to understand the political world in which they live. The effects of formal education, even beyond the specific civics education curriculum of the earlier grades, make an important positive contribution to an individual's political socialization.

The Media

Americans spend a great deal of time accessing news information and being entertained by the mass media. It is not surprising, then, that the media act as an important agent of political socialization as well. Information that citizens glean from media news coverage about political events and political campaigns has an impact on their values, beliefs, and opinions. Research has shown that heavy users of the news media are more politically informed than lighter users;[17] they are also more supportive of basic American values, such as individualism, equality, and free speech rights.

The media's impact as a socialization agent extends beyond the provision of news information. Entertainment television, the movies, talk radio, and other media forms also inspire various types of political learning. Studies have shown, for example, that entertainment television tends to promote negative stereotypes of women and minorities, which may reinforce negative attitudes about race or affirmative action. Use of Internet websites and blogs may also help shape a person's political outlook.

Social networking sites are very new and constitute a medium that may socialize people in a way like no other medium. Social network users can select whether to allow or shut out those who want to communicate with them. The audience for each user is a familiar one. A user's network of friends is likely to be more trusted, more connected, and more likely to be open and receptive to others' views. Although this medium is too new for research to explore its impact on socialization, social networking seems to have at least a tremendous potential as an agent of socialization, considering that a recent Pew Center survey found that more than one-third of social network users around the world use this medium to express political views.[18]

Religion

Throughout American history, religious organizations have played an important role in the political socialization process. The values of individualism and hard work were important influences in establishing a capitalist economy and continue to underpin economic policy in the United States. These values, based on the Protestant work ethic, continue to influence the socialization process. More recently, the Christian-based fundamentalist movement has utilized religious teaching to influence opinions about political issues. The Catholic Church's opposition to abortion affects many Catholics' position on that issue.

10-6 | How Is Public Opinion Measured?

public opinion poll A method of measuring the opinions of a large group of people by asking questions of a subset of the larger group and then generalizing the findings to the larger group.

When Americans think about the term *public opinion* in contemporary politics, they often focus on the results of public opinion polls. A **public opinion poll** is a method of measuring the opinions of a large group of people by selecting a subset of the larger group, asking them a set of questions, and generalizing the findings to the larger group.

Public opinion polls are not the only way that public opinion in America is either expressed or understood, but polls have become the most obvious and important instrument for gauging public opinion. Polls provide information that elected leaders use in making public policy, thus providing an important way for public sentiment to influence public policy. Polls have also become a centerpiece of elections, used both by the candidates to shape a winning strategy and by journalists to provide news coverage of campaigns.

Polling has become a huge industry in the United States. To the public, the most visible polls are those that are regularly conducted by media organizations, asking Americans what they think about a variety of topics, such as whom they plan to vote for in an upcoming election, how they rate the job the president is doing, how they feel about the condition of the economy, and many other topics. Media polls are conducted with the purpose of broadcasting results as news stories. However, the polling industry extends far beyond media polls. Candidates at all levels conduct polls to identify strategies for

The Supreme Court and the U.S. Census

Department of Commerce v. U.S. House of Representatives (1999)

Every 10 years, official census workers scatter around the country with clipboards and pencils to help determine the number of people who live in various towns, cities, and states, as well as changes in the overall population. Although many citizens respond to census forms by mail, census takers must fill in the gaps left by those without permanent addresses, or who otherwise go uncounted. Why does the census take place? An accurate counting of people is compelled by the U.S. Constitution's census clause, which requires an "actual enumeration" of the public once per decade to provide an accurate basis for apportioning congressional representation. To address the growing problem of undercounting of certain identifiable groups, including certain minorities, children, and renters in poor neighborhoods, the U.S. Census Bureau of the Department of Commerce proposed to use a form of statistical sampling in 2000. These methods would essentially adjust for undercounting in the actual enumeration process. Critics of the plan countered that the Constitution requires "actual counting" of the population. Who was right? The critics of sampling won the argument. By a 5–4 decision, the U.S. Supreme Court in *Department of Commerce v. U.S. House of Representatives* (1999) held that the use of statistical sampling does not alter the constitutional requirement of "actual enumeration" and the census act that implements it. Accordingly, college students (who tend to be among the most transient citizens) may want to be on the lookout for census takers knocking on their doors—the number crunchers will not be replacing them any time soon.

For Critical Thinking and Discussion

1. Scientific sampling was not available at the time the U.S. Constitution was written. If sampling were available, do you think the Founders might have considered it as an alternative to a full census?

2. If sampling can provide a more accurate demographic portrait of America, do you think the Constitution should be amended to replace the census with a sample?

waging a successful election campaign. Federal, state, and local government agencies conduct polls to evaluate the successes and failures of public programs. Interest groups conduct polls to promote their agendas.

Even though polls have come to play an important and visible role in American politics, the manner in which they are conducted is often misunderstood, and questions about their accuracy are often raised. What makes a poll "scientific"? How is it possible to interview 1,000 Americans and conclude how more than 200 million Americans think? How can two polls be conducted on the same topic and produce different findings? An understanding of polling techniques can help answer these questions.

The History of Political Polling

The immediate predecessor to modern scientific polling in the United States dates back to the 1824 presidential campaign. Newspapers such as the *Boston Globe*, *New York Herald*, and *Harrisburg Pennsylvanian* attempted to gauge voter attitudes about the presidential candidates and predict the election outcome that year by conducting what has come to be known as the **straw poll**. A straw poll gathers the opinions of people who are conveniently available in a particular gathering place. (Today, many refer to these polls as "convenience" polls.) Back in 1824, the newspapers sent "counters" to public places (such as taverns and public meetings) to ask patrons and attendees whom they planned to vote for in the upcoming election. Newspaper publishers quickly found a hearty appetite among readers for stories that attempted to predict the outcome of political races—an appetite modern media executives continue to find quite strong today.

Early straw polls assumed that the accuracy of polls was based on the total number of respondents included in each poll. The larger the number of respondents, the more accurate the results, so it was thought. Straw polls remained the basic methodology for conducting polls for more than a century.[19]

straw poll An unscientific poll that gathers the opinions of people who are conveniently available in a gathering place, such as a shopping center.

By the early 1930s, the most famous national straw poll was the *Literary Digest* poll. In addition to conducting straw polls on policy issues, this poll correctly predicted the winners of the 1920, 1924, 1928, and 1932 presidential elections. The *Literary Digest* conducted its polls by mailing ballots to millions of people. Mailing addresses were obtained from the *Digest*'s own readership lists as well as telephone directories and automobile registration lists. The *Digest* assumed its accuracy in predicting election outcomes was based on the large number of ballots that it counted from voters across the country.

In the 1936 election between Franklin Roosevelt and Alfred Landon, the *Literary Digest* collected ballots from more than 2 million people and confidently predicted that Landon would receive 55 percent of the vote, Roosevelt would get 41 percent, and the remaining 4 percent would go to Union Party candidate William Lemke. The actual election results stunned the *Literary Digest* and its many readers. Roosevelt won the election with a whopping 61 percent of the popular vote. Landon garnered 36.5 percent, whereas Lemke won less than 2 percent. The missed projection put the *Literary Digest* out of business.

This widely publicized missed call by the *Literary Digest* is explained by the faulty assumption of the straw-poll methodology—the assumption that the greater the number of respondents, the more accurate the poll. The number of interviews in a poll is only one of a number of factors that affect poll accuracy. In 1936, the United States was still fighting the effects of the Great Depression, when many Americans had difficulty making ends meet. Those Americans with telephones, automobiles, and subscriptions to the *Literary Digest* (the sources of the mailing addresses for the ballots) tended to be wealthier, less affected by the Depression, and disproportionately less likely to support the liberal economic policies of FDR's New Deal.

At the time, the *Literary Digest* debacle was aptly explained by several researchers who had already begun to conduct polls with more accurate methodologies. Chief among these was Dr. George Gallup, who was applying probability sampling methods to the polls he conducted. During the 1936 campaign, Gallup argued that the *Literary Digest* methodology was producing faulty results. His cries fell on many deaf ears until after the election, when his advice sowed the seeds for a healthy polling industry based on more scientific methods. However, his scientific methods of polling would quickly become adopted as standards of the polling industry in the decades to come. Figure 10.4 shows the remarkable accuracy of the Gallup Poll in predicting winners of presidential elections over the past eight decades.

scientific sample A randomly selected subgroup drawn from a population using probability theory.

Scientific Sampling

The polling procedures popularized by Gallup in the aftermath of the 1936 election relied on the principles of probability theory and focused on the sampling of the population under study.[20] A *sample* is a subgroup of people from a population who are studied for the purpose of learning something about the whole population. Based on the laws of probability, it is possible to draw a sample from a population, administer a set of questions to those in the sample, and understand something about the entire population, within a known level of error.

A **scientific sample** is one that uses probability theory as a guide to selecting people from the population who will compose the sample. Random selection of respondents in the sample is key to achieving a scientific, or representative, sample. *Random sampling* is achieved by giving each possible respondent in the population a known chance of being selected in the sample. There are a number of ways of achieving a random sample.

The polls projected Thomas Dewey would defeat President Harry Truman in 1948. The polls were wrong, but they led many newspapers across the country to prematurely project Truman's defeat as they went to press.

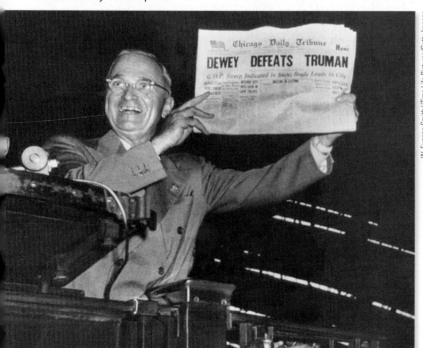

W. Eugene Smith//Time Life Pictures/Getty Images

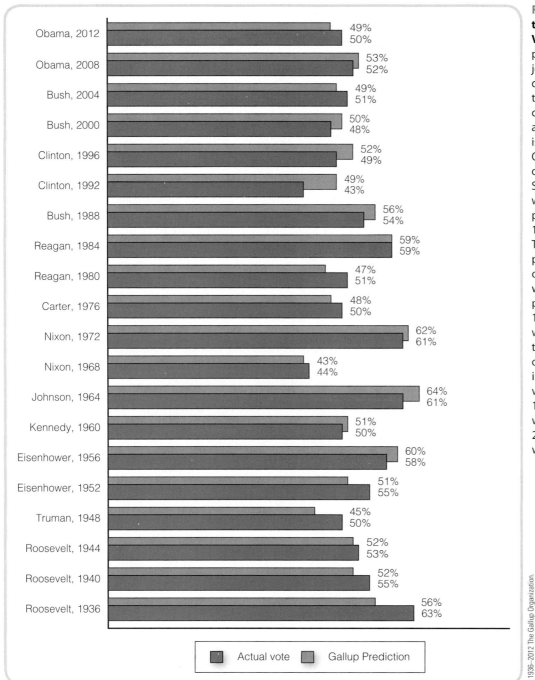

FIGURE 10-4 Accuracy of the Gallup Poll in Predicting Voter Behavior Preelection polls offer candidates, journalists, and voters detailed information on the dynamics of an election contest. How well the polls actually predict vote choices is a frequently voiced concern. One of the best known opinion polls in the United States is the Gallup Poll, which has been conducting preelection polls since the 1936 presidential election. This figure shows Gallup's prediction for the percentage of the vote that the winner would receive in each presidential election from 1936 to the present, along with the actual percentage of the vote that the winner got on Election Day. Gallup made incorrect predictions of the winner in two elections: in 1948 it predicted that Dewey would defeat Truman and in 2012 it predicted Romney would defeat Obama.

Unscientific Polls

In a scientific poll, the results of the poll are generalizable to a population that is represented by the sample of people who are interviewed. **Unscientific polls** differ from scientific ones in that the sample of people who are interviewed is not representative of any group beyond those who register their opinion. There are many examples of unscientific polls in politics. What makes a poll unscientific is the way respondents are selected for

unscientific poll A poll in which the sample of people interviewed is not representative of any group beyond those who register their opinion.

The Presidential Honeymoon

When President Donald Trump took the oath of office to become the nation's 45th chief executive, he enjoyed a level of support that—while hardly universal—was likely to stand as among the highest recorded during his first term in office. The "presidential honeymoon period" refers to the early portion of a new president's term in office when public opinion tends to rally in support of the new chief executive. Despite partisan differences, Americans offer large-scale support with the hope that the new president might successfully move the nation in a positive direction. The honeymoon period generally reflects higher-than-normal approval ratings from Americans as he is given the benefit of the doubt as his term commences. Generally, this translates into initial policy successes.

The Gallup Organization has been measuring presidential approval from the start through the end of each president's term since Harry Truman became president in 1945. From Truman through Obama, that's 13 presidents in all. Figure 10-5 shows the "honeymoon" approval rating (i.e., the approval rating as the new president took office) as well as the "overall average" approval rating through the presidents' full term in office:

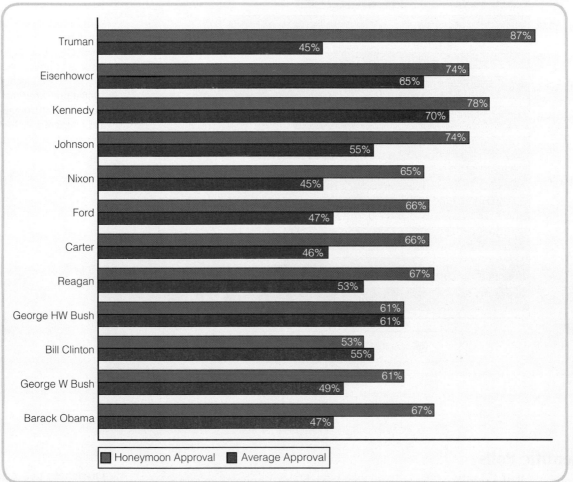

Honeymoon Approval ■ **Average Approval**

Source: www.gallup.com/poll/124922/presidential-job-approval-center.aspx

FIGURE 10-5 Presidential Approval Rating

For Critical Thinking and Discussion

1. Often, the approval rating at the start of a president's term ranks among the highest ratings that he receives, due to the "honeymoon effect." What other factors might boost a president's rating *after* the honeymoon?

2. Figure 10-5 shows that some presidents enjoy honeymoons with higher approval ratings than other presidents. What explains this?

the sample. If the vast majority of people in a population are given a chance of being sampled, then the poll is scientific. If not, then the sample represents nothing beyond itself. In an unscientific sample, some individuals in the population have no chance of being included. Many unscientific polls are conducted even today. A good example is the television call-in poll. Often television news shows that deal with political topics will offer viewers an opportunity to call an 800 or 900 number to answer a poll question. These polls are unscientific because only those people who are viewing the show have an opportunity to respond. E-mail surveys conducted by CNN.com and ESPN.com are similarly unscientific surveys. The sample of people who call in is not representative of any group beyond the callers themselves. Other examples of unscientific polls include the following:

- **Log-in polls.** A poll question pops up as you enter your computer's web browser with the question: Do you think Sarah Palin would make a good president? Click here for "yes" or click here for "no." Many services, such as Yahoo!, Netscape, and MSN, include questions such as these on their home page and then present a tally of the results. This type of poll is an unscientific one because only those people who click on the browser and decide to take the time to answer the question have their opinion registered. The poll question shown in Image 10-6 from CNN's website is another example.

- Those who don't have a computer (for example, poorer and older people), those who don't have Internet access, and those who are less interested in politics have no chance or far fewer chances of being selected for such a poll. The results of those polls represent nothing more than the people who answer the question.

- **SLOPs, or self-selected listener opinion polls.** Television and radio news/talk shows sometimes conduct polls during the course of a broadcast by offering an 800 or 900 phone number for registered listeners to call and express their opinion on some topic. SLOPs are also known as "call-in" polls. These polls are unscientific because only those people who happen to be tuned in to the broadcast have any opportunity to be included in the sample.

- **CRAPs, or computerized response audience polling.** This kind of poll is often used by local news organizations. Telecommunications equipment places a call, and automated voice systems ask the poll questions. Respondents are asked to use the keypad of their telephone to register their answers to the questions. The extremely high rate of refusal (for example, most people hang up when they hear the automated voice) renders them highly unscientific.

- **Intercept polls.** Have you ever been in a shopping mall when someone with a clipboard comes up to you and asks if you would answer some questions? If so, you've been solicited to participate in an intercept poll (that is, an interviewer "intercepted" you). Respondents in such polls are conveniently selected into the sample because they are spotted by the interviewer. Because people who are at shopping malls or other public places are not representative of all people, this is regarded as an unscientific type of poll.

The *Literary Digest* mishap highlights the problem with unscientific samples—those people who have no chance of being included in the sample may be very different from those who are included. Voters who had no car or published telephone number had no chance of being selected in the *Literary Digest* sample described earlier. Even though the total number of people in the sample was quite high (more than 2 million), it was not representative of the population of voters because less-well-off people had little to no chance of being included in the sample. Today's reliance on telephone surveys to gauge public opinion has come under attack on the basis that cell phone numbers are not sampled and thus such polls systematically exclude younger Americans from the sampling (because younger people are more likely to rely on cell phones).

Pseudo-Polls

Recently, some unscrupulous political campaigns and political action committees (PACs) have been disguising themselves as pollsters for the purpose of planting messages with voters, rather than measuring public opinion. Some of these campaigns or PACs present themselves as pollsters for the purpose of fund-raising as well. These phone calls have come to be known as **pseudo-polls**. As the term implies, there is no polling going on with a pseudo-poll. Pretending to be pollsters, callers often contact tens of thousands of voters and ask hypothetical (that is, untrue) questions about their political opponents—such as "Did you happen to know that John Smith is reported to have beaten his wife in the past—does this make you any less likely to support him in his race for senator?" Respondents to the call believe they are being interviewed by a legitimate polling firm and take away from the conversation a contrived and false message about a political candidate. This type of pseudo-poll is called a "push poll" because the intention of the call is to "push," or influence, people to vote a particular way.

Another type of pseudo-poll is referred to as "FRUGing," or fund-raising under the guise of polling. This is an unethical practice that tricks people into thinking they are being polled by a legitimate organization, when they are really being set up for a fund-raising attempt. "SUG-ing," or selling under the guise of polling, is a pseudo-poll that engages in telemarketing. The individual—who will ultimately receive a sales pitch at the end of the call—believes that she or he is answering a legitimate poll.

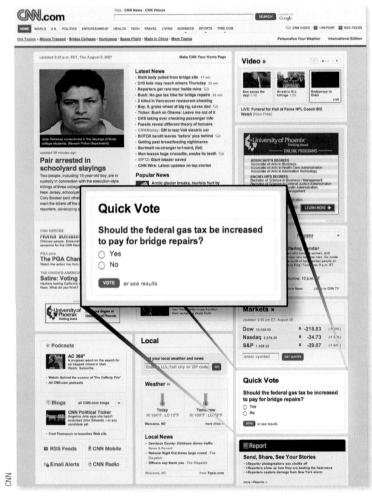

An unscientific poll as it appears to those who visit CNN's website.

pseudo-poll Phone calls from members of political campaigns or PACs who present themselves as pollsters for the purpose of planting messages with voters rather than measuring public opinion.

sampling error The amount of error in a poll that results from interviewing a sample of people rather than the whole population under study; the larger the sample, the less the sampling error.

Sample Size

A fundamental characteristic of a scientific public opinion poll is the nature of the procedures used to draw a sample from the population. The size of the sample is also a factor in poll quality. **Sampling error** is the term used to indicate the amount of error in the poll that results from interviewing a sample of people rather than the whole population under study. Sampling error is largely a function of sample size: the larger the sample size, the less sampling error with the poll. However, there is a law of diminishing returns associated with increasing the size of the sample.

For example, a national scientifically drawn sample of 200 Americans has a sampling error of about $+/-7$ percent at the 95 percent level of confidence. This means that with a sample of 200, chances are 95 in 100 that the sample will produce results within 7 points above or below the survey result. By increasing the sample size by 400 respondents, from 200 to 600, the sampling error is reduced to $+/-4$ percent. An additional 600 respondents in the sample, bringing the sample size to 1,200, reduces the sampling error to $+/-3$ percent.

Media organizations that report poll findings often attempt to convey information about the poll to help the reader/audience understand the sampling error associated with the results. Typically, a news report on a poll will include a statement like this: "The survey was conducted by telephone with a random sample of 1,200 American adults. Sampling error for the survey is +/−3 percent at the 95 percent level of confidence."

What does this statement mean? Suppose the poll found that 60 percent of the respondents approved of the job that Barack Obama was doing as president. The statement indicates that there was a "random sample" of American adults. This means that the poll was a scientific poll and the results can be generalized to the full American adult public.

With any scientific poll, there is sampling error, and probability theory allows us to calculate what the sampling error might be. This calculation is thus expressed as a "confidence interval," or range, which is reported to be +/−3 percent of the poll result (or a 6-point range). The level of confidence typically reported is at the "95 percent level of confidence" (meaning that 95 out of 100 similarly conducted polls would produce results in this range). Thus, what the statement says, then, is that we can be 95 percent confident that the approval rating for President Obama is somewhere between 57 and 63 percent.

In addition to random selection and sample size, the quality of the sample is affected by "nonresponse" error. Once a sample is selected, it is necessary to contact and conduct interviews with those in the sample. Rarely is it possible to obtain an interview with 100 percent of those sampled. Some people refuse to be interviewed, some are not home when contacts are made, and others screen their phone calls through an answering machine or caller ID system. Nonresponse is problematic when those who do not respond tend to answer the questions differently than those who do respond. The goal is to achieve as high a response to the poll as possible in order to limit possible nonresponse error.

Modern-day scientific polls of Americans and voters typically use a probability technique known as **random-digit dialing (RDD)** to obtain scientific telephone samples. RDD uses known information about telephone area codes and exchanges and randomly assigns the last four digits to these. RDD sampling, however, only covers landline telephones. Pollsters using RDD now generally supplement their RDD samples with randomly selected cell phone numbers so that the sampling adequately reflects the growing number of Americans who use cell phones exclusively.

random-digit dialing (RDD) A probability technique for scientific telephone polling that randomly assigns the last four digits to known information about telephone area codes and exchanges.

Asking Questions on Polls

Accurate and reliable polls require not only scientific sampling procedures, but also significant attention to the way in which polling questions are asked. The way in which a question is worded can have a large impact on the type of answers that are given by survey respondents. Consider the following example of a question asked on a national survey conducted by the Roper Organization in 1993: "Does it seem possible or does it seem impossible to you that the Nazi extermination of the Jews never happened?" More than one in five respondents to the poll indicated that he or she thought it was possible that the Holocaust never happened. The results from this question led to a series of news stories expressing concern that nearly one-quarter of the American public questioned the reality of the Holocaust. However, researchers noted an important problem with the wording of the question; namely, it included a double negative. It is difficult for respondents, particularly in a telephone interview (where they are not looking at the words of the question), to interpret what it means to "seem impossible" that something "never happened." The confusing question led to the exaggerated survey result. To test the notion that the question was confusing, the Gallup organization instead asked this question in a 1994 survey: "In your opinion, did the Holocaust definitely happen, probably happen, probably not happen, or definitely not happen?" In this form of the question, only 2 percent said that the Holocaust probably did not happen, and 0 percent said that it definitely did not happen.

Another example of how wording can influence the responses to a question involves two questions, on separate surveys, intended to measure attitudes about the legality of flag burning. A CBS/*New York Times* poll asked, "Should burning or destroying the American flag as a form of political protest be legal or should it be against the law?"

The Diversity Dilemma

Are Minority Voters Counted in Exit Polls?

Political pollsters aim to follow rules for scientific polls, which include specifications on sampling so that results can be generalizable to the general public. Unfortunately, traditional polling sometimes provides results that may be more generalizable to the national white population than to the wider population, which includes significant numbers of racial and ethnic minorities. Professor Gary Segura of Stanford University has cautioned the news media and the public to be especially wary of The National Exit Poll in particular, as it may not accurately capture the minority vote.[21] Dr. Segura urges that reporters raise three different questions when presented with exit polls of Latinos and other minority populations:

1. *How do the pollsters select the precincts for surveys?*
   Segura warns that traditional exit polls have selected precincts that do not have sizeable racial/ethnic minority populations.
2. *What share of these surveys are done in the respondents' native language?*
   Immigrant-based groups, like Latinos and Asians, include some foreign-born individuals who prefer to be interviewed in their dominant language. Yet the traditional pollsters generally rely on English.
3. *How reflective is the exit poll of the true population?*
   Segura warns that traditional exit polls generally overrepresent minority populations that are more middle-class and highly educated.

For Critical Thinking and Discussion

1. Do you ever question the results of national exit polls when they are disseminated to the general public?
2. What are the ramifications of national exit polls that provide results that misrepresent the racial and ethnic minority vote?

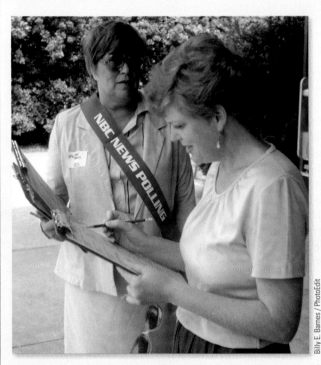

A pollster from the NBC News polling unit administering a questionnaire to a voter who just cast her ballot.

Billy E. Barnes / PhotoEdit

Fourteen percent said it should be legal and 83 percent said it should be against the law. A Gallup Poll asked the question this way: "The Supreme Court ruled that burning the American flag, though highly offensive, is protected under the free speech guarantee of the First Amendment to the Constitution. Do you agree or disagree?" Thirty-eight percent agreed that flag burning should be legal based on this question—fully 24 percentage points higher than what was found with the CBS/*New York Times* question. In this case, the context in which Gallup framed the question—that the Supreme Court said flag burning was legal based on the First Amendment—produced the different result.

The polling community of practitioners and scholars has, over the years, conducted a number of experiments to test how question wording can influence the results of polls. Listed here are some of the key recommendations for guidelines in constructing good poll questions:[22]

1. **Avoid double negatives in questions** (as in the Holocaust question example cited earlier).

2. **Keep the question as simple as possible, using words that people with a limited vocabulary might understand.**

3. **Don't include more than one question within a question**—such an error is called a **double-barreled question.** An example of a double-barreled question is, "Do you approve or disapprove of the job that President Obama is doing in handling the economic and domestic affairs of the nation?" Respondents might have different answers to the president's performance in economic versus other domestic affairs.

4. **The questions should not lead the respondent to a particular answer.** The following is an example of a leading question: "Do you approve of the job that Barack Obama is doing as president?" Because only the "approve" option is stated in the question, some respondents might likely answer "yes, they approve," when they might have answered that they "disapprove" had that option been provided as well.

5. **Don't expect honest answers to socially unacceptable response questions.** For example, using illegal drugs is not only illegal but regarded as socially unacceptable. So one should not necessarily expect all drug users to answer honestly a question about their own use of drugs.

Many polls conducted in the United States are intended to provide information for public consumption. These polls are referred to as "public polls." The *USA Today*/CNN/Gallup Poll and the *New York Times*/CBS Poll are just a few of the organizations that regularly conduct polling intended for public consumption.

There are so many polling organizations, people often have a hard time ascertaining the quality of a poll. The National Council on Public Polls (NCPP) is an association of organizations that regularly conduct public polls. Members of NCPP have articulated the following list of items that should be disclosed about any poll that is released publicly, as a way to help the poll consumer evaluate the quality of the poll:

- The name of the organization that sponsored or paid for the poll
- The dates of interviewing
- The method for obtaining the interviews (for example, telephone, e-mail, in-person)
- A definition of the population that was sampled
- The size of the sample (that is, the number of interviews conducted)
- The size and description of subsamples, if the poll relies primarily on less than the total sample
- The complete wording of questions on which the poll results are based
- The percentages from the poll on which conclusions are based

10-7 | Interpreting Public Opinion Data

Understanding public opinion requires attention not only to the scientific aspects of sampling and the wording of questions, but also to the analysis and interpretation of the results of a poll. In assessing results, analysts are concerned with three important characteristics of public opinion data: direction, intensity, and continuity.[23]

To understand the **direction** of public opinion, the analyst seeks to find which position or preference a majority of people hold as their opinion. On most topics, there are two possible directions in which public opinion might lean—a positive direction or a negative direction. For example, with respect to presidential approval, respondents might either approve or disapprove of the job the president is doing. Similarly, the public might either trust or distrust their political leaders; or they might support or oppose a proposal for a policy that makes it more difficult to buy a handgun. On any given opinion question, direction is a basic characteristic that the analyst seeks to gauge.

Intensity is also an important characteristic of public opinion. Often, the analyst seeks not only to find the direction of opinion but also to determine how strongly or how committed the public feels about the opinion that it holds. Consider the responses to the following question asked to a national sample of Americans in 2000: "Do you

direction (of public opinion) A tendency toward a particular preference, usually (though not always) characterized as either positive or negative.

intensity (of public opinion) The degree of strength or commitment the public feels about the opinion it holds.

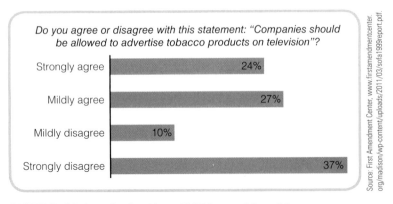

Do you agree or disagree with this statement: "Companies should be allowed to advertise tobacco products on television"?

Strongly agree	24%
Mildly agree	27%
Mildly disagree	10%
Strongly disagree	37%

Source: First Amendment Center, www.firstamendmentcenter.org/madison/wp-content/uploads/2011/03/sofa1999report.pdf.

FIGURE 10-6 Attitudes About TV Tobacco Advertising

agree or disagree with this statement—companies should be allowed to advertise tobacco products on television?" Those polled were asked a follow-up question: "Do you strongly or mildly (agree/disagree) with this?" The results are shown in Figure 10-6.

The direction of opinion in this case only marginally swings in agreement that companies should be able to advertise tobacco on TV. Fifty-one percent, a bare majority, agreed with this statement, and 47 percent disagreed. The direction of opinion only modestly endorses the statement. However, the follow-up question sheds additional light on the intensity of opinion. Among those who agree, they are about evenly divided, 24 percent to 27 percent, between strongly and mildly agreeing. Those who disagree are much more intense in their feelings, with 37 percent strongly and only 10 percent mildly disagreeing.

continuity (in public opinion) A tendency for political preferences to remain generally stable over time.

Continuity is a third important characteristic of public opinion. Political preferences may remain very stable over time, they may gradually change, or they may fluctuate wildly over short periods of time. Continuity (or "changeability," its opposite) is often an important dimension of public opinion. The presidential approval rating is often analyzed from the context of the continuity/change dimension. When major political events occur, we often see change. Figure 10-7 shows the changing views of Americans on their concerns about environmental protection from 2007 through 2011. The percentage feeling that environmental issues are "very serious and should be a priority for everyone" decreased over this period, the likely result of enhanced concerns about the American economy through the recessionary years.

Public opinion plays an important role in any system of government. Even authoritarian regimes such as the French government under King Louis XVI in the late eighteenth century, the Soviet Union in the late twentieth century, and the Egyptian dictatorship of Hosni Mubarak in 2011 were susceptible to being overthrown by the forces of the popular will. But in a democratic society, public opinion is freely expressed and willingly heeded by those running the government. In contemporary American politics, there are a variety of ways in which public opinion may be expressed. Presidents have learned that public opinion can change drastically over the course of their term in office, keeping chief executives and other public officials continuously accountable to the popular will. In 2014 President Obama's deteriorating approval rating significantly curbed his ability to achieve legislative goals. Modern technology and the advancement of social science research have enabled political scientists, journalists, political candidates, and elected leaders to measure accurately and understand better not only what public opinion is, but also how and why it changes. Modern presidents have the resources of scientific public opinion polls at their disposal and use them quite extensively. But although the scientific opinion poll is a modern phenomenon, the importance of public opinion has always been central to the life of American politics.

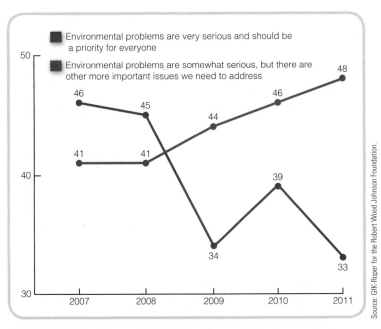

Environmental problems are very serious and should be a priority for everyone

Environmental problems are somewhat serious, but there are other more important issues we need to address

Source: GfK-Roper for the Robert Wood Johnson Foundation.

FIGURE 10-7 Change in Attitudes About the Environment

From Your Perspective

Using Social Networking to Express Your Political Opinions

The use of social networking has spread around the world like a wildfire, and young adults with a college education are more likely than any other demographic to adopt it. That's your demographic! A 2012 survey across 23 countries found that the United States ranked #2 in usage of social networks (Britain was #1). The study found that many social networkers are making use of this new medium to express their political views (34 percent), although sharing views on music, movies, and sports is even more popular:

Certainly, social networks like Facebook and Twitter provide a unique forum for the expression of public opinion: a familiar audience, a selective audience, an audience more likely to take expressed views seriously, and an audience that can opt to engage in the conversation or express its like or dislike with the opinion. As social networking grows in popularity, it is certain that this format for political expression will become even more popular.

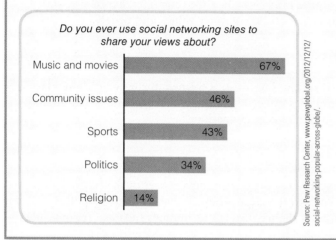

Do you ever use social networking sites to share your views about?

Music and movies — 67%
Community issues — 46%
Sports — 43%
Politics — 34%
Religion — 14%

Source: Pew Research Center, www.pewglobal.org/2012/12/12/social-networking-popular-across-globe/.

For Critical Thinking and Discussion

1. Have you ever expressed your opinion about politics on Facebook, Twitter, or another social networking site? If so, did you get feedback from your friends? Would you have expressed those views if social networks were not available?
2. Do your friends often express their political opinions? How much do you think your own opinions are influenced by what your friends say on social networking sites?

Summary

10-1 Public Opinion in American Politics

- Public opinion plays an important role in ensuring that citizens' beliefs are embraced in a democracy; public opinion also plays a tactical role for political officials, influencing the outcome of many important political battles.

10-2 How Is Public Opinion Expressed?

- Public opinion may be expressed through a variety of means, including public opinion polls, voting, free speech and assembly, political blogging, the support of particular candidates for political office, and the contribution of time and effort to interest groups. The news media also serve as an outlet for public opinion, whether by publishing articles about important individuals' opinions or by sponsoring their own public opinion polls on politics and policy issues. Still, many members of the public prefer to express their opinions directly to elected officials through letters, phone calls, or e-mails. Blogs have become an increasingly popular way for individuals to express their views on issues.

10-3 The Levels of Public Opinion

- Public opinion exists at its most abstract level in the form of values and beliefs; it exists in a more specific form through political orientations, which translate values and beliefs into a systematic way of assessing political realities, and in an even more specific way in the form of particular political preferences.

10-4 How Informed Is Public Opinion?

- Many noted scholars in the early and mid-twentieth century argued that the public lacks the necessary knowledge for their opinions to provide value. Contemporary surveys continue to confirm that the public maintains a low interest in politics generally, and that most Americans are uninformed about basic political facts. By contrast, numerous other scholars, beginning with V. O. Key Jr. in the 1960s, have argued that regardless of its specific knowledge of politics, the public as a whole behaves quite rationally over the long haul, expressing stable opinions that move (if at all) in logical and meaningful directions based on their values and beliefs.

10-5 How Does Public Opinion Form?

- Individuals' opinions are shaped in part by political socialization; impressions formed during youth often last well into adulthood. Opinions are also shaped by demographics (race, ethnicity, gender, age, and so on), family members, friends and peer groups, schools, the media, and religious organizations.

10-6 How Is Public Opinion Measured?

- Public opinion polls measure the opinions of a large group of people by selecting a subset of the larger group and then generalizing the findings from the small group back to the large group. To ensure that the poll is scientific, the sample must be chosen randomly using probability theory through techniques such as random-digit dialing. Unscientific polls can produce misleading results.
- The way in which questions on a poll are worded is also an important factor in assessing the quality of a poll. Misleading questions, whether intentional or unintentional, may produce faulty results.

10-7 Interpreting Public Opinion Data

- The proper interpretation of public opinion data requires attention to the direction, intensity, and continuity of the public's expressions. With regard to the third characteristic, political preferences may fluctuate wildly over short periods of time.

Key Terms

agents of political socialization (p. 271)
conservative ideology (p. 268)
continuity (in public opinion) (p. 284)
direction (of public opinion) (p. 283)
intensity (of public opinion) (p. 283)
liberal ideology (p. 268)
political ideology (p. 268)

political orientations (p. 267)
political preferences (p. 269)
political socialization (p. 271)
primacy tendency (p. 271)
pseudo-poll (p. 280)
public opinion (p. 265)
public opinion poll (p. 274)

random-digit dialing (RDD) (p. 281)
sampling error (p. 280)
scientific sample (p. 276)
straw poll (p. 275)
unscientific poll (p. 277)
values and beliefs (p. 266)

Test Yourself

1. Which of the following people argued in an influential book entitled *Semisovereign People* that "public opinion can emerge as a key factor in any political context"?
   a. James Madison
   b. V. O. Key
   c. E. E. Schattschneider
   d. Abraham Lincoln

2. V. O. Key argued that public opinion is not merely the summation of individual opinions. What else, according to Key, was necessary for "public opinion" to be present?

3. The legal guarantees protecting protests as a form of public opinion may be found in the
   a. Declaration of Independence.
   b. First Amendment.
   c. Preamble to the Constitution.
   d. Fourth Amendment.

4. Elections are an expression of public opinion. When the Constitution was first adopted, which of the following provided a direct link between popular preferences and federal officeholders?
   a. Presidential elections
   b. House elections
   c. Senate elections
   d. Elections of Supreme Court justices

5. Identify five specific ways that public opinion may be expressed in the American political system.

6. Over the past 50 years, which of the following partisan groups has increased proportionately?
   a. Democrats
   b. Independents
   c. Republicans
   d. Socialists

7. The broadest and most abstract level of public opinion that forms the basis for American political culture is
   a. values and beliefs.
   b. political orientations.
   c. preferences on policy issues.
   d. preferences for political candidates.

8. Distinguish between the "liberal" and "conservative" ideologies in contemporary politics.

9. Which of the following books used scientific surveys to document the low level of political knowledge among ordinary American citizens?
   a. *Federalist Papers*
   b. *The American Voter*
   c. *The Decline of America*
   d. *Jay-Walking in America*

10. Despite low levels of political knowledge among Americans, V. O. Key argued that "voters are not fools." How does he justify this claim?

11. The "primacy tendency" has its greatest impact through which of the following agents of political socialization?
    a. Family
    b. Friends
    c. Religion
    d. The media

12. How does entertainment television programming act as a factor that influences one's socialization to politics?

13. Phone calls initiated by political campaigns that pretend to be conducting a poll but actually intend to send negative messages about political opponents are known as
    a. intercept polls.
    b. push polls.
    c. log-in polls.
    d. self-selected listener opinion polls.

14. Most scientific telephone opinion polls use which of the following techniques in selecting a sample of respondents?
    a. Random sampling from phone directories
    b. Internet recruiting via e-mail
    c. Call-ins from news television shows
    d. Random-digit dialing

15. What distinguishes a scientific poll from an unscientific one?

16. The strength of commitment that the public feels about the job performance of the president is a measure of
    a. the direction of opinion.
    b. the intensity of opinion.
    c. the continuity of opinion.
    d. change in opinion.

17. How has public opinion changed regarding concerns about the environment from 2007 through 2011? Why has this change occurred?

---

1. c (LO 10-1); 3. b (LO 10-2); 4. b (LO 10-2); 6. b (LO 10-3); 7. a (LO 10-3); 9. b (LO 10-4); 11. a (LO 10-5); 13. b (LO 10-6); 14. d (LO 10-6); 16. b (LO 10-7)

LEARNING OBJECTIVES

11-1 Pluralism and the Interest-Group System
- Assess the function of interest groups as a mechanism by which groups of people attempt to influence government to advance shared goals
- Define pluralism as the theory that public policy is largely the product of a variety of different interest groups competing with one another to promote laws that benefit members of their respective groups
- Compare and contrast both the benefits and criticisms of the interest-group system in the United States

11-2 Interest Groups in Action
- Identify the reasons for the growth of interest groups in the United States over the past few decades
- Evaluate the critical role interest groups play in influencing policymaking through iron triangles and issue networks

- Distinguish between the three types of benefits that are derived from group membership: material, solidary, and purposive
- Assess the factors that contribute to each interest group's level of influence on policy

11-3 Types of Interest Groups
- Distinguish between economic interest groups and noneconomic interest groups according to their primary purpose
- Explain the "free rider" problem that many interest groups face

11-4 How Interest Groups Achieve Their Goals
- Identify the activities interest groups engage in to achieve their goals and influence public policy

11

Interest Groups

The U.S. political system provides numerous opportunities for people to influence public policy. Voting in elections to choose leaders offers one such opportunity. The guarantees of freedom of speech to speak one's mind about political issues and freedom of the press to critically assess issues and leaders' performance are others. Public opinion polls are yet another mechanism that solicits input from the masses. But perhaps the most natural—and arguably the most influential—form of public input arrives by way of the activities of interest groups. Interest groups today play a central role in making laws, regulating industries, and even influencing court decisions. The vast influence of interest groups makes them a target of criticism, particularly when scandals emerge. Thus, a persistent issue regarding interest-group activities is just how far we should allow such groups to press their interests. At what point do interest groups become a negative force in democracy? This chapter assesses the workings and performance of American politics from the perspective of interest-group activity. What are interest groups? How do they work? Who belongs to them? Which ones are more and less powerful? How do they exert influence on what government does?

Have You Contributed to an Interest Group?

Approximately four in five Americans identify themselves as members of at least one interest group. Many participate in interest group politics by making direct monetary donations to the group. When someone feels strongly about a cause, he or she often makes a financial contribution to an interest group whose activities support that cause. The impact of money and interest groups on elections and lawmaking, however, has come under increased scrutiny over the years. Much of the concern focuses on how well-funded interest groups might unethically or inappropriately impact election outcomes and public policy in the United States. As a way to both protect the right of individuals to participate in interest groups, while at the same time ensuring that the process is fair, Congress has passed a number of laws regarding interest-group activity. One set of laws requires that individual contributions of money to any interest group, political organization, or candidate must be reported, and those reports must be publicly available.

An organization called the Center for Responsive Politics (which is itself an interest group) has created a website (opensecrets.org) that compiles all of the data on individual contributions reported to the federal government by interest groups, political organizations, and individual candidates since 1989. Opensecrets.org not only summarizes the amounts contributed and spent, but allows users to search for the names of individual contributors and the amounts of their contribution. As you can see on the homepage below, you can navigate to the Politicians and Elections tab to locate the Donor Lookup area and search for anyone who has made a contribution. So if you ever have or ever will make a contribution yourself, anyone can access that information on this site.

Homepage of OpenSecrets.org

- Have you, your friends, your parents, or your professors made a contribution to an interest group or a political organization? If you (or they) have, you can easily look it up by going to the individual donor page at www.opensecrets.org/indivs.

To see how your answers compare to others, take the **Who Are You?** poll in MindTap!

11-1 | Pluralism and the Interest-Group System

An influential form of public input into policymaking arrives by way of the activities of interest groups. James Madison, in Federalist No. 10, admonished that "the latent causes of faction are thus sown in the nature of man."[1] By faction, Madison was referring to what we now term interest groups. Madison was concerned about the potential influence of factions on the government. But at the same time, he understood that people were drawn by nature toward the organization of collective interests and the use of that organization to influence government. Madison expected that if enough interest groups vied to influence policy, they would act as checks on each other.

What Is an Interest Group?

An **interest group** (also referred to as a *pressure group* or *organized interest*) is an organization of people with shared goals that tries to influence public policy through a variety of activities. Every individual has interests, and interest groups are a mechanism for people with shared goals to protect or advance their own interests. People can try to influence government on their own—such as by calling or writing their elected representatives to voice their opinion or by voting in an election. Another way that people can influence government is by joining a group that is organized to accomplish an objective.

Senior citizens, for example, have a shared interest in securing cost-of-living adjustments (COLAs) in the Social Security system that disburses checks to them each month. Each year, the president and Congress determine the percentage rate increase in the COLA. The larger the increase, the higher will be an individual's monthly Social Security check. Each individual senior citizen might call his or her representatives in Congress to try to influence the vote for a larger COLA increase. Another way senior citizens may try to influence government is by joining and supporting the AARP (formerly the American Association of Retired Persons), an interest group that, among other activities, tries to influence government to approve large increases in the annual COLA for Social Security. AARP is large, with many resources and lobbyists to influence legislators. Although an individual citizen's call to a representative may carry some weight, it is no match for the vast resources and activities of the AARP.

Interest groups link people with government policies. The linkage created by interest groups is constitutionally protected by the First Amendment, which guarantees the people's right "to peaceably assemble, and to petition the Government for redress of grievances." People assembling in groups that carry out activities to foster group members' goals is a common activity in Washington, in the 50 state capitals, and in thousands of local governments.

Alexis de Tocqueville, a Frenchman who toured the United States in the early 1830s and observed the early workings of the U.S. political system, was struck by the extent to which group association and activity dominated the American system. In his now-classic 1835 book titled *Democracy in America*,[2] de Tocqueville praised the extent to which group activity underpins American democracy:

> The [citizen] of the United States learns from birth that he must rely on himself to combat the ills and trials of life. . . . If some obstacle blocks the public road halting . . . traffic, neighbors at once form a deliberative body; this improvised assembly produces an authority which remedies the trouble before anyone has thought of the possibility beyond that of those concerned . . . associations are formed to combat moral troubles. Public security, trade and industry, and morals and religion all provide the aims for associations in the United States. There is no end to which the human will despair of attaining by the free action of the collective power of individuals.

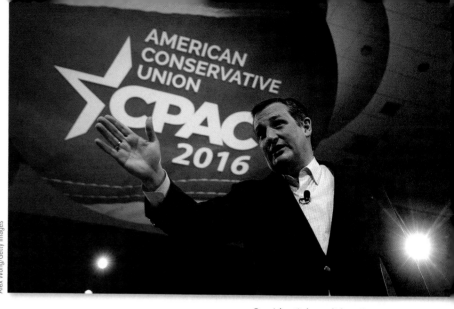

Alex Wong/Getty Images

Presidential candidate Senator Ted Cruz (R-TX), a strong social conservative, courted CPAC (the Conservative Political Action Committee) members for their support and donations during the 2016 GOP primaries.

interest group An organization of people with shared goals that tries to influence public policy through a variety of activities.

When a political association is allowed to form centers of action at certain important places in the country, its activity becomes greater and its influence more widespread.

More than his fellow French citizens and other Europeans that he observed, de Tocqueville found that Americans were particularly prone to organize in groups and use their associations to influence the political process.

Pluralism refers to the theory that public policy largely results from a variety of interest groups competing with one another to promote laws that benefit members of their respective groups. By contrast, **majoritarianism** refers to the theory that public policy is a product of what majorities of citizens prefer. Whereas the majoritarian perspective focuses on public opinion, voting results, and mass representation to describe how democracy in America actually works, the pluralist perspective suggests that in fact the majority rarely rules.

Political scientist Robert Dahl, an architect of pluralist ideas, suggested in *A Preface to Democratic Theory*[3] that the American people are represented in government primarily through interest-group activity. The products of public policy are largely a function of support for and membership in interest groups that compete for influence through activities such as lobbying, which is discussed later in this chapter. The U.S. political system, according to Dahl, offers a number of "access points" for any given group to provide input. These access points include Congress, executive branch offices, the courts, elections, and the news media. David B. Truman, another political scientist, has advanced the notion that group activity and mobilization are natural consequences of shared concerns.[4] The free and open competition among groups advances the democratic system, just as a free and open marketplace of ideas promotes the adoption of the best ideas in society.

pluralism The theory that public policy largely results from a variety of interest groups competing with one another to promote laws that benefit members of their respective groups.

majoritarianism The theory that public policy is a product of what majorities of citizens prefer.

The Pros and Cons of Interest Groups

The political power of group organization for the purpose of influencing government outputs can be quite strong. "Are interest groups good or bad for American democracy?" is a question akin to the old cliché "Is the glass half full or half empty?" The answer, of course, depends on one's perspective. Madison himself recognized that interest groups were powerful and that they could be dangerous. But he also acknowledged that factions could not be eliminated. Channeling them into productive devices for promoting public input was a primary challenge his generation faced in framing the government.

Interest groups in America invite criticism from some circles and praise from others. Listed next are the primary arguments for the advantages and disadvantages of interest-group activity.

The Pros. Many observers today sing the praises of an interest-group system that advances the interests of the people. Their arguments in support of interest groups include the following:

- Interest groups provide all groups in society with an opportunity to win support for their ideas and positions. The vast number of interest groups represents a wide array of political opinions, economic perspectives, and social class differences.
- By their very nature, humans seek out others who have ideas similar to their own. Joining groups and working for the interests of the group are natural inclinations of citizens and should be encouraged as a method of representation in our democracy.

Former lobbyist Jack Abramoff is a recent example of a corrupt lobbyist whose actions contribute to negative feelings about lobbying generally. Abramoff illegally spent millions of dollars to influence elected officials by offering them extravagant meals, vacations, and professional sporting events tickets, among other things. He was prosecuted by the federal government and eventually pled guilty to an array of charges.

AP Photo/Gerald Herbert

- The right of association is a basic right protected implicitly by the First Amendment to the U.S. Constitution, which affords individuals the right "peaceably to assemble."
- A wide array of diverse groups in society—rich and poor, urban and nonurban, male and female, northern and southern, liberal and conservative—potentially may organize and attempt to influence government. The system is fair in that it gives all groups an opportunity to compete.

The Cons. Many other observers of the U.S. political system are quite critical of the power exerted by interest groups. In *The Power Elite*, C. Wright Mills[5] characterizes interest groups as a tool of the political elite rather than a system that enables broad participation in influencing public policy. Along this line, many criticize the ability of wealthy corporations and individuals to exert disproportionate influence on government through well-financed interest-group activities. John Heinz and his colleagues argue further that the influence of interest groups is contingent on a number of factors and that their influence may be quite limited.[6] Other criticisms of interest groups include the following:

- Use of interest groups to make public policy is unfair because groups supported by the wealthy have far greater resources to promote their interests in the political system.
- Large corporations exist to maximize profits. They dominate the interest-group system and tend to be ruthless in achieving their policy goals. The interest-group system thus promotes the advancement of interests that do not always strive for the common good.
- The amount of interest-group activity is so great that it has made it difficult to get things done in government. Too many groups are operating, slowing down the policymaking process to a state of gridlock in many arenas.
- Interest-group leaders are not elected, distinguishing them from many of the policymaking institutions that have been constitutionally ordained—such as Congress and the executive branch. Thus, interest-group dominance of the political system is an affront to democracy.
- Interest groups work to concentrate benefits for the few while distributing costs to the many.

Interest Groups and Political Parties

Political parties also link people to government policies. However, parties differ from interest groups in two important ways. First, parties today mainly focus on elections by endorsing candidates and working for their election to office. Most interest groups do not run candidates for office as parties do (although interest groups often endorse candidates). Interest groups commonly find other access points of government to accomplish their goals—access points such as the courts, the committee system in Congress, and executive agencies.[7]

A second important difference between interest groups and political parties is that groups tend to focus narrowly on special issues or sets of issues (hence the term *special interests*), whereas major parties are generally all-encompassing and are guided by broader ideological approaches to governing, rather than by a specific policy position. In short, the major parties are generalist whereas interest groups are focused. Consequently, there are few political parties, but many, many interest groups. Groups do not try to appeal to as many individuals as possible; rather, they appeal to those whose special interests are advocated by the group. For example, the National Rifle Association (NRA) does not try to recruit gun control advocates because they are less likely to help promote the group's interests. Conversely, parties try to appeal to as many people as possible to optimize their electoral success.

Interest Groups and Social Movements

Numerous **social movements** have been identified in American history, such as the civil rights, consumer safety, women's rights, and environmental movements of the 1960s and 1970s. These large informal groupings of individuals were often spawned directly from particular interest groups. The consumer protection movement, for example, was driven by the activities of the group Public Citizen, formed by consumer activist Ralph Nader. The American drive toward equality has produced a number of important social movements that utilized organized interests.

Movements have been political (for example, women's suffrage in the early 1900s), economic (for example, labor rights in the late 1800s and early 1900s), and social (for example, the civil rights movements of the 1960s). These movements have all been propelled by the activities of interest groups.

11-2 | Interest Groups in Action

Interest groups have always played an important role in American politics. Even in the colonial period, groups such as the Sons of Liberty gathered members, collected donations, and organized protests to achieve the goal of American freedom from British taxation. The Sons of Liberty were successful in their aims because they tied their actions to the economic interests of their members. As Madison acknowledged, economic interests tend to be the type of concerns that are most salient to people and thus move them to collective action.

In 1886, the American Federation of Labor (AFL) was formed as the first broad-based national labor union. The AFL was originally established to advocate the rights of craft unions and ensure the terms of union contracts. Organized and led by Samuel Gompers for 40 years, it attracted many members and raised funds to promote laws benefiting organized labor. The AFL was the principal advocate for establishing a cabinet department, the U.S. Department of Labor, to administer labor programs. This department continues to serve as one of the largest executive departments in the nation. In the 1950s, the AFL merged with the Congress of Industrial Organizations (CIO) to create the AFL-CIO, an interest group still very active in promoting the labor agenda.

The National Association of Manufacturers (NAM) was organized in 1885 for the purpose of advancing the interests of the manufacturing businesses. Though

Women and children in 1890 labor at a food processing plant.

Lewis W. Hine/Time Life Pictures/Getty Images

setting protective tariffs was its core objective, the NAM also became a primary opponent of the AFL and other labor interest groups. The goals of organized labor (such as higher wages for workers, better working conditions, increased benefits, and job security) and the goals of business owners (maximizing profits) often came into conflict.

Tensions between labor and business interests intensified with the tremendous growth of the American economy beginning in the late 1800s and continued to mount as the economy expanded. Large companies, focusing on maximizing profits (which in turn appealed to shareholders), opposed laborers' demands for increased wages, better working conditions, and worker benefits. Today, labor and business interest groups continue to be among the largest and most powerful interest groups in the nation.

The Growth of Interest Groups

Perhaps the most significant factor leading to an increase in the number of interest groups has been the overall growth in government. Interest groups attempt to advance their agenda by influencing various aspects of government. As the number of government programs and agencies has expanded, along with their reach, opportunities for influencing what government does through interest-group activities have expanded as well.

The New Deal programs of the 1930s and the Great Society programs of the 1960s led to tremendous growth in the federal government and huge increases in the federal budget. Government began to assume a more active role not only in promoting its economic policies but in promoting social policies as well. In response, a vast number of interest groups formed. Both proponents and opponents of a more active government organized interest groups to advocate their views. As the number of interest groups advocating economic issues expanded, so too did the number of groups promoting ideological perspectives, positions on single issues, and political reforms.

Although interest groups have been part of the American system since its beginning, the number of groups has increased dramatically over the past half-century. Between 1960 and 2000, the number of official associations increased by 400 percent (from 5,843 to 23,298); the total amount of lobbying spending in Washington increased from $1.45 billion in 1998 to $3.22 billion in 2015; and from 1998 through 2015 the total number of registered lobbyists in Washington, D.C., increased from 10,405 to 11,514.[8] Major political developments, such as the antiwar movement, the civil rights movement, and the Watergate scandal of the Nixon administration, mobilized a better-educated mass public to become increasingly concerned about political issues. This heightened concern about social and political issues fostered a significant amount of new interest-group activity. The sophisticated use of mass-media technologies such as television, the computer, and the Internet has facilitated the ability of groups to emerge and flourish.

Another factor contributing to the increase in interest-group activity has been the escalating cost of financing political campaigns. As costs have increased, interest groups have come to play a greater role in supporting political parties and the election of candidates. The Federal Election Campaign Act of 1971 placed limits on individual and corporate contributions to political campaigns. As a means of financing campaigns through alternative methods, interest groups have formed **political action committees (PACs)**, which raise money from individuals and provide a source of funding for candidates and political parties. PACs also engage in "soft money" spending on advertising and other political work independent of candidates and parties. Recently the Supreme Court ruled in *Citizens United v. Federal Election Commission* (2010)[9] that corporations, like individuals, may make contributions to PACs. In 2012 this controversial opinion facilitated the rise of the so-called super-PACs. As we will see in Chapter 14, PACs are a source of much controversy.

political action committee (PAC) The political arm of an interest group that promotes candidates in election campaigns primarily through financial contributions.

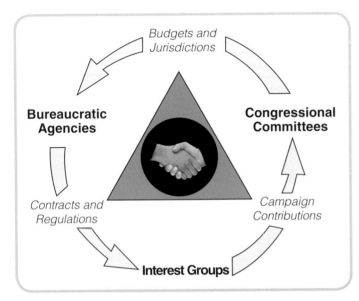

FIGURE 11-1 The Iron Triangle of Policymaking

iron triangle A three-sided network of policymaking that includes congressional committees (and subcommittees) in a specific policy area, executive agencies with authority over that area, and private interest groups focused on influencing that area.

issue network The broad array of actors (beyond just the iron triangle) that try to collectively influence a policy area in which they maintain a vested interest.

Iron Triangles, Issue Networks, and the Influence of Groups

The influence of interest groups is buoyed by the process in which public policy is created and modified. As shown in Figure 11-1, in any policy area, three key sets of actors interact to produce public policy: (1) congressional committees and subcommittees assigned to a specific policy area, (2) executive agencies of government that have the authority to administer policies in a particular area, and (3) private interest groups that have an interest in influencing that policy area. Members of congressional committees, managers of agencies, and leaders of interest groups all have vested interests in the specific policy area. As political scientist Theodore Lowi has noted, although these parties may not always agree on particular positions, they all seek to promote policies favorable to their interests, and they come to depend on one another for support and influence. Together, this network of actors dominates the development of public policies. This durable and seemingly impenetrable three-sided network has come to be known as the **iron triangle** of policymaking.[10]

The development of U.S. defense policy illustrates how iron triangles work. The armed services and defense committees and subcommittees in Congress are responsible for appropriating funds for defense contracts (such as for the building of new military aircraft). Members of Congress on these committees are committed to maintaining a strong national defense, and they control the purse strings for developing new defense systems. Leaders in the U.S. Department of Defense are responsible for implementing defense systems under the orders of the president and rely on congressional committees to fund strong systems. Private contractors such as Pratt & Whitney (an airplane engine manufacturer) employ the engineers and researchers to design superior systems and provide valuable information to the congressional committees and the defense department.

The committees and the Department of Defense depend on Pratt & Whitney for advanced engine technologies, advice on aircraft design, and the capacity to produce cutting-edge aircraft engines. Pratt & Whitney benefits from winning federal contracts to produce defense systems. The congressional committees, Defense Department managers, and corporate leaders and lobbyists from Pratt & Whitney are familiar with one another, depend on one another, and use one another in the development of defense systems. The iron-triangle approach to public policymaking has institutionalized the role of interest groups in the exercise of American democracy.

Although an iron triangle refers to the interdependent relationship between legislators, bureaucrats, and lobbyists in a particular policy area, it is also possible to identify a broader set of actors who all have a vested interest in an area of public policy and try to collectively influence their policy area. Political scientists have used the term **issue networks** to describe this broader array of actors beyond legislators, bureaucrats, and lobbyists who try to influence a particular policy area. These include congressional staff people, journalists or other members of the media who often report on the policy area, and researchers who have done work on and are experts in the policy area.[11]

Membership in Groups

Many Americans belong to interest groups, and many businesses, nonprofit organizations, and public entities belong to interest groups as well. It is estimated that about four in five citizens belong to at least one interest group. Many of the more common groups Americans belong to include labor unions (such as the AFL-CIO, which boasts a total of about 11 million members), professional associations (such as the 240,000 physicians and medical students who belong to the American Medical Association), and organizations such as the AARP, to which many of the nation's senior citizens belong. As many as 3 million businesses across the United States belong to the U.S. Chamber of Commerce.[12]

Although the number of Americans who belong to interest groups is high, certain types of people are more likely than others to engage in interest-group activity. Americans with higher incomes and greater resources, and those who are better educated and employed in professional occupations, are much more likely to belong to groups. Those with more financial resources tend to better appreciate the utility of group membership and interest groups' impact on the political process; wealthier individuals are also more likely to have the resources to support interest-group activities. Thus, many critics of interest-group politics charge that the pluralist model of democracy favors the upper middle class and upper class of society. Because those with more resources can and do support interest groups, they are more likely to influence public policy to their financial advantage.

Various reasons have been proposed to explain why people or organizations might join and support certain interest groups. One is that they receive specific, tangible benefits from membership. These are referred to as **material benefits**[13] of group membership. For instance, local units of the National Education Association (NEA) work for its teacher members to win salary increases, and so the benefits of membership often produce a favorable material benefit to teachers in the form of higher wages. Many interest groups provide their members with other material benefits such as health and auto insurance discounts, magazine subscriptions, and free products.

Another reason why interest groups are appealing is the **purposive benefits** (or expressive benefits) of membership.[14] Purposive rewards are those that do not directly benefit the individual member but benefit society more generally. Some interest groups, for example, are committed to the goal of improving the environment and promoting policies that better protect the natural environment. The Sierra Club is one such organization that endorses these goals, and members of the Sierra Club receive purposive benefits from membership and support of the group's activities.

A third type of incentive for interest-group membership is the **solidary benefits**[15] of membership, or the satisfaction that individuals receive from interacting with like-minded individuals for a cause. Solidary rewards derive less from the interest group's goals and more from the process of interacting with others to achieve a goal. For example, a union worker who attends a labor rally to support increases in a new contract may receive satisfaction from simply being with colleagues in support of a cause.

material benefits (of group membership) The specific, tangible benefits individuals receive from interest-group membership, such as economic concessions, discounts on products, and so forth.

purposive benefits (of group membership) Rewards that do not directly benefit the individual member, but benefit society as a whole.

solidary benefits (of group membership) Satisfaction that individuals receive from interacting with like-minded individuals for a cause.

What Makes Some Groups More Powerful Than Others?

Although there are thousands of interest groups operating in the United States, some groups are more successful than others in promoting their cause and affecting public policy. There are three general characteristics of an interest group that may have significant bearing on how powerful that group's influence will be in Washington:

1. **The size of the membership.** There is, undoubtedly, power in numbers. The larger the number of members of an interest group, the more powerful that group will be. Large membership alone makes elected leaders responsive to a group's concerns. An interest group with a large number of members can increase its power and influence by convincing its members to vote for a candidate or candidates. The Christian Coalition of America (CCA) is a Christian political advocacy group that includes fundamentalists, evangelicals, Pentecostals, and many members of mainline Protestant churches as well. Officials of the CCA often communicate with the organization's huge membership regarding the endorsement of political candidates. Not

The Supreme Court and Interest Groups

Citizens United v. FEC (2010)

One of the most controversial cases to emerge from the U.S. Supreme Court in recent memory was *Citizens United v. FEC* (2010). For as much passion as the decision has generated on both ends of the political spectrum, it may be one of the most poorly understood cases that the justices have ever handed down. The controversy began in 2008 when a conservative nonprofit interest group, Citizens United, produced a documentary highly critical of U.S. Senator Hillary Clinton, who was then running for president. Citizens United sought to show a video entitled *Hillary: The Movie*, on cable TV right before the Democratic primaries in 2008. At the time, such an "electioneering communication" was illegal under the Bipartisan Campaign Reform Act of 2002, which banned such communications within 30 days of an election. A district court agreed with the Federal Election Commission that there was "no reasonable interpretation [of the movie] other than as an appeal to vote against Senator Clinton" and so upheld the fine against Citizens United.

On appeal, the U.S. Supreme Court accepted the interpretation of the movie as an electioneering communication by a corporation acting as a political interest group, but nevertheless struck down as unconstitutional all those provisions of the 2002 Act that barred corporations and unions from making independent expenditures and electioneering communications. Writing for a narrowly divided 5–4 majority, Justice Kennedy wrote that the First Amendment keeps the government from interfering in the marketplace of ideas, which includes independent political speech by such organized interests as corporations or unions. "If the First Amendment has any force, it prohibits Congress from fining . . . associations of citizens [including corporations] for simply engaging in political speech." (Of course, the Act's provisions requiring disclosure of expenditures and limiting direct contributions to candidates remains applicable to corporations and unions, just as it does to individuals.)

For Critical Thinking and Discussion

1. Most Americans believe that media corporations like *The New York Times* are organized interests that should enjoy some First Amendment rights. Given that, would it be fair to deny First Amendment rights to other types of corporations, as the FEC suggests?

2. Critics of *Citizens United* argue that the decision will bring even more money from heavily financed interest groups into the political process. On the other hand, it also adds some measure of transparency to the election process. On balance, would you trade the increase in campaign money for more transparency? Why or why not?

---

surprisingly, the CCA attracts the attention of candidates as well as officeholders who plan on running for another term. Groups with large numbers of members also have an advantage in raising funds to support their activities. With many members, the potential for fund-raising is great. And funding goes a long way in advancing the effectiveness of interest-group activities. A good example of a group that exhibits strength through numbers is the American Farm Bureau Federation (AFBF), which boasts 4.7 million members and has proven especially effective at promoting policies that provide large subsidies and other benefits to American farmers. A bilateral trade agreement between the United States and Russia in late 2006 was a testament to AFBF influence, as it substantially expanded the export market for U.S. farmers.

2. **The wealth of the members.** The number of members is an important indicator of the potential amount of money that interest groups might be able to raise. But just as important is the wealth of the membership. Certain interest groups enjoy a huge advantage when it comes to the average wealth of members. For example, the American Trial Lawyers Association (ATLA) is made up of trial lawyers, who, by virtue of their occupation, are quite wealthy when compared to average Americans. Thus, whereas the number of members of the ATLA is only about 60,000, the wealth of its membership and the consequent level of financial contributions from members provide sufficient resources to make it an especially powerful interest group in Washington.

3. **The dedication of members to the goals of the group.** In addition to the number of members and wealth of members, groups that have a loyal following based

on member commitment to the cause of the group can be a powerful resource.[16] The National Right to Life Committee (NRLC) is a good example. The NRLC organized and began to solicit members and contributions in 1973, after the *Roe v. Wade*[17] decision legalized abortion. NRLC's members tend to be dedicated to right-to-life positions and willing to contribute much time, effort, and resources to advance its pro-life agenda.

11-3 | Types of Interest Groups

Although interest groups represent a wide array of interests in American society, there are two basic types of interest groups: economic groups and noneconomic groups. Many groups engage in both economic and noneconomic pursuits, but most can be classified as either primarily economic or noneconomic in nature.

Economic Groups

Although the specific goals of different interest groups vary greatly, the vast majority of groups in America have goals that are economic in nature. Two out of every three interest groups in America are **economic interest groups**, or groups that exist to promote favorable economic conditions and economic opportunities for their members. Economic groups also tend to be the largest and most powerful groups because members of such groups maintain a vested personal financial stake in having the group achieve its goals.

economic interest group An organized group that exists to promote favorable economic conditions and economic opportunities for its members.

As well as being the most numerous, economic groups also tend to be the best organized and most influential interest groups. Because economic interests are those that generally inspire more concern from businesses and citizens alike, they tend to feature greater individual involvement, commitment, resources, and organization.

There are thousands of interest groups that focus primarily on advancing the economic goals of members. These groups include private businesses, labor unions, business and industry associations, and professional associations.

Business Groups. The largest companies in the nation and the world typically maintain internal units that function as an interest group for the company. Very large companies, such as General Motors (GM) and IBM, for example, have their own interest groups. Such companies typically have wide and varied interests. GM, for example, is affected by environmental laws (tougher air pollution laws often require GM to spend more on technologies to reduce emissions from its cars), labor laws (increases in the minimum wage require higher pay for some workers), and product safety laws (increased safety standards might increase the cost of assembling a car). GM needs a well-staffed interest group to try to influence these and many other types of legislation.

Most businesses belong to associations, and often these associations engage in interest-group activities to advocate for the interests of their members. Some associations are very broad in scope, such as the U.S. Chamber of Commerce, with its 3 million members. These businesses range from small neighborhood auto mechanics to large billion-dollar financial institutions. The Chamber seeks to broadly advance the interests of business owners.

Another type of business association is a **trade association**. A trade association typically focuses on one particular industry, and members of the association are drawn exclusively from that industry. Businesses in a particular trade often face similar types of concerns, and the trade association looks out for the specific interests of a classification of businesses. For example, the American Society of Travel Agents (ASTA) is a trade association whose 24,000 member institutions include travel agencies, hotels, airlines, car rental agencies, and the like. ASTA promotes legislation and regulations favoring the travel industry.

trade association A business association that focuses on one particular industry, with membership drawn exclusively from that industry.

Businesses, business associations, and trade associations have an advantage over associations and other organizations whose members are individual citizens or consumers.

Businesses quickly see the advantage of joining an association, which collectively advocates for the interests of like businesses. Individuals, however, are less likely to join and contribute to an association that advocates for such things as consumer protection. Because there are so many consumers, an individual consumer is less likely to see a benefit in his or her own contribution. But because there are fewer businesses that belong to any given trade association, businesses are more likely to perceive a benefit from participating in the organization. As Mancur Olson, a well-known scholar on interest groups, put it, smaller groups are more likely to organize and associate because members can more readily see the benefits and "logic of collective action."[18] That is, people with common interests working together in groups are more effective than the same number of people working independently.

Certainly members of smaller groups are more likely to perceive direct benefits from their membership; smaller groups are also less likely to suffer from the free-rider problem. **Free riders** are those individuals who do not join or contribute to an interest group that is representing their interests. Thus, they enjoy the benefits of membership without paying for the costs. The free-rider problem is more common in larger groups, which may have trouble convincing individuals to contribute due to each individual's perception that others will work to achieve the group's goal.

Labor Unions. Whereas business groups promote the interests of companies and corporations, labor unions promote the interests of American workers. Initially, labor unions emerged from the expansion of the U.S. economy in the late 1800s and early 1900s. The new technologies that resulted from the Industrial Revolution led to the rapid growth of large-scale farming and manufacturing and created many new jobs. Many business owners exploited their laborers, providing low pay, few benefits, and often poor and unsafe working conditions. Workers then organized into unions, using the threat of a strike to improve their conditions.

In the early 1940s, as many as 35 percent of workers in America were union members. Over the years, however, the percentage of union workers has declined. Today only about 13 percent of workers belong to a union. An important reason for this decline relates to changes in the type of jobs that Americans hold. Skilled and unskilled laborers are most likely to be unionized, but these types of jobs represent an increasingly smaller proportion of the workforce. Professional and service jobs, which are less likely to be unionized, now dominate the American workforce, and so union membership has declined. Rather than unionizing, professionals tend to organize and join professional associations. Some professionals, however, have unionized. The largest union in the United States today is a teachers' union, the National Education Association.

Unions differ from professional associations in that the laws provide certain bargaining rights to unions. Union membership may be required for all employees as well. State laws vary on this issue. Some states are **open shop**, which means that employees in that state maintain the option of whether or not to join a certified union. Of course, in open-shop states, workers who do not join the union may benefit from union activities without "paying the price"—another form of the free-rider problem. Since 1947, the federal Taft-Hartley Act has technically banned the **closed shop**, which requires union membership as a condition of employment in a unionized workplace. Still, unions have successfully convinced some state legislatures that because all workers enjoy the benefits of union advocacy (for example, promoting pay increases and so on), all workers should at least be required to pay dues to the union. Thus, many states allow so-called

free rider An individual who does not join or contribute to an interest group that is representing his or her interests.

open shop The law that allows employees the option of joining or not joining the certified union at a unionized workplace.

closed shop The law that requires employees to become members of the union as a condition of employment in unionized workplaces.

Secretary of Defense Leon Panetta (right) meets with Imad Hamad, the director of the interest group the Arab-American Anti-Discrimination Committee.

AP Images/Carlos Osorio

union shops, which require that employees in unionized workplaces either join the union or pay the equivalent of union dues to it after a set period of time.

Professional Associations. Higher levels of education and advances in technology have transformed the American workforce over the past half-century. One of the major changes has been an increase in professional, technical, and service jobs and a decrease in the number of skilled and unskilled labor jobs. Professionals have organized to promote and protect their economic interests through membership in professional organizations, which lobby on their behalf.

Two large and growing classes of professionals are lawyers and medical doctors, both of which have high-profile and powerful interest groups—the American Bar Association (ABA) for lawyers and the American Medical Association (AMA) for doctors. The medical and legal professions are regulated by state governments, and the AMA and ABA have been quite successful in influencing the regulatory process—for example, by establishing licensing requirements for doctors and lawyers.

Another large and influential professional association is the National Association of Realtors (NAR), with a total membership of over 700,000; an annual budget of over $60,000,000; and an organizational staff of more than 400 people. The size, budget, and organization of the NAR provide it with ample resources to advocate the interests of the nation's real estate agents.

Noneconomic Groups

Economic groups exist primarily to advance the commercial and financial interests of their members. Whereas economic interests (as demonstrated in Table 11-1) dominate pluralist activities, many other interest groups advocate for primarily noneconomic concerns. Three general categories of **noneconomic interest groups** are public-interest groups, issue or ideological groups, and government groups.

union shop The law that requires that employees in unionized workplaces either join the union or pay the equivalent of union dues to it after a set period of time.

noneconomic interest group An organized group that advocates for reasons other than its membership's commercial and financial interests.

TABLE 11-1	Who Spends the Most on Lobbying?

Each year, interest groups spend more than $3 billion on lobbying activities in Washington, D.C. This table shows the biggest spenders from 1998 through 2013.

Organization	Total
U.S. Chamber of Commerce	$1,018,910,680
American Medical Association	297,960,000
General Electric	295,057,500
American Hospital Association	249,433,008
Pharmaceutical Research and Manufacturers of America	246,386,420
National Association of Realtors	245,760,858
AARP	229,932,064
Blue Cross/Blue Shield	220,956,832
Northrop Grumman	202,685,253
Exxon Mobil	193,022,742
Verizon	164,424,841

Source: Center for Responsive Politics, www.opensecrets.org

public-interest group An organized group that promotes the broad, collective good of citizens and consumers.

Public-Interest Groups. Public-interest groups promote the broad, collective good of citizens and consumers. Many public-interest groups seek to promote political reforms that enhance the role of the public in the political process. The League of Women Voters is one such group. Initially formed as an interest group that promoted women's suffrage, the League has become a leading advocate for improving turnout among all citizens in elections. The League of Women Voters has also taken the lead in promoting candidate engagement on issues of importance to the voters by sponsoring campaign debates.

Another highly active public-interest group is Common Cause. This group's literature describes itself in the following way: "Common Cause is a nonprofit, nonpartisan citizen's lobbying organization promoting open, honest and accountable government. Supported by the dues and contributions of over 200,000 members in every state across the nation, Common Cause represents the unified voice of the people against corruption in government and big money special interests."[19]

Common Cause promotes reforming the political system in ways that enhance the role of the average citizen. Thus, it supports laws limiting elected officials from taking gifts from special interests, banning large speaking honoraria for members of Congress, and reforming the presidential campaign finance system. Ironically, Common Cause is an interest group that tries to limit the role of interest groups.

Ralph Nader and the various citizens' advocacy groups he helped to start (including Public Citizen and the Center for Auto Safety) are among the nation's leading public-interest groups. Nader's best-selling book *Unsafe at Any Speed: The Designed-in Dangers of the American Automobile*[20] forced the president of General Motors to publicly admit to the U.S. Senate that the company ignored automobile safety problems. Nader's Raiders, the name later given to the hundreds of young activists who arrived in Washington, D.C., to help Nader investigate government corruption, were highly influential in pushing automobile safety legislation in the late 1960s, which dramatically raised safety standards for cars and trucks. Their efforts effectively launched a widespread consumer movement, which remains strong. Today these groups advocate campaign finance reform, monitor the health care industry, and promote consumer safety and consumer rights, among other public-interest activities.

issue and ideological group An organized group that focuses on specific issues and ideological perspectives.

Issue and Ideological Groups. Interest groups that focus on specific issues and ideological perspectives are known as **issue and ideological groups**. Abortion, women's rights, and the environment are just a few of the policy issues that have produced interest groups such as the National Right to Life Committee (pro-life), Americans for Free Choice (pro-choice), the National Organization for Women (NOW; women's rights), and the Sierra Club and the Nature Conservancy (both environmental groups). Each of these groups maintains effective lobbies on behalf of its positions.

Some groups have a broader focus than a particular issue or set of policy issues. These are known as ideological groups, and they promote a more general ideological approach on how government should deal with a host of issues. Both liberal and conservative ideological groups operate in the American pluralist system. Americans for Democratic Action (ADA), for example, is an interest group that promotes government policies with a liberal orientation. Since 1947, the voting records of members of Congress on certain issues have served as the standard measure of political liberalism. The ADA supports candidates for office whose votes on key issues score a high liberal quotient.

The American Civil Liberties Union (ACLU) is an interest group that advocates for the civil rights and liberties of American citizens. Specifically, the ACLU adamantly supports the rights of the accused, free speech rights, free press rights, religious liberty rights, and many other liberties guaranteed by the Bill of Rights. The ACLU has also become a strong advocate for students' rights, the rights of workers, lesbian/gay rights, and immigrants' rights.

The Christian Coalition of America (CCA) is another ideological group that has become a lobbying powerhouse in recent decades; it offers a vehicle to become involved in influencing public policy. The CCA's agenda advocates pro-life positions, promotes

Contemporary Movements for Civil Rights

We are now witnessing a new force in American politics: the proliferation of identity-based social movements that have organized to advocate for civil rights and to provide brand new avenues for increased political participation. Groups such as Black Lives Matter (BLM) and the DREAMers exemplify this phenomenon, which you can see from their two websites: blacklivesmatter.com and unitedwedream.org.

DREAMers began in the early 2000s as an immigrant youth network that worked on behalf of immigrant rights. The network developed out of stalled congressional efforts to pass the "Dream Act," which would have provided a path to citizenship for undocumented youth brought to the United States as young children. The network eventually grew to encompass the largest youth-led organization in the country, which "runs programs to advocate for access to higher education; stops deportations of undocumented youth and their parents; and strengthens

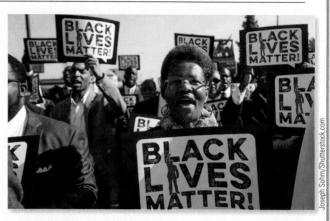

Members of Black Lives Matter march at the annual Martin Luther King Day parade in Los Angeles in January 2015.

alliances and support for DREAMers at the intersection of queer and immigrant rights."[21]

BLM is a chapter-based national organization that works for black civil rights. The organization was created in 2012 following George Zimmerman's acquittal for the death of Trayvon Martin. The organization aims to broaden the "conversation around state violence to include all of the ways in which Black people are intentionally left powerless at the hands of the state."[22] Both movements aim to advocate for human rights and unite people in social action.

For Critical Thinking and Discussion

1. How do BLM and DREAMers differ from more traditional groups or movements?
2. Do you think these new identity-based groups can be successful advocating for political and social change? What advantages, if any, do they offer?

Members of the group DREAMers protest in front of the US Citizenship and Immigration Services building in Fairfax, VA.

the role of religion as a part of what government does, favors reducing tax burdens on families, and supports victims' rights.

Government Interest Groups. Most interest-group activity organizes private concerns (of either individuals or businesses) for the purpose of influencing public policy. But private interests are not the only ones represented in the pluralist system. Groups representing the interests of governments also operate in this complex system.

Cities and states across the nation have organized to exert influence on the federal government. Most states and large cities employ their own lobbyists in Washington, D.C. But states, cities, and other governments also organize collectively through a variety of interest groups, which are generally referred to as **intergovernmental lobbies**. The National League of Cities, for example, is an interest group that advocates for the broad interests of local governments. Another intergovernmental lobby advancing the cause of the nation's cities is the U.S. Conference of Mayors. The Council of State Governments and the National Governors Association lobby on behalf of the states' interests.

intergovernmental lobby Any interest group that represents the collective interests of states, cities, and other governments.

Not only do state and local governments lobby in Washington, D.C., but foreign governments also organize and lobby. Many nations have embassies in the Washington, D.C., area, and many of these embassies engage in interest-group activities of their own.

11-4 | How Interest Groups Achieve Their Goals

Interest groups engage in a number of activities to advance the goals of the group and influence public policy. These activities usually involve lobbying, supporting candidates and parties in election campaigns, litigating, and mounting persuasion campaigns.

Lobbying

lobbying The means by which interest groups attempt to influence government officials to make decisions favorable to their goals.

Interest groups attempt to influence elected and other public leaders to make decisions that are favorable toward the group's goals. **Lobbying** is the term used to describe how interest groups go about influencing government officials. Lobbyists are the professionals who do the lobbying.

Lobbyists provide information to public officials, with the hope that the information will convince the official to vote or act in a manner favorable to the group's interest. Lobbyists perform a valuable function to public officials by providing not only information and perspectives on issues, but expertise as well. In the iron-triangle system, lobbyists seek access to members of Congress and to managers in executive agencies in a particular policy area. Public officials come to depend on the lobbyists for information and knowledge. For example, managers in the Department of Defense and members of Congress on the Armed Services Committee rely on lobbyists from Pratt & Whitney for information on emerging jet engine technologies, engine performance data, and other information, which allows the military to plan and improve the nation's defenses.

Similarly, the congressional committees responsible for workplace safety standards and the Occupational Safety and Health Administration (OSHA), the executive agency responsible for administering those standards, depend on the lobbyists representing labor unions and product safety groups for data and information on workplace hazards and for recommendations for remediation. Of course, these same public officials are likely to be lobbied by business interests concerned about the increased costs associated with remediation of hazards.

Lobbyists communicate with public officials in many different ways, including formal presentations, written memos and policy papers, informal e-mails or notes, face-to-face meetings, and informal discussions over a meal or a drink. The most effective lobbyists are those who provide valuable, truthful information on policy issues and who make persuasive arguments. Having a good working relationship with public officials and a quality reputation provides the lobbyist with access to officials, which is crucial to the lobbyist's success.

A common depiction of lobbying is that of an individual offering money, gifts, trips, or other goods in return for a favorable action, such as a congressperson's vote on a particular bill. Though such activities do take place, in modern times they have become the exception rather than the rule. The activities of lobbyists today are strictly regulated by federal and state governments. Lobbyist gift-giving and bribery of public officials are illegal in most states and can be prosecuted. States require lobbyists to provide financial statements, report expenses, and maintain official registration for interest groups and individuals who provide lobbying services.

Lobbyists are regularly seen in the halls of the Capitol building and the House and Senate office buildings. They are also common fixtures in the halls and offices of the state capitol buildings. Many lobbyists own their own lobbying firms and contract with interest groups to provide services, similar to the way that an organization might hire a law firm to conduct legal work. More commonly, however, lobbyists are employed by

The Political Power of the NRA

The National Rifle Association (NRA) has demonstrated time and time again how a powerful interest group can impact public policy. Its political work in 1968 and 2013 are examples of how a well-organized interest group created very real policy consequences.

Then

After the gun assassinations of President John F. Kennedy in 1963, civil rights leader Martin Luther King Jr. in April of 1968, and presidential candidate Robert Kennedy in June of 1968, many congressional leaders felt the time was right for new gun control legislation. A Gallup poll conducted at the time found that as many as half of all Americans explicitly favored the banning of all handguns, whereas just 44 percent opposed such a law. Maryland Senator Joseph Tydings, a personal friend and colleague of Senator Robert Kennedy, took Kennedy's place on NBC's *Meet the Press* a few days after the assassination to announce that he would be introducing a new bill into Congress, the Firearms Registration and Licensing Act. If passed, the bill would have mandated the registration of all guns and created licensing requirements to keep guns out of the hands of criminals. The reaction to Tydings's bill was initially favorable, winning public praise from the Kennedy family as well as many commentators. The bill made it out of committee and onto the Senate floor. Then, as Tydings later lamented,

"the NRA (National Rifle Association) got to work." The NRA, under the direction of its president Franklin Orth, used its vast resources to lobby Congress and engage in a public campaign that eventually not only defeated the bill in the Senate, but also defeated Tydings in his 1970 bid for reelection. At least for the time being, the powerful NRA had thwarted any measure to control the registration and licensing of guns.

Franklin Orth, president of the NRA, in 1969.

Now

In the wake of the December 2012 shootings of 20 children and staff at the Sandy Hook Elementary School in Newtown, Connecticut, public opinion polls showed that Americans were ready for new gun control laws. The Newtown event followed the 2011 gunning down of five people at an Arizona shopping center; included among the victims was Congressperson Gabby Giffords, who suffered a chronic brain injury in the incident. After the Newtown shooting, a Gallup poll found that 58 percent of Americans favored stricter gun control laws and nearly 9 in 10 favored stricter recordkeeping requirements for gun purchasers. California Senator Diane Feinstein took to the airwaves on *Meet the Press* a few days after the Newtown incident to try to convince Americans that new control measures were needed to curb the senseless gun violence. Several weeks later she introduced into Congress the Assault Weapons Ban of 2013, which would have stopped the sale, manufacturing, and transfer of military-style assault weapons such as the ones used in the Newtown murders. The bill won praise from President Obama, the families of many of the Newtown victims, and Rep. Giffords herself. The tide of public opinion and support from political elites, however, proved no match for the powerful

NRA. Within a few months from the time the bill was introduced into Congress, it began to die in the Senate. A well-orchestrated public information campaign by the NRA under the direction of Wayne LaPierre, along with strong lobbying efforts, helped to amass enough votes to halt the gun ban legislation in its tracks.

Wayne LaPierre, CEO of the NRA, in 2013.

For Critical Thinking and Discussion

1. Why do you think the NRA has been so successful in pressing for its agenda?
2. If a large segment of the public favors gun regulations, why do they find it so hard to match the NRA's organization and lobbying efforts?

businesses, associations, or other organizations to lobby for that employer alone. Large organizations and businesses have the resources to hire full-time lobbyists; contract lobbyists often work for smaller organizations that do not have the resources to hire their own full-time lobbying staff.

A form of lobbying that has been used more frequently in recent years is known as **grassroots lobbying**. The idea behind grassroots lobbying is that interest groups communicate with government officials by mobilizing public opinion to exert influence on government action. Because elected leaders are often quite sensitive to the opinions of voters, if a group can demonstrate that public opinion supports a particular position or that the public is willing to contact officials to express their view, officeholders will respond favorably because they want to enhance their chances of being reelected to office. Interest groups with a large number of members are particularly effective at grassroots lobbying, mainly because they can produce large numbers of potential votes in a given election. The AARP, with more than 40 million members, has successfully used grassroots methods of lobbying to put pressure on Congress to protect the Social Security and Medicare systems—two primary goals of the AARP.

grassroots lobbying Communications by interest groups with government officials through the mobilization of public opinion to exert influence on government action.

Supporting Candidates and Parties in Elections

Interest groups are also quite active in electoral politics, providing resources for candidates and parties that support the interest groups' goals. Table 11-2 lists the groups that have contributed the most money to political campaigns over the past quarter century. PACs, described earlier in this chapter, are an important instrument through which interest groups provide financial support to candidates and political parties.

TABLE 11-2 Big Givers to Campaigns

These 11 organizations were the biggest contributors to American political campaigns between 1989 and 2012. AT&T, the National Association of Realtors, and Goldman Sachs gave about equally to Democrats and Republicans, whereas the remaining top 11 givers heavily tilted toward giving to Democratic Party candidates. None of the top 11 tilted toward the GOP.

Organization	Contributions
ActBlue	$58,511,226
AT & T, Inc.	48,196,209
American Federation of State, County and Municipal Employees	47,347,798
National Association of Realtors	41,687,376
Service Employees International Union	38,083,375
National Education Association	37,937,019
Goldman Sachs	37,343,517
American Association for Justice	35,673,179
International Brotherhood of Electrical Workers	34,821,537
American Federation of Teachers	32,833,966
Laborers Union	32,409,200

Source: Center for Responsive Politics, February 2012.

In addition to providing financing to support candidates, groups can play an important role in campaigns in other ways as well. For example, a labor union might endorse a candidate and communicate that endorsement to its members, urging members to vote for the candidate. A group might also use its resources to hire a phone bank to make "get out the vote" phone calls on behalf of a candidate or slate of candidates. Groups have also provided support by drafting speeches for candidates on policy matters or hosting rallies for office seekers.

Business groups tend to support Republican candidates, largely because Republicans are more likely to agree with their goals. Similarly, labor unions tend to support Democratic candidates because Democrats are likely to support labor's positions on many issues, such as increases in the minimum wage and family leave laws. On social issues, Republican candidates tend to receive the support of conservative groups, such as pro-life groups and groups advocating stiffer crime-control measures. Groups that advocate a more liberal social agenda (such as the ACLU and Sierra Club) tend to support Democratic candidates, whose issue agenda is more consistent with the groups' goals.

Litigation

Interest groups have also become quite adept at using the court system as a means of achieving their goals. Groups regularly initiate lawsuits, request injunctions, defend members, and file briefs. Consumer product safety groups, for example, regularly file for injunctions in courts seeking to order companies to cease the sale of products that are unsafe.

Some interest groups focus primarily on the courts to achieve their goals. For example, the ACLU regularly initiates lawsuits in circumstances in which it believes the government is compromising individual civil liberties. The ACLU is very active in litigating gender discrimination cases. One of the advantages of interest-group litigation is its capitalization of interest groups' financial resources; average citizens do not have sufficient resources to initiate so many lawsuits. Also, because interest groups often specialize in particular kinds of lawsuits, they are able to litigate more skillfully.

Another way interest groups use the court system to exert influence is by the filing of amicus curiae ("friend of the court") briefs, which are companion briefs supporting an argument or set of arguments in an existing Supreme Court case.[23] Although the interest group is not a direct litigant in a matter, it can use an amicus brief to further or better articulate a position and thus aid litigants in their respective case.

Interest groups have also influenced the court system by engaging in lobbying activities to influence the appointment of judges. Pro-life and pro-choice groups are very active in supporting or opposing particular judicial nominees, based on the nominees' position and past decisions on abortion cases. The American Bar Association uses a rating system to rank individuals nominated for federal judgeships that has become extremely influential in the appointment process.

Persuasion Campaigns

Many interest groups run media campaigns to persuade the public to support their position on issues. Some of this persuasion occurs during election campaigns when groups create and place ads intended to help a political candidate or political party achieve victory. But increasingly, groups have run such campaigns outside of election campaigns to persuade or educate others to the group's way of thinking.

Groups have developed sophisticated public relations operations to communicate their positions. They use tactics such as targeted mass mailings, in which they mail a pamphlet or other document to a large list of individuals that the group is attempting to influence. For example, the Americans for Democratic Action (ADA) group maintains a list of voters who are not registered with any particular political party. The ADA often

ACLU attorney Ruth Bader Ginsburg in 1977. Sixteen years later Ginsburg became an associate justice on the U.S. Supreme Court.

sends mailings to those on the list to try to persuade them to support the ADA's position on a particular issue. In addition to mass mailings, groups regularly use television, radio, newspapers, magazines, or even billboards to communicate positions and try to persuade. They also use the Internet to send messages to the wider public.

Interest groups have become firmly entrenched within the American political landscape. Their influence is both certain and controversial. More than two centuries ago, James Madison expressed concerns about the influence of "factions." Today, many observers of American politics continue to express concerns about the influence of groups and the value of pluralism as a mode of governance. Nevertheless, interest groups offer an important and unique linkage between American citizens' varied interests and public policy. This does not diminish the importance of other linkages, such as free and open elections. But the linkage offered by interest groups is unique in that it allows citizens to exert influence by interacting with one another and collectively attempting to influence what government does. Few would argue with the premise that interest groups have been responsible for leading the charge in promoting political and social policies that have significantly improved the lot of millions of Americans.

 ## From Your Perspective

"Before the Lecture Begins, Students from PIRG Have an Announcement . . ."

If you have spent significant time on a college campus, you have probably heard about PIRG (Public Interest Research Group). PIRG is a federation of state-based public interest groups that, in the words of its website, "stand up to powerful special interests on behalf of the American public."[24]

The PIRG model of a national campus network was proposed by public-interest advocate Ralph Nader in 1970 and now has expanded to include 30 state-based organizations.

State PIRGs are particularly active in recruiting students on college campuses. At the start of the semester, student members of PIRG ask professors for a few minutes of class time to pitch PIRG-related activities to the class. For many students, this is their first exposure to an interest group. Those who join will quickly get involved in PIRG's public-interest causes and sometimes even become interns and get course credit for the experience.

For Critical Thinking and Discussion

1. Does PIRG operate on your campus? If so, how effective has it been in influencing state legislative decisions?
2. Take a look at your campus PIRG's website or that of another campus if PIRG is not active at your institution. What positions does it advance on which issues? Do you personally support its lobbying efforts, or do you oppose its lobbying efforts?

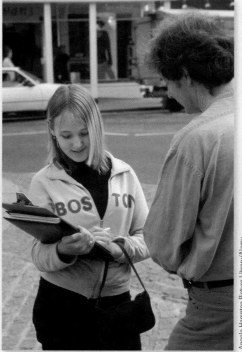

A college student in Florida solicits signatures on a petition for Florida PIRG.

Angela Hampton Picture Library/Alamy

Summary

11-1 Pluralism and the Interest Group System

- Interest groups are a popular mechanism by which groups of people attempt to influence government to advance their shared goals.
- Pluralism is the theory that public policy largely results from a variety of interest groups competing with one another to promote laws that benefit members of their respective groups.
- Many praise the interest-group system in the United States because it provides all groups in society with access and a fair opportunity to compete for influence over public policy. By contrast, critics of the interest group system say that it allows wealthy corporations and individuals a disproportionate influence on public policy, encourages many groups to promote their own causes even if they run counter to the public interest, and significantly slows down the policymaking process.

11-2 Interest Groups in Action

- The growth of interest groups in the United States during the twentieth century was a product of the tremendous growth of government in general over that same period and the increased concerns about political issues that are expressed by a better-educated mass public.
- Interest-group influence over public policy is theoretically informal; in reality, interest-group participation has become ingrained in the process through structures such as iron triangles and issue networks.
- Individuals tend to join or support interest groups in order to receive material benefits, purposive benefits (those that benefit society more generally), and solidary benefits based on individuals' satisfaction from interacting with like-minded people in pursuit of a goal.
- The most successful interest groups tend to maintain a large membership of individuals, at least some of whom are wealthy, as well as a loyal following based on members' commitment to the cause.

11-3 Types of Interest Groups

- Economic interest groups that pursue favorable monetary benefits for their members include business groups such as industry trade associations, labor unions, and professional associations. Noneconomic interest groups that pursue goals other than the commercial interests of their members include public-interest groups, issue or ideological groups, and government interest groups.
- Large interest groups must always concern themselves with the problem of "free riders," those who benefit from the groups' activities without ever joining or contributing to the groups.

11-4 How Interest Groups Achieve Their Goals

- Interest groups achieve their goals through lobbying activities, supporting candidates in election contests, litigating, and mounting persuasion campaigns.

Key Terms

closed shop (p. 300)
economic interest group (p. 299)
free rider (p. 300)
grassroots lobbying (p. 306)
interest group (p. 291)
intergovernmental lobby (p. 303)
iron triangle (p. 296)
issue and ideological group (p. 302)
issue network (p. 296)

lobbying (p. 304)
majoritarianism (p. 292)
material benefits (of group
   membership) (p. 297)
noneconomic interest group (p. 301)
open shop (p. 300)
pluralism (p. 292)
political action committee
   (PAC) (p. 295)

public-interest group (p. 302)
purposive benefits (of group
   membership) (p. 297)
social movement (p. 294)
solidary benefits (of group
   membership) (p. 297)
trade association (p. 299)
union shop (p. 301)

Test Yourself

1. What theory suggests that the competition between interest groups is responsible for policymaking?

    a. Elitism

    b. Majoritarianism

    c. Pluralism

    d. Liberalism

2. The argument that interest groups are a tool of the political elite and are thus used to advance the views of the wealthy and powerful was first set forth by

    a. C. Wright Mills.

    b. Robert Dahl.

    c. Alexis de Tocqueville.

    d. David Truman.

3. What distinguishes an interest group from a political party?

4. If an individual joins an interest group as a way of advancing his or her own economic interests, what type of benefits is that individual seeking?

    a. Material

    b. Purposive

    c. Solidary

    d. Instrumental

5. An "iron triangle" does NOT include which of the following entities?

    a. A federal court

    b. An interest group

    c. A bureaucratic agency

    d. A congressional committee

6. The American Trial Lawyers Association is a successful interest group primarily because

    a. its members are dedicated to a cause.

    b. it contains millions of members.

    c. its members tend to be quite wealthy.

    d. most members of Congress are lawyers.

7. Distinguish between an "iron triangle" and an "issue network."

8. Two out of every three interest groups are

    a. public-interest groups.

    b. economic-based groups.

    c. single-issue groups.

    d. ideological groups.

9. A unionized workplace that requires employees to join the union by state law is known as a(n)

    a. closed shop.

    b. open shop.

    c. union shop.

    d. mixed shop.

10. What type of interest group is the PIRG on your campus (or another campus in your state if PIRG is not active at your institution)? Why would you classify it that way?

11. If an interest group files an "amicus curiae" brief, it is engaging in what type of activity?

    a. Persuasion campaign

    b. Litigation

    c. Election support

    d. Grassroots lobbying

12. Which of the following Supreme Court justices was once an important official with the ACLU?

    a. Antonin Scalia

    b. Anthony Kennedy

    c. Clarence Thomas

    d. Ruth Bader Ginsburg

13. Why is the AARP so successful at using grassroots lobbying campaigns to achieve its goals?

1. c (LO 11-1); 2. a (LO 11-1); 4. a (LO 11-2); 5. a (LO 11-2); 6. c (LO 11-2); 8. b (LO 11-3); 9. a (LO 11-3); 11. b (LO 11-4); 12. d (LO 11-4)

Scott Kowalchyk/CBS/Getty Images

LEARNING OBJECTIVES

12-1 The Media in American Politics
- Describe the purpose and evolution of the Federal Communications Commission
- Compare and contrast the various functions that the media serve in the American political system

12-2 Historical Development of the Media
- Assess the evolution from a partisan press to a media focused on objectivity
- Explain how changes in technology have transformed the nature of the media

12-3 The Mass Media Today
- Identify the large variety of media that cover news and provide opinion about government and politics, including both traditional media and "new" media

- Appraise changes in audience and readership patterns, and the impact of those changes on news coverage
- Describe how the ownership of media organizations is concentrated in large corporations

12-4 The Effects of the Media
- Compare and contrast the different theories that have been developed to explain the effect that exposure to news has on viewers/readers

12-5 Criticisms of the News Media
- Critique media coverage of politics, including bias, sensationalism, and the concentration of corporate ownership

12

The Media and American Politics

T he news media serve a number of important political functions in the United States, operating through a large and growing number of outlets. Voters' primary source of information about political candidates and political issues is the news media, and political leaders constantly monitor and attempt to influence the content of news stories to their political advantage. The technologies of television and the Internet both allow citizens to observe events on the battlefield, look into the eyes of presidential candidates, and watch tragedies unfold. Further, social media have facilitated the ability of anyone—so-called citizen journalists—to publish the news in real time as it is happening in front of them. Events, and government's reaction to those events, now unfold live before a worldwide audience at the flip of a switch or click of a mouse. Not only do the media serve as an important information source, but they also help set the political agenda, provide perspective and commentary on issues and political candidates, and help keep the government accountable to the people.

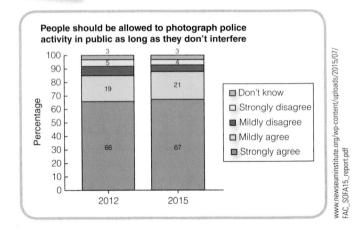
Are You a "Citizen Journalist?"

New technology, such as smartphones and social media, have created a new type of news reporter—the so-called citizen journalist. These technologies allow anyone to play a role in gathering, analyzing, and reporting news and information. Prior to the emergence of these new technologies, only journalists employed at news organizations had the capability to gather and report the news to mass audiences through television, radio, and newspapers. But today, any citizen with a camera-equipped smartphone and a Facebook or Twitter account can gather news by taking videos and pictures and simply "tweeting" (or even re-tweeting) what they have viewed or experienced.

Some of the more salient national news stories that have been reported recently include reporting from citizen journalists, such as video of questionable police use of force in Brooklyn and South Carolina. Far more common on social media and local news media are pictures and video of events that citizens record as they see it happen. Surveys indicate that most Americans endorse the right to engage in citizen journalism, as depicted in the following graphic:

People should be allowed to photograph police activity in public as long as they don't interfere

(Percentage)

	2012	2015
Don't know	3	3
Strongly disagree	5	4
Mildly disagree	19	21
Mildly agree		
Strongly agree	66	67

www.newseuminstitute.org/wp-content/uploads/2015/07/FAC_SOFA15_report.pdf

- Have you ever practiced citizen journalism?
- Have you gathered information on a breaking event on your smartphone and posted it on social media, or provided it to a news media outlet?
- If you were to witness a news event live, would you take a picture and post it for your friends to see?

To see how your answers compare to others, take the **Who Are You?** poll in MindTap!

12-1 | The Media in American Politics

Consider the following facts about media use in the United States: More than 160 million Americans use Facebook (1.4 billion worldwide), and each user has an average of over 300 "friends"; the average American spends more time (about three hours per day) watching television than working or going to school; all forms of media considered, the average person is engaged in media consumption for 3,500 hours each year—that's almost 40 percent of the 8,760 hours that exist in a year. There are even more TV sets per household than there are toilets. The media clearly have a pervasive presence in the everyday life of most Americans. From watching the political comedy of *Late Night with Stephen Colbert*, to listening to the political commentary of Rush Limbaugh, to catching up on the latest news from around the world on cable TV's CNN or Politico on the Internet, Americans make ample use of media sources available to them for getting political information.

Most news media organizations in the United States are owned by private companies, which, like most other private companies, seek to make a profit. Unlike other industries, however, the media enjoy a special constitutionally granted protection. The First Amendment to the U.S. Constitution specifically provides that "Congress shall make no law . . . abridging the freedom . . . of the press." When the First Amendment was adopted in 1791, the press was mostly a small collection of newspapers and magazines. Over the years, the press, now more commonly referred to as the media, has expanded to include radio, television, book publishers, music producers, the Internet, and motion pictures.

One early event that helped shape America's perspective on freedom of the press was the trial in 1735 of newspaper printer Peter Zenger, who in the *New York Weekly Journal* published a series of articles highly critical of the British-appointed governor of New York. Zenger was arrested on charges of criminal libel. He was defended by Philadelphia lawyer Andrew Hamilton, who won the case with his argument that Zenger had printed the truth and the truth cannot be considered libelous. Hamilton's argument thus established the principle of truth as a defense against libel.

The argument for a free press in the United States today largely rests upon the concept of the "free marketplace of ideas," a phrase coined by Supreme Court Justice Oliver Wendell Holmes in his dissenting opinion in *Abrams v. United States* (1919),[1] which suggests that allowing people to freely communicate their ideas will provide a larger variety of ideas to consider. Encouraging the publication and dissemination of a wide variety of political ideas offers citizens a diversity of opinions and perspectives and facilitates the free flow of information about local, national, and global events. Of course, for ideas to flow freely, government must be prevented from using its power to stifle perspectives with which it disagrees.

Government Regulation of the Media

Congress created the Federal Communications Commission (FCC) in 1934 to regulate the electronic media (primarily radio and eventually television) through licensing broadcasters and creating rules for broadcasters to follow. The FCC does not have authority to regulate the print media, such as newspapers. In fact, regulation of print media is rare, and courts have consistently treated the right of print media to publish free of government regulation. Some electronic media require broadcast frequencies that are scarce and thus need to be regulated to ensure the orderly transmission of programs.

Among the tools that the FCC may employ to regulate the activities of broadcasters is the threat of revoking a license or fining a station for violating its rules. The FCC has used these tools to limit the language and type of sexual material that broadcasters might use. For example, the FCC imposed fines on the owners of radio stations that broadcast "shock jock" Howard Stern. Stern's program often included graphic descriptions of sexual acts and sex games, as well as language that the FCC deems unacceptable. Some of those stations fined then dropped the Stern show from their program schedule. To avoid further legal battles with the FCC, in 2005 Stern moved his show to a satellite radio station, which is not subject to FCC regulations because satellite radio is purchased by users and does not rely on the publicly controlled airwaves.

One of the most visible instances of the FCC clamping down on material in broadcast transmission involved comedian George Carlin's "Seven Dirty Words" skit, which satirized attitudes toward vulgar language. In the skit, Carlin continually repeated the seven words that you can't say on TV or radio. The piece was played on a radio station licensed to the Pacifica Foundation. Prior to playing the piece, the announcer warned the audience about its content. Nevertheless, a listener complained to the FCC, and the FCC in turn warned the radio station not to replay the piece. The station challenged the FCC's authority to regulate programming content, and the case made its way to the U.S. Supreme Court in *FCC v. Pacifica Foundation* (1978).[2] In that case, the Supreme Court upheld the FCC's power to regulate the broadcast media on the criteria of indecent material.

The Supreme Court and Student Media Organizations

Hazelwood School District v. Kuhlmeier (1988)[3]

In 1983 the principal of Hazelwood East High School in St. Louis County, Missouri, found two articles in that high school's newspaper that he deemed to be "inappropriate": one concerned the use of birth control among students and the other considered how a student was handling his parents' divorce. The principal immediately barred the two articles from publication. Cathy Kuhlmeier and two other students on the newspaper staff subsequently brought suit, arguing that the principal's actions violated their First Amendment rights. Eventually the case made it all the way to the U.S. Supreme Court.

On January 13, 1988, the Supreme Court decided that schools must be able to set high standards for speech disseminated under their supervision and that schools, as part of their educational mission, maintain the right to refuse to support speech that is "inconsistent with the shared values of a civilized social order" in their school-supported newspapers or media outlets. High school and college journalists who depend on

their schools for financial support better take notice. Although some forms of censorship may be deemed "incomprehensible" as a means of meeting pedagogical concerns, the ultimate decision over publication more often than not belongs to school administrators in this context.

For Critical Thinking and Discussion

1. What types of articles and/or editorials in a student newspaper might be so important or central to the educational mission as to be immune from censorship under this standard?
2. What if a student newspaper attempted to print an article detailing the harmful effects of bus diesel fumes on students? Could the principal justify barring such an article as "inappropriate" or "inconsistent with the shared values of a civilized social order"? Why or why not?

---

equal time rule The FCC mandate that radio and TV broadcast stations offer equal amounts of airtime to all political candidates who want to broadcast advertisements.

The FCC's **equal time rule** mandates that radio and TV broadcast stations must offer equal amounts of airtime to all political candidates who want to broadcast advertisements. This rule also now includes a provision requiring that if a station broadcasts the president's State of the Union message, then that station must also provide free airtime for the opposing political party to broadcast a response.

From 1950 through the late 1980s, the FCC also enforced the so-called fairness doctrine, requiring broadcasters to set aside time for public affairs programming. The proliferation of news sources and technologies for transmitting electronic messages during the 1980s effectively ended the FCC's fairness doctrine requirements. These changes in technologies also resulted in the passage of the 1996 Telecommunications Act, which shifted the emphasis of government policy from regulating to facilitating competition. This law deregulated cable television providers, eliminated monopolies held by local phone companies, and allowed local phone companies to provide long-distance phone services. The Telecommunications Act transformed the FCC from a regulator of the telecommunications industry into an aggressive supporter of competition within that industry.

Functions of the Media in American Politics

Throughout the history of the United States, the media have come to serve a number of functions in the political system, all of which promote the free flow of information to the public. Principal functions of the media include (1) providing objective coverage of events, (2) facilitating public debate, and (3) serving as government watchdog.

Providing Objective Coverage of Events. The media's most basic role involves monitoring events around the nation and the world and communicating those events to the public. Through modern communications technologies, the media have become proficient at reporting major events as they happen. Live coverage of presidential addresses, campaign debates, war operations, prominent trials, natural disasters, and other important world events have made their way almost instantaneously onto front-page headlines and into television's round-the-clock news coverage.

Providing information about news and events is perhaps the most basic and most important function of the media. Factual news information is an essential component of evaluating events and forming political opinions. Operating free of government control, the U.S. media can provide objective coverage of events to the American public. **Objectivity** refers to the media reporting events factually, accurately, fairly, and equitably—an important goal for many journalists. In addition to providing factual information about events, objective journalism requires signaling when important events occur and providing perspectives on all sides of an issue or policy debate. The goal of objectivity, however, is itself the subject of some debate. Objectivity is hard to define and measure, and journalists sometimes take a shortcut by trying to give equal weight to all sides without making any judgments of their own. This approach permitted Senator Joseph McCarthy to falsely but very publicly accuse people of being communists in the 1950s; it let cigarette companies get away with denying that smoking causes cancer; and it is prolonging the current national debate on global warming. Journalism professor Philip Meyer has advocated for a science-based definition of objectivity by getting journalists to seek more independent verification of facts.[4]

Numerous media formats strive to provide objective coverage of news information. Most of the content of newspapers (with the notable exception of the editorial pages) is aimed at objectively covering news events and politics at the global, national, and local levels.

The 24-hour cable news channels, such as CNN, Fox News, and MSNBC, provide news of events on a continuous basis. Many other formats are aimed at providing an objective look at news information to readers and viewers.

Moreover, the proliferation of cable television has broadened the role of the media as provider of information. Channels like the Biography Channel, the History Channel, local government access channels, and C-SPAN now offer programming that gives historical context to local, national, and international events.

Facilitating Public Debate. In addition to monitoring and reporting events, the media also facilitate public dialogue and debate on important political issues. By helping frame issues, offering perspectives on how a problem might be solved, and providing context and commentary on political campaigns, the media serve a vital role in a democratic system that depends heavily on voters to make informed choices in elections.

The media facilitate public debate through a variety of forms, both print and electronic. Newspaper editorials provide perspectives on policy debates and political candidates. Websites, such as the left-leaning *Huffington Post* and the right-leaning *Townhall.com*,

objectivity The journalistic standard that news reporting of events must be factual, accurate, fair, and equitable.

TABLE 12-1   Top 5 Political Blogs

Here are the 10 most popular political sites in 2015 according to *eBizMBA Rank*

1. The Huffington Post (www.huffingtonpost.com)

2. The Blaze (www.theblaze.com)

3. The Drudge Report (www.drudgereport.com)

4. Newsmax (www.newsmax.org)

5. Politico (www.politico.com)

Based on data from technorati.com/blogs/op100/.

MSNBC talk show host Rachel Maddow provides a more liberal perspective on the issues of the day for her audience.

offer their respective partisan audiences a source of online political information. Syndicated columnists, such as conservative Charles Krauthammer and liberal Thomas Friedman, publish columns in numerous newspapers around the nation on a regular basis, presenting their own perspectives on issues. Most newspapers dedicate space on their editorial pages for citizens to write opinion pieces ("op-eds") and letters to the editor offering their point of view. Many news magazines adhere to a liberal or conservative approach to discussing issues or evaluating candidates for office. *The Nation*, for example, has a liberal perspective, whereas *The National Review* presents a conservative perspective. Even magazines devoted to one perspective or another, however, usually offer a forum for readers to assess issues. Radio talk shows that offer perspectives on politics, such as those of conservative radio talk show host Rush Limbaugh or liberal political commentator Ed Schultz, also facilitate public debate, as do television programs like MSNBC's *Hard Ball with Chris Matthews* and Fox News' *Hannity's America*, which often feature debates between the anchors and their ideological opponents.

These media formats go beyond objectively reporting news to analyzing events and presenting arguments from varying ideological perspectives that readers and viewers can evaluate and use in forming their own opinions about public policies and political candidates.

Government Watchdog. Since the founding of the nation, American political culture has been characterized by a healthy skepticism about government. To govern is to have power, and power (in the minds of many) corrupts. The federal system that divides power between the federal government and state and local governments; the system of shared power among the legislative, executive, and judicial branches of government; and the system of checks and balances among these three branches are mechanisms that help guard against the potential abuse of government power. The news media also help prevent the abuse of government power through their role as government watchdog. In this role, the media are sometimes referred to as the fourth branch of government, or the "fourth estate," checking the power of the other branches. Rooting out corruption and abuses of power through investigative journalism is a core function of the American media, no less important today than it was two centuries ago.

More than a century ago, a group of journalists, who came to be known as "muckrakers"[5] (they were given this name by one of their top admirers, President Theodore Roosevelt), investigated and exposed corporate and political corruption in American life, including the corrupting effect of corporate contributions on presidential candidates who won office. In the late 1800s, corporate wealth was concentrated in a handful of companies in the railroad and banking industries, and those companies bought favors and influence with various presidential administrations. The muckrakers exposed the rash of influence peddling and by doing so helped spawn new laws curbing corporate contributions to federal campaigns.

Perhaps the most well-known case of the media uncovering and exposing government corruption was the investigative reporting of *Washington Post* reporters Bob Woodward and Carl Bernstein in the early 1970s concerning the Watergate corruption scandal of President Richard M. Nixon's administration. Their work led in part to the resignation of President Nixon in 1974 for his role in covering up the details of the Republican-led break-in of the Democratic National Headquarters in the Watergate Hotel during the 1972 presidential campaign.[6] Woodward and Bernstein largely depended on an anonymous administration source, who came to be known as "Deep Throat," for information that ultimately exposed the White House cover-up of a number of criminal activities in Nixon's 1972 campaign for reelection.

Fox News conservative talk show host Bill O'Reilly draws a very high audience for his nightly cable TV show, The O'Reilly Factor.

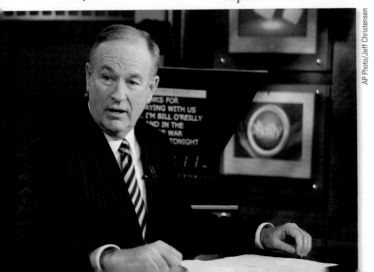

The media also exercise their watchdog function through television programs such as *60 Minutes*, *Dateline*, and *Meet the Press* and through Internet websites set up by groups like Common Cause, which provides data on the negative influence of corporate donations on political campaigns. The media also carry out their watchdog function through books. For example, a 2014 book (*Duty: Memoirs of a Secretary at War*) by Robert Gates, former Secretary of Defense to presidents George W. Bush and Barack Obama, criticized the Obama administration's foreign policy decision making.

Bettmann/Corbis

Pulitzer Prize–winning investigative reporters Carl Bernstein and Bob Woodward in 1973. Woodward and Bernstein investigated the Watergate scandal of the Nixon administration from 1972 through 1974 for the Washington Post.

12-2 | Historical Development of the Media

Before the American Revolution, the news media consisted of a handful of newspapers that were published by printers.[7] The main job of the printer was not to publish a newspaper, but rather to prepare official documents (such as marriage licenses, deeds to land, and government documents), political pamphlets, and religious books. Newspapers of the time mostly featured notices of public events and advertisements for local merchants. These early newspapers carried little information about politics or news events.

The political events that led up to the American Revolution and the events of the Revolution itself changed the nature and functions of the colonial newspapers. Many colonists were intensely interested in the disputes with Great Britain and eager for news about the battles of the Revolution. Newspapers responded to these interests with news stories about the events. Stories about the economic turmoil of the post-Revolution period, particularly the bitter partisan fight between the Federalists and Anti-Federalists over ratification of the Constitution, also appeared in the nation's early newspapers.

The Era of the Partisan Press

The Federalist/Anti-Federalist battle ushered in the **partisan press era**, a period characterized by newspapers supporting a particular political party. This period lasted from the late 1700s through the mid-1850s. Newspapers advocating the Federalist position that favored a stronger central government included John Fenno's *Gazette of the United States* and Noah Webster's *American Minerva*. The Anti-Federalists and later the Jeffersonian-Republicans, who supported states' rights, had their own partisan newspapers, such as the *National Gazette* and the *National Intelligencer*.

Partisan newspapers appealed mostly to readers who already agreed with the political positions advocated by those publications. Partisan-oriented news eventually became big business, and government printing contracts to partisan publications became a regular part of the spoils system.

During the early nineteenth century, a number of technological developments had a significant impact on the newspaper business. The invention of the rotary press in 1815 enabled the mass production of newspapers. The invention of the telegraph and the development of the telegraph system across the United States in the 1840s provided for the widespread electronic dissemination of news information. The expansion of the railroad system across the nation facilitated the mass distribution of newspapers across the

partisan press era The period from the late 1700s to the mid-1800s when newspapers typically supported a particular political party.

continent. These developments allowed newspapers to print news events more quickly and distribute their publications to a larger number of people in a shorter period of time. These technologies also helped reduce production costs, making newspapers affordable for most Americans. The term *penny press* aptly described the low cost of newspapers during the early to mid-nineteenth century.

By the 1850s, newspapers found that they could increase their circulation by distancing themselves from particular partisan positions. Eyeing ever-larger markets, newspapers began to appeal to all Americans. Journalists began to tout the goals of objective reporting of the facts, rather than providing a biased or partisan perspective on events. By the end of the nineteenth century, the technological innovations and the desire of newspaper publishers to reach larger numbers of readers and maximize profits through the selling of advertisements had transformed the newspaper industry from a mostly partisan press to one focused on objective reporting of the news.

The Emergence of Electronic Media

The development of the radio in the early twentieth century provided a new means for Americans to get information about politics. Most notably, communication from the media source to the audience was instantaneous. In addition, the technology allowed political leaders to directly communicate with the American people. The first radio station was KDKA in Pittsburgh, established in 1923. The first network of radio stations, which was established in 1926 as the National Broadcasting Company (NBC), provided common programming and newscasts that were made available to the first truly mass audiences.

Franklin Delano Roosevelt, elected president in 1932, used the radio to deliver comforting and inspiring messages to the nation, then suffering in the midst of the Great Depression. FDR's weekly radio addresses, which the president called "fireside chats," represented the first significant use of this medium by a political leader to communicate to the nation's people. In addition to FDR's fireside chats, radio commentators such as Father Charles Coughlin (Detroit's anti-Semitic "fighting priest") and Louisiana Senator Huey Long popularized radio as a medium that could provide a great deal of political commentary and debate. During World War II, Americans eager for news about the progress of the war turned to the radio for information. Edward R. Murrow's live radio reports from London during the Nazi bombings of that city and from other battle sites captivated the nation.

In the 1950s, Joe Pyne of radio station KABC hosted the first political talk radio show. Pyne challenged the status quo political views of the times, invited call-in questions from listeners, and promoted confrontation and debate. Pyne's style and format laid the foundation for many of today's popular political talk radio shows.

Numerous technological advancements have had a large impact on the scope and importance of the news media through American history, but none has had a more profound influence than the invention of television. In the post–World War II boom of the American economy, the nation quickly adopted TV as its primary medium for getting news about politics and the world. NBC and CBS developed the standard TV news show format in the early 1950s with a 15-minute daily news program. The program featured a news anchor reading the news, supported by film footage and reporters. This format—now modified into a half-hour program produced each evening—continues to be widely used today by all the major networks. In the 1950s, TV networks

President Franklin Delano Roosevelt, delivering one of his famous "fireside chats" in 1933.

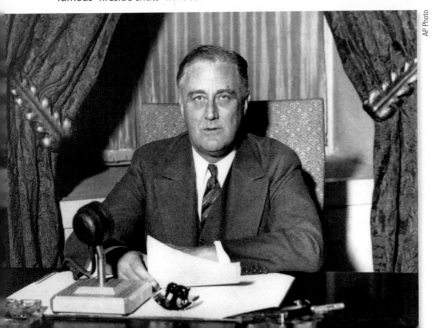

broadcast the Army–McCarthy hearings of the U.S. Senate that exposed Senator Joseph McCarthy as a crude bully and resulted in his censure for ethical misconduct. Live television coverage of the Republican and Democratic national conventions set the standard for live broadcasts of major political events. The networks also sold advertising time to the major party candidates in the presidential election of 1952, revolutionizing the way in which candidates would wage their bids for elective office.

Presidential Debates and the Power of Television. A defining moment in revealing the political power of electronic media was the live television broadcast of the debates between Republican Richard Nixon and Democrat John Kennedy, candidates in the presidential election of 1960. For the first time, all Americans were able to watch a live debate between the candidates. Many observers credit Kennedy's favorable TV performance as an important factor contributing to his razor-thin victory over Nixon in the November election. During the first of three televised debates, Kennedy won over the audience with his relaxed and self-assured manner before the camera; by contrast, Nixon seemed nervous and uncomfortable.

Republican presidential candidates Dr. Ben Carson, Sen. Marco Rubio (R-FL), Donald Trump, Sen. Ted Cruz (R-TX) and Gov. John Kasich (R-OH) at the Republican presidential primary candidate debate sponsored by CNN and Telemundo at the University of Houston on February 25, 2016.

Nixon prepared for the debate by studying briefing documents but spent little time practicing debate style. Kennedy, on the other hand, spent a great deal of time practicing answers to questions out loud. For the two days prior to the first debate, Kennedy and his inner circle of advisers didn't leave the practice session in their hotel room. On the night of the debate, a tanned Kennedy looked strong and healthy. He wore a navy blue suit that contrasted sharply with the light walls of the TV studio. Nixon, on the other hand, looked ill and underweight. Just before the debate he had been hospitalized with an infection, exhausted from a hard week of campaigning. He wore makeup to cover up his five o'clock shadow and dressed in a light gray suit that blended into the background.

The candidates debated the important issues and both did well in articulating their positions. But TV analysts reported that Kennedy won the debate. His stage presence, practice addressing the camera, tanned complexion, hand gestures, and commanding appearance compared favorably to the somber, pale Nixon. It was a lesson that no future presidential candidate would forget.

Interestingly, research on this debate[8] reveals that those who listened to the debate on the radio thought Nixon won, whereas those who watched the debate on TV tended to think that Kennedy won, proving that the medium through which events are communicated can indeed influence the way in which people evaluate those events. That the medium itself may have an important effect on the way in which people receive and perceive news was suggested by communications researcher Marshall McLuhan, who summarized this idea with his memorable phrase "the medium is the message."[9]

Live televised debates between the candidates for president did not occur again until 1976, when Republican President Gerald Ford and Democratic challenger Jimmy Carter met. This time both candidates were well prepared to convey the image they wanted to the American viewing audience. Dressed to coordinate with the set background, prepped with numerous practice sessions, and made up to ensure a favorable skin color tone, both Carter and Ford sought to communicate a positive image. Live broadcasts of presidential campaign debates have been a part of every presidential election contest since 1976.[10]

Television has transformed virtually every aspect of political campaigns and government policymaking. Prior to TV, the vast majority of voters never saw more than a still picture of the candidates, and most learned about them from reading newspaper accounts of their statements, speeches, and activities. Television, however, has allowed viewers to observe candidates live and in action, and to see how they deliver a speech and respond to questions. Television has also given candidates the opportunity to develop an "image" through carefully planned media appearances and strategically designed political advertisements.

Presidential Press Conferences. The power of televised images has also altered the governing process. Whereas President Woodrow Wilson was the first to hold regular and formal presidential news conferences, President Dwight D. Eisenhower was the first to hold regular news conferences as we know them today, as a means of explaining his administration's policies and appealing directly to the public for support. Before Eisenhower, the news media's access to the president was primarily through appointments that the chief executive would give to favored reporters. Eisenhower opened up the press conference to reporters from all types of news organizations. The questions were not prescreened, and Eisenhower addressed whatever topics were on reporters' agendas. This format for addressing the nation, coupled with the capability of television to show Americans the event, opened up the presidency to the public.

Eisenhower's successor, President John F. Kennedy, quickly mastered the art of the presidential press conference. He made events seem even more dramatic and intriguing by allowing TV to broadcast them live. Kennedy's preparedness on issues, strong intellect, charismatic personality, and sense of humor made his press conferences interesting and successful events. President Lyndon B. Johnson continued the press conference tradition set by his predecessors, but such events became more difficult for Johnson as America's involvement in the Vietnam War escalated, with press questions increasingly focused on war casualties and military ineffectiveness.

Eisenhower, Kennedy, and Johnson averaged about two press conferences every month, but Presidents Nixon, Ford, Carter, and Reagan held fewer—less than one per month. Nixon, Ford, and Carter each dealt with crisis situations (Vietnam, Watergate, a severe energy crisis, and the Iranian hostage crisis), which led to uncomfortable open questioning from journalists, and so each president cut back on the number of conferences. Reagan, despite his acting background and ease in front of a camera, had a difficult time dealing with reporters' questions in a press conference setting, and so he began a weekly radio address as a regular means of communicating with the American public. All presidents since Reagan have used this form of weekly address to speak to the nation.

President Bill Clinton increased the number of presidential press conferences to an average of two per month, based on his ability to use this format quite effectively. However, the number of Clinton press conferences was reduced sharply during the period when he faced his biggest crisis in office, over his relationship with White House intern Monica Lewinsky. President George W. Bush, who like Reagan was often ill at ease at responding to questions in a press conference situation, averaged only one press conference per year. Staged events, one-on-one interviews with reporters, televised speeches, and the weekly radio address were Bush's preferred means of communicating to the public through the media. Like his predecessor, President Obama has also held few press conferences, preferring public appearances, staged events, and use of his White House web page to communicate with the public. As indicated at the opening of this chapter,

President Obama holds a press conference at the White House.

Obama's use of the Internet to influence both public and elite opinion is credited with the passage of the health care reform law, which was passed in 2010.

With each successive presidential administration, White House staffs have become better equipped at using the media to influence the public through direct communication. Press conferences, presidential addresses, and carefully staged presidential appearances are typical of the means by which the White House uses the media to muster support for the president's agenda.

12-3 | The Mass Media Today

Today's mass media include a variety of channels of communication through which news content is disseminated to audiences. Channels of communication may be either print or electronic. Print media largely include newspapers, magazines, and books. Electronic media include television, radio, the Internet, and movies. In addition, forms of content on any medium may be classified as either news or entertainment. In newspapers, for example, the first section of most publications is entirely devoted to news stories and editorials. Subsequent sections might include other news such as sports news or business news. Typically, there is an entertainment section that includes movie reviews, comics, crossword puzzles, recipes, and so forth. Television stations also provide news programming in the forms of news broadcasts, investigative reporting shows, and political talk shows, and entertainment programming in the form of sitcoms, soap operas, reality TV programs, and drama shows.

Even media sources that are intended primarily to provide entertainment programming sometimes include content that may fall within the realm of politics. One very popular show that combines news with comedy is *The Daily Show*, hosted by political comedian Trevor Noah. During recent presidential elections, the cable television station MTV broadcast programming that attempted to increase voter turnout among young people.

Courtesy of Rock the Vote

Rock the Vote is a non-profit organization that uses media campaigns to encourage young people to participate in elections and politics.

The Print Media

The modern print media mostly include newspapers, magazines, and books. Use of these print media has declined in recent decades, as consumers of news increasingly turn to the Internet and television as sources of information. These and other news magazines often rely on photojournalism to support their longer stories to engage readers.

Books also enjoy an important place in American journalism. *Plan of Attack*, a 2004 book by Bob Woodward, documented the role of the Bush administration in preparing for the second Iraq War. Woodward, through interviews with top White House sources, including the president and the secretary of state, concluded that the Bush administration had actively begun preparations for war long before the U.S. invasion and well before notifying Congress of its intentions. Woodward's work became an important topic during the 2004 presidential campaign. Thirty years earlier, in a book called *All the President's Men*, co-written with Carl Bernstein, Woodward documented the Nixon administration's role in the Watergate affair.

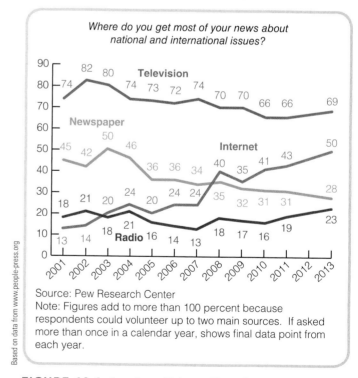

Based on data from www.people-press.org

Where do you get most of your news about national and international issues?

Source: Pew Research Center
Note: Figures add to more than 100 percent because respondents could volunteer up to two main sources. If asked more than once in a calendar year, shows final data point from each year.

FIGURE 12-1 Americans' Primary News Sources

A century ago there were about 2,200 newspapers published daily; today there are only about 1,300 daily newspapers—a 30 percent decline—purchased by about 76 million readers. Once the prime source of news for Americans, newspapers now take a backseat to television as the nation's main news source (see Figure 12-1). Just as the number of newspaper readers has declined steadily since the 1950s, today the Internet seems to be becoming a more popular source of news and, as a result, the number of newspaper readers is falling at an even greater rate than before. The youngest generation of news consumers—those in high school—are most likely to be using digital media to get their news and information, as demonstrated in Figure 12-2. As the American population ages, it is likely that the trend toward greater use of the Internet and lesser use of traditional media such as newspapers will continue.

The vast majority of newspapers are regional metropolitan and suburban publications. They range from those that cover large metropolitan areas, such as the *Chicago Tribune*, the *Miami Herald*, the *Dallas Morning News*, and the *San Francisco Chronicle*, to those covering much smaller towns. A handful of newspapers such as the *New York Times, The Wall Street Journal*, and *USA Today* are considered national dailies and are designed to appeal to a national readership. The *New York Times* trumpets its supposed status as the "paper of record" of events from around the world; *The Wall Street Journal* has the niche of being the nation's leading newspaper on financial markets and commerce; *USA Today*'s format of brief stories along with colorful graphics and pictures has helped it attract a nationwide following.

Wire services provide a clearinghouse for news as it is occurring. The largest wire service by far is the Associated Press (AP). The AP employs a large number of reporters throughout the nation and around the world to write stories on news events. Newspapers and television and radio stations that are members of the AP share the news services it produces. Using the AP as their news source allows smaller regional newspapers and

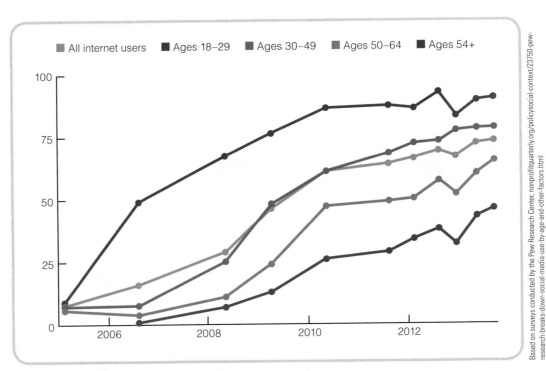

FIGURE 12-2 **The Generational Divide in Use of Social Media** Recent studies from the Pew Research Center show that as of September of 2013, 73 percent of all online adults are currently using social media. While the data show that within every age group social media usage has increased, the data also show the large differences between age groups.

The Diversity Dilemma

The Media Gender Gap

Have you noticed the lack of diversity on your nightly news program? We occasionally hear about the lack of diversity at key events, such as the annual announcement of Oscar nominees. However, a lack of diversity is also evident when one examines various types of media sources. The Women's Media Center (WMC) publishes an annual report to highlight the status of women in U.S. media. Their findings are pretty bleak: In 2014, there was a sizeable news gender gap, with men generating 62.1 percent and women generating 37.3 percent of the news.[11] In fact, U.S. political news stories are far more likely to be reported by men (65 percent) than women (35 percent). Overall, the WMC report warns that gender inequality among journalists can be found across all media outlets and across most issues. The media gender gap is further exacerbated by the disproportional number of white men holding key leadership and management posts across media organizations, which in turn plays a key role in agenda-setting. In particular, the WMC report highlights the lack of diversity in staffing of newspaper newsrooms, where men (about 56 percent white and 7 percent minority) continue to dominate key positions, as compared to women (about 31 percent white and 6 percent minority).

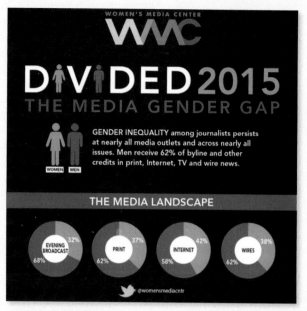

Infographic from the Women's Media Center.

For Critical Thinking and Discussion

1. What are the ramifications of such wide gender and racial gaps in our media?

2. Do we need more diversity in the news media to ensure the availability of different perspectives? Why or why not?

---

local TV and radio stations to cover events from around the world in an efficient, informative, and cost-effective manner.

The Electronic Media

The major electronic media are television, radio, and the Internet. Television and radio have played an important role in American politics for many decades, and the Internet has been responsible for more recent changes in the news and the way in which Americans use the news. The Internet along with other relatively **new media** technologies such as smartphones, satellites, and cable TV, have come to be known as the *digital media*, which have revolutionized the news business at every level.

Television. With its mass adoption by households in the early 1950s, television became and has remained the primary source of news for most Americans. More than 98 percent of households in the United States report having at least one television set. News programming on TV is provided mostly by broadcast television networks and their local affiliates. The broadcast networks include ABC, CBS, and NBC. Cable television stations, such as CNN, Fox News, and MSNBC, provide 24-hour news programming as well. Other cable stations, such as C-SPAN and local public access stations, provide specialized coverage—for example, the live broadcast of congressional debates and committee meetings.

new media Media outlets that rely on relatively newer technologies for communicating, such as the Internet, DVDs, fax machines, cell phones, satellites, cable TV, and broadband.

The defining characteristic of television is its visual nature.[12] The implied "reality" of seeing video of events, or live broadcasts of events, can be quite powerful, as civil rights demonstrators learned in the mid-1960s. Compared to the written word, the spoken word, or even still pictures, video communicates events "as they are," and so is regarded by viewers as more trustworthy and "real." Many argue that film footage of reporters covering the Vietnam War contributed to the erosion of public support for America's involvement there. The daily barrage of video showing dead soldiers brought new meaning to Americans' understanding of war and helped influence President Lyndon Johnson's decision not to seek reelection in 1968. In 2012, video of terrorist attacks at the U.S embassy in Benghazi, Libya, killing four American diplomats captured a great deal of attention and reduced support for the Obama administration's foreign policy. Likewise, vivid pictures of American mistreatment of Iraqi detainees at Abu Ghraib prison did not help the Bush administration's effort to defeat the Iraqi insurgents.

New satellite technologies further facilitate the live and instantaneous coverage of events not only around every corner of the globe, but also from the moon, Mars, and Jupiter. The new high-tech satellites provide an opportunity for people to view events as they occur even from the outer reaches of the universe, such as the live pictures sent back from satellites on the 2004 U.S. spaceship mission to Mars.

Radio. Contemporary radio largely programs commercial music, with several minutes of each hour allotted for news, sports, traffic reports, and weather forecasts. These short news reports are an important source of information (particularly for commuters who use their cars to get to and from work or school) about news events and politics. Many radio stations carry a specialized form of radio programming referred to as **talk radio**, in which one or more hosts provide commentary and often invite listeners to call in to the show and offer their own opinions. Talk radio steadily gained popularity in the late 1980s and early 1990s, marked by a growing interest in political talk shows, as increasing numbers of commuters with cell phones began to take time while sitting in traffic to listen to these shows and call in to offer their own views.

Some of the more popular call-in shows focus on politics. The hosts often provide an ideological perspective on policies, issues, and political candidates and campaigns. Listeners of a particular ideological persuasion enjoy hearing what the host and others have to say, and small numbers call in to offer their own views. Many local radio stations provide political talk radio programs, ranging from very modestly ideological debates to extremely partisan ones. Several nationally syndicated shows have also attracted an especially large listening audience, such as conservative commentator Rush Limbaugh's show.

A trend in ownership of radio is the purchase of smaller, local radio stations by large media organizations. Critics of this trend contend that the large corporate owners typically impose standardized programming through satellite feeds, thus depriving them of their local character.

The Internet. In 1993, a group of students at the University of Illinois developed MOSAIC, the first graphical Internet browser. MOSAIC allowed users to view pictures and color images on the World Wide Web. MOSAIC soon went commercial and became Netscape, and by the mid-1990s it was attracting tens of millions of users. Coupled with huge worldwide increases in sales of personal computers through the 1990s, the ease and user-friendliness of accessing the Internet made the medium an attractive source of news and information for people around the world.

The Internet's rise as a mass medium has many implications for news, information, and the American political system. One such effect is the way in which people use the Internet compared to other news sources. From the viewers' perspective, TV watching is a passive activity. Once they've tuned into a particular channel, viewers have no other choice but to get whatever news is being presented. They cannot ask

talk radio A specialized form of radio programming in which one or more hosts provide commentary and often invite listeners to call in to the show and offer their own opinions.

questions or seek specific answers to questions they might have. Likewise, listening to a radio broadcast is a fairly passive activity for listeners unless, of course, they choose to call in to the show. While reading a newspaper, people can pick and choose the articles they prefer to read. However, newspapers are also limited in the amount of content they can provide, and readers cannot query a newspaper to get answers on specific questions they might have.

The Internet, however, allows users to pursue exactly the kind of news and information they are interested in. Search engines such as Google and Yahoo allow Internet users to find whatever they are looking for. Furthermore, most news websites include a "search" feature that allows users to search the website and/or newspaper database for information relevant to a particular query.

Scott Pelley anchors the CBS Evening News, the network's flagship news program.

Unlike other media, the Internet also enables individual users to be their own mass publisher, largely through social media such as Facebook and Twitter. Most word processing packages include the option to "save as Web page." A simple set of keystrokes enables users to place information, data, and graphics on their own webpage. Web design software enables users to put a web page on a server and thus make that page available to millions of other Internet users to access. In this way, Internet users can publish material that is accessible to a mass audience.

Most newspapers and television stations maintain websites that include the organization's news content and links to other sources, such as the Associated Press. Many of these sites also include a searchable database of archived news stories. Some of the most-used news websites are CNN (www.cnn.com) and *The New York Times* (www.nytimes.com). With searchable indices to past stories, links to other sites, online forums, and audio and video files, these sites offer a broad array of content that users can easily access.

The Internet has transformed the flow of news and information about politics in other ways as well. It has become a common source of information about political campaigns because candidates for office often create web pages and post them on servers for voters to access. Widely varying "chat rooms" and online forums serve as venues for users to post their opinions, ask questions, and engage in dialogue on political issues. **Blogs** (derived from the term *weblogs*) are also popular among many Internet users. In 2008 and 2012, for example, the significant amount of fund-raising and voter communication by Obama supporters substantially buoyed that campaign's success. Blogs provide a combination editorial page, personal web page, and online diary offering personal observations in real time about news events and issues. Some of the more popular blogs are published by journalists and political commentators.

blogs Internet sites that include a combination of editorial page, personal web page, and online diary of personal observations in real time about news events and issues.

The so-called social media in particular may be having a particularly transformative effect on media and politics. Increasingly, Americans say that they get more and more of their news and information about politics from places like Facebook, Twitter, and YouTube. Although these media are still very new and so research into their impact is largely not yet available, some preliminary work suggests that the social media may potentially be significant. One early study found that use of social media increases understanding and support for constitutional values.[13] Another study conducted on Election Day 2010 found that use of Facebook increased voter turnout.[14] As use of social media for political news and information continues to grow, their potential impact on American politics will grow as well.

digital divide The large differences in usage of the Internet between older and younger people, lower- and middle-/upper-class people, lesser and better educated people, and minority groups and nonminority groups.

Another issue that is of concern to some is that those who use the Internet are more likely to be younger, middle and upper class, better educated, and nonminority—a disparity that has been referred to as the **digital divide**. Greater access to the Internet facilitates access to news and information, and those who have access clearly enjoy an advantage. However, as computers and Internet access costs decline, and as younger generations with computer skills replace older generations, the digital divide is likely to become less and less pronounced. Public libraries have provided another remedy to the digital divide. In 1996, 28 percent of all libraries had public access to the Internet. Today, 95 percent of libraries offer Internet access to patrons. Because they are eager to gain access, the number of visitors to public libraries has increased by nearly 20 percent over the past six years.

Ownership of the Media

The Framers of the Constitution were clearly committed to the freedom of the press. Government ownership of the press was then and is today regarded as a threat to the basic freedoms that Americans enjoy. If government controls the news and the flow of information to citizens, it holds too much power. Private ownership of the media allows for the free and open exchange of ideas. Ironically, some today argue that the concentration of ownership of the news media by large nonmedia corporations, such as Comcast Corporation and the Disney Corporation, has stifled diversity in news content and blurred the line between what is news and what is entertainment. One large corporation that owns multiple media outlets has become the norm, whereas in the past most media outlets were independently owned. It is also argued that ownership of media organizations by a conglomerate such as Comcast Corporation might compromise the objectivity of the news. When NBC, which is owned by Comcast, reports on a story about Comcast, might that story be biased?

The big-three television networks—ABC, CBS, and NBC—have dominated television viewership since the early 1950s. By 1956, more than 9 in 10 stations were affiliated with one of these networks. Over the past several decades, the growing popularity of cable and satellite TV has challenged the predominant position of the three networks. With hundreds of channels now available, the three networks' share of the viewing market continues to shrink. This competition led the networks to focus on greater efficiencies in the day-to-day operation of their businesses. By the mid-1980s, all three networks had experienced a change in corporate ownership, and all three now are part of "vertically integrated" corporations that are involved in video production as well as national and local distribution. In the late 1980s, competition between the networks further increased with the addition of the Fox Network. Figure 12-3 suggests the extent to which these three corporate owners control other media.

NBC is currently owned by the megacorporation Comcast; the CBS network, formerly owned by Viacom, is now its own corporation; the Disney Corporation owns and operates the ABC network; and Fox, the newest of the major networks, is owned by the News Corporation.

Not all television and radio stations in the United States are privately owned. The Public Broadcasting Act of 1967 created the Corporation for Public Broadcasting (CPB), which is responsible for distributing federal funds to support public, noncommercial radio and television stations. These stations have had a difficult time surviving economically in a marketplace dominated by commercial interests. CPB funds the Public Broadcasting Service (PBS), which was formed in 1969 to distribute programming to the nation's public television stations. CPB-funded radio programs are distributed by National Public Radio (NPR), American Public Media, and Public Radio International to member stations.

The 1967 law provided much-needed support for noncommercial TV and radio and has established a rather impressive network of stations that provide some very popular programming. *Morning Edition* and *All Things Considered* are highly regarded

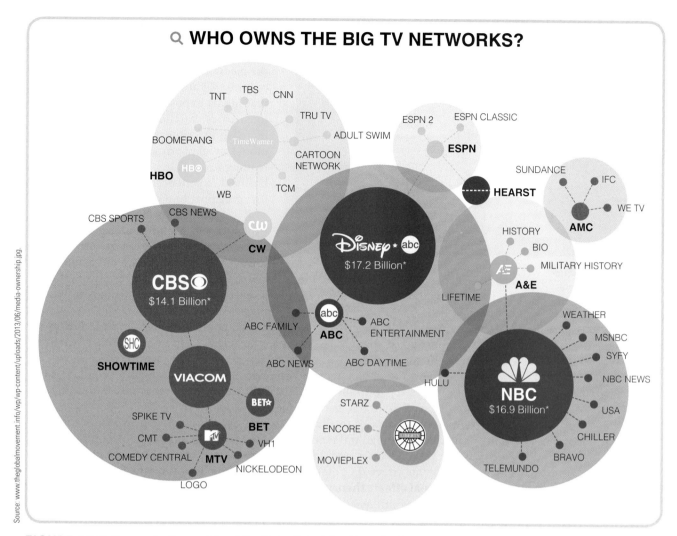

FIGURE 12-3 Corporate Ownership of the Major Television News Outlets

radio news shows with a very loyal following; the same goes for the PBS-supported *NewsHour*. *Frontline* is a popular, award-winning investigative reporting program supported by PBS. Documentary series on the Civil War, produced by Ken Burns, and other such topics have been well received by large audiences. PBS has also supported a significant amount of children's educational programming, including *Sesame Street*.

PBS and NPR member stations do not generally engage in commercial advertising. They rely instead on funds from the CPB and on donations from businesses and individuals to support their broadcasting operation. For example, in 1999 General Motors provided a major 10-year commitment of support to PBS to finance productions by Burns, including documentaries on Major League Baseball and jazz music. Individual pledges of support are typically solicited through on-air membership drives and corporate underwriting of programming. There are nearly 400 PBS television stations, many of which are aligned with communications departments in colleges and universities across the nation.

An important assumption underlying federal support for public broadcasting is that government is obligated to ensure that offerings are diverse and that ample numbers of educational programs are developed. Federal support for public TV and radio, however, is often a political hot potato. Conservatives claim that public television has a liberal bias, and many have attempted, unsuccessfully, to curb federal funding for CPB.

Andrew Lipovsky/NBC/NBCU Photo Bank/Getty Images

As a way to show their lighter side, presidential candidates have become regular guests on late night comedy shows. Pictured here is GOP Senator Ted Cruz, making an appearance on Jimmy Fallon's The Tonight Show during the 2016 GOP primary campaign.

12-4 | Effects of the Media

There is no doubt that Americans rely on the media for news and information about politics. What is less clear is the influence that media exposure has on citizens' opinions (Does watching a news story on the increase in crime rates make the viewer more fearful of crime?) and behavior (Does reading an article about Donald Trump's business experiences lead a reader to vote for or against him on Election Day?).

Researchers can quite easily gauge the exposure and use of the media. It is much more difficult, however, to identify the impact of media exposure on opinions and behavior. Citizens are constantly bombarded by news stories from a variety of different media. Isolating how one news story, or even several stories in one medium, influences opinions or behaviors is very hard to determine.

Despite the difficulty of proving media effects, political leaders and candidates for election certainly act as though the effects are powerful. Leaders constantly try to influence campaign stories and news stories to favor their own positions. Presidents use press conferences to send messages and attempt to win public support. Candidates buy advertising time to try to influence voters. Political parties orchestrate events at party conventions to send favorable partisan messages to voters.

Early research studies of media effects examined how citizen exposure to media content during a campaign influenced how they voted. In classic books on the subject (such as *The Voter Decides* and *The American Voter*), the media were credited with having little or no effect on voters' decisions. These studies, which led to a theory known as **minimal effects theory**, found that deep-seated, long-term political attitudes had a much greater influence on the vote decision.[15] Such enduring and preexisting attitudes lead to selective perception and retention of news content. People evaluate news material from their own partisan perspectives (selective perception) and tend to process and remember the material more consistent with their preexisting attitudes (selective retention).[16]

minimal effects theory The theory that deep-seated, long-term political attitudes have much greater influence on an individual's vote decisions than does news media coverage.

Moreover, preexisting attitudes often influence what kinds of news people choose to pay attention to in the first place (selective exposure). Psychologists suggest that people's desire to achieve cognitive consistency and avoid cognitive dissonance explains why they process new information in such a way as to assimilate with existing attitudes. These early studies that found "minimal effects" were largely focused on partisan elections and attempted to evaluate the effects of media exposure on the vote decision.

Subsequent research, although not refuting the findings of the media's minimal effects on partisan behavior, examined other areas where media exposure might have an impact. **Social learning theory**, for example, argued that viewers imitate what they view on television through observational learning.[17] Television's focus on sex and violence has led to a large number of studies that try to assess whether exposure to such material leads viewers to become more violent, with reduced moral standards. Some of this research suggests that viewers do learn negative, antisocial behavior from TV.

social learning theory The theory that viewers imitate what they view on television through observational learning.

Some communications researchers have advanced the notion of *priming*,[18] which suggests that the activation of one thought also activates other thoughts, and exposure to media provides cues to people on this thought-activation process. For example, watching the Road Runner beat up on Wile E. Coyote in the old Warner Brothers cartoon may make one child act violently against another child after watching the cartoon. The rash of injuries related to the show *Jackass* is another example of the priming theory in action.

Critics of media often use social learning and priming theories to advocate for government controls of the media. The Telecommunications Act of 1996, for example, required television set manufacturers to include a V-chip in new units to allow parents to block programs they did not wish their children or families to view. Another law, passed in 1997, required the television industry to develop a rating system for television shows based on the show's level of sex, violence, and profanity. Studies that demonstrated a connection between TV exposure and negative behavior were important pieces of evidence used to promote support for the V-chip requirement and the TV ratings system.

The **cultivation theory** of media effects suggests that heavy television exposure helps develop an individual's overall view of the world.[19] According to this theory, the emphasis on violence and crime in both news and entertainment programming would lead the heavy viewer to overestimate and be disproportionately concerned about the extent of crime and violence.

A final theory of media effects is best known as **agenda-setting theory**. This theory suggests that although the effects of exposure may be minimal or difficult to gauge, the media are quite influential in telling the public what to think about. For example, Monica Lewinsky's affair with President Bill Clinton was a lead story in the news throughout 1998, and the prominent placement of that story in numerous media outlets helped to keep it a popular topic of conversation. Daily news coverage of the number of soldiers and civilians killed in Iraq focuses public attention on the U.S. military engagement there.

The media set the public agenda for the issues and activities that many Americans choose to think about and talk about. Prominently placed and frequently repeated headlines in newspapers, lead stories on television news shows and on talk radio, and highlighted stories on well-trafficked websites set the stage for public discourse. Citizens pick up a newspaper or flip on an all-news TV station to become informed about what is happening in their community, the nation, and the world. In this sense, the news media have a powerful impact on public debate.[20] As news media scholar Doris Graber has noted, "When media make events seem important, average people as well as politicians discuss them and form opinions. This enhances the perceived importance of these events and ensures even more public attention and, possibly, political action."[21]

cultivation theory The theory of media effects that suggests that heavy television exposure helps develop an individual's overall view of the world.

agenda-setting theory The theory holding that although the effects of television exposure may be minimal or difficult to gauge, the media are quite influential in telling the public what to think about.

12-5 | Criticisms of the News Media

Although Americans rely on the media for information about what is going on in the nation and around the world, the news media are also the subject of a number of criticisms. For example, despite the vast array of news sources available, most news programming follows a standard format that makes it appear the same to the public. Many newspapers are owned by a handful of publishers (such as "tronc" [formerly known as Tribune Publishing Company] and Gannett) and follow a standard format for news. Similarly, just a few companies own many of the nation's radio stations and TV stations and employ a similar format in their programming. Critics charge that this concentration in ownership could result in a handful of companies promoting their own political objectives.

Polls have also demonstrated that there has been a decline in the percentage of Americans who say that news reporting is fair and accurate. Figure 12-4 demonstrates this erosion in public sentiment over the past three decades.

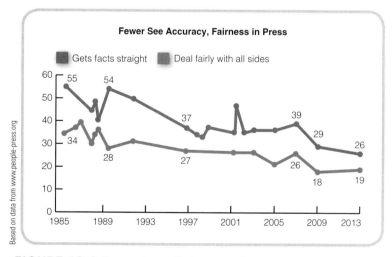

FIGURE 12-4 **Perceptions of Fairness and Accuracy in the Media**

Another criticism of the private ownership of the media stems from the premise that the media, like most other privately owned companies, are in business primarily to make money. For the media, increasing profits requires attracting larger audiences and more readers, and as many media companies have found, providing higher-quality news programming on politically important topics does not always guarantee increased audience ratings or numbers of readers. Rather, news that provides more entertainment tends to get larger audience shares.

Often, the result is news that is characterized by sensationalized content. Stories that highlight or exploit crime, violence, disasters, personal conflicts, competition, and scandals tend to increase the sale of newspapers and improve the ratings of TV news programs. Thus, the profit motive of private ownership drives companies in the news business to disproportionately cover events that include sensationalized content. Stories about the untimely deaths of Michael Jackson and Prince, and the extramarital affairs

Then & Now

Using New Media to Change Public Policy

Throughout American history, presidents have taken advantage of new and emerging technologies to advance their policy agendas.

Then

In 1964, President Lyndon Johnson used the relatively new medium of television to accomplish civil rights reforms that had eluded his predecessors. Past presidents had tried and failed to pass civil rights laws: In 1947 President Truman was rebuffed in his hopes for legislation that addressed segregation. President Eisenhower pursued a centrist agenda on civil rights, but the best he could achieve was to establish a bipartisan civil rights commission and a civil rights division in the Justice Department; the 1957 Civil Rights Act had such a narrow impact that it proved a disappointment to civil rights leaders. Johnson's ambitious civil rights agenda might have met a similar fate had the plight of African Americans in the South not been seen by the rest of the nation through extensive and unprecedented television coverage. Footage from television cameras allowed viewers at home to witness police officials directing full-pressure water hoses on African American school children, police dogs set loose on civil rights demonstrators, and numerous brutal beatings. Donations to the civil rights movement increased dramatically once the public outside the South became an eyewitness to these dramatic events, and legislative leaders from both parties soon felt public pressure to overcome the objections of opponents. After waiting out a 54-day filibuster, the Senate eventually joined the House in approving major civil rights legislation. On July 2, 1964, President Lyndon Johnson signed the Civil Rights Act into law. Clearly, the "small screen" had played a large role in the process.

A still shot from a television report showing a Birmingham fireman hosing down protesters in 1963.

Charles Moore/Black Star/Alamy

(Continued)

of John Edwards, Tiger Woods, New York Governor Elliot Spitzer, and South Carolina Governor Mark Sanford, all received a tremendous amount of coverage at the expense of other, more important and politically relevant stories.

Sensationalism extends to coverage of elections as well. Studies of election coverage have found that most news dwells more on stories about the candidates' personal background than on their positions on the issues. Political scientists note that this emphasis on covering "character" issues rather than policy positions characterizes modern presidential election campaign news. For example, in 2004, significant coverage targeted the military service of the candidates, including Bush's "questionable" military record in the Alabama Air National Guard and John Kerry's record as a Vietnam War soldier and protester. Also, in 2008, a significant amount of coverage focused on Barack Obama's association both with his outspoken pastor Jeremiah Wright and with William Ayers, a cofounder of the Weather Underground, a radical leftist organization. Critics of election

Then & Now (continued)

Now

Civil rights reform was not the only legislation that benefitted from a president's use of a new communications medium. Early in his presidency, Barack Obama was determined to achieve legislative success on a subject that had proved elusive to so many of his predecessors: comprehensive health care reform. Franklin Roosevelt in 1935, Harry Truman in 1951, and Bill Clinton in 1994 all saw their major health care reform proposals defeated by well-organized opposition. In these earlier battles, the American Medical Association and other opponents used media campaigns to prey upon public fears that the legislation might separate individuals from their own doctors. The Obama administration's efforts to pass health care reform would overcome similar opposition campaigns by embarking on a successful media effort of its own, using the Internet. Obama's forces effectively used the newest communications medium to bring the full debate over health care out into the open, exposing backroom deals and revealing opponents' exaggerations about negative consequences of the reform proposals. Through a continuous bombardment of information released over the Internet, Obama successfully justified the plan to many of the millions of Americans lapping up news on the Internet. The legislation eventually overcame all obstacles in its path, including a Republican party-line filibuster. Had the public not been privy to the immense amounts of information pouring forth from the Internet, the arguments against the administration's plan might once again have proven too difficult to overcome.

The Obama White House web page in 2009, promoting the health care reform bill.

For Critical Thinking and Discussion

1. How much does the media type influence the message received by citizens?
2. In your opinion, would civil rights reforms have progressed so quickly in the 1960's if the civil rights movement had been covered exclusively by radio? If President Obama had been restricted to more traditional media sources like print, would the Affordable Care Act (aka Obamacare) have even passed? Why or why not?

coverage also charge that there is too much focus on preelection polls and the competitiveness of the "horse race," which crowds out the more substantive coverage of the issues and the candidates' positions on them.

Another common criticism of the news media is that they are politically biased. Some critics, for example, charge that corporate owners of media organizations are more likely to hold a conservative ideology, which is reflected in their news products. Others cite studies indicating that journalists and reporters tend to hold a more liberal philosophy, and that this orientation seeps into their stories. Certainly there is evidence to support the assertions that owners and managers are more conservative than the citizenry as a whole, and that journalists are more liberal. But the issue of whether personal ideology or partisanship is reflected in news stories is less clear. In some elections, research has demonstrated that newspapers and TV news programs have shown a pro-Republican bias, whereas in others it has found a pro-Democratic bias.[22]

The media serve a number of important functions in the American political system. In addition to providing information, signaling events, and "watchdogging" what government does, the media also provide an infrastructure that leaders use to communicate

From Your Perspective

Do You Use Social Media to Participate in National Political Discussions?

Social media have significantly changed the way that people across the country participate in American politics. They offer anyone with a computer and access to the Internet the opportunity to publish their political opinions in the mass media, to share ideas and perspectives with others, to recommend the views of others by providing cross-links, and to debate and challenge the positions of those with whom they disagree. Social media sites, such as Facebook, Twitter, and Instagram, are used by 200 million Americans, and billions of people worldwide, to express their opinions and perspectives on politics and to try to convince their "friends" to vote or support a particular policy position.

A citizen journalist uses a smartphone to capture an interview of activist Capt. Songklod Chuenchupol after his arrest during an anti-amnesty bill rally on Aug 7, 2013 in Bangkok, Thailand.

Americans between the ages of 18 and 35 have been especially active in contributing their ideas in this particular media marketplace. Some of their efforts have had a significant impact on political events. For example, during a Virginia Senate campaign, a supporter of Democratic candidate Jim Webb was following Webb's opponent, incumbent Senator George Allen, with a video camera. Annoyed at being followed, Allen referred to the Webb supporter as a "Macaca," a term that refers to a species of monkey and is considered an ethnic slur. The videotaper, S. R. Sidarth, was also a blogger and immediately posted the video of Allen's slur on YouTube. Many other blogs and national news organizations began to cover the clip of Allen's slur. The posting is credited with clinching Webb's narrow victory in the race.

Another way people have used social media to influence politics is through the "moneybomb," a blog-driven grassroots fund-raising campaign that is usually generated over a short period of time: Supporters use the blogs to create a frenzied atmosphere to quickly raise money.

For Critical Thinking and Discussion

1. Search for a blog or Facebook page that aligns with your own political interests or attitudes and read at least a week's worth of postings and comments. What do you notice? Do opinions tend to get debated or echoed within that blog?

2. What are the advantages and disadvantages of engaging in this form of political participation?

with citizens. In the examples used at the outset of this chapter, we saw how Presidents Johnson and Obama took advantage of relatively new media (television and the Internet, respectively) to successfully win long-term political struggles to pass civil rights and health care reform legislation. Technological innovations have served to change the forms and nature of the media throughout the course of American history. These changes have opened up new opportunities for presidents and other leaders to help shape a political agenda and successfully bring important policy ideas to fruition. These changes have also had the effect of bringing news and information to audiences with more and more speed and efficiency. The American media remain as important a political institution as any in our system of government. Americans' demand for information, the appetite of journalists to keep tabs on government performance, and political leaders' reliance on the media to communicate with citizens all serve to make the media stronger today than they have ever been.

Summary

12-1 The Media in American Politics

- The media serve a number of important functions in the political system, all of which promote the free flow of information to the public. These functions include providing objective coverage of events, facilitating public debate, and serving as government watchdog.

- Congress created the Federal Communications Commission (FCC) in 1934 to regulate the electronic media through licensing broadcasters and creating rules for broadcasters to follow. The FCC does not have authority to regulate the print media because the courts have consistently treated the right of print media to publish free from government regulation.

12-2 Historical Development of the Media

- From the nation's founding through the 1850s, news in America was largely provided by a partisan press, made up of newspapers supported by a particular political party. Over the past 150 years, however, the standards for news reporting have become less focused on serving political party interests and more focused on "objectivity."

- Technological change has greatly altered the news media. The invention of the rotary press in 1815 facilitated the mass printing of papers; the railroad system provided for speedy distribution of papers; the invention of the radio provided instantaneous coverage of events as they unfolded; and television brought taped and live footage of news events into people's homes.

12-3 The Mass Media Today

- Politics and political events, such as presidential campaigns, debates, and news conferences, are widely covered by media organizations. Today's mass media comprise large and varied types of news outlets, including radio, television, books, newspapers, and magazines. They also include the so-called new media facilitated by the Internet, satellites, cell phones, broadband, and other newer technologies.

- Although the big-three television networks—ABC, CBS, and NBC—have dominated television viewership since the early 1950s, with the growing popularity of the Fox Network, as well as cable and satellite TV, additional networks have begun to offer stiff competition.

- Corporate ownership of news media outlets today is characterized by large nonmedia corporations such as Comcast and the Disney Corporation. Some argue that this concentration of large corporate ownership has stifled diversity in news content and blurred the line between what is news and what is entertainment.

12-4 The Effects of the Media

- The effects of exposure to news on readers/viewers are the subject of much debate. A number of theories—including social learning, minimal effects, cultivation, and agenda setting—seek to explain how the news media influence what people think about politics.

12-5 Criticisms of the News Media

- Media performance is often the subject of criticism. Some of the major sources of discontent with media performance include the concentration of corporate ownership of media outlets, sensationalized coverage of relatively unimportant events, and ideological bias in news reporting.

Key Terms

agenda-setting theory (p. 331)
blogs (p. 327)
cultivation theory (p. 331)
digital divide (p. 328)

equal time rule (p. 316)
minimal effects theory (p. 330)
new media (p. 325)
objectivity (p. 317)

partisan press era (p. 319)
social learning theory (p. 330)
talk radio (p. 326)

Test Yourself

1. The FCC has the authority to regulate all of the following, *except*
   a. political stories in *The New York Times*.
   b. NBC entertainment shows.
   c. your local radio station.
   d. ABC's political talk shows.

2. The FCC's "equal time rule" applies to
   a. newspapers.
   b. the Internet.
   c. magazines.
   d. television networks.

3. What are the primary functions that the news media provide in American democracy?

4. The "partisan press era" refers to
   a. the post–Revolutionary War era through the mid-1800s.
   b. the Civil War through the Industrial Revolution.

   c. World War I and World War II.
   d. the modern era of cable news shows.

5. The president who most effectively communicated his positions through press conferences was
   a. Franklin Roosevelt.
   b. John Kennedy.
   c. George W. Bush.
   d. Barack Obama.

6. What did Marshall McLuhan mean when he penned "the medium is the message"?

7. The medium that most Americans say is their primary source of news is
   a. newspapers.
   b. the Internet.
   c. radio.
   d. television.

8. MOSAIC, the first graphical Internet browser, was developed by
   a. Microsoft.
   b. IBM.

c. students at the University of Illinois.

d. the Central Intelligence Agency.

9. Which of the following is a news program produced by the Corporation for Public Broadcasting?

a. *NewsHour with Jim Lehrer*

b. *Hannity's America*

c. *Hard Ball with Chris Matthews*

d. *Nightly News with Brian Williams*

10. What do critics cite as a problem with the concentration of media outlets owned by a few large corporations?

11. The theory of media effects suggesting that viewers imitate what they view on television through observational learning is

a. agenda setting.   c. minimal effects.

b. cultivation.   d. social learning.

12. The theory of media effects suggesting that the media are influential in telling people what to think about is

a. agenda setting.   c. minimal effects.

b. cultivation.   d. social learning.

13. Media coverage of which presidential candidate focused a great deal of attention on his association with the controversial Reverend Jeremiah Wright?

a. Bill Clinton   c. John McCain

b. George W. Bush   d. Barack Obama

14. What are the main criticisms of the media in their coverage of politics in America?

1. a. (LO 12-1) 2. d. (LO 12-1); 4. a. (LO 12-2); 5. b. (LO 12-2); 7. d. (LO 12-3); 8. c. (LO 12-3); 9. a. (LO 12-3); 11. d. (LO 12-4); 12. a. (LO 12-4); 13. d. (LO 12-5)

Anadolu Agency/Getty Images

LEARNING OBJECTIVES

13-1 The Development of Political Parties in the United States
- Explain the historical development of the modern Democratic and Republican Parties
- Define "critical elections" and party realignment and dealignment in the United States and cite examples of their occurrence

13-2 The Functions of Political Parties
- Identify and explain the four broad functions of political parties

13-3 Why a Two-Party System?
- Describe the historical and legal factors that contributed to the development of the two-party system in the United States
- Assess the role that third parties have played in U.S. elections

13-4 Party Organizations
- Illustrate how party organizations operate at the national, state, and local levels and how they help their candidates win elections

13-5 Are Parties in Decline?
- Analyze the decline in political parties over the past few decades and assess the future prospects for the parties

13-6 Voting
- Assess the role of state governments in managing elections
- Evaluate the effect of constitutional amendments on the expansion of voting rights in the United States
- Distinguish between the wide array of voter registration systems implemented in the 50 states

13-7 Exercising the Franchise
- Assess the influence of different factors in influencing voter turnout, including personal demographics and the type of election contest
- Analyze the trends in U.S. voter turnout over time and how turnout in the United States compares to that in other democracies

13-8 Participation Beyond Voting
- Explain the many forms of political participation beyond voting

13

Political Parties and Voting

Although they merit no mention at all in the Constitution, political parties have become the lifeblood of American politics. New laws are enacted through the debate and negotiation of party leaders in government, and individuals are recruited and promoted as political candidates through the apparatus of the political party structure. At the national, state, and local levels, the two major political parties set the tone, control the agenda, and run the government. The electoral successes and failures of the Democrats or the Republicans, and competition within the majority party to set the national agenda, define the nature of public policy. Further, political parties provide the framework through which citizens participate in American politics; they remain the primary cue that voters use to understand and participate in politics.

Are You a Democrat, a Republican . . . or Something Else?

There are two major political parties in the United States today: the Democratic Party and the Republican Party. These two parties have dominated the political system since the Civil War. Today, about four in five Americans say they identify with—or at least lean toward—one of these two parties. Which political party do you identify with?

Christos Georghiou/Shutterstock.com

People may identify with either political party for a variety of reasons. On fiscal issues, those who prefer lower taxes and less government regulation (especially of business) tend to favor the GOP; while those who support a larger role for government in regulating the activities of business, providing a social safety net for the less fortunate, and raising taxes on the rich to pay for it tend to favor the Democrats. On social issues, those supporting abortion rights, a larger role for government in preserving the environment, LGBT rights, and stricter guns control laws lean to the Democratic Party; meanwhile, gun rights activists, pro-life supporters, school prayer advocates, and those believing in more traditional family values tend to sway Republican.

For some, one or two important issues lead them to identify with a party. For others, a party's set of positions across a host of issues is the deciding factor. For still others, the attractiveness of a particular political candidate or the party their parents associated with leads them to a specific party.

- What is your party affiliation? Are you a Democrat? A Republican? An independent? Or something else (such as a Libertarian or Socialist)? Look up the Democratic Party and Republican Party platforms online and read about them. Then make up your mind, if you haven't already done so.

To see how your answers compare to others, take the **Who Are You?** poll in MindTap!

13-1 | The Development of Political Parties in the United States

More than 60 years ago, the American Political Science Association (APSA) focused the scholarly community's attention on what it referred to as responsible party government.[1] The "responsible party government" model depicts the proper role of parties as organizations that offer clear programs and policy positions to voters. Voters make choices on the basis of those programs, and when victorious in elections, the party works toward achieving those programs and policies. At the time of the next election cycle, voters hold the party accountable for what it has accomplished.

The extent to which parties actually resemble the responsible party model has been the subject of much debate over the past half century. Moreover, despite the large role parties play in the American political system, many observers argue that parties are organizationally weak, particularly when compared to parties in other democracies around the world. Whereas most European parties have clearly defined constituencies based on social class and regional, ethnic, or religious divisions, American political parties are often ideologically vague, aligning with broader constituencies and gravitating toward more centrist positions on issues. And despite their prevalence in politics, there are indications that the influence of parties is on the decline.

The Founders who drafted the Constitution designed a federal system without political parties. They envisioned a system that would be run by independent-minded people who served out of a sense of civic virtue. James Madison's famous Federalist No. 10 deplores "factions," as he calls them. Madison and his colleagues largely looked upon parties (the equivalent of extremely large factions) as tools of the politically ambitious that would tend to promote corruption and bias in the political system.

Despite the Founders' disdain for political parties, they have become central to the American political system. E. E. Schattschneider, a well-regarded student of American politics, observed in 1942 that "democracy is unthinkable, save in terms of the parties."[2] The Democratic and Republican Parties not only have become important political institutions in their own right, but they play a central role in running government at all levels, and they organize and provide context to voters.

Political parties are organizations that seek to win elections for the purpose of influencing the outputs of government. They are typically guided by a political philosophy, rooted in particular values and an ideological approach to governing. The philosophy, values, and ideological approach generally lead to specific issue positions espoused by leaders of a party and the candidates who run for office under a party's label. Some minor parties focus less on the unrealistic assumption that they might win elections and more on articulating an ideological approach to governing and supporting particular issue positions. As in any organization, parties include leaders as well as citizens. In American politics, parties provide an important link between citizens and their leaders, playing a key role in recruiting citizens and relying on them for support at election time.

Even though the Founders frowned on political parties and made no provision for them in the federal government they designed, not long after the first government under the new U.S. Constitution took office in 1791, some of the architects of the Constitution became strong advocates of particular parties.[3] Perhaps more than anything else, this contradiction serves to highlight not only the importance of political parties to the practice of democracy, but also the necessity of parties. In the United States, competition between the political parties has kept any one group or "faction" from becoming too powerful for too long. The Constitution provides various safeguards against the accumulation of power in the form of checks and balances. Paradoxically, although parties are not mentioned at all in the Constitution, competition between political parties has proven to be a significant check against tyranny.

political parties
Organizations that seek to win elections for the purpose of influencing the outputs of government.

The First Parties in America

The history of political parties in the United States traces back to colonial America, when supporters of the English Crown aligned with the British Tory Party, and advocates of a new independent American nation aligned themselves with the British Whig Party. Benjamin Franklin and other Founders still considered themselves Tories up through the early 1770s, and during the American Revolution colonists who supported Britain were

Parties are also important in other democracies around the globe. Left: Former British Prime Minister David Cameron of the Conservative Party. Right: Israeli Prime Minister Benjamin Netanyahu of the Likud Party.

called Tories or Loyalists. The period following the war ushered in new challenges as leaders of the new American nation debated the relationship that should exist between the national government and the state governments. Ultimately, this debate created two new parties (or "factions," as many still called them in the eighteenth century). The U.S. Constitution that replaced the Articles of Confederation significantly enhanced the structure, power, and importance of the national government. The debate over ratification of the new Constitution pitted the Federalists, who supported a stronger federal government, against the Anti-Federalists, who opposed a strong federal government and supported state sovereignty.[4]

More formal, identifiable political parties emerged and began to assume the critical function of supporting candidates for elective office during the first administration of George Washington. Once again, the issue that spurred the emergence of parties as vehicles for nominating candidates was the distribution of power between the federal and state governments under the Constitution. The Federalists continued to support a stronger federal government and the policies of the Washington administration, which promoted the power of the national government. Most Federalists also favored maintaining close ties with Great Britain. President Washington did not consider himself a member of the Federalist Party; he despised parties and refused to endorse their presence in the politics of the new country. Yet many of Washington's supporters, led by Alexander Hamilton, organized the Federalist Party and used the organization to recruit candidates for office.

The Federalist Party was soon challenged by the Democratic-Republican Party, which asserted that the Washington administration was assuming greater powers than those the Constitution granted the federal government. It also criticized the federal government's favorable relations with Britain, preferring France as a closer European ally. As early as 1792, the Democratic-Republicans were organized and led by Thomas Jefferson and James Madison—the same Madison who 10 years earlier had authored in Federalist No. 10 perhaps the most eloquent argument *against* factions that has ever been written. In the congressional elections of 1792, Democratic-Republican candidates won a majority of seats in the House of Representatives. George Washington was unopposed for president, but the Democratic-Republicans backed George Clinton against Federalist John Adams for the vice presidency. Adams, however, won reelection to the vice presidency by an electoral-vote margin of 77 to 50.

Every presidential and congressional election since 1796 has featured some form of party competition. In this early period of American political parties, the Federalists drew most of their support from the northern states, whereas the Democratic-Republicans had greater support in the southern and mid-Atlantic states. Sectional differences in partisan support have characterized American politics for much of the nation's history. In the first competitive presidential election of 1796, the Federalists endorsed John Adams and the Democratic-Republicans endorsed Thomas Jefferson. Adams won 71 electoral votes and Jefferson won 68 votes, making Adams president and Jefferson vice president. Not anticipating political parties, the Constitution allowed for the election of a president and vice president who stood very far apart on critical issues of the day.

By the time of the election of 1800, the parties were highly organized. Each of the two political parties endorsed a slate of candidates for president and vice president to

In 2016, Donald Trump, who never held elective office, was selected by GOP voters to represent their party in the general election for President.

Jeff Swensen/Getty Images

avoid the problem of having two separate parties occupy those offices. The party organization selected presidential electors, who dutifully cast their constitutionally granted two votes to their party's candidates. The Federalists nominated both John Adams and Charles Pinckney, whereas the Democratic-Republicans endorsed Thomas Jefferson and Aaron Burr. Jefferson and Burr each received 73 electoral votes, thus producing an electoral college tie for the presidency. By the provisions of the Constitution, the election was then to be decided by the House of Representatives. After a fair amount of debate and politicking, the House eventually selected Jefferson on the 36th ballot. Clearly, the system of selecting the president needed to be modified from one that did not recognize the importance of political parties in the electoral process to one that did.

The Twelfth Amendment deferred to the reality of parties in presidential elections. Ratified prior to the election of 1804, this amendment formally separated the electoral college vote for president and vice president. Rather than having electors cast two ballots for president, electors were now to cast separate votes for president and vice president. This modification in the electoral process helped avoid the problem that had occurred in 1796 of having a president and vice president locked in partisan struggle, as well as the problem in the 1800 election that resulted in two candidates from the same party tied for the presidency.

The election of 1800 marked the beginning of the end for the Federalist Party. The Federalists would never again win a presidential election, and their strength in Congress diminished steadily over the next two decades. The Democratic-Republicans enjoyed party dominance to such an extent that the Federalists were virtually extinct after the election of 1820. Interestingly, this lack of competition from the Federalists during the first two decades of the nineteenth century had the effect of fragmenting the Democratic-Republicans. In 1824, the Democratic-Republican Party put forth several sectional candidates, but no candidate received a majority of electoral votes. (Andrew Jackson won 99 votes, John Quincy Adams took 84, and another 74 votes were scattered among other candidates.) Eventually, the House of Representatives decided in favor of Adams. The result was a Democratic-Republican Party in disarray.

A Second Party System Emerges

Disillusioned by the outcome of the 1824 election, Andrew Jackson eventually formed a new political party, the Democratic Party, which remains one of the two major parties still competing in American politics today. Jackson's support in 1824 derived from many of the new states that had been added to the Union as a result of westward expansion. Many such states, including Jackson's home state of Tennessee, allowed voters to choose presidential electors directly, rather than following the traditional practice of authorizing the state's congressional delegation (known as the *congressional caucus*) to choose electors. Because he received more popular votes than John Quincy Adams in 1824, Jackson felt the presidency was rightfully his that year. However, Henry Clay, the fourth-place candidate, allied himself with Adams, thereby giving Adams enough votes for victory. When Adams became president, he appointed Clay as secretary of state. Jackson and his supporters accused Clay of making a "corrupt bargain" by trading his votes to Adams in exchange for his appointment as secretary of state. Those who remained loyal to John Quincy Adams began calling themselves the National Republicans. The next presidential election would be a contest essentially between two splinter groups (Democrats and National Republicans) of the now defunct Democratic-Republicans.[5]

Jackson took his case directly to the people and ran for president again in 1828, this time as a Democrat. He ran a populist campaign, arguing that the people should have a greater say in selecting the president, and developed his campaign theme around the Adams–Clay "corrupt bargain." Jackson's theme caught fire with the voters, and the nation's continuing westward expansion, along with voting reforms and increased suffrage in eastern states, suddenly expanded the role of voters in selecting presidential electors. Thus, in a campaign that was essentially decided by the people, puritanical John Quincy Adams proved no match for the flamboyant Jackson, still revered as the general who led American forces to victory in the Battle of New Orleans, the final military engagement of the War of 1812. And Jackson's newly established Democratic Party emerged as a national force to be reckoned with.

The election of 1828 also permanently changed the nature of campaigns, and, with them, the nature of parties. The precedent for a presidential election influenced by the masses was now set, and the era of congressional delegations selecting presidential electors was over. Parties quickly recognized the need to organize in states and localities to accommodate the new process of selecting presidential electors. Party organizations became larger and more powerful as they developed into critical instruments in campaigns. This era also established the tradition of holding **national party conventions**. These conventions drew together party delegates from across the states for several purposes. First, the delegates were responsible for choosing the party's presidential candidate and vice presidential candidate. Second, the delegates articulated their **party platform**, a document outlining the party's position on important policy issues. Third, the conventions coordinated the activities of parties across the states. National party conventions remain a central event both in the presidential selection process and in the organization of modern political parties in general.

The Democratic Party held its first national party convention in 1832, once again nominating Andrew Jackson for president. The National Republicans again nominated Henry Clay, who lost to Jackson in the November election. Several years later, a new political party, the Whigs, which was made up of a coalition of National Republicans and other groups, emerged as a principal competitor to the Democrats. By the 1840s, the Democrats and Whigs dominated not only election contests, but also leadership and committee assignments in Congress. Soon those two parties became the primary vehicles through which legislation was sponsored and then shepherded through the Congress.

From 1836 through 1856, the Whigs and the Democrats shared the presidency and the vast majority of seats in Congress. Both parties were truly national parties, with organizations in each of the states. The issue of slavery, however, soon became the principal issue on the American political agenda. The Civil War would transform American politics forever, and a product of this transformation was the demise of the Whig Party. Within the Whigs, there were strong differences of opinion over the slavery issue, which led to the decline of the Whigs as a national force by the late 1850s. New, smaller parties emerged, such as the Free Soil and Know-Nothing parties, but none of those parties was able to attract large numbers of voters over an extended period of time. By the late 1850s, a new Republican Party had emerged to

national party convention A large meeting that draws together party delegates from across the nation to choose (or formally affirm the selection of) the party's presidential and vice presidential candidates.

party platform A document outlining the party's position on important policy issues.

Jackson Forever!
The Hero of Two Wars and of Or'eans!
The Man of the People!
HE WHO COULD NOT BARTER NOR BARGAIN FOR THE
PRESIDENCY!

Who, although "*A Military Chieftain*," valued the purity of Elections and of the Electors, **MORE** than the Office of **PRESIDENT** itself! Although the greatest in the gift of his countrymen, and the highest in point of dignity of any in the world,

BECAUSE
It should be derived from the
PEOPLE!

No Gag Laws! No Black Cockades! No Reign of Terror! No Standing Army or Navy Officers, when under the pay of Government, to browbeat, or

KNOCK DOWN
Old Revolutionary Characters, or our Representatives while in the discharge of their duty. To the Polls then, and vote for those who will support

OLD HICKORY
AND THE ELECTORAL LAW.

© Bettmann/CORBIS

Election poster in 1828 for Andrew Jackson's presidential campaign. Jackson is the founder of today's Democratic Party.

absorb these smaller parties and replace the Whigs as the major opposition party to the Democrats.

The Modern Party System in America: Democrats versus Republicans

The year 1856 marked the first presidential election when the precursors to the modern Democratic and Republican Parties faced off for office. Democratic nominee James Buchanan defeated Republican candidate John Fremont by 174 to 114 electoral votes. Since 1856, every presidential election but one has featured the Democrats and Republicans as the only two major political parties in serious contention for the White House.

In 1860, Democratic Party support for states' rights and Republican Party support for national power and preservation of the Union divided the parties over the issue of slavery. Republican Abraham Lincoln's successful campaign that year helped his party capture the presidency and a majority in both houses of Congress. It also precipitated the Civil War. With the eventual secession of 11 Democrat-heavy states in the South, the Republican Party came to dominate politics for the next decade.

Like the election of 1828, the election of 1860 is considered by many scholars to be a **critical election**. The theory of critical elections, developed by political scientist V. O. Key Jr., posits that certain elections can be characterized as producing sharp changes in patterns of party loyalty among voters.[6] This occurred in 1860 when voter support for parties realigned along the issue of slavery, based primarily on a North-versus-South division. Until 1860, the Democratic Party had enjoyed support from urban and industrial areas in both the North and the South and the demographic and social groups associated with those regions. The Civil War shifted these alignments to a North-South division, thus rendering the 1860 contest a critical election. The theory of critical elections suggests that every such election is accompanied by some type of electoral realignment,[7] a lasting reconfiguration of how certain groups of voters align with the parties.

When the last of the former Confederate states was readmitted to the Union in 1870, the Democratic Party once again began to assert itself in national politics. The Civil War had cemented a "solid South" stronghold for the Democratic Party that would continue for a century. Republicans remained the favored party in the northern and midwestern states, although some major cities in the North (including New York City) tended toward the Democratic Party. Republicans dominated the presidency for the remainder of the century, winning six of the next eight presidential contests.

A third realigning election occurred in 1896. That election did not result in a clear shifting of voter preferences from one party to another; rather, it marked the rise of the Republican Party to a near total consolidation of power and voter support in the northern and western states, as well as the continued Democratic Party dominance in southern states. Republican candidate William McKinley won the 1896 election, and with it a realignment of new allegiances to the Republican Party. Indeed, the only Democrat to capture the presidency between 1896 and 1932 was Woodrow Wilson, and Wilson's initial success was more a consequence of Theodore Roosevelt's split with the Republican Party than it was a result of an expanded Democratic base. Roosevelt, a Republican president from 1901 to 1909, formed the Progressive "Bull Moose" Party and ran as its presidential candidate in 1912. He in effect split the Republican vote, handing Democrat Woodrow Wilson an electoral college victory.

In 1912, the Republican Party's progressive and conservative wings split, giving the Democrats the White House and a majority in both houses of Congress. Within six years, however, Republicans regained control of Congress and were well positioned to retake the White House in 1920.

During the 62-year period from 1870 to 1932, the two major parties developed their party organizations and shored up their voting coalitions. They institutionalized their

critical election An election that produces sharp changes in patterns of party loyalty among voters.

President Franklin Delano Roosevelt, a Democrat, campaigning for reelection in Hartford, Connecticut, in 1936.

power in Congress by creating the party caucuses and electing party leaders. Also, during this period, the Democrats and Republicans developed party organizations so strong that the two-party Democrat–Republican system would become permanently institutionalized in American politics.

A fourth realigning election resulted from shifting party allegiances in the midst of the Great Depression. Republican President Herbert Hoover was elected in 1928, less than a year before the stock market crash of 1929 sent the economy into a tailspin. Hoover and the Republicans adopted some limited measures to deal with the economic disaster, but they maintained their party's traditional conservative faith in the dynamics of the market to solve economic problems. Franklin Delano Roosevelt, the Democratic candidate opposing Hoover in 1932, advocated a substantially larger and more activist role for government in dealing with the Depression. Roosevelt's pledge of a "New Deal" and an activist government won the support of the urban working class, people of lower socioeconomic status, new immigrants, and many Catholics and Jews. The shift in allegiances from the Republican Party to the Democratic Party in 1932 (FDR carried 42 states and 60 percent of the vote) had a lasting impact on voters. Adding the "New Deal coalition" to the "solid Democratic South" resulted in Democratic Party domination of American politics for at least the next 36 years. The policies of Democratic Presidents Roosevelt, Harry Truman, John F. Kennedy, and Lyndon Johnson during this era, supported by large Democratic majorities in Congress, were the product of the powerful New Deal coalition established in 1932.

Since 1968, however, both the New Deal coalition and the Democrats' solid grip on the South have declined.[8] At the same time, the century-long southern hostility toward the Republican Party of Abraham Lincoln has diminished, as many conservatives in the South have become attracted to the Republican Party and its socially conservative agenda. Between 1969 and 2016, the Democrats controlled the White House for just 19 years, whereas the Republicans held the White House for 28 years. During that same period, the Democrats controlled both chambers of Congress for 24 years and the Republicans for 12 years, with 11 years of split majorities in the House and Senate. No clear critical elections appear to have occurred over this time frame, and few patterns in voter realignment are obvious. Indeed, some political scientists have argued that the term **dealignment**[9] best describes the behavior of voters since the 1960s. Dealignment refers to the decline in voter attachment to both parties.

dealignment A decline in voter attachment to parties and in clarity of party coalitions.

The 2008, 2010, 2012, 2014, and 2016 election results provided new evidence of the electorate's lack of attachment to either of the two major political parties. After successive election cycles in which the Democratic Party took significant strides toward reestablishing itself as a lasting majority, many independents and disaffected Republicans who had voted for Democrats in 2006 and 2008 returned to the Republican fold in 2010. As a result, the Republicans retook control of the House and reduced the Democrats' margin of control in the Senate to just six seats. Yet the pendulum swung back once again in 2012, as voters opted for divided government: They returned President Obama to the White House, gave the Democrats a slightly expanded majority in the Senate, and maintained the GOP's sizeable majority in the House. Two years later, in the 2014 midterm elections, majority control in the Senate once again shifted to the GOP, and has remained there since.

As the Democrats and Republicans struggle with their long-term political identities, conflicting electoral outcomes will continue to hold their feet to the fire, threatening the long-term party attachments that had been so prevalent in the past.

13-2 | The Functions of Political Parties

Political parties serve a number of critical functions in the American political system at the national, state, and local levels of government. They give organizational coherence to both the operations of popular elections and the management of government. The functions that political parties serve have become inseparable from the principles that define how Americans choose leaders and how elected leaders formulate and administer public policies.

Contesting Elections

Free and open elections are the hallmark of the American republican form of government. With winning elections as their principal goal, political parties promote the prominence, competitiveness, and significance of elections in America. By winning elections and occupying seats in the government, members of the party can influence public policy. The larger the number of elective seats that a party controls, the greater will be the party's potential influence on policy outcomes. Thus, contesting elections lies at the core of a political party's functions.

To contest elections most effectively, the two major parties in the United States have developed a large set of party organizations. These organizations, which operate at the national, state, and local levels, are engaged in a number of activities directed toward winning elections. These activities include fund-raising, organizing events and meetings, providing funding to candidates who are running for office, recruiting and organizing volunteers who want to work for the election of candidates, and purchasing services (for example, polling services, political advertisements, campaign materials such as bumper stickers, direct mail to homes, and so forth) to promote the election of candidates. Many election contests feature a candidate from the party currently in office (the incumbent candidate) defending his or her record against an alternative candidate from the party out of power. The fact that political parties are organized to contest elections and offer alternative proposals for making public policy promotes the responsiveness of elected officials to the voters: By offering voters alternative candidates more in line with public opinion, parties provide an effective mechanism for voters to remove leaders from office through elections. The alternative candidates offered by the Democratic and Republican Parties also serve to organize the process of competitive elections in the United States because the vast majority of elections feature a Democratic candidate and a Republican candidate running against each other. Some elections include independent or third-party candidates, and in some elections a Democratic candidate or a Republican candidate runs unchallenged. But most election contests feature some form of competition between candidates from the two major parties.

Among the 17 candidates who sought the Republican presidential nomination in 2016 were business executive Carly Fiorina and Senator Marco Rubio (FL), pictured here at a GOP primary debate.

Recruiting and Nominating Candidates

Political parties are the main vehicles through which candidates for office are recruited and screened. The fact that parties exist to win elections gives them the incentive to recruit candidates to run for office under the party label. Parties want to find candidates who will represent the party well, and thus they provide a "weeding-out" process that results in higher-quality candidates.

ROBYN BECK/AFP/Getty Images

Most recruiting and promoting of candidates begins at the local party level. Individuals interested in politics often donate their time and efforts to working for political parties by, among other things, attending and participating in party meetings, distributing campaign literature, and driving candidates to campaign events. Local organizations tend to reward this service work with nominations for local offices, such as a seat on a local school board or a planning and zoning board. Successful candidates for these local offices often move up through the ranks of the local party organization to earn the endorsement and nomination of their party for higher office.

Providing a Framework for Voters to Make Vote Choices

Political parties also provide a useful framework for voters who must choose among candidates for elective office. Without even knowing the names of particular candidates for office, voters may be cued in to those candidates' political, ideological, and policy perspectives on the basis of a candidate's party. Most voters associate the political parties with at least broad approaches to governing, if not positions on specific policy issues. For example, on the role that government should play in fixing economic problems, most voters perceive the Democratic Party to be more likely to support an active role for government, whereas Republicans are perceived as having a more "hands-off" approach, preferring economic problems to correct themselves through the free market.

The organizational framework for voters to assess candidates is the political party. This framework helps voters more easily process and evaluate campaign information. Party labels thus offer voters an efficient shortcut mechanism for choosing among candidates. For instance, the Democratic Party and candidates running under that label are often regarded by voters as being more liberal or left of center in their position on issues, whereas candidates under the Republican Party label are viewed as being more conservative or right of center. Party identification is the psychological connection that voters have with a political party that influences other attitudes (such as one's position on gun control) as well as voting behavior. **Party identification**, an individual's feeling of attachment to a particular political party, is a political attitude that begins to form early in a person's life and generally remains quite stable throughout his or her lifetime. The authors of *The American Voter*,[10] a classic book on American voting behavior, described party identification as "generally a psychological identification which can persist without legal recognition or evidence of formal membership." Party identification serves an important role in forming attitudes on particular issues and making vote decisions.

Scientific surveys usually measure party identification by asking questions such as: "Generally speaking, do you think of yourself as a Republican, a Democrat, an independent, or what?" Scholars began measuring party identification in the 1950s, and research on the concept has revealed several important findings. First, although the number of independents has grown slightly over the years, there are many more party identifiers than there are independents. Indeed, the majority of Americans today identify with a political party. Second, whereas the Democratic Party had more identifiers than the Republican Party from the mid-1940s to the

party identification The psychological attachment that an individual has to a particular party.

FIGURE 13-1 Party Identifiers Who Said They Would Support the Party Line in 2016
Results of a preelection poll conducted by Quinnipiac University in September 2016.

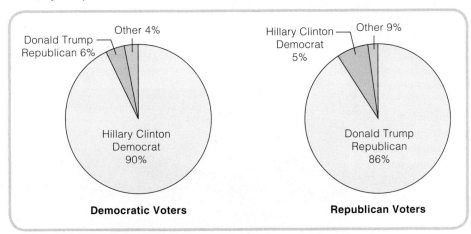

1980s, the number of Democrats and Republicans is nearly equal today. As a consequence, the two major parties enjoy pretty much equal amounts of support from the American public. Third, despite these shifts, party identification in the electorate is quite resistant to change. Thus, from one election to another, voting patterns remain remarkably stable and rarely deviate from either a Democratic or Republican victory. Fourth, party identification plays a very important role in helping voters make voting decisions: As shown in Figure 13-1, the vast majority of Republican identifiers vote for Republican candidates and the vast majority of Democratic identifiers vote for Democratic candidates.[11]

In addition to providing an important cue to voting habits, party identification also serves as an important influence on the policy positions that individuals hold. For example, Figure 13-2 shows the results of a Gallup Poll depicting the stark differences between Democrats and Republicans on activities that might be considered morally acceptable.

Party identification is also an important concept for candidates and party leaders in plotting campaign strategies and contesting elections. As political scientist Phillip Converse has noted, a **normal vote**[12] can be expected for any given election contest. That is, a certain percentage of voters can be expected to cast a ballot for the Democrats, whereas another

normal vote The percentage of voters that can be expected with reasonable certainty to cast a ballot for each of the two major political parties.

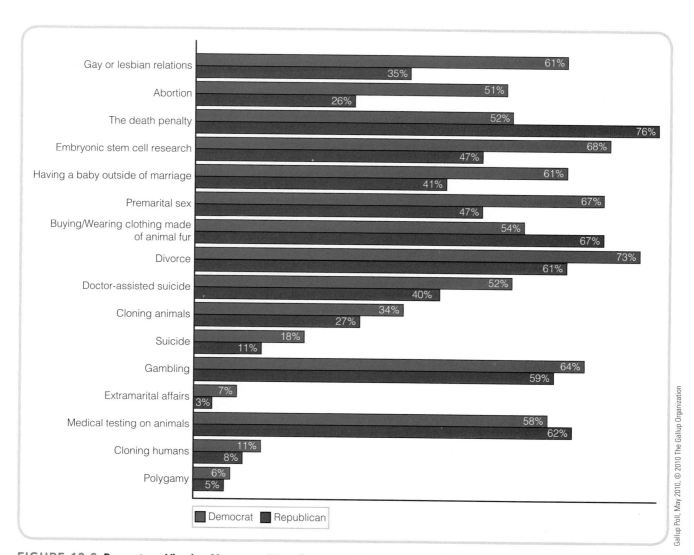

FIGURE 13-2 **Percentage Viewing Matters as "Morally Acceptable," by Party ID (Democrat vs. Republican)**

Top 10 Democratic States		Top 10 Republican States	
State	Democratic advantage	State	Democratic advantage
	Pct. pts.		Pct. pts.
District of Columbia	75	Utah	−23
Rhode Island	37	Wyoming	−20
Massachusetts	34	Idaho	−15
Hawaii	34	Alaska	−11
Vermont	33	Nebraska	−7
New York	27	Kansas	−2
Connecticut	26	Alabama	−1
Maryland	26	Arizona	0
Illinois	24	South Carolina	0
Delaware	23	Three tied at	1

The Gallup Poll, www.gallup.com/poll/114016/state-states-political-party-affiliation.aspx

FIGURE 13-3 Party Identification: The Most Democratic States and the Most Republican States Based on Party Registration

predictable percentage can be expected to vote for the Republicans. The strategy designed to win an election, and the chances that the strategy will result in a victory, largely depend on the normal vote distribution. The larger the margin of one party's normal vote, the less competitive the race. The competitiveness of the race can also be influenced by the number of the nonpartisan voters.

An important caveat about the "normal vote" is that states vary widely in their distribution of Democrats and Republicans. In other words, what is normal for one state may be very abnormal when compared to another state. Figure 13-3 depicts the large variety in Democratic and Republican Party identifiers from state to state. For example, whereas in Rhode Island, Massachusetts, Hawaii, and Vermont Democratic party identifiers largely outnumber Republicans, the opposite is especially true in Utah, Wyoming, Idaho, and Alaska.

Although party identification is defined as a psychological attachment that an individual has to a particular political party and is regarded by political scientists as an attitude, formal membership in a political party is generally associated with the process of voter registration. In addition to making a citizen eligible to vote, the voter registration process in many states includes registering as a member of a political party. In some states, membership in a political party is a necessary precondition for voting in that political party's primary elections to select the candidates who will represent the party in a general election. States with open primaries do not limit the nomination process to voters of one party. State laws govern how a citizen becomes a member of a political party and thus eligible to vote in the party's primary election contests. In most states, it is possible to register to vote without being a member of any particular party. The rules for becoming a member of a party vary widely from state to state.

Providing Organization for the Operations of Government

The majority party organizes its respective institution to accomplish the task of governing.[13] The leadership organization in the House and Senate is based primarily on majority-party leadership. The top leadership position in the House of Representatives is the Speaker of the House, who is always chosen by the majority-party caucus of the House. The chief leadership position in the Senate is the majority leader, who is selected by the majority-party caucus in the Senate. Members of the majority party chair committees in both houses of Congress. Leaders in Congress then try to implement the campaign pledges and platforms advocated by their party during the previous election campaigns. The executive branch, headed by the president, includes various departments and agencies that conduct the work of the federal government. Partisanship and loyalty

The Diversity Dilemma

Gender Trends in Party Support

The most recent presidential elections have demonstrated the huge electoral impact of specific groups, including racial/ethnic minorities and women. In particular, there was considerable attention paid to the "women's vote" in 2012 and 2016. Both parties focused on the critical gender gap in U.S. politics, defined as the difference between men's and women's support for the winning candidate. In the 2012 election, 55 percent of women supported Democratic candidate President Obama, which was 10 points higher than the male support he received. In 2016, 54 percent of women voters supported Democrat Hillary Clinton, a 13 point gap.* This partisan gender gap has been evident in the United States since 1980, when women voters started to consistently support the Democratic presidential candidate by at least 7 to 10 points. The modern gender gap also includes women voting at higher rates than men, which in turn motivates both political parties to strategically appeal to the important "women's vote" through their policy stances and candidate selections.

Most of the focus on this modern gender gap is on the white majority population; however, the parties have also placed increasing importance on the gender gap among racial/ethnic minority voters as well. In terms of partisan identity and support, racial/ethnic minorities also provide a majority of their support to the Democratic Party. In fact, the modern partisan gender gap is now reinforced by the political behavior of racial/ethnic minority women. In 2012, black women and Latina voters overwhelmingly supported President Obama, by 9 to 11 points, respectively, which was considerably greater than the support from their male counterparts. This partisan gender gap for black women and Latinas even exceeded the gender gap for whites, which was 7 points. In 2016, the gender gap in support of Clinton was 14 points among blacks and 15 points for Latinos.† Meanwhile, the gender gap was 12 points among whites, with the majority of white women supporting the Republican candidate.

*www.cnn.com/election/results/president
†www.latinodecisions.com/files/8614/7866/3919/National_2016__Xtabs.pdf

For Critical Thinking and Discussion

1. Why do you think the Democratic Party has been more successful in attracting the majority of the women's vote in recent presidential elections?
2. What policy issues have most influenced women's partisan support?

---

to the president's political party are important factors that influence whom the president appoints to lead these agencies and departments.

The policy agenda and important policy decisions are largely the result of the political party organization and partisan leadership of these key branches of government. The greater a party's control over the key governing institution, the more power that party has in influencing public policy. When the Democratic Party has a majority in both the House and the Senate and occupies the presidency, the Democratic Party has virtual control over what laws get passed. For example, the 1932 elections brought FDR, a Democrat, into the White House and resulted in increased Democratic majorities in both houses of Congress. The result of this dominance was passage of numerous laws promoting active government involvement in dealing with the Great Depression.

Divided government,[14] on the other hand, refers to split-party control of Congress and the presidency. Because both houses of Congress are required for passing new laws, when the majority party in at least one house of Congress differs from the party occupying the presidency, a form of divided government exists. For example, the last six years of Democratic President Obama's term were characterized by GOP control of either one or both houses of Congress. This presence of divided government made it difficult for either party to advance its policy goals and objectives.

Whereas the first 150 years of the republic were mostly characterized by one party controlling both branches of government, the last half century has been dominated by divided government. Seven of the last nine presidents have experienced at least some form of divided government during their term in office. Many observers of American politics question the rationality of an American electorate that so often sends one party to the presidency, yet keeps the opposite party in control of Congress. The stalemate or

divided government
Split-party control of Congress and the presidency.

gridlock that may result from divided government is problematic to some. Still, many Americans believe that divided government has its benefits; certainly divided control tends to intensify the checks and balances on power envisioned by the framers of the Constitution.

13-3 | Why a Two-Party System?

Political parties are an integral part of many of the world's democracies. Contemporary party systems are largely a product of the unique characteristics, history, issues, and social class structure of any given nation.

Although party systems in a democracy vary in numerous ways, they may generally be classified into one of two types: (1) two-party systems and (2) multiparty systems. The United States features a two-party system, dominated by the Democratic and Republican Parties.[15] The vast size and organizational structure of the two major parties, coupled with the fact that these two parties win the great majority of elections, appropriately classify the United States as a **two-party system**. Other democracies feature as many as 10 parties of relatively equal stature. The nations with **multiparty systems** typically include parties organized on the basis of political ideologies (such as the Socialist Party or Conservative Party), particular economic interests (such as the Agricultural Party or the Industrial Party), religion, geography, or positions on a single issue or set of issues.

In the United States, there is a wide range of ideological views, economic interests, religious orientations, ethnic groups, and geographic disparities. Other nations with such a wide diversity of interests typically rely on multiple parties to represent these different components of the population. However, in the United States, a two-party model has persisted now for more than two centuries.

Reasons for the Two-Party System in the United States

What are the factors that contribute to the American two-party model? A key factor is the electoral college system for selecting the president of the United States. In order to win the presidency, a candidate must obtain a majority, not simply a plurality, of votes in the Electoral College. Naturally, this requirement encourages groups of voters to align with one of the major political parties, lest their votes be wasted. Minority groups, such as blue-collar union members, which have no chance of achieving a majority of votes as a single unified party, have found it in their best interest to support one of the two major parties in a presidential election. Being part of a winning coalition yields more influence than being in a smaller unified group with no chance of winning.

A second important factor that promotes the two-party system is the winner-take-all process that prevails in selecting members of Congress. In U.S. congressional elections, only the candidate with the most votes in a single district wins the seat. For example, in a race for a Senate seat, if the Democratic candidate receives 40 percent of the vote, the Republican 35 percent, the Reform Party 15 percent, and the Green Party 10 percent, the Democratic candidate with the 40 percent plurality is elected to Congress. By contrast, in other democracies, such as Israel, France, and Germany, forms of **proportional representation** are used. Under this system, the percentage of the vote that a party receives is reflected in the number of seats that that party occupies in the national legislature. In Israel, for example, a party that receives as little as 1.5 percent of the vote nationally is entitled to at least one seat in the 120-seat Knesset (the Israeli legislature). Whereas a proportional representation system gives minor parties representation in the legislature, the winner-take-all system does not. A third party must win the most votes in any given election contest to win a seat. The winner-take-all system promotes the two-party system and prevents smaller parties from achieving even minimal representation in the national legislature.

two-party system A party system dominated by two major parties that win the vast majority of elections.

multiparty system A political system in which many different parties are organized on the basis of political ideologies, economic interests, religion, geography, or positions on a single issue or set of issues.

proportional representation A system of electing a national legislature in which the percentage of the vote that a party receives is reflected in the number of seats that the party occupies.

A third factor promoting the two-party system is the ideological nature of public opinion in America. Most Americans are ideologically centrist, or moderate, with few considering themselves strong ideologues. The lack of strong ideological differences helps explain why only two parties dominate American politics. Neither the Democratic nor the Republican Party can afford to be too strongly ideological because to be so would risk building a winning coalition in elections.

A fourth factor promoting the two-party system is the laws and regulations that govern campaigns in United States, which tend to benefit the major parties at the expense of third parties. For example, in order to qualify for matching federal funds for presidential

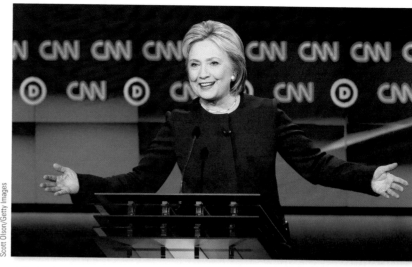

Hillary Clinton speaks during the CNN Democratic Presidential Primary Debate on March 6, 2016 in Flint, Michigan. Clinton was the Democratic Party's nominee in the 2016 presidential race.

campaigns and many state gubernatorial campaigns, candidates must demonstrate a minimum level of support in prior elections and/or primary elections. Most minor parties, however, are eligible to receive such funds only after the election is over. They receive public funding in federal elections, for example, if (1) they receive 5 percent of the popular vote and (2) they appear on the ballot in at least 10 states. Because money to finance a campaign is necessary during, rather than after, the campaign, third parties are at a serious disadvantage. The lack of a history and lack of public interest in third-party primary elections precludes most from receiving federal or state funding in these elections. For a third party's candidate to appear on election ballots in the states, the party must meet a number of criteria, including petitions supporting the candidate and often significant fees.

Minor and Third Parties

Despite the dominance of the Republican and Democratic Parties over the past century and a half, third parties occasionally have contested elections in the United States. In 2016, two third-party candidates (Libertarian Gary Johnson and the Green Party's Jill Stein) together received 4% of the vote. Most third-party candidates fail to register even one percentage point of the popular vote in presidential elections, and few third-party candidates are found in the U.S. Congress, in state legislatures or governorships, or in local government. For the past 160 years, not one president has been elected who did not run as either a Democrat or Republican.

Even the few-and-far-between third-party candidacies that have attracted a sizeable percentage of popular votes in presidential elections have experienced only short-lived success (see Table 13-1). The Progressive or "Bull Moose" Party of Theodore Roosevelt, for example, garnered 27 percent of the vote in 1912 but failed to establish itself as a permanent threat to the two major parties. Its success was largely based on Roosevelt's personal stature and popularity, and by 1916 Roosevelt had returned to the Republican fold. Likewise, Ross Perot, running as an independent in the 1992 presidential race, captured nearly 20 percent of the popular vote. But his attempt to match his 1992 success met with disappointment in his 1996 bid, when he took only 9 percent of the popular vote. By 2000, Perot's Reform Party showed up as barely a blip in the vote totals.[16]

Third parties face a number of obstacles in their attempt to become viable. First, their mostly negligible chance of winning at the outset leads many voters to sense that

TABLE 13-1 Important Third-Party Candidacies in Presidential Races

Third parties are by no means a new phenomenon in American politics. Despite their tendency to be short-lived and their relative lack of success in capturing elective office, third-party movements endure, often affecting which major-party candidate wins office. The following is a select list of third parties, their respective candidates, and the percentage of their vote totals in presidential elections.

Year	Party	Candidate	% of Popular Vote
1832	Anti-Masonic	William Wirt	8
1856	Know-Nothing	Millard Fillmore	22
1892	Populist	James Weaver	9
1912	Bull Moose	Theodore Roosevelt	27
1912	Socialist	Eugene V. Debs	6
1924	Progressive	Robert La Follette	17
1948	States' Rights	Strom Thurmond	2
1948	Progressive	Henry Wallace	2
1968	American Independent	George Wallace	14
1980	National Unity	John Anderson	7
1992	United We Stand America	Ross Perot	19
1996	Reform	Ross Perot	9
2000	Green	Ralph Nader*	3
2004	Independent	Ralph Nader	1
2016	Libertarian	Gary Johnson	3
2016	Green	Jill Stein	1

* Nader was technically the Green Party candidate for president in 1996 as well, but he was only on 22 state ballots that year, and his candidacy labored under a self-imposed spending limit of $5,000. In the 2004 presidential election, the Green Party candidate was Texas attorney David Cobb; Nader ran as an independent in 2004.

a vote for a third party would be wasted. The strong historical and cultural institutionalization of the American two-party system is another obstacle third parties face. The sizeable number of voters who identify themselves as either a Democrat or Republican inclines most voters to support major-party candidates in elections. In addition to the legal barriers already discussed, media coverage of campaigns also plays a role; the media tend to focus most coverage on the two major parties, with little attention given to third-party candidacies.

Still, third parties persist. Table 13-2 lists and describes the most active third parties in the United States today. Despite their limited success in winning important government positions, they often have substantial influence on the outcome of elections. Third-party candidates in hotly contested presidential races have on occasion siphoned off enough votes from one of the major-party candidates to provide an electoral college victory to the other major party. Twice since 1832 a third party has won more than 20 percent of the popular vote in a presidential race, and five times during this period a third party has won at least 10 percent of the popular vote.

TABLE 13-2 Third Parties Today

Despite the lack of electoral success by third parties, many continue to operate in the United States today. Listed here are a few of them, along with a description of their reason for being.

Party	Description
1. Natural Law Party	This party advocates all-party government, which its website defines as "bringing together the best ideas, programs, and leaders from all political parties and the private sector to solve and prevent problems." The party argues that bringing the individual lives of people and national policies into harmony with the natural law will best solve the nation's problems.
2. Constitution Party	This party bases the foundation of its political activities on religious principles of Christianity. It argues on its web page that the U.S. Constitution established a "republic under God, rather than a democracy."
3. Reform Party	Ross Perot ran as a candidate in the 1992 presidential election under the organization United We Stand America. He ran to protest the leadership of both the Republican and Democratic Parties and won 19 percent of the popular vote. In 1996, Perot reorganized under the Reform Party name and won 9 percent of the popular vote. Former Republican Pat Buchanan was a Reform Party candidate for president in 2000, receiving 0.5 percent of the popular vote.
4. Libertarian Party	This party endorses the notion that government should be small and limited, interfering as little as possible with the lives of citizens. The Libertarian Party argues on its web page that "individuals have the right to exercise sole dominion over their own lives [and] they have the right to live in whatever manner they choose so long as they do not interfere with the rights of others." Libertarians place a premium on individual liberties and personal responsibility.
5. Socialist Party	Whereas the Libertarians support a very limited role for government, the Socialist Party supports active government involvement in providing equitable distributions of resources in society. Socialists endorse a strong government role in providing health care, jobs, housing, and education, among other public programs. Although Bernie Sanders won election in 2006 as a U.S. senator from Vermont running as a self-described Democratic Socialist, he does not belong to the Socialist Party.
6. Green Party	The foundation of the Green Party rests on pro-environmentalist positions like Green parties in other democracies, such as Germany and France. In the United States, the Green Party is also identified with a number of social justice causes, including feminism, promotion of diversity, and global responsibility.

13-4 | Party Organizations

Political parties exist through party organizations at the national, state, and local levels. Although most elected government officials are members of the Democratic or Republican Parties, political parties also exist as organizations outside of the government. These party organizations, which often count millions of volunteers among their members, articulate positions on issues; enlist members from the public at large; recruit candidates who will run under the party label for elective office; raise money from individuals, corporations, and interest groups; and provide organizational and campaign services to candidates who are running for office.

Andrew Jackson is regarded as the father of the **national party organization**. Up until the election of 1828, a party's candidates for president and vice president were nominated by the party congressional caucus. Jackson changed this process by establishing a

national party organization The institution through which political parties exist at the national, state, and local levels, primarily focused on articulating policy positions, raising money, organizing volunteers, and providing services to candidates.

In 2016, the chair of the Republican National Party was Reince Priebus (left) and the chair of the Democratic National Party was Debbie Wasserman-Schultz (right). Wasserman-Schultz resigned as chair the day before the Democratic convention opened, amidst accusations that she favored Hillary Clinton over Bernie Sanders.

national party convention to be held several months before a presidential election. The convention brings together state and local party leaders to nominate the party's candidates for president and vice president. In addition to party leaders, the national conventions today include delegates from the states elected by members of the party in presidential primary elections.

Since the middle of the nineteenth century, both the Democratic and Republican national party organizations have been run by a **national committee**, which oversees the conduct of the presidential campaign and develops strategy for each party's congressional elections as well. The national committees, consisting of state and local party representatives, are run by a **national committee chair** chosen soon after the presidential election has concluded.

national committee The committee that oversees the conduct of a party's presidential campaign and develops strategy for congressional elections.

national committee chair The head of the national committee for one of the two major parties.

At the national level, the committees, chairs, and party organization largely provide a supportive role during the presidential campaign. Once providing a core advisory role to a presidential candidate, the national organizations today are more involved in helping their candidate raise money and campaign for office. Strategy, planning, and advising are now handled mostly by the candidate's own campaign staff, which typically includes a media consultant, a pollster, a campaign manager, and various other campaign consultants. The modern-day national party organization is also less influential in determining who the nominee will be and more responsive to the victorious candidate's personal campaign staff. They maintain greater influence in assisting state and local party efforts to win elections by providing polling and media consulting services, campaign management services, and financial resources.

In the modern era, state and local party organizations tend to be more influential in the nomination of candidates, in developing and organizing campaigns, and in providing a cue to voters about their vote selections. Voters pay less attention to campaigns in state and local elections and therefore depend more on partisan cues in their choice of candidates. State legislative and local election campaigns generally have limited resources to mount significant image-building campaigns for candidates. Candidates are thus more dependent on the resources of the state and local party organizations for financing. Local party organizations provide "get out the vote" services by funding phone banks to contact voters directly. State and local organizations also fund and make available polling services and media consulting services to candidates in less visible races. Because they benefit from these services, candidates for local and state offices may feel the need to be more responsive to the party organizations.

Local party organizations also provide the grassroots manpower for soliciting mass participation in political activities. These activities include implementing voter registration drives, organizing political fund-raisers and rallies, and staffing phone banks to make direct contact with voters urging them to vote for their party's candidates. Local organizations also provide the mechanism for identifying and recruiting talented citizens to become candidates for elective office. They provide the "farm team" for potential candidates for higher offices, such as governor, member of Congress, and senator.

13-5 | Are Parties in Decline?

Many political scientists contend that the political party is in a state of decline in America. Bolstering this claim is the dealignment thesis described earlier in this chapter, which holds that voters today are less attached to parties and tend to be more independent-minded than they were up through the 1960s. Political scientist Martin Wattenberg[17] argues that increased negativity toward the parties has contributed to party decline. Wattenberg suggests further that the mass media have contributed to this decline by neglecting to cover parties. Prior to the 1960s, voters depended mainly on parties to provide information about political issues and candidates; now voters turn to the media as the prime information source. Furthermore, the medium of television allows candidates today to bypass parties and appeal directly to the public for support. Many candidates now run campaigns that de-emphasize parties and focus primarily on the candidate's image.

Scholars have also noted a decline in the organizational linkages between officeholders and the political parties. Patronage, the practice by which victorious parties offer loyal party members jobs in government, declined substantially during the past century. Under the patronage system, parties were able to retain the strong support of many of their members by offering the prospect of a good government job if the party was victorious. The civil service and other reforms seriously limited a political party's ability to offer jobs or other favors in return for supporting the party. Although these reforms have eroded the power of parties, they have also improved the quality of government officials and reduced corruption in government affairs.

Changes in the way candidates are nominated by a party have also reduced the power of party organizations. Until recently, parties exerted powerful control over the process by which an individual becomes a candidate wearing the party label in a general election. Without endorsement of the party organization, candidates for president, Congress, and state and local office once were virtually precluded from running under the party label. However, reforms in the 1960s and 1970s reduced the party organization's role in the nomination process. The **direct primary election**, which provides for the nomination of a candidate based on an open election among all party members, has empowered rank-and-file party members rather than party leaders to choose the party's nominees. Direct primaries make it easier for candidates who are not necessarily approved by the party organization to wear the party label in a general election. Donald Trump's successful drive for the Republican presidential nomination in 2016 occurred to a large extent over the wishes of party officials, rather than as a result of their support—that type of success would not have been possible as little as a half century ago.

> **direct primary election** An open election, rather than an election by party leaders, to choose candidates for the general election.

Some scholars, however, are not so convinced that parties are on the decline. They argue that although certain aspects of parties are declining, in other ways parties are showing a resurgence in relevance.[18] For example, parties have adapted quite well to candidate-centered campaigns by servicing candidate organizations. Party-line voting in the House and the Senate has been highly disciplined in recent years. In the 110th Congress (2007–2008), for example, senators voted with their party's position on legislation an average of 83 percent of the time. Not much changed during the 111th and 112th Congresses. When health care reform came up for a series of final votes in the Senate in late 2009 and early 2010, all 100 senators voted down the line with their party leadership's position on the issue. Discipline on major congressional votes remains highly partisan in the current 113th Congress.

Whether they are declining or not, at the moment parties remain alive and quite active in American politics. Even though voter partisanship may have waned, party identification still remains a strong determinant of vote choice. Although the parties may be less visible to voters, they continue to exert considerable influence over voting decisions. The Democratic and Republican Party organizations are well funded and include millions of party workers. Party organizations provide money and expertise to candidates to help them achieve electoral success. The president remains the recognized leader of the party label he wears, and the party with a majority of seats in each house of Congress maintains clear control of the legislative agenda. Although the power of the party may have declined, it is clear that "the party" is far from over in American politics.

13-6 | Voting

representative democracy System of government in which citizens elect the individuals who are responsible for making and enforcing public policy.

elections The political mechanism that ensures that the majority will rule.

franchise The right to vote.

Political participation takes many forms in American politics. At the core of participation is the act of voting. Open and free elections held on a regular basis are the hallmark characteristic of a democratic government. Voting provides the critical linkage between citizens' preferences and governmental authority. The United States is not a direct democracy in which every citizen is invited to deliberate the issues and vote on public policy. Rather, the U.S. system is a **representative democracy**, sometimes referred to as an indirect democracy or republican form of government, in which citizens choose the individuals who are then responsible for making and enforcing public policy. The people do not directly rule, but they have the opportunity to exercise power vicariously by choosing as their leaders those whom they prefer.

The core principle underlying representative democracy is majoritarianism, or majority rule, which means that among the choices presented to voters, the choice that is supported by the most voters (that is, receives the most votes) is the choice that prevails. When a majority makes its choice, the consent of the governed is satisfied. Given the diversity of opinions and interests among people in our society, it is unrealistic to assume that all, or even most, voters will agree on one choice. But the will of the people is accomplished when the majority decides.

Voting in **elections** is the mechanism that ensures that the majority will rule. Times change, and so do people's opinions and preferences. Therefore, representative democracy not only requires an election in the selection of leadership, but also requires that elections occur on a regular basis so that the government's authority reflects changing majority views. Regular and periodic elections allow the majority of voters to continue to exercise ultimate control over the direction of public policy.

FIGURE 13-4 **The Hispanic Vote in Presidential Elections, 1990–2012**
The growing number of Hispanic voters, fully 25.2 million in 2012, has played to the advantage of Democratic Party presidential candidates. Latinos voted for President Obama over Governor Romney in 2012 by a margin of 72 percent to 27 percent.
Notes: Winner in **bold**. Independent and other third-party candidates not shown. In 1992, the independent candidate Ross Perot received 14 percent of the Hispanic vote; "Democratic advantage" calculated after rounding.

(Percentage of Hispanic voters casting ballots for the ...)

Year	Democratic candidate	Republican candidate	Democratic advantage
1980	Jimmy Carter, 56%	**Ronald Reagan, 35%**	+21
1984	Walter Mondale, 61%	**Ronald Reagan, 37%**	+24
1988	Michale Dukakis, 69%	**George H.W. Bush, 30%**	+39
1992	**Bill Clinton, 61%**	George H.W. Bush, 25%	+36
1996	**Bill Clinton, 72%**	Bob Dole, 21%	+51
2000	Al Gore, 62%	**George W. Bush, 35%**	+27
2004	John Kerry, 58%	**George W. Bush, 40%**	+18
2008	**Barack Obama, 67%**	John McCain, 31%	+36
2012	**Barack Obama, 71%**	Mitt Romney, 27%	+44

Pew Hispanic Center analysis of national exit roll data, 1980–2012

The Legal Structure for Voting in the United States

The **franchise**, or suffrage, is the right to vote. When speaking about majority rule, it is important to ask, "majority of whom?"

Article I, Section 4 of the U.S. Constitution assigns the system of voting, including the definition of who is granted suffrage, to the states. Voting registration, voter eligibility, methods of casting ballots, and the tallying of official results are all functions reserved for states. The original Constitution prescribes eligibility requirements for federal officeholders (representatives, senators, and the president) and lays out the system for selection of the president and vice president, but it says nothing about who can vote in the elections for these officials. Constitutional amendments have been ratified and federal laws have been passed that prevent states from discriminating in granting suffrage rights, but, technically, there exists no absolute constitutional right to vote in the first place.

Toward Universal Suffrage

The states have exercised significant authority in defining who is eligible to vote. For many years, states regularly denied minorities, women, young adults, Native Americans, and the poor the right to vote for officeholders at the local, state, and national levels of government. In addition, a number of states prescribed property ownership requirements that prevented many people from being eligible to vote. Some states at various points in the nation's early history sought to broaden the right of suffrage. New Jersey, for example, allowed women the right to vote in the early 1800s, and some northern states provided for black suffrage prior to the Civil War.[19] But the goal of **universal suffrage**—or the right of all citizens to vote—has been an elusive one throughout American history. Restrictions on voting rights have systematically denied the right of particular groups of people to participate in choosing their leaders.

universal suffrage The idea that all citizens in a nation have the right to vote.

Two centuries of government under the Constitution, however, have been marked by steady progress toward the goal of extending the franchise to all Americans. In the first federal elections in 1788, voting rights were limited to white men who owned property, whereas in the most recent federal elections of 2012, all citizens of the United States aged 18 or older (who were not otherwise prohibited from voting due to a felony conviction or some similar offense) enjoyed the legal right to vote. Enfranchisement was not achieved quickly, nor did it happen as the result of one or two events. Rather, the process of extending the right to vote to all American adults occurred over centuries of time, and with much opposition.

The Civil War presented the first major challenge to the disenfranchisement of a particular class of people, namely, African Americans. Prior to the Civil War, African American slaves not only did not have the right to vote, they had no rights at all. In the infamous U.S. Supreme Court decision *Dred Scott v. Sandford* (1857),[20] the Court ruled that slaves were property, that they had no rights under the law, and that they were not and could never become legal citizens of the United States. Immediately after the surrender of Confederate forces in 1865, President Abraham Lincoln gave an address suggesting that freed slaves be given the franchise. The idea met with some resistance, even among the Northern states. However, the so-called Civil War amendments to the Constitution not only ended the institution of slavery (the Thirteenth Amendment) and granted citizenship to former slaves (the Fourteenth Amendment), but the **Fifteenth Amendment**, passed in 1870, guaranteed that "[t]he right of citizens of the United States to vote shall not be denied or abridged by the United States or by any State on account of race, color, or previous condition of servitude." The Fifteenth Amendment was the first formal action granting the federal government the power to enforce voting rights over the states.

Fifteenth Amendment The amendment to the Constitution that guaranteed the franchise regardless of race, color, or previous condition of servitude.

The Fifteenth Amendment, however, did not deter some officials from the former Confederate states from finding ways to deny African Americans their newly won voting rights after Reconstruction ended in 1877. Threats, beatings, destruction of property, and other intimidation tactics, often ignored by local police, effectively kept blacks from coming to the polls on Election Day.[21] In addition, some states sought legal means to

poll tax The requirement that individuals pay a fee before being allowed to vote.

literacy test The requirement that individuals prove that they can read and write before being allowed to vote.

Twenty-fourth Amendment The constitutional amendment that outlaws poll taxes.

Nineteenth Amendment The constitutional amendment that guarantees women equal voting rights.

Twenty-third Amendment The constitutional amendment providing electoral votes to the District of Columbia, thus giving District residents the right to vote in presidential elections.

Twenty-sixth Amendment The constitutional amendment that lowered the voting age to 18 in all local, state, and federal elections.

prevent blacks from voting. They passed laws instituting a **poll tax** that required individuals to pay a fee before being allowed to vote; they required potential voters to pass a **literacy test** to prove that they could read and write. Because most blacks were poor, they were often unable to pay the poll tax (usually about $30). Blacks also tended to have less education (in some states it had been illegal to teach slaves to read and write), so they frequently could not pass the literacy tests, which were often deliberately difficult and unfairly applied to minorities to prevent them from voting. From the late 1800s through the first half of the twentieth century, these methods posed a substantial barrier to black turnout in federal elections, which typically was about 10 percent. These laws also depressed turnout of poor people in general.

The civil rights movement of the 1960s addressed the problems associated with the disenfranchisement of blacks. Two important products of this movement were the Twenty-fourth Amendment and the Voting Rights Act of 1965. The **Twenty-fourth Amendment**, passed in 1964, outlawed poll taxes by making unconstitutional any law that made payment of a tax a voting eligibility requirement in federal elections.[22] The Voting Rights Act of 1965 denied states the right to use literacy tests as a requirement for voting; it also provided African Americans with protection from intimidating tactics that had been used to keep them away from the polls.

The past century also witnessed the enfranchisement of women. Although passage of the Fifteenth Amendment in 1870 granted African American men the legal right to vote, women would not receive the same constitutional guarantee until 1920 with the passage of the **Nineteenth Amendment**. In 1848, some 200 delegates—women and men—met in Seneca Falls, New York, to issue a call for women's rights, including the right to vote. The Civil War years diverted the nation's attention from women's rights to other pressing problems.[23] Attempts to include a women's right to vote in the Fifteenth Amendment proved unsuccessful, although women began voting in some states well before passage of the Fifteenth Amendment. By the late nineteenth century, some of the new western states, such as Utah, Wyoming, Colorado, Idaho, Washington, and California, enacted women's suffrage laws. Despite continued opposition from leaders, including President Woodrow Wilson, and many states in the Northeast, popular sentiment and a well-organized lobbying effort eventually led to the passage of the Nineteenth Amendment.

Three other groups have successfully won the right to vote through federal legislation and constitutional amendment. Until the early twentieth century, Native Americans had neither citizenship nor voting rights, but federal laws passed in 1924 made it illegal for states to deny Native Americans the franchise. In 1961, the **Twenty-third Amendment** to the Constitution gave residents of the District of Columbia the right to vote in presidential elections. Because the District is not a state, its residents had not been allowed to participate in presidential elections. The Twenty-third Amendment allocates electoral votes to the District using the same formula by which electoral votes are allocated to a state: the total number of representatives it would have in the House, if it were a state, plus two. Today, the District of Columbia has a total of three electoral votes. In 1971, in the midst of the Vietnam War when many young Americans were dying in battle, Congress passed and the states ratified the **Twenty-sixth Amendment**, which lowered the voting age to 18 in all local, state, and federal elections.

Although the administration of election and voting rules is largely controlled by the states, significant numbers of federal laws and constitutional amendments have extended voting rights in the United States. Collectively, these laws prevent states from discriminating against particular groups of citizens with respect to their right to vote. Unfortunately, racism and other forms of discrimination continue to exist and thus continue to affect voting rights in America. Subtle forms of discrimination, including intimidation tactics by groups such as the Ku Klux Klan, may scare individuals into not voting. But more overt discriminatory tactics, supported by some state and local laws, have largely been erased. As a society, the United States, over many years, has progressed toward the democratic ideal of universal suffrage. Today in the United States, the only adults legally disenfranchised are convicted felons in prison (47 states), on probation (29 states), and on parole (32 states).

Voter Registration Laws

Just as the extension of the franchise has evolved over the years, so has the system of voter registration. Most states today have voter registration systems in which individuals must qualify in order to become eligible to vote. The responsibility for qualifying lies with the individual. States do not compile and maintain a list of individuals who are eligible to vote. Rather, individuals must take it upon themselves to demonstrate their qualifications and file the appropriate paperwork to become eligible.

Massachusetts, in 1800, was the first state to require individuals to register to vote.[24] A handful of states followed Massachusetts's lead, but not until after the Civil War did most states adopt voter registration systems. Many of the voter registration systems that were adopted between the 1870s and the early 1900s made it harder for immigrants, the less educated, and those less familiar with the political system to vote. A leading force behind the institution of voter registration systems was the populist movement of the late nineteenth century, which largely included white, middle-class, native-born Americans. In the northern states, registration laws were intended to make it more difficult for new European immigrants to vote; in the West, the intention was to make voting by new Chinese and Japanese immigrants more difficult; in the South, registration was aimed at limiting the black vote; and the source of concern in the Southwest was Mexican immigrants. Most states today still rely on some form of self-initiated voter registration, which continues to present an obstacle to voting for some people.

A person must first find out how to register, remember to register in advance of Election Day, and then spend time registering. Many states require proof of age and citizenship, and many also impose a length-of-residence qualification, requiring a potential voter to prove that he or she has resided in the state for a specified period of time.[25]

Numerous organizations and public-interest groups have lobbied state legislatures and Congress to simplify and ease voter registration requirements in order to allow more people to vote on Election Day, including those who fail to register in advance of the election. North Dakota is the only state that does not currently require registration, and three states—Maine, Minnesota, and Wisconsin—permit voters to register on Election Day. The National Voter Registration Act of 1993, often called the **Motor Voter law**, mandates that when an individual applies for or renews a state driver's license, the state must also provide that individual with voter registration materials. The idea behind the law is that combining the process of registering to vote with the more routine task of obtaining a driver's license makes voter registration easier. Research suggests that although this law has increased voter registration, it has not increased actual turnout.[26]

Motor Voter law The federal law mandating that when an individual applies for or renews a state driver's license, the state must also provide that individual with voter registration materials.

13-7 | Exercising the Franchise

A number of factors explain why people decide to cast a ballot on Election Day. An individual's interest in politics is one important factor. People who are more interested in politics tend to follow news about campaigns to a much greater degree than those who are less interested, and those who are more interested are more likely to vote.

The Angry Voter Rises Again. . . and Again.

Many presidential candidates hope to run a positive campaign, appealing to the average voter's hopes and promises for a better future. The candidate hailing from the incumbent party in particular benefits from happy and contented voters who wish to keep the party in power just where it is. Just as often, however, the winning candidate appeals to voter discontent and frustration with the economy, the nation's foreign policy, or any of a host of problems afflicting the nation. And in some cases the victor will actually seek to stoke the discontent of an angry electorate with the promise that everything will be better once we "kick the bums out" and "clean up Washington." Two of the many elections that fit the latter description are:

Then

The **1968** presidential campaign was a tumultuous one. Not only were Americans seriously divided over continued U.S. involvement in the Vietnam War, but racial divisions produced riots across the country and unrest on the nation's college campuses. Richard Nixon, the Republican presidential nominee, ran a campaign based on a "Southern strategy"—win over white Democratic voters in the South by promising to restore "law and order" to American communities. He also promised to redirect the military effort at winning the war. At campaign rallies Nixon spoke of returning to a "forgotten America," the label he gave to a nation of citizens who "obey the law, pay their taxes, go to church, send their children to school, love their country and demand new leadership." (A year later, he would popularize the term "silent majority" to describe these target voters.) Meanwhile, Hubert Humphrey, the Democratic candidate who was the sitting Vice President, was forced with considerable difficulty to defend the status quo. Nixon effectively tapped into voter anger to gain a narrow win in the popular vote, and a convincing 301–191 electoral college victory that fall.

Now

In 2016, outsider candidate Donald Trump, a businessman who had never before held public office, proved the ideal messenger for millions of citizens who were angry with a federal government that seemingly did not care about them. Trump campaigned on the promise to "Make America Great Again," which appealed to the voters' sense that America was no longer great, and that we should return to an earlier time when things were better. Critics of Trump's candidacy complained that his appeal harkened back to Nixon's "Southern strategy" by reaching out to poor and uneducated white voters who had suffered economic hardships under the Democrats. When polls in September showed him trailing significantly behind his Democratic opponent, former Secretary of State Hillary Clinton,

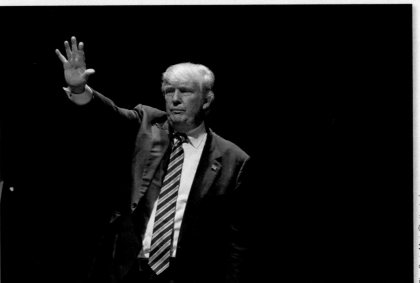

The GOP nominee tapped into voter anger about the direction of the country to win the presidential election in 2016.

Trump spoke of his own "silent majority of voters" who would bring Midwestern states back into the Republican fold. This strategy proved on the mark: On Election Day he scored a startling upset victory thanks to millions of silent voters who the pollsters had missed. Though Trump narrowly lost the popular vote, he managed to win a clear Electoral College victory thanks to stunning victories in Michigan, Wisconsin and Pennsylvania, just as he had promised.

Interest in politics, however, is only one factor that leads people to vote. Another is a person's sense of "civic duty," or the belief that being a good citizen requires one to vote. Many people who are not very interested in politics show up to vote nonetheless because they have a sense of civic duty.[27] From a young age, most Americans are socialized to believe that participating in elections is characteristic of the good democratic citizen, and so they feel an obligation to cast a vote even though they may not be particularly interested in elections and campaigns.

Another factor that influences some people to vote is the perception that their vote can have an impact on the outcome of an election. Individuals who feel strongly about a particular issue, a set of issues, or a candidate may want to vote on the theory that if the election is close, their vote might actually make a difference in the outcome. Indeed, the sense that one's vote can make a difference contributes to higher turnout in elections that are perceived to be close.

Finally, for some people, social group pressure can be a motivating factor in deciding to vote. Voting is often regarded as the "right" thing to do, and some people feel that casting a ballot is expected of them by others. This sense of social pressure to do what is acceptable by society's standards can increase the likelihood that a person will vote.

Who Turns Out to Vote?

An individual's interest in politics and attentiveness to news about politics and campaigns, sense of civic duty, and sense of political efficacy (that is, the belief that one's vote can make a difference) all lead to higher rates of **voter turnout**, which is the percentage of eligible voters who show up to vote on Election Day. In addition to these "political" factors that help to distinguish between citizens who are more or less likely to vote, there are a number of demographic characteristics that also help to explain turnout. A person's gender, age, race/ethnicity, and level of education are all related to the decision to vote (see Figure 13-5).

voter turnout The number of people who turn out to vote as a percentage of all those eligible to vote.

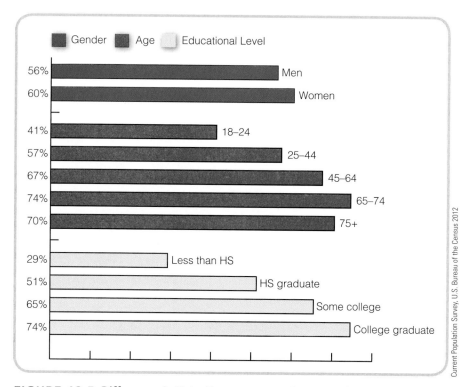

FIGURE 13-5 **Differences in Voter Turnout among Demographic Groups in the 2012 Presidential Election**

In many elections, younger people tend to pass up the opportunity to vote at greater rates than middle-aged and older people do. Youth nonvoting is often attributed to the more transient nature of younger people's lives.[28] At about age 18, many young people leave their parents' home to go to college, take a job, or start their careers. Younger Americans are less rooted in a community, have had less time to register to vote, and are experiencing major changes in their social and personal situations. Voting tends to be less of a priority under these changing circumstances. As people age, buy a home, have a family, and reside in a particular community for a period of time, they become more socially attached and are more likely to vote.

Two other demographic groups are substantially more likely to vote: better-educated Americans[29] and wealthier Americans.[30] These two factors are related because higher levels of education also lead to higher relative affluence and social status. The process of being educated sharpens a person's mind, improves the individual's ability to understand problems in society, and equips him or her to deal with complex information, such as the issues discussed in political campaigns. Education also enhances a person's appreciation for democracy and sense of civic duty. A better understanding of the issues and appreciation for the democratic process encourage higher levels of voter participation.

Racial and ethnic minority groups typically turn out to vote at lower rates compared to the white population, but the 2016 election marked the most diverse electorate in U.S. history. Thirty-one percent of eligible voters came from racial and ethnic minority groups, a net increase of 7.5 million voters.* In contrast, the share of the white non-Hispanic eligible voters hit an all-time low of 69 percent. The growing Latino population, in particular, has begun to wield major political influence. As depicted in Figure 13-6, Hispanics nearly quadrupled in voting strength over the last 30 years to 27.3 million eligible voters, the largest increase of any racial/ethnic group.† Both major parties have sought the endorsement of this large and growing portion of the American electorate, but Democrats have proven more successful in capturing Latino interest, especially in national races. In the last three presidential elections, Democratic candidates won a substantial portion of the Latino vote: 67% in 2008 and 72% in 2012 supported Barack Obama; 79% supported Hillary Clinton in 2016.‡ Hispanic voting dips, however, in midterm elections (see Figure 13-7), such as in 2010 (when the GOP won back the House of Representatives) and 2014 (when Republicans won control of the Senate), muting the Democratic advantage provided by the Hispanic vote in presidential contests. Both parties know that the great untapped prize will come in the form of

*www.pewresearch.org/fact-tank/2016/02/03/2016-electorate-will-be-the-most-diverse-in-u-s-history/
†www.pewresearch.org/fact-tank/2016/11/09/hillary-clinton-wins-latino-vote-but-falls-below-2012-support-for-obama/
‡www.latinovote2016.com/app/

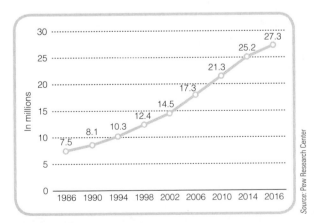

FIGURE 13-6 A Record Number of Latinos Are Eligible to Vote . . .
Note: Eligible voters are U.S. citizens ages 18 and older.

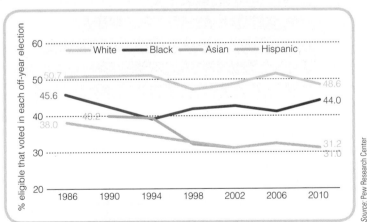

FIGURE 13-7 Latino Voter Turnout Rates Consistently Below Whites, Blacks in Midterm Elections
Note: Hispanics are of any race. Whites, blacks, and Asians include only non-Hispanics. Data for non-Hispanic Asians were not available in 1986.

younger Hispanic voters aged 18–29, who make up a third of all eligible Hispanic voters but lag behind most other groups in turnout. And as the Hispanic population on the whole continues to grow, the next great ruling coalition in American politics may have Latino voters at its core.

Of course this modern surge in the size of the Hispanic electorate is hardly the first case of an immigration trend impacting the American political landscape. From 1880 through 1920, a surge in immigration from southern and eastern Europe occurred, as Italians, Hungarians, Poles, and Greeks (among others) left the economic and political strife of Europe seeking jobs and opportunities in America.

This new immigrant population settled mostly in cities, which suffered disproportionately from the Great Depression. Neither party rushed to embrace America's newest citizens at the outset, yet it was the Democratic Party that was first to formulate policies aimed at these city dwellers. In 1932, Americans with eastern and southern European roots formed the core of Franklin D. Roosevelt's New Deal coalition, which came to dominate the American policy agenda for the next half century.

Stagnation in economic conditions for today's working and middle-class Hispanics has been a source of frustration for this growing population. Exaggerating their frustration is the current gridlock in Washington over immigration reform, which Latino voters identify as their chief policy concern. Obama's endorsement of immigration reform in his second term was particularly popular among Hispanics. Just as early 20th century immigrants found a home in FDR's New Deal coalition, the modern Democratic Party's willingness to embrace immigration reform sent a warning to Republicans: Ignoring this group's policy concerns may leave your party on the outside looking in on the next great ruling coalition in American politics. Republicans in 2016 had an opportunity to place a Hispanic on their presidential ticket, in Senators Marco Rubio of Florida and Ted Cruz of Texas. The choice of Donald Trump, however, with his anti-Latino and anti-immigrant rhetoric, signaled a huge step backward in GOP attempts to attract the Latino vote.

Why Don't More People Vote?

Despite the numerous factors that motivate people to vote, many in fact do not vote. Voter turnout is a measure of how engaged Americans are in voting in any given election contest. High turnout is considered a healthy sign for a democratic system. It implies that people are engaged in political issues, spend the time to contribute to the system, and take responsibility for selecting leaders. Lower turnout is often viewed as a by-product of alienation, mistrust, and lack of confidence in the political system.

Economist Anthony Downs originally offered an explanation for nonvoting based on a theory known as *rational choice*.[31] He argued that voters might decide not to vote because they reason that the costs of obtaining and understanding information about candidates and campaigns outweigh the benefits of making a vote choice. It is a rational choice, therefore, to decide not to vote, or to vote on the basis of certain "shortcuts" such as a candidate's political party.

Elections are plentiful in the United States and are held for many different offices at many different levels of government. Turnout varies from one type of election to another. Some elections draw much more media attention and thus engender more interest than others. Some feature much more political advertising and so provide more cues to voters. Some elections are inherently viewed as more important and so inspire a greater sense of civic duty among voters.

In 1966, political scientist Angus Campbell and his colleagues identified five factors that distinguish between "high-stimulus" elections (in which turnout tends to be higher) and "low-stimulus" elections (in which turnout is generally lower).[32] The factors that characterize a high-stimulus election are (1) greater levels of media coverage, (2) higher significance of the office, (3) campaigns in which voters assign high importance to an issue, (4) more attractive candidates, and (5) perceptions of a close race. Campbell and his colleagues argue that events external to voters may stimulate interest in elections and thus increase the likelihood that individuals will turn out to vote on Election Day. For example, when big issues such as war and peace are at stake, people are more likely to take an interest in the election and vote.

Presidential elections tend to produce the highest levels of turnout because (1) they are heavily covered by the media; (2) there is more spending on political advertisements, particularly on television, thus making the campaign more visible to voters; and (3) the presidency is the most significant office in the U.S. political system. In presidential races where an issue important to many voters is at stake, such as problems with the economy in 1992, the Vietnam War in 1968, or the war with Iraq and terrorism in 2004, turnout tends to be especially high. Races for higher office typically deal with bigger issues and feature candidates who are more attractive to voters. For these reasons, turnout in presidential races, and to a lesser extent in contests for U.S. senators and state governors, tends to be higher than turnout in elections for lower state offices and local races.

A well-documented trend from 1960 through 2000 was the declining rate of voter turnout in U.S. elections. Prior to 2004, turnout hovered around 50 percent for eight presidential elections. In fact, the election of 1996 marked the first time since 1908 that turnout actually dipped below the 50 percent mark, with only 49.1 percent of Americans of voting age going to the polls. For the past three presidential elections, however, voter turnout has trended upward (60 percent in 2004, 61 percent in 2008, and approximately 58 percent in 2012). Voter turnout is usually much lower in midterm congressional elections (that is, the congressional elections that occur midway through a president's term). Forty-one percent of American adults cast a ballot in the 2006 elections.

Figure 13-8 depicts the trend in voter turnout for presidential elections covering the past half century. It shows that the downward trend in turnout from 1960 through 2000 has been reversed, with turnout in 2004 reaching the 60 percent level.

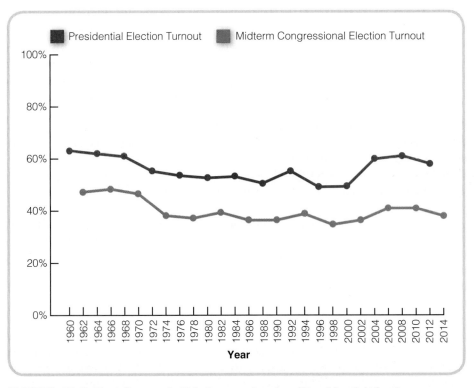

FIGURE 13-8 Voter Turnout in U.S. Congressional and Presidential Elections
Trends in voter turnout from 1960 through 2014 for presidential year elections and midterm congressional elections.

Voting in the United States Compared with Other Democracies

Many observers of elections note that voter turnout rates are lower in the United States than they are in other democracies. From 1992 through 2000, the average turnout rate in the United States for presidential elections was 52 percent. Over the same period, the average turnout rate in all federal elections (including midterm congressional races) was 45 percent. During roughly the same period of time, turnout in other nations, as shown in Figure 13-9, was much higher.[33]

Several explanations have been offered to account for both the lower turnout rates in the United States compared to other democracies as well as the trend toward declining rates of turnout in the United States over the past half century:

1. **There are a large number of elections in America, making the opportunity to participate less of a novelty.** U.S. turnout rates may be lower than those in other democracies of the world simply because there are so many elections held in the United States.[34] The U.S. system of federalism produces several layers of government: national, state, and local. At the federal level, elections are held for president, the Senate, and the House of Representatives. At the state level, there are gubernatorial races as well as elections for other statewide offices, including attorney general, state treasurer, and other state agency heads. At the local level, there may be elections for mayor, city council, sheriff, local judges, and so on. Furthermore, for many of these offices there are two elections: a primary election to elect the party candidate and a general election to determine the office winner. Also, in many states and localities there are often special elections on referendum questions and bond issues. Opportunities for participation in elections in the United States are so plentiful that they have become commonplace events. The vast number of elections may help explain lower rates of voting in any one contest. Switzerland, which also has a large number of elections, also has relatively low turnout compared to other democracies.

2. **Tuesdays are workdays.** Traditionally, most elections in the United States have been held on Tuesdays. Most working people work on Tuesday, and so it may be inconvenient or difficult for many voters to find the time to vote on this day. People report having less and less free time in our society, which can account in

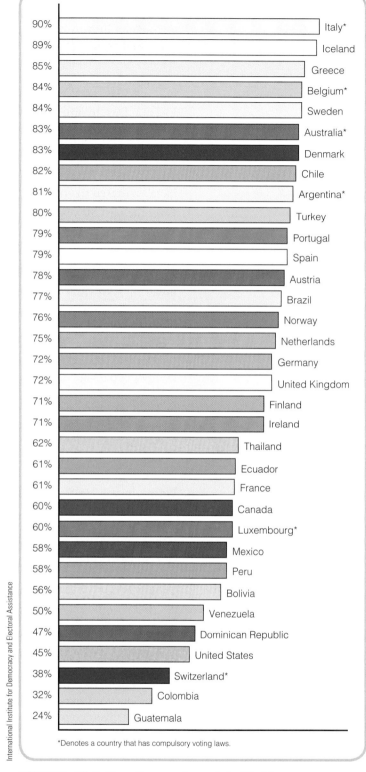

*Denotes a country that has compulsory voting laws.

International Institute for Democracy and Electoral Assistance

FIGURE 13-9 Voter Turnout Around the World
Voter turnout varies a great deal from one country to another. This figure depicts average voter turnout from 1991 through 2000 in a number of the world's democracies. The turnout rates are expressed as the percentage of the voting-age population that actually voted in national elections. For the United States, the percentage includes both presidential and midterm congressional elections.

part for declining turnout. In many other countries, elections are held on weekends or over a period of a number of days, making it easier for people to find the time to cast a vote. In May of 2016, President Barack Obama called for Election Day to be a national holiday; Congress's determination to retain state control over the election process makes such a reform unlikely, at least in the short term.

3. **Voting in the United States usually requires advance registration.** As described earlier in this chapter, voters in most U.S. states are required to register to vote prior to Election Day. In other countries, voter registration is often automatic; that is, citizens of legal age are automatically registered to vote. Thus, voters simply need to show up at the voting place on Election Day. In countries where registration is automatic, 100 percent of eligible voters are thus registered; in the United States, where registration is usually a separate process, typically about 70 percent of eligible individuals have registered to vote.

4. **Over the past 50 years, perceptions both that participation can make a difference in what government does (that is, voters' sense of "internal efficacy") and that government is responsive to the people ("external efficacy") have declined.** Many researchers have concluded that the decline in political efficacy,[35] which is accompanied by declines in political trust and in confidence in political institutions, has produced lower rates of voter turnout. As people come to feel that they are less able to influence the system and that the system is less responsive to them, they may become less likely to vote.

5. **Extensions of the franchise lead to short-term declines in turnout.** Ironically, events that have expanded the franchise have been followed by lower rates of voter turnout. Following passage of the Fifteenth Amendment in 1870, which enfranchised former male slaves, the turnout rate dropped in 1872; passage of the Nineteenth Amendment in 1920, granting women the right to vote, led to an overall drop in turnout; and passage of the Twenty-sixth Amendment in 1971 that lowered the voting age to 18 led to lower turnout rates. One explanation for this phenomenon is that many newly eligible voters are not yet registered to vote and may require some time and socialization to get into the habit of voting.

6. **Voting in the United States is not compulsory.** Some democracies, including the United States, regard the franchise as a right. Accordingly, citizens have the opportunity to exercise their right to vote or they may choose not to vote. By contrast, some democracies have compulsory voting laws requiring citizens to vote. These nations assert that voting is a citizen's responsibility. Belgium, in 1892, was the first country to adopt compulsory voting. According to the International Institute for Democracy and Electoral Assistance, 32 countries have compulsory voting laws on the books. Twenty-four countries enforce these laws to some degree, and of them, nine—Australia, Belgium, Cyprus, Fiji, Luxembourg, Nauru, Singapore, Switzerland, and Uruguay—have strict enforcement policies.

Punishments for not voting in countries with compulsory voting laws include large fines, possible imprisonment (although imprisonment is generally the punishment for not paying a fine), and disenfranchisement. In Belgium, individuals who do not vote in four elections over a 15-year period are stripped of their voting rights. In Bolivia, voters are given vouchers after they vote, and these vouchers are needed to receive a salary from a bank during a three-month period after an election. In Greece, it is very difficult to get a passport or driver's license without showing proof of having voted.

Many arguments can be made in favor of or against compulsory voting laws, but one thing is certain: countries with compulsory voting laws have much higher turnout rates than countries without such laws. In Italy, for example, where lists of nonvoters are publicized, turnout has been around 90 percent. Though compulsory voting laws certainly increase turnout, many critics argue that the right to vote implicitly

The Supreme Court and the Electoral Process

Bush v. Gore (2000)[36]

The presidential election of November 7, 2000, stands among the most hotly contested races in American history. After initially conceding the race late on election night to Texas Governor George W. Bush, Vice President Al Gore withdrew that concession just a short time later. Hanging in the balance were the 25 electoral votes of Florida: whichever candidate nabbed that prize would become the next president of the United States. With Bush leading Gore by just a few hundred votes, a series of recounts was initiated in counties throughout Florida. Not surprisingly, lawyers for Governor Bush attempted to stop the recounts, first by appeal to the Florida courts and then to the U.S. Supreme Court. Would the high Court interfere in state election procedures and stop the recounts? More than a month after Election Day, the public nervously awaited a final verdict on who would be sworn in as the nation's 43rd president in January.

The answer came on December 12, 2000. By a 5–4 vote, the Supreme Court held that determination of the controversy by proper, constitutionally valid recounts could not occur by the legal date required for reporting final electoral votes; accordingly all recounts had to be halted. (Seven of the nine justices agreed that the use of different counting standards in different counties violated the equal protection clause, but that larger bloc split 5–2 on the issue of whether there was enough time to correct the problem.) The media took special note of the Court's division: the five most conservative justices sided with the conservative Republican George W. Bush's position, while the four more liberal justices sided with the Democrat Al Gore. Regardless, the U.S. Supreme Court's ruling effectively made George W. Bush the president-elect. So much for what Alexander Hamilton predicted would be "the least dangerous branch" of government.

For Critical Thinking and Discussion

1. Should the courts ever interfere with a presidential election, and, if so, under what circumstances?
2. Are you bothered by the seemingly partisan lines dividing the Court? Does it make the final decision seem less legitimate?

---

includes the right not to vote, just as the right to practice the religion of one's choice also includes the right not to practice a religion.

7. **The decline in "social capital."** Political scientist Robert Putnam has noted a general decline in **social capital**, which is the extent to which individuals are socially integrated into their community.[37] Over the past half century, Americans have become less socially connected because they are not as likely to be members of organizations such as political parties, labor unions, civic groups, or even bowling leagues. As reasons for this decline, Putnam cites the increase of women in the workforce and corresponding reduction in the amount of time that women have available to spend on social and community activities. Other factors for the decline include the increase in residential mobility and technological innovations such as radio, television, and the Internet. People today are more likely to stay home and watch TV or surf the Internet and less likely to engage in social activities with other people. Voting is, in part, a social activity. The decline in social capital may be responsible, at least in part, for the general decline in voting.

> **social capital** The "social connectedness" of a community, or the extent to which individuals are socially integrated into their community.

Is Nonvoting a Problem?

Although turnout has declined, the American political culture encourages people to vote. Over the years, voting has evolved from a privilege offered to a relatively few number of people to a right enjoyed by all. The League of Women Voters, Common Cause, and other groups regularly engage in campaigns to increase voter registration and stimulate turnout on Election Day. Candidates often stress the importance of voting, and the nation's educational system promotes the values of exercising the franchise, even to those not yet of age to vote. Even the television station MTV invested time and money into the popular "Rock the Vote" campaign to encourage young people to vote. These efforts are predicated on the assumption that voting is important and that, conversely, nonvoting is problematic.

So to what extent is low voter turnout a problem in our democracy? Two main arguments support the contention that nonvoting is problematic. The first holds that low voter turnout rates are a symptom of a weak democracy. The essence of what makes a democracy is the link between what a majority of citizens prefer and those who are given the authority to govern. Voting is the mechanism that creates this link. With low turnout, majorities of all citizens do not rule. When barely 50 percent of eligible voters cast ballots, successful candidates can hardly claim to have captured majority support. George W. Bush won the 2000 presidential election, for example, but less than 25 percent of all American adults voted for him.

The second argument contends that low turnout awards distinct advantages to the affluent, higher-socioeconomic groups in our society. As we have seen, turnout rates are lower among less-educated and lower-income groups. Thus, nonvoting affords better-educated and wealthier groups of people more power in determining the winner of a political race.

There are also reasons, however, as to why nonvoting may not be a cause for concern. Perhaps nonvoting produces an electorate that is more informed, more aware of the important issues, and better able to make vote choices for the candidates who most deserve election to office. Former Senator Sam Ervin once said, "I don't think it's a problem that apathetic, lazy people don't vote." Voting simply for the sake of voting may not produce good choices. Although ideally all citizens should become informed and cast a vote based on their information, many people lack the capacity or interest to cast a truly meaningful vote.

Another reason why nonvoting may not be a problem rests on the premise that voting is a voluntary right, just as the rights of free speech, religious choice, and peaceful assembly are voluntary. Our society does not compel citizens to speak out on issues, to declare a religious affiliation, or to contribute time or money to any particular cause or political party. So why should it expect people to exercise their right to vote? Furthermore, for many people, nonvoting may be their expression of satisfaction with the status quo.

13-8 | Participation Beyond Voting

Participation in American politics extends far beyond the act of voting. As Figure 13-10 shows, many Americans volunteer to help out on political campaigns, contribute money to a candidate or party, try to influence others how to vote, and sign petitions endorsing a position on an issue. In addition, attending political rallies or participating in political protests are common ways of engaging in American politics.

One recent protest movement that gained a national following is the so-called Tea Party movement. Beginning in early 2009, a series of anti-tax protests emerged in response to the federal government's increase in spending to combat the economic recession. The Tea Party protests challenged the Barack Obama–Democratic Party policies of deficit spending and proposals to reform the nation's health care insurance system. The term *Tea Party* was chosen strategically to reference the Boston Tea Party, whose goal was to protest Britain's taxation policies toward the colonies during the American Revolutionary period. "TEA" is also used as an acronym for "taxed enough already." In addition to organizing protest rallies across the nation (annually on April 15, or "tax day," for example), Tea Party organizers were particularly active during the 2010 midterm elections and are credited with the large-scale GOP victories in the 2010 congressional contests.

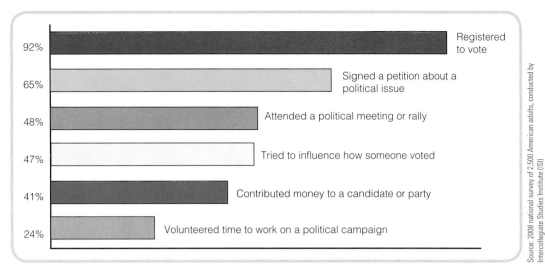

Source: 2008 national survey of 2,500 American adults, conducted by Intercollegiate Studies Institute (ISI)

FIGURE 13-10 **The Ways in Which Americans Participate in Politics**
Some of the more common methods of political participation, along with the percentage of Americans who have engaged in each type of activity.

Another protest movement that became popular in 2011 was the "Occupy Wall Street" protest movement. Beginning as a protest rally in New York City's financial district near Wall Street, many supporters of the movement organized rallies around the nation to voice their concerns about the growing division in economic equality between the top 1 percent of wealth and the remaining 99 percent. They blame the growing economic inequality on the greed and corruption of large financial institutions and demand reforms in public policy to reverse this inequality.

Protests can take one of three forms: legal protests in which citizens play by the "rules of the game" to speak out against a government policy, acts of nonviolent civil disobedience, and illegal protest activities that often include violence.

Marches, sit-ins, and rallies are forms of legal protests; such activities are designed to call attention to an issue that the protesters feel is not receiving adequate attention in the standard political process. Protesters are exercising their First Amendment right "peaceably to assemble, and to petition the Government for a redress of grievances." Many legal peaceful protests have raised awareness of an issue to a level that forces the normal legislative process to address it. A number of protest movements paved the way for substantial changes in public policy. Protests against the Vietnam War, for example, during the late 1960s and early 1970s led, in part, to American withdrawal from the Vietnam War. After World War I, protests among women's groups demanding the right of women to vote led to the adoption in 1920 of the Nineteenth Amendment granting women suffrage. Successful protests are often begun by small groups of individuals who feel strongly about an issue and are willing to spend the time and effort to make their case.

Protests make for good television because they generally feature conflict, a grievance, and individuals who are outspoken about the particular cause. Well-organized groups that engage in protests on hot-button issues, such as environmental groups, pro-life or pro-choice groups, and anti-death penalty groups, have become adept at informing the news media about the protests ahead of time and engaging articulate speakers to make their case. The media attention often provides protesters an opportunity to ensure that their causes reach the policy agenda of governing institutions.

The second type of protest behavior, *civil disobedience*, involves protesters engaged in illegal but nonviolent activity. The goal of the protesters is to break laws that they feel are unjust, and the protesters willingly accept the consequences for breaking the law. Blacks protesting segregation laws in the southern states during the 1950s and 1960s

Occupy Wall Street demonstrators march outside of the New York Stock Exchange in November 2011.

would intentionally break those laws as a way of drawing attention to the problem of segregation.

Finally, a third type of protest behavior involves violent protests. In 1992, a number of rioters in south central Los Angeles took to the streets after a jury acquitted several white police officers in a case where the officers had been caught on videotape brutally beating a black man they had stopped for a traffic violation. The rioters were protesting accusations of racial bias in the Los Angeles criminal justice system. The protesters looted businesses, stopped traffic, pulled a white truck driver out of his vehicle and severely beat him, and caused much damage to property.

The Founders never intended for a two-party system to take hold in the republic they so carefully designed; and yet two-party systems have dominated U.S. politics for over two centuries, beginning with the rivalry between Federalists and the Democratic-Republicans in the 1790s and extending all the way up to the present, in which Democrats and modern-day Republicans take turns controlling our government. Sometimes both major parties—despite all their built-in political advantages—lose touch with passionate strains of popular opinion. This is most likely to occur when the public grows increasingly skeptical about government as a whole. In such instances, an upstart political movement may suddenly arrive on the scene, connecting with the interests of a segment of the electorate that seeks a brand new means of influencing government. In the 1890s it was the "People's Party" (also known as the Populists) that made its voice heard; in 2010 and then again in 2014, the Tea Party movement lent its support to numerous anti-government candidates and helped to shift party control of Congress in the process. If history is a guide, those movements tend to be short-lived, exerting significant influence in a series of election cycles before one or both of the major parties bring the movement's energetic set of followers into their own party's fold. Will the major political party that is most successful in this regard be willing to incorporate the upstart movement's ideas into its policy agenda as well? That was the dilemma that faced the Democratic Party in the 1890s, and that faces the Republican Party today.

From Your Perspective

Youth Voting in 2012 and 2016 Made the Difference

Mitt Romney, the Republican nominee in 2012, decisively won the middle-aged and senior vote (i.e., age 30 and over). His problem was the youth vote (voters age 18 to 29), where he lost to President Barack Obama by an overwhelming 60 percent to 37 percent. A study by the Center for Information and Research on Civic Learning and Engagement at Tufts University (CIRCLE) found that youth voting for Obama in four key battleground states (Florida, Pennsylvania, Ohio, and Virginia) tipped the outcome to an Obama win. Without the youth block in those states, Romney would have taken them and thus the election.

In response to the study, Heather Smith, president of Rock the Vote, was quoted in politico.com as saying, "I think we've now established a fairly decent pattern that this generation is different from their older brothers and sisters, and we can put those rumors of apathy to bed." On a conference call with reporters, Smith added: "This voting bloc can no longer be an afterthought to any party or campaign."[38]

In 2016, Hillary Clinton won the 18 to 29 year old age group by an impressive margin of 55% to 37% over Donald Trump. Still the youth vote for Clinton was not large enough to impact the electoral college victory for Trump.

Voters in Hermosa Beach, California, wait to cast their ballots at a polling place in a lifeguard station.

For Critical Thinking and Discussion

1. Why do you think that President Obama so handily won the youth vote in 2012, and Hillary Clinton in 2016?
2. What issue positions and/or perspectives of young voters swayed them to these candidates?
3. What do you think about Heather Smith's comment regarding an established pattern that young voters today are different from their older cohorts? Was there a real difference in 2016?

Summary

13-1 The Development of Political Parties in the United States

- Despite the fact that the Founders frowned on political parties and did not plan for them in the Constitution, every presidential and congressional election since 1796 has featured some form of party competition. National party conventions and national party organization originated during Andrew Jackson's presidency. The Democratic and Republican Parties have dominated since 1856.

- Certain elections, such as those of 1860, 1896, and 1932, are considered "critical elections" because they produced sharp and lasting changes in patterns of party loyalty among voters. Some political scientists have termed the era since 1968 as a period of dealignment, characterized by a decline in voter attachment to parties and in clarity of party coalitions.

13-2 The Functions of Political Parties

- There are four primary functions of political parties: recruiting and nominating candidates to run for office, providing organization and resources to help win elections, providing structure for voters as they make vote choices, and running the government.

13-3 Why a Two-Party System?

- The U.S. party system has been dominated by Democrats and Republicans since the election of 1856. This two-party system is perpetuated by several factors, including the need for a majority of Electoral College votes (not just a plurality) to win the presidency outright and a winner-take-all system that makes it especially hard for third parties to succeed to any degree.

- Third-party candidates rarely attract a significant percentage of popular votes in presidential elections because voters perceive that votes for such a candidate would be wasted and because various legal barriers make it hard for third-party candidates to receive government funding.

13-4 Party Organizations

- The two major political parties have organizations at the national level, at the state level in all 50 states, and at the local level in most cities and towns across the nation. These organizations are active in developing party platforms, recruiting candidates to run for office, and providing financial support and other resources to aid the candidates electorally.

13-5 Are Parties in Decline?

- The decline of patronage and the prevalence of the direct primary election have contributed to the belief that parties are now in decline. Regardless, party identification remains an especially strong determinant of vote choice in America today.

13-6 Voting

- Traditionally, the states and not the federal government have had authority in running elections. However, state attempts to disenfranchise certain groups have been thwarted by constitutional amendments and federal laws. Although the goal of universal suffrage may not be fully realized today, over the centuries the United States has moved closer to this goal.

- The constitutional amendments that have limited states' ability to disenfranchise voters include the Fifteenth Amendment (guaranteeing African American men the franchise), Nineteenth Amendment (women's suffrage), Twenty-fourth Amendment (outlawing poll taxes), and Twenty-sixth Amendment (guaranteeing the vote to those eighteen years of age).

- States are responsible for maintaining a system of voter registration, and the systems vary widely from state to state. Only one state (North Dakota) does not require voters to register to vote as a prequalification to voting. Through the Motor Voter law, the federal government has tried to encourage higher levels of voter registration.

13-7 Exercising the Franchise

- Among the factors that have been identified as relating to a citizen's propensity to vote are interest in politics, sense of civic duty, the perception that one's vote can make a difference, level of education, level of income, age, and social group pressure. The nature of the times and type of political campaign can also influence turnout. High-stimulus elections, in which the issues are very important or the races are more visible, tend to produce higher voter turnout. Presidential elections generally promote the highest levels of turnout, and the less visible local races inspire the lowest levels of turnout.

- Although there has been a general declining trend in voter turnout in the United States over the past six or seven decades, recent presidential and midterm congressional elections have seen a modest increase in voting.
- Voter turnout in the United States tends to be lower than turnout in other democracies. Reasons that account for the lower U.S. turnout are the fact that there is no compulsory voting in the United States, the wide variation in states' voter registration requirements, the vast number of U.S. elections, and the tradition of holding elections on one weekday.

13-8 Participation Beyond Voting

- Americans participate in politics in many ways beyond voting, including contributing time and money, participating in rallies and protests, and contacting their elected officials.

Key Terms

critical election (p. 345)
dealignment (p. 346)
direct primary election (p. 357)
divided government (p. 351)
elections (p. 358)
Fifteenth Amendment (p. 359)
franchise (or suffrage) (p. 358)
literacy test (p.360)
Motor Voter law (p. 361)
multiparty system (p. 352)

national committee (p. 356)
national committee chair (p. 356)
national party convention (p. 344)
national party organization (p. 355)
Nineteenth Amendment (p. 360)
normal vote (p. 349)
party identification (p. 348)
party platform (p. 344)
political parties (p. 341)
poll tax (p. 360)

proportional representation (p. 352)
representative democracy (p. 358)
social capital (p. 369)
Twenty-fourth Amendment (p. 360)
Twenty-sixth Amendment (p. 360)
Twenty-third Amendment (p. 360)
two-party system (p. 352)
universal suffrage (p. 359)
voter turnout (p. 363)

Test Yourself

1. In 1796 and 1800, Thomas Jefferson ran for president as a candidate from which political party?

   a. Federalists

   b. Democratic-Republicans

   c. Republicans

   d. Whigs

2. The modern Democratic Party's first successful attempt to win the presidency occurred in

   a. 1796 with the victory of John Adams.

   b. 1824 with the victory of John Quincy Adams.

   c. 1828 with the victory of Andrew Jackson.

   d. 1932 with the victory of Franklin Roosevelt.

3. All of the following are considered to be critical realigning elections *except*

   a. Jefferson's victory in 1800.

   b. Lincoln's victory in 1860.

   c. McKinley's victory in 1896.

   d. Roosevelt's victory in 1932.

4. Distinguish between a "realigning" election and a "dealignment."

5. Party identification is measured by asking voters

   a. which party they are registered with.

   b. whether they belong to a third party.

   c. which party best represents their issue preferences.

   d. which party they support.

6. The condition when American government is characterized by split-party control of Congress and the presidency is known as

   a. gridlock government.

   b. partisan government.

   c. divided government.

   d. locked government.

7. What are the implications of the "normal vote" concept for presidential candidates as they try to develop winning strategies?

8. Governments that rely on proportional representation as a means of selecting a national legislature and ruling government most typically have what type of party system?

   a. Single-party system

   b. Two-party system

   c. Multiparty system

   d. No party system

9. The most successful third party in U.S. presidential election history, whose candidate received more votes than the Republican Party candidate, was

   a. Ross Perot's Reform Party in 1996.

   b. Ralph Nader's Green Party in 2000.

   c. Theodore Roosevelt's Bull Moose Party in 1912.

   d. George Wallace's American Independent Party in 1968.

10. What are the factors that contribute to the fact that the United States is dominated by a two-party model?

11. In the modern era of elections, which level of party organization has the *least* amount of influence in nominating candidates for office?

    a. National parties

    b. State parties

    c. County/parish parties

    d. Local parties

12. Which of the following makes it easier for candidates to bypass the parties in a pathway to the party nomination?

    a. Party caucuses

    b. Direct primary elections

    c. Political party machines

    d. State election laws

13. What evidence has been used recently to suggest that political parties are not in a state of decline?

14. Which amendment to the U.S. Constitution declares "[t]he right of citizens of the United States to vote shall not be denied or abridged by the United States or by any State on account of race, color, or previous condition of servitude"?

    a. Tenth Amendment

    b. Thirteenth Amendment

    c. Fifteenth Amendment

    d. Twentieth Amendment

15. The 1857 U.S. Supreme Court ruling that slaves were property and could not become legal citizens of the United States, thus precipitating the Civil War, was

    a. *Scott v. Sandford.*

    b. *Plessy v. Ferguson.*

    c. *McCulloch v. Maryland.*

    d. *Brown v. Board of Education.*

16. What is the "Motor Voter" law, and how does it improve voter registration?

17. Members of which one of the following demographic groups are most likely to turn out to vote in an election?

    a. Men

    b. Women

    c. 18- to 24-year-olds

    d. 65- to 75-year-olds

18. Which of the following is *not* an example of a "high-stimulus" election?

    a. A race believed to be very close

    b. A presidential race

    c. A mayoral race

    d. A race with a high level of media coverage

19. What are the explanations for why voter turnout in the United States tends to be lower than voter turnout in other democracies?

1. b. (LO 13-1); 2. c. (LO 13-1); 3. a. (LO 13-1); 5. d. (LO 13-2); 6. c. (LO 13-2); 8. c. (LO 13-3); 9. c. (LO 13-3); 11. a. (LO 13-4); 12. b. (LO 13-5); 14. c. (LO 13-6); 15. a. (LO 13-6); 17. d. (LO 13-7); 18. c. (LO 13-7)

LEARNING OBJECTIVES

14

Campaigns and Elections

The U.S. Constitution calls for a presidential election every four years and congressional elections every two years. Without skipping a beat, the United States has met this constitutional requirement for more than two centuries. Through a Civil War, two world wars, and several major economic depressions, elections—the hallmark of American democracy—have taken place like clockwork. In designing this representative democracy, the Founders intended a system that demanded accountability from elected officials. Elections for president and Congress provide this accountability. Regular and free elections are the linchpin underlying democracy in America. Every year Americans are invited to cast ballots in elections for many local, county, and statewide races, but no election receives more attention than the race for the presidency.

Who Did You Vote For in the 2016 Presidential Election?

WHO ARE YOU?

Was it Republican Donald Trump? Democrat Hillary Clinton? Libertarian Gary Johnson? Or the Green Party's Jill Stein? The race between Trump and Clinton was very close: Clinton took 48% of the vote and Trump earned 47% (Trump won because he won more electoral votes than Clinton). While their percentages are small, Johnson received over 4 million votes and Stein got more than one million.

Are you a "typical" Trump or Clinton voter? Thanks to the exit polls, we know quite a bit about the kinds of people who voted for each of the major party candidates. Clinton did much better among younger voters and Trump did better with men. White voters were more likely to opt for Trump while non-whites mostly supported Clinton. 18 to 29 year old whites tended to vote for the Republican, while African Americans in that age group overwhelmingly picked Clinton.

Democrat Hillary Clinton

Republican Donald Trump

- Who did you vote for in the 2016 presidential election?
- Answer the question, then take a look at the exit poll breakdowns and see if you are a "typical" or "atypical" Trump or Clinton voter.

To see how your answers compare to others, take the **Who Are You?** poll in MindTap!

14-1 | American Presidential Elections in Historical Perspective

The U.S. Constitution says nothing about the process by which individuals become candidates for the presidency. The Founders assumed that electors, chosen by the states (and heavily influenced by the House of Representatives), would identify and evaluate potential candidates, and then the electoral college would select the chief executive.[1] The selection of president was intended to be the product of a select group of rational, wise men making choices at a lofty level above partisan politics.

Although their intentions for presidential selection were noble, the Founders' expectations about how a president would actually be chosen proved to be quite naïve. Political parties have provided the framework for every presidential election since 1796. Each of the two major parties holds nomination contests in the 50 states to select the party's candidate in the general election; the party nominees then compete in the general election.

The modern presidential selection process is long and complex. The manner in which the 2016 selection process occurred is not based on some elaborate constitutional design. Rather, this complicated and quirky process is the result of more than 225 years of evolution. Over the years, two distinct phases of the presidential selection process have developed: the nomination phase and the general election phase.

The Nomination Phase

In the nomination phase, the political parties select specific people to run as the presidential and vice presidential candidates in the general election. This duo is referred to as the *party ticket*. The Constitution did not account for a nomination phase because the Founders did not anticipate that a two-party system would emerge. The first two presidential elections did not even include political parties. Rather, the electors from the states all agreed that George Washington should be president in 1789 and again in 1792. Nevertheless, divisions within the federal government erupted and political alliances began to form during Washington's administration. These alliances resulted in the first two major political parties, the Federalists and their opponents, who eventually became known as the Democratic-Republicans. In 1796, when Washington decided not to seek a third term, each of these parties sought to win the presidency by recruiting and supporting candidates.[2]

The Federalists in Congress supported John Adams and the Democratic-Republicans threw their support to Thomas Jefferson. Electors, who were largely chosen by state legislatures, followed the cues of their partisan leadership in casting their electoral votes, and Adams, the Federalist-supported candidate, won the general election with 71 electoral votes, whereas Jefferson received 68 electoral votes. The nomination process in 1796 reflected a significant level of party discipline in the casting of ballots among electors. In the elections of 1800, 1804, and 1808, both the Federalists and the Democratic-Republicans used informal meetings and discussions to choose a party nominee. Democratic-Republicans dominated electoral politics from 1812 through 1828, as the Federalist Party eventually disappeared.

In 1824, however, a significant split occurred within the Democratic-Republican Party. Andrew Jackson, who had the support of many common people, challenged party favorite John Quincy Adams. Jackson won both the popular vote and a plurality of the electoral vote, but no candidate received a majority of electoral votes. By constitutional provision, the election was sent to the House of Representatives, which voted Adams the victor. Jackson then founded a new party, the Democratic Party,[3] which is, of course, one of the two major parties still in existence today. Jackson and his followers believed in the enfranchisement of all white men, rather than just the propertied class—during what became known as the Jacksonian era, white male suffrage was dramatically expanded throughout the country. Specifically, more and more state political parties adopted open caucuses, in which party members formally met to provide input as to who their party should nominate for elective office.

Electoral reforms during the Progressive Era of the early 1900s opened participation in the nomination process to a greater number of Americans. The direct primary gave voters an opportunity to cast a ballot for delegates, who would in turn be sent to a national convention for the purpose of choosing a presidential nominee. The state of Florida was the first to hold a direct primary in a presidential election, in 1900. Although direct primaries did allow greater numbers of people the opportunity to help select delegates, until the 1960s it was still the political elite of a party (governors, mayors, party chairs, and other

Latino candidates make their mark on the 2016 GOP nomination race. Two of the earliest contestants in the race for the Republican Party's nomination were Florida Senator Marco Rubio (left) and Texas Senator Ted Cruz (right).

AP Photo

officials) that selected most of the delegates and thus had the most input in choosing the party's presidential nominee.

The political unrest of the 1960s, spurred by anti-Vietnam War activism, led to further changes that gave voters in primaries even more weight in selecting party nominees. Benefiting from the increased percentage of convention delegates chosen through open primaries, Jimmy Carter, the little-known governor of Georgia, won the Democratic Party's nomination in 1976. A political outsider, Carter was able to appeal directly to average voters. Carter not only won the nomination, but he also went on to win the presidency that year. His victory demonstrated to candidates in both the Democratic Party and the Republican Party that securing sufficient numbers of delegates to win the nomination requires direct appeals to voters, whether through party caucuses or, more likely, through party primary contests. Today this pattern persists: to win a party's nomination, a candidate must win a majority of delegates who are primarily chosen by voters in the state primaries and caucuses.

The General Election Phase

The unanticipated emergence of political parties not only established a party nomination process, but it also forced a change in the Founders' design for the electoral college. The Founders intended the state legislatures to pick well-qualified "electors," who would meet on a specified day in their state to decide who was the best choice to become president. At the end of the day, these electors would then cast votes for president. The states then sent their vote totals to the president of the U.S. Senate (the sitting vice president), who counted the votes before Congress. The candidate with a majority of votes became president and the second-place finisher became vice president. If no one candidate received a majority of the votes, the election was to be decided by the House of Representatives, with each state delegation having one vote to select the new president. The Senate was to select the vice president.

In the 1800 presidential race, nearly all of the Federalists voted for John Adams and Charles Pinckney (65 and 64 votes, respectively), and all of the Democratic-Republicans voted for Jefferson and Aaron Burr, each of whom received 73 votes. Although it was generally agreed that Jefferson was the leader of the Democratic-Republican ticket, Burr challenged Jefferson in the House (because the election was a tie, the House state delegations had to choose the new president). Ultimately, the House decided in favor of Jefferson, who became president, with Burr then becoming vice president. It was clear that the presidential election system needed fixing.[4]

The Twelfth Amendment to the Constitution, passed in 1804, provided for separate balloting for president and vice president by requiring that electors designate one of their two votes for president and the second of their two votes for vice president. This amendment greatly reduced the possibility that future elections would end in a tie.

Several other amendments to the Constitution have altered the presidential selection process. The Twenty-second Amendment, ratified in 1951, limits presidents to two 4-year terms in office (or 10 years if a vice president serves out the term of a president). The Twenty-third Amendment, ratified in 1961, provides the District of Columbia with three electoral votes. Because the District is not a state, it previously had no electoral votes.

The modern presidential selection system, then, is an amalgamation of the Founders' design, modified by constitutional amendments and changes that occurred over time. This all makes for a complex system of picking a president. Although there are many caveats and exceptions to the rules, the contemporary presidential selection process generally consists of five stages:

1. **The prenomination campaign.** After a new president is selected, potential candidates for the next presidential election (four years hence) begin to explore the

possibility of running. The ability to raise money, garner support from key leaders in the party, and attract the attention of the news media all contribute to each candidate's decision of whether to enter the race.

2. **The nomination campaign.** From January through June of the presidential election year, parties in each state hold either a primary or caucus (a handful of states actually hold both) in which the party delegates from the state commit to candidates. Each party has different criteria for allocating the number of delegates that a state will get. The candidate who receives a majority of delegates wins the party nomination.

3. **The national conventions.** Each political party holds a national convention during the summer to showcase its candidate. Prior to the convention, the party nominees select their vice presidential running mates. Although the conventions used to play an important role in defining the party platform and selecting the party's nominee, today the conventions are largely publicity events for the ticket and other stars in the party, as well as an opportunity to critique the opposing party.

4. **The general election campaign.** Because national party conventions today generally affirm rather than choose party nominees, presidential candidates usually begin waging their general election campaigns before the conventions, as soon as it becomes clear who the two major-party nominees will be. (These decisions generally occur in the spring of the election year.) Most recent campaigns have included a series of televised debates between the presidential and the vice presidential candidates, a significant amount of advertising and campaigning in key states, and, more recently, strong efforts to appeal to voters through the social media.

5. **The electoral college decision.** The winner of the presidential election is decided on the basis of the vote count in the electoral college. The number of electoral votes for each state is equivalent to the state's allotment of House members plus two (for the state's two U.S. senators). In all but two states, the candidate who wins the popular vote automatically receives all of the electoral votes from that state. (Currently in Maine and Nebraska, the votes for president are counted for each congressional district; candidates get one elector for each district they win, and the candidate who wins the state overall gets an additional two electors.) Nationwide, the candidate who receives an outright majority of electoral votes wins the election.

14-2 | The Prenomination Campaign

Although the presidential campaign officially begins with the first state contest for delegates in January of the election year, the real campaign for president actually begins much earlier, soon after the previous presidential election has concluded. As part of the **prenomination campaign**, behind-the-scenes candidates who are thinking about making a run often begin to "test the waters" by talking to party insiders, shoring up early commitments of support, lining up a campaign staff, beginning a fund-raising operation, traveling around the country making speeches and appearances, setting up "exploratory committees" to assess the feasibility of making a formal declaration of official candidacy, and then making the official announcement. Shortly after the 2012 election, for example, former Secretary of State Hillary Clinton, New Jersey Governor Chris Christie, and former Florida Governor Jeb Bush, among others, all established exploratory committees and began testing the waters to wage a bid for their party's nomination.

The prenomination campaign also marks the beginning of the "weeding-out" process. Early on, many would-be candidates find insufficient support from party insiders. Others cannot raise sufficient funds to be competitive. Some tire too quickly of the arduous and time-consuming schedule necessary for launching a run for the presidency.

prenomination campaign The political season in which candidates for president begin to explore the possibility of running by attempting to raise money and garner support.

Patrick T. Fallon/Bloomberg/Getty Images

Prior to the Iowa caucus in 2016, 17 candidates sought the GOP nomination, a field so large that organizers split the first GOP debate: an "undercard" for the bottom 8 in the polls, and the "main event" in primetime featuring the top nine (pictured above).

invisible primary The competition among candidates seeking the party nomination for frontrunner status prior to the primaries and caucuses.

presidential primary A statewide election to select delegates who will represent a state at the party's national convention.

open primary An election that allows voters to choose on the day of the primary election the party in which they want to vote.

closed primary An election that requires voters to declare their party affiliation ahead of time.

caucus A method of choosing party nominees in which party members attend local meetings at which they choose delegates committed to a particular candidate.

These and other obstacles begin the process of narrowing the field of candidates.

The **invisible primary** is the competition between candidates seeking the party nomination for frontrunner status. A candidate gains frontrunner status by winning broad support from important people within the party, raising more money than others, and achieving the top position in the public polls conducted by leading news organizations. Frontrunners tend to receive more coverage in the news, thus promoting their name recognition and popularity as candidates. The 2016 prenomination process began with 17 Republican candidates and 5 Democrats. By the time the first of the primaries was being held, the number of viable candidates had already been whittled down to 3 Democrats and 5 Republicans.

14-3 | The Nomination Campaign

The invisible primary may go a long way toward winnowing the field down to a handful of realistic contenders for major-party nominations. Still, contenders for the party nomination must ultimately deliver victories in state primaries and caucuses or risk seeing their financial and volunteer support dry up in a hurry. Given the reduced importance of party conventions in influencing nomination decisions in the modern era, success in the early primaries and caucuses is crucial.

Primaries and Caucuses

The nomination of a candidate by a political party is the product of state-to-state contests in which delegates are committed to those candidates seeking the party's nomination. There are two basic methods by which states allocate delegates: presidential primary elections and caucuses.[5] A **presidential primary** is a statewide election to select delegates who will represent a state at the party's national convention.[6] In this election, voters choose among delegates who are committed to a particular candidate. The delegates who win go to the national convention and cast their vote for a party nominee to run in the general election. In 2016, 45 states used the presidential primary method of delegate selection. There are two types of primaries held by states. The less common approach is the **open primary**,[7] in which voters can show up at the voting booth on the primary Election Day and declare whether they want to vote in the Democratic Party primary or the Republican Party primary; they then cast their vote in the primary they have chosen. A **closed primary**[8] election, by contrast, requires voters to declare a party affiliation ahead of time. When the voters show up to vote on primary Election Day, they are eligible to vote only in the party in which they are registered. Many states that use the closed primary have modified their requirements by allowing voters who have previously declared no party affiliation to show up at the polls on Election Day and declare a party, and thus vote in that party's primary.

A handful of states, including Iowa, Nevada, and Maine, do not hold presidential primary elections; instead they use the caucus method to select delegates for the national party convention. In the **caucus** method, party members are invited to attend local meetings at which they choose delegates who make a commitment to a

"It Was the Most Negative Campaign in the History of American Presidential Elections"

President Barack Obama famously proclaimed that "Elections have consequences." Certainly politicians of all stripes pour in considerable time, effort and money into presidential campaigns in hopes that those consequences will be favorable ones. Often the stakes in election outcomes are so high and the will to win so strong that campaigns take a negative tone. Living through a negative campaign can leave voters with the sense that "politics has never been so negative." However, the reality is that in the history of American presidential elections, campaigns are often quite negative.

Then

In 1828, incumbent John Quincy Adams, the sixth president of the U.S., was embroiled in an intense re-match against Andrew Jackson, a general and war hero. Jackson had won a plurality of votes in the 1824 race, and enjoyed a slight edge over Adams in the Electoral College count as well. Yet because Jackson did not achieve a majority within the Electoral College, the race was thrown into the House of Representatives where a questionable behind-the-scenes deal led to Adams winning the presidency. Four years later the stakes were high, as the United States economy was struggling. Debates over tariffs in international trade were especially intense, and the tone of the campaign turned negative. At one point Adams called Jackson's wife "a convicted adultress" and his mother "a common prostitute." Jackson responded by accusing Adams of having premarital sex with his wife and acting as a pimp. Voters in 1828 were left with the feeling that politics could not get much worse. Many involved in that campaign were not around to see the highly negative campaign of 1800 waged between two of America's founding fathers.

"Jackson is to be President. and you will be HANGED."

A cartoon during the 1828 campaign, accusing Andrew Jackson of lynching his opponents.

Now

We all lived through **the 2016 campaign**—few of us will soon forget the negative, bitter tone that was reported by the media on a near daily basis. America's intense ideological divide over Obamacare, taxes, immigration and the war on terrorism fueled this negativity. At one point in the campaign Hillary Clinton referred to Donald Trump supporters as "a basket of deplorables," adding that they are "sexist, racist, homophobic, xenophobic, islamophobic" people. Trump, for his part fueled the negativity with claims that "Bill Clinton has actually abused women and Hillary has bullied, attacked, shamed and intimidated his victims." To be sure, the 2016 campaign was filled with vitriolic and personal attacks, but it was one of many such negative elections in American history.

US President-elect Donald Trump arrives at his celebration party on November 8, 2016.

candidate for the party nomination. These delegates in turn attend more regionalized meetings and select delegates from that group. Depending on the size of the state and the number of regions, this process continues until a slate of delegates attends a statewide convention, or caucus. At this statewide caucus, attendees again vote for a slate of delegates, who are committed to a candidate, to send to the party's national convention.

The first state contest for delegates, normally the Iowa caucus, launches the process by which delegates from the states commit to candidates for the party nomination. About one week after the Iowa caucus comes the New Hampshire

Harold Stassen holds the record for most attempts to win a party nomination—10. Stassen, a Republican governor of Minnesota, first attempted to win the Republican nomination in 1948. His 10th and final attempt was in 1992. In only two elections (1956 and 1972) between his first and last attempts was Stassen not a contender for the Republican nomination. Pictured here are Stassen supporters at the 1948 Republican convention.

nomination campaign The political season in which the two major parties hold primaries and caucuses in all the states to choose party delegates committed to specific candidates.

frontloading The recent trend of states moving their primaries and caucuses to earlier in the year to attract greater attention from the candidates and the media.

primary,[9] which has traditionally been the first state primary election in which delegates commit to candidates.[10] Each of the 50 states (along with the District of Columbia, the U.S. Virgin Islands, American Samoa, and Guam) holds either a caucus or primary election, and in each of these contests delegates commit to candidates. The calendar of state caucuses and primaries, beginning in February and extending into June, is referred to as the nomination campaign. Through the **nomination campaign**, a candidate attempts to win a majority of delegates in the caucus and primary contests to lay claim to be the winner of the party's nomination.

The Traditional Importance of the Iowa and New Hampshire Contests

Iowa and New Hampshire are small states with relatively few delegates. The Iowa caucus in 2016 had just 28 delegates at stake, and the 2016 New Hampshire primary had a mere 23 delegates at stake. To win the nomination campaign, the successful Republican candidate needed to amass support from at least 2,137 total delegates. In pure delegate count, larger states, such as California with 170 delegates and New York with 95, are, of course, much more important. Why, then, do Iowa and New Hampshire enjoy such disproportionately great influence in the nomination process? The answer is timing: Iowa and New Hampshire have traditionally been the first two contests held. The news media thus focus a tremendous amount of attention on these initial competitions. Winners of the Iowa and New Hampshire contests receive a great amount of attention in the news, whereas losers tend to get written off as "unelectable."

The importance of the early contests has led to a phenomenon known as **frontloading**,[11] a trend that has occurred over the past six or seven presidential elections in which states have moved their primary or caucus contests earlier in the year to attract greater attention from the candidates and the media. A state that holds its contest early makes itself more important in the nominee selection process. In 1988, the time between the Iowa caucus and the date by which most states had chosen their convention delegates was more than 20 weeks.

In 2016, most delegates from both parties were selected within a six-week period, from early February to late March.

In 2012 and 2016, both major political parties agreed to stall, if not reverse, the frontloading process. Thus, no primary or caucus occurred prior to the Iowa caucuses held

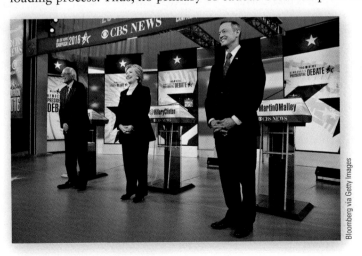

Senator Bernie Sanders (left), Secretary Hillary Clinton (center) and Governor Martin O'Malley (right) pose for photos prior to a debate held just a few days before the 2016 Iowa Caucuses.

on February 1. States that allocated their delegates proportionate to the vote outcome were permitted to hold contests as early as the first Tuesday in March, as a way to encourage greater voter turnout. States that allocated all delegates to the contest winner (the "winner-take-all" states) were allowed to hold contests beginning on the first Tuesday in April. This plan was intended to spread out the primaries and caucuses, giving candidates more time to campaign in more states, and at the same time preserve the unique role that Iowa and New Hampshire have played in the nomination process.

For the 2016 Democratic Party nomination, Hillary Clinton, Vermont Senator Bernie Sanders, former Maryland Governor Martin O'Malley, former Virginia Governor Jim Webb, and former Rhode Island Senator and Governor Lincoln Chaffee all threw their hats in the ring early on. All but Clinton and Sanders dropped out shortly after the primaries began. Sanders stayed in the race until the last of the primaries, but fell short of Clinton by a final tally of 2,807 to 1,894 delegates.

Senator Marco Rubio (left), Donald Trump (center) and Senator Ted Cruz were 3 of the 5 Republicans whose campaigns survived to Super Tuesday on March 1, 2016.

On the GOP side, fully 17 candidates entered the race. By March of 2016, five candidates had survived: billionaire real estate developer Donald Trump, Texas Senator Ted Cruz, Ohio Governor John Kasich, Florida Senator Marco Rubio, and former Florida Governor Jeb Bush. Though dismissed by most pundits initially, Trump campaigned furiously against the GOP establishment and appealed to frustrated Republican voters who had elected large majorities to Congress, only to be stymied by the Democratic president. Trump's message gained steam as the campaign wore on, and by June of 2016 he had secured enough delegates to take the nomination.

The Nominating Conventions

The national conventions for the Democratic and Republican Parties were once used to discuss the party platform and, most important, to choose the candidate who would represent the party in the general election. The images of the smoke-filled back rooms where deals were cut and delegates were lobbied to throw their support behind a particular candidate were very real. For most of our nation's history, the major parties selected candidates for the presidency in this way. Much of the brokering and deal making took place by skilled political operators at the national conventions.

The 1968 Democratic national convention, held in Chicago, was characterized by a great deal of divisiveness and discord, much of which was captured on national network television. Vietnam War protesters outside of the convention hall were beaten by Chicago police under the direction of Chicago mayor and "political boss" Richard J. Daley. Tension reigned inside the convention center as well, with antiwar supporters of Eugene McCarthy and George McGovern clashing with the party regulars supporting Hubert Humphrey. Television brought the negative images of the divided Democratic Party into American homes, seriously damaging the Democratic ticket. Four years later, television coverage again captured a disunited Democratic Party at the national convention in Miami, where delegates fought into the wee hours of the morning to nominate a party candidate (George McGovern finally won the nomination). The Democrats were not the only party to suffer discord and division. In 1976, grassroots support for Ronald Reagan spoiled any momentum incumbent President Gerald Ford hoped to generate at the Republican national convention.

By the mid-1980s, both major political parties, recognizing the influential role that television was playing in election politics, had begun to adjust their agenda for the

Chicago has been a frequent host to national party conventions. Twenty-five national conventions have been held in the Windy City, 11 Democratic and 14 Republican. The second most frequent hosting city is Baltimore, which has seen 10 conventions. The 1968 Democratic convention in Chicago was characterized by violent protests over the Vietnam War.

national conventions. With the frontloading process allowing candidates to capture a majority of delegates prior to the national convention, the parties began to choreograph their conventions and use them as advertisements for the party ticket. Today's conventions tend to avoid airing any intraparty differences. Instead, they are "anointing" ceremonies for the party ticket. They feature popular members of the party endorsing the nominees and include prerecorded videos highlighting the nominees' record of public service and family values.[12]

The 2016 GOP and Democratic nominating conventions were important political events. Rather than playing a crucial role in selecting the party nominee and debating the policy positions of the party, however, these conventions provided a week-long forum for the parties and their nominees to introduce themselves to voters and to formally kick off the general election campaign.

The Democrats held their convention in Philadelphia. Prime time speakers were fiery liberal Senator Elizabeth Warren, First Lady Michelle Obama, President Obama, Vice President Joe Biden, President Bill Clinton and Senator Bernie Sanders. A number of popular performers appeared, including Alicia Keys, Paul Simon, Katy Perry and Lenny Kravitz. The convention provided Clinton with a 7% bounce in the polls.

The GOP convention was held in Cleveland, Ohio, and was less unified than the Democratic convention. A number of high profile Republicans did not attend, including most of Donald Trump's sixteen primary competitors. His most serious challenger,

Hillary Clinton, appearing at the 2016 Democratic National Convention, accepts the Party's nomination.

Ted Cruz, spoke at the convention but refused to endorse Trump. Still, family members and other who spoke on Trump's behalf provided a short-lived 4% bounce in the polls.

14-4 | The General Election Campaign

A number of factors provide context for understanding general election campaigns in the American political system. These include whether or not an incumbent is running, the candidate's pick for the number-two spot on the ticket, the strategy for achieving a winning coalition of states, the presidential debates, political advertisements, and, finally, the vote in the electoral college.

Incumbent Race versus Open Election

General election campaigns for president are highly visible, very well funded, and among the most noteworthy of events in the American political system. Sometimes the contest is an **incumbent race** pitting a sitting president against a challenger, such as the 2012 contest between President Obama and challenger Mitt Romney. In an incumbent race, the focus of the campaign tends to revolve around the performance of the incumbent over the past four years. In this sense, incumbent races are often viewed as a referendum on the performance of the current occupant of the White House.

incumbent race General election race pitting a person currently holding the office against a challenger.

In all, there have been 11 incumbents who lost their bids for another term. Five of these incumbent losses occurred over the past 100 years: in 1912 Woodrow Wilson defeated President William Howard Taft; in 1932 Franklin Delano Roosevelt defeated President Herbert Hoover; in 1976 Jimmy Carter defeated President Gerald R. Ford; in 1980 Ronald Reagan beat President Carter; and in 1992 Bill Clinton defeated President George H. W. Bush.

In **open elections**, neither candidate is an incumbent. In 2016, for example, President Barack Obama was constitutionally prohibited from running for a third term. Former First Lady, U.S. senator and Secretary of State Hillary Clinton was the Democratic Party's nominee, and billionaire businessman Donald Trump was the Republican Party's candidate in the general election. Clinton took credit for her work in the Obama administration and Trump criticized Clinton's association with Obama. However, the focus of the race was more on the personality characteristics (and flaws) of these two candidates with far less discussion of President Obama's record.

open election General election race in which neither candidate is the incumbent. (Open elections for Congress are normally called *open-seat elections*.)

A charismatic Democratic Governor from a Southern state, Bill Clinton (with then-Arkansas First Lady Hillary Clinton), would defeat incumbent George H.W. Bush in 1992 and serve two terms as the 42nd president.

Mark Reinstein / Getty Images

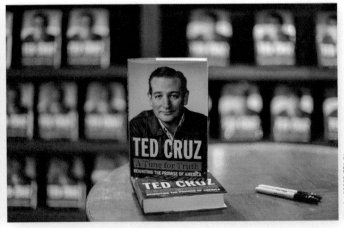

In recent decades a number of presidential candidates have authored books as a way of bringing attention to their candidacies. Among the authors contending in the 2016 race were Hillary Clinton and Ted Cruz.

The Choice of a Vice Presidential Candidate

Another important aspect of campaign strategy is the selection of the vice presidential running mate. Significant amounts of thought and fanfare go into this selection. Vice presidential candidates are quite visible on the campaign trail and can provide a boost to the ticket. The choice of running mate often attempts to balance the ticket geographically; John Edwards, for example, was from the southern state of North Carolina, a factor deemed important by the 2004 Democratic nominee, John Kerry, who was from Massachusetts, a New England state. Vice presidential candidates are often chosen on the basis of their ideological leanings. In 1980 Ronald Reagan selected George H. W. Bush as his running mate in part because Reagan was viewed as far to the political right and needed a running mate who was more moderate. By contrast, the more moderate Bob Dole chose the ideologically conservative Jack Kemp as his choice for vice president in 1996 to mobilize conservative Republican voters, as did Donald Trump with his selection of Indiana Governor Mike Pence in 2016.

Governor Mike Pence of Indiana (right) disagrees with Senator Tim Kaine of Virginia at the 2016 debate between the two major party hopefuls for Vice President. Vice Presidents in the modern era have played increasingly influential roles as policy makers in government.

Much of the scrutiny that surrounds the selection of a vice presidential running mate is negative, as some have turned out to be significant liabilities for the ticket. In 1972, when it was revealed that Senator Thomas Eagleton had been hospitalized for nervous exhaustion and had received electroshock therapy, an embarrassed George McGovern quickly replaced him on the ticket with the former U.S. Ambassador to France, Sargent Shriver. Similarly, it became clear in 1988 that George H. W. Bush's selection of Dan Quayle as his running mate was problematic after disclosure of Quayle's attempts to avoid the military draft during the Vietnam War. Bush kept Quayle on the ticket, however, and went on to win the 1988 election. Many observers questioned George W. Bush's decision to keep Vice President Dick Cheney on the ticket in 2004, given the perception that Cheney was the driving influence behind the decision for early and swift American military action in Iraq, where weapons of mass destruction were never found.

In 2008, John McCain's selection of the relatively unknown Alaska governor, 44-year-old Sarah Palin, earned him plaudits from social conservatives. But the choice also led to excessive scrutiny of McCain's choice after Palin stumbled in several interviews with the mainstream media. Palin was also regarded by some as being too inexperienced to sit just "a heartbeat away" from the presidency. By comparison, Barack Obama's selection of Senator Joseph Biden of Delaware received relatively little scrutiny.

In 2012, Mitt Romney selected Wisconsin Representative Paul Ryan as his running mate. Ryan, the chair of the House Budget Committee, was an outspoken critic of the Obama administration's handling of the national debt crisis, a cornerstone position of the Romney campaign.

In 2016, Democrat Presidential nominee Hillary Clinton selected as her running mate Senator Tim Kaine of Virginia. This choice was at least in part based on Kaine's reputation as a moderate Democrat (thus appealing to Independent voters) and the fact that he was popular in the battleground state of Virginia, where he had once served as Governor. Republican Donald Trump selected Governor Mike Pence of Indiana. Pence's popularity among social conservatives served as the basis for this choice, along with the fact that Pence had plenty of experience in elective office (something Trump lacked).

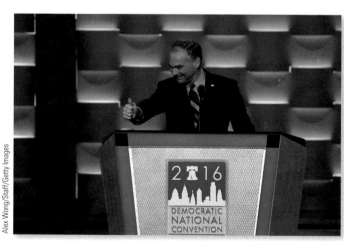

U.S. Senator Tim Kaine of Virginia, the Vice Presidential choice of Democrat Hillary Clinton in 2016.

Governor Mike Pence of Indiana, Donald Trump's running mate in 2016.

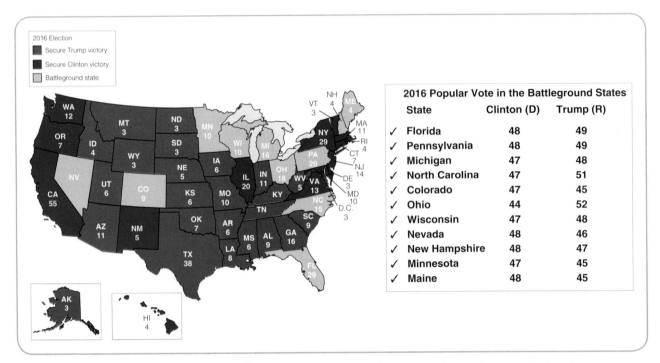

FIGURE 14-1 **Top Battleground States in 2016** In the presidential campaign of 2016, the vast majority of states saw relatively little activity in terms of candidate appearances and television advertising. Instead, the candidates for both major parties targeted a few select states for concentrated activity. They spent most of their resources of time and money on these battleground states because, as each candidate knew well ahead of time, these were where the election outcome would be decided.

Gathering a Winning Coalition of States

A central feature of any general election campaign is each candidate's plan to put together a coalition of states sufficient to win a majority of electoral votes. At the outset of the campaign, states may be divided into three categories: reliably Republican states, reliably Democratic states, and the so-called **battleground** (or "swing") **states**, those that either candidate has a reasonable chance of winning. The map in Figure 14-1 (above) depicts this categorization of states for the 2016 presidential campaign. The blue states were considered safely Democratic and the red were considered safely Republican; the gold states were the ones up for grabs.

In 2016 both the Republican nominee, Donald Trump, and the Democratic nominee, Hillary Clinton, set their sights on 11 battleground states (see Figure 14-1): Colorado, Florida, Minnesota, Michigan, Nevada, New Hampshire, Maine, North Carolina, Ohio, Pennsylvania, and Wisconsin. Trump won six of them and five went to Clinton. The six that went for Trump were the larger states, and so his path to electoral college victory included the large number of electoral votes in these swing states. Interestingly, in four of the six, Trump's margin of victory was one percentage point or less.

The Presidential Debates

The media and the public have come to expect that a presidential campaign will feature debates between the presidential candidates, and sometimes between the vice presidential candidates as well. Candidates may not believe it is in their strategic

battleground states States identified as offering either major-party candidate a reasonable chance for victory in the electoral college.

interest to debate their opponents (for example, a candidate who is ahead in the polls might prefer to play it safe and not run the risk of losing a debate and perhaps the lead in the campaign). Still, both major-party candidates usually agree to debate so that they aren't portrayed as being afraid to do so. The expectation of a set of debates, however, is a relatively recent phenomenon in presidential elections. The first debates that generated a high level of interest and scrutiny were those between John F. Kennedy and Richard M. Nixon in the 1960 election campaign. Some political scientists today credit Kennedy's victory as partly the result of his strong performance in the debates.[13]

The next set of debates occurred in 1976, between Gerald Ford and Jimmy Carter. Each presidential campaign since then has included debates between the presidential candidates and sometimes also between the vice presidential candidates. (The presidential debates are discussed in further detail in Chapter 12.) The schedule of debates and the rules governing their conduct are the product of intense negotiation between the campaigns. In 2016, the detailed set of rules for the three presidential debates included instructions that the candidates could not cross over a line on the stage separating them and time limits on answering questions and offering rebuttals.

The 2016 general election campaign featured 3 fiery debates between Donald Trump and Hillary Clinton. Pictured here, they square off in the first debate at Hofstra University.

Despite the large amount of attention both the campaigns and the media pay to the debates, the impact that debates have on the election outcome is unclear. Many researchers have documented that those who tend to watch the debates already have moderate to strong convictions regarding who they want to win, and these convictions often shape how an individual voter evaluates the candidate's performance in the debates. Although polls sometimes show that the voters tend to identify a debate "winner," there is far less evidence to show that this has any impact on voter intentions. The first of the debates often gets the most attention, and yet many of the media-dubbed "winners" of first debates, whether Walter Mondale in 1984, Michael Dukakis in 1988, Ross Perot in 1992, or John Kerry in 2004, have ended up on the short side of the electoral vote count on election day. More evidence of this pattern emerged in the 2012 race, as Republican challenger Mitt Romney was widely regarded as the winner of the first debate against President Barack Obama. Yet it was Obama who secured the overall victory on Election Day. Some observers of elections indicate that although debates may not have a direct impact on vote intentions, they can change the dynamics of a campaign, which in turn may influence the outcome.[14]

Presidential candidate Donald Trump speaks during a campaign rally on April 27, 2016, at the Indiana State Fairgrounds in Indianapolis.

The Advertising

Television advertisements have become a staple of presidential campaign strategies.[15] They are used to heighten name recognition, communicate core messages to voters, and offer reasons why one should vote for (or against) a particular candidate. Television advertising uses a variety of different techniques to accomplish these goals. The most controversial of these techniques is the attack or "negative" ads that candidates often use to portray their opponents in a bad light.[16] Television ads can be very effective at convincing voters to support a candidate—particularly voters who are undecided on any particular candidate or who are politically independent rather than identifying themselves as a Democrat or a Republican. Whereas other forms of campaign communication (such as televised debates, political news columns, political talk shows on radio and TV, and news broadcasts) are provided in formats that appeal to voters who are interested in the campaign and have already made up their minds about who they will vote for, televised advertisements may be placed during certain shows or at certain times when independents and undecided voters are tuning in. The unsuspecting audience is captive to the short advertisement, which provides a unique opportunity for a campaign to attract votes.

The Electoral College Vote

Unlike elections for most public offices in the United States, the outcome of the popular vote does not determine who wins the presidential election. The winner of the presidential election is the candidate who receives a majority of the 538 votes in the **electoral college**. In the highly controversial 1876 and 2000 presidential elections, the popular vote winner lost the presidential race. Similarly, John Quincy Adams won the 1824 election despite losing the popular vote, as did Benjamin Harrison in 1888.

How does the electoral college work? The Constitution allocates to each state a certain number of electoral votes, based on the sum of the number of senators (two) plus representatives (currently anywhere from 1 to 53) that a state has in the U.S. Congress. The Twenty-third Amendment to the Constitution allocated three electoral votes to the District of Columbia. The number of seats a state has in the House of Representatives may change as a result of the official census conducted every 10 years. Thus, the number of electoral votes that a state has may change as well. The total number of electoral votes remains fixed at 538, and a candidate must receive a majority—270—to win the presidency (see Figure 14-1).

The minimum number of electoral votes allotted to any one state is three because the Constitution guarantees to each state exactly two senators and at least one House member. Vermont, Wyoming, North Dakota, South Dakota, Alaska, Montana, and Delaware all have three votes. California currently has the largest number of electoral votes with 55 (53 members of the House and 2 senators).

Even small states with as few as three electoral votes can influence the outcome of an election. In 2000, George Bush received 271 electoral votes, only one vote more than the 270 majority he needed to win. Had just one of the small states that gave Bush its three electoral votes voted for Gore, Bush would not have won the election.

Over the past 60 years the U.S. population has shifted, with the southern and western states gaining population and most of the northeastern and midwestern states losing. Consequently, the numbers of electoral votes in states such as Florida, California, Texas, and Arizona have grown, and the number of votes allocated to states such as New York, Pennsylvania, Ohio, and Illinois has declined. Based on figures from the 2010 U.S. Census, the 2016 electoral vote count in Texas swelled from 34 to 38. Florida gained two electoral votes, and a number of states gained at least one electoral vote: Arizona, Georgia, Nevada, South Carolina, Utah, and Washington. By contrast, each of the following states lost at least one electoral vote: Illinois, Iowa, Louisiana, Massachusetts, Michigan, New Jersey, and Pennsylvania. Ohio and New York lost two each. As a result of this trend, the southern and southwestern states have become more influential in the presidential selection process.

Article II of the Constitution gives the state legislature of each state the authority to appoint **electors**, one for each electoral vote that a state has been allocated. During the first few presidential elections, most states used the state legislature to select the individuals who would be the state's electors.[17] By 1860, however, states gradually shifted to using the popular vote outcome in the state to allocate electors, or the so-called **unit rule**. The unit rule (or "winner-take-all" system) means that the candidate who receives the most votes among the popular votes cast for president in a state will receive all the electoral votes from that state. At present, only two states, Maine and Nebraska, do not

electoral college The constitutional mechanism by which presidents are chosen. Each state is allocated electoral college votes based on the sum of that state's U.S. senators and House members.

electors Individuals appointed to represent a state's presidential vote in the electoral college; in practice, voters in presidential elections vote for a slate of electors committed to a particular candidate, rather than voting directly for the candidate.

unit rule The system in 48 states by which the candidate who wins the most votes among popular votes cast for president in a state receives all the electoral votes from that state; also known as the "winner-take-all" system.

use the unit rule. Rather, in those states the popular vote winner in each congressional district receives the electoral vote from that district, and the two votes that derive from the state's Senate seats are awarded to the statewide popular vote winner.

In practice, the voters in a presidential election vote not for the actual candidate but for the slate of electors who commit to the candidate for whom the voters cast their ballots. Interestingly, the electors who pledge themselves to a candidate are under no legal obligation to actually cast their electoral vote for that candidate. In fact, electors do sometimes break their pledge. In 7 of the last 15 presidential elections, at least one individual elector has not voted for the candidate who won the popular vote in his or her state.

The most recent deviation occurred in 2004, when a Minnesota elector pledged to vote for John Kerry cast his presidential vote for "John Ewards " [sic] instead. That vote may have been an accident. By contrast, in 2000, Washington, D.C., elector Barbara Lett-Simmons, while pledged to vote for Democrats Al Gore and Joe Lieberman, intentionally cast no electoral votes as a protest against the District of Columbia's lack of statehood. To date, however, these rare broken promises (or mistakes) have not had an impact on an election outcome—and only 9 of the 21,829 electoral votes cast since 1796 deviated from the vote that was expected of an elector.[18]

The significance of the unit rule is illustrated by the outcome of the 2000 presidential election. In Florida, which had 25 electoral votes, the popular vote distribution between Bush and Gore was very close. For nearly one month after election day in 2000, controversies surrounding the vote count and the ballot in Florida left uncertain which candidate won the most popular votes in the state. What loomed in the balance was all of Florida's 25 electoral votes—and the election victory. Without Florida, Gore had 267 electoral votes—just 3 votes shy of victory, whereas Bush had 246. Because the unit rule applied to Florida's 25 votes, all 25 would be allocated on the basis of which candidate received the most popular votes.

The Founders' original intent in creating the electoral college was to keep the presidential selection process out of the direct hands of the people. They felt that the people were best represented by the House of Representatives, whose members were elected directly by voters. But the Founders questioned the ability of the general public to select the chief executive. Rather, they believed that the more knowledgeable, wise, and politically thoughtful members of each state's legislature should be empowered with the authority to appoint electors who would choose from the best of the best.

But as the meaning of democracy changed and as American politics opened up to greater political participation, states began to use the popular vote as a means of allocating their electoral votes. Further, public opinion polls strongly endorse presidential selection based on the national popular vote, rather than the electoral vote. For example, a Gallup Poll conducted in 2011 favored the popular vote over the electoral vote system as a way of selecting the president by a margin of 62 to 35 percent.

If Americans strongly prefer the selection of a president based on the total national popular vote rather than by the electoral vote, why, then, do we continue to use this rather complicated, indirect system for voters to choose their president? Why not simply use the sum total of the popular vote to choose a winner? The most basic answer is explained by politics, not necessarily logic. The electoral college system benefits smaller states. For example, Wyoming's population of approximately 500,000 represents 0.17 percent of the potential popular vote. But its three electoral votes constitute 0.56 percent of the electoral vote total. Because every state starts off with two electoral votes (for its two U.S. senators), smaller states end up with disproportionately more voting power in the electoral college than in the popular vote. In recent years, the states that benefit from the electoral college system have tended to be dominated by Republican legislatures. Because changing the electoral college system requires a constitutional amendment, and because amendment procedures require approval by three-fourths of the state legislatures, any attempt to change the system is unlikely to win the support of a sufficient number of state legislatures, enough of which are small enough to benefit from the electoral college. Despite the many proposals that have been offered to reform or eliminate the electoral college, it seems likely, at least for the foreseeable future, that the electoral college is here to stay.

14-5 | Making a Vote Choice

Although the electoral college system muddies the connection between popular vote choice and the election outcome, voter decisions are still the basis upon which candidates win. It's not so surprising, then, that in covering American politics the news media spend a tremendous amount of time and resources analyzing how voters will vote in a contest, particularly in presidential elections. For this reason, preelection polling has become a centerpiece of American political campaign strategy as well as news coverage. Years before a presidential election takes place, media polls query American voters on the potential candidates and assess the level of support voters offer these candidates. Months before the election, daily tracking polls monitor how voters are thinking and how opinions are changing from one day to the next.

Likewise, political scientists' primary focus of research on American political behavior is on how voters make up their minds about who they will vote for. In 2008, 2012, and 2016, for example, the age of voters had a significant relationship with vote choice (the youth vote from 2016 is depicted in Figure 14-2). Research has identified a number of different factors that act as cues to individual voters in helping them make a vote decision. Collectively, these factors are referred to as *determinants of vote choice*.

Candidate Familiarity

The most basic voting cue is simple name recognition and familiarity with a candidate. Many voters pay little attention to politics and political campaigns. Recognizing the name of a candidate on a ballot, then, offers an important voting cue. If voters recognize one candidate's name and no others, they are much more likely to vote for the name they recognize. Likewise, the more familiar voters are with a candidate, the more likely they are to vote for that candidate. In lower-visibility elections, such as primaries and local elections, name recognition plays a large role in the voting decision. However, even in statewide and presidential races (particularly presidential primaries), familiarity with a candidate can be an important cue to voters. High name recognition and voter familiarity, for example, propelled Hillary Clinton, former first lady, senator, and secretary of state, to frontrunner status early on in the race for the 2016 Democratic presidential nomination. In many congressional House races, incumbents tend to win reelection at rates in excess of 90 percent, in large part because voters recognize their names and are less familiar with the challengers.

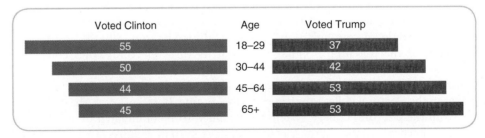

FIGURE 14-2 The Youth Vote in the 2016 Presidential Race

The Supreme Court and Voter ID Laws

Crawford v. Marion County Election Board (2008)[19]

While the public's attention during a presidential election contest often focuses on character issues, ideological differences, and media strategies, political insiders believe the final outcome of close contests turns far more often on the issue of turnout. Stated simply, each side has a vested interest in mobilizing its core constituencies to appear at the polls on election days. The Democratic party, which in recent decades has attracted significant support from lower-income voters, faces a daunting challenge in this regard, as those voters are far less likely to come to the polls than more well-off citizens. Should legal drivers and those who possess driver's licenses have an easier time voting? The recent proliferation of state voter ID laws that require voters to present a government-authorized photo ID card at the polls has raised this question anew. Do photo ID requirements discriminate against lower-income groups that are statistically less likely to possess photo IDs in the form of driver's licenses?

In *Crawford v. Marion County Election Board* (2008), the U.S Supreme Court considered the constitutionality of an Indiana law that required all voters casting a ballot in person to present a U.S. or Indiana photo ID—voters lacking such as an ID could cast a provisional ballot and then visit a designated government office within 10 days to either (1) bring a photo ID or (2) sign a statement saying they couldn't afford one. In a 6–3 decision, the Supreme Court upheld the law: in seeking to reduce fraud, it placed burdens on only a small percentage of the population. At least 12 states now require voters to show some form of voter ID, with many others pursuing such legislation during recent election cycles.

For Critical Thinking and Discussion

1. A 2016 study by University of California, San Diego, researchers found that strict voter photo ID laws "have a differentially negative impact on the turnout of Hispanics, Blacks, and mixed-race Americans in primaries and general elections." If that is the case, can the interest in addressing voter fraud still be justified? In short, does it matter that the impact of the law falls so heavily on certain racial minorities?

2. Critics of the voter ID laws claim that most of the laws have originated in states with Republican-dominated legislatures. If Democratic turnout is disproportionately impacted by such laws, does that undermine their validity?

Party Identification

Political parties play many important roles in the American political system. Often voters form a psychological attachment to a party that helps them organize their political information and offers an important cue to vote choice. As discussed in Chapter 13, *party identification* is the term for this psychological attachment to a political party. Party identification tends to be a long-term predisposition—once it is formed, it usually remains with an individual over the course of his or her life. Party identification, then, is an important determinant of vote choice.[20]

Party identification is particularly powerful in influencing a vote decision in lower-profile political races: those in which no particularly serious issues are at stake, the candidates are not well known, and the news media pay little attention to covering the race. In such contests, those who identify with a political party are most likely to turn out to vote, and those who turn out usually vote for the candidate associated with their political party.[21]

For example, elections for the House of Representatives tend to be lower-profile events than presidential or Senate races. Among the 435 congressional districts across the country, more than 350 are considered to be "safe seats" for one of the two major parties. Safe seats are districts where the party affiliation of the voters is so one-sided that the candidate who wears that party's label is virtually assured of victory.

It should be noted, however, that overall party identification and its impact on vote choice have been in a state of decline.[22] Over the past 50 years, voters have become less likely to identify as either a Democrat or a Republican, and more likely to say that they are independent. Decline in confidence in the political parties, campaigns

Role of Diversity in Vote Choice

An increasingly important campaign dynamic has been the role that descriptive characteristics of individual candidates have on voters. You may have noticed that certain candidates are more "familiar" to you, whether because their name or photo rings a bell. Many of us identify with candidates based on some shared descriptive characteristics such as gender, race, ethnicity, age, religion, or sexual orientation—we then vote based on that familiarity and disregard other factors such as ideology and policy position. Some political scientists have identified clear voter preferences for political candidates that share some of their own descriptive characteristics.

Voters may be assuming that if they share some of the same descriptive characteristics with the candidate, they might also share some of the same previous experiences, perspectives, and policy interests. Accordingly, these voter affinities may politically advantage some diverse candidates, while serving as a potential disadvantage for others due the biases some of these voters hold. In the 2016 presidential campaign, gender became a focal point, as Donald Trump accused Hillary Clinton of playing the "women's card," which he argued was the only reason she was doing well among voters. (You can see Clinton's campaign response in the tweeted image.)

Screenshot of Hillary Clinton 2016 campaign tweet advertising an official 'woman's card.'

For Critical Thinking and Discussion

1. Which candidates did you support in the 2016 presidential election and might shared descriptive characteristics have influenced your decision? Can you explain why?
2. If shared characteristics do indeed play a significant role in voter decision making, racial/ethnic minority candidates may find it more difficult to win elections in majority white voter districts, while enjoying significant political advantages in districts with heavy racial/ethnic minority populations. Is this a healthy development for our democracy? Why or why not?

---

that are more focused on the candidates than on the candidate's party, and increased television news coverage of campaigns are cited as primary reasons for the drop in party identification.

Still, two-thirds of voters continue to identify with one of the major parties, and thus party identification remains the single best predictor of how an individual might vote in an election. Identifying with a partisan perspective provides a shortcut for voters in making candidate choices. More broadly, party identification enables people to more readily make sense of their political world.

Issue Voting

For voters who identify as Democrats, the Democratic Party's candidate is likely to hold an issue position that they favor; the same is true for voters who identify as Republicans. For voters who identify themselves as independents, however, a candidate's party does not serve as a determinant of vote choice. For these voters, a candidate's position on a particular issue or set of issues is a voting cue.

Voting on the basis of issues is more likely to occur in certain types of elections.[23] First, when a particular issue captures the attention of many people in the electorate, voters are more likely to use a candidate's position on that issue to form a vote decision.

For example, in the 1968 presidential race, American involvement in the Vietnam War was a central concern for many voters, and many voted on the basis of the two candidates' positions on the war.[24]

Second, issue voting occurs more often when an issue is of particular personal concern to a voter. In 2012, for example, American voters were concerned about a poorly performing economy, and thus many cast a vote on the basis of President Obama's performance in dealing with the "Great Recession" and Mitt Romney's proposed alternatives for addressing the economic crisis. Third, issue voting is much more likely to occur when the candidates hold clearly distinct positions on issues.

Anthony Downs's rational-choice approach to understanding voting turnout also applies to making a vote choice.[25] Downs suggested that in making a choice, voters examine the issue positions of the candidates and assess how close they are to the voters' own positions. The candidate whose positions on the issues are closer to the voter's earns the vote.

Issue voting is often regarded as the most sophisticated type of voting behavior. Notions of the "ideal democratic citizen" describe such a person as someone who is informed about issues, has developed a position on those issues, and then compares that position to the positions of the candidates. Voting on the basis of such a calculation requires political knowledge and attentiveness to campaigns. Although issues remain important to many voters and take on higher levels of importance under certain circumstances, most research indicates that other shortcut factors, such as party identification, are more commonly used to make choices.

Retrospective Voting

In issue voting, a voter assesses the candidates' issue positions and casts a vote based on which candidate the voter thinks will do a better job in dealing with that issue in the future. However, a voter's past experience with a candidate or a political party also can be an important determinant of vote choice. **Retrospective voting**, a concept developed by political scientist Morris Fiorina, posits that evaluations of incumbents' past performance in office provide important cues for voters in deciding whether to vote for that incumbent.[26] Voters who believe that an incumbent has done a good job are likely to vote for the officeholder, whereas if they judge that an incumbent's job performance has been poor, they are likely to vote against the officeholder. Voter assessments of the economy and the performance of the president in handling economic conditions are especially important in a voter's retrospective evaluation of an incumbent. Bill Clinton's victory over incumbent George H. W. Bush in the 1992 presidential election was largely the result of voters' negative evaluations of Bush's handling of the nation's economy. Likewise, Ronald Reagan's defeat of incumbent President Jimmy Carter in 1980 was based on voters' perception that Carter performed poorly in dealing with economic problems and the Iranian hostage crisis.

In retrospective voting, the evaluation of the incumbent provides the determination of vote choice. In other words, a voter's assessment of the incumbent's job performance provides a shortcut decision rule on voting for or against the incumbent. Pollsters often measure this assessment through a question on "job approval rating." The percentage of voters who approve of the incumbent's job performance often reflects the percentage of the vote that the incumbent receives in a reelection bid.

Candidates for office often try to encourage voters to think retrospectively, if it is in their strategic interest to do so. In the 1980 presidential campaign, while the nation was experiencing economic problems and an extended international crisis with hostages being held in Iran, challenger Ronald Reagan defeated incumbent Jimmy Carter in part by asking the voters, "Are you better off today than you were four years ago [before Carter took office]?" Similarly, in 1992, challenger Bill Clinton questioned the integrity of President George H. W. Bush by repeating a TV clip of the president saying, "Read my lips, no new taxes"—a pledge Bush had made in 1988 but did not keep.

retrospective voting A theory on voting behavior suggesting that voter evaluations of an incumbent's past performance provide important cues to voters in deciding whether to vote for that incumbent again.

Candidate Image Voting

The image, personal traits, and other characteristics of the particular candidates in a campaign can also influence the way people vote. Especially in higher-stimulus elections, where candidates make ample use of television advertisements to build an image, voter perceptions of candidates' qualities are important. Perceptions of candidate image include such characteristics as honesty, trustworthiness, leadership ability, concern for voters, integrity, intelligence, and sense of humor. Candidates for office who have more favorable images than their opponents among voters tend to fare much better in election contests. In 11 of the 13 presidential elections between 1952 and 2000, the candidate who had the higher "image score" from questions asked on the American National Election Survey won the election. The two exceptions were 1960, when John Kennedy and Richard Nixon shared an identical score in a very close election that Kennedy won, and 1984, when Walter Mondale and Ronald Reagan shared an identical score (Reagan went on to a decisive victory).

In today's media age, candidates have found that image development is an efficient means of persuading swing voters how to vote. Thus, candidates often use television advertising to build their own favorable image or, conversely, to depict their opponents as having negative image characteristics. Visual images on television are useful in conveying symbolic, image-oriented messages. Bill Clinton in 1996 built a successful campaign around a theme that he would continue to improve the nation's economic future (his theme was captured in the slogan "building a bridge to the twenty-first century"). Ronald Reagan in 1984 cemented his strong leadership image in his campaign for reelection with the TV ad slogan "It's morning again in America."

14-6 | Campaign Funding

Waging a political campaign, particularly a presidential campaign, is becoming increasingly expensive.[27] In 2012 the campaigns of President Barack Obama and Governor Mitt Romney combined to raise over $2 billion. That figure does not include money raised or held by the two candidates' "victory funds," which are joint fund-raising committees that distribute funds to the campaigns and party committees. President Obama, in particular, focused on individual contributors for support, even though their individual donations were limited to $2,500 by campaign finance laws. The 2012 figures thus dwarfed all previous figures. In 2008, all the candidates together raised more than $1.7 billion, nearly double the amount raised in 2004, and more than four times the amount raised in 2000 (see Figure 14-3). Barack Obama's campaign alone raised $745 million.

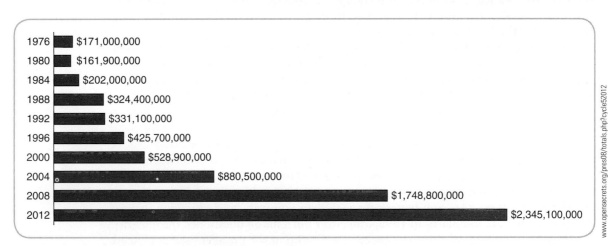

FIGURE 14-3 **Total Fundraising by Presidential Candidates, 1976–2012**

Campaign financing, then, is one of the most important functions of a political campaign. Hiring a professional staff to develop and implement a successful campaign, producing and airing TV commercials and radio spots, renting campaign headquarters office space, conducting polls to monitor the course of the campaign, and producing buttons, bumper stickers, and signs all cost money. Good candidates have demonstrated a high capacity for raising money to wage a campaign.

Sources of Funding

Where do campaigns find financial support? They find money from individual citizens, from interest groups and political action committees, and from political parties. Companies, groups, and individuals all have vested interests in the political system, and each may provide support (including monetary contributions) to promote candidates who advocate their own positions on issues. Our system of politics encourages people and groups to participate in the political process, and this participation includes financial contributions to campaigns. Indeed, giving money to candidates may be seen as a healthy sign that people are engaged in the political process and want to participate in making a difference.

Beginning in the 1970s, parties and candidates turned to political action committees (PACs) to address the new realities of political campaigns, particularly regarding fund-raising and limits on individual contributions. PACs are the arms of interest groups that raise and give money to political candidates. Any group that wishes to participate in financing campaigns must create a PAC and register it with the Federal Elections Commission (FEC). There are more than 4,000 PACs currently registered with the federal government (see Figure 14-4). Of the $1 billion raised by House and Senate campaigns in 2004, about 30 percent came from the fund-raising efforts of PACs.

In addition to individual and PAC contributions, the political parties play an important role in financing political campaigns. Both major parties have national and statewide committees, which raise money to fund campaigns. In 2000, the national party committees each collected and spent about $200 million to help fund their candidates. Typically, the parties support House and Senate candidates, particularly those who have a competitive chance of winning.

Another important source of campaign funding comes from the individual candidates' House and Senate campaigns. Members of Congress who hold safe seats are very effective at raising money for their own campaigns. These campaigns, because they are for safe seats, tend not to need a great deal of funding. So the incumbents use their campaign war chests to help fund the campaigns of their colleagues in more competitive races. Often they do so through the formation of a PAC.

Although not the norm, some federal candidates for office use their own personal wealth to fund their campaigns. In 1992 and 1996, independent presidential candidate Ross Perot spent millions of dollars of his own personal fortune (Perot's personal wealth is in the billions of dollars). Similarly, Democratic Senator Jon Corzine from New Jersey spent more than $50 million of his own money to win a Senate seat in 2000 (his Republican competitor spent over $30 million of his own money).

The federal government and a handful of state governments (including those of Arizona, Connecticut, North Carolina, and Maine) maintain some form of public campaign financing as well. Although candidates cannot be forced to participate in public financing schemes, which restrict their expenditures, the government may entice their participation by offering them significant public funds in return for their agreement to abide by personal campaign spending limits. The federal government's presidential election financing system allows major-party candidates to draw on funds received when taxpayers check a box on their tax returns agreeing to donate to the fund. In 2004, presidential candidates were eligible to receive approximately

Harold W. Stanley and Richard G. Niemi, *Vital Statistics on American Politics 2004–2005*, 103 (Washington, DC: CQ Press, 2006). Data for 2005–2012 are from www.fec.gov/press/pre ss2009/20090415pac/20090424pac.shtml.

FIGURE 14-4 **The Growth of Political Action Committees** The federal campaign finance legislation of the 1970s was the first vigorous attempt to monitor and regulate the money that was raised and spent on political campaigns. These laws applied to the regulation of hard money, which was money raised directly by and spent by the political candidates. They influenced the creation of political action committees (PACs), which raise and spend soft money—funds for political campaigning independent of the political candidates. In 1974, there were only 608 PACs registered with the federal government; by 2002, 4,027 PACs were registered. This figure shows the total amount of receipts and expenditures of all PACs registered with the federal government from the 1975–1976 election cycle to the 2011–2012 election cycle.

$70 million each if they agreed to limit their campaign expenditures. Yet neither of the two major-party candidates in 2004, George W. Bush and John Kerry, elected to participate in the federal financing scheme. By rejecting the use of such public financing, they were able to freely spend throughout the primaries and general election campaign without regard to any federally imposed limits. In 2008, John McCain accepted the $85 million he qualified for in public financing to fund his general election campaign. Barack Obama, however, declined public financing and continued to privately raise funds through the general election—a decision based on his widespread success in raising campaign money during the primaries. The 2012 general election between

Barack Obama and Mitt Romney marked the first time that *both* major candidates turned down public financing so they could continue unlimited fundraising activities after their respective conventions. Similarly in 2016, neither major party candidate accepted public financing, opting to raise and spend much more than pubic financing normally provides.

In recent presidential election cycles, candidates have been able to take advantage of the Internet as yet another means of fund-raising. In 2000, Bill Bradley raised more than $2 million via the Internet for his campaign for the Democratic presidential nomination. (He ended up losing his bid for the nomination to Al Gore.) Then, in the 2004 race for the Democratic presidential nomination, a little-known former governor from the small state of Vermont, Howard Dean, waged an impressive campaign by tapping into the vast potential of the Internet and online fund-raising. His followers, who came to be known as "Deaniacs," tended to be younger Americans, a group much more inclined to use the Internet, to IM (instant message), and to blog. The Dean campaign translated this orientation of his followers into the most successful Internet fund-raising campaign that American politics had ever seen.

Dean raised an unprecedented $40 million in his campaign for the nomination. This amount exceeded that of all his competitors for the nomination, and the vast bulk of his campaign war chest was derived from small, individual donations solicited through the Internet. Although Dean's campaign collapsed after the candidate suffered unexpected losses in Iowa and New Hampshire and although most of his $40 million war chest was depleted by the first primary contest, Dean's success at Internet fund-raising was nonetheless quite impressive. Then, in 2008, Barack Obama's campaign substantially raised the stakes in fund-raising through the Internet by raising over $200 million through that medium, and in 2012 the Obama reelection campaign proved groundbreaking in this regard, leveraging micro-donations by raising money online from over 3 million separate donors. His appeal to voters through the Internet represents a significant achievement in the use of this technology in campaign politics. Today, political parties as well as individual candidates use the Internet as a fund-raising tool. As Americans increasingly come to rely on the Internet, it is likely that more and more political candidates will follow Dean's and Obama's examples and harness this technology for fund-raising and other campaigning.

Bernie Sanders successfully raised millions of small donations during his nomination run in 2016 using the Internet.

Regulating Campaign Financing

Congress and the states have passed many and varied laws to regulate the conduct of campaign contributions. These laws are not intended to prevent individuals or groups from giving money. Rather, they attempt to prevent a "quid pro quo," or a donation in return for an elected official voting or acting in a certain way in direct response to accepting the campaign gift.

The first significant piece of federal legislation aimed at regulating campaign financing was the **Federal Election Campaign Act (FECA)**, passed in 1971 and amended in 1974. The law required that all federal candidates accurately disclose campaign contributions and document all campaign expenditures. Subsequent amendments to FECA imposed legal limits on campaign contributions by individuals ($1,000 to each candidate per election cycle; $5,000 to PACs per year; and $20,000 to national party committees per year). Additionally, FECA imposed an outright ban on certain

Federal Election Campaign Act (FECA) The federal legislation passed in 1971 that established disclosure requirements and restricted individual campaign contributions.

hard money Donations made directly to political candidates and their campaigns that must be declared with the name of the donor (which then becomes public knowledge).

soft money Money not donated directly to a candidate's campaign, but rather to a political advocacy group or a political party for "party-building" activities.

Federal Election Commission (FEC) The agency created in 1974 to enforce federal election laws.

independent campaign expenditures Political donations that PACs or individuals spend to support campaigns but do not directly contribute to the campaigns.

Buckley v. Valeo (1976) The 1976 Supreme Court opinion that held that spending money to influence elections is protected First Amendment speech and that prohibited limitations on independent expenditures or personal money spent by candidates on their own campaigns.

campaign contributions by corporations, unions, national banks, and foreign nationals, among others.

All these provisions targeted so-called **hard money** contributions that go directly to candidates and their campaign committees. Although the Supreme Court in 2014 struck down attempts to limit the *total amount* an individual can contribute to federal candidates as a whole in a two-year cycle, the federal government still imposes limits on how much an individual can contribute to a single candidate in primaries and general elections. Meanwhile, FECA did little to stem the influx of **soft money** funds to political parties and political advocacy groups that are not contributed directly to candidate campaigns and that do not expressly advocate the election of a particular candidate. In the two decades following FECA, the two major political parties have strategically spent soft money on administrative and party-building activities, as well as on issue ads that do not specifically promote an individual candidate, but that nevertheless attempt to affect the election outcome.

The **Federal Election Commission (FEC)** was established in 1974 to enforce all campaign financing rules and regulations, including limits on campaign contributions. Today, the FEC is the federal agency in charge of enforcing election laws. Provisions for public funding of presidential campaigns were subsequently passed in 1976 and 1979.

Critics have voiced a number of complaints about the system of campaign finance regulations. For one thing, the original limits on individual contributions—fixed by legislation in the 1970s—were never indexed to inflation. This oversight was addressed in legislation in 2002 mandating that limits be indexed for inflation every two years. For example, in 2005–2006 individuals were able to give up to $2,100 to candidates and up to $26,700 to national party committees.

Another complaint concerns the failure of the system to adapt to modern campaign dynamics. As a result of frontloading, presidential primary elections are now bunched up earlier and earlier in the general election campaign; yet the strict limits on expenditures imposed on those who accept public financing do not really account for these new campaign realities, which compel candidates to spend a considerable amount of their money during a relatively short period of time.

In recent years, advocates of campaign finance reform have focused their greatest criticism on soft money in the form of **independent campaign expenditures**. These are monies that PACs or individuals spend to support political campaigns but that do not directly contribute to them. FECA banned the unlimited use of independent expenditures to directly support the election of one candidate or the defeat of another candidate, but those funds could still be used to build the party as a whole. For example, a PAC can produce and support a political advertisement that endorses a particular party's position on an issue and pay for the airtime to broadcast that ad on television. The money for the ad is not donated to a campaign per se, but instead is spent on services that support the campaign; thus, the money spent is considered an "independent" expenditure. The U.S. Supreme Court in **Buckley v. Valeo (1976)** [28] ruled that Congress could limit campaign contributions consistent with the First Amendment, but that it could not limit independent campaign expenditures or personal money spent by candidates on behalf of their own campaigns. Nearly 30 years later, in *McConnell v. F.E.C.* (2003),[29] the Court extended that ruling to apply to spending by political parties as well. Thus, political parties themselves often sponsor television ads that talk more generally about issues facing the country without mentioning any individual candidate or race; of course, most political experts acknowledge that these ads may have a significant impact on individual campaigns.

The most recent reform attempts have focused on soft money and independent campaign expenditures. Senators John McCain (R-AZ) and Russell Feingold (D-WI) were particularly critical of the loopholes in campaign financing that have allowed soft money to go unregulated by the FEC. They cosponsored legislation designed to better regulate the way campaigns are financed and how the money is spent. In 2002, Congress passed the **Bipartisan Campaign Reform Act (BCRA) of 2002**, popularly known as the McCain-Feingold Act, which prohibited national parties and candidates for federal office from accepting soft money (i.e., that which is not subject to regulation by the FEC). The BCRA also raised limits on contributions to a particular candidate for federal office from $1,000 to $2,000. The U.S. Supreme Court, in the highly controversial decision of **Citizens United v. FEC (2010)**,[30] struck down as unconstitutional several other provisions of the BCRA, including certain limits on corporate and union funding of broadcast ads right before an election. Although President Obama has been openly critical of that Supreme Court opinion, his 2012 presidential campaign benefitted to a degree from the new rules, as labor unions helped to bankroll super PACs that favored his reelection. And although the Obama campaign refused to accept corporate or PAC donations for the Democratic Party convention, the president's advisers pressed labor unions to help close financial shortfalls stemming from the convention.

14-7 | Congressional Campaigns and Elections

Although presidential elections typically receive the most attention from the media and the public, many other elections also occur regularly, including those that send members to the two houses of Congress. In each presidential election year, all 435 seats in the House of Representatives are contested, as are one-third of the seats in the Senate. Midway between successive presidential elections are the **midterm congressional elections**, in which all 435 House seats are contested again and another one-third of the Senate seats are voted on (senators serve six-year terms, and the 100 Senate elections are staggered so that about one-third of the seats are contested every two years).

Midterm elections for Congress differ from presidential-year elections in important ways.[31] First, voter turnout tends to be lower in the midterm contests. Without the large-scale attention the presidential race receives, voter interest and engagement in the midterm elections are lower, and thus turnout tends to suffer. Even in the highly charged midterm elections of 2010, voter turnout was just 43 percent, almost 15 percentage points below voter turnout figures for the preceding presidential election.

Second, midterm elections fail to offer congressional candidates what has come to be known as the **coattail effect**. In a presidential election year, the names of candidates for Congress typically are listed below the name of their party's candidate for president on the ballot. Thus, voters' selection of congressional candidates may be influenced by their choice for president. The congressional candidates, in effect, ride the coattails of the presidential candidate.[32] For the coattail effect to be apparent, the outcome of the presidential race typically needs to be a landslide victory for the winner, such as in 1984 when President Ronald Reagan soundly defeated Democrat Walter Mondale. For the first time in decades, the 1984 elections ushered in a Republican majority to the U.S. Senate. By contrast, George W. Bush's narrow victory in 2004 did not appear to produce a coattail effect.

Third, in midterm elections there has been a discernible trend—although often not very strong—that favors congressional candidates in the party opposite the president's party in midterm contests. When a president wins, especially by a large margin, the coattail effect distorts what would normally occur in any given congressional race. Yet in midterm elections, without the president's name at the top of the ballot, the absence of the coattail gives the advantage to the opposing party. In the modern era, the party in opposition to the president has managed to regain control of Congress

Bipartisan Campaign Reform Act (BCRA) of 2002 Also called the McCain-Feingold Act, the federal legislation that (1) restricted soft money spent by political parties, (2) regulated expenditures on ads that refer to specific candidates immediately before an election, and (3) increased limits on hard money donated directly to candidates and their campaigns.

Citizens United v. FEC (2010) The 2010 Supreme Court opinion that held that government restrictions on independent political spending by corporations, unions, and other associations violate the First Amendment. Critics of the decision predicted the ruling would bring about a new era of corporate influence in politics. In fact, the bulk of large expenditures has come from so-called Super PACs dominated by a small group of billionaires; this development more than anything else has shifted significant power away from the political parties and toward the donors themselves.

midterm congressional elections Congressional elections held midway between successive presidential elections.

coattail effect The potential benefit that successful presidential candidates offer to congressional candidates of the same political party during presidential election years.

only in the midterm elections when the president's popularity is waning. Thus, in 1946 and then in 1994, the Republicans wrestled both houses of Congress back from the Democrats at midterm elections during the presidencies of Democrats Harry Truman and Bill Clinton, respectively. In 2006, voters upset about the state of the war in Iraq dealt a devastating blow to the Republicans' control of Congress: although many Republican incumbents in the House and Senate were ousted from office that year, not one Democratic House member or senator lost a seat in the 2006 midterm elections. The Democrats successfully rode the public's antiwar sentiment to regain control of both houses of Congress midway through the second term of Republican President George W. Bush.

True to form, the 2010 midterm elections once again offered a rebuke to the political party holding the White House. Running on a platform that opposed Democratic spending initiatives and promised to rein in the size of government, Republican House candidates transformed a 178-seat minority into a 240-seat majority. By taking more than 60 seats away from the Democrats, Republicans enjoyed a level of midterm election success not seen by either party in decades. Republicans were also successful in the Senate, shrinking the Democrats' 18-seat margin of control down to just 6 seats. While the Democrats won back a few seats in the Senate in 2012, the 2014 midterm elections saw a wave of GOP victories. This time President Obama's sinking approval ratings would provide no coattails for his Democratic candidates in Congress. The GOP won back majority control in the Senate and enhanced its majority in the House.

More important than presidential coattails or any other factor in congressional elections, however, is the **power of incumbency**. Incumbent members of Congress, particularly those in the House, are returned to office by voters at amazingly high rates. In a normal year of House races, an incumbent who is running for reelection stands a better than 90 percent chance of being returned to office.[33] What accounts for such a high return rate? First, name recognition of the candidate is a significant factor in lower-profile congressional races, and incumbents, because they have been in office, tend to have higher name recognition than do challengers. Second, the vast majority of congressional districts—and thus the vast majority of seats in Congress—are dominated by either the Republican Party or the Democratic Party. Congressional seats from districts that include either a high percentage of Democratic voters or a high percentage of Republican voters are dominated by their respective majority party and are referred to, as noted earlier, as **safe seats**. A far smaller number of districts tend to have similar numbers of Democratic and Republican voters and are known as **marginal seats**. In the redistricting of congressional districts that periodically takes place, the political parties try to configure districts to their own partisan advantage. This maneuvering tends to create a large number of safe seats and often very few marginal seats (see Table 14-1).

Finally, incumbent members of Congress enjoy financial advantages, such as the **franking privilege**, which allows members to mail materials to their constituents without paying postage.

Elections and campaigns are central features of the republican form of government in the United States. The number of elections is many; the cost of campaigns is high; and the process for selecting the nation's chief officeholder, the president of the United States, is long and complex. U.S. presidential elections evoke a great deal of passion, engage the interest of millions of voters, persuade vast numbers of citizens and groups to contribute large amounts of money, and focus attention on the great issues of the day. Thus, campaigns and elections duly serve their purpose in providing an important connection between Americans and their government.

power of incumbency The phenomenon by which incumbent members of Congress running for reelection are returned to office at an extremely high rate.

safe seat A congressional seat from a district that includes a high percentage of voters from one of the major parties.

marginal seat A seat in a congressional district that has relatively similar numbers of Democratic and Republican voters.

franking privilege The traditional right of members of Congress to mail materials to their constituents without paying postage.

TABLE 14-1 Safe Seats in Congress

The vast majority of the 435 seats in the House of Representatives, each of which is contested every two years, and the 100 U.S. Senate seats, each of which is contested every six years, are safe seats for incumbents who are running for reelection. Even if there is no incumbent running for reelection, most of these seats tend to be safe for one of the two major political parties. The 2010 midterm elections proved to be a bit of an anomaly, as 51 Democratic House incumbents in all lost their general reelection bids.

   The following table shows the number of incumbents defeated and the number of seats that switched from one party to another in each congressional election since 1980.[*] Keep in mind that in each election year, 435 House races and 33 or 34 Senate races are usually contested.

Year	House of Representatives			Senate		
	Incumbents Defeated	Open Seats Where Party Changed	Total Changes	Incumbents Defeated	Open Seats Where Party Changed	Total Changes[*]
1980	30	11	41	9	3	12
1982	23	8	31	2	2	4
1984	16	6	22	3	1	4
1986	6	15	21	7	3	10
1988	6	3	9	4	3	7
1990	15	6	21	1	0	1
1992	24	19	43	4	0	4
1994	35	26	61	2	6	8
1996	21	14	35	1	3	4
1998	6	11	17	3	3	6
2000	6	12	18	6	2	8
2002	4	8	12	3	1	4
2004	5	5	10	1	7	8
2006	22	9	31	6	0	6
2008	17	13	30	5	3	8
2010	53	10	63	2	4	6
2012	23	4	27	1	3	4
2014	13	6	19	3	1	4

[*]Figures include only shifts from one major party to the other party.

Harold W. Stanley and Richard G. Niemi, *Vital Statistics on American Politics 2005–2006* (Washington, DC: CQ Press, 2006), 48-49. Copyright © 2006 CQ Press, a division of Sage Publications; updated by authors.

Getting Involved in Political Campaigns

Politics is very much on the minds of college-age Americans today. In 2008, a record 35.6 percent of first-year college students said that they had frequently discussed politics in the past year.[34] (The previous high was 33.6 percent in 1968, at the

Iowa State University students at a Bernie Sanders campaign stop in Ames, Iowa.

height of the Vietnam War.) In the 2012 and 2016 presidential campaigns, college students were more interested and more active than ever before. Students who work on election campaigns may find themselves performing such simple tasks as stuffing envelopes or walking door to door to distribute leaflets. Those who are technologically savvy may assist campaigns in other ways—for example, by helping to create Facebook profiles or fan pages on the Internet. About 11 percent of first-year college students in 2008 said they were active in election campaigns. (This figure was up by about 3 percentage points from 2004.) More first-year college students also report that they are likely to engage in a political protest (6.1 percent in 2008, as compared to 4.9 percent in 1966).

For Critical Thinking and Discussion

1. Why do you think your peers were so energized about the 2008, 2012, and 2016 presidential elections? What do you think about youth energy for future elections—will the trend toward greater interest in politics continue to rise?

2. Do you think college students' participation made a difference in the election outcome in 2016?

Summary

14-1 American Presidential Elections In Historical Perspective

- From 1796 up through the 1830s, the presidential nomination process was dominated by officials of the two major parties who chose party nominees based on informal discussions; by the twentieth century, electoral reforms such as the direct primary gave voters in many states a formal opportunity to cast a ballot for delegates, who would in turn choose their party's nominees at a national convention. For the general election, the electoral college began as a mechanism for the political elite to select the chief executive and has evolved into a complex system where voters select the president.

14-2 The Prenomination Campaign

- Modern presidential elections begin with a prenomination campaign waged by potential candidates to raise money and gain the support of key party leaders. A candidate's failure to raise sufficient funds in this "invisible primary" may cause him or her to drop out of the race before any formal primaries or caucuses have been held.

14-3 The Nomination Campaign

- Nomination campaigns focus on attaining victories in presidential primaries and caucuses. The Iowa caucus and the New Hampshire primary have traditionally come at the beginning of the nomination calendar, and so they tend to disproportionately influence final outcomes. In recent elections, many states have attempted to move their primaries and caucuses up on the calendar in a process known as frontloading.

- National party conventions used to play an important role in helping choose party nominees; today they are mostly made-for-television affairs, anointing the party ticket with speeches offering testimonials to the nominees.

14-4 The General Election Campaign

- General election races may be either incumbent races (pitting a sitting president against a challenger) or open elections (with no incumbent in the race). In the former, the election often amounts to a referendum on the performance of the president over the previous four years.

- Presidential candidates choose their running mates (the vice presidential candidates) strategically to address specific weaknesses of the presidential candidate or to boost the ticket's prospects in certain geographical areas.

- To win the presidency, a candidate must put together a coalition of states sufficient to win a majority of the 538 electoral college votes, which are allocated to each state based on the sum of the number of senators and the number of representatives. The candidate who does well in battleground states will normally win the 270 or more votes necessary to secure a majority.

14-5 Making A Vote Choice

- A number of factors contribute to voter decision making at the polls. These include candidate familiarity, party identification, candidate issue positions, a candidate's image, and retrospective evaluations of the candidates and the parties.

14-6 Campaign Funding

- Campaign funding is critical to the success of individual candidates. Election laws since 1974 have limited the amount individuals or organizations can give to candidates (hard money). The Bipartisan Campaign Reform Act (BCRA) of 2002 went a step further, restricting expenditures to political parties or advocacy groups that are theoretically independent of specific candidates or campaigns (soft money). The Federal Election Commission enforces all such limitations that have been upheld as constitutional by the U.S. Supreme Court.

14-7 Congressional Campaigns and Elections

- In congressional elections, the power of incumbency is more important than any other factor. Unlike midterm elections, congressional elections that coincide with presidential elections tend to garner greater voter turnout, and members of the successful presidential candidate's party sometimes benefit from the coattail effect.

Key Terms

battleground states (p. 392)

Bipartisan Campaign Reform Act (BCRA) of 2002 (p. 405)

Buckley v. Valeo (1976) (p. 404)

caucus (p. 384)

Citizens United v. FEC (2010) (p. 405)

closed primary (p. 384)

coattail effect (p. 405)

electoral college (p. 394)

electors (p. 394)

Federal Election Campaign Act (FECA) (p. 403)

Federal Election Commission (FEC) (p. 404)

franking privilege (p. 406)

frontloading (p. 386)

hard money (p. 404)

incumbent race (p. 389)

independent campaign expenditure (p. 404)

invisible primary (p. 384)

marginal seat (p. 406)

midterm congressional elections (p. 405)

nomination campaign (p. 386)

open election (p. 389)

open primary (p. 384)

power of incumbency (p. 406)

prenomination campaign (p. 383)

presidential primary (p. 384)

retrospective voting (p. 399)

safe seat (p. 406)

soft money (p. 404)

unit rule (p. 394)

Test Yourself

1. In the presidential election of 1800, Thomas Jefferson and which other candidate had the same number of electoral votes, thus sending the election to the House of Representatives?

   a. John Adams

   b. Alexander Hamilton

   c. Aaron Burr

   d. Andrew Jackson

2. The state that held the first direct primary election for the party nomination was

   a. California.

   b. New York.

   c. Texas.

   d. Florida.

3. Which of the following amendments to the Constitution limits the office of president to two terms?

   a. Thirteenth Amendment

   b. Fifteenth Amendment

   c. Twenty-second Amendment

   d. Twenty-seventh Amendment

4. What are the five discernable stages in modern presidential election races?

5. The 2012 prenomination campaign for the GOP included all of the following candidates *except*

   a. Mitt Romney.

   b. John McCain.

   c. Rick Santorum.

   d. Newt Gingrich.

6. Why is the invisible primary called the "invisible" primary?

7. A state nomination contest in which party members are invited to attend local meetings at which they choose delegates who make a commitment to a candidate for the party nomination is a(n)

   a. open primary.

   b. closed primary.

   c. caucus.

   d. general election.

8. Which of the following states holds the first caucus of the presidential nominating process?

   a. Iowa

   b. New Hampshire

   c. Florida

   d. South Carolina

9. Who was the political boss in Chicago who used police force against protesters during the 1968 Democratic National Convention?

   a. Hubert Humphrey

   b. George McGovern

   c. Rahm Emanuel

   d. Richard J. Daley

10. Distinguish between an open primary and a closed primary.

11. The vice presidential candidate chosen to run with President Barack Obama was

    a. Sarah Palin.

    b. Dick Cheney.

    c. Al Gore.

    d. Joe Biden.

12. Which of the following was a battleground state in the 2012 presidential election?

    a. Texas

    b. Ohio

    c. New York

    d. California

13. Which of the following states gained the most net votes in the electoral college as a result of the 2010 census?

    a. Texas

    b. Florida

    c. Ohio

    d. Pennsylvania

14. What is the "unit rule," and how does it impact presidential elections?

15. Donations made directly to political candidates and their campaigns that must be declared with the name of the donor are known as

    a. hard money.

    b. soft money.

    c. hot money.

    d. cold money.

16. What did the Bipartisan Campaign Reform Act accomplish, and which of its provisions was struck down as unconstitutional by the Supreme Court?

17. An incumbent member of Congress who is running for reelection on average stands about what chance of being reelected?

    a. 30 percent

    b. 50 percent

    c. 70 percent

    d. 90 percent

18. The electoral benefit that a presidential candidate provides to congressional candidates of the same party during a presidential election is known as the

    a. executive effect.

    b. incumbency effect.

    c. safe-seat effect.

    d. coattail effect.

19. What factors contribute to the power of incumbency?

1. c. (LO 14-1); 2. d. (LO 14-1); 3. c. (LO 14-1); 5. b. (LO 14-2); 7. c. (LO 14-3); 8. a. (LO 14-3); 9. d. (LO 14-3); 11. d. (LO 14-4); 12. b. (LO 14-4); 13. a. (LO 14-4); 15. a. (LO 14-6); 17. d. (LO 14-7); 18. d. (LO 14-7)

LEARNING OBJECTIVES

15

American Domestic Policy

In the 1950s, Yale Professor Charles E. Lindblom described U.S. domestic policymaking as the "science of muddling through."[1] Lindblom's view challenged what had been the prevailing model of policymaking: a rational and comprehensive process in which decision makers utilized scientific analysis and logic to develop public policy. Lindblom's theory introduced the human element and expressly partisan factors into the process. Today we view public policy—whether in the form of small, incremental shifts or in the form of landmark, sweeping legislation—as the product of reluctant compromises entered into between the president, Congress, and other political actors based on the immediate political environment. Indeed, the very term "public policy" in the United States has come to be associated today with the coordinated response of public institutions to immediate events and conditions, a nod to the often messy reality of modern policymaking. Whether the government is enacting economic policy, social policy, or foreign policy, imperfect solutions to significant problems are a given, and the final outcome rarely garners widespread satisfaction. So long as the political (and often highly partisan) branches of government engage in some form of conflict, such "muddling through" to landmark legislation may offer the best policy process to which we can realistically aspire.

How Much Economic Regulation Is Desirable?

Many Americans still view their nation's economic system as the last great bastion of capitalism, standing proudly for free enterprise in contrast to the many government-managed economic systems that prevail elsewhere. In truth, the U.S. economy is highly regulated. Government policy impacts interest rates and determines personal income and corporate taxes, as well as a wide range of other economic policies. Since the Great Depression of the 1930s revealed the extreme dangers that an unregulated economy can pose, even the more conservative, libertarian politicians have accepted some degree of government control over the economy.

The question of income disparities and economic equality is relevant in this context. Some economists theorize that an unregulated economy would allow the wealthiest to increase their wealth at the expense of others. Beyond ensuring that the overall economy is doing well, does government have an obligation to redistribute wealth to reduce the economic disparities between the richest and poorest Americans?

Job seekers wait in line to speak with agents at the problem resolution office of Michigan's Unemployment Insurance Agency.

Ask the following questions of yourself:

- Do you think that the distribution of money and wealth in this country is fair? If not, should the government do more to reduce the gap between the rich and the poor in this country?
- In general, would you favor or oppose increasing taxes on wealthy Americans and large corporations in order to help reduce income inequality in the United States?

To see how your answers compare to others, take the **Who Are You?** poll in MindTap!

15-1 | An Overview of the Policymaking Process

public policy The set of laws, regulations, and rules that affect the whole of society.

Public policy refers to the set of laws, regulations, and rules that affect the whole of society. Because the responsibilities and interests of private and public institutions often overlap, some battles that are waged primarily among private parties may still fall under the general subject of public policy—after all, government may seek to enact laws or regulations aimed at monitoring such disputes. Antitrust laws, for example, offer a public policy response to disputes that arise between competing private companies such as Amazon and Apple. In April 2012, the Department of Justice brought an antitrust action against Apple and five major book publishers for allegedly colluding to raise prices for e-books after Apple had launched its iPad. (Amazon wanted to charge $9.99 for most e-books available on its website; the publishers and Apple eventually settled the lawsuit by agreeing to pay over $166 million to aggrieved consumers.) More than anything, the government regulators feared that such collusive practices had prevented market forces from establishing what should be the fair price for digital books. Thus, the regulation of Apple and the book publisher defendants became a matter of public policy, even though the alleged agreement to raise prices was entered into by private entities.

Meanwhile, **social policy**—a subset of public policy—refers to the rules, regulations, and policymaking pertaining to the quality of life, welfare, and relations of human beings in the United States. There are many different types of social policy, and this chapter will review some of the major ones: crime policy, welfare policy, Social Security policy, and health care policy.

social policy Rules, regulations, and policymaking pertaining to the quality of life, welfare, and relations of human beings in the United States.

Although the policymaking process tends to vary considerably from one subject area to another, most policies unfold in five separate stages:

- The recognition/definition stage, in which objectives to be fulfilled and goals to be pursued through policy are first identified and defined according to how the problem fits within existing policy categories, and *then* prioritized;
- The formulation stage, in which various alternative courses for this policy are considered, and a preferred course is selected;
- The adoption (or legitimation) stage, in which the policy under consideration assumes the authority of law through ratification by Congress or through regulations issued by the relevant administrative agencies;
- The implementation stage, in which a bureaucratic agency translates law into action through the adoption of administrative regulations and the dedication of agency resources to carry out the policy; and
- The evaluation stage, in which the policy is assessed for its worth and effectiveness in meeting its original objectives and goals.

Numerous actors and institutions are involved in making policy in the United States. Bureaucrats in administrative agencies often play a key role at every stage of the policymaking process, helping to define the problem and identify the possible options, proposing alternatives and implementing the preferred course, and assisting in collecting information necessary to evaluate the policy.[2] The Department of Commerce, for example, in addition to the Secretary of Commerce, employs at least six undersecretaries responsible for overseeing the formulation of numerous policy initiatives on behalf of the agency. Just one of those commerce officials, the Undersecretary for the National Oceanic and Atmospheric Administration, oversees a $5.54 billion bureaucracy that supervises the National Marine Fisheries Service, the National Ocean Service, and the National Weather Service, among other ocean-related agencies.

Congress and the president are most directly involved in the recognition, formulation, and adoption stages of policymaking, when media attention is most intense; their influence over the other stages is limited by the practical need to delegate administrative details to agencies with the resources and expertise to handle such matters. The courts may play a role in ensuring that all proper procedures are followed in the formulation of policy and in interpreting rules, regulations, and policies that emerge from the policymaking process.[3]

Interest groups and think tanks (policy research institutes) tend to focus on influencing program choices and decisions, where they have the opportunity to make significant gains on behalf of their members.[4] For example, the Sierra Club lobbies bureaucrats at the EPA and members of Congress on environmental committees to ensure that the Clean Air Act is successfully updated to meet new challenges. The specialized committee structure of Congress encourages interest groups to focus their resources on those legislators and members of legislative staffs who have authority over relevant issue areas. Think tanks are organizations that do intensive research and problem solving, either on behalf of other entities or on their own (see Table 15-1). Normally, a think tank staffed by researchers and policy analysts will produce an elaborate report detailing the implications of the problem it has studied; as with interest groups, it then seeks to publicize its findings, whether by

TABLE 15-1 Influential Policy Think Tanks

Institute	Date Established	Philosophy/Goals
American Enterprise Institute	1943	A conservative think tank dedicated to preserving "limited government, private enterprise . . . and a strong foreign policy and national defense."
The Brookings Institution	Roots trace back to 1916	A more liberal policy institute (once targeted by the Nixon administration) that aims to improve "the performance of American institutions and the quality of public policy" through the use of social science.
The Cato Institute	1977	Mostly libertarian; seeks to broaden the parameters of public policy debate to allow consideration of "the traditional American principles of limited government, individual liberty, free markets, and peace."
The Heritage Foundation	1973	Seeks "to formulate and promote conservative public policies based on the principles of free enterprise, limited government, individual freedom, traditional American values, and a strong national defense."
The Progressive Policy Institute	1989	Affiliated with the Democratic Leadership Council; maintains as its mission the definition and promotion of a new progressive politics in America. Its work rests on three ideals: equal opportunity, mutual responsibility, and self-governing citizens and communities.
The RAND Corporation	1945	Seeks to provide policy analysis and solutions that address challenges facing the nation and the world, including education, poverty, crime, and the environment, as well as a range of national security issues.

holding a press conference, sponsoring a symposium or panel discussion, or some other means.

Economic policymaking encompasses all the legislative and rule-making initiatives that affect the management of wealth and resources within this country. For much of its history, the United States maintained one of the world's most entrepreneurially free economies, with minimal government regulation. The government's mostly hands-off approach to economic matters survived until the early part of the twentieth century, when the federal government began to insert itself more regularly in the economy. At first, government involvement was directed at antitrust matters and corporate abuses such as the employment of child labor; by the 1930s government involvement had begun to take a variety of new forms, as federal agencies actively oversaw the monetary system, supported struggling businesses, regulated the stock and bond markets, and otherwise reinforced the economic infrastructure as a whole. Indeed, immediately following the frightening events on Wall Street that occurred in September 2008, few from either political party questioned the wisdom of increasing government oversight of Wall Street. Today the government's role in managing the economy is significant—elections are often decided by voter perceptions of success or failure in this area. Overseeing the economy includes two distinct forms of policymaking: fiscal policymaking and monetary policymaking.

fiscal policy Decisions by the federal government that relate to raising revenue through taxation and spending the revenue that is thereby generated.

15-2 | Theories and Practice in Fiscal Policy

Fiscal policy is concerned with how to raise revenue through taxation and how to spend the revenue generated. Many economists believe that the nation's fiscal policy has direct implications for unemployment, measured as the percentage of the workforce that wants to work and is not currently employed, and **inflation**, or consistent increases in the prices of goods and services. The primary instrument by which the federal government manages fiscal policy is the *federal budget*, a comprehensive plan laying out what the government will spend for its various programs during the coming fiscal years and how it expects to raise the money to pay for them.

Fiscal policy can be thought of as lying on a spectrum. At one end of the spectrum is the policy of minimal government interference in the economy, in which the government exercises little or no budget-making power by authorizing only minimal spending, taxation, and regulation of private business practices. At the opposite end of the spectrum is the policy of considerable government intervention in the economy, perhaps by taxing citizens or by offering subsidies to farmers in return for their agreement not to overproduce certain commodities.

Various economic theories explain the decision to craft fiscal policy at a given point along the fiscal policy spectrum. For example, the economic doctrine known as **laissez-faire** (a French phrase meaning literally "leave us alone") **economics** guided the fiscal policy that prevailed for much of the eighteenth and nineteenth centuries in the United States.[5] Laissez-faire favors less intervention in the economy, allowing businesses to conduct their affairs more or less free from governmental regulation. The theory came under attack toward the end of the 1800s, when increasing industrialization led to more frequent financial panics, bouts of severe unemployment, corrupt business practices, and the abuse of workers, especially in big cities. Government's involvement in the economy gradually increased, and in the 1930s widespread public support for President Franklin Delano Roosevelt's New Deal programs, enacted to address the problems of the Great Depression, effectively spelled the end of laissez-faire theory as the guiding principle for the nation's fiscal policy.

Many of FDR's New Deal policies were based on **Keynesian economic theory**, named for the British economist John Maynard Keynes. Keynesian theory argues that the government should increase spending when economic times are bad as a way of raising total demand. Total demand for goods and services, according to this theory, is the key determinant of whether the economy is performing well.[6] The economic recovery that occurred during World War II, when federal military spending increased significantly, is often used to support the validity of Keynesian theory. Administrations that attempted to draw on the theory quickly learned that although government spending may forestall or even end a **recession**—defined as an economic slowdown characterized by higher unemployment, reduced productivity, or some other negative economic indicators—it may also bring about other economic problems such as inflation and chronically high deficits. Barack Obama's administration also adopted a Keynesian approach to addressing the financial crisis of 2007–2010. President Obama adopted that approach while aware of the risks that higher deficits might pose to his reelection chances in 2012. (Obama was reelected despite those huge deficits).

Supply-side economics is an alternative to Keynesian economics, arguing that rather than increasing government spending, cutting taxes (and cutting the government spending such taxes help to fund) is the preferred way to increase economic productivity and spur the economy. According to supply-side theory, high taxes take money out of the economy that would otherwise be invested in goods and services; thus, by decreasing taxes, money flows back into the economy, stimulating business, new jobs, and overall productivity. While campaigning for the presidency in 1980, Ronald Reagan seized on this theory to propose that a program of implementing tax cuts and spending cuts and balancing the budget was the best means to get the economy out of recession. (As president, Reagan did secure passage of a large tax cut, but federal spending and deficits also multiplied during his eight years in office.[7])

inflation The overall general upward price movement of goods and services in an economy, normally measured by the consumer price index (CPI).

laissez-faire economics Fiscal policy theory that favors minimal intervention in the nation's economy.

Keynesian economic theory Fiscal policy theory that favors government taxation and spending during difficult economic times.

recession An economic slowdown characterized by high unemployment, reduced productivity, or other negative economic indicators.

supply-side economics Economic theory that favors cutting taxes as a way of increasing economic productivity.

Assessing the Economy's Performance

Just as different economic theories guide the crafting of fiscal policy, different measures are used to assess whether the nation's fiscal policy has been a success. Following are several economic measures regarded as especially significant indicators of general economic performance:

gross domestic product (GDP) An estimate of the total money value of all the goods and services produced in the United States in a one-year period.

- **Gross domestic product (GDP)** is an estimate of the total money value of all the goods and services produced in the United States in a given one-year period. When GDP improves, workers are producing more in fewer hours, allowing employers in turn to increase wages without raising prices. By contrast, declining productivity signals higher labor costs and, ultimately, higher prices for consumers. Measured in constant dollars (that is, adjusting for inflation), the GDP enjoyed its highest one-year increase during the past half century in 1984, when it rose by 6.8 percent. The GDP has actually fallen in constant dollars in five separate years over that same 50-year time span.

consumer price index (CPI) An index of prices for goods and services regularly traded in the U.S. economy.

- The **consumer price index (CPI)** is an index of prices for goods and services regularly traded in the U.S. economy. A sustained rise over time in the CPI indicates that inflation is on the rise and consumers' buying power is on the decline. Although critics argue that the CPI overstates inflation by at least 1 percent per year, the government still heavily relies on the CPI in defining tax brackets and spending for certain entitlement programs, such as cost-of-living adjustments for Social Security recipients. In 1980, the CPI increase for urban consumers was 13.5 percent, the highest figure recorded in more than three decades. Since 1983, the CPI has not increased by more than 6 percent in any given year.

- The unemployment rate measures the percentage of people unemployed and actively looking for work in the U.S. labor market. Although a major goal of the economic programs of most Western governments (including the United States) is to keep unemployment relatively low, full employment remains an elusive goal due to seasonal factors, voluntary job changes, and routine shifts in economic conditions (such as the rise in interest rates) that assist some businesses (e.g., apartment rental firms) and hinder others (e.g., construction companies and home loan financing companies). In recent years, a rate of 5 percent has been considered a realistic minimum for unemployment in the United States. That rate is certainly better than the unemployment rate of about 10 percent recorded for a short period during 2009.

budget deficit The amount of money spent by the U.S. government beyond that which it collects in taxes and other revenue in a single year.

budget surplus The amount by which the U.S. government's revenue exceeds its spending in a given fiscal year.

- The **budget deficit** is the amount of money spent by the U.S. government over and above what it collects in taxes and other revenue in a single year. A **budget surplus**, on the other hand, is the amount by which the U.S. government's revenue exceeds its spending in a given fiscal year. The federal government has posted annual budget surpluses just 11 times since 1931, including four straight years from 1998 through 2001. Prior to 1998, the last surplus recorded was in 1969, the first year of Richard Nixon's presidency. Although budget deficits are often compelled by national crises that require the quick allotment of funds for some specific purpose (such as responding to the September 11, 2001, terrorist attacks), critics argue that continued budget deficits beyond a short period of time can lead to politically unpopular remedies such as tax increases or spending cuts, or, alternatively, to a burgeoning national debt that can slow economic growth in the long run. The Obama administration's attempts to address the nation's economic problems in 2009 contributed to record deficits. According to the Congressional Budget Office, the deficit forecast for fiscal year 2016 will exceed $534 billion, or about 2.9 percent of the nation's economic output.

national debt The total sum of the federal government's outstanding debt obligations.

- The **national debt** is the total sum of the outstanding debt obligations of the U.S. government, largely generated through the sale of interest-bearing U.S.

savings bonds, U.S. treasury notes, and U.S. treasury bills to individuals or organizations. It represents the accumulated total of all government budget surpluses and deficits of past years as well.[8] In April of 2016, the debt reached the $19-trillion mark for the first time; it will likely continue to escalate by at least $1 trillion per year for the foreseeable future. Consequently, the government must pay in excess of $430 billion per year in interest costs alone. That means to meet interest obligations on the debt, the government must annually pay out the equivalent of more than $2,000 for every man, woman, and child in the country.

- The Dow Jones Industrial Average is perhaps the most widely used indicator of the overall condition of the stock market, where publicly owned companies are actively traded each business day. "The Dow" is actually just a price-weighted average of 30 actively traded blue-chip stocks (that is, from large companies), but its prominence on network newscasts each evening testifies to the important status it holds in the minds of consumers. Other stock market indexes include the Standard & Poor's 500 Index, which encompasses a broader range of large company stocks, and the NASDAQ, an index of high-tech company stocks.

- Housing starts are a measure of the number of U.S. residential building construction projects begun during a specific period of time. Many experts believe that a decline in housing starts is one of the first signs of an approaching economic downturn, and thus it is one of the first indicators consulted by those trying to assess the overall direction of the economy.

- The consumer confidence index (CCI) measures the public's evaluation of the economy by asking a representative sample of Americans how they feel about the current condition of the economy, their personal financial situation, and their prediction about the future of the economy. As shown in Figure 15-1, the CCI underwent dramatic changes between January of 2000 and the beginning of the Great Recession of 2007–2010. By the end of 2015, the CCI had returned to its highest levels in a decade; still, these more recent numbers do not approach the near-record-high numbers last seen in 2000.

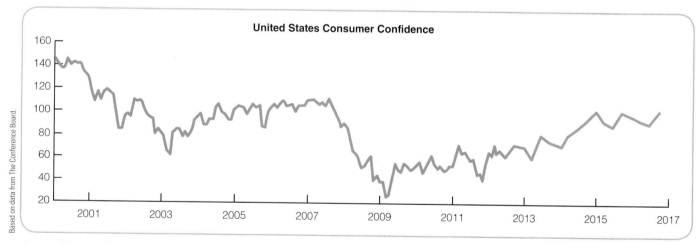

FIGURE 15-1 Consumer Confidence in the United States, 2000–2017

- Balance-of-trade figures (also called net exports) measure the sum of the money gained by a given economy by selling exports, minus the cost of buying imports. When a country exports more than it imports, the country has a trade surplus, whereas the reverse situation denotes a trade deficit. The United States has posted an annual trade deficit dating back to the 1970s; this is perhaps a testament to the rising purchasing power American consumers enjoy around the world. Economists often debate whether such chronic trade deficits are a bad thing; regardless, because especially large trade deficits or surpluses may be a sign of some other economic problems, economists keep a watchful eye on these measures.

In an effort to gauge the state of the economy as a whole, economists have attempted to combine these measures and others into some all-purpose economic indicator. For example, the misery index, measured by adding the inflation rate to the unemployment rate, is a rough indicator of how badly the economy is performing. Jimmy Carter capitalized on an exceedingly high misery index for 1975 to defeat incumbent President Gerald Ford, only to be victimized by an even higher misery index in 1979, which may well have cost Carter reelection in 1980.

Although most observers agree that presidents actually exert only a marginal impact on the economy, economic performance can still be a crucial factor in determining which party wins a presidential election.[9] The U.S. economy normally runs in cycles. The onset of a recession tends to deliver a "one-two punch" against the economy: first, federal revenues decline as profits decrease and fewer people work; then federal expenditures increase as people claim more and more *entitlements* (guaranteed government benefits such as food stamps and welfare) to get them through the jobless period. A recession is eventually followed by an economic recovery, marked by an upswing of positive economic indicators.

The Federal Budget-Making Process

Once considered to be little more than a document detailing sums of money to be spent for particular purposes, the federal budget today has become the primary instrument of federal fiscal policy. The Budget and Accounting Act of 1921 made the president formally responsible for initially formulating the national budget. Today, the president's budget establishes the position around which all subsequent budget battles will be fought. With passage of the Employment Act of 1946, Congress permanently committed the federal government to use the budgetary process to promote maximum employment, production, and purchasing power. Together, these two acts obligate the president to craft budgets strategically to strengthen the economy.

The budget process begins when federal agencies formulate their budget requests and pass them on to the Office of Management and Budget (OMB). A part of the Executive Office of the President, the OMB determines whether the agency's budget proposals are in accord with the president's program and then uses those proposals to prepare an overall budget for the coming fiscal year, setting guidelines for estimating revenue and allotting spending.[10]

After receiving the president's proposals, Congress offers its own budget resolution for the fiscal year, based on its own projections for revenue. The appropriations committees of the House and the Senate are primarily responsible for such budget formulation. Each of the two committees plans overview hearings during which the OMB director and representatives of federal agencies discuss the president's budget priorities. Each of the appropriations committees must eventually pass 10 to 12 appropriations bills to keep the government running. House appropriations bills generally cover the following topic areas, with some variations from year to year:

- Agriculture, Rural Development, Food and Drug Administration, and related agencies
- Commerce, Justice, science, and related agencies
- Defense
- Transportation, Housing and Urban Development, and related agencies
- Energy and water development
- State, foreign operations, and related programs
- Homeland Security

- Interior, Environment, and related agencies
- Labor, Health and Human Services, and Education
- Financial Services and general government
- Legislative branch
- Military construction and Veterans Affairs

All appropriations bills originate in the House; after the House Appropriations Committee has reported the bills to the full House, and after the full House has passed each measure, the Senate Appropriations Committee takes its turn revising the House version. After Senate subcommittee work has been completed on the House bills, the Senate Appropriations Committee marks up its own versions of the bills and reports them to the Senate for floor action.

Congress created separate House and Senate budget committees during the 1970s to oversee the budget process. The Budget and Impoundment Act of 1974 required Congress to set a maximum spending figure for the total budget and for each of several broad funding categories based on projections of future revenue. These figures are prepared by the Congressional Budget Office (CBO), which reports to Congress, and the OMB, which reports to the president. When the CBO and the OMB differ widely on estimates, as has happened frequently in recent years, Congress tends to side with its own agency. The House and Senate budget committees may require cuts in spending to ensure that the overall budget targets can be reached. Eventually the House and Senate must reconcile their competing versions of the budget and secure additional votes from their members for approval of the final budget bill, which is then presented to the president for signature.

All these legislative obstacles must be navigated over a period of eight months, extending from the first Monday in February (when the president's budget proposal is delivered to Congress) through October 1, when the new fiscal year begins. If Congress and the president cannot agree on a final budget over this period of time, Congress may be forced to pass *continuing resolutions* to allow the government to keep running while final budget negotiations continue.[11]

Occasionally, Congress and the president are at such loggerheads that a budget showdown becomes inevitable. In late 1995, the Republican Congress, led by House Speaker Newt Gingrich, insisted that President Bill Clinton sign a budget bill with spending cuts that Clinton's administration had strenuously opposed. When Congress refused to keep passing continuing resolutions, the resulting impasse led to two government shutdowns totaling 27 days, during which all federal government institutions and buildings were forced to close.[12] President Barack Obama and the Republican-controlled House of Representatives have undergone similar budget battles since 2011. Most recently in October 2013, a band of Republicans in Congress shut down the government when the Obama administration refused to defund or delay the controversial Obamacare law. The Speaker of the House at that time, Republican John Boehner, emphasized his party's position that the national debt had grown out of control; President Obama and leading Democrats countered that the budget process was not the appropriate venue to reconsider Obamacare. After a 16-day shutdown, the third longest in American history, the House Republicans eventually conceded defeat, joining with more moderate Republicans in the Senate to pass a compromise bill through both houses of Congress.

Even though the Senate and House budget committees have brought more fiscal restraint to the budget process, some within and outside Congress attempted to introduce bolder budgetary reforms in response to the $200-billion deficits of the mid-1980s. The Gramm-Rudman-Hollings Act of 1985 set annual targets for reducing the deficit and required the General Accounting Office (renamed the Government Accountability Office in 2004; GAO) to determine whether automatic spending cuts would take effect if Congress passed budgets that missed the established deficit target. In 1986, the Supreme Court struck down the act as unconstitutional because the GAO, accountable only to

Congress, could not legally perform what were essentially "executive" acts.[13] The Budget Enforcement Act of 1990 set deficit targets that could be adjusted due to unforeseen economic changes; however, the act did not compensate for unexpected spending increases by requiring offsetting cuts elsewhere.

Of course, the central problem of the budget process—that it allows the federal government to spend more money than it takes in—remained in place even with such reforms. Thus, as shown in Figure 15-2, the total U.S. debt continues to grow by leaps and bounds, with little end in sight. In recent years, Congress has debated passing a balanced budget amendment to the Constitution, which would at least require that annual federal spending be kept at or below revenue collected during the year. Proponents of the amendment argue that it would force free-spending lawmakers to become accountable: just as many taxpayers must live off their income (or even considerably less), the government should be expected to do likewise. Opponents of the amendment counter that the government might—in accordance with Keynesian principles—want to engage in deficit spending during times of recession as a method of economic stimulation. They also note that the federal government must be able to spend freely to defend the national security of the United States, even if that means running up large deficits. (Although recent versions of the amendment would allow Congress to

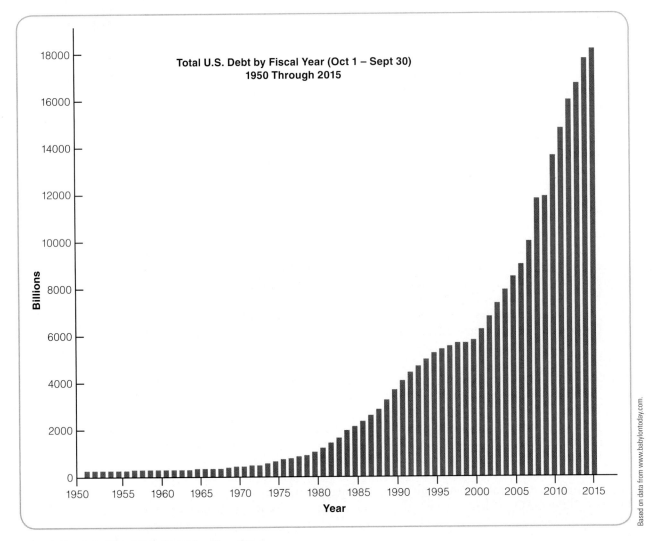

FIGURE 15-2 **Total U.S. Debt by Fiscal Year**

waive the requirement in case of war or military conflict, critics argue that even more flexibility is necessary.) The Balanced Budget Amendment has been passed in one house but defeated in the other on five separate occasions since 1982. In 1995 and again in 1997, the amendment failed by a single vote in the U.S. Senate. More recently in 2011, the House of Representatives voted down a balanced-budget amendment because it did not impose a supermajority requirement on tax increases.

Taxation Policy

Taxation policies tend to fall into one of two general categories. **Redistributive tax policies** aim to provide a social safety net to meet the minimum physical needs of citizens. Such policies accomplish this end by following Robin Hood's principle of "taking from the rich and giving to the poor." For example, taxes that are channeled directly into public assistance programs are redistributive. **Distributive tax policies**, on the other hand, are intended to promote the interests of all economic classes equally. Taxes that are directed toward the maintenance of national parks or the national highway system theoretically benefit all citizens.

All governments need revenue to pay the salaries of government workers and to fund various activities. In July 1789, just four months after the creation of the new government, Congress passed its first revenue-raising bill: specifically, it levied tariffs, which are taxes on imported foreign goods. Up until the Civil War, tariffs provided approximately 90 percent of the federal government's revenue; yet as that war evolved into a long-lasting conflict, the Union needed far greater revenues than even high tariffs could provide. The exponential growth of the federal government after the Civil War exacerbated these demands further. Thus, in the late nineteenth and early twentieth centuries, the federal government was forced to look elsewhere for major sources of funding. Eventually it started to draw more heavily on internal sources of revenue, including payroll taxes, corporate income taxes, and individual income taxes.

The Sixteenth Amendment to the U.S. Constitution authorizes Congress to tax an individual's increase in wealth, whether that wealth comes from wages, benefits, bonuses, or any other form of income. The fairness of individual income taxes, which now provide nearly half of all revenue that flows into the U.S. treasury, remains a subject of contentious debate. The federal government has traditionally imposed a **progressive tax** on incomes. With a progressive tax, the tax rate on an individual's income increases as the amount of income gets larger. Though President Reagan signed tax reform legislation in 1986 to cut top rates and close various loopholes, the personal income tax system still remained mostly progressive—in 2015 the tax system featured rates that went up in several stages to a high of 39.6 percent for all wages (earned by an individual) that exceed $413,200.

Conversely, a tax that charges all individuals the same amount, regardless of income, is called a **regressive tax** because it exacts a larger percentage of income from the lower-wage earner than it does from the high-income earner. Most state sales taxes are regressive because they apply equally to every purchaser: for example, both a poor person and a wealthy person pay the same amount of sales tax for a gallon of gasoline, but that amount constitutes a higher percentage of the poor person's income.

Some people confuse regressive taxes with **flat taxes**. Unlike regressive taxes, flat taxes tax all entities at the same rate *as a proportion of income*. Thus, with a flat tax, a rich person may pay far more in total taxes than a poor person, although the two are still being taxed at the same percentage rate. In 1996 and 2000, presidential candidate Steve Forbes proposed that the federal government impose a flat tax of 15 percent on all income earned in the United States. Forbes argued that such a system would spread the tax burden more evenly, stop penalizing Americans for working harder to earn more, and dramatically simplify the current system.[14] Forbes's proposals have not fared well in the political arena; currently, neither of the two major parties is putting its weight behind a truly flat income tax for Americans.

redistributive tax policies Taxation policies that aim to provide a social safety net to meet the minimum physical needs of citizens.

distributive tax policies Taxation policies intended to promote the interests of all classes equally.

progressive tax A tax whose effective rate on an individual's income increases as the person's income rises.

regressive tax A tax that charges individuals the same amount, regardless of income.

flat tax A tax that draws money from all entities at the same proportion of their income.

Social Security taxes (a tax on personal income and on employers) contribute on average 35 percent to the federal government's overall revenues. Created in 1935, the Social Security system is primarily a self-supporting, "pay-as-you-go" program: payments to current retirees come from current worker payments (dedicated payroll taxes taken directly out of workers' paychecks). In recent decades, Social Security has become the largest expenditure in the federal budget. If and when near-term revenue from payroll taxes proves insufficient to fund near-term benefits, the government may eventually be forced to alleviate the shortfalls either by cutting benefits payments or by passing tax increases. Neither approach would be popular with the public.

During the past century Congress has also imposed corporate income taxes, which today make up approximately 11 percent of the government's revenues. Other important revenue sources include federal taxes on gasoline, communications services, estates, large financial gifts, and customs duties. And if these revenue sources fall short of projected expenditures in the form of a deficit, the federal government must make up the difference by borrowing money in the form of issuing U.S. savings bonds, treasury bills, and the like.

Americans commonly complain about the high taxes they pay, and politicians do not like to be perceived as favoring tax increases; in 1984, Democratic presidential candidate Walter Mondale promised to raise taxes in response to skyrocketing deficits, a promise that all but doomed his hopes of unseating President Ronald Reagan, the candidate more closely identified with lower taxes.

At the Republican national convention in 1988, Vice President George H. W. Bush—having just been named his party's presidential nominee for the upcoming fall—sought to associate himself with the economic policies of the Reagan administration and its emphasis on tax cutting. In his speech accepting the nomination, Bush predicted that if elected president, the Democratic Congress would come to him, pushing him to raise taxes . . .

> *. . . and I'll say no, and they'll push, and I'll say no, and they'll push again, and I'll say to them: "READ MY LIPS: NO NEW TAXES."*

Bush's promise seemed politically astute at the time it was issued, and he coasted to victory that fall. But in 1990, with an economic recession firmly in place, Bush signed the Revenue Reconciliation Act, which aimed to reduce the federal deficit by $500 billion over the next five years. To accomplish that goal, the act called for $125 billion in new taxes, inviting charges that the president had flip-flopped on his 1988 pledge of "no new taxes." In the 1992 presidential campaign, Democratic candidate Bill Clinton attempted to capitalize on the flip-flop. Bush's defeat in the 1992 election was attributed in part to the lack of enthusiasm his candidacy had generated among conservatives, many of whom were still frustrated by the president's decision to sign that infamous tax bill in the first place. James Carville, chief political consultant to Clinton's 1992 presidential campaign, called it "the most famous broken promise in the history of American politics."

Despite all the complaints about high taxes, Americans' tax burden is quite low when compared with the tax burdens of other developed countries. Although U.S. citizens pay an income tax rate somewhere between 10 percent and 39.6 percent, citizens of Sweden pay twice that amount—between 33 percent and 60 percent of their income—to the Swedish government. Taxes paid by citizens in France, Germany, and Great Britain also tend to be higher (as a percentage of their income) than those paid by citizens of the United States. Of course, such comparisons are not altogether

President Barack Obama and New Jersey Governor Chris Christie visit the Jersey Shore to witness firsthand the devastation caused by Hurricane Sandy in October 2012. Since 2008, Congress has allotted to the Federal Emergency Management Agency (FEMA) nearly $6 billion per year in disaster relief funds. FEMA then dispenses those funds to victims of natural disasters across the United States.

fair—for example, Sweden, as part of its welfare system, provides all its citizens with an extensive tax-funded public child care system, dental care, and a ceiling on health care costs. England's tax-funded national health care service offers its citizens "free" services as well.

Still, politicians are reluctant to ignore perceptions that the American tax system is overly burdensome or unfair. In the 2012 and 2014 elections, President Barack Obama and the Democrats sought to redirect the issue to tax fairness and the growing income gap between the rich and the middle class. They argued that the highest income earners—many of whom take advantage of tax breaks on real estate and capital gains to pay an effective tax rate considerably lower than 35 percent—should pay the same or a higher rate than lower-income earners. His administration thus proposed the so-called Buffet plan, named after wealthy investor Warren Buffet, who had argued publicly for higher income tax rates on wealthy individuals such as himself. The Buffet plan would have applied an absolute minimum effective tax rate of 30 percent on earnings of more than $1 million annually. High-profile Republicans, including House Budget Chairman Paul Ryan and 2012 Republican presidential candidate Mitt Romney, criticized the proposal as a form of class warfare that would negatively impact job creation and investment. Tax fairness promises to be a front-burner issue in national elections for the foreseeable future.

Spending Policies—Dividing the Pie

Budget surpluses are a rarity in modern American politics because the federal government has demonstrated time and again its capacity to spend taxpayer money—U.S. government spending topped $3.3 trillion in fiscal year 2015 alone. Although the president is legally responsible for proposing budgets and has the power to veto spending decisions, Article I of the Constitution grants the Congress exclusive power to lay and collect duties "to pay the Debts and provide for the common Defence and general Welfare of the United States." In reality, Congress allots funds from the U.S. treasury to federal departments and agencies and then gives them **budget authority**, which allows them to incur obligations to spend or lend that money. Budget authority for a fiscal year is essentially like the permission for an agency to enter a contract; it is not the same thing as how much the agency will spend in that fiscal year—that amount is called **outlays**.

Where does taxpayer money go? The truth about government spending might surprise you. Spending tends to fall into two general categories. **Mandatory spending** refers to spending not controlled by annual budget decisions—these funds are automatically obligated by virtue of previously enacted laws and may not be modified by annual budget decisions (although they can be modified by repeal or modification of the original legislation). Most mandatory spending occurs in the form of entitlements: government spending such as Social Security, Medicare (national health insurance for seniors), and veterans benefits that must be paid to anyone meeting specific eligibility requirements. President Franklin Delano Roosevelt's New Deal programs and President Lyndon Johnson's Great Society programs substantially expanded the number of entitlements, forcing future lawmakers to grapple with those entitlements when they considered reforms of their own. Since 1995, nearly two-thirds of all government spending has been mandatory, almost double the percentage of mandatory spending outlays of the early 1960s (see Figure 15-3).

Discretionary spending encompasses all those spending categories that Congress does have the power to modify or eliminate in a given year. Budgeting is normally a give-and-take process between Congress and the president concerning the most appropriate levels of discretionary spending. Most federal spending on education, the environment, and national defense is based on discretionary spending outlays. When an administration's critics accuse the president of not being fiscally conservative enough with government spending, their criticisms usually focus on government spending as a whole; in fairness, however, only discretionary spending really lays within the president's

budget authority The power of federal departments and agencies to incur obligations to spend or lend money.

outlays The amount of money a government agency will actually spend during a fiscal year.

mandatory spending Federal government spending that is not controlled by annual budget decisions; includes entitlements such as Medicare and Social Security.

discretionary spending Forms of federal government spending that Congress can modify or eliminate in any given year, including spending on education, the environment, and national defense.

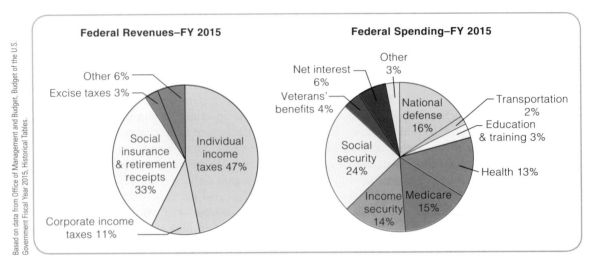

FIGURE 15-3 Where Do Federal Tax Dollars Come from and Where Do They Go?
Mandatory spending (required by law) represents such a large percentage of the budget (approximately two-thirds of all government spending) that lawmakers often complain that their hands are tied as they wrestle with ways to cut costs. Unlike most spending on our national defense, which Congress authorizes each year at its discretion, entitlements such as Social Security, Medicare, and the food stamp program are examples of mandatory spending categories. The two pie charts shown here illustrate sources of federal revenues and the allocation of federal spending in fiscal year 2015.

immediate influence. In the eight years the Clinton administration was responsible for the federal budget (1994 through 2001), discretionary spending increased by an annual average of 3.4 percent; during the George W. Bush administration, discretionary spending increased by an average of 10.5 percent annually. Discretionary spending in the final years of the Obama administration amounted to approximately 30 percent of the overall budget.

Year in and year out, one particular mandatory spending category—Social Security spending—tops all the other categories. In fiscal year 2015, the federal government spent over $888 billion on the program, and Social Security expenditures of over $900 billion are anticipated by fiscal year 2017. Among the discretionary program outlays, national defense has traditionally constituted the largest part of the budget. In 1962, the federal government allotted $52.4 billion to defense, almost 10 times the amount earmarked to any other discretionary program category. More than a half century later, in 2015, nearly $600 billion was allotted to national defense. The growth in discretionary spending during the past 15 years can be attributed in part to the George W. Bush administration's desire to increase spending on defense and homeland security in the wake of the terrorist attacks of September 11, 2001, as well as to the Obama administration's willingness to continue most of those same defense policies as well as to increase military spending in Afghanistan.

monetary policy Regulation of the money supply and interest rates by a central bank, such as the U.S. Federal Reserve Board, in order to control inflation and stabilize the currency.

15-3 | Theories and Practice In Monetary Policy

Monetary policy is the means by which the government controls the supply and price of money in the economy. Although this may seem like a nonpolitical, technical function, the exercise of monetary policy can have profound implications on unemployment rates and inflation, and thus is the focus of considerable political interest.

Diversity Dilemma

Diversity in America's Classrooms

America's increasingly diverse population has brought a new set of challenges and opportunities to its various educational systems. Indeed, the demographic makeup of the nation's classrooms has been transformed. The 2014–2015 academic school year marked the first time in U.S. history that a majority of students (50.2 percent) in pre-kindergarten through 12th grade were nonwhite. The National Center for Education Statistics (NCES) projects that by 2023, our country's schools will include about 45 percent white and 55 percent nonwhite students.[15] The NCES also provides evidence that this population diversity is not likely to be reflected in the makeup of our school teachers and administration, as at least 82 percent of classroom teachers are currently non-Hispanic white.[16] This teacher-to-student disparity has significant ramifications for students' sense of well-being in schools, and even for various measures of academic achievement. In addition, this changing demographic picture has raised critical questions concerning educational policy, such as (1) How do schools incorporate more diverse curricula and recruit more teachers from a variety of backgrounds? (2) How do schools address academic achievement gaps among racial/ethnic groups? (3) How do schools address the high incidence of racial and income-related school segregation across the country? The next decade or so promises to be a challenging era indeed for educational reformers charged with addressing the needs of our changing American population.

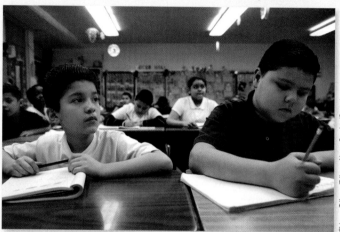

Students work on their math in a fourth grade classroom at Carman-Buckner Elementary School in Waukegan, Illinois.

Chicago Tribune/Tribune News Service/Getty Images

For Critical Thinking and Discussion

1. Have you thought about a career in education?
2. What opportunities do the challenges of a changing student population offer to incoming new teachers?

With few exceptions, the **Federal Reserve System**, which is headed by the **Federal Reserve Board** ("the Fed"), determines monetary policy in the United States. Since 1913, this independent agency has acted as the nation's central bank, supervising and regulating all of the nation's banks and providing financial information to the public. In addition to the Federal Reserve Board, Congress established 12 nonprofit Federal Reserve Banks to serve as the operating arms of the central banking system. By law, all member banks in the United States (which includes all national banks and many state banks) must maintain fractional reserves—a portion of their deposits that must be kept on hand or at the Fed to satisfy any demands for withdrawal. (Most fractional reserves are kept in accounts at the Federal Reserve Banks.) The Federal Reserve Banks in turn issue stock and pay dividends to member banks as partial compensation for the lack of interest they pay on member banks' required reserves. The Federal Reserve Board sets all rules and regulations for the Federal Reserve Banks.[17]

Perhaps the single most important responsibility of the Federal Reserve is to set the **discount rate** that all member banks and other depository institutions will be charged to borrow short-term funds. A high discount rate makes it more expensive for member banks to borrow money from the Federal Reserve Banks, but more profitable for banks to lend money (because they'll secure a greater interest on their investment). The opposite is true when the Federal Reserve lowers the discount rate: Banks are more apt to borrow

Federal Reserve System The central banking system of the United States, which controls the nation's money supply.

Federal Reserve Board The Federal Reserve System's Board of Governors, which votes on monetary policy in the United States, supervises the nation's banks by setting rules for the 12 Federal Reserve Banks, and engages in open market operations.

discount rate The rate (expressed as a percentage) that all Federal Reserve member banks and other depository institutions will be charged by the Federal Reserve Banks to borrow short-term funds.

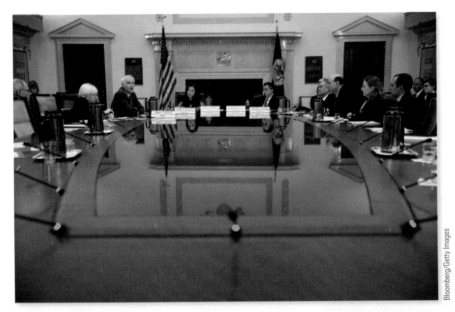

Federal Reserve Chairperson Janet Yellen (seated at the table, second from the left) confers with other Board members at a recent Federal Reserve Board meeting.

open market operations The buying and selling of government securities by the Federal Reserve Board as a means of controlling the national money supply.

reserve requirement The minimum liquid assets each bank must keep on hand to back customer loans.

money because it is cheaper, whereas lending money to others becomes less profitable. A second important function of the Federal Reserve is its engagement in **open market operations**, in which it buys and sells government securities as a means of controlling the national money supply—buying bonds increases the amount of money in circulation, whereas selling has the opposite effect. Finally, the Federal Reserve sets the **reserve requirements** of member banks, determining the minimum liquid assets each bank must keep on hand to back customer loans. Any of these actions has the effect of either tightening or loosening the overall money supply.

In recent years, it has become common for investors to eagerly anticipate the Federal Reserve's next announcement that it plans to adjust the interest rate up or down.[18] Although hardly an exact science, the Federal Reserve's setting of a new discount rate can affect the economy in profoundly important ways. Why would the Federal Reserve choose to raise the discount rate? The primary goal of the Federal Reserve is to stabilize the economy and prevent dangerously wide fluctuations that can upset the economy. Although politicians may benefit in the short run from a quickly growing economy, the Federal Reserve may fear the eventual onset of high inflation. Under such circumstances, it may seek to tighten the money supply (the total amount of money available in the economy at a particular point in time) by increasing the discount rate. Such a move may be politically unpopular because interest rates throughout the economy tend to rise along with the discount rate, making it harder for individuals to borrow money for houses and consumer goods. Investments by businesses may similarly be curtailed.

On the flip side, the Federal Reserve may choose to lower the discount rate as a way to stimulate investment and spur the economy forward. Lower interest rates allow individuals to borrow and invest more for consumer goods and real estate and businesses to borrow more money for capital investment. Some economists believe lower interest rates also keep unemployment at a minimum because businesses are better able to maximize their production capacity.

When Congress enacted the Federal Reserve Act in 1913, it sought to ensure that the Federal Reserve could act independently of partisan political considerations, which often demand short-term fixes to the economy. Each of the Fed's seven members serves a term of 14 years. Once appointed and confirmed, a board member may not be removed from office except through a cumbersome impeachment process for serious criminal violations. The president also determines (with the consent of the Senate) who will serve as Federal Reserve chair for a period of four years, although in practice the chair is often reappointed several times.

Few officials in history have faced a more daunting challenge than Ben Bernanke, the Federal Reserve chair who presided over the Board from 2006 through 2014. Bernanke replaced Alan Greenspan, the legendary chairman who presided over an unprecedented period of high economic growth and low inflation during his 19 years at the helm of the Fed. Yet the new chairman's challenge grew significantly in late 2008 when he presided over the biggest economic collapse since the Great Depression. Bernanke approached the crisis by proposing initiatives designed to save the world economy rather than simply to shape U.S. monetary policy. Under his leadership, the Federal Reserve Bank ratcheted interest rates down to zero; lent money to mutual funds, hedge funds, foreign banks, investment banks, manufacturers, insurers, and other borrowers; and jump-started stalled credit markets and revolutionized housing finance in the United States by purchasing mortgage bonds in bulk. *Time* magazine named Bernanke its "Person of the Year" in 2009 for these efforts, and President Obama reappointed Bernanke to a second four-year term in 2010.

In 2014 Bernanke gave way to his successor as Board chairman, economist Janet Yellen. Making history as the first female ever to hold that position, Yellen immediately faced questions about what the Board might do to address the slumping housing market, among other troubling warning signs. The first Democratic nominee to run the Federal Reserve in nearly three decades, Yellen chaired the Federal Reserve in 2015, when it increased its key interest rate for the first time since 2006.

15-4 | The Nature and Practice of Crime Policy

Perhaps the most fundamental way in which modern societies manage relations among human beings residing within their jurisdictions is through the use of a comprehensive criminal justice system. Democratic systems must strike a careful balance between maintaining public order and protecting individual freedom—the rules and practices of the criminal justice system determine where and how that balance will be struck. For example, especially severe and strict forms of law enforcement could prove effective at making citizens safe, but only at a very high cost in taxpayers' money and possibly some loss of individual freedom as well.

In 1968, social scientist Herbert Packer defined two different models of criminal justice policymaking: the "crime control model" and the "due process model."[19] The **crime control model** views the controlling of criminal behavior as the most important function of criminal justice. Packer depicts the crime control model as a type of "assembly-line justice" because it tries to move cases quickly and efficiently though the system. The process requires that police and prosecutor make crucial judgments about defendants' guilt early in the process; the crime control model thus relies extensively on negotiations between defense attorneys and state prosecutors early on to avoid the uncertainty and high costs associated with a full-blown trial. In theory, the guilty will be routinely pressed to enter plea bargains, whereas the innocent should hope to see their indictments dismissed early in the process. Of course, the quick nature of this process increases the likelihood that public officials and defense attorneys will not always make the best judgments.

crime control model Criminal justice policymaking model that views the controlling of criminal behavior as the system's most important function.

due process model Criminal justice policymaking model that views the attainment of justice—which includes protection of the innocent—as the principal goal of the system.

A defendant being arraigned in one of the nation's criminal courtrooms.

By contrast, in the **due process model**, the principal goal is justice, which focuses just as much on acting to protect the innocent as it does on convicting the guilty. Stressing the adversarial process and the need for hearings, the model endeavors to guarantee that all criminal justice decisions will be based on reliable information at every stage of the process, with the government forced to meet far higher standards than the accused along the way. By placing a premium on protecting the rights of individuals, some guilty defendants may go free simply because the state has not met its high burden of proving guilt "beyond a reasonable doubt."[20]

The American system of criminal justice can be characterized as a tug-of-war between both of these models, with no-name,

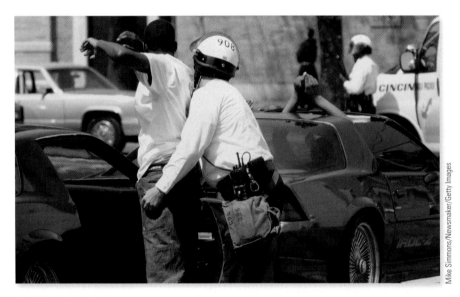

An African American man being arrested. Racial profiling authorizes stopping and interrogating members of racial minorities because their racial characteristics are similar to those of others who have committed crimes.

relatively run-of-the-mill, usually poor defendants generally falling into the crime control "assembly line," whereas bigger-name, higher-profile, and wealthy defendants are far more likely to experience the due process model.

Critics of the criminal justice system charge that racial disparities have become the norm, with African Americans, Hispanics, and other racial and ethnic minorities entering the system in numbers disproportionate to their representation in the general population.[21] They point also to the controversy surrounding police use of racial profiling, in which African Americans in particular are often stopped and interrogated simply because they possess the same racial characteristics as others who have committed crimes. Defenders of the system contend that racial minorities commit a larger percentage of crimes, perhaps a product of their relative economic disadvantage in society as a whole. That defense does not take into account alarming statistical trends showing that race figures directly into sentencing decisions. For example, a famous 1990 study demonstrated that killers of whites in Georgia were 4.3 times more likely to be sentenced to death than killers of African Americans.[22] Because racism remains a problem in American society as a whole, judicial sentencing and racial stereotyping may well be tainted by feelings of racism that lie below the surface.

Up through the 1980s, criminal justice policymaking mostly occurred within state and local governments. In recent decades, however, Congress has acted to criminalize and/or increase sentences for a host of unlawful activities at the federal level.[23] Passage of the federal Gun-Free School Zones Act of 1990 outlawing the possession of guns within a specified proximity of a school building, a 1996 federal carjacking statute, and federal crime bills that expand the death penalty to cover certain federal crimes are all representative of this modern policymaking trend.[24] Congress has also been actively involved in the "war on drugs," passing numerous statutes outlawing the possession, use, and sale of certain illegal drugs. As a result, federal drug laws today account for over 30 percent of all drug offenders' sentences.

Occasionally Congress has overstepped its constitutional bounds in passing crime laws—in 1995 the Supreme Court struck down the Gun-Free School Zones Act as an unconstitutional usurpation of each state's prerogative to criminalize acts that take place solely within its jurisdiction.[25] Additionally, many of these federal laws duplicate existing state criminal laws. Still, given the public's favorable response to such laws, it is tough to imagine Congress withdrawing from this area of policymaking any time soon.

15-5 | The Welfare State and Programs for the Poor

welfare state Social system in which the state assumes a considerable degree of responsibility for citizens in matters of health care, employment, education, and retirement income.

The term **welfare state** refers to a social system in which the state assumes a considerable degree of responsibility for citizens in matters of health care, employment, education, and retirement income. In its ideal form, a welfare state is expected to do more than merely guarantee a minimum level of subsistence in these matters; thus, welfare states do not simply ensure a "safety net" for their citizens. (Naturally, these welfare states require higher levels of taxation than do more strictly capitalist systems.) The actual amount of welfare provided varies widely from nation to nation. Nearly all modern welfare states sit

The Supreme Court And Health Care Policy

King v. Burwell (2015)[26]

When the Patient Protection and Affordable Care Act of 2010 (aka Obamacare) narrowly survived the Supreme Court's constitutional scrutiny in 2012, President Obama and the law's supporters breathed a major sigh of relief. Still, Obamacare has remained a ripe target for legal challenge. After all, its provisions extend for 2,700 pages, with an additional 20,000 pages of associated regulations. Critics eventually found within those many pages a technicality that could unravel the entire legal regime: language that on its face appeared to technically provide eligibility for tax credits only to those living in states with "state-operated exchanges" that provide reasonably priced health care insurance. If that was the case, patients in the 34 states that did not set up their own exchanges (and thus relied on federal exchanges instead) would lose their tax credits, and with them their health insurance coverage. By challenging this essential foundation of Obamacare, the legal claim might well spell the end of the entire legislative regime.

Perhaps that is why a 6–3 Supreme Court majority in *King v. Burwell* (2015), rejected the legal challenge. According to the Court, the only way to resolve the somewhat ambiguous language of the statute was by looking at the purpose of the overall statute, which was to have subsidies available for all federally run exchanges as well. Otherwise, "it would destabilize the individual insurance market in any State with a Federal Exchange, and likely create the very 'death spirals' that Congress designed the Act to avoid." Much to the chagrin of its critics, President Obama's landmark legislation had once again survived to live another day. Rather than puncturing the law, the Supreme Court allowed the controversial policy to continue.

For Critical Thinking and Discussion

1. Assuming a major domestic policy has survived constitutional scrutiny, what role should the judiciary play in interpreting its provisions? Should judges interpret the law in ways likely to enhance its success, or offer more technical interpretations that could undermine political compromises carefully achieved elsewhere?

2. In his dissent in *King v. Burwell*, the late Justice Antonin Scalia ridiculed the majority for adopting an absurd interpretation, and thus renamed "Obamacare" as "Scotuscare." By helping to save a law, is the Court essentially advocating for the policy choices that underlie it? Why or why not?

---

somewhere on a spectrum between pure **capitalism** (an economic system in which all or most of the means of production are privately owned under competitive conditions) and **socialism** (an economic system in which all or most of the means of production are owned by the community as a whole). Most welfare states have this much in common: They ensure that whatever welfare is provided is done so in universal fashion—in short, they tend to cover every person who meets welfare standards as a matter of right, rather than discretion.

The form of the modern welfare state dates back to the late nineteenth and early twentieth centuries. Germany under Chancellor Otto von Bismarck in the 1880s was the first nation in history to provide social insurance for its citizens.[27] In the early part of the twentieth century, Scandinavian countries were among the first to establish comprehensive welfare states—Sweden, for example, provided for child care, maternity and paternity leave, a ceiling on health care costs, free education at all levels, and retirement pensions. Many other Western European nations, including Ireland, Britain, and France, soon followed suit.

Fiercely protective of its capitalist origins, the U.S. government vigorously resisted assuming broad welfare state functions up until the 1930s, when the Great Depression exposed the harsh realities that unfettered capitalism can occasionally impose on the masses. Still, although Franklin Delano Roosevelt's New Deal is accurately credited with establishing the modern welfare state in America with its provisions for assisting the poor, his program actually featured few express provisions that directly ensured better education or health care for the masses, to name just two examples.[28] Even the Social Security Act of 1935, which established the Social Security system, was billed at the time not as a welfare program, but as a system of forced savings that would benefit only those in wage-earning families. It wasn't until the Great Society legislation of the mid-1960s that the federal government actively expanded the reach of the welfare state to

capitalism Economic system in which all or most of the means of production are privately owned under competitive conditions.

socialism Economic system in which all or most of the means of production are owned by the community as a whole.

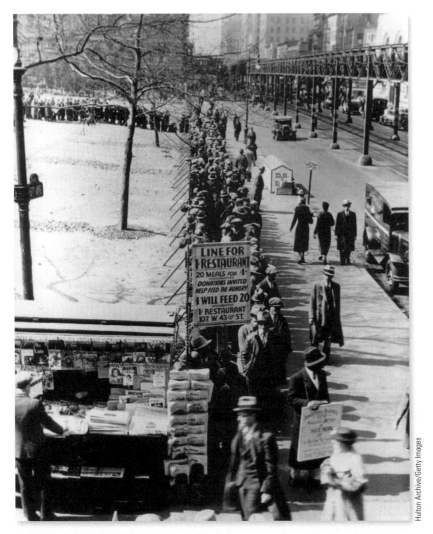

Long lines of people in New York City waited patiently for handouts during the Great Depression.

include the provision of education, health care, and assistance to the poor.

Compared with other Western democracies in Europe and elsewhere that have embraced the welfare state on behalf of their citizens, the U.S. welfare state model is far less comprehensive and ambitious. Why the reluctance to go further? Welfare continues to be seen as "taking something" without contributing in return, so the notion of a state built around this premise remains objectionable to many Americans. Indeed, many Americans (and the political parties that curry favor with them) view welfare recipients as going against the grain of the work ethic, and thus getting a "free ride" based on the efforts of others. Although the miserable conditions associated with the Great Depression went a long way toward debunking the belief that the poor are always responsible for their own plight, Americans are still reluctant to see the federal government install a system of social welfare similar to what has been established in many European democracies.

Poverty has always been a problem in the United States, but until the middle part of the twentieth century, true welfare programs—defined as those programs that maintain the economic and physical well-being of society's poorest members— were primarily the responsibility of local communities and private organizations, including churches. The federal government acted only when circumstances seemed to dictate a potential crisis: For example, the Freedmen's Bureau provided rudimentary education and work opportunities for former slaves in the late 1860s and early 1870s; similarly, industrial abuses led to limited federal aid to poor mothers and children during the initial decades of the twentieth century. But in general, public resistance to a substantial federal welfare role held fast, at least up until the 1930s.

The Great Depression created a significant change in attitudes about welfare programs and led directly to broader government involvement. New Deal programs such as the Works Progress Administration and the Federal Emergency Relief Administration provided public jobs and emergency aid. Aid to Dependent Children (later called Aid to Families with Dependent Children, or AFDC) supplemented existing state programs by providing money to poor single mothers unable to work and partake in federal jobs programs.[29] More a public charity than an entitlement, AFDC money went to the extremely poor, and its benefits were often below prevailing minimum wages.

President Lyndon Johnson's Great Society program of the mid-1960s substantially expanded federal welfare programs. As part of his administration's "war on poverty," a federal food stamps program was initiated in 1964; the federal government also gave money to community service programs such as Legal Aid, medical clinics in poor neighborhoods, and the Head Start preschool education program for disadvantaged children. The **Medicare** program was created to provide health insurance for the elderly in general, whereas **Medicaid** became the first federal program to provide limited health care services

Medicare Federal program that provides health insurance for the elderly.

Medicaid Federal program that provides limited health care services to the poor.

to the poor.[30] Mismanagement slowed the progress of the war on poverty; the outbreak of riots and crimes in the inner cities—where much of the antipoverty legislation was targeted—further doomed legislative support for the expansion of such programs.

Once established into law, the welfare reforms of the mid-twentieth century were not free of controversy. Activists complained that AFDC benefits were not high enough to bring poor families out of poverty, trapping them in their economic plights for the foreseeable future. Additionally, approximately 25 percent of those defined as poor by federal law were still not receiving any form of federal benefits under the current program. Conservatives were also frustrated, charging that the incentives of the welfare system encouraged poor mothers to stay home without actively seeking employment, or even to have more children as a means of increasing government payments.

As a presidential candidate in 1992, Bill Clinton promised to "end welfare as we know it"; four years later, with the Republicans firmly in control of Congress, President Clinton was presented with legislation that held him to those very words. In 1996, Congress passed and Clinton signed into law the Personal Responsibility and Work Opportunity Reconciliation Act, which replaced AFDC with the Temporary Assistance to Needy Families (TANF) program. TANF devolved much of the former AFDC program back to the states, scaled back the food stamps program, and required welfare recipients to work, or at least actively look for work. The law also imposed a five-year limit on receiving benefits, overthrowing the previous system of providing indefinite benefits to those who met federal eligibility requirements.[31] In its first few years, the program succeeded in decreasing state caseloads by as much as 50 percent. Still, critics charged that it penalizes the truly needy; additionally, because "last-hired" individuals tend to be the first ones fired during more difficult times, many have returned to welfare in the last 15 years, increasing caseloads for state governments to manage.

15-6 | The Social Security System

Social Security has frequently been called the "third rail" of American politics—any politician who touches it is sure to get shocked into submission.[32] The specter of millions of older Americans living in poverty as a result of the Great Depression led to the establishment of Social Security in 1935 as a sort of national pension system. The system was originally intended to be a self-sufficient, "pay-as-you-go" system: Workers and their employers would pay dedicated Social Security taxes, and these funds would then be disbursed in the form of pension payments to current retirees. During its early years, the Social Security system often ran surpluses because the ratio of workers to beneficiaries remained high. In the 1950s, Congress even broadened the system's coverage and raised minimum benefits to lower-income contributors.

Unfortunately, the severe economic strains of the 1970s, including high inflation, substantially eroded the Social Security trust fund, which contains securities redeemable to make payments to retirees whenever contributions are not sufficient to pay benefits. Minor reforms have been implemented to increase Social Security taxes and raise the retirement age, shoring up the trust fund for the time being. Still, some economists fear that the Social Security system will become weaker in the years ahead.[33] Thus, by the year 2025, when all baby boomers are eligible for Social Security, the system may start to face serious solvency issues. Indeed, according to the Social Security Board of Trustees, the cost will continue to rise such that by 2035, taxes will be enough to pay for only 75 percent of scheduled benefits.

Social Security thus represents a conundrum for politicians: Many recognize the need for large-scale reform of the system, but public opinion and interest groups that favor the current system have proven just as stubborn. The broad political support Social Security enjoys is based largely on the premise that the system is not simply another form of welfare; although lower-income contributors do receive some breaks, rich and poor employees alike pay into the system and receive its benefits.

Because of the concern over the long-run solvency of the Social Security system, many future retirees have been forced to adjust their savings strategies to plan for a future without any guarantee of Social Security. Traditionally, government employees and people who work for larger companies or organizations have enjoyed conventional pension plans that guarantee a monthly benefit after retirement. Unfortunately, employees normally have no control over the investment of pension funds—many employees learn that their company's pension fund has been depleted by unwise investments only after the damage has been done. Additionally, most pension plans provide significant benefits only for employees who work at a particular organization for the long haul—perhaps for 25 or 30 years. In an increasingly mobile economy such as ours, fewer and fewer workers fit this description.

Through the use of tax incentives, the federal government has recently played a role in encouraging people to put aside extra savings for retirement. As a result, millions today directly invest a substantial portion of their savings in the stock market through the use of tax-favored retirement vehicles such as individual retirement accounts (IRAs) and 401(k) plans. Not only do such vehicles help provide an extra retirement cushion, they also have helped to ensure that a stream of investment capital continues to flow into publicly traded companies on the stock market, which in turn contributes to the well-being of the economy.

15-7 | Health Care Policy

universal health care National health care system in which full access to health care is provided to citizens at government expense.

Patient Protection and Affordable Care Act of 2010 (PPACA, aka "Obamacare") The main federal legislation passed in 2010 that overhauled the health care system by expanding Medicaid and guaranteeing health care coverage for select groups of citizens.

The U.S. health care system differs in important ways from the public-run systems found in other modern industrial nations. France, Great Britain, and other European democracies have all adopted systems of **universal health care**, in which full access to health care is provided to citizens at government expense. In the United States, health care has remained a privately operated activity, in which patients secure health care insurance and enter into relationships with physicians largely outside of government control. The **Patient Protection and Affordable Care Act of 2010 (PPACA, aka "Obamacare")** and subsequent legislation passed by Congress (most notably the Health Care and Education Reconciliation Act of 2010) feature an "individual mandate" that penalized most citizens who do not obtain health care insurance by 2014.

The PPACA proved successful at decreasing the percentage of Americans who remain uninsured. By the end of 2014, several different sources reported that the number of uninsured had declined by at least 25 percent, and a well-known Henry J. Kaiser Family Foundation study placed the number of uninsured in the United States at just 10 percent during that same time frame. Still, the controversial law has not been without problems. Because insurers are required to charge the same premiums to individuals regardless of health status, they are often incentivized to leave the best doctors and the best hospitals out of their networks to keep costs down. Additionally, provisions of the PPACA that mandate preventive care without any deductible or co-payment make it impossible to give enrollees financial incentives to use non-doctor services, which would in turn expand the supply of care without sacrificing quality. Finally, some low-income families have not qualified for subsidies under the law because the definition of "affordable" employer-based coverage only takes into account the cost of individual plans and not family plans. (Critics call this the "family glitch.")

Even supporters of Obamacare have called for improvements to the controversial legislation. During the 2016 presidential campaign, Democratic contender Hillary Clinton advocated reforms to "deal with the high cost of deductibles" by lowering the maximum percentage of income that makes families eligible for premium subsidies to 8.5 percent. Others complain that the legislation does not provide any form

Then and Now

States as "Laboratories of Democracy" that Point the Way for National Domestic Policy

State legislators who sponsor innovative new programs in their respective jurisdictions may—if the programs are successful—start a movement of similar initiatives in other states. They may also offer a model of sorts for the federal government to enact a similar program on a national scale some time later. In this way, state governments and their laws can fulfill an even greater purpose in a democracy: As Supreme Court Justice Louis Brandeis argued in 1932, states provide the nation as a whole with true "laboratories for democracy." Consider two such laboratories in action:

Then

In 1930, with a severe economic crisis bearing down on states across the country, New York Governor Franklin Delano Roosevelt urged passage of legislation to provide so-called old-age pensions. Such laws had been practically nonexistent before the onset of the Great Depression; yet 30 separate states passed some form of elderly assistance legislation between 1930 and 1935, including legislatures in California, Massachusetts, and New York. Thus, when President Franklin Delano Roosevelt proposed the national system of Social Security legislation in 1935, he was able to learn and borrow from states' experiences, including his own. Unlike failed programs in other states, California and Massachusetts did not require counties to "opt in" to the program to participate; all counties were enrolled automatically. Roosevelt

also learned that many of the failed state programs had trouble enrolling older citizens who were reluctant to "go on welfare"; the more successful state policies billed themselves instead as variations on employee savings programs. Accordingly, the national Social Security program passed in 1935 was mandatory, and it too would be financed by payroll taxes, distinguishing it further from more traditional welfare programs. The state governments had performed a valuable service with their experimental policies, pointing the way to a national program that survives nearly 85 years later. Roosevelt must have been especially proud, as the Old Age Pension Act of New York that he had signed into law as governor of that state helped pave the road to the Social Security Act he signed into law as president just a few years later.

Now

In 2010, the Obama administration settled for half a loaf rather than no loaf at all. Although the comprehensive health care policy passed by Congress and signed into law on March 23, 2010, significantly expanded health care coverage to uninsured individuals across the country, it stopped short of the "universal coverage" Obama and Democratic leaders had once advocated. Supporters of universal health care coverage should have been forewarned: progressive state legislatures had debated the merits of their own health care initiatives in recent decades, and a handful had even made significant strides, but none had succeeded in guaranteeing complete universal coverage. Hawaii was the true pioneer in this regard: In the 1970s, its legislature enacted a law that mandated employer-based health insurance for all employees not covered by collective bargaining. Later, in 1989, the Aloha state went a step further, subsidizing insurance coverage for Hawaiians unable to pay. Even so, 5 percent of Hawaii's population remained uninsured. Meanwhile the Massachusetts Health Care Reform Law of 2006 had a bit more success, lowering the number of insured in that state significantly during its first four years of implementation.

Five thousand miles away in Boston, Massachusetts, the state legislature in 2006 passed legislation requiring all residents to purchase health insurance or face stiff legal penalties. Once again, however, ambiguous definitions of the term *affordable* meant that at least some Massachusetts residents would continue to be uninsured. Several state governments had expanded health care coverage, but they had failed to

Massachusetts Governor Mitt Romney, signing that state's health care reform law in 2006. As the Republican nominee for president in 2012, Romney struggled to distinguish his state's health care laws from the federal program passed by President Obama and the Democrats, which borrowed heavily from the Massachusetts model.

enact universal coverage for their populations. Like its state forbearers, the national government's health care reform plan similarly expanded coverage for millions, but it too failed to provide universal coverage.

For Critical Thinking and Discussion

1. Are some states so different in culture and character from the nation as a whole that they make poor "laboratories" for experimentation? In considering national legislation, can we really learn much from Hawaii, Alaska, or Wyoming, to name just a few places?
2. How can the federal government do more to encourage state-level policy innovations?

of public-sponsored health care plans (other than "health insurance exchanges" that organize the marketplace for the purchase of private health insurance in more cost-efficient ways).

Ensuring that society's oldest and poorest citizens receive adequate health care was a primary concern of U.S. health care laws even before the 2010 legislative reforms. Since 1965, the Medicare program has provided health insurance as a Social Security benefit to retirees; amendments to the program in 2003 limited the costs of prescription drugs for seniors. More recently, the federal government extended the reach of Medicare to small, rural hospitals and facilities. The poor sometimes receive health insurance through grants to the states as part of the Medicaid program; the PPACA expanded Medicaid eligibility as well. Beginning in 2014, persons with income levels up to 133 percent of the poverty line will qualify for coverage. Additionally, federal legislation dictates the rules to be followed by **health maintenance organizations (HMOs)**, which are prepaid group practice arrangements that attempt to limit costs through flat monthly rates.[34] Yet the defining characteristic of health care in the United States—patients' reliance on private, voluntary health plans—continues, with government incentives and penalties playing a major role in the process.

Significant criticisms of the health care system in the United States remain. Most of those who do have health insurance receive it through group plans offered by their employers, and the 2010 legislation did little to reverse that reality. Thus, when employees change jobs, their health insurance coverage is normally disrupted. Additionally, in 2009 one in seven Americans under age 65 still did not have health insurance. Although the PPACA is expected to significantly lower this figure, it will not guarantee universal coverage by any means.

Finally, health insurance is not the same as actual health care. Many continue to be hindered by a lack of access to primary care: More than 20 million people in the United States live in rural areas or inner-city neighborhoods that have a shortage of physicians to meet their basic health care needs.[35] Rural residents are particularly disadvantaged; according to the U.S. Department of Health and Human Services, residents of rural areas maintain the highest death rates for unintentional injuries generally and for motor-vehicle injuries specifically, due in large part to the shortage of physicians in such areas. Thus, health care delivery practices will continue to be a problem, no matter how far government extends the scope of health care insurance coverage.

Domestic policy in the United States has been a source of continued frustration for many. This nation's status as one of the richest nations in the world over the past century might imply a responsibility on the part of the government to spread around those riches so that each person is assured at least a minimum level of subsistence and welfare. At the same time, the U.S. capitalist system tends to foster a culture of "pull yourself up by your bootstraps," which is at odds with policy efforts leading to the systematic provision of goods and services to needy people. In the modern era, the U.S. government has attempted to strike a balance between these two positions, to the satisfaction of few. Prior to the New Deal, the government's role in providing social welfare was quite limited. Since the 1930s, and especially since the 1960s, the government's social welfare functions have increased substantially.

Unfortunately, the course of public policy is rarely a smooth one, and frustrations can weigh down even the most well-intentioned domestic programs. Toxic waste dumps at Love Canal and elsewhere became a local health hazard and a nightmare for

health maintenance organizations (HMOs) Prepaid group practice arrangements entered into by doctors and other health professionals that attempt to limit costs by charging customers flat monthly rates with little or no deductibles.

Realistic Options for National Service

In the early 1960s, young people in the United States who wanted to help change the world considered joining the Peace Corps, a government agency charged with "increasing international mutual understanding." More than 200,000 have taken up that call, working for the Peace Corps in 139 different countries. But for all the opportunities the Peace Corps provided for international service, it lacked an outlet to serve the United States at home. That changed in 1993 when the National Community and Service Trust Act created AmeriCorps. Since its creation, AmeriCorps has sent over a quarter of a million young people to communities in the United States to support the start-up of innovative new national programs, including City Year, Public Allies, and Teach for America. It also brought vital resources to established programs, including the Boys and Girls Clubs, Big Brothers and Big Sisters, Justicecorps, and the American Red Cross.

Like any government program, AmeriCorps has its share of critics. Some have alleged that the program diverts young people participating in the program from attaining higher levels of education on their own behalf or that it delays the start of their careers. Critics also charge that AmeriCorps sends the wrong message by implying that volunteers should be paid for community service work (full-time members who complete their service earn a Segal AmeriCorps Education Award of up to $5,775 as well as an annual stipend of $10,000).

A volunteer for Habitat for Humanity pitches in to rebuild a house in New Orleans in the wake of Hurricane Katrina.

For Critical Thinking and Discussion

1. Would you consider joining AmeriCorps or some other form of national service before embarking on your own career? Why or why not?
2. Should AmeriCorps "volunteers" be paid even a minimal scholarship amount? How would such payments influence the makeup and character of students?

---

public officials during the 1970s; the Superfund legislation enacted in 1980 addressed the problem in theory, but its enforcement scheme was riddled with problems, generating its own form of opposition. Similarly, President Obama hoped the stresses on America's health insurance system would be eased with the passage of Obamacare in 2010. Yet here too the reality of passing landmark legislation offered no guarantee of a smooth rollout and implementation. Early visitors to the healthcare.gov website encountered numerous technical difficulties, and barely 1 percent of those interested visitors were able to sign up for health insurance during the initial weeks of operation. The website was ill-equipped for the traffic that arrived, and Obama's critics had a field day lamenting yet another failed big-government initiative. Clearly, Charles Lindblom's "science of muddling through" is a policymaking process for the patient and determined only, even in the case of policy reforms that are considered groundbreaking in many respects.

Summary

15-1 An Overview of the Policymaking Process

• The policymaking process generally unfolds in five stages: a recognition/definition stage, a formulation stage, an adoption stage, an implementation stage, and an evaluation stage. Bureaucrats in administrative agencies, interest groups (including think tanks), Congress, and the president are all actively involved throughout the process.

15-2 Theories and Practice in Fiscal Policy

• Fiscal policy is concerned with the raising of revenue through taxation and the spending of whatever revenue has been generated. Laissez-faire capitalism, which favors minimal government interference in the economy, dominated the U.S. economy for much of the eighteenth and nineteenth centuries; in the 1930s, the government began to apply the principles of Keynesian economic theory, which favors government spending during difficult economic times. Finally, during the past quarter century, some presidents have turned to supply-side economics, whereas others have returned to Keynesian economic theory once again.

• The federal budget, which lays out a comprehensive plan of government spending, is the primary means by which government carries out fiscal policy. Today's budget-making process is dominated by the president, who proposes an initial budget that will serve as the framework for all budget negotiations. Congress responds initially through its appropriations and budget committees, which in turn formulate budget proposals based on their own projections for future revenue.

• Taxation policies may be redistributive (benefiting the poor at the expense of the rich) or distributive (promoting the interests of all economic classes equally). A large percentage of taxpayer funds goes to mandatory spending (usually in the form of entitlements such as Medicare and Social Security) that is unaffected by annual budget decisions. Discretionary spending categories include defense, education, and the environment.

15-3 Theories and Practice in Monetary Policy

• The Federal Reserve supervises the nation's monetary policy by setting the discount rate that its Federal Reserve Banks may charge member banks to receive loans and by determining the minimum assets banks must keep on hand, called the reserve requirements. When the Federal Reserve lowers the discount rate, it may stimulate economic investment, but it risks setting off higher inflation rates.

15-4 The Nature and Practice of Crime Policy

• Democratic governments must strike a delicate balance between maintaining public order and protecting individual freedom. Whereas the crime control model of crime policy emphasizes, above all else, the need to control criminal behavior that threatens society, the due process model emphasizes the rights of the accused, the need for justice, and the protection of the innocent.

15-5 The Welfare State and Programs for the Poor

• The welfare state is a social system in which the state assumes a considerable degree of responsibility for citizens in matters of health care, employment, education, and retirement income. The actual amount of welfare provided varies widely from nation to nation. Most Western democracies feature welfare systems that sit on the end of the spectrum closer to pure socialism, whereas the U.S. welfare state mixes elements of socialism and capitalism in its regulatory schemes that protect citizens.

15-6 The Social Security System

- Social Security has provided retirement income for millions of retirees since 1935. Although many economists predict that the system will eventually be forced to pay out significantly more than it brings in, to date the U.S. Congress has enacted no major policy changes, putting off all discussion of privatization for the time being. The U.S. government encourages private retirement investing through tax-free investment vehicles such as IRAs and 401(k) plans.

15-7 Health Care Policy

- The U.S. health care system contrasts sharply with systems found in other Western democracies that feature universal health care. The controversial 2010 federal legislation, entitled the Patient Protection and Affordable Care Act, addressed various inequities in the insurance industry, but it did not guarantee universal health care for all, and it failed to address these access-to-care issues.

Key Terms

budget authority (p. 425)
budget deficit (p. 418)
budget surplus (p. 418)
capitalism (p. 431)
consumer price index (CPI) (p. 418)
crime control model (p. 429)
discount rate (p. 427)
discretionary spending (p. 425)
distributive tax policies (p. 423)
due process model (p. 429)
Federal Reserve Board (p. 427)
Federal Reserve System (p. 427)
fiscal policy (p. 416)
flat tax (p. 423)

gross domestic product (GDP) (p. 418)
health maintenance organizations (HMOs) (p. 436)
inflation (p. 417)
Keynesian economic theory (p. 417)
laissez-faire economics (p. 417)
mandatory spending (p. 425)
Medicaid (p. 432)
Medicare (p. 432)
monetary policy (p. 426)
national debt (p. 418)
open market operations (p. 428)
outlays (p. 425)

Patient Protection and Affordable Care Act of 2010 (PPACA) (p. 434)
progressive tax (p. 423)
public policy (p. 414)
recession (p. 417)
redistributive tax policies (p. 423)
regressive tax (p. 423)
reserve requirement (p. 428)
social policy (p. 415)
socialism (p. 431)
supply-side economics (p. 417)
universal health care (p. 434)
welfare state (p. 430)

Test Yourself

1. The stage of the policymaking process where the proposed policy assumes the authority of law is the _____ stage.
   a. definition
   b. formulation
   c. adoption
   d. implementation

2. The federal bureaucracy is primarily responsible for which stage of the policymaking process?
   a. Definition stage
   b. Formulation stage

   c. Adoption stage
   d. Implementation stage

3. What are the various stages of policymaking process, and do they oversimplify the actual process in practice?

4. The fiscal theory that favors stimulus spending by government as a way to spark economic activity is
   a. supply-side economics.
   b. Keynesian economics.
   c. laissez-faire economics.
   d. Reaganomics.

5. The total money value of all goods and services produced in the United States in a given one-year period is the

    a. gross domestic product.

    b. consumer price index.

    c. consumer confidence index.

    d. Dow Jones industrial index.

6. A tax that exacts a larger percentage of income from lower-wage earners than higher-wage earners is a _____ tax.

    a. progressive

    b. regressive

    c. flat

    d. unfair

7. Distinguish between federal "mandatory" spending and "discretionary" spending, and give an example of each.

8. Which of the following determines monetary policy?

    a. Office of Management and Budget

    b. Department of Treasury

    c. Congressional Budget Office

    d. Federal Reserve Board

9. The minimum liquid assets that banks must keep on hand to back customer loans are called the

    a. discount rate.

    b. open market mandate.

    c. savings rate.

    d. reserve requirement.

10. How is the Federal Reserve designed to operate independent of partisan politics?

11. The model of criminal justice policymaking that emphasizes the rights of the accused is the

    a. crime control model.

    b. First Amendment model.

    c. due process model.

    d. equal protection model.

12. What are the most common criticisms leveled at the criminal justice system today?

13. Which of the following is true of the Medicaid program?

    a. Its funding comes exclusively from the federal government.

    b. People become eligible for benefits at age 65.

    c. It is a health insurance system.

    d. It provides money for health services for those in poverty.

14. The 1996 Welfare Reform Law that replaced AFDC with TANF did which of the following?

    a. Placed a five-year limit on welfare payments

    b. Required welfare recipients to work

    c. Scaled back the food stamps program

    d. All of the above

15. What distinguishes a capitalist economic system from a socialist economic system?

16. The Social Security system was created under the administration of which president?

    a. Franklin Delano Roosevelt

    b. Lyndon Baines Johnson

    c. Ronald Reagan

    d. Bill Clinton

17. The Social Security system is funded through

    a. payroll taxes on employers and employees.

    b. taxes on individuals earning over $1 million annually.

    c. corporate income taxes.

    d. taxes on imported goods.

18. Beyond Social Security, what programs has Congress put in place to encourage American workers to save money for retirement?

19. The element of the 2010 health care reform laws that requires the purchase of health insurance is known as the

    a. universal requirement.

    b. individual mandate.

    c. single-payer duty.

    d. public option.

20. What are HMOs, and how do they control health care costs?

1. c. (LO 15-1); 2. d. (LO 15-1); 4. b. (LO 15-2); 5. a. (LO 15-2); 6. b. (LO 15-2); 8. d. (LO 15-3); 9. d. (LO 15-3); 11. c. (LO 15-4); 13. d. (LO 15-5); 14. d. (LO 15-5); 16. a. (LO 15-6); 17. a. (LO 15-6); 19. b. (LO 15-7)

LEARNING OBJECTIVES

16

American Foreign Policy

U.S. foreign policy comprises all of the nation's activities directed at conducting relations with other countries, including military operations and diplomatic activities. The establishment of trade practices, the entering of treaties, and the decision to lend arms to another country in battle are but some of the many elements that make up the nation's extensive foreign policy apparatus. Unlike other types of government authority that are subject to frequent jurisdictional squabbles, few dispute the federal government's status as the sole authority in charge of U.S. foreign policy. Of course, with that undisputed power come significant responsibility and accountability. In fact, the list of presidential administrations that have seen their domestic policy successes overshadowed (if not outright negated) by foreign policy failures is a long one indeed. No president can afford to ignore the importance that Americans place on the country's leading role in the world as an economic and military superpower.

Choosing the Candidate with the Right Military Policy

WHO ARE YOU?

Though no one questions the importance foreign policy holds for the nation, conflicts over foreign policy issues—including the nation's approach to national defense—rarely decide the outcome of presidential elections. There are some notable exceptions: FDR won a fourth term in 1944 because voters favored his steady hand during wartime; George W. Bush's strong response to the 9/11 attacks played a key role in his successful reelection bid in 2004. Yet these instances tend to be few and far between; while the public wants the president to be a competent commander-in-chief, most elections turn instead on the state of the economy, law and order issues, and other domestic concerns.

A central question thus arises: Do candidate differences in military policy positions even matter? Polling results would indicate so. When these issues are isolated for Americans to consider, differences over military and defense issues often generate especially strong responses. Consider four hypothetical candidates running for president and their contrasting positions on military policy:

Candidate A

- Opposes any and all increases in defense spending; would decrease spending on nuclear weapons in the post-Cold War era
- Wants to challenge the Pentagon to justify its spending, as it has "avoided real scrutiny for decades."
- Opposed the troop surges both in Iran (2007) and in Afghanistan (2009)
- Opposes sending U.S. ground troops into the Middle East under nearly all circumstances

Candidate B

- Seeks to renew the current military budget at its current levels, including spending on nuclear weapons
- Seeks to shift more resources to take better care of the military and their families
- Supports military interventions in the Middle East (including with ground troops) so long as the action is authorized by the UN
- Seeks to hold China accountable on cybersecurity issues, and to deter Russian aggression

Candidate C

- Seeks to significantly increase military spending
- Supported U.S. intervention in the Middle East in the past but based on recent failures in that region, now opposes any future interventions
- Openly questions America's continued participation in NATO; believes it is an outdated instrument that ignores specific American goals and interests
- Seeks to require long-time allies that rely on U.S. military protection to pay their "fair share" of military costs or "go it alone"

Candidate D

- Believes in "peace through strength," and thus would raise military spending to record highs, including building a brand new generation of aircraft and improved ballistic missile defense systems
- Seeks to strengthen alliances with Egypt and Saudi Arabia, despite their respective records on human rights, to combat global threats
- Favors returning a U.S. Army Special Operations Group to Europe to counter Russian aggression.

For Critical Thinking and Discussion

- Of the four presidential candidates described above, which one holds the position on military issues that most closely aligns with your own positions?
- Are the differences among these candidates on military issues significant enough to lead you to vote on that basis, notwithstanding differences you might have on domestic issues? Why or why not?
- Why do you think these issues do not garner even more attention in presidential elections that do not occur during wartime?

To see how your answers compare to others, take the **Who Are You?** poll in MindTap!

16-1 | The Constitutional Framework of American Foreign Policy

Two of the three original cabinet departments created by Congress in 1789 were the Department of State and the Department of War, a sign of just how important these two functions would be to the young nation. Article I of the Constitution gives Congress the exclusive power to declare war, raise armies, punish maritime crimes, and regulate foreign commerce. Under Article II, the president is empowered as commander-in-chief to conduct the course of war. The Founders' intent in separating the power to command from the power to fund the military was to check the war power from being abused. The Constitution also gives the president the authority to negotiate treaties and to appoint and receive ambassadors.

Perhaps the most basic elements of foreign policy during the eighteenth and nineteenth centuries were the treaties the United States entered into with foreign nations. Because the Senate alone was vested with the authority to ratify such treaties (by a two-thirds vote), many expected that this small legislative body (there were just 26 senators at the outset) would exert a strong influence over the nation's foreign policy.

Within the next two centuries, control over foreign affairs, including the power to make war, would shift from Congress to the White House. Fundamental changes in America's role in world affairs during the twentieth century spurred this transfer of power. America's ascendancy to superpower status in the early part of the twentieth century led to U.S. involvement in world affairs. The presidency was well suited to respond to these new demands on America's attention; within the three branches of government, the single chief executive is best positioned to respond to sudden changes in circumstances around the globe in a quick and forceful manner. Unlike Congress, the president can use the "bully pulpit" of the office to communicate policies and generate support for the administration's goals. Highly activist presidents, including Theodore Roosevelt, Woodrow Wilson, and Franklin Delano Roosevelt, capitalized on these assets by communicating frequently with world leaders and their own publics on pressing affairs around the world.

Although the Constitution appears to give Congress primary authority over foreign and military affairs, the large and often unwieldy Congress has proven no match for modern presidents on the world stage. Political scientist Aaron Wildavsky's **two presidencies theory** posits the existence of a more powerful presidency in foreign affairs and a more limited presidency in the domestic sphere.[1] Of course, the president's dominance over foreign affairs hasn't stopped Congress from at least trying to reassert its authority in this realm.

In 1973, with public opinion shifting against military involvement around the globe, Congress passed the **War Powers Resolution**, overriding President Richard Nixon's veto in the process. The resolution theoretically restricted the president's power to engage in war to instances in which Congress had declared war or specifically granted the president permission to use armed forces, or to cases where the nation was under attack. The resolution required the president to report to Congress whenever American forces were entered into hostilities and attain congressional permission to engage those forces for more than 60 days. Every president since Nixon has either evaded or ignored the War Powers Resolution, arguing that it unconstitutionally infringes on the president's war powers. In fact, no court to date has ever ruled definitively on whether the president must comply with the law's provisions.

With some exceptions, the rise of the president to become the key actor in foreign affairs was a twentieth-century development. Initially, the Founders' hopes for an American foreign policy built on consensus among the political branches of government were for the most part realized. But this new decision-making apparatus faced severe tests in the decades following the American Revolution.

two presidencies theory Theory articulated by political scientist Aaron Wildavsky that posits the existence of a more powerful presidency in foreign affairs and a more limited presidency in the domestic sphere.

War Powers Resolution Largely ignored congressional policy that restricts the president's power to engage in war except (1) when Congress has declared war, (2) when Congress has specifically granted the president permission to use armed forces, or (3) when the nation is under attack. The resolution further requires the president to report to Congress whenever American forces are entered into hostilities.

16-2 | The Roots of American Foreign Policy

As a new nation with a limited military, the United States was at first heavily dependent on maintaining good foreign relations to avoid disadvantageous military engagements. Fortunately, the great distance that separated America from Western European super-powers provided a measure of protection from frequent threats and incursions. More than two centuries later, the nation's status as a military superpower affords it far more leverage in its relations with foreign powers. Still, with advances in communications and transportation effectively shrinking the size of the global community, the United States must expend considerable resources and energy to successfully navigate through an increasingly complex foreign policy landscape. American foreign policy has always stood front and center in the list of U.S. government priorities.

The Isolationist Tradition and the Monroe Doctrine

The successful transition of the former British colonies in America into an independent nation was the product of astute foreign policy initiatives by some high-profile figures. George Washington's Continental army struggled for victories throughout the war for American independence; American fortunes in the war were raised only after Benjamin Franklin helped convince France in 1778 to join the war on the side of the colonies. Indeed, many historians and analysts attribute the Americans' victory over Britain to this crucial Franco-American alliance, which provided the colonies with resources to threaten British ships off the waters near the Atlantic Coast. However, under the leadership of President George Washington, the newly formed United States of America set aside the alliance with France and declared formal neutrality when England and revolutionary France went to war in 1793. In his farewell address to the nation in 1796, Washington urged his fellow Americans to steer clear of permanent alliances of any kind.

During the nation's early years, the United States maintained a foreign policy marked by **isolationism**, defined as opposition to both (1) interventions in distant wars (that is, outside the Western hemisphere) and (2) involvement in permanent military alliances. The policy of isolationism dominated America's foreign affairs for nearly a century and a half, preserving America's freedom to refuse to act until the very last

isolationism Foreign policy doctrine that opposes intervention in distant wars and involvement in permanent military alliances.

A napalm strike erupts in a fireball near U.S. soldiers in Vietnam in 1966.

AP Images

minute, and in most cases allowing it to forgo intervention altogether. Isolationism is distinguished from **pacifism**, a policy that refuses to sanction *any* military conflict and opposes all war making. Consistent with its general policy of isolationism, during the nineteenth century, the United States fought wars in lands that bordered the nation or lay within U.S. boundaries in 1812 (against Britain), in 1846 (against Mexico), and in 1898 (against Spain in the Caribbean). Finally, the policy of military isolationism did not mean complete isolation from the world's culture or commerce, as Americans enthusiastically learned from other nations and welcomed visitors and products from abroad throughout this period.

America's brand of military isolationism never applied to the Western hemisphere. On December 2, 1823, President James Monroe declared the nation's commitment to a foreign policy that would eventually become known as the **Monroe Doctrine**. Specifically, Monroe proclaimed that both North and South America should not be considered "as subjects for future colonization by any European power," and that the United States would consider any efforts by Europeans to colonize these areas "as dangerous to our peace and safety." The implications of the Monroe Doctrine were profound: America would consider any new colonization efforts on its side of the Atlantic Ocean as tantamount to an act of war against the United States. This doctrine did not cause much controversy for most of the nineteenth century. Yet the degree to which European nations actually deferred to the United States because of the doctrine (as opposed to deferring because it was in their interests to do so) is difficult for historians to assess.

With the rise of European imperialism at the end of the nineteenth century, the United States eventually took action on its own to invoke the Monroe Doctrine. In 1895, the United States intervened in a dispute between Great Britain and Venezuela over the boundaries between Venezuela and British Guiana (present-day Guyana). In the early twentieth century, the United States prevented European nations from interfering in the affairs of debt-ridden Latin American countries by taking over the struggling economies of the Dominican Republic (1907) and Nicaragua (1911). Concerned about German influence over the Republic of Haiti, the United States even occupied that small country in 1915. The United States also actively encouraged the revolt of Latin American nations against Spain in the early part of the twentieth century, even though Spanish possession of these territories predated the Monroe Doctrine.

Expansionism and the Birth of a Superpower

U.S. opposition to further European colonization in the Western hemisphere helped the nation to establish itself as the preeminent power in the Americas. Meanwhile, the United States practiced a policy of expansionism on the North American continent. **Expansionism** is the doctrine of expanding the territory or economic influence of one's own country. The policy began as a systematic effort to pursue what many American officials viewed as the nation's defining ideology: its **manifest destiny** to acquire lands and occupy the entire continent from the Atlantic to the Pacific Ocean. America's purchase of the massive Louisiana Territory from the French in 1803 more than doubled the land size of the United States at the time. The federal government went on to annex Florida after conquering Spanish holdings there between 1817 and 1819. Resolution of border conflicts with Great Britain in the 1840s established the northeastern boundary of Maine and of the Oregon territory. The United States annexed the independent Republic of Texas in 1845, and following a successful war against Mexico in 1846–1848 gained all of present-day California, Nevada, and Utah and parts of present-day Arizona, New Mexico, Colorado, and Wyoming.

Adherence to isolationism in principle also did not preclude the United States from setting its imperial sights on territories in the Pacific Ocean and the Caribbean Sea. In the late 1890s, Congress annexed Hawaii around the same time that it fought the

pacifism Doctrine of foreign relations that refuses to sanction any military conflict and that opposes all war making.

Monroe Doctrine U.S. foreign policy that proclaimed North and South America unavailable for future colonization by any European power and that declared that any such colonization would be viewed as an act of war on the United States.

expansionism Doctrine that favors a country expanding its own territory and influence.

manifest destiny U.S. policy of the mid-nineteenth century that advocated acquiring lands and occupying the entire American continent from one ocean to the other.

Spanish-American War to free Cuba from Spain. The United States gained possession of the Philippine Islands as a result of the Philippine-American War of 1898–1902. Although the United States mostly discontinued its quest for territorial acquisitions abroad after the turn of the century, it continued to play an active role in opposing the imperialist designs of other nations.

America's increasing willingness to intervene militarily in foreign affairs signaled a potential shift in the traditional balance of powers, as the United States increasingly found itself a major player on the world stage. Nevertheless, up until World War I, the United States remained primarily separate from the rest of the world militarily. Even the outbreak of World War I in 1914 produced no immediate change in U.S. foreign policy; President Woodrow Wilson openly proclaimed U.S. neutrality in the dispute and between 1915 and 1917 continually attempted mediation among the warring parties. Only when those efforts to settle the war failed, and Germany began to relentlessly attack U.S. vessels in 1917, did America enter the war on the side of the Allies—Great Britain, France, Italy, and Russia.

By the end of World War I, the European Allies owed more than $11 billion to the United States, making America a creditor nation for the first time in its history. Other world powers looked to the United States for guidance and resources to help construct a new international order, and together with President Wilson, in 1919 they drafted the Treaty of Versailles, which established a system of reparations and called for the creation of a League of Nations, which was intended to arbitrate international disputes and thereby avoid future wars. Yet preferences for a policy of isolationism still ran strong throughout America. After an overconfident Wilson engaged in a series of political missteps in selling the Treaty of Versailles to the public, the Republican-controlled U.S. Senate balked at the risk that the League of Nations might force the U.S. president to engage in unwarranted military action; the Senate wanted Wilson to modify those aspects of the League covenant, but he refused. Facing an unyielding president on the issue, the Senate voted against U.S. membership in the League, which thereafter proved ineffective in maintaining peace and preventing aggression and was eventually dissolved in 1946. Thus, American isolationism continued to prevail in the years between the two world wars.

A cartoon satirizing President Theodore Roosevelt's approach to foreign policy: "Speak softly and carry a big stick."

Universal History Archive/Getty Images

As a second world war approached in the late 1930s and early 1940s, President Franklin Roosevelt made clear where the sympathies of the U.S. government lay, first by utilizing a lend-lease program with Britain that supplied that country with arms at little or no cost and, later, by increasing economic pressures on the Japanese in the Pacific.[2] The Japanese attack on Pearl Harbor on December 7, 1941, propelled the United States into the war against Germany, Japan, and Italy.

U.S. involvement in World War II proved critical to the final outcome: American manpower and resources were an important component in the success of the D-Day invasion of France and much of Western Europe in 1944. The United States detonated two atomic bombs over Japan in August 1945, forcing the Japanese to surrender. After the war, the European victors looked to the United States again to help keep international peace. This time they were not disappointed, as they had been when the U.S. Senate refused to support the League of Nations three decades earlier. In 1945, the United States joined the newly created **United Nations (UN)**, an international organization formed to promote and maintain international security and peace.

After World War II, America's prevailing foreign policy changed from one marked by isolationism to one featuring **internationalism**—the United States now actively participated in a process that collectively secured the political independence and territorial boundaries of other countries by a system of economic and military sanctions against aggressor nations. In fact, America went even further than other nations in this regard. The **Marshall Plan** (formally the European Recovery Program), introduced by Secretary of State George Marshall in 1947, provided $13 billion in loans to Western European countries whose economies had been ravaged by World War II. Some countries used the money to combat inflation or retire state debts; others (defeated Germany, Austria, and Italy among them) used the assistance to buy food. Proponents of the plan deemed it a humanitarian policy intended to alleviate suffering, whereas critics argued that the aid had a more strategic purpose: to increase European dependence on the United States and discourage potential new alliances with the Soviet Union.[3]

Out of the wreckage of World War II emerged two global military and political superpowers, the United States and the Soviet Union, locked in what would become a half-century-long struggle called the **Cold War**.[4] This conflict over ideological differences (the promotion of democracy by the United States versus the promotion of communism by the Soviet Union) lasted from 1945 until the dissolution of the Soviet Union in 1991 and was carried on by a variety of methods, including economic warfare, arms build-ups, and tense diplomacy. Postwar leaders in the United States believed that the nation had fought in World War II to protect self-determination and open trade, and together with other Western European nations, including Great Britain and France, it formed military, political, and, at times, economic alliances. Formally created in 1949, the **North Atlantic Treaty Organization (NATO)** bound the United States to the military defense of Western Europe. Meanwhile, the Soviet Union in the late 1940s dominated its Eastern European neighbors, including Poland and Romania. In 1955, those nations and others within the Soviet sphere formed the **Warsaw Pact**. Germany, divided in two following World War II, was split between the two alliances, with West Germany as a model democratic nation in NATO and East Germany serving as a western outpost for Soviet communism in the Warsaw Pact.

In 1947, President Harry Truman articulated the **Truman Doctrine**, which provided money and resources to sustaining noncommunist governments in areas strategically vital to the United States, such as the Mediterranean and the Middle East. American foreign policy during the Cold War generally adhered to a policy of **containment**—restricting Soviet power to its current geographical sphere and resisting any efforts to expand communist influence. When the Soviets in 1949 blockaded the city of Berlin (a West German city located entirely within Soviet-controlled East German territory), the United States airlifted supplies to the city for nearly a year. Aerial reconnaissance

United Nations (UN) International organization formed after World War II to promote and maintain international security and peace.

internationalism Doctrine that favors active participation of the nation in collective arrangements that secure the political independence and territorial boundaries of other countries.

Marshall Plan The 1947 U.S. policy that provided loans and aid to Western European countries whose economies had been ravaged by World War II.

Cold War The nearly half-century struggle over ideological differences between the United States and the Soviet Union. Waged through economic warfare, arms build-ups, and tense diplomatic talks, the Cold War never broke out into a sustained military engagement between the two nations and ended with the dissolution of the Soviet Union in 1991.

North Atlantic Treaty Organization (NATO) A military, political, and economic alliance of nations formally bound to protect self-determination and open trade in Western Europe.

Warsaw Pact Formal alliance of nations within the Soviet sphere during the Cold War.

Truman Doctrine Doctrine articulated by President Harry Truman in the late 1940s by which money and resources were provided to support and sustain noncommunist governments in areas strategically vital to the United States.

containment U.S. foreign policy that sought to restrict Soviet power (and communist influence) to its existing geographical sphere.

allowed the Cold War adversaries to keep a more careful eye on each other beginning in the 1950s. It also led to the Cuban missile crisis in October 1962, when President John F. Kennedy's demands that the Soviet Union remove missiles from nearby Cuba led to a tense standoff with the Soviets and nearly ignited a nuclear war. U.S. military involvement in both the Korean and Vietnam Wars was spurred by U.S. government fears of a total communist takeover of those two countries. Most U.S. presidents during the Cold War subscribed to some version of the **domino theory**, which posited that communist takeovers of these Southeast Asian countries would be followed by takeovers of Taiwan, India, Iran, and possibly other nations as well.

The American military failure in the Vietnam War in particular led officials at every level of the American government to revisit some of the most fundamental premises of U.S. foreign policy, including the theory of containment.[5] The American phase of that war, extending from 1964 until 1973, proved longer lasting and more divisive than any other war involving the United States up to that point.[6] The conflict eventually left 58,000 Americans dead or missing and cost the U.S. government more than $167 billion. Despite all the bloodshed, none of the U.S. aims in the war—to repel North Vietnam aggression, help negotiate a lasting peace, and encourage South Vietnam as a self-sufficient republic—were accomplished. The final peace agreement allowed for extrication of U.S. forces and return of prisoners of war, but little else; and by 1975 South Vietnam had fallen to the communists.[7] The decade-long Vietnam quagmire struck a blow against the domino theory. Future military interventions would require that administrations present some additional evidence of a direct threat to America's strategic interests abroad or at home.

During the 1970s, the United States and the Soviet Union engaged in a period of somewhat eased tensions, or limited détente. During this time, they agreed on several strategic arms limitation treaties (SALT I and SALT II) that set restrictions on nuclear missiles.[8] But such détente proved short-lived, as confrontations in underdeveloped Third World nations continued to inject tensions into the Cold War landscape. President Ronald Reagan, denouncing the Soviet Union as an "evil empire," outlined a new defense plan, the controversial **Strategic Defense Initiative (SDI)**, an antimissile system based on the use of lasers and particle beams to shoot down Soviet nuclear missiles in outer space.[9]

East-West tensions eased with the ascension of reform-minded Mikhail Gorbachev to the leadership of the Soviet state in 1985. Gorbachev's reforms aimed at restructuring the faltering Soviet economy with greater competition and at liberalizing dissent by introducing press freedoms could not be reconciled with a continuation of the costly arms race with the United States. The Cold War formally came to a close in 1991, when Gorbachev resigned his position with the Soviet government amid extremely difficult economic times. In addition to the former Soviet-bloc countries, 10 former Soviet republics, including Russia, declared their independence.[10] Following the end of the Cold War, U.S. leaders redirected their foreign policy thinking toward a new world order characterized by conflicts in the Third World, a war on terrorism, and threats of nuclear attack from both terrorists and rogue nations.

domino theory The theory that held that communist takeovers of countries in Southeast Asia and elsewhere would be followed by subsequent communist takeovers of nearby countries.

Strategic Defense Initiative (SDI) A theoretical antimissile system based on the use of lasers and particle beams to shoot down Soviet nuclear missiles in outer space.

Bettmann/CORBIS

A distraught President Ronald Reagan and Soviet leader Mikhail Gorbachev leaving their unsuccessful arms limitations talks in Reykjavik, Iceland, in October 1986.

New World Order and New World Disorder

U.S. responsibilities around the world have not decreased much at all in the aftermath of the Cold War. In his January 1991 State of the Union speech, President George H. W. Bush spoke of the onset of a **new world order**, in which numerous nations would work together for the purpose of securing collective peace, security, freedom, and the rule of law.[11] Maintaining this new world order has been a challenge for American political leaders ever since.

Further complicating the foreign affairs landscape was the looming presence of China. Still a communist nation, China is a crucial market for U.S. goods and products, given that it contains one-fifth of the world's population. In the 1990s, both Presidents George H. W. Bush and Bill Clinton emphasized the need for liberalization of global trade, and in 1993 Congress approved the North American Free Trade Agreement (NAFTA), which lifted trade barriers such as protective tariffs and investment restrictions between the United States, Canada, and Mexico. With the U.S. economy increasingly intertwined with the global economy, economic relations with East Asia, Europe, and other countries in the Western hemisphere continue to be a central factor in American foreign policy. Of course, economic concerns do not eliminate other interests—tragic human rights abuses in Somalia and Bosnia put pressure on the George H. W. Bush and Clinton administrations to intervene on humanitarian grounds in those countries. The balance both presidents struck in those instances, providing limited aid but no military assistance, prompted criticisms that they had failed to wield America's superpower status in the most appropriate fashion.[12]

new world order President George H. W. Bush's description of the post–Cold War world, in which nations would work together for the purpose of securing collective peace, security, freedom, and the rule of law.

The U.S. Government Confronts the Middle East

Although the Cold War has ended, among the current generation of policymakers the specter of the Vietnam War continues to cast a large shadow on foreign policy deliberations. Discussions of American military intervention since the early 1970s have occurred with the lessons of the Vietnam War looming ominously in the background. Some hawkish conservatives even complain of what they call a "Vietnam syndrome," in which the problems of Vietnam produce an undesirable pacifism on the part of American leaders. Politicians live in fear of supporting yet another war in which public support is flimsy, the military objectives are unclear, and an exit strategy remains ill-defined. American interventions in the Balkans and Somalia in the 1990s were limited by fears that increased U.S. involvement in those countries would escalate into another Vietnam. During the first Persian Gulf War of 1991, Joint Chiefs of Staff Chairman Colin Powell urged the nation to avoid Vietnam-like entanglements in which fear of escalation placed the military in an essentially unwinnable conflict.

President George W. Bush's administration faced inevitable comparisons between the Vietnam War and the U.S. intervention in Iraq in 2003. When the military failed to unearth the weapons of mass destruction cited as partial justification of the war, critics of the Iraqi intervention argued that U.S. interests in the region were just as unclear as they had been in Southeast Asia during the 1960s. Furthermore, the U.S. military's failure to contain rebel insurgents even after taking control of Baghdad invited comparisons to guerrilla war in North Vietnam. In response, President Bush proclaimed that the Iraqi invasion had both removed a brutal dictator, Saddam Hussein, from power and restored a democratic government, in the form of duly held elections, to the previously oppressed nation.

Militarily, the greatest threats to U.S. security during the first decade of the twenty-first century appear to be in two areas of the world: the Middle East and North Korea. More of the U.S. government's attention in recent decades has been focused on the former locus of conflict. Since it first recognized the newly created independent nation of Israel in 1948, the United States has been committed in its support for that country as a political haven for Jews. Meanwhile, Israel has emerged as a modernized democratic presence in a region of the world dominated by Arab countries largely hostile to Western economic power and its cultural domination. U.S. support for Israel has assured the United States of a friendly ally in the Middle East, yet it has also at times run counter to fundamental principles of self-determination, as U.S. officials have been forced to confront another dilemma—what to do with the tens of thousands of Palestinian refugees uprooted from their homes in the years following Israel's occupation of former Palestinian territory.

President Jimmy Carter's successful mediation of disputes between Israel and Egypt in 1978 demonstrated that the United States can play a role in resolving conflicts, but long-term peace between Israel and its neighbors has remained elusive despite such efforts. The George H. W. Bush administration encouraged negotiations between Palestinian Liberation Organization head Yasser Arafat and the Israeli government—the resulting Oslo accords of 1993 called for the exchange of Israeli territory and ultimate Palestinian self-determination for the guarantee of peace. Unfortunately, the accords left unclear the precise boundaries and the specific characteristics of Palestinian rule. Right-wing Israeli extremists murdered Israeli Prime Minister Yitzhak Rabin two years later, and both sides hardened against the accords. The Clinton administration attempted to renew negotiations between the two sides in the late 1990s, and the Obama Administration's Secretary of State, John Kerry, pressed forward with peace talk in 2013. Yet none of these negotiations produced long-term improvements in the region, and so an impasse continues today, with Palestinian suicide bombers and Israeli government bombings becoming a routine feature of Israeli and Palestinian daily life in the early part of the twenty-first century.

Distrust of the United States by many Middle East countries has intensified in the wake of the U.S. government's strong support for Israel and the continued presence of the U.S. military in the Middle East, facilitated by the granting of military bases to the United States in Saudi Arabia and Kuwait. Activities by revolutionary forces have occasionally fomented in the region, threatening U.S. interests directly and indirectly. In 1979, the new fundamentalist Iranian regime under Ayatollah Khomeini seized the U.S. Embassy and held U.S. hostages for more than a year. In late 1990, Iraq President Saddam Hussein invaded Kuwait, threatening U.S. economic interests in the region and spurring the first Bush administration to militarily expel Hussein's army from Kuwait in early 1991.

Navigating the New World Order After the September 11 Attacks

The events of September 11, 2001, refocused the U.S. government's foreign policy energies toward a global war on terrorism. After a short-lived war in Afghanistan that purportedly expelled the Al Qaeda terrorist network from that country, the George W. Bush administration turned its attention back to Saddam Hussein's government in Iraq, which it accused of supporting terrorism abroad and concealing weapons of mass destruction. After less than six weeks of fighting, American military forces liberated the country of Hussein's dictatorial government during the spring of 2003.

Yet the aftermath of the Iraqi invasion proved highly problematic, with insurgent forces in and around the nation's cities posing a threat to the more than 150,000 American troops who remained there for years as part of the occupation phase of the operation.[13] By early 2007, over 3,000 Americans had died in Iraq, and Congress began putting pressure on the Bush administration to lay out a timetable and plan for eventual American withdrawal. Rejecting those entreaties, in early 2007 President Bush increased by over 20,000 the number of troops deployed to Iraq in what came to be known as the "Iraq war troop surge of 2007." As one of the first moves of his young presidency, Barack Obama announced an 18-month withdrawal window for combat forces, with approximately 50,000 troops remaining in the country after 2011 to advise and train Iraqi security forces and to provide intelligence and surveillance. Those final troops exited the country on December 18, 2011, marking the end of America's military presence in that country.

President Obama's announcement did not spell a pullback from the Middle East as a whole, however. In December 2009, he confirmed plans for a surge of his own: He escalated U.S. military involvement in Afghanistan by deploying an additional 30,000 troops in that region. The Obama administration cited the recent strengthening of the Taliban, a Sunni Islamist political movement that has supported terrorist training camps in the region, as the reason for increasing America's military presence in that country. More than four years later, in May of 2014, Obama announced that after more than 13 years of fighting in Afghanistan, the United States would draw down its armed forces to less than 10,000 by the close of the calendar year. Thus on December 28, 2014, the United States and NATO formally ended their combat operations in Afghanistan and transferred full security responsibility to the Afghan government.

Meanwhile, Iraq experienced a significant upsurge in violence shortly after the American withdrawal in 2011. Once the terrorist organization known by the acronyms ISIS ("The Islamic State of Iraq and Al-Sham") or ISIL ("The Islamic State of Iraq and the Levant") began attacking government targets at will, the United States responded by offering limited air support and humanitarian relief to the besieged Iraqi government. None of these actions has stopped the rapid growth of ISIS/ISIL: Since establishing a base of operation in Iraq, it has carried out executions of both men and women accused of various acts against Islam such as sodomy, adultery, usage and possession of contraband, and even witchcraft. These executions have taken various forms including beheading and burning people alive, which has invited outrage from the international human rights community. International journalists from Tunisia and elsewhere have also suffered at the hands of ISIS. Even more recently, the gunman responsible for killing almost 50 people at an Orlando nightclub in June of 2016 had previously sworn allegiance to ISIS. Given the organization's willingness to recruit those who live elsewhere, the threat of terror from ISIS will know few boundaries in the years to come.

In other parts of the Middle East, terrorists continue to operate underground with some success. In one notable incident in September 2012, Islamic militants attacked the American diplomatic mission at Benghazi, in Libya, killing the U.S. ambassador and three other government workers. The use of chemical weapons is an ongoing concern in that region as well. U.S.-Syria relations hit an all-time low when U.S. officials uncovered evidence that the Syrian government had used deadly sarin nerve gas against some of its own citizens in August 2013; that evidence—supported by the United Nations in a subsequent report—pushed the United States to the brink of launching retaliatory strikes against Syria. The conflict was averted only when Russia entered the fray, brokering an agreement by which Syria would remove or destroy its chemical weapon arsenal.

Finally, North Korea has also emerged as a potential nuclear threat in the past decade. Since 2006 the North Korean government has conducted at least four underground nuclear tests, drawing sanctions from the UN Security Council. Critics charge that the end of the Cold War has in fact ushered in a "new world disorder," featuring ever-shifting alliances and grave terrorist threats from entities not formally associated with any specific nation.

Within this constantly shifting international terrain, America continues to search for its role and identity in the twenty-first-century world. In *Colossus: The Rise and Fall of the American Empire*, British-born Harvard University Professor Niall Ferguson argues

Sean Adair/Reuters/Corbis Wire/CORBIS

The September 11 terrorist attacks on the World Trade Center towers shifted the focus of American foreign policy to fighting terrorism in the Middle East and elsewhere.

that like the great British empire of old, the United States needs to embrace its imperial character and commit to more securely establishing the types of democratic institutions around the world that foster long-term prosperity.[14] In another influential book, *Soft Power: The Means to Success in World Politics*, Joseph Nye argues that rather than relying on unilateralism and military power, the United States should endeavor to win the voluntary cooperation of foreign governments.[15] Is the United States an empire? Does it want to be? In light of the difficulties U.S. military forces have faced in postwar Iraq, many of these questions will continue to be debated in the years ahead.

Then & Now

Assassinating Foreign Leaders

On December 4, 1981, President Ronald Reagan signed Executive Order 12333. Part 2.11 of that order reiterated a general prohibition on U.S. intelligence agencies sponsoring or carrying out assassinations. President Reagan's order reaffirmed several previous presidents' bans on assassinations in general, and the assassination of foreign leaders in particular. On one hand, the targeted assassination of a mass murderer or frequent violator of human rights might be justified as in the public interest. Still, two factors counsel in favor of such a prohibition: (1) The contradiction inherent in the United States trumpeting its efforts to serve as "moral conscience" of the world, while at the same time participating in the act of murder, and (2) the occasional failure of targeted assassinations (including even successful ones) to actually create positive regime change. That said, the U.S. government's involvement in past plots to assassinate foreign leaders is now a matter of public record.

Then

In 1960, two Central Intelligence Agency (CIA) officials were asked by superiors to assassinate Patrice Lumumba, the prime minister of the Congo suspected of being a communist. (Lumumba denied having any communist ties.) Poisons were sent to the Congo and some exploratory steps were taken, but Lumumba was killed first by his own local Congolese rivals.

Between 1960 and 1965, according to a 1975 Senate Committee chaired by Senator Frank Church (D-ID), U.S. government personnel plotted to kill Cuban communist leader Fidel Castro on at least eight occasions. According to the Church committee, some of the plots were of the "James Bond variety": poisoned pills, an exploding seashell, and a planned gift of a diving suit contaminated with toxins. None proved successful, and Castro remained in power as President of Cuba until 2008, when his younger brother Raul Castro succeeded him.

In 1961, Dominican Republic leader Rafael Trujillo was shot by Dominican dissidents supported by the U.S. government (at least three carbines and three pistols were furnished by U.S. officials). Trujillo's government was charged with brutally oppressing actual or perceived members of the opposition. As worldwide opinion against Trujillo rose to a fever pitch in the 1950s, he became an embarrassment to the United States, which had initially supported Trujillo's anticommunist regime.

Cuban communist revolutionary and politician Fidel Castro survived at least eight CIA-led assassination plots.

Owen Franken/Historical/CORBIS

16-3 | The Structure of American Foreign Policymaking

The Constitution designates specific roles for the president and the Senate in making U.S. foreign policy. Yet over the course of two centuries, the president of the United States and the executive branch that reports to the president have assumed an increasingly significant role in the process, rendering Congress, interest groups, and citizens themselves less significant in foreign policymaking.

Many actors and institutions attempt either formally or informally to influence American foreign policy. The president of the United States sits squarely at the center of foreign policymaking—within the federal government, the president often dictates its terms with little interference from the other branches.[16] On the positive side, presidential dominance of foreign policy allows the U.S. government to act immediately and decisively in response to developments abroad. The quick reactions

Charlie Rose, host of PBS's The Charlie Rose Show, interviews controversial Syrian President Bashar al Assad at his presidential palace in Damascus.

← Then & Now (*Continued*)

Now

Al Qaeda founder Osama bin Laden was killed by U.S. Special Forces on May 2, 2011.

In 2011, Al Qaeda leader Osama bin Laden, mastermind of the 9/11 terrorist attacks, was killed by a U.S. Special Forces military unit pursuant to Operation Neptune Spear. Unlike the assassinations just described in which the United States sought to evade responsibility for the outcome, President Barack Obama authorized the killing through orders given to the CIA. Amnesty International, among other organizations, questioned two aspects of the killing: (1) the decision not to take bin Laden into custody given that he was unarmed and (2) the decision to not release any photographic or DNA evidence of bin Laden's death to the public. By contrast, the United Nations and the leaders of most other countries issued statements welcoming the news.

For Critical Thinking and Discussion

1. Can one justify the assassination of foreign leaders (military or otherwise) *other than* those recognized by the international community to be mass murderers? Are there any foreign leaders in place today whose assassination would be welcomed worldwide? If so, who are they?
2. Some defenders of selective assassinations contend that the trial of individuals like Castro or bin Laden would offer nothing more than a "show trial" with little hope of real justice. Do you think a prisoner of Castro's or bin Laden's infamy could ever hope to achieve justice in such a forum? What obstacles would he or she face?

Source: Senate Committee to Study Governmental Operations, Interim report on "Alleged Assassination Plots Involving Foreign Leaders," 94th Congress, 1st sess., November 20, 1975.

Diversity Challenges in U.S. Refugee Policy

The United Nations defines a "refugee" as someone who, "owing to a well-founded fear of being persecuted for reasons of race, religion, nationality, membership of particular social group or political opinion, is outside the country of his nationality, and is unable to, or owing to such fear, is unwilling to avail himself of the protection of that country." UN member nations, including the United States, must devise appropriate refugee policies that include a formal determination of how many refugees can eventually gain admission into their respective boundaries. Such a foreign policy determination must take into account the ethnic, racial, and religious conflicts or biases present within the host country.

Many well-meaning nations with relatively liberal refugee policies were put to the test by the recent refugee crisis caused by the Syrian war—more than 9 million Syrian refugees have fled that country since 2011. Accusations have been leveled at countries that instituted a policy of selective acceptance, which included religion-specific selection criteria for refugee resettlement. In particular, Saudi Arabia and other Muslim countries were accused of accepting predominantly Muslim refugees into their country, while other nations limited refugee relocations in their country to non-Muslims.[17] Many of these refugees faced additional discrimination during resettlement due to their religious or racial identities.

The United States has admitted nearly 3 million refugees into its borders during the last four decades; still, by the end of 2015 it had accepted approximately 2,300 refugees from the Syrian civil war. While President Obama pledged to accept at least 10,000 Syrian refugees into the country, others have opposed his efforts, arguing against the United States accepting Muslim refugees from Syria on the grounds that they may raise security concerns. During the 2016 presidential campaign, the Republican frontrunner Donald Trump called for a temporary ban on all non-citizen Muslims entering the United States. Clearly, these issues will continue to arise, no matter who serves as president going forward.

For Critical Thinking and Discussion

1. What criteria should the United States apply when establishing a refugee resettlement policy? How, if at all, should the government account for racial, ethnic, or religious diversity in articulating its policy?

2. How is your state responding to the resettlement of Syrian refugees in the United States?

---

to the bombing of Pearl Harbor, the threat of nuclear missiles in Cuba, and the 9/11 terrorist attacks might not have been possible had the principal decision makers been a legislative body or council. At the same time, more controversial foreign policy forays such as America's involvement in the Vietnam War, the trading of arms for hostages with Iran in the 1980s, and military intervention in Iraq without proof of weapons of mass destruction might well have been avoided had so much power not been vested in one individual. Although the president is at the center of foreign policymaking, other executive branch departments and agencies help formulate and implement foreign policy.

The **Department of State**, headed by the secretary of state, maintains primary responsibility for many foreign policy programs. State Department programs include diplomatic missions to other countries, foreign aid to developing nations, and contributions to **international organizations** (official entities of international scope or character, usually established by treaty, such as the World Bank and the International Monetary Fund). During the latter half of the twentieth century, the secretary of state emerged as a principal spokesperson for the U.S. government on all foreign policy matters.

In recent times, the position of secretary of state has been held by individuals with political star power that rivals that of the president. Colin Powell, the secretary of state during George W. Bush's first term in office, served a decade earlier as the first African American chairman of the Joint Chiefs of Staff under President George H. W. Bush. In that capacity, Powell articulated the framework for intervention in the

Department of State Executive branch agency that is primarily responsible for most foreign policy programs within the executive branch, including diplomatic missions, foreign aid, and contributions to international organizations.

international organization Entity of international scope or character, usually established by treaty, such as the World Bank or the International Monetary Fund.

first Gulf War, later termed the "Powell Doctrine": Military action should be used as a last resort, and then only with clear popular support, overwhelming force, and a clear exit strategy. After flirting with a presidential run of his own, Powell eventually landed at the State Department, where he failed in his efforts to line up many of America's European allies behind the George W. Bush administration's threat to engage in a second Iraq war.[18] Hillary Rodham Clinton, a former first lady and the Democratic nominee for president in 2016, first served on the international stage as Barack Obama's initial secretary of state. Performing in that role, she is credited with shifting America's foreign policy toward a greater emphasis on diplomacy and foreign aid, in line with President Obama's stated goals.

Military power is an important factor in U.S. foreign relations. The **Department of Defense** plays a critical role in helping formulate and implement U.S. foreign policy by managing the nation's military. The secretary of defense is the principal civilian adviser to the president on military matters. On the military side, the president is advised by the **Joint Chiefs of Staff (JCS)**, which consists of the chief officers of the four branches of the armed forces (U.S. Army, Navy, Air Force, and Marines) as well as the JCS chair and vice chair. The JCS delivers the president's orders to the military commands involved in a particular operation. During the 2003 war in Iraq, Secretary of Defense Donald Rumsfeld emerged as the principal spokesman for the administration, holding frequent press conferences to report on the operation's progress and reaffirm the administration's objectives. Three years later, several retired army officers complained that when the decision was made to go to war in Iraq, Rumsfeld bypassed the advice of the Joint Chiefs of Staff. Rumsfeld resigned in November 2006, at which point he was already the second-longest-serving defense secretary in American history (only Robert McNamara, who served during the 1960s for the Kennedy and Johnson administrations, served longer).

In 1947, the National Security Act established the **National Security Council (NSC)** as an advisory body to the president, coordinating information about foreign, military, and economic policies that affect national security. By law, the NSC must include the president, vice president, and the secretaries of state and defense. But recent presidents have also appointed a national security adviser to supervise the council and monitor the implementation of national security decisions made by the president. Dating back to the 1960s, the national security adviser has served as both a key adviser and policymaker for most modern presidents.[19]

With three executive branch officials (the secretary of defense, the secretary of state, and the national security adviser) in a position to advise the president on foreign policy, some conflicts are inevitable. During George W. Bush's first term as president, National Security Advisor Condoleezza Rice, Secretary of State Colin Powell, and Secretary of Defense Donald Rumsfeld all served as critical advisers in helping the president formulate national security policy in the wake of the 9/11 terrorist attacks. The war in Afghanistan that followed generated widespread support throughout the country, and among these officials as well. But when the Bush administration turned its attention to a possible war in Iraq, sharp divisions among the three officials emerged. Although such terms may be oversimplified, the

REUTERS/Brendan Smialowski/Poo

Secretary of State John Kerry meets with Saudi Arabia's King Abdullah in January 2014 to discuss U.S.-Saudi relations.

Department of Defense Executive branch agency that is responsible for managing the nation's military and advising the president on all military matters.

Joint Chiefs of Staff (JCS) Group of chief officers of the four branches of the armed forces as well as a JCS chair and vice chair, which advises the president on military matters and delivers the president's orders to the military.

National Security Council (NSC) Advisory body to the president charged with coordinating information about foreign, military, and economic policies that affect national security.

hawks Members of the president's administration who call for aggressive military actions wherever hostile forces may be found.

realists Members of the president's administration who advocate diplomacy as the primary means of protecting U.S. interests abroad.

administration's **hawks**—who called for aggressive military action wherever hostile forces might be found—were led by Rumsfeld, Rice, and Vice President Dick Cheney. On the other side of this divide were the **realists**, led by Powell, who counseled diplomacy as the primary means of protecting U.S. interests abroad. Powell was particularly concerned that a military attack on Iraq might reduce support for democratic reforms in Saudi Arabia and strain relationships with important Western European allies such as France and Germany. Ultimately the hawks won the day, as the Bush administration waged the 2003 war in Iraq without support from the United Nations and many of its allies.

Although not directly responsible for formulating the administration's overall foreign policy direction, other agencies and executive branch officials also influence aspects of foreign policy. In the aftermath of the 9/11 terrorist attacks, the Bush administration sought to create a unified security structure to coordinate the protection of U.S. citizens against terrorist threats within the nation's own borders. Accordingly, Congress in 2002 established the **Department of Homeland Security (DHS)**. Various governmental divisions responsible for U.S. security have been brought under DHS control, including border and transportation security, infrastructure protection, the U.S. Coast Guard, the U.S. Secret Service, the Federal Emergency Management Agency (FEMA), and the Bureau of Citizenship and Immigration Services. The DHS secretary is responsible for overseeing the efforts of more than 180,000 government employees in the department's efforts to strengthen U.S. borders, provide for intelligence analysis and infrastructure protection, and improve the use of science and technology to combat terrorist threats. The DHS is also responsible for formulating a comprehensive response and recovery capability in the event of an unexpected threat.

Department of Homeland Security (DHS) Executive branch agency established in 2002 to coordinate government entities in protecting U.S. citizens against terrorism within the nation's borders.

The National Security Act of 1947 created the **Central Intelligence Agency (CIA)** to correlate, evaluate, and disseminate intelligence information from throughout the world that affects national security. Unlike the NSC, the CIA is also responsible for disseminating propaganda or performing public relations functions on behalf of the U.S. government and for engaging in overt or covert activities at the direction of the president.

Central Intelligence Agency (CIA) Federal agency charged with evaluating and disseminating intelligence information, performing public relations functions that affect international perceptions of the United States, and engaging in overt and covert operations at the direction of the president.

Since the fall of the Soviet Union in 1991, the CIA has struggled to define its role in the post-Cold War era, particularly with regard to the Middle East and the recent war on terrorism. The first CIA director during the George W. Bush administration, George Tenet, came under heated criticism both for the failure of his agency to coordinate information about the Al Qaeda terrorist network in advance of the 9/11 attacks and for mistakenly allowing President Bush to make false claims about Iraq's nuclear capabilities during a State of the Union address.

With the continued need for information about activities in the Middle East, the Balkans, and North Korea, the CIA still plays a critical role in helping American leaders craft foreign policy.[20] Congress has increasingly pressed the agency to improve its operations and justify its specific operations. A House-Senate Intelligence Committee investigating the 9/11 attacks complained that the traditional post of Director of Central Intelligence was outdated and poorly suited to coordinate intelligence coming from so many different parts of government; accordingly, it recommended the establishment of a new cabinet-level post on intelligence matters. In 2004, the Bush administration created the new position of Director of National Intelligence, charged with leading the intelligence community across all government agencies.

Other Foreign Policy Actors and Interests

Although generally more oriented toward domestic affairs, Congress possesses various constitutional powers that give it some stake in crafting U.S. foreign policy. Although presidents have committed troops to battle more than a hundred times in our nation's history without a formal declaration of war from Congress—including most notably in Korea and Vietnam—modern chief executives have learned that there may be some political benefits to asking for a congressional resolution to support military action. Congressional approval of such actions can help rally public support and possibly provide some political cover should those military operations fail. In October 2002, for example, Congress passed a resolution backing the use of military force in Iraq. In the months that followed the invasion when guerrilla warfare continued to threaten American soldiers, many Democratic senators who voted for the resolution were hard-pressed to criticize the president's decision to invade.

Legislators on the Foreign Relations committees of the Senate and the House may take the lead in initiating investigations into a broad range of foreign policy initiatives undertaken by the executive branch.[21] The secretary of state reports regularly to both committees, which oversee relations with foreign nations, executive agreements in foreign affairs, international organizations, and foreign interventions. The secretary of defense reports regularly to the House and Senate Armed Services committees, which are responsible for overseeing defense and national security issues. The diffusion of power among so many separate committees and individual legislators tends to hamstring congressional efforts to encourage the executive branch to consult with the committees before taking some action. Further, the possibility that members of congressional committees might leak information provides the White House with the incentive to conceal information by claiming executive privilege. The Senate's constitutionally vested power to ratify all treaties may also thwart a president eager to move forward. For example, when the Senate in the late 1970s ratified two treaties guaranteeing that the United States would transfer control of the Panama Canal to Panama, senators offered no fewer than 145 amendments to the treaties.

Groups of legislators frequently tour other nations to learn firsthand the nature of particular foreign policy problems. In rare cases, individual legislators may choose to act on their own to influence foreign policy, sometimes causing headaches for White House officials determined to present a unified front to foreign nations. For example, during the 1980s, Representative Charlie Wilson (D-TX), a maverick congressman from East Texas, worked behind the scenes to help the CIA arm and sustain a rebel Afghanistan group, the Mujahidin, in its revolt against military occupation by the Soviet Union.[22] In November 2005, the late Congressman John Murtha (D-PA), a former U.S. Marine and noted war hawk, spoke out forcefully against the war in Iraq. After attempts to paint Murtha as an extremist failed, Bush administration officials, including Vice President Dick Cheney, scrambled to respond to Murtha's comments with specific plans for the occupation.

Certainly some private citizens may be in a position to pursue similar initiatives on their own; before making his first presidential bid in 1992, millionaire Ross Perot helped rescue two employees of his corporation from an Iranian prison.[23] Yet most Americans seeking to influence foreign policy organize themselves into special interest or "pressure" groups for the purpose of doing so. The power that the so-called pro-Israel lobby wields in Congress is well known: The American-Israel Public Affairs Committee (AIPAC) has influenced important appropriation decisions on Capitol Hill during the past 30 years, helping to ensure the continuation of American aid to Israel. AIPAC's tactics have included letter-writing campaigns and active involvement in election campaigns to assist members of Congress who it believes are sympathetic to Israel.

Private-sector interest groups have been especially active with regard to most aspects of general trade policy. Textile manufacturers' lobbies have fought to limit imports of foreign garments, whereas farmers' lobbies have pressured the government to pass tariffs on agricultural products imported from other countries. U.S. business interests seeking to export high-tech goods, such as computer and software firms and aerospace manufacturers, have opposed all efforts to impose trade restrictions and sanctions on large potential markets such as China. Is it appropriate for such interest groups to attempt to influence foreign affairs? Critics contend that the lobbying activities of these pressure groups may inadvertently undermine American foreign policy or even threaten American national security interests. Despite these concerns, interest groups continue to play an active and aggressive role in the process.

military-industrial complex The vast network of defense industries in America (including manufacturers of weapons, missiles, aircraft, and so forth) and their allies in the federal bureaucracy.

The term **military-industrial complex** refers to the vast network of defense industries in America, such as manufacturers of weapons, missiles, aircraft, submarines, and so forth, and their bureaucratic allies. The complex as a whole maintains a keen interest in foreign policymaking that is concerned with defense and national security. These industries expanded during the Cold War as U.S. defense budgets rose to as much as 40 percent of annual federal spending. In the late 1990s, defense spending amounted to just 15 percent of the budget, generating ever-more-feverish efforts by members of the military-industrial complex to either increase that allotment or shift the focus of defense spending to weapons and resources that meet their own areas of expertise. One of the by-products of the terrorist attacks of 9/11 was a renewed commitment to military and national security spending; 10 years after the tragedy, America's military spending had leveled to approximately 20 percent of the overall U.S. budget.

American Foreign Policy and Public Opinion

Public opinion on foreign policy issues is a central concern for key actors in the U.S. foreign policymaking arena, including the president, in part because those actors won't keep their jobs for long if they ignore popular sentiments. When the public punishes officials at the polls for their ill-advised foreign policy decisions, observers are quick to criticize those officials for ignoring the will of the people.[24] Yet when President George W. Bush ordered a "surge" of 20,000 more U.S. forces in Iraq in early 2007, he was not responding to public opinion as much as he was hoping to shift it in a pro-war direction. President Obama assumed the intervention in Afghanistan would be well received, although, as shown in Figure 16-1, the public saw little success there occurring during President Obama's first term in office. Moreover, many political defeats occur because officials have misinterpreted public attitudes, rather than ignoring them outright. Even Lyndon Johnson, whose Vietnam policy proved so unpopular that he was forced to drop out of the presidential election race in 1968, was known to have carried in his pajama pockets the results of public opinion polls about foreign policy.

Part of the challenge facing U.S. officials is that public attitudes toward foreign affairs often defy easy analysis and interpretation. Modern presidents have managed to generate considerable public support for foreign policy objectives that protect American jobs, control illegal immigration, or counter the illegal drug trade. Foreign policy initiatives that promote human rights or advance democracy abroad have been far less likely to garner support. The 1991 Persian Gulf War generated public support from the outset because an adversary had engaged in aggressive military action against a U.S. ally. By contrast, the Clinton administration fought an uphill battle against public opinion in its Operation Restore Hope to counter widespread famine in Somalia and in its limited military interventions in Bosnia. Political scientist John Mueller offered the following four propositions to describe American public opinion concerning foreign policy:

1. Americans will tolerate a substantial loss of American lives only if the enemy is seen to be truly powerful and set on jeopardizing vital American interests.

2. The advantage to a president of a success in minor foreign policy ventures is marginal; the disadvantage to a president of a failure in such a venture is more than marginal.

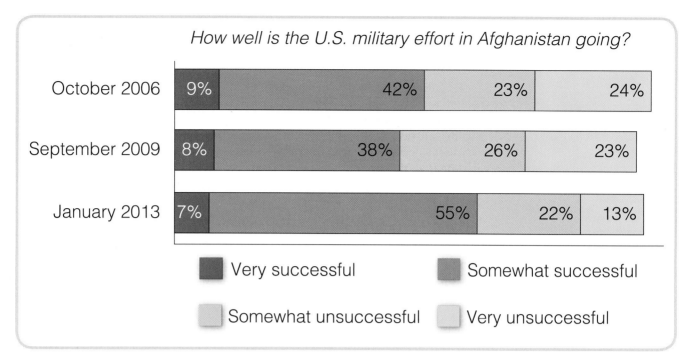

How well is the U.S. military effort in Afghanistan going?

	Very successful	Somewhat successful	Somewhat unsuccessful	Very unsuccessful
October 2006	9%	42%	23%	24%
September 2009	8%	38%	26%	23%
January 2013	7%	55%	22%	13%

FIGURE 16-1 Failing to Win over the Public in Afghanistan When President Barack Obama elected to turn the military's focus away from Iraq and toward Afghanistan in 2009, he expected the decision to be controversial. Still, the new president was no doubt surprised to learn that the decision to increase troops in that country would initially create perceptions of failure, rather than success, in that region. It was only in 2013, after four more years of fighting there, that public perceptions finally turned more optimistic on Afghanistan. Consider the NBC/*Wall Street Journal* poll that asked: *"Do you think the war in Afghanistan against the Taliban and Al Qaeda has been very successful, somewhat successful, somewhat unsuccessful, or very unsuccessful?"*

Based on data from NBC News/*Wall Street Journal* Poll, Study #13018, conducted by the polling organizations of Peter Hart (D) and Bill McInturff (R), January 12–15, 2013. N 5 1,000 adults nationwide.

3. If they are not being killed, American troops can remain in peacekeeping or other ventures virtually indefinitely with little public criticism.

4. Although few concerns can turn the public's attention to foreign affairs, nuclear weapons retain the capacity to arrest the public's attention, and the same may hold for biological and chemical weapons.[25]

Once again it was the events of September 11, 2001, that turned the attention of Americans to foreign policy like few other events of the past 30 years. The George W. Bush administration sought to characterize its foreign policy initiatives in Afghanistan, Iraq, and elsewhere in terms designed to be acceptable to public opinion. The war on terrorism is framed in terms of a worldwide threat of seismic proportions. Officials may have delayed the 2003 war to lay the groundwork for clear-cut and unambiguous military success. Even after the formal military engagement of that war was concluded, President Bush continued to couch the threat in terms of intelligence received that Iraq possessed nuclear capabilities. More recently, President Obama faced an uphill battle in generating public support for his decision to increase troop levels for the war in Afghanistan: Nearly a decade after the terrorist attacks of 9/11, the war no longer seemed so pressing to a majority of the American population. Indeed, polls indicated that the public remained split during the summer of 2010 on whether fighting that war was even the right thing to do.

The thorny politics of foreign occupation that occurs following most military battles—when the victors must (at least temporarily) control the area that has been seized by military force—can weigh especially heavily in the court of public opinion. Public support for the war tends to tail off once the opposing armies have been defeated. If the occupation fails, the defeated or other hostile entities may seize the opportunity to reverse the war's outcome. America's military history features numerous successful military occupations, such as that over West Germany and Japan in the aftermath of World War II. By contrast, the George W. Bush administration invested more than $1 billion per day in the occupation of Iraq; yet far more American troops were killed during the occupation than during the brief six-week military conflict.

16-4 | Foreign Policy Dilemmas for the Twenty-First Century

Some foreign policy dilemmas of the twenty-first century, such as the problematic occupation of Iraq by U.S. forces after the 2003 Iraq war, represent new versions of age-old challenges that the U.S. government has faced on an intermittent basis since the nation's founding. Others represent unforeseen obstacles produced by circumstances unique to the modern, post-Cold War world. Regardless, American officials must always be on the lookout for foreign policy challenges that arise with little or no warning and that can overshadow all other aspects of the federal government's agenda if they are not kept under control. Officials must also be prepared to justify their actions according to some theory or well-articulated rationale, lest they be accused of conducting foreign policy "on the fly" with little real reason for endangering American resources and, in some instances, for putting American troops in harm's way.

Is the "Preemption Doctrine" Justifiable?

Only a year after the collapse of the Soviet Union in 1991, the first hint of a dramatic transformation in America's foreign policy could be seen. In 1992, several Pentagon planners working in the George H. W. Bush administration drafted a policy statement asserting that the American government should assume a far more activist role in foreign affairs, especially in the Middle East. Their statement specifically reserved the right of the U.S. military to use advance strikes to stop rogue states from developing weapons of mass destruction. Later termed the **preemption doctrine**, this statement sparked considerable controversy after it was leaked to *The New York Times*. In 1997 one of its original authors, Paul Wolfowitz, joined Donald Rumsfeld and other conservative foreign policy advocates to warn President Bill Clinton that America's containment of Iraq had failed. They urged the government to shift its focus to the outright removal of Iraqi leader Saddam Hussein, who had remained in power even through the American military's conquering of his country during the Persian Gulf War of 1991.

With George W. Bush's election as president in 2000 and the more intense focus on international terrorism that followed the September 11, 2001, attacks, the emphasis on preemption became ingrained in U.S. policy. Rumsfeld, who had become secretary of defense, joined others in pressing the administration to exercise its military power, unilaterally if necessary, to confront hostile states bent on acquiring weapons of mass destruction. Bush named Wolfowitz as deputy secretary of defense, a platform from which he more forcefully stressed the merits of a strategic preemption doctrine.

Even advocates of this doctrine do not dispute that preemption carries with it some significant risks. The fundamental paradox of preemption is that it can be effectively applied only to a country that lacks the capacity to retaliate. Although

preemption doctrine
Doctrine of war making that reserves the right of the U.S. military to use advance strikes to stop rogue states from developing weapons of mass destruction.

Iraq suffered from preemptive American attacks in the spring of 2003, North Korea and Iran—two nations similarly charged with posing international threats—are less likely to be targets of a U.S. preemptive attack because neither is viewed as so weak or vulnerable as was Saddam Hussein's regime. Critics of the preemption doctrine also charge that although this policy may be justified in the rare instance when a rival power's attacks are imminent, it cannot be justified to prevent attacks in the distant and more ambiguous future.

Cultivating Relations with Russia

Although many now view America as the world's lone remaining superpower, the fall of the Soviet Union did not eliminate all threats to the United States from that part of the globe. The Russian Federation headed by Vladimir Putin controls a landmass of more than 6.5 million square miles, nearly twice the size of the United States. It also maintains one of the world's most powerful military threats because most of the nuclear capabilities of the former Soviet Union were passed on to Russia (see Table 16-1 for a run-down of the nations that currently maintain some form of nuclear capability). Although U.S. foreign policy must address each of the 12 independent nations of the former Soviet Union on its own merits, the Russian Federation continues to capture the bulk of attention from American foreign policymakers.

Concerns around the world have been raised about Russia's continued use of military force. For example, over a decade ago, it subdued the smaller Republic of Chechnya, the site of the bloody Chechen-Russian War of 1994–1996. Then, in August 2008, Russia temporarily occupied the nearby country of Georgia by force after months of skirmishes

TABLE 16-1 Who Is in the Nuclear Club?

The list of states that have successfully detonated nuclear weapons—often termed the "nuclear club"—continues to grow in the post-Cold War era. Only five members of the club are considered "nuclear weapon states" under the terms of the Nuclear Non-Proliferation Treaty (NPT), a landmark international treaty first established in 1970 between states that possess such weapons and 190 nations that do not. Four other states in the club do not subscribe to the NPT, but they are known or believed to possess nuclear weapons. Just one state (South Africa) has actually dropped out of the club, dissembling its arsenal before joining the NPT. The current list of states in the nuclear club is as follows:

Recognized Nuclear Weapon States Under the Terms of the NPT	Year of First Test
1. The United States	1945
2. Russia (successor state to the Soviet Union)	1949
3. United Kingdom	1952
4. France	1960
5. China	1964
Other States Believed to Have Nuclear Weapons (non-signatories to the NPT)	
6. India	1974
7. Pakistan	1998
8. North Korea	2006
9. Israel	1979*

*Year is disputed; Israel neither confirms nor denies that it has conducted nuclear tests.
Based on data from National Resources Defense Council Archive of Nuclear Data, www.nrdc.org/nuclear/nudb/datainx.asp.

and increasing tensions between the two nations. More recently, in February of 2014, pro-Russian forces (including Russian military servicemen fighting without insignia) occupied the Crimean peninsula—formerly under Ukrainian control—in the aftermath of the Ukrainian revolution. On March 16, 2014, Russia and Crimea signed a treaty of accession. Despite a UN resolution declaring Russia's incorporation of Crimea as illegal, in July of 2015, Russian Prime Minister Dmitry Medvedev confirmed that Crimea had been fully integrated into Russia in every respect.

Russia's recent military incursions have led to a further deterioration in U.S.-Russian relations. In 2013 things got even worse when Russia offered a form of temporary asylum to Edward Snowden, the former CIA systems administrator and private intelligence contractor who admitted to disclosing thousands of classified documents while working as a National Security Agency contractor in June 2013. Snowden's leaked documents uncovered the existence of theretofore secret global surveillance programs. Although the U.S. government continues to seek Snowden's appearance in federal court, Russia's decision to grant Snowden a residency permit in August 2014 appears to have negated those efforts, at least in the short term. As it stands, Snowden has willingly responded to some American media interviews and at the time of this writing, he continues to speak regularly to his million-plus followers on Twitter.

Despite all these tensions, both American and Russian officials still have strong incentives to cultivate friendly relations with each other. Russia's efforts to establish itself as a member of the club of democratic nations in good standing require it to demonstrate to the world that it can conduct responsible foreign policy with the United States.

Meanwhile, the United States needs Russian cooperation to allow the stationing of U.S. forces in distant sites, such as the central Asian republic of Tajikistan, in order to combat terrorist threats in that part of the globe. A stronger relationship between Russia and the United States would also have important implications for American foreign policy: Specifically, it might encourage some of America's allies, particularly France and Germany, to go along with American military operations. Consider that Russia's refusal to support the 2003 war in Iraq may have helped embolden those two Western European countries to withhold support for the American-led war.

What Role Does Foreign Aid Play in the New International Order?

The American government's legacy of providing monetary aid to struggling nations and allies was first established on a monumental scale with the Marshall Plan to help Western European nations recover after World War II. Although humanitarian concerns continue to influence such aid, U.S. economic and national security interests also affect foreign aid decisions. Expanded foreign markets would purchase domestic products and agricultural goods, boosting the U.S. economy. New states would also be more likely to join the expanding capitalist world economy if U.S. aid contributed to their recovery and encouraged them to reject anti-capitalist economic systems.

Because the dissolution of the Soviet Union has weakened some of the strategic rationale for foreign aid, there have been substantial reductions in such aid during the past decade. Critics of foreign aid also charge that much of the money provided by America goes to elites in the recipient nations, rather than to those who need help. Defenders of aid respond that even when elites control a sizeable portion of the aid, the recipient nation is able to expand its national output, which leads to higher living standards for all. But this "trickle-down" theory of foreign aid has been cast aside in recent years by experts such as economist Peter Boone of the London School of Economics. After assessing the experience of nearly 100 nations, Boone concluded that because foreign transfers only tend to increase government consumption (which has no positive effect on growth), foreign aid has had little or no impact on the recipient country's overall investment levels.[26]

The United States continues to be a leading contributor to such international aid institutions as the World Bank, which since 1945 has extended credit to nations for building and economic development. America also contributes substantially to the International Monetary Fund, which helps to maintain the value of foreign currencies during times of crisis. But the heyday of foreign aid—when it served as a critical instrument of U.S. foreign relations—appears to be a thing of the past.

President Barack Obama, speaking to the United Nations in September 2014, asks for support to back a U.S.-led campaign against militants in Iraq and Syria.

Does the United Nations Still Serve an Important Function?

The United Nations, founded at the conclusion of World War II, is structured around five separate governing bodies: (1) the General Assembly, which is made up of all member states (at present there are 192 member states); (2) the Economic and Social Council, which is made up of 54 members chosen by the General Assembly and serves primarily as an advisory body to the General Assembly on matters of international economic and social cooperation; (3) the Secretariat, which supports the other UN bodies and carries out tasks as directed by those bodies; (4) the International Court of Justice, the UN's judicial organ that has jurisdiction to try certain international war criminals and settles disputes submitted to it by duly authorized international entities; and (5) the Security Council, which maintains peace and security among nations by issuing resolutions that (at least in theory) are binding on UN members. The separation of the Security Council from the larger General Assembly is significant. As currently constituted, the Security Council consists of 5 permanent members (China, France, the Russian Federation, the United States, and Great Britain) and 10 nonpermanent rotating members. Each of the five permanent members maintains the absolute right to veto decisions of the all-important Security Council, the only UN body with the power to authorize economic sanctions or military force. However, the General Assembly retains the exclusive power to enforce Security Council decisions.

The United States dominated the UN on all security issues during its first 40 years, but as U.S. influence over the body has declined, calls have increased within Congress to reduce American aid to the organization and to ignore its dictates whenever American security interests are at issue. In 2003, America went to war in Iraq even though the UN Security Council was unwilling to offer advance authorization for any such military action. Yet immediately after the war with Iraq had concluded, the UN began relief and reconstruction activities in the war-torn nation, and began pushing for a resolution that would broaden international control over the region. Thus, in the twenty-first century, the UN seems destined to play at least a limited role in international affairs, asserting its authority most strongly during peacekeeping and relief missions that follow military action.

From Your Perspective

Is the American Military Draft a Thing of the Past?

The U.S. government discontinued use of compulsory military service in 1973, much to the relief of a generation of young Americans that had grown increasingly hostile to America's military involvement in Vietnam. Since then, Americans have marveled at the degree to which America's comparative advantage in military technology has helped to reduce (although certainly not eliminate) casualties of U.S. military incursions. Yet is the move to an all-voluntary military force permanent? Critics of the Bush administration's invasion of Iraq argue that America's active military force of nearly 1.5 million soldiers was stretched far too thin between 2003 and 2008. Several high-profile members of Congress at the time, including Charles Rangel (D-NY), even called for the draft to be reinstated as a means of ensuring that service would be spread equally between the rich and the poor (those from poor families are more apt than those from wealthier families to voluntarily enlist for military service). President Barack Obama's decision to upgrade the nation's military presence in Afghanistan reopened those same questions yet again.

Should college-age students anticipate that the draft might come again in the near future? On one hand, the political platforms of both parties have consistently opposed reinstatement of the draft. On the other hand, since 1980 all male U.S. citizens age 18 or older have been required by law to register with the selective service, in case emergency manpower needs in a time of national crisis require conscription once again.

An official at Selective Service Headquarters in Washington, D.C., draws labeled ping-pong balls to determine the rank order of birthdates in the first nationally televised draft lottery on December 2, 1969. All 19-year-old male citizens with birthdays chosen early in the process would become the first draftees in the Vietnam War.

For Critical Thinking and Discussion

1. Do you believe America's selective service system—the agency that maintains information on those who may be subject to a military draft—is unfair? Should it apply only to male U.S. citizens, or to others as well?
2. Given the advanced state of military technology, can involuntary conscription still be justified in the 21ˢᵗ century?

Summary

16-1 The Constitutional Framework of American Foreign Policy

- The president is the commander-in-chief and has the power to negotiate treaties and appoint and receive ambassadors; Congress has the power to declare war, raise armies, and regulate foreign commerce, among its other functions.

16-2 The Roots of American Foreign Policy

- Over two centuries, the practical power to make war has shifted from Congress to the president. The United States adhered to a policy of isolationism from the time of its founding until the late nineteenth century, generally forgoing intervention in foreign wars during that period. With its entry into World War I and World War II, the United States rose to the status of a world superpower emphasizing internationalism, by which it participated in a system of collective security.

- The Cold War, pitting the United States against the Soviet Union from 1945 until 1991, was waged through economic warfare, arms build-ups, and moments of tense diplomacy that fell short of direct military engagements between the two superpowers. The demise of Soviet-run regimes in Russia and elsewhere beginning in the late 1980s failed to decrease U.S. involvement around the world.

- The U.S. military overthrew the governments of Afghanistan and Iraq in 2001 and 2003, respectively, as part of the war on terrorism. Although the continued occupation of Iraq by U.S. forces after the Iraq war was a source of debate among political officials between 2003 and 2008, President Obama accomplished a drawdown of forces in Iraq; the Obama administration sought instead to redirect U.S. military strength to Afghanistan and elsewhere. Unfortunately, the recent upsurge in violence in Iraq makes it impossible for the United States to completely separate itself from that troubled nation.

16-3 The Structure of American Foreign Policymaking

- In formulating foreign policy, the president is assisted by the secretary of state, the secretary of defense, the Joint Chiefs of Staff, the national security adviser, and the Director of National Intelligence. The Department of Homeland Security, created by an act of Congress in 2002, is responsible for border and transportation security, intelligence analysis, infrastructure protection, and all activities that protect against terrorist threats in the United States.

- Congress oversees foreign policy through its Foreign Relations committees, which receive regular reports from the secretary of state and the secretary of defense. Public opinion concerning American foreign policy often defies easy interpretation, as some presidents have been punished at the polls for ill-advised foreign policy decisions, whereas others have rescued their presidencies by engaging in successful foreign policy initiatives.

16-4 Foreign Policy Dilemmas for the Twenty-First Century

- Foreign policy dilemmas facing American officials in the twenty-first century include questions about when (if at all) a preemptive military attack is justified.

- U.S. foreign policy today is further complicated by the determination of what role (if any) the United States should play in supporting the United Nations, questions as to whether the United States should increase or decrease foreign aid in general, and increasingly tense relations between the United States and Russia. Russia's role as a broker in recent U.S.-Syria relations, and its military incursion in Crimea, make that nation and its leadership impossible to ignore as a factor in the post-Cold War international order.

Key Terms

Central Intelligence Agency (CIA) (p. 458)

Cold War (p. 449)

containment (p. 449)

Department of Defense (p. 457)

Department of Homeland Security (DHS) (p. 458)

Department of State (p. 456)

domino theory (p. 450)

expansionism (p. 447)

hawks (p. 458)

international organization (p. 456)

internationalism (p. 449)

isolationism (p. 446)

Joint Chiefs of Staff (JCS) (p. 457)

manifest destiny (p. 447)

Marshall Plan (p. 449)

military-industrial complex (p. 460)

Monroe Doctrine (p. 447)

Test Yourself

1. The U.S. Constitution grants which of the following the power to declare war?
   a. The president
   b. Congress
   c. The U.S. Supreme Court
   d. The secretary of defense

2. The "two presidencies theory" suggests that presidents
   a. have more power in influencing domestic policy.
   b. have more power in influencing foreign policy.
   c. should have the power to declare war.
   d. lack the ability to negotiate treaties with other nations.

3. Why did Congress pass the War Powers Resolution in 1973?

4. Which of the following best characterizes U.S. foreign policy prior to the twentieth century?
   a. Pacifism
   a. Internationalism
   a. Isolationism
   a. Colonialism

5. The policy that the United States would consider any European colonization of the Americas as an act of war is known as
   a. the Marshall Plan.
   b. the Monroe Doctrine.
   c. the Truman Doctrine.
   d. manifest destiny.

6. The Cold War ended when
   a. the United States defeated South Vietnam in 1973.
   b. the United States forced the Soviets to withdraw missiles from Cuba in 1962.
   c. Soviet leader Mikhail Gorbachev resigned amid the economic collapse of soviet nations in 1991.
   d. President Nixon negotiated the SALT agreements with the Soviets in 1973.

7. What dangers would the U.S. government face if it were to move to a more isolationist policy in the modern era?

8. The U.S. cabinet department primarily responsible for protecting the United States from a terrorist attack is the
   a. Department of State.
   b. Department of Defense.
   c. Department of Interior.
   d. Department of Homeland Security.

9. Those who advocate diplomacy as the initial means of protecting U.S. interests abroad are known as
   a. hawks.
   b. doves.
   c. realists.
   d. diplomats.

10. Which of the following presidents ordered a "surge" in U.S. military activities, despite opposition in the public opinion polls, to defeat insurgents in Afghanistan?

a. George H. W. Bush

b. Bill Clinton

c. George W. Bush

d. Barack Obama

11. What are the four propositions, developed by political scientist John Mueller, that describe public opinion about foreign policy?

12. The modern foreign policy position that states the United States may use advance military strikes to prevent rogue nations from developing weapons of mass destruction is

a. the advance option.

b. the Clinton doctrine.

c. containment.

d. the preemption doctrine

13. How is the United Nations structured, and which five nations have disproportionate power in that structure?

1. b. (LO 16-1); 2. b. (LO 16-1); 4. c. (LO 16-2); 5. b. (LO 16-2); 6. c. (LO 16-2); 8. d. (LO 16-3); 9. c. (LO 16-3); 10. d. (LO 16-3); 12. d. (LO 16-4)

APPENDIX

Declaration of Independence

In Congress, July 4, 1776.
A DECLARATION
By the Representatives of the United States of America,
In General Congress Assembled.

When in the Course of human Events, it becomes necessary for one People to dissolve the Political Bands which have connected them with another, and to assume among the Powers of the Earth, the separate and equal Station to which the Laws of Nature and of Nature's God entitle them, a decent Respect to the Opinions of Mankind requires that they should declare the causes which impel them to the Separation.

We hold these Truths to be self-evident, that all Men are created equal, that they are endowed by their Creator with certain unalienable Rights, that among these are Life, Liberty, and the Pursuit of Happiness—That to secure these Rights, Governments are instituted among Men, deriving their just Powers from the Consent of the Governed, that whenever any Form of Government becomes destructive of these Ends, it is the Right of the People to alter or abolish it, and to institute new Government, laying its Foundation on such Principles, and organizing its Powers in such Form, as to them shall seem most likely to effect their Safety and Happiness. Prudence, indeed, will dictate that Governments long established should not be changed for light and transient Causes; and accordingly all Experience hath shewn, that Mankind are more disposed to suffer, while Evils are sufferable, than to right themselves by abolishing the Forms to which they are accustomed. But when a long Train of Abuses and Usurpations, pursuing invariably the same Object, evinces a Design to reduce them under absolute Despotism, it is their Right, it is their Duty, to throw off such Government, and to provide new Guards for their future Security. Such has been the patient Sufferance of these Colonies; and such is now the Necessity which constrains them to alter their former Systems of Government. The History of the present kind of Great Britain is a History of repeated Injuries and Usurpations, all having in direct Object the Establishment of an absolute Tyranny over these States. To prove this, let Facts be submitted to a candid World.

He has refused his Assent to Laws, the most wholesome and necessary for public good.

He has forbidden his Governors to pass Laws of immediate and pressing importance, unless suspended in their Operation till his Assent should be obtained; and when so suspended, he has utterly neglected to attend to them.

He has refused to pass other Laws for the Accommodation of large Districts of People, unless those People would relinquish the Right of Representation in the Legislature, a Right inestimable to them, and formidable to Tyrants only.

He has called together Legislative Bodies at Places unusual, uncomfortable, and distant from the Depository of their public records, for the sole Purpose of fatiguing them into Compliance with his Measures.

He has dissolved Representative Houses repeatedly, for opposing with many Firmness his Invasions on the Rights of the People.

He has refused for a long Time, after such Dissolutions, to cause others to be elected; whereby the Legislative Powers, incapable of Annihilation, have returned to the People at large for their exercise; the State remaining in the mean time exposed to all the Dangers of Invasion from without, and Convulsions within.

He has endeavoured to prevent the Population of these States; for that Purpose obstructing the Laws for Naturalization of Foreigners; refusing to pass others to encourage their Migrations hither, and raising the Conditions of new Appropriations of Lands.

He has obstructed the Administration of Justice, by refusing his Assent to Laws for establishing Judiciary Powers.

He has made Judges dependent on his Will alone, for the Tenure of their Offices, and the Amount and Payment of their Salaries.

He has erected a Multitude of new Offices, and sent hither Swarms of Officers to harass our People, and eat out their Substance.

He has kept among us, in Times of Peaces, Standing Armies, without the consent of our Legislatures.

He has affected to render the Military independent of and superior to the Civil Power.

He has combined with others to subject us to a Jurisdiction foreign to our Constitution, and unacknowledged by our Laws; giving his Assent to their Acts of pretended Legislation:

For quartering large Bodies of Armed Troops among us:

For protecting them, by a mock Trial, from Punishment for any Murders which they should commit on the Inhabitants of these States:

For cutting off our Trade with all Parts of the World:

For imposing Taxes on us without our Consent: For depriving us, in many Cases, of the Benefits of Trial by Jury:

For transporting us beyond Seas to be tried for pretended Offences:

For abolishing the free System of English Laws in a neighbouring Province, establishing therein an arbitrary Government, and enlarging its Boundaries, so as to render it at once an Example and fit Instrument for introducing the same absolute Rule into these Colonies:

For taking away our Charters, abolishing our most valuable Laws, and altering fundamentally the Forms of our Governments:

For suspending our own Legislatures, and declaring themselves invested with Power to legislate for us in all Cases whatsoever.

He has abdicated Government here, by declaring us out of his Protection and waging War against us.

He has plundered our Seas, ravaged our Coasts, burnt our Towns, and destroyed the Lives of our People.

He is, at this Time, transporting large Armies of foreign Mercenaries to compleat the Works of Death, Desolation, and Tyranny, already begun with circumstances of Cruelty and Perfidy, scarcely paralleled in the most barbarous Ages, and totally unworthy the Head of a civilized Nation.

He has constrained our fellow Citizens taken Captive on the high Seas to bear Arms against their Country, to become the Executioners of their Friends and Brethren, or to fall themselves by their Hands.

He has excited domestic Insurrections amongst us, and has endeavoured to bring on the Inhabitants of our Frontiers, the merciless Indian Savages, whose known Rule of Warfare, is an undistinguished Destruction, of all Ages, Sexes and Conditions.

In every stage of these Oppressions we have Petitioned for Redress in the most humble Terms: Our repeated Petitions have been answered only by repeated Injury. A Prince, whose Character is thus marked by every act which may define a Tyrant, is unfit to be the Ruler of a free People.

Nor have we been wanting in Attentions to our British Brethren. We have warned them from Time to Time of Attempts by their Legislature to extend an unwarrantable Jurisdiction over us. We have reminded them of the Circumstances of our Emigration and Settlement here. We have appealed to their native Justice and Magnanimity, and we have conjured them by the Ties of our common Kindred to disavow these Usurpations, which, would inevitably interrupt our Connections and Correspondence. They too have been deaf to the Voice of Justice and of Consanguinity. We must, therefore, acquiesce in the Necessity, which denounces our Separation, and hold them, as we hold the rest of Mankind, Enemies in War, in Peace, Friends.

We, therefore, the Representatives of the UNITED STATES OF AMERICA, in GENERAL CONGRESS, Assembled, appealing to the Supreme Judge of the World for the Rectitude of our Intentions, do, in the Name, and by Authority of the good People of these Colonies, solemnly Publish and Declare, That these United Colonies are, and of Right ought to be, FREE AND INDEPENDENT STATES; that they are absolved from all Allegiance to the British Crown, and that all political Connection between them and the State of Great-Britain, is and ought to be totally dissolved; and that as FREE AND INDEPENDENT STATES, they have full Power to levy War, conclude Peace, contract Alliances, establish Commerce, and to do all other Acts and Things which INDEPENDENT STATES may of right do. And for the support of this Declaration, with a firm Reliance on the Protection of divine Providence, we mutually pledge to each other our Lives, our Fortunes, and our sacred Honor.

John Hancock

Georgia:

Button Gwinnett

Lyman Hall

George Walton

North Carolina:

William Hooper

Joseph Hewes

John Penn

South Carolina:

Edward Rutledge

Thomas Heyward, Jr.

Thomas Lynch, Jr.

Arthur Middleton

Maryland:

Samuel Chase

William Paca

Thomas Stone

Charles Carroll of Carrollton

Virginia:

George Wythe

Richard Henry Lee

Thomas Jefferson

Benjamin Harrison

Thomas Nelson, Jr.

Francis Lightfoot Lee

Carter Braxton

Pennsylvania:

Robert Morris

Benjamin Rush

Benjamin Franklin

John Morton

George Clymer

James Smith

George Taylor

James Wilson

George Ross

Delaware:

Caesar Rodney

George Read

Thomas McKean

New York:

William Floyd

Philip Livingston

Francis Lewis

Lewis Morris

New Jersey:

Richard Stockton

John Witherspoon

Francis Hopkinson

John Hart

Abraham Clark

New Hampshire:

Josiah Bartlett

William Whipple

Massachusetts:

Samuel Adams

John Adams

Robert Treat Paine

Elbridge Gerry

Rhode Island:

Stephen Hopkins

William Ellery

Connecticut:

Roger Sherman

Samuel Huntington

Oliver Wolcott

New Hampshire:

Matthew Thornton

Annotated Constitution of the United States of America

Annotated Constitution

OF THE UNITED STATES OF AMERICA

The Constitution of the United States of America

We the people of the United States, in order to form a more perfect union, establish justice, insure domestic tranquility, provide for the common defense, promote the general welfare, and secure the blessings of liberty to ourselves and our posterity, do ordain and establish this Constitution for the United States of America.

As a statement containing the essential reasons for drafting the Constitution and the purposes of the new central government, the Preamble theoretically does not confer any actual power on government. Nevertheless, on numerous occasions the Supreme Court has cited the preamble to illustrate the origin, scope, and purposes of the Constitution, as well as to help discern the meaning of certain constitutional provisions that follow it. Most notably in McCulloch v. Maryland *(1819), Chief Justice John Marshall quoted from the Preamble at length to confirm that the Constitution comes directly from the people, and not from the states.*

Article I

Section 1. All legislative powers herein granted shall be vested in a Congress of the United States, which shall consist of a Senate and House of Representatives.

The placement of provisions for congressional power in Article I confirms what the Founders undoubtedly assumed to be true: that Congress would be the preeminent branch of the new central government. Section 1 established two important principles. First, by specifying "powers herein granted," it declared that the national government is one of enumerated powers. Despite the broadening of powers implied by the necessary and proper clause of Section 8, this statement of Section 1 still means that Congress theoretically cannot do whatever it wants to do. Rather, it must ground its exercise of power (whether explicitly stated or implied) in a specific provision of Article I. Second, Section 1 established the principle of bicameralism—the presence of two separate but equally powerful legislative bodies—as a further safeguard against government tyranny.

Section 2. The House of Representatives shall be composed of members chosen every second year by the people of the several states, and the electors in each state shall have the qualifications requisite for electors of the most numerous branch of the state legislature.

No person shall be a Representative who shall not have attained to the age of twenty five years, and been seven years a citizen of the United States, and who shall not, when elected, be an inhabitant of that state in which he shall be chosen.

Representatives and direct taxes shall be apportioned among the several states which may be included within this union, according to their respective numbers, which shall be determined by adding to the whole number of free persons, including those bound to service for a term of years, and excluding Indians not taxed, three fifths of all other Persons. The actual Enumeration shall be made within three years after the first meeting of the Congress of the United States, and within every subsequent term of ten years, in such manner as they shall by law direct. The number of Representatives shall not exceed one for every thirty thousand, but each state shall have at least one Representative; and until such enumeration shall be made, the state of New Hampshire shall be entitled to chuse three, Massachusetts eight, Rhode Island and Providence Plantations one, Connecticut five, New York six, New Jersey four, Pennsylvania eight, Delaware one, Maryland six, Virginia ten, North Carolina five, South Carolina five, and Georgia three.

When vacancies happen in the Representation from any state, the executive authority thereof shall issue writs of election to fill such vacancies.

The House of Representatives shall choose their speaker and other officers; and shall have the sole power of impeachment.

Section 2 of Article I establishes a House of Representatives as the lower House of the Congress. The membership of the U.S. House of Representatives is apportioned according to each state's population; the so-called Three-Fifths Compromise (only three-fifths of the population of slaves would be counted for enumeration purposes) helped resolve an impasse at the Convention between Southern states, which wanted slaves to count as more, and Northern states, which wanted them to count as less. Although the number of House members has grown with the population, since 1911 it has been fixed by statute at 435. As constituted, the House is as powerful as the U.S. Senate, and in one respect is even more powerful: the House has the sole power to originate revenue bills. Section 2 also lays out the two-year-term rule and qualifications for each House member, as well as providing procedures for apportionment and filling vacancies. Finally, it authorizes the House to choose top officials, including the Speaker.

Section 3. The Senate of the United States shall be composed of two Senators from each state, chosen by the legislature thereof, for six years; and each Senator shall have one vote.

Immediately after they shall be assembled in consequence of the first election, they shall be divided as equally as may be into three classes. The seats of the Senators of the first class shall be vacated at the expiration of the second year, of the second class at the expiration of the fourth year, and the third class at the expiration of the sixth year, so that one third may be chosen every second year; and if vacancies happen by resignation, or otherwise, during the recess of the legislature of any state, the executive thereof may make temporary appointments until the next meeting of the legislature, which shall then fill such vacancies.

No person shall be a Senator who shall not have attained to the age of thirty years, and been nine years a citizen of the United States and who shall not, when elected, be an inhabitant of that state for which he shall be chosen.

The Vice President of the United States shall be President of the Senate, but shall have no vote, unless they be equally divided.

The Senate shall choose their other officers, and also a President pro tempore, in the absence of the Vice President, or when he shall exercise the office of President of the United States.

The Senate shall have the sole power to try all impeachments. When sitting for that purpose, they shall be on oath or affirmation. When the President of the United States is tried, the Chief Justice shall preside: And no person shall be convicted without the concurrence of two thirds of the members present.

Judgment in cases of impeachment shall not extend further than to removal from office, and disqualification to hold and enjoy any office of honor, trust or profit under the United States: but the party convicted shall nevertheless be liable and subject to indictment, trial, judgment and punishment, according to law.

Just as Section 2 does for the House of Representatives, Section 3 establishes various powers and procedures for the U.S. Senate. Individual senators may be more powerful than their counterparts in the House because of the longer length of their terms (six years) and because there are far fewer members in the body; however, there is no constitutional basis for the claim that the Senate is a superior chamber. Although the vice president theoretically presides over the Senate as its president, and the president pro tempore serves in the vice president's absence, in actual practice the president pro tempore usually deputizes a more junior senator to preside over most Senate business. The provisions of Clause 1 and Clause 2 that state legislatures choose senators have been overturned by the Seventeenth Amendment, which now provides that senators are chosen by popular election.

Section 4. The times, places and manner of holding elections for Senators and Representatives, shall be prescribed in each state by the legislature thereof; but the Congress may at any time by law make or alter such regulations, except as to the places of choosing Senators.

The Congress shall assemble at least once in every year, and such meeting shall be on the first Monday in December, unless they shall by law appoint a different day.

According to Article I, Section 4, states can regulate the time, place, and manner of all federal elections, but Congress can still establish a single uniform date for federal elections (and it has done so on the first Tuesday following the first Monday in November).

Section 5. Each House shall be the judge of the elections, returns and qualifications of its own members, and a majority of each shall constitute a quorum to do business; but a smaller number may adjourn from day to day, and may be authorized to compel the attendance of absent members, in such manner, and under such penalties as each House may provide.

Each House may determine the rules of its proceedings, punish its members for disorderly behavior, and, with the concurrence of two thirds, expel a member.

Each House shall keep a journal of its proceedings, and from time to time publish the same, excepting such parts as may in their judgment require secrecy; and the yeas and nays of the members of either House on any question shall, at the desire of one fifth of those present, be entered on the journal.

Neither House, during the session of Congress, shall, without the consent of the other, adjourn for more than three days, nor to any other place than that in which the two Houses shall be sitting.

Section 6. The Senators and Representatives shall receive a compensation for their services, to be ascertained by law, and paid out of the treasury of the United States. They shall in all cases, except treason, felony and breach of the peace, be privileged from arrest during their attendance at the session of their respective Houses, and in going to and returning from the same; and for any speech or debate in either House, they shall not be questioned in any other place.

No Senator or Representative shall, during the time for which he was elected, be appointed to any civil office under the authority of the United States, which shall have been created, or the emoluments whereof shall have been increased during such time: and no person holding any office under the United States, shall be a member of either House during his continuance in office.

Article I, Section 6 extends to members of Congress various immunities. The speech and debate clause of Section 6 prevents House members or senators from being sued for slander during congressional debates, committee hearings, or most other official congressional business. In deference to the principle of separation of powers, Clause 2 ensures that members of Congress cannot hold another civil office while retaining their legislative seats.

Section 7. All bills for raising revenue shall originate in the House of Representatives; but the Senate may propose or concur with amendments as on other Bills.

Every bill which shall have passed the House of Representatives and the Senate, shall, before it become a law, be presented to the President of the United States; if he approve he shall sign it, but if not he shall return it, with his objections to that House in which it shall have originated, who shall enter the objections at large on their journal, and proceed to reconsider it. If after such reconsideration two thirds of that House shall agree to pass the bill, it shall be sent, together with the objections, to the other House, by which it shall likewise be reconsidered, and if approved by two thirds of that House, it shall become a law. But in all such cases the votes of both Houses shall be determined by yeas and nays, and the names of the persons voting for and against the bill shall be entered on the journal of each House respectively. If any bill shall not be returned by the President within ten days (Sundays excepted) after it shall have been presented to him, the same shall be a law, in like manner as if he had signed it, unless the Congress by their adjournment prevent its return, in which case it shall not be a law.

Every order, resolution, or vote to which the concurrence of the Senate and House of Representatives may be necessary (except on a question of adjournment) shall be presented to the President of the United States; and before the same shall take effect, shall be approved by him, or being disapproved by him, shall be repassed by two thirds of the Senate and House of Representatives, according to the rules and limitations prescribed in the case of a bill.

Article I, Section 7 is often referred to as the presentment clause. It establishes the procedures by which Congress presents bills to the president for approval; it also lays out the process by which the president may veto legislation, either by refusing to sign it and sending it back, or by keeping the bill for a period of 10 days without signing it while Congress has adjourned in the interim (referred to as a pocket veto). In 1996, Congress passed the Line Item Veto Act, which allowed the president to veto specific expenditures at the time of signing; the Supreme Court declared the Line Item Veto Act unconstitutional in Clinton v. City of New York *(1998) because it gave the president the power to repeal parts of duly enacted statutes in a manner different from the "finely wrought and exhaustively considered procedure" described in this section.*

Section 8. The Congress shall have power to lay and collect taxes, duties, imposts and excises, to pay the debts and provide for the common defense and general welfare of the United States; but all duties, imposts and excises shall be uniform throughout the United States;

To borrow money on the credit of the United States;

To regulate commerce with foreign nations, and among the several states, and with the Indian tribes;

To establish a uniform rule of naturalization, and uniform laws on the subject of bankruptcies throughout the United States;

To coin money, regulate the value thereof, and of foreign coin, and fix the standard of weights and measures;

To provide for the punishment of counterfeiting the securities and current coin of the United States;

To establish post offices and post roads;

To promote the progress of science and useful arts, by securing for limited times to authors and inventors the exclusive right to their respective writings and discoveries;

To constitute tribunals inferior to the Supreme Court;

To define and punish piracies and felonies committed on the high seas, and offenses against the law of nations;

To declare war, grant letters of marque and reprisal, and make rules concerning captures on land and water;

To raise and support armies, but no appropriation of money to that use shall be for a longer term than two years;

To provide and maintain a navy;

To make rules for the government and regulation of the land and naval forces;

To provide for calling forth the militia to execute the laws of the union, suppress insurrections and repel invasions;

To provide for organizing, arming, and disciplining, the militia, and for governing such part of them as may be employed in the service of the United States, reserving to the states respectively, the appointment of the officers, and the authority of training the militia according to the discipline prescribed by Congress;

To exercise exclusive legislation in all cases whatsoever, over such District (not exceeding ten miles square) as may, by cession of particular states, and the acceptance of Congress, become the seat of the government of the United States, and to exercise like authority over all places purchased by the consent of the legislature of the state in which the same shall be, for the erection of forts, magazines, arsenals, dockyards, and other needful buildings;—And

To make all laws which shall be necessary and proper for carrying into execution the foregoing powers, and all other powers vested by this Constitution in the government of the United States, or in any department or officer thereof.

Article I, Section 8 may be the most heavily cited clause in the original Constitution, as it lays out all the enumerated powers of Congress. The 18th clause listed, the necessary and proper clause, was the source of significant controversy in the early republic. In McCulloch v. Maryland (1819), Chief Justice John Marshall interpreted the clause as essentially aiding Congress in carrying out its expressed powers. Combining the powers granted by the 18th clause with other powers allows Congress to exercise implied powers not explicitly listed in the Constitution, so long as those powers offer a theoretical means of achieving the enumerated powers. Thus, Congress successfully incorporated a bank of the United States because it was deemed necessary and proper to achieve the power to coin money and regulate its value (Clause 5), as well as other powers. No wonder the necessary and proper clause has also been called the elastic clause: it gives Congress the power to enact laws on almost any subject it desires. The power to regulate interstate commerce under Clause 3 has been especially useful in this regard. Citing the commerce clause, Congress since 1937 has regulated minimum wages of state employees, outlawed loan sharking, and passed numerous civil rights laws, among other legislation. The modern limits to that practice were outlined by the Supreme Court in United States v. Lopez (1995), United States v. Morrison (2000), and NFIB v. Sebelius (2012)—the law in question must regulate affirmative activities that are directly economic in nature. By comparison, the Supreme Court recently held that Congress may regulate even inactivity (e.g., a refusal to purchase health insurance) under its power to collect taxes in Clause 1.

Section 9. The migration or importation of such persons as any of the states now existing shall think proper to admit, shall not be prohibited by the Congress prior to the year one thousand eight hundred and eight, but a tax or duty may be imposed on such importation, not exceeding ten dollars for each person.

The privilege of the writ of habeas corpus shall not be suspended, unless when in cases of rebellion or invasion the public safety may require it.

No bill of attainder or ex post facto Law shall be passed.

No capitation, or other direct, tax shall be laid, unless in proportion to the census or enumeration herein before directed to be taken.

No tax or duty shall be laid on articles exported from any state.

No preference shall be given by any regulation of commerce or revenue to the ports of one state over those of another: nor shall vessels bound to, or from, one state, be obliged to enter, clear or pay duties in another.

No money shall be drawn from the treasury, but in consequence of appropriations made by law; and a regular statement and account of receipts and expenditures of all public money shall be published from time to time.

No title of nobility shall be granted by the United States: and no person holding any office of profit or trust under them, shall, without the consent of the Congress, accept of any present, emolument, office, or title, of any kind whatever, from any king, prince, or foreign state.

Section 9 places some explicit limits on congressional power, including restrictions on the power to ban the import of slaves (at least through 1808), the power to bestow titles of nobility, and the power to lay direct taxes not apportioned to the states' populations. This last restriction was effectively

removed by ratification of the Sixteenth Amendment in 1913. It also pro-
hibits Congress from issuing bills of attainder (legislative acts that inflict
punishment without a judicial trial) and from passing ex post facto laws
(criminal laws that apply retroactively to acts committed in the past).

Section 10. No state shall enter into any treaty, alliance, or confederation; grant letters of marque and reprisal; coin money; emit bills of credit; make anything but gold and silver coin a tender in payment of debts; pass any bill of attainder, ex post facto law, or law impairing the obligation of contracts, or grant any title of nobility.

No state shall, without the consent of the Congress, lay any imposts or duties on imports or exports, except what may be absolutely necessary for executing its inspection laws: and the net produce of all duties and imposts, laid by any state on imports or exports, shall be for the use of the treasury of the United States; and all such laws shall be subject to the revision and control of the Congress.

No state shall, without the consent of Congress, lay any duty of tonnage, keep troops, or ships of war in time of peace, enter into any agreement or compact with another state, or with a foreign power, or engage in war, unless actually invaded, or in such imminent danger as will not admit of delay.

The final section of Article I limits states from exercising powers reserved exclusively to the federal government. Most controversial of these clauses was the contracts clause, which prohibits states from impairing the obligation of contracts. Added to the Constitution largely to prevent state laws that undermined the collection of valid debts, it was later used to protect certain franchises or special privileges that corporations had received from state legislatures. Thus, the Supreme Court held in Trustees of Dartmouth College v. Woodward *(1819) that the charter given to Dartmouth by a colonial legislature in 1769 could not be changed without Dartmouth's consent. State legislatures complained that the contracts clause unduly restricted their ability to legislate; thus, the Supreme Court over the course of two centuries has narrowed the meaning of the clause to allow states greater freedom to operate, relying on the theory that such contracts are by implication the laws of the state and thus may be modified by the state. The Court has also upheld state bankruptcy laws when the laws are applied to debts incurred after passage of the law.*

Article II

Section 1. The executive power shall be vested in a President of the United States of America. He shall hold his office during the term of four years, and, together with the Vice President, chosen for the same term, be elected, as follows:

Each state shall appoint, in such manner as the Legislature thereof may direct, a number of electors, equal to the whole number of Senators and Representatives to which the State may be entitled in the Congress: but no Senator or Representative, or person holding an office of trust or profit under the United States, shall be appointed an elector.

The electors shall meet in their respective states, and vote by ballot for two persons, of whom one at least shall not be an inhabitant of the same state with themselves. And they shall make a list of all the persons voted for, and of the number of votes for each; which list they shall sign and certify, and transmit sealed to the seat of the government of the United States, directed to the President of the Senate. The President of the Senate shall, in the presence of the Senate and House of Representatives, open all the certificates, and the votes shall then be counted. The person having the greatest number of votes shall be the President, if such number be a majority of the whole number of electors appointed; and if there be more than one who have such majority, and have an equal number of votes, then the House of Representatives shall immediately choose by ballot one of them for President; and if no person have a majority, then from the five highest on the list the said House shall in like manner choose the President. But in choosing the President, the votes shall be taken by States, the representation from each state having one vote; A quorum for this purpose shall consist of a member or members from two thirds of the states, and a majority of all the states shall be necessary to a choice. In every case, after the choice of the President, the person having the greatest number of votes of the electors shall be the Vice President. But if there should remain two or more who have equal votes, the Senate shall choose from them by ballot the Vice President.

The Congress may determine the time of choosing the electors, and the day on which they shall give their votes; which day shall be the same throughout the United States.

No person except a natural born citizen, or a citizen of the United States, at the time of the adoption of this Constitution, shall be eligible to the office of President; neither shall any person be eligible to that office who shall not have attained to the age of thirty five years, and been fourteen Years a resident within the United States.

In case of the removal of the President from office, or of his death, resignation, or inability to discharge the powers and duties of the said office, the same shall devolve on the Vice President, and the Congress may by law provide for the case of removal, death, resignation or inability, both of the President and Vice President, declaring what officer shall then act as President, and such officer shall act accordingly, until the disability be removed, or a President shall be elected.

The President shall, at stated times, receive for his services, a compensation, which shall neither be increased nor diminished during the period for which he shall have been elected, and he shall not receive within that period any other emolument from the United States, or any of them.

Before he enter on the execution of his office, he shall take the following oath or affirmation:—'I do solemnly swear (or affirm) that I will faithfully execute the office of President of the United States, and will to the best of my ability, preserve, protect and defend the Constitution of the United States.'

Article II, Section 1 lays out the manner by which the president and vice president are selected, the qualifications for those two offices, and the means for removal and succession. (Clause 2 on presidential elections has been replaced by the Twelfth Amendment.) Section 1 begins with the vague declaration that the "executive power shall be vested in a president of the United States of America." Does this clause serve as a source of independent power for the chief executive? Beginning in the twentieth century, the Supreme Court has held that the president possesses broad "inherent powers" to exercise certain powers not specifically enumerated in the Constitution. These vast executive powers included, for example, Franklin Roosevelt's various executive agreements extending the scope of the federal government during the 1930s. On the other hand, the Supreme Court ruled in Youngstown Sheet and Tune Co.

v. Sawyer *(1951) that a president's inherent powers did not include President Truman's attempt to seize the steel mills to avert a strike without congressional approval; similarly, in* United States v. Nixon *(1974), the Court held that the chief executive's inherent powers did not encompass President Richard Nixon's refusal to turn over important documents in a criminal matter.*

Section 2. The President shall be commander in chief of the Army and Navy of the United States, and of the militia of the several states, when called into the actual service of the United States; he may require the opinion, in writing, of the principal officer in each of the executive departments, upon any subject relating to the duties of their respective offices, and he shall have power to grant reprieves and pardons for offenses against the United States, except in cases of impeachment.

He shall have power, by and with the advice and consent of the Senate, to make treaties, provided two thirds of the Senators present concur; and he shall nominate, and by and with the advice and consent of the Senate, shall appoint ambassadors, other public ministers and consuls, judges of the Supreme Court, and all other officers of the United States, whose appointments are not herein otherwise provided for, and which shall be established by law: but the Congress may by law vest the appointment of such inferior officers, as they think proper, in the President alone, in the courts of law, or in the heads of departments.

The President shall have power to fill up all vacancies that may happen during the recess of the Senate, by granting commissions which shall expire at the end of their next session.

Article II, Section 2 is striking for how few expressed powers are granted to the president, as compared to the long list of powers granted to Congress in Article I, Section 8. In the twentieth century the powers granted to the president expanded to create a far more powerful presidency than the Founders envisioned. Thus, invoking their power as commander-in-chief, modern presidents have deployed troops around the world in military battles even without a formal declaration of war by Congress. Recent presidents have occasionally terminated treaties without the consent of the Senate. Presidents have also asserted the power to terminate officers of the United States without cause. The combined Supreme Court precedents of Myers v. United States *(1926) and* Humphrey's Executor v. United States *(1935) authorize them to do so in the case of purely executive officers, but not in the case of independent agency heads.*

Section 3. He shall from time to time give to the Congress information of the state of the union, and recommend to their consideration such measures as he shall judge necessary and expedient; he may, on extraordinary occasions, convene both Houses, or either of them, and in case of disagreement between them, with respect to the time of adjournment, he may adjourn them to such time as he shall think proper; he shall receive ambassadors and other public ministers; he shall take care that the laws be faithfully executed, and shall commission all the officers of the United States.

Article II, Section 3 lists numerous presidential responsibilities, including the obligation to give a report on the "state of the union" to Congress (today this occurs in the form of a yearly address), and the duty to "take care that laws be faithfully executed." Citing this latter phrase, presidents have asserted the power to impound money appropriated by Congress and to suspend the writ of habeas corpus. Although reluctant to afford the chief executive such unbridled authority, the Supreme Court has upheld nearly all efforts by the president to call upon the military to assist in faithfully executing the law. President Eisenhower, for example, exercised this power when he used federal troops to enforce desegregation decrees in Arkansas and Mississippi in the late 1950s.

Section 4. The President, Vice President and all civil officers of the United States, shall be removed from office on impeachment for, and conviction of, treason, bribery, or other high crimes and misdemeanors.

Article II, Section 4 lays out the process of impeachment and conviction of civil officers, but the phrase "high crimes and misdemeanors" is vague and subject to conflicting interpretations. Regardless, the House of Representatives has asserted its authority to decide on its own how to define the term. Only two chief executives have ever been formally impeached under this section: Andrew Johnson in 1868 and Bill Clinton in 1998. However, in both cases, the U.S. Senate failed to provide the required two-thirds vote necessary for conviction.

Article III

Section 1. The judicial power of the United States, shall be vested in one Supreme Court, and in such inferior courts as the Congress may from time to time ordain and establish. The judges, both of the supreme and inferior courts, shall hold their offices during good behaviour, and shall, at stated times, receive for their services, a compensation, which shall not be diminished during their continuance in office.

Section 2. The judicial power shall extend to all cases, in law and equity, arising under this Constitution, the laws of the United States, and treaties made, or which shall be made, under their authority;—to all cases affecting ambassadors, other public ministers and consuls;—to all cases of admiralty and maritime jurisdiction;—to controversies to which the United States shall be a party;—to controversies between two or more states;—between a state and citizens of another state;—between citizens of different states;—between citizens of the same state claiming lands under grants of different states, and between a state, or the citizens thereof, and foreign states, citizens or subjects.

In all cases affecting ambassadors, other public ministers and consuls, and those in which a state shall be party, the Supreme Court shall have original jurisdiction. In all the other cases before mentioned, the Supreme Court shall have appellate jurisdiction, both as to law and fact, with such exceptions, and under such regulations as the Congress shall make.

The trial of all crimes, except in cases of impeachment, shall be by jury; and such trial shall be held in the state where the said crimes shall have been committed; but when not committed within any state, the trial shall be at such place or places as the Congress may by law have directed.

Section 3. Treason against the United States, shall consist only in levying war against them, or in adhering to their enemies, giving them aid and comfort. No person shall be convicted of treason unless on the testimony of two witnesses to the same overt act, or on confession in open court.

The Congress shall have power to declare the punishment of treason, but no attainder of treason shall work corruption of blood, or forfeiture except during the life of the person attainted.

Article III establishes a U.S. Supreme Court, spells out the terms of office of its members, and lists the various cases to which its judicial power extends. Just as important, it provides the basis for a more elaborate judicial system featuring numerous levels of courts, which Congress may establish at its discretion. Note how vague and general this article is compared to Articles I and II: only one court (the Supreme Court) is specifically mentioned, and there are no provisions that specify the size or composition of the court. Congress subsequently established that federal judges on the courts of appeals and the district courts, like justices of the Supreme Court, are appointed by the president and confirmed by the Senate. They too serve for indefinite terms on good behavior, which provides the equivalent of life tenure to federal judges on those three levels of courts. Article III does not specifically grant the Supreme Court the power of judicial review, that is, the power to review the actions of other branches for their constitutionality. The Supreme Court seized that power for itself in Marbury v. Madison *(1803), and it remains a fundamental precept of the federal judicial system today.*

Article IV

Section 1. Full faith and credit shall be given in each state to the public acts, records, and judicial proceedings of every other state. And the Congress may by general laws prescribe the manner in which such acts, records, and proceedings shall be proved, and the effect thereof.

Section 2. The citizens of each state shall be entitled to all privileges and immunities of citizens in the several states.

A person charged in any state with treason, felony, or other crime, who shall flee from justice, and be found in another state, shall on demand of the executive authority of the state from which he fled, be delivered up, to be removed to the state having jurisdiction of the crime.

No person held to service or labor in one state, under the laws thereof, escaping into another, shall, in consequence of any law or regulation therein, be discharged from such service or labor, but shall be delivered up on claim of the party to whom such service or labor may be due.

Section 3. New states may be admitted by the Congress into this union; but no new states shall be formed or erected within the jurisdiction of any other state; nor any state be formed by the junction of two or more states, or parts of states, without the consent of the legislatures of the states concerned as well as of the Congress.

The Congress shall have power to dispose of and make all needful rules and regulations respecting the territory or other property belonging to the United States; and nothing in this Constitution shall be so construed as to prejudice any claims of the United States, or of any particular state.

Section 4. The United States shall guarantee to every state in this union a republican form of government, and shall protect each of them against invasion; and on application of the legislature, or of the executive (when the legislature cannot be convened) against domestic violence.

Article IV describes the responsibilities states have to one another under the Constitution, and the obligations of the federal government to the states. It also provides the procedures for admitting new states to the union (no state has been admitted since the entry of Alaska and Hawaii in 1959). In recent decades, the most controversial aspect of Article IV has been the full faith and credit clause of Section 1, which theoretically binds states to respect the public acts and proceedings of other states, including child custody rulings and the granting of drivers' licenses. Initially that clause did not deter the federal government (through the Defense of Marriage Act) and various states from seeking to evade the recognition of gay marriages sanctioned elsewhere through legislation. However, the Supreme Court rendered the controversy moot when it upheld the right of same-sex couples to marry in all 50 states. See Obergefell v. Hodges (2015).

The ambiguous privileges and immunities clause of Article IV, Section 2 requires that states not discriminate against citizens of other states in favor of their own citizens, although the Supreme Court has allowed states to establish more favorable terms for in-state residents when distributing certain recreational rights such as amateur fishing licenses or permits to use state parks; taxes on commuters, by contrast, may be unconstitutional if they penalize out-of-state residents who work or do business in the state. The requirement in Section 4 that the United States guarantee to every state a republican form of government was invoked in the 1840s when President John Tyler threatened the use of federal troops after a rebellion occurred in Rhode Island. Today that provision is obscure and seldom used.

Article V

The Congress, whenever two thirds of both houses shall deem it necessary, shall propose amendments to this Constitution, or, on the application of the legislatures of two thirds of the several states, shall call a convention for proposing amendments, which, in either case, shall be valid to all intents and purposes, as part of this Constitution, when ratified by the legislatures of three fourths of the several states, or by conventions in three fourths thereof, as the one or the other mode of ratification may be proposed by the Congress; provided that no amendment which may be made prior to the year one thousand eight hundred and eight shall in any manner affect the first and fourth clauses in the ninth section of the first article; and that no state, without its consent, shall be deprived of its equal suffrage in the Senate.

Article V spells out the process for amending the Constitution. By far the most common form of constitutional amendment has been by congressional proposal, with state legislatures ratifying the proposal. Twenty-six of the 27 amendments have been adopted in this way. The sole exception was the Twenty-first Amendment, which was ratified by specially chosen state ratifying conventions to assure that farmer-dominated state legislatures would not undermine the effort to repeal Prohibition. The procedure by which the requisite number of state legislatures (two-thirds) applies to Congress to call a convention for proposing amendments has never been used. Article V does not provide a deadline for considering proposed amendments, although Congress has the power to set such deadlines in the language of the proposed amendment. Congress did not do so in the case of the Twenty-seventh Amendment, which received the approval of the required three-fourths of states necessary for ratification in 1992—fully 203 years after the amendment was first proposed.

Article VI

All debts contracted and engagements entered into, before the adoption of this Constitution, shall be as valid against the United States under this Constitution, as under the Confederation.

This Constitution, and the laws of the United States which shall be made in pursuance thereof; and all treaties made, or which shall be made, under the authority of the United States, shall be the supreme law of the land; and the judges in every state shall be bound thereby, anything in the Constitution or laws of any State to the contrary notwithstanding.

The Senators and Representatives before mentioned, and the members of the several state legislatures, and all executive and judicial officers, both of the United States and of the several states, shall be bound by oath or affirmation, to support this Constitution; but no religious test shall ever be required as a qualification to any office or public trust under the United States.

Article VI establishes that the Constitution, laws, and treaties are to be the supreme law of the land. In interpreting this supremacy clause, the U.S. Supreme Court has countenanced little resistance. Thus, the Supreme Court has consistently struck down attempts by states to control federal institutions, and it has reminded state governments that even state constitutions are subordinate to federal statutes. Even more important, in Cooper v. Aaron (1957), the U.S. Supreme Court stated in no uncertain terms that its own rulings are to be treated as if they are the words of the Constitution itself, heading off attempts by some state governments to resist Supreme Court rulings on desegregation by offering their own interpretations of the federal Constitution as authority.

Article VII

The ratification of the conventions of nine states, shall be sufficient for the establishment of this Constitution between the states so ratifying the same. Done in convention by the unanimous consent of the states present the seventeenth day of September in the year of our Lord one thousand seven hundred and eighty seven and of the independence of the United States of America the twelfth. In witness whereof We have hereunto subscribed our Names,

G. Washington—Presidt. and deputy from Virginia

New Hampshire
John Langdon
Nicholas Gilman

Massachusetts
Nathaniel Gorham
Rufus King

Connecticut
Wm. Saml. Johnson
Roger Sherman

New York
Alexander Hamilton

New Jersey
Wil. Livingston
David Brearly
Wm. Paterson
Jona. Dayton

Pennsylvania
B. Franklin

Thomas Mifflin
Robt. Morris
Geo. Clymer
Thos. FitzSimons
Jared Ingersoll
James Wilson
Gouv Morris

Delaware
Geo. Read

Gunning Bedford jun
John Dickinson
Richard Bassett
Jaco. Broom

Maryland

James McHenry
Dan of St Thos. Jenifer
Danl Carroll

Virginia

John Blair—
James Madison Jr.

North Carolina

Wm. Blount
Richd. Dobbs Spaight
Hu Williamson

South Carolina

J. Rutledge
Charles Cotesworth
  Pinckney
Charles Pinckney
Pierce Butler

Georgia

William Few
Abr Baldwin

Amendments to the Constitution of the United States

The Bill of Rights, ratified in 1791, consists of the first 10 amendments to the Constitution. Since that time, 17 additional amendments have been ratified by the states. Originally the Bill of Rights applied only to the federal government and not to the state governments; however, through a process known as incorporation, the Supreme Court has ruled that the Fourteenth Amendment (adopted in 1868) made most of the provisions found in the Bill of Rights applicable to the states as well. Subsequent amendments have extended the franchise, established (and repealed) Prohibition, and clarified important procedures that the federal government must follow.

Amendment I (1791)

Congress shall make no law respecting an establishment of religion, or prohibiting the free exercise thereof; or abridging the freedom of speech, or of the press; or the right of the people peaceably to assemble, and to petition the government for a redress of grievances.

Although many provisions of the original Bill of Rights are based on aspects of English law, the extensive guarantees found in the First Amendment have no true English equivalent. The First Amendment offered one of the first written guarantees of religious freedom, and it formed the basis for extensive free speech and free press protection as well. Yet its unqualified language notwithstanding, the First Amendment has never conveyed absolute freedom to Americans. Whether it was the Alien and Sedition Acts of 1798, the aggressive application of the Espionage Act during World War I, or the "red scare" of the late 1940s, government has often found ways to evade the First Amendment, especially during times of crisis. The Supreme Court has also specifically exempted obscenity, libel, fighting words, and incitement from free speech protections. Nor has the separate and independent provision for the freedom of the press been interpreted to give members of the press any more protection than is afforded to ordinary citizens. Finally, as noted, although the first word of the amendment implies that its protections apply only against actions of the federal government, today the First Amendment offers protection against the state governments as well.

Amendment II (1791)

A well regulated militia, being necessary to the security of a free state, the right of the people to keep and bear arms, shall not be infringed.

The Second Amendment originated as a compromise in the debate between those who feared mob rule by the people and those committed to give the people everything they need to fight governmental tyranny. In 2008, the U.S. Supreme Court ruled for the first time that certain gun-control laws may violate an individual's Second Amendment right to "bear arms." Two years later it went a step further, applying those protections against all 50 state governments and their subdivisions. See District of Columbia v. Heller, 554 U.S. 570 (2008); and McDonald v. Chicago, 561 U.S. 742 (2010).

Amendment III (1791)

No soldier shall, in time of peace be quartered in any house, without the consent of the owner, nor in time of war, but in a manner to be prescribed by law.

The Third Amendment has been all but lost to history. The Quartering Act, which required the American colonists to provide shelter and supplies for British troops, was one of the grievances that provoked the Declaration of Independence and ultimately the Revolution. Many colonists resented having to house British soldiers in private homes. The Third Amendment aimed to protect private citizens from such intrusions.

Amendment IV (1791)

The right of the people to be secure in their persons, houses, papers, and effects, against unreasonable searches and seizures, shall not be violated, and no warrants shall issue, but upon probable cause, supported by oath or affirmation, and particularly describing the place to be searched, and the persons or things to be seized.

Like the First Amendment, the Fourth Amendment is a uniquely American right. It arose out of colonists' anger over the warrantless searches and so-called General Warrants by which British authorities would conduct raids of colonists' homes virtually at their own discretion. The Fourth Amendment guarantees that with certain carefully specified exceptions (consent of the owner, urgent circumstances, etc.), government authorities can conduct searches only when they possess a reasonably specific warrant demonstrating probable cause. Enforcement of the Fourth Amendment occurs primarily through application of the controversial exclusionary rule, which excludes from trial all evidence seized in violation of a defendant's constitutional rights.

Amendment V (1791)

No person shall be held to answer for a capital, or otherwise infamous crime, unless on a presentment or indictment of a grand jury, except in cases arising in the land or naval forces, or in the militia, when in actual service in time of war or public danger; nor shall any person be subject for the same offense to be twice put in jeopardy of life or limb; nor shall be compelled in any criminal case to be a witness against himself, nor be deprived of life, liberty, or property, without due process of law; nor shall private property be taken for public use, without just compensation.

The Fifth Amendment is a collection of various rights, most of which are important primarily to those accused of a crime. Those who "take the Fifth" under oath are normally invoking the privilege against self-incrimination; under current precedents they can invoke that privilege in other contexts as well, such as whenever they are being questioned by police or other authorities. The grand jury requirement has never been incorporated to apply against state governments. The requirement against double jeopardy prevents defendants who have been acquitted from being retried for the same offense by the same government. The due process clause of the Fifth Amendment was later duplicated in the Fourteenth Amendment and applied to states as well. Finally, the takings clause limits the traditional power of eminent domain by requiring that the government must pay compensation whenever it takes private property for public use.

Amendment VI (1791)

In all criminal prosecutions, the accused shall enjoy the right to a speedy and public trial, by an impartial jury of the state and district wherein the crime shall have been committed, which district shall have been previously ascertained by law, and to be informed of the nature and cause of the accusation; to be confronted with the witnesses against him; to have compulsory process for obtaining witnesses in his favor, and to have the assistance of counsel for his defense.

The Sixth Amendment offers the accused numerous constitutional protections. The need for a speedy and public trial dates back to concerns raised by imprisoned enemies of the British Crown who were detained indefinitely and without notice. The right to a jury trial—considered a sacred aspect of the American political culture—is not all-encompassing either: it applies only to nonpetty offenses (punishable by more than six months of prison).

Amendment VII (1791)

In suits at common law, where the value in controversy shall exceed twenty dollars, the right of trial by jury shall be preserved, and no fact tried by a jury, shall be otherwise reexamined in any court of the United States, than according to the rules of the common law.

The Seventh Amendment is the only amendment in the Bill of Rights that focuses on elements of civil trials exclusively. It preserves the distinction the English system draws between courts of common law (in which juries grant monetary relief) and courts of equity (in which a judge grants nonmonetary relief, such as an injunction).

Amendment VIII (1791)

Excessive bail shall not be required, nor excessive fines imposed, nor cruel and unusual punishments inflicted.

The Eighth Amendment offers protections that come directly from the English Bill of Rights. The prohibition against excessive bail was established to prevent judges from keeping the accused indefinitely imprisoned while waiting for trials on minor offenses; it has subsequently been interpreted to allow judges to deny bail in instances where the charges are sufficiently serious, or where preventative detention is warranted for the safety of the community. The prohibition against cruel and unusual punishment forbids some punishments entirely (drawing and quartering, burning alive, and other forms of torture), while forbidding other punishments only when they are excessive compared to the crime. Aside from the four-year period from 1972 through 1976, the Supreme Court has consistently held that with proper safeguards, capital punishment is not cruel and unusual punishment. However, consistent with this clause, it may not be imposed for rape or crimes lesser than murder, and it may not be imposed against mentally handicapped or juvenile offenders.

Amendment IX (1791)

The enumeration in the Constitution, of certain rights, shall not be construed to deny or disparage others retained by the people.

The Ninth Amendment has been nicknamed "the Madison Amendment" in deference to James Madison's general concerns about the Bill of Rights. During debates over ratification of the Constitution, Anti-Federalists called for a Bill of Rights to protect the people against a potentially abusive new central government. In correspondence with Thomas Jefferson, Madison expressed the fear that by listing exceptions to congressional powers, such a Bill of Rights would effectively deny the existence of rights that did not happen to appear on the list. Eventually, as a member of the House of Representatives in the First Congress, Madison sponsored passage of the Bill of Rights, but he included this amendment as a way to ensure that the listing of certain rights did not mean that other rights were denied. As interpreted, the Ninth Amendment has not had much impact on the constitutional landscape. Likened by some to an "inkblot," it has been most commonly viewed not as a source of rights, but rather as a loose guideline on how to interpret the Constitution.

Amendment X (1791)

The powers not delegated to the United States by the Constitution, nor prohibited by it to the states, are reserved to the states respectively, or to the people.

The Tenth Amendment lays out in explicit terms that the federal government is limited only to the powers granted to it in the Constitution. For most of the twentieth century, the Supreme Court regarded this amendment largely as a redundant truism, adding little to the Constitution as it was originally ratified. In the early 1990s, the Supreme Court began to put teeth into the amendment, interpreting it as a prohibition on attempts by Congress to force states to participate in federal programs.

Amendment XI (1798)

The judicial power of the United States shall not be construed to extend to any suit in law or equity, commenced or prosecuted against one of the United States by citizens of another state, or by citizens or subjects of any foreign state.

The Eleventh Amendment was ratified to modify the Supreme Court's controversial decision in Chisholm v. Georgia *(1793), which upheld the authority of federal courts to hear lawsuits brought by citizens of*

*one state against another state. The Supreme Court has ruled that the
Eleventh Amendment provides states with some form of sovereign
immunity, which means that it generally protects states from civil or
criminal prosecution. The Supreme Court has also determined that under
the Eleventh Amendment, a state cannot be sued by one of its own citizens.*

Amendment XII (1804)

The electors shall meet in their respective states and vote by ballot for President
and Vice-President, one of whom, at least, shall not be an inhabitant of the same
state with themselves; they shall name in their ballots the person voted for as President, and in distinct ballots the person voted for as Vice-President, and they shall
make distinct lists of all persons voted for as President, and of all persons voted for
as Vice-President, and of the number of votes for each, which lists they shall sign
and certify, and transmit sealed to the seat of the government of the United States,
directed to the President of the Senate;—The President of the Senate shall, in the
presence of the Senate and House of Representatives, open all the certificates and
the votes shall then be counted;—the person having the greatest number of votes
for President, shall be the President, if such number be a majority of the whole
number of electors appointed; and if no person have such majority, then from the
persons having the highest numbers not exceeding three on the list of those voted
for as President, the House of Representatives shall choose immediately, by ballot,
the President. But in choosing the President, the votes shall be taken by states, the
representation from each state having one vote; a quorum for this purpose shall
consist of a member or members from two-thirds of the states, and a majority of
all the states shall be necessary to a choice. And if the House of Representatives
shall not choose a President whenever the right of choice shall devolve upon them,
before the fourth day of March next following, then the Vice-President shall act as
President, as in the case of the death or other constitutional disability of the President. The person having the greatest number of votes as Vice-President, shall be
the Vice-President, if such number be a majority of the whole number of electors
appointed, and if no person have a majority, then from the two highest numbers on
the list, the Senate shall choose the Vice-President; a quorum for the purpose shall
consist of two-thirds of the whole number of Senators, and a majority of the whole
number shall be necessary to a choice. But no person constitutionally ineligible
to the office of President shall be eligible to that of Vice-President of the United
States.

*The Twelfth Amendment altered the Constitution's original procedures for
holding presidential elections. Under Article II, the winner of a majority of
electoral college votes would become president, and the runner-up would become vice president. The election of 1800 exposed the peculiarity that if every
member of the electoral college voted for both members of a party ticket, each
member of the most popular ticket would receive the same number of votes,
resulting in a deadlock. The Twelfth Amendment cured that flaw by requiring electors to cast separate votes for president and vice president, and by
ensuring that if a deadlock occurred anyway and the House of Representatives
failed to choose a president, then the candidate who received the highest*

number of votes on the vice presidential ballot would act as president (thus, all vice presidents must be constitutionally eligible to serve as president).

Amendment XIII (1865)

Section 1. Neither slavery nor involuntary servitude, except as a punishment for crime whereof the party shall have been duly convicted, shall exist within the United States, or any place subject to their jurisdiction.
Section 2. Congress shall have power to enforce this article by appropriate legislation.

The Thirteenth Amendment was the first of the three Civil War Amendments. It officially prohibited slavery in all states, and with certain exceptions (such as in the case of convicts) involuntary servitude. Immediately prior to its ratification in December 1865, slavery remained legal in only two states, Kentucky and Delaware. (Slavery in the former confederate states had been outlawed by the Emancipation Proclamation of 1863.)

Amendment XIV (1868)

Section 1. All persons born or naturalized in the United States, and subject to the jurisdiction thereof, are citizens of the United States and of the state wherein they reside. No state shall make or enforce any law which shall abridge the privileges or immunities of citizens of the United States; nor shall any state deprive any person of life, liberty, or property, without due process of law; nor deny to any person within its jurisdiction the equal protection of the laws.
Section 2. Representatives shall be apportioned among the several states according to their respective numbers, counting the whole number of persons in each state, excluding Indians not taxed. But when the right to vote at any election for the choice of electors for President and Vice President of the United States, Representatives in Congress, the executive and judicial officers of a state, or the members of the legislature thereof, is denied to any of the male inhabitants of such state, being twenty-one years of age, and citizens of the United States, or in any way abridged, except for participation in rebellion, or other crime, the basis of representation therein shall be reduced in the proportion which the number of such male citizens shall bear to the whole number of male citizens twenty-one years of age in such state.
Section 3. No person shall be a Senator or Representative in Congress, or elector of President and Vice President, or hold any office, civil or military, under the United States, or under any state, who, having previously taken an oath, as a member of Congress, or as an officer of the United States, or as a member of any state legislature, or as an executive or judicial officer of any state, to support the Constitution of the United States, shall have engaged in insurrection or rebellion against the same, or given aid or comfort to the enemies thereof. But Congress may by a vote of two-thirds of each House, remove such disability.
Section 4. The validity of the public debt of the United States, authorized by law, including debts incurred for payment of pensions and bounties for services in suppressing insurrection or rebellion, shall not be questioned. But neither the United States nor any state shall assume or pay any debt or obligation incurred in aid of insurrection or rebellion against the United States, or any claim for the loss or emancipation of any slave; but all such debts, obligations and claims shall be held illegal and void.

Section 5. The Congress shall have power to enforce, by appropriate legislation, the provisions of this article.

The Fourteenth Amendment was ratified in an attempt to secure rights for freed slaves by broadening the definition of national citizenship and offering all persons equal protection of the law as well as due process of law from state governments. In the Slaughterhouse Cases *(1873), the Supreme Court held that the privileges and immunities of national citizenship are actually quite limited: they include visiting the seat of government, petitioning Congress, using the nation's navigable waters, and other narrow privileges. By contrast, beginning in the twentieth century, the equal protection clause provided the basis for dismantling legally enforced segregation in* Brown v. Board of Education *(1954) and other cases. It has been used to extend equal protection to African Americans and other racial and ethnic minorities, women, and most recently, gays and lesbians. Of equal significance, the Supreme Court has also interpreted the equal protection clause to require states to apportion their congressional districts and state legislative seats on a "one-person, one-vote" basis.*

The due process clause has been interpreted to provide procedural safeguards before the government deprives a person of life, liberty, or property. More controversially, in the early part of the twentieth century, the Supreme Court in Lochner v. New York *(1905) interpreted the clause as providing substantive protection to private contracts and other economic agreements. In later rulings, the clause sparked considerable controversy when the Court used it as the basis for protecting substantive privacy rights not explicitly spelled out in the Constitution, such as that of a woman's right to an abortion (in the Court's 1973* Roe v. Wade *decision), and of homosexual sodomy (in its 2003 ruling in* Lawrence v. Texas*).*

Amendment XV (1870)

Section 1. The right of citizens of the United States to vote shall not be denied or abridged by the United States or by any state on account of race, color, or previous condition of servitude.

Section 2. The Congress shall have power to enforce this article by appropriate legislation.

The Fifteenth Amendment was ratified in order to enfranchise all the former male slaves. (As was the case with all women, former female slaves would have to wait for passage of the Nineteenth Amendment to gain the franchise.) Unfortunately, the promise of the franchise was subsequently undermined in many states by the proliferation of rigorous voter qualification laws, including literacy tests and poll taxes. Not until passage of the Voting Rights Act of 1965 and the elimination of poll taxes did the franchise become a reality for African American voters in many parts of the South.

Amendment XVI (1913)

The Congress shall have power to lay and collect taxes on incomes, from whatever source derived, without apportionment among the several states, and without regard to any census of enumeration.

The Sixteenth Amendment was ratified in response to the Supreme Court's controversial decision in Pollack v. Farmer's Loan & Trust Co. *(1895), which held that a tax on incomes derived from property was a "direct tax." Prior to the Pollack case, income taxes had been considered "indirect" taxes, and thus well within the powers given to Congress by the Constitution. "Direct taxes," by contrast, could be imposed only if they were apportioned among the states according to each state's population (Article I, Section 9). The effect of the Pollack decision was to make an income tax all but impractical; the Sixteenth Amendment remedied the situation by placing income taxes back in the category of "indirect taxes."*

Amendment XVII (1913)

The Senate of the United States shall be composed of two Senators from each state, elected by the people thereof, for six years; and each Senator shall have one vote. The electors in each state shall have the qualifications requisite for electors of the most numerous branch of the state legislatures.

When vacancies happen in the representation of any state in the Senate, the executive authority of such state shall issue writs of election to fill such vacancies: Provided, that the legislature of any state may empower the executive thereof to make temporary appointments until the people fill the vacancies by election as the legislature may direct.

This amendment shall not be so construed as to affect the election or term of any Senator chosen before it becomes valid as part of the Constitution.

The Seventeenth Amendment changed the method by which U.S. senators were elected, overturning the provisions in Article I, Section 3. The amendment was the culmination of an extended effort of Progressive Era reformers at the beginning of the twentieth century, who frequently targeted institutions marked by economic privilege and corrupt politics. Eventually they demanded that U.S. senators should be more responsive to the public will—the best way to accomplish that goal was to require that senators should be chosen by popular election, rather than by state legislatures. Prior to the amendment's ratification, many states had already amended their primary laws to allow a popular vote for party nominees, and a handful of states had bound their respective legislatures to select the candidate who received the highest number of popular votes in the general election. The Seventeenth Amendment soon followed, receiving the approval of the required number of states (three-fourths) less than a year after it was first introduced.

Amendment XVIII (1919)

Section 1. After one year from the ratification of this article the manufacture, sale, or transportation of intoxicating liquors within, the importation thereof into, or the exportation thereof from the United States and all territory subject to the jurisdiction thereof for beverage purposes is hereby prohibited.

Section 2. The Congress and the several states shall have concurrent power to enforce this article by appropriate legislation.

Section 3. This article shall be inoperative unless it shall have been ratified as an amendment to the Constitution by the legislatures of the several states, as provided in the Constitution, within seven years from the date of the submission hereof to the states by the Congress.

> *The Eighteenth Amendment slipped into the Constitution on the strength of efforts by the Anti-Saloon League and members of other groups who believed that intoxicating liquors were harmful and sinful. The amendment was proposed immediately after the end of World War I, and the Prohibition era began a year after its formal ratification on January 16, 1919.*

Amendment XIX (1920)

The right of citizens of the United States to vote shall not be denied or abridged by the United States or by any state on account of sex.

Congress shall have power to enforce this article by appropriate legislation.

> *The Nineteenth Amendment was a reform spurred by the Progressive movement. Although women had been fighting for their right to vote since before the Civil War, the drive for woman suffrage started achieving success only with the entry of western states such as Wyoming, which extended the right to vote to women upon its admission to the Union in 1890. (Five other western states followed suit in subsequent decades.) By concentrating their efforts on a federal constitutional amendment guaranteeing women the right to vote, woman suffrage activists brought immediate pressure to bear on Congress and the president to support the movement. With momentum clearly on its side, the Nineteenth Amendment was ratified less than 15 months after it was first proposed.*

Amendment XX (1933)

Section 1. The terms of the President and Vice President shall end at noon on the 20th day of January, and the terms of Senators and Representatives at noon on the 3d day of January, of the years in which such terms would have ended if this article had not been ratified; and the terms of their successors shall then begin.

Section 2. The Congress shall assemble at least once in every year, and such meeting shall begin at noon on the 3d day of January, unless they shall by law appoint a different day.

Section 3. If, at the time fixed for the beginning of the term of the President, the President elect shall have died, the Vice President elect shall become President. If a President shall not have been chosen before the time fixed for the beginning of his term, or if the President elect shall have failed to qualify, then the Vice President elect shall act as President until a President shall have qualified; and the Congress may by law provide for the case wherein neither a President elect nor a Vice President elect shall have qualified, declaring who shall then act as President, or the manner in which one who is to act shall be selected, and such person shall act accordingly until a President or Vice President shall have qualified.

Section 4. The Congress may by law provide for the case of the death of any of the persons from whom the House of Representatives may choose a President whenever the right of choice shall have devolved upon them, and for the case of the death of any of the persons from whom the Senate may choose a Vice President whenever the right of choice shall have devolved upon them.

Section 5. Sections 1 and 2 shall take effect on the 15th day of October following the ratification of this article.

Section 6. This article shall be inoperative unless it shall have been ratified as an amendment to the Constitution by the legislatures of three-fourths of the several states within seven years from the date of its submission.

> *The Twentieth Amendment brought an end to the excessively long period of time between the November election and the March inauguration of a new president. Given advances in transportation and communications systems over the previous century, such a delay in the president taking office—with the out-going president reluctant to act even during times of crisis—could no longer be justified. The amendment also limited Congress's lame-duck sessions that followed the November elections: newly elected members of Congress could now begin their service to constituents in early January, rather than waiting 13 months until the following December. Finally, the amendment authorized Congress to provide for a line of succession in the event that neither a president-elect nor a vice president–elect qualified to serve by the January 20th date.*

Amendment XXI (1933)

Section 1. The eighteenth article of amendment to the Constitution of the United States is hereby repealed.

Section 2. The transportation or importation into any state, territory, or possession of the United States for delivery or use therein of intoxicating liquors, in violation of the laws thereof, is hereby prohibited.

Section 3. This article shall be inoperative unless it shall have been ratified as an amendment to the Constitution by conventions in the several states, as provided in the Constitution, within seven years from the date of the submission hereof to the states by the Congress.

> *The Twenty-first Amendment repealed Prohibition. The enforcement of the Eighteenth Amendment had proven too difficult and expensive, as thousands of illegal sources arose to meet the continuing public demand for alcohol. Crime gangs involved in the illegal liquor trade spread violence and bloodshed throughout the nation, which pressured politicians to end Prohibition. Finally, when both political parties came out in favor of repeal during the 1932 election, Prohibition's days were clearly numbered. After the Twenty-first Amendment was ratified on December 5, 1933, states would thereafter have the exclusive power to prevent the import and use of liquor in their respective jurisdictions.*

Amendment XXII (1951)

Section 1. No person shall be elected to the office of the President more than twice, and no person who has held the office of President, or acted as President, for more than two years of a term to which some other person was elected President shall be elected to the office of the President more than once. But this article shall not apply to any person holding the office of President when this article was proposed by the Congress, and shall not prevent any person who may be holding the office of President, or acting as President, during the term within which this article becomes operative from holding the office of President or acting as President during the remainder of such term.

Section 2. This article shall be inoperative unless it shall have been ratified as an amendment to the Constitution by the legislatures of three-fourths of the several states within seven years from the date of its submission to the states by the Congress.

Franklin Roosevelt's election to a record fourth term as president in 1944 sent politicians clamoring for a means of restoring the unwritten two-term tradition originally established by George Washington. Within two years of FDR's death, Congress proposed the Twenty-second Amendment, and it was adopted soon thereafter. In addition to setting a limit on the number of terms (two) to which a president may be elected, the amendment also sets a maximum of 10 years less one day for a president to serve in the event he or she also succeeds to a part of another president's term. The amendment was worded so as not to apply to the then-sitting president, Harry S. Truman, but it has applied to Dwight Eisenhower and all other presidents since.

Amendment XXIII (1961)

Section 1. The District constituting the seat of government of the United States shall appoint in such manner as the Congress may direct:

A number of electors of President and Vice President equal to the whole number of Senators and Representatives in Congress to which the District would be entitled if it were a state, but in no event more than the least populous state; they shall be in addition to those appointed by the states, but they shall be considered, for the purposes of the election of President and Vice President, to be electors appointed by a state; and they shall meet in the District and perform such duties as provided by the twelfth article of amendment.

Section 2. The Congress shall have power to enforce this article by appropriate legislation.

The Twenty-third Amendment cured the anomaly of U.S. citizens being denied the right to vote for federal officials (including president of the United States) so long as they remained permanent residents of the District of Columbia. Since ratification of the amendment in 1961, DC residents have been entitled to vote for presidential and vice presidential candidates, but the amendment did not authorize residents of DC to elect members to either branch of Congress. Nor did it provide DC residents with home rule or the power to run their own local government. Since 1973 Congress has authorized the DC government to be run primarily by locally elected officials, subject to the oversight and supervision of Congress.

Amendment XXIV (1964)

Section 1. The right of citizens of the United States to vote in any primary or other election for President or Vice President, for electors for President or Vice

President, or for Senator or Representative in Congress, shall not be denied or abridged by the United States or any state by reason of failure to pay any poll tax or other tax.

Section 2. The Congress shall have power to enforce this article by appropriate legislation.

> *The Twenty-fourth Amendment eliminated yet another vestige of legally enforced racism in the South and elsewhere. Many states had already eliminated the requirement that voters pay a tax before voting, a restriction that created an undue hardship on lower economic classes, including disproportionate numbers of racial/ethnic minorities. Still, as late as 1964, five states (Alabama, Arkansas, Mississippi, Texas, and Virginia) continued to tie a poll tax to the voting privilege. In 1966 the Supreme Court ruled in* Harper v. Board of Education *that poll taxes also violated the equal protection clause of the Fourteenth Amendment.*

Amendment XXV (1967)

Section 1. In case of the removal of the President from office or of his death or resignation, the Vice President shall become President.

Section 2. Whenever there is a vacancy in the office of the Vice President, the President shall nominate a Vice President who shall take office upon confirmation by a majority vote of both Houses of Congress.

Section 3. Whenever the President transmits to the President pro tempore of the Senate and the Speaker of the House of Representatives his written declaration that he is unable to discharge the powers and duties of his office, and until he transmits to them a written declaration to the contrary, such powers and duties shall be discharged by the Vice President as Acting President.

Section 4. Whenever the Vice President and a majority of either the principal officers of the executive departments or of such other body as Congress may by law provide, transmit to the President pro tempore of the Senate and the Speaker of the House of Representatives their written declaration that the President is unable to discharge the powers and duties of his office, the Vice President shall immediately assume the powers and duties of the office as Acting President.

Thereafter, when the President transmits to the President pro tempore of the Senate and the Speaker of the House of Representatives his written declaration that no inability exists, he shall resume the powers and duties of his office unless the Vice President and a majority of either the principal officers of the executive department or of such other body as Congress may by law provide, transmit within four days to the President pro tempore of the Senate and the Speaker of the House of Representatives their written declaration that the President is unable to discharge the powers and duties of his office. Thereupon Congress shall decide the issue, assembling within forty-eight hours for that purpose if not in session. If the Congress, within twenty-one days after receipt of the latter written declaration, or, if Congress is not in session, within twenty-one days after Congress is required to assemble, determines by two-thirds vote of both Houses that the President is unable to discharge the powers and duties of his office, the Vice President shall continue to discharge the same as Acting President; otherwise, the President shall resume the powers and duties of his office.

The Twenty-fifth Amendment clarified several ambiguous aspects of presidential succession. At the outset, it formalized an unwritten precedent first established by John Tyler, who succeeded to the presidency upon the death of William Henry Harrison in 1841: If the office of president becomes vacant because of the president's death or resignation, the vice president becomes president and assumes all powers and duties of the office. If the vice presidency is vacant, the amendment establishes new procedures for filling the position between elections: the president nominates a successor, to be confirmed by a majority vote of both houses of Congress. Since its adoption in 1967, two vice presidents have been selected in this manner: Gerald Ford in 1973 and Nelson Rockefeller in 1974. When Gerald Ford succeeded to the presidency upon the resignation of Richard Nixon in 1974, he became the first—and to date, the only—president in American history to hold that office without being formally elected to either the presidency or the vice presidency.

The amendment also addresses the vexing problem of presidential disabilities. In the early twentieth century, Woodrow Wilson was an invalid for more than a year of his presidency; in the 1950s, Dwight Eisenhower suffered a stroke once during each of his two terms in office. The Twenty-fifth Amendment addresses the problem of presidential disability by providing procedures for the president to temporarily discharge the duties and powers of the office to the officer next in line (normally the vice president), who then becomes "acting president." This has happened only twice: in 1985, when Vice President George H. W. Bush received a transmission of power temporarily while President Ronald Reagan underwent a minor medical procedure, and in 2002, when President George W. Bush temporarily transferred his powers to Vice President Dick Cheney while he underwent a colonoscopy. The amendment further authorizes the vice president and certain members of the executive branch to declare the president disabled or incapacitated, subject (within 27 days) to Congress upholding the finding of incapacity. This final provision has never been invoked.

Amendment XXVI (1971)

Section 1. The right of citizens of the United States, who are 18 years of age or older, to vote, shall not be denied or abridged by the United States or any state on account of age.

Section 2. The Congress shall have the power to enforce this article by appropriate legislation.

The Twenty-sixth Amendment extended suffrage to those age 18 and older. At the time of its passage, soldiers under the age of 21 were fighting in Vietnam, creating intense pressure on Congress and state legislatures to extend the vote to all those who were old enough to fight. The amendment does not apply to the denial of rights other than voting to those who are between 18 and 21 years of age. Thus, the National Minimum Drinking Age Act of 1984 obliges states to establish a 21-year-old drinking age or risk the loss of federal highway funds. Additionally, Utah and Alaska have established 19 as the minimum age for tobacco use.

Amendment XXVII (1992)

No law, varying the compensation for the services of the Senators and Representatives, shall take effect, until an election of Representatives shall have intervened.

The Twenty-seventh Amendment was intended to serve as a restraint on the power of Congress to raise its own pay—it may only do so if the raise takes effect after a subsequent general election. Although the Supreme Court has never ruled on the issue, lower courts have held that this amendment does not prevent Congress from receiving cost-of-living adjustments immediately.

FEDERALIST NO. 10

November 23, 1787

TO THE PEOPLE OF THE STATE OF NEW YORK

AMONG the numerous advantages promised by a well-constructed Union, none deserves to be more accurately developed than its tendency to break and control the violence of faction. The friend of popular governments never finds himself so much alarmed for their character and fate, as when he contemplates their propensity to this dangerous vice. He will not fail, therefore, to set a due value on any plan which, without violating the principles to which he is attached, provides a proper cure for it. The instability, injustice, and confusion introduced into the public councils, have, in truth, been the mortal diseases under which popular governments have everywhere perished; as they continue to be the favorite and fruitful topics from which the adversaries to liberty derive their most specious declamations. The valuable improvements made by the American constitutions on the popular models, both ancient and modern, cannot certainly be too much admired; but it would be an unwarrantable partiality, to contend that they have as effectually obviated the danger on this side, as was wished and expected. Complaints are everywhere heard from our most considerate and virtuous citizens, equally the friends of public and private faith, and of public and personal liberty, that our governments are too unstable, that the public good is disregarded in the conflicts of rival parties, and that measures are too often decided, not according to the rules of justice and the rights of the minor party, but by the superior force on an interested and overbearing majority. However anxiously we may wish that these complaints had no foundation, the evidence of known facts will not permit us to deny that they are in some degree true. It will be found, indeed, on a candid review of our situation, that some of the distresses under which we labor have been erroneously charged on the operation of our governments; but it will be found, at the same time, that other causes will not alone account for many of our heaviest misfortunes; and, particularly, for that prevailing and increasing distrust of public engagements, and alarm for private rights, which are echoed from one end of the continent to the other. These must be chiefly, if not wholly, effects of the unsteadiness and injustice with which a factious spirit has tainted our public administrations.

By a faction, I understand a number of citizens, whether amounting to a majority or a minority of the whole, who are united and actuated by some common impulse of passion, or of interest, adversed to the rights of other citizens, or to the permanent and aggregate interests of the community.

There are two methods of curing the mischeifs of faction: the one, by removing its causes; the other, by controlling its effects.

There are again two methods of removing the causes of faction: the one, by destroying the liberty which is essential to its existence; the other, by giving to every citizen the same opinions, the same passions, and the same interests.

It could never be more truly said than of the first remedy, that it was worse than the disease. Liberty is to faction what air is to fire, an aliment without which it instantly expires. But it could not be less folly to abolish liberty, which is essential to political life, because it nourishes faction, than it would be to wish the annihilation of air, which is essential to animal life, because it imparts to fire its destructive tendency.

The second expedient is as impracticable as the first would be unwise. As long as the reason of man continues fallible, and he is at liberty to exercise it, different opinions will be formed. As long as the connection subsists between his reason and his self-love, his opinions and his passions will have a reciprocal influence on each other; and the former will be objects to which the latter will attach themselves. The diversity in the faculties of men, from which the rights of property originate, is not less an insuperable obstacle to a uniformity of interests. The protection of these faculties is the first object of government. From the protection of different and unequal faculties of acquiring property, the possession of different degrees and kinds of property immediately results; and from the influence of these on the sentiments and views of the respective proprietors, ensues a division of the society into different interests and parties.

The latent causes of faction are thus sown in the nature of man; and we see them everywhere brought into different degrees of activity, according to the different circumstances of civil society. A zeal for different opinions concerning religion, concerning government, and many other points, as well of speculation as of practice; an attachment to different leaders ambitiously contending for pre-eminence and power; or to persons of other descriptions whose fortunes have been interesting to the human passions, have, in turn, divided mankind into parties, inflamed them with mutual animosity, and rendered them much more disposed to vex and oppress each other than to co-operate for their common good. So string is this propensity of mankind to fall into mutual animosities, that where no substantial occasion presents itself, the most frivolous and fanciful distinctions have been sufficient to kindle their unfriendly passions and excite their most violent conflicts. But the most common and durable source of factions has been the various and unequal distribution of property. Those who hold and those who are without property have ever formed distinct interests in society. Those who are creditors, and those who are debtors, fall under a like discrimination. A landed interest, a manufacturing interest, a mercantile interest, a moneyed interest, with many lesser interests, grow up of necessity in civilized nations, and divide them into different classes, actuated by different sentiments and views. The regulation of these various and interfering interests forms the principal task of modern legislation, and involves the spirit of party and faction in the necessary and ordinary operations of the government.

No man is allowed to be a judge in his own case, because his interest would certainly bias his judgment, and, not improbably, corrupt his integrity. With equal, nay with greater reason, a body of men are unfit to be both judges and parties at the same time; yet what are many of the most important acts of legislation, but so many judicial determinations, not indeed concerning the rights of single persons, but concerning the rights of large bodies of citizens? And what are the different classes of legislators but advocates and parties to the causes which they determine? Is a law proposed concerning private debts? It is a question to which the creditors are parties on one side and the debtors on the other. Justice ought to hold the balance between them. Yet the parties are, and must be, themselves the judges; and the most numerous party, or, in other words, the most powerful action must be expected to prevail. Shall domestic manufactures be encouraged, and in what degree, by restrictions on foreign manufactures? are questions which would be differently decided by the landed and the manufacturing classes, and probably by neither with a sole regard to justice and the public good. The apportionment of taxes on the various descriptions of property is an act which seems to require the most exact impartiality; yet there is, perhaps, no legislative act in which greater opportunity and temptation are given to a predominant party to trample on the rules of justice. Every shilling with which they overburden the inferior number, is a shilling saved to their own pockets.

It is in vain to say that enlightened statesmen will be able to adjust these clashing interests, and render them all subservient to the public good. Enlightened statesmen will not always be at the helm. Nor, in many cases, can such an adjustment be made at all without taking into view indirect and remote considerations, which will rarely prevail over the immediate interest which one party may find in disregarding the rights of another or the good of the whole.

The inference to which we are brought is, that the *causes* of faction cannot be removed, and that relief is only to be sought in the means of controlling its *effects*.

If a faction consists of less than a majority, relief is supplied by the republican principle, which enables the majority to defeat its sinister views by regular vote. It may clog the administration, it may convulse the society; but it will be unable to execute and mask its violence under the forms of the Constitution. When a majority is included in a faction, the form of popular government, on the other hand, enables it to sacrifice to its ruling passion or interest both the public good and the rights of other citizens. To secure the public good and private rights against the danger of such a faction, and at the same time to preserve the spirit and form of popular government, is then the great object to which our inquiries are directed. Let me add that it is the great desideratum by which this form of government can be rescued from the opprobrium under which it has so long labored, and be recommended to the esteem and adoption of mankind.

By what means is this object attainable? Evidently by one of two only. Either the existence of the same passion or interest in a majority at the same time must be prevented, or the majority, having such coexistent passion or interest, must be rendered, by their number and local situation, unable to concert and carry into effect schemes of oppression. If the impulse and the opportunity be suffered to coincide, we well know that neither moral nor religious motives can be relied on as an adequate control. They are not found to be such on the injustice and violence of individuals, and lose their efficacy in proportion to the number combined together, that is, in proportion as their efficacy becomes needful.

From this view of the subject it may be concluded that a pure democracy, by which I mean a society consisting of a small number of citizens, who assemble and administer the government in person, can admit of no cure for the mischiefs of faction. A common passion or interest will, in almost every case, be felt by a majority of the whole; a communication and concert result from the form of government itself; and there is nothing to check the inducements to sacrifice the weaker party or an obnoxious individual. Hence it is that such democracies have ever been spectacles of turbulence and contention; have ever been found incompatible with personal security or the rights of property; and have in general been as short in their lives as they have been violent in their deaths. Theoretic politicians, who have patronized this species of government, have erroneously supposed that by reducing mankind to a perfect equality in their political rights, they would, at the same time, be perfectly equalized and assimilated in their possessions, their opinions, and their passions.

A republic, by which I mean a government in which the scheme of representation takes place, opens a different prospect, and promises the cure for which we are seeking. Let us examine the points in which it varies from pure democracy, and we shall comprehend both the nature of the cure and the efficacy which it must derive from the Union.

The two great points of difference between a democracy and a republic are: first, the delegation of the government, in the latter, to a small number of citizens elected by the rest; secondly, the greater number of citizens, and greater sphere of country, over which the latter may be extended.

The effect of the first difference is, on the one hand, to refine and enlarge the public views, by passing them through the medium of a chosen body of citizens, whose wisdom may best discern the true interest of their country, and whose patriotism and love of justice will be least likely to sacrifice it to temporary or partial considerations. Under such a regulation, it may well happen that the public voice, pronounced by the representatives of the people, will be more consonant to the public good than it pronounced by the people themselves, convened for the purpose. On the other hand, the effect may be inverted. Men of factious tempers, of local prejudices, or of sinister designs, may, by intrigue, by corruption, or by other means, first obtain the suffrages, and then betray the interests, of the people. The question resulting is, whether small or extensive republics are more favorable to the election of proper guardians of the public weal; and it is clearly decided in favor of the latter by two obvious considerations:

In the first place, it is to be remarked that, however small the republic may be, the representatives must be raised to a certain number, in order to guard against the cabals of a few; and that, however large it may be, they must be limited to a certain number, in order to guard against the confusion of a multitude. Hence, the number of representatives in the two cases not being in proportion to that of the two constituents, and being proportionally greater in the small republic, it follows that, if the proportion of fit characters be not less in the large than in the small republic, the former will present a greater option, and consequently a greater probability of a fit choice.

In the next place, as each representative will be chosen by a greater number of citizens in the large than in the small republic, it will be more difficult for unworthy candidates to practice with success the vicious arts by which elections are too often carried; and the suffrages of the people being more free, will be more likely to centre in men who possess the most attractive merit and the most diffusive and established characters.

It must be confessed that in this, as in most other cases, there is a mean, on both sides of which inconveniences will be found to lie. By enlarging too much the number of electors, you render the representatives too little acquainted with all their local circumstances and lesser interests; as by reducing it too much, you render him unduly attached to these, and too little fit to comprehend and pursue great and national objects. The federal Constitution forms a happy combination in this respect; the great and aggregate interests being referred to the national, the local and particular to the State legislatures.

The other point of difference is, the greater number of citizens and extent of territory which may be brought within the compass of republican than of democratic government; and it is this circumstance principally which renders factious combinations less to be dreaded in the former than in the latter. The smaller the society, the fewer probably will be the distinct parties and interests composing it; the fewer the distinct parties and interests, the more frequently will a majority be found of the same party; and the smaller the number of individuals composing a majority, and the smaller the compass within which they are placed, the more easily will they concert and execute their plans of oppression. Extend the sphere, and you take in a greater variety of parties and interests; you make it less probable that a majority of the whole will have a common motive to invade the rights of other citizens; or if such a common motive exists, it will be more difficult for all who feel it to discover their own strength, and to act in unison with each other. Besides other impediments, it may be remarked that, where there is a consciousness of unjust or dishonorable purposes, communication is always checked by distrust in proportion to the number whose concurrence is necessary.

Hence, it clearly appears, that the same advantage which a republic has over a democracy, in controlling the effects of faction, is enjoyed by a large over a small republic,— and is enjoyed by the Union over the States composing it. Does the advantage consist in the substitution of representatives whose enlightened views and virtuous sentiments render them superior to local prejudices and schemes of injustice? It will not be denied that the representation of the Union will be most likely to possess these requisite endowments. Does it consist in the greater security afforded by a greater variety of parties, against the event of any one party being able to outnumber and oppress the rest?

In an equal degree does the increased variety of parties comprised within the Union, increase this security. Does it, in fine, consist in the greater obstacles opposed to the concert and accomplishment of the secret wishes of an unjust and interested majority? Here, again, the extent of the Union gives it the most palpable advantage.

The influence of factious leaders may kindle a flame within their particular States, but will be unable to spread a general conflagration through the other States. A religious sect may degenerate into a political faction in a part of the Confederacy; but the variety of sects dispersed over the entire face of it must secure the national councils against any danger from that source. A rage for paper money, for an abolition of debts, for an equal division of property, or for any other improper or wicked project, will be less apt to pervade the whole body of the Union than a particular member of it; in the same proportion as such a malady is more likely to taint a particular county or district, than an entire State.

In the extent and proper structure of the Union, therefore, we behold a republican remedy for the diseases most incident to republican government. And according to the degree of pleasure and pride we feel in being republicans, ought to be our zeal in cherishing the spirit and supporting the character of Federalists.

PUBLIUS

Federalist No. 51

February 8, 1788

TO THE PEOPLE OF THE STATE OF NEW YORK

TO WHAT expedient, then, shall we finally resort, for maintaining in practice the necessary partition of power among the several departments, as laid down in the Constitution? The only answer that can be given is, that as all these exterior provisions are found to be inadequate, the defect must be supplied, by so contriving the interior structure of the government as that its several constituent parts may, by their mutual relations, be the means of keeping each other in their proper places. Without presuming to undertake a full development of the important idea, I will hazard a few general observations, which may perhaps place it in a clearer light, and enable us to form a more correct judgment of the principles and structure of the government planned by the convention.

In order to lay a due foundation for that separate and distinct exercise of the different powers of government, which to a certain extent is admitted on all hands to be essential to the preservation of liberty, it is evident that each department should have a will of its own; and consequently should be so constituted that the members of each should have as little agency as possible in the appointment of the members of the others. Were this principle rigorously adhered to, it would require that all the appointments for the supreme executive, legislative, and judiciary magistracies should be drawn from the same fountain of authority, the people, through channels having no communication whatever with one another. Perhaps such a plan of constructing the several departments would be less difficult in practice than it may in contemplation appear. Some difficulties, however, and some additional expense would attend the execution of it. Some deviations, therefore, from the principle must be admitted. In the constitution of the judiciary department in particular, it might be inexpedient to insist rigorously on the principle: first, because peculiar qualifications being essential in the members, the primary consideration ought to be to select that mode of choice which best secures these qualifications; secondly, because the permanent tenure by which the appointments are held in that department, must soon destroy all sense of dependence on the authority conferring them.

It is equally evident, that the members of each department should be as little dependent as possible on those of the others, for the emoluments annexed to their offices. Were the executive magistrate, or the judges, not independent of the legislature in this particular, their independence in every other would be merely nominal.

But the great security against a gradual concentration of the several powers in the same department, consists in giving to those who administer each department the necessary constitutional means and personal motives to resist encroachments of the others. The provision for defense must in this, as in all other cases, be made commensurate to the danger of attack. Ambition must be made to counteract ambition. The interest of the man must be connected with the constitutional rights of the place. It may be a reflection on human nature, that such devices should be necessary to control the abuses of government. But what is government itself, but the greatest of all reflections on human nature? If men were angels, no government would be necessary. If angels were to govern men, neither external nor internal controls on government would be necessary. In framing a government which is to be administered by men over men, the great difficulty lies in this: you must first enable the government to control the governed; and in the next place oblige it to control itself. A dependence on the people is, no doubt, the primary control on the government; but experience has taught mankind the necessity of auxiliary precautions.

This policy of supplying, by opposite and rival interests, the defect of better motives, might be traced through the whole system of human affairs, private as well as public. We see it particularly displayed in all the subordinate distributions of power, where the constant aim is to divide and arrange the several offices in such a manner as that each may be a check on the other—that the private interest of every individual may be a sentinel over the public rights. These inventions of prudence cannot be less requisite in the distribution of the supreme powers of the State.

But it is not possible to give to each department an equal power of self-defense. In republican government, the legislative authority necessarily predominates. The remedy for this inconveniency is to divide the legislature into different branches; and to render them, by different modes of election and different principles of action, as little connected with each other as the nature of their common functions and their common dependence on the society will admit. It may even be necessary to guard against dangerous encroachments by still further precautions. As the weight of the legislative authority requires that it should be thus divided, the weakness of the executive may require, on the other hand, that it should be fortified. An absolute negative on the legislature appears, at first view, to be the natural defense with which the executive magistrate should be armed. But perhaps it would be neither altogether safe nor alone sufficient. On ordinary occasions it might not be exerted with the requisite firmness, and on extraordinary occasions it might be perfidiously abused. May not this defect of an absolute negative be supplied by some qualified connection between this weaker department and the weaker branch of the stronger department, by which the latter may be led to support the constitutional rights of the former, without being too much detached from the rights of its own department?

If the principles on which these observations are founded be just, as I persuade myself they are, and they be applied as a criterion to the several State constitutions, and to the federal Constitution it will be found that if the latter does not perfectly correspond with them, the former are infinitely less able to bear such a test.

There are, moreover, two considerations particularly applicable to the federal system of America, which place that system in a very interesting point of view.

First. In a single republic, all the power surrendered by the people is submitted to the administration of a single government; and the usurpations are guarded against by a division of the government into distinct and separate departments. In the compound republic of America, the power surrendered by the people is first divided between two distinct governments, and then the portion allotted to each subdivided among distinct and separate departments. Hence a double security arises to the rights of the people. The different governments will control each other, at the same time that each will be controlled by itself.

Second. It is of great importance in a republic not only to guard the society against the oppression of its rulers, but to guard one part of the society against the injustice of the other part. Different interests necessarily exist in different classes of citizens. If a majority be united by a common interest, the rights of the minority will be insecure. There are but two methods of providing against this evil: the one by creating a will in the community independent of the majority that is, of the society itself; the other, by comprehending in the society so many separate descriptions of citizens as will render an unjust combination of a majority of the whole very improbable, if not impracticable. The first method prevails in all governments possessing an hereditary or self-appointed authority. This, at best, is but a precarious security; because a power independent of society may as well espouse the unjust views of the major as the rightful interests of the minor party, and may possibly be turned against both parties. The second method will be exemplified in the federal republic of the United States. Whilst all authority in it will be derived from and dependent on the society, the society itself will be broken into so many parts, interests, and classes of citizens, that the rights of individuals, or of the minority, will be in little danger from interested combinations of the majority. In a free government the security for civil rights must be the same as that for religious rights. It consists in the one case in the multiplicity of interests, and in the other in the multiplicity of sects. The degree of security in both cases will depend on the number of interests and sects; and this may be presumed to depend on the extent of country and number of people comprehended under the same government. This view of the subject must particularly recommend a proper federal system to all the sincere and considerate friends of republican government, since it shows that in exact proportion as the territory of the Union may be formed into more circumscribed Confederacies, or States oppressive combinations of a majority will be facilitated: the best security, under republican forms, for the rights of every class of citizens, will be diminished; and consequently the stability and independence of some member of the government, the only other security, must be proportionately increased. Justice is the end of government. It is the end of civil society. It ever has been and ever will be pursued until it be obtained, or until liberty be lost in the pursuit. In a society under the forms of which the stronger faction can readily unite and oppress the weaker, anarchy may as truly be said to reign as in a state of nature, where the weaker individual is not secured against the violence of the stronger; and as, in the latter state, even the stronger individuals are prompted, by the uncertainty of their condition, to submit to a government which may protect the wear as well as the more powerful. It can be little doubted that if the State of Rhode Island was separated from the Confederacy and left to itself, the insecurity of rights under the popular form of government within such narrow limits would be displayed by such reiterated oppressions of factious majorities that some power altogether independent of the people would soon be called for by the voice of the very factions whose misrule had proved the necessity of it. In the extended republic of the United States, and among the great variety of interests, parties, and sects which it embraces, a coalition of a majority of the whole society could seldom take place on any other principles than those of justice and the general good; whilst there being thus less danger to a minor from the will of a major party, there must be less pretext, also, to provide for the security of the former, by introducing into the government a will not dependent on the latter, or, in other words, a will independent of the society itself. It is no less certain than it is important, notwithstanding the contrary opinions which have been entertained, that the larger the society, provided it lie within a practical sphere, the more duly capable it will be of self-government. And happily for the *republican cause*, the practicable sphere may be carried to a very great extent, by a judicious modification of mixture of the *federal principle*.

PUBLIUS

Presidents of the United States

Name of President	Dates of Service	Political Party Affiliation	Vice President(s)	Major Party Candidate(s) Defeated in General Election
George Washington	1789–97		Adams	
John Adams	1797–1801	Federalist	Jefferson	Jefferson
Thomas Jefferson	1801–09	Democratic-Republican	Burr/Clinton	Adams, Pinckney
James Madison	1809–17	Democratic-Republican	Clinton/Gerry	Pinckney, D. Clinton
James Monroe	1817–25	Democratic-Republican	Tompkins	King
John Quincy Adams	1825–29	Democratic-Republican/ Democratic	Calhoun	Jackson
Andrew Jackson	1829–37	Democratic	Van Buren	J. Q. Adams, Clay
Martin Van Buren	1837–41	Democratic	Johnson	Harrison
William Harrison	1841	Whig	Tyler	Van Buren
John Tyler	1841–45	Whig	vacant	
James Polk	1845–49	Democratic	Dallas	Clay
Zachary Taylor	1849–50	Whig	Fillmore	Cass
Millard Fillmore	1850–53	Whig	vacant	
Franklin Pierce	1853–57	Democratic	King/vacant	Scott
James Buchanan	1857–61	Democratic	Breckinridge	Fremont
Abraham Lincoln	1861–65	Republican	Hamlin/Johnson	Breckinridge, Douglas, McClellan
Andrew Johnson	1865–69	Democratic	vacant	
Ulysses S. Grant	1869–77	Republican	Colfax/Wilson/vacant	Seymour, Greeley
Rutherford B. Hayes	1877–81	Republican	Wheeler	Tilden
James Garfield	1881	Republican	Arthur	Hancock
Chester Arthur	1881–85	Republican	vacant	
Grover Cleveland	1885–89	Democratic	Hendricks/vacant	Blaine
Benjamin Harrison	1889–93	Republican	Morton	Cleveland
Grover Cleveland	1893–97	Democratic	Stevenson	Harrison
William McKinley	1897–1901	Republican	Hobart	Bryan
Theodore Roosevelt	1901–09	Republican	vacant/Fairbanks	Parker
William Taft	1909–13	Republican	Sherman/vacant	Bryan

Name of President	Dates of Service	Political Party Affiliation	Vice President(s)	Major Party Candidate(s) Defeated in General Election
Woodrow Wilson	1913–21	Democratic	Marshall	T. Roosevelt, Taft, Hughes
Warren G. Harding	1921–23	Republican	Coolidge	Cox
Calvin Coolidge	1923–29	Republican	vacant/Dawes	Davis
Herbert Hoover	1929–33	Republican	Curtis	Smith
Franklin D. Roosevelt	1933–45	Democratic	Garner/Wallace/Truman	Hoover, Landon, Wilkie, Dewey
Harry Truman	1945–53	Democratic	vacant/Barkley	Dewey
Dwight Eisenhower	1953–61	Republican	Nixon	Stevenson
John F. Kennedy	1961–63	Democratic	Johnson	Nixon
Lyndon Johnson	1963–69	Democratic	vacant/Humphrey	Goldwater
Richard Nixon	1969–74	Republican	Agnew/vacant/Ford	Humphrey, McGovern
Gerald Ford	1974–77	Republican	vacant/Rockefeller	
Jimmy Carter	1977–81	Democratic	Mondale	Ford
Ronald Reagan	1981–89	Republican	G. H.W. Bush	Carter, Mondale
George H. W. Bush	1989–93	Republican	Quayle	Dukakis
William Clinton	1993–2001	Democratic	Gore	G. H. W. Bush, Dole
George W. Bush	2001–2009	Republican	Cheney	Gore, Kerry
Barack Obama	2009–2017	Democratic	Biden	McCain, Romney
Donald Trump	2017–present	Republican	Pence	H. Clinton

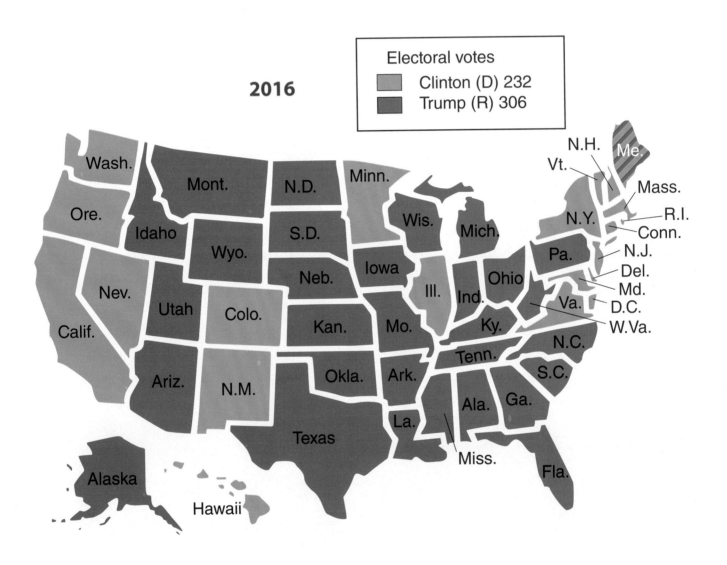

2016

Electoral votes

Clinton (D) 232

Trump (R) 306

2012

2008

2004

*A Minnesota elector pledged to Kerry cast a ballot for John Ewards [sic].

2000

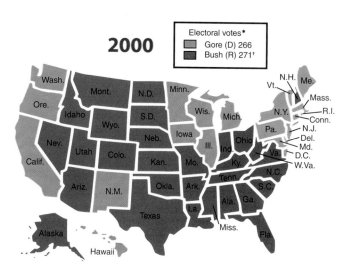

*A District of Columbia elector pledged to Gore cast no ballot as a protest against the District of Columbia's lack of representation in the U.S. Congress.

†The state of Florida certified Bush the winner on November 26, a result that Gore contested in court.

GLOSSARY

A

administrative discretion The freedom of agencies to decide how to implement a vague or ambiguous law passed by Congress.

administrative law A law that relates to the authority of administrative agencies and the rules promulgated by those agencies.

affirmative action Programs, laws, or practices designed to remedy past discriminatory hiring practices, government contracting, and school admissions.

agenda-setting theory The theory holding that although the effects of television exposure may be minimal or difficult to gauge, the media are quite influential in telling the public what to think about.

agents of political socialization Factors that have a significant impact on an individual's socialization to politics.

amendments Modifications or additions to the U.S. Constitution passed in accordance with the amendment procedures laid out in Article V.

amicus curiae briefs Written documents filed by outside parties in the case with an interest in the outcome of the litigation expressing their own views on how the Court should decide a particular case.

anarchy A state of lawlessness and discord in the political system caused by lack of government.

Anti-Federalists Those who opposed ratification of the proposed constitution of the United States between 1787 and 1789.

appellate jurisdiction The authority of a court to review decisions handed down by another court.

Articles of Confederation The document creating a "league of friendship" governing the 13 states during and immediately after the war for independence; hampered by the limited power the document vested in the legislature to collect revenue or regulate commerce, the Articles eventually proved unworkable for the new nation.

authoritarianism A form of government in which one political party, group, or person maintains such complete control over the nation that it may refuse to recognize and may even suppress all other political parties and interests.

authority The ability of public institutions and the officials within them to make laws, independent of the power to execute them.

B

bail An amount of money determined by a judge that the accused must pay to a court as security against his or her freedom before trial.

battleground states States identified as offering either major-party candidate a reasonable chance for victory in the electoral college.

bicameral legislature A legislature composed of two separate chambers.

bill A proposed law presented for consideration to a legislative body.

bill of attainder An act of a legislature declaring a person (or group) guilty of some crime, and then carrying out punishment without a trial. The Constitution denies Congress the ability to issue a bill of attainder.

Bill of Rights The first 10 amendments to the U.S. Constitution, which protect various rights of the people against the new federal government.

Bipartisan Campaign Reform Act (BCRA) of 2002 Also called the McCain-Feingold Act, the federal legislation that (1) restricted soft money spent by political parties, (2) regulated expenditures on ads that refer to specific candidates immediately before an election, and (3) increased limits on hard money donated directly to candidates and their campaigns.

block grants Grants from the federal government to the states that may be used at the discretion of states to pursue more generalized aims.

blogs Internet sites that include a combination of editorial page, personal web page, and online diary of personal observations in real time about news events and issues.

briefs Written documents filed by parties in an appealed case arguing why constitutional or statutory law weighs in favor of their respective positions.

***Brown v. Board of Education* (1954)** The 1954 U.S. Supreme Court decision that declared school segregation to be unconstitutional.

***Buckley v. Valeo* (1976)** The 1976 Supreme Court opinion that held that spending money to influence elections is protected First Amendment speech and that prohibited limitations on independent expenditures or personal money spent by candidates on their own campaigns.

budget authority The power of federal departments and agencies to incur obligations to spend or lend money.

budget deficit The amount of money spent by the U.S. government beyond that which it collects in taxes and other revenue in a single year.

budget surplus The amount by which the U.S. government's revenue exceeds its spending in a given fiscal year.

bureaucracy An organization set up in a logical and rational manner for the purpose of accomplishing specific functions.

bureaucratic adjudicating Determining the rights and duties of particular parties within the scope of an agency's rules or regulations.

C

cabinet The collection of the principal officers in each of the executive departments of the federal government who serve as key advisers to the president.

cabinet departments Those federal agencies that qualify as the major administrative organizations of the executive branch.

capitalism Economic system in which all or most of the means of production are privately owned under competitive conditions.

casework The direct assistance that a member of Congress provides to a constituent, community group, or local or state official.

caucus A method of choosing party nominees in which party members attend local meetings at which they choose delegates committed to a particular candidate.

Central Intelligence Agency (CIA) Federal agency charged with evaluating and disseminating intelligence information, performing public relations functions that affect international perceptions of the United States, and engaging in overt and covert operations at the direction of the president.

checks and balances A system of limits imposed by the Constitution that gives each branch of government the limited right to change or cancel the acts of other branches.

Citizens United v. FEC (2010) The 2010 Supreme Court opinion that held that government restrictions on independent political spending by corporations, unions, and other associations violate the First Amendment. Critics of the decision predicted the ruling would bring about a new era of corporate influence in politics. In fact, the bulk of large expenditures has come from so-called Super PACs dominated by a small group of billionaires; this development more than anything else has shifted significant power away from the political parties and toward the donors themselves.

civil law This term has two meanings: (1) legislative codes, laws, or sets of rules enacted by duly authorized lawmaking bodies such as Congress, state and local legislatures, or any executive authority entrusted with the power to make laws; and (2) the body of noncriminal laws of a nation or state that deal with the rights of private citizens.

civil liberties Those specific individual rights that are guaranteed by the Constitution and cannot be denied to citizens by government. Most of these rights are in the first 10 amendments to the Constitution, known as the Bill of Rights.

civil rights Those positive rights, whether political, social, or economic, conferred by the government on individuals or groups.

Civil Rights Act of 1964 The federal law that banned racial discrimination in all public accommodations, including those that were privately owned; prohibited discrimination by employers and created the Equal Employment Opportunity Commission to investigate complaints of discrimination; and denied public funds to schools that continued to discriminate on the basis of race.

Civil Rights Act of 1968 The federal law that banned race discrimination in housing and made interference with a citizen's civil rights a federal crime.

civil service The system whereby workers in the federal bureaucracy are supposed to be immune from partisan political maneuvering.

Civil Service Reform Act of 1978 The federal act that replaced the Civil Service Commission (the agency that oversaw federal hiring and firing practices) with the Office of Personnel Management (OPM) and the Merit Systems Protection Board (MSPB).

Civil War Amendments The Thirteenth Amendment (ratified in 1865) banished slavery from all states and U.S. territories. The Fourteenth Amendment (ratified in 1868) granted full U.S. and state citizenship to all people born or naturalized in the United States and guaranteed to each person "the equal protection of the laws." The Fifteenth Amendment (1870) forbade the denial or abridgement of the right to vote by any government on account of race.

class action lawsuit A lawsuit filed by a large group of people with clearly defined common interests.

closed primary An election that requires voters to declare their party affiliation ahead of time.

closed rule A rule of procedure adopted by the House Rules Committee that severely limits the ability of members of Congress to amend a bill.

closed shop The law that requires employees to become members of the union as a condition of employment in unionized workplaces.

cloture A Senate debate procedure that permits that body to end debate and force a vote on a bill by a vote of 60 senators.

coattail effect The potential benefit that successful presidential candidates offer to congressional candidates of the same political party during presidential election years.

Cold War The nearly half-century struggle over ideological differences between the United States and the Soviet Union. Waged through economic warfare, arms build-ups, and tense diplomatic talks, the Cold War never broke out into a sustained military engagement between the two nations and ended with the dissolution of the Soviet Union in 1991.

common law Judge-made law handed down through judicial opinions, which over time establish precedents.

complaint A document written by the plaintiff arguing why the court is empowered to hear the case and explaining why the plaintiff is entitled to some form of relief under the current law.

concurrent powers Those powers shared by the federal and state governments under the Constitution.

concurring opinion The opinion of one or more justices that agrees with the end result reached by the majority but disagrees with the reasons offered for the decision.

confederation A system of government (or "league") in which two or more independent states unite to achieve certain specified common aims.

conference committee A joint committee of Congress appointed by the House of Representatives and the Senate to resolve differences on a particular bill.

congressional agencies Government bodies formed by and relied on by Congress to support members of Congress in performing their functions.

congressional committee staff A group of workers assigned to congressional committees to support each committee's legislative work.

congressional district A geographic region (either a state itself or a region located entirely within one state) whose residents select one member to represent it in the House of Representatives.

congressional oversight Congress's exercise of its authority to monitor the activities of agencies and administrators.

congressional personal staff A group of workers who assist an individual member of Congress in performing his or her responsibilities.

conservative ideology A political orientation that generally favors government activism in defense of more traditional values on social issues but favors government restraint in economic redistribution.

Constitutional Convention Meeting of delegates from 12 states in Philadelphia during the summer of 1787, at which was drafted an entirely new system to govern the United States.

consumer price index (CPI) An index of prices for goods and services regularly traded in the U.S. economy.

containment U.S. foreign policy that sought to restrict Soviet power (and communist influence) to its existing geographical sphere.

continuity (in public opinion) A tendency for political preferences to remain generally stable over time.

cooperative federalism The doctrine of federalism that affords Congress nearly unlimited authority to exercise its powers through means that often coerce states into administering and/or enforcing federal policies.

crime control model Criminal justice policymaking model that views the controlling of criminal behavior as the system's most important function.

critical election An election that produces sharp changes in patterns of party loyalty among voters.

cultivation theory The theory of media effects that suggests that heavy television exposure helps develop an individual's overall view of the world.

D

dealignment A decline in voter attachment to parties and in clarity of party coalitions.

Declaration of Independence Formal document listing colonists' grievances and articulating the colonists' intention to seek independence; formally adopted by the Second Continental Congress on July 4, 1776.

defendant The target of a plaintiff's complaint.

delegated congressional power Congress's transferring of its lawmaking authority to the executive branch of government.

democracy Form of government in which the people, either directly or through elected representatives, hold power and authority. The word *democracy* is derived from the Greek *demos kratos,* meaning "rule by the people."

Department of Defense Executive branch agency that is responsible for managing the nation's military and advising the president on all military matters.

Department of Homeland Security (DHS) Executive branch agency established in 2002 to coordinate government entities in protecting U.S. citizens against terrorism within the nation's borders.

Department of State Executive branch agency that is primarily responsible for most foreign policy programs within the executive branch, including diplomatic missions, foreign aid, and contributions to international organizations.

deregulation The elimination of government oversight and government regulation of certain activities.

devolution The transfer of power and responsibilities for certain regulatory programs from the federal government back to the states.

digital divide The large differences in usage of the Internet between older and younger people, lower- and middle-/upper-class people, lesser and better educated people, and minority groups and nonminority groups.

direct democracy A system of government in which all citizens participate in making policy, rules, and governing decisions.

direct primary election An open election, rather than an election by party leaders, to choose candidates for the general election.

direction (of public opinion) A tendency toward a particular preference, usually (though not always) characterized as either positive or negative.

discount rate The rate (expressed as a percentage) that all Federal Reserve member banks and other depository institutions will be charged by the Federal Reserve Banks to borrow short-term funds.

discovery A stage of pretrial litigation in which the plaintiff and defendant have the right to learn what information the other side has about the case by requesting documents or materials, access to property, and/or examinations, or by offering answers to questions about the litigation either in written form or verbally at a deposition.

discretionary spending Forms of federal government spending that Congress can modify or eliminate in any given year, including spending on education, the environment, and national defense.

dissenting opinion The opinion of one or more justices who disagree with the result reached by the majority.

distributive tax policies Taxation policies intended to promote the interests of all classes equally.

divided government Split-party control of Congress and the presidency.

domino theory The theory that held that communist takeovers of countries in Southeast Asia and elsewhere would be followed by subsequent communist takeovers of nearby countries.

double jeopardy clause The constitutional protection that those accused of a crime cannot be tried twice for the same crime.

dual federalism The doctrine of federalism that holds that state authority acts as a significant limit on congressional power under the Constitution.

due process model Criminal justice policymaking model that views the attainment of justice—which includes protection of the innocent—as the principal goal of the system.

E

economic equality May be defined as providing all groups the equality of opportunity for economic success, or as the equality of results. In the United States, the latter has been the more common understanding of economic equality.

economic interest group An organized group that exists to promote favorable economic conditions and economic opportunities for its members.

election The political mechanism that ensures that the majority will rule.

electoral college The constitutional mechanism by which presidents are chosen. Each state is allocated electoral college votes based on the sum of that state's U.S. senators and House members.

electors Individuals appointed to represent a state's presidential vote in the electoral college; in practice, voters in presidential elections vote for a slate of electors committed to a particular candidate, rather than voting directly for the candidate.

enumerated powers Express powers explicitly granted by the Constitution, such as the taxing power specifically granted to Congress.

equal time rule The FCC mandate that radio and TV broadcast stations offer equal amounts of airtime to all political candidates who want to broadcast advertisements.

establishment clause The clause in the First Amendment that prohibits government from enacting any law "respecting an establishment of religion." Separationist interpretations of this clause affirm that government should not support any religious activity. Accommodationists say that support for a religion is legal provided that all religions are equally supported.

ex post facto law A law that punishes someone for an act that took place in the past, at a time when the act was not illegal. The Constitution denies government the ability to write laws ex post facto.

exclusionary rule The legal rule requiring that all evidence illegally obtained by police in violation of the Bill of Rights must be "excluded" from admission in a court of law, where it might have assisted in convicting those accused of committing crimes.

executive agreement A pact reached between the president and a foreign government that does not require the consent of Congress.

Executive Office of the President The staffers who help the president of the United States manage the rest of the federal bureaucracy.

executive orders Rules or regulations issued by the chief executive that have the force of law and do not require the consent of Congress.

expansionism Doctrine that favors a country expanding its own territory and influence.

F

Federal Election Campaign Act (FECA) The federal legislation passed in 1971 that established disclosure requirements and restricted individual campaign contributions.

Federal Election Commission (FEC) The agency created in 1974 to enforce federal election laws.

Federal Register The journal that publishes regulations that implement federal programs.

Federal Reserve Board The Federal Reserve System's Board of Governors, which votes on monetary policy in the United States, supervises the nation's banks by setting rules for the 12 Federal Reserve Banks, and engages in open market operations.

Federal Reserve System The central banking system of the United States, which controls the nation's money supply.

federalism The doctrine underlying a system of government in which power is divided between a central government and constituent political subunits.

Federalist Papers A series of articles authored by Alexander Hamilton, James Madison, and John Jay that argued in favor of ratifying the proposed constitution of the United States; the Federalist Papers outlined the philosophy and motivation of the document.

Federalists Those who supported ratification of the proposed constitution of the United States between 1787 and 1789.

Fifteenth Amendment The amendment to the Constitution that guaranteed the franchise regardless of race, color, or previous condition of servitude.

filibuster The action by a single senator or a minority of senators to block a bill from passage by refusing to end discussion.

fiscal policy Decisions by the federal government that relate to raising revenue through taxation and spending the revenue that is thereby generated.

flat tax A tax policy that draws money from all entities at the same proportion of their income.

franchise The right to vote.

franking privilege The traditional right of members of Congress to mail materials to their constituents without paying postage.

free exercise clause The religious freedom clause in the First Amendment that denies government the ability to prohibit the free exercise of religion. Debate over the clause has largely focused on whether government laws can force adherents of a certain religion to engage in activities that are prohibited by their religious beliefs or prevent them from performing acts that are compelled by their religious beliefs.

free rider An individual who does not join or contribute to an interest group that is representing his or her interests.

frontloading The recent trend of states moving their primaries and caucuses to earlier in the year to attract greater attention from the candidates and the media.

full faith and credit clause The provision in Article IV, Section 1 of the Constitution that forces states to abide by the official acts and proceedings of all other states.

G

gerrymandering The drawing of House district boundaries to the benefit of one political party over another. The term is named for Elbridge Gerry, a Massachusetts delegate to the Constitutional Convention, who (as governor) redrew districts in this fashion to favor the Democratic-Republicans.

Gibbons v. Ogden (1824) The Supreme Court case that held that under the Constitution, a federal license to operate steamboats overrides a state-granted monopoly of New York water rights.

good faith exception An exception to the exclusionary rule stating that if a search warrant is invalid through no fault of the police, evidence obtained under that warrant may still be admitted into court.

government The collection of public institutions in a nation that establish and enforce the rules by which the members of that nation must live.

government corporations Units in the federal bureaucracy set up to run like private companies that depend on revenue from citizens to provide their services.

grand jury A jury whose duty it is to hear the evidence offered by a prosecutor and determine whether a trial is justified.

grants-in-aid Grants from the federal government to states that allow state governments to pursue specific federal policies, such as highway construction.

grassroots lobbying Communications by interest groups with government officials through the mobilization of public opinion to exert influence on government action.

Great Compromise A proposal also known as the "Connecticut Compromise" that provided for a bicameral legislature featuring an upper house based on equal representation among the states and a lower house whose membership was based on each state's population; approved by a 5–4 vote of the state delegations.

Great Society A set of aggressive federal domestic policies proposed by President Lyndon Johnson and passed by Congress in the 1960s that further enhanced the role of the presidency.

gross domestic product (GDP) An estimate of the total money value of all the goods and services produced in the United States in a one-year period.

H

hard money Donations made directly to political candidates and their campaigns that must be declared with the name of the donor (which then becomes public knowledge).

hawks Members of the president's administration who call for aggressive military actions wherever hostile forces may be found.

health maintenance organizations (HMOs) Prepaid group practice arrangements entered into by doctors and other health professionals that attempt to limit costs by charging customers flat monthly rates with little or no deductibles.

I

impeachment The first step in a two-step process outlined in Article II, Section 4, of the U.S. Constitution to remove a president or other high official from office. The House of Representatives, by majority vote, may impeach if the official has committed "Treason, Bribery, or other high Crimes and Misdemeanors." The second step requires a conviction in the Senate by a two-thirds vote.

incorporation The process by which the U.S. Supreme Court used the due process clause of the Fourteenth Amendment to make most of the individual rights guaranteed by the

Bill of Rights also applicable to the states. Incorporation provided that state and local governments, as well as the federal government, could not deny these rights to citizens.

incumbent race General election race pitting a person currently holding the office against a challenger.

independent agency A department that focuses on a narrower set of issues than do higher-status cabinet departments.

independent campaign expenditures Political donations that PACs or individuals spend to support campaigns but do not directly contribute to the campaigns.

indictment A decision by a grand jury authorizing the government to proceed to trial against the defendant.

individualism The value that individuals are primarily responsible for their own lot in life and that promotes and rewards individual initiative and responsibility. This value underlies America's reliance on a capitalist economy and free market system.

inflation The overall general upward price movement of goods and services in an economy, normally measured by the consumer price index (CPI).

intensity (of public opinion) The degree of strength or commitment the public feels about the opinion it holds.

interest group An organization of people with shared goals that tries to influence public policy through a variety of activities.

intergovernmental lobby Any interest group that represents the collective interests of states, cities, and other governments.

international organization Entity of international scope or character, usually established by treaty, such as the World Bank or the International Monetary Fund.

internationalism Doctrine that favors active participation of the nation in collective arrangements that secure the political independence and territorial boundaries of other countries.

invisible primary The competition among candidates seeking the party nomination for frontrunner status prior to the primaries and caucuses.

iron triangle A three-sided network of policymaking that includes congressional committees (and subcommittees) in a specific policy area, executive agencies with authority over that area, and private interest groups focused on influencing that area.

isolationism Foreign policy doctrine that opposes intervention in distant wars and involvement in permanent military alliances.

issue and ideological group An organized group that focuses on specific issues and ideological perspectives.

issue networks The broad array of actors (beyond just the iron triangle) that try to collectively influence a policy area in which they maintain a vested interest.

J

Jim Crow laws Laws used by some southern states that required segregation of nonwhites and whites in public schools, railroads, buses, restaurants, hotels, theaters, and other public facilities. The laws excluded nonwhites from militias and denied them certain education and welfare services.

Joint Chiefs of Staff (JCS) Group of chief officers of the four branches of the armed forces as well as a JCS chair and vice chair, which advises the president on military matters and delivers the president's orders to the military.

joint committee A committee composed of members of both the House and the Senate that is investigative in nature.

judicial review The power of a court to declare acts of the other branches of government or of a subordinate government to be unconstitutional and thus invalid.

K

***Katz* test** The legal standard that requires the government to attain a warrant demonstrating "probable cause" for any "search" that violates a person's actual and reasonable expectation of privacy.

Keynesian economic theory Fiscal policy theory that favors government taxation and spending during difficult economic times.

L

laissez-faire economics Fiscal policy theory that favors minimal intervention in the nation's economy.

layer-cake federalism Description of federalism as maintaining that the authority of state and federal governments exists in distinct and separate spheres.

legitimacy The extent to which the people afford the government the authority and right to exercise power.

***Lemon* test** The legal test that determines if a government statute aiding public or private schools is an unconstitutional violation of the establishment clause. The statute is unconstitutional if the statute has no secular purpose, if its principal or primary effect advances or inhibits religion, or if it fosters "an excessive government entanglement with religion."

libel Printing or disseminating false statements that harm someone.

liberal ideology A political orientation that favors a more assertive role in the redistribution of economic resources but emphasizes individual freedom on a range of social issues.

limited government The value that promotes the idea that government power should be as restricted as possible.

literacy test The requirement that individuals prove that they can read and write before being allowed to vote.

litigation Any judicial contest, including all the events that lead up to a possible court event.

lobbying The means by which interest groups attempt to influence government officials to make decisions favorable to their goals.

logrolling The trading of influence or votes among legislators to achieve passage of projects that are of interest to one another.

loose construction Constitutional interpretation that gives constitutional provisions broad and open-ended meanings.

M

majoritarianism The theory that public policy is a product of what majorities of citizens prefer.

majority caucus The members of the party that has the majority of seats in a particular chamber.

majority leader In the Senate, the controlling party's main spokesperson who leads his or her party in proposing new laws and crafting the party's platform. The Senate majority leader also enjoys the power to make committee assignments. In the House, the majority leader is the controlling party's second in command, who helps the Speaker to oversee the development of the party platform.

majority opinion The opinion of a majority of members of the U.S. Supreme Court, which carries the force of law.

majority rule The notion that the will of the majority should guide decisions made by American government.

majority-minority district A congressional district drawn with geographic boundaries that promote the chances of electing a minority member to represent that district.

mandatory spending Federal government spending that is not controlled by annual budget decisions; includes entitlements such as Medicare and Social Security.

manifest destiny U.S. policy of the mid-nineteenth century that advocated acquiring lands and occupying the entire American continent from one ocean to the other.

marble-cake federalism Description of federalism as intertwining state and federal authority in an inseparable mixture.

marginal seat A seat in a congressional district that has relatively similar numbers of Democratic and Republican voters.

Marshall Plan The U.S. policy that provided loans and aid to Western European countries whose economies had been ravaged by World War II.

Martin v. Hunter's Lessee **(1816)** The Supreme Court case that established that state governments and state courts must abide by the U.S. Supreme Court's interpretation of the federal Constitution.

material benefits (of group membership) The specific, tangible benefits individuals receive from interest-group membership, such as economic concessions, discounts on products, and so forth.

McCulloch v. Maryland **(1819)** The Supreme Court case that established that Congress enjoys broad and extensive authority to make all laws that are "necessary and proper" to carry out its constitutionally delegated powers.

Medicaid Federal program that provides limited health care services to the poor.

Medicare Federal program that provides health insurance for the elderly.

Mendez v. Westminster **(1947)** The federal court decision that ended the segregation of Mexican Americans in California primary schools.

merit system A system of appointing and promoting civil service personnel based on merit rather than political affiliation or loyalty.

midterm congressional elections Congressional elections held midway between successive presidential elections.

military-industrial complex The vast network of defense industries in America (including manufacturers of weapons, missiles, aircraft, and so forth) and their allies in the federal bureaucracy.

minimal effects theory The theory that deep-seated, long-term political attitudes have much greater influence on an individual's vote decisions than does news media coverage.

minority caucus The members of the party that has a minority of seats in a particular chamber.

minority leader The leader of the minority party in each chamber.

Miranda **warning** The U.S. Supreme Court's requirement that an individual who is arrested must be read a statement that explains the person's right to remain silent and the right to an attorney.

monarchy A form of government in which one person, usually a member of a royal family or a royal designate, exercises supreme authority.

monetary policy Regulation of the money supply and interest rates by a central bank, such as the U.S. Federal Reserve Board, in order to control inflation and stabilize the currency.

Monroe Doctrine U.S. foreign policy that proclaimed North and South America unavailable for future colonization by any European power and that declared that any such colonization would be viewed as an act of war on the United States.

Motor Voter law The federal law mandating that when an individual applies for or renews a state driver's license, the state must also provide that individual with voter registration materials.

multiparty system A political system in which many different parties are organized on the basis of political ideologies, economic interests, religion, geography, or positions on a single issue or set of issues.

N

national committee chair The head of the national committee for one of the two major parties.

national committee The committee that oversees the conduct of a party's presidential campaign and develops strategy for congressional elections.

national debt The total sum of the federal government's outstanding debt obligations.

national party convention A large meeting that draws together party delegates from across the nation to choose (or formally affirm the selection of) the party's presidential and vice presidential candidates.

national party organization The institution through which political parties exist at the national, state, and local levels, primarily focused on articulating policy positions, raising money, organizing volunteers, and providing services to candidates.

National Security Council (NSC) Advisory body to the president charged with coordinating information about foreign, military, and economic policies that affect national security.

national supremacy doctrine Chief Justice John Marshall's interpretation of federalism as holding that states have extremely limited sovereign authority, whereas Congress is supreme within its own sphere of constitutional authority.

natural law According to John Locke, the most fundamental type of law, which supersedes any law that is made by government. Citizens are born with certain natural rights (including life, liberty, and property) that derive from this law and that government cannot take away.

necessary and proper clause The clause in Article I, Section 8 of the Constitution that affords Congress the power to make laws that serve as a means to achieving its expressly delegated powers.

New Deal A set of aggressive federal domestic policies proposed by President Franklin Delano Roosevelt in the 1930s and passed by Congress as a response to the Great Depression; it ultimately transformed the presidency into an institution marked by permanent bureaucracies and well-established repositories of power.

New Jersey Plan A proposal known also as the "small states plan" that would have retained the Articles of Confederation's principle of a legislature where states enjoyed equal representation.

new media Media outlets that rely on relatively newer technologies for communicating, such as the Internet, DVDs, fax machines, cell phones, satellites, cable TV, and broadband.

new world order President George H. W. Bush's description of the post–Cold War world, in which nations would work together for the purpose of securing collective peace, security, freedom, and the rule of law.

Nineteenth Amendment The constitutional amendment that guarantees women equal voting rights.

nomination campaign The political season in which the two major parties hold primaries and caucuses in all the states to choose party delegates committed to specific candidates.

noneconomic interest group An organized group that advocates for reasons other than its membership's commercial and financial interests.

normal vote The percentage of voters that can be expected with reasonable certainty to cast a ballot for each of the two major political parties.

North Atlantic Treaty Organization (NATO) A military, political, and economic alliance of nations formally bound to protect self-determination and open trade in Western Europe.

O

objectivity The journalistic standard that news reporting of events must be factual, accurate, fair, and equitable.

oligarchy A form of government in which a small exclusive class, which may or may not attempt to rule on behalf of the people as a whole, holds supreme power.

open election General election race in which neither candidate is the incumbent. (Open elections for Congress are normally called *open-seat elections*.)

open market operations The buying and selling of government securities by the Federal Reserve Board as a means of controlling the national money supply.

open primary An election that allows voters to choose on the day of the primary election the party in which they want to vote.

open rule A rule of procedure adopted by the House Rules Committee that permits amendments to a bill.

open shop The law that allows employees the option of joining or not joining the certified union at a unionized workplace.

original jurisdiction The authority of a court to be the initial court in which a legal decision is rendered.

outlays The amount of money a government agency will actually spend during a fiscal year.

overriding (a veto) The power of the Congress to enact legislation despite a president's veto of that legislation; requires a two-thirds vote of both houses of Congress.

P

pacifism Doctrine of foreign relations that refuses to sanction any military conflict and that opposes all war making.

pardon The president's constitutional authority to relieve an individual of both the punishment and the guilt of violating the law.

partisan press era The period from the late 1700s to the mid-1800s when newspapers typically supported a particular political party.

party identification The psychological attachment that an individual has to a particular party.

party platform A document outlining the party's position on important policy issues.

Patient Protection and Affordable Care Act of 2010 (PPACA) The main federal legislation passed in 2010 that overhauled the health care system by expanding Medicaid and guaranteeing health care coverage for select groups of citizens.

patronage The act of appointing people to government positions in return for their partisan and/or political support.

Pendleton Civil Service Reform Act The law that created a merit system for hiring many federal workers, protected them from being fired for partisan reasons, and set up a Civil Service Commission to oversee the hiring and firing process.

plaintiff The party that chooses to initiate formal legal proceedings in a civil case.

plea bargain A pretrial negotiated resolution in a criminal case in which the defendants seek to reduce their jail sentences by pleading guilty and in return prosecutors are willing to trade down the severity of the punishment.

***Plessy v. Ferguson* (1896)** The Supreme Court case that upheld a Louisiana segregation law on the theory that as long as the accommodations between the racially segregated facilities were equal, the equal protection clause was not violated. The Court's ruling effectively established the constitutionality of racial segregation and the notion of "separate but equal."

pluralism The theory that public policy largely results from a variety of interest groups competing with one another to promote laws that benefit members of their respective groups.

pocket veto The indirect veto of a bill received by the president within days of the adjournment of Congress, effected by the president's retaining the bill unsigned until Congress adjourns.

policy implementation The process of carrying out laws, and the specific programs or services outlined in those laws.

political action committee (PAC) The political arm of an interest group that promotes candidates in election campaigns primarily through financial contributions.

political culture The values and beliefs about government, its purpose, and its operations and institutions that are widely held among citizens in a society; it defines the essence of how a society thinks politically and is transmitted from one generation to the next.

political equality A condition in which members of different groups possess substantially the same rights to participate actively in the political system. In the United States, these rights include voting, running for office, petitioning the government for redress of grievances, free speech, free press, and the access to an education.

political ideology A philosophical guide that people use to help translate their values and beliefs into political preferences.

political orientation The translation of values and beliefs into a systematic way of assessing the political environment.

political parties Organizations that seek to win elections for the purpose of influencing the outputs of government.

political preferences The attitudes people maintain regarding the performance of political leaders and institutions, their candidate preferences in elections, and specific policy issues.

political socialization The process by which an individual acquires values, beliefs, and opinions about politics.

politics The way in which the institutions of government are organized to make laws, rules, and policies, and how those institutions are influenced.

poll tax The requirement that individuals pay a fee before being allowed to vote.

popular sovereignty The idea that the ultimate source of power in the nation is held by the people.

pork-barrel legislation A government project or appropriation that yields jobs or other benefits to a specific locale and patronage opportunities to its political representative.

power of appointment The president's constitutional power to hire and fire those charged with administrative authority to help execute federal laws, such as ambassadors; federal judges, including those on the Supreme Court; and all other federal officers under the president's charge. Most of these appointments require the consent of the Senate.

power of incumbency The phenomenon by which incumbent members of Congress running for reelection are returned to office at an extremely high rate.

power The ability to get individuals to do something that they may not otherwise do, such as pay taxes, stop for red lights, or submit to a search before boarding an airplane.

preemption doctrine Doctrine of war making that reserves the right of the U.S. military to use advance strikes to stop rogue states from developing weapons of mass destruction.

preemption The constitutional doctrine that holds that when Congress acts affirmatively in the exercise of its own granted power, federal laws supersede all state laws on the matter.

prenomination campaign The political season in which candidates for president begin to explore the possibility of running by attempting to raise money and garner support.

president pro tempore In the absence of the vice president, the senator who presides over the Senate session. By tradition, this is usually the senator from the majority caucus who has served the longest number of consecutive years in the Senate.

presidential primary A statewide election to select delegates who will represent a state at the party's national convention.

primacy tendency The theory that impressions acquired while an individual is younger are likely to be more influential and longer lasting.

prior restraint The government's requirement that material be approved by government before it can be published.

privatization The process of replacing government-provided services with services provided by the private sector.

progressive tax A tax whose effective rate on an individual's income increases as the person's income rises.

proportional representation A system of electing a national legislature in which the percentage of the vote that a party receives is reflected in the number of seats that the party occupies.

pseudo-poll Phone calls from members of political campaigns or PACs who present themselves as pollsters for the purpose of planting messages with voters rather than measuring public opinion.

public opinion The summation of individual opinions on any particular issue or topic.

public opinion poll A method of measuring the opinions of a large group of people by asking questions of a subset of the larger group and then generalizing the findings to the larger group.

public policy The set of laws, regulations, and rules that affect the whole of society.

public-interest group An organized group that promotes the broad, collective good of citizens and consumers.

purposive benefits (of group membership) Rewards that do not directly benefit the individual member, but benefit society as a whole.

R

racial profiling The law enforcement practice of taking race into account when identifying possible suspects of crimes.

random-digit dialing (RDD) A probability technique for scientific telephone polling that randomly assigns the last four digits to known information about telephone area codes and exchanges.

realists Members of the president's administration who advocate diplomacy as the primary means of protecting U.S. interests abroad.

reapportionment The allocation of a fixed number of House seats to the states.

recession An economic slowdown characterized by high unemployment, reduced productivity, or other negative economic indicators.

redistributive tax policies Taxation policies that aim to provide a social safety net to meet the minimum physical needs of citizens.

redistricting The act of redrawing congressional boundaries to achieve equal representation in each of the congressional districts.

regressive tax A tax that charges individuals the same amount, regardless of income.

regulations Rules or other directives issued by government agencies.

regulatory agency A government body responsible for the control and supervision of a specified activity or area of public interest.

reporting legislation The exclusive power of standing committees to forward legislation to the full House or Senate. Neither chamber can vote on a bill unless the committee votes to approve it first.

representative democracy A form of government designed by the U.S. Constitution: Free, open, and regular elections allow voters to choose those who govern on their behalf; it is also referred to as *indirect democracy* or a *republican* form of government.

representative democracy System of government in which citizens elect the individuals who are responsible for making and enforcing public policy.

reprieve The president's constitutional authority to reduce the severity of a punishment without removing the guilt for those who have violated the law.

reserve requirement The minimum liquid assets each bank must keep on hand to back customer loans.

reserved powers Those powers expressly retained by the state governments under the Constitution.

retrospective voting A theory on voting behavior suggesting that voter evaluations of an incumbent's past performance provide important cues to voters in deciding whether to vote for that incumbent again.

Rules Committee A committee in the House of Representatives that determines the rules by which bills will come to the floor, be debated, and so on.

S

safe seat A congressional seat from a district that includes a high percentage of voters from one of the major parties.

sampling error The amount of error in a poll that results from interviewing a sample of people rather than the whole population under study; the larger the sample, the less the sampling error.

scientific sample A randomly selected subgroup drawn from a population using probability theory.

select committee A committee established by a resolution in either the House or the Senate for a specific purpose and, usually, for a limited time.

Senior Executive Service (SES) Since the late s, a defined group of approximately career professionals in the federal bureaucracy who provide continuity in the operations of the bureaucracy from one presidential administration to the next.

separation of powers The principle that each branch of government enjoys separate and independent powers and areas of responsibility.

Shays's Rebellion Armed uprising by debt-ridden Massachusetts farmers frustrated with the state government.

SLAPS test A standard that courts established to determine if material is obscene based in part on whether the material has serious literary, artistic, political, or scientific value. If it does, then the material is not obscene.

social capital The "social connectedness" of a community, or the extent to which individuals are socially integrated into their community.

social contract From the philosophy of Jean-Jacques Rousseau, an agreement people make with one another to form a government and abide by its rules and laws, and, in return, the government promises to protect the people's rights and welfare and promote their best interests.

social equality Equality and fair treatment of all groups within the various institutions in society, both public and private, that serve the public at large, including in stores, theaters, restaurants, hotels, and public transportation facilities, among many other operations open to the public.

social learning theory The theory that viewers imitate what they view on television through observational learning.

social movement A large informal grouping of individuals and/or organizations focused on specific political or social issues.

social policy Rules, regulations, and policymaking pertaining to the quality of life, welfare, and relations of human beings in the United States.

socialism Economic system in which all or most of the means of production are owned by the community as a whole.

soft money Money not donated directly to a candidate's campaign, but rather to a political advocacy group or a political party for "party-building" activities.

solicitor general The lawyer representing the U.S. government before the U.S. Supreme Court.

solidary benefits (of group membership) Satisfaction that individuals receive from interacting with like-minded individuals for a cause.

South Dakota v. Dole **(1987)** The Supreme Court case that allowed Congress to coerce state governments to pass state laws by conditioning grants to those states, so long as the requirements are related to the overall spending in question.

sovereignty The supreme political power of a government to regulate its affairs without outside interference.

Speaker of the House The leader of the House of Representatives, responsible for assigning new bills to committees, recognizing members to speak in the House chamber, and assigning chairs of committees.

spoils system The postelection practice of rewarding loyal supporters of the winning candidates and party with appointive public offices.

standing committee A permanent committee that exists in both the House and Senate; most standing committees focus on a particular substantive area of public policy, such as transportation, labor, foreign affairs, and the federal budget.

standing The requirement that a party must be uniquely or singularly affected by a controversy in order to be eligible to file a lawsuit.

State of the Union address An annual speech that the president delivers to Congress laying out the status of the nation and offering suggestions for new legislation.

Strategic Defense Initiative (SDI) A theoretical antimissile system based on the use of lasers and particle beams to shoot down Soviet nuclear missiles in outer space.

straw poll An unscientific poll that gathers the opinions of people who are conveniently available in a gathering place, such as a shopping center.

strict construction Constitutional interpretation that limits the government to only those powers explicitly stated in the Constitution.

strict scrutiny A legal standard set in *Brown v. Board of Education* for cases related to racial discrimination that tends to invalidate almost all state laws that segregate racial groups.

supply-side economics Economic theory that favors cutting taxes as a way of increasing economic productivity.

supremacy clause The provision in Article VI, Clause 2 of the Constitution that provides that the Constitution and federal laws override any conflicting provisions in state constitutions or state laws.

symbolic speech Nonspoken forms of speech that might be protected by the First Amendment, such as flag burning, wearing armbands at school to protest a war, or camping out in public parks to protest the plight of the homeless.

T

talk radio A specialized form of radio programming in which one or more hosts provide commentary and often invite listeners to call in to the show and offer their own opinions.

theocracy A form of government in which a particular religion or faith plays a dominant role in the government.

Three-Fifths Compromise A compromise proposal in which five slaves would be counted as the equivalent of three free people for purposes of taxes and representation.

Title IX The section of the Federal Educational Amendments Law of that prohibits the exclusion of women from an educational program or activity receiving financial assistance from the federal government. Courts have interpreted those provisions to force colleges and universities to provide as many athletic teams for women as they do for men.

trade association A business association that focuses on one particular industry, with membership drawn exclusively from that industry.

Truman Doctrine Doctrine articulated by President Harry Truman in the late s by which money and resources were provided to support and sustain noncommunist governments in areas strategically vital to the United States.

Twenty-fourth Amendment A constitutional amendment that banned poll taxes in federal elections.

Twenty-fourth Amendment The constitutional amendment that outlaws poll taxes.

Twenty-second Amendment Passed in , this constitutional amendment restricts any one person from being elected to the presidency "more than twice," or from acting as president for longer than two and a half terms.

Twenty-sixth Amendment The constitutional amendment that lowered the voting age to in all local, state, and federal elections.

Twenty-third Amendment The constitutional amendment providing electoral votes to the District of Columbia, thus giving District residents the right to vote in presidential elections.

Two Presidencies Theory Theory articulated by political scientist Aaron Wildavsky that posits the existence of a more powerful presidency in foreign affairs and a more limited presidency in the domestic sphere.

two-party system A party system dominated by two major parties that win the vast majority of elections.

U

union shop The law that requires that employees in unionized workplaces either join the union or pay the equivalent of union dues to it after a set period of time.

unit rule The system in states by which the candidate who wins the most votes among popular votes cast for president in a state receives all the electoral votes from that state; also known as the "winner-take-all" system.

unitary system of government A system of government in which the constituent states are strictly subordinated to the goals of the central government as a whole.

United Nations (UN) International organization formed after World War II to promote and maintain international security and peace.

universal health care National health care system in which full access to health care is provided to citizens at government expense.

universal suffrage The idea that all citizens in a nation have the right to vote.

unscientific poll A poll in which the sample of people interviewed is not representative of any group beyond those who register their opinion.

V

values and beliefs The broad principles underlying the American political culture that citizens support and adhere to.

veto The constitutional procedure by which the president refuses to approve a bill or joint resolution and thus prevents its enactment into law.

Virginia Plan A proposal known also as the "large states plan" that empowered three separate branches of government, including a legislature with membership proportional to population.

voter turnout The number of people who turn out to vote as a percentage of all those eligible to vote.

Voting Rights Act of 1965 The federal law that invalidated literacy tests and property requirements and required select states and cities to apply for permission to the Justice Department to change their voting laws. As a consequence, millions of African Americans were effectively reenfranchised in the South.

W

War Powers Resolution Largely ignored congressional policy that restricts the president's power to engage in war except (1) when Congress has declared war, (2) when Congress has specifically granted the president permission to use armed forces, or (3) when the nation is under attack. The resolution further requires the president to report to Congress whenever American forces are entered into hostilities.

warrant A document issued by a judge or magistrate that allows law enforcement to search or seize items at a home, business, or anywhere else that might be specified.

Warsaw Pact Formal alliance of nations within the Soviet sphere during the Cold War.

welfare state Social system in which the state assumes a considerable degree of responsibility for citizens in matters of health care, employment, education, and retirement income.

whip (majority and minority) Member of Congress elected by his or her party to count potential votes and promote party unity in voting.

White House chief of staff The manager of the White House staff, which serves the president's organizational needs, including speechwriting, advance work for presidential appearances, scheduling, congressional relations, public relations, and communications.

White House Office of Legislative Affairs A presidential office that serves as a liaison between the president and Congress. This office helps the president develop the strategy used to promote passage of the president's legislative agenda.

White House press secretary The person on the White House staff who plays an especially important role in briefing the press, organizing news conferences, and even briefing the president on questions that may be asked.

writ of certiorari The formal term for an order by which the Supreme Court acts in its discretion to review a case from a lower court.

NOTES

CHAPTER 1

1. www.people-press.org/2015/04/30/a-different-look-at-generations-and-partisanship/

2. See Thomas Hobbes, *Leviathan* (London: A. Crooke, 1651).

3. For a collection of Rousseau's work, see Jean-Jacques Rousseau, *The Social Contract and Discourses*, translation and commentary by G. D. H. Cole (London: Guernsey Press, 1983).

4. Harold Lasswell, *Politics: Who Gets What, When and How* (New York: McGraw-Hill, 1936).

5. John Locke, *Two Treatises of Government*, ed. Peter Laslett (Cambridge: Cambridge University Press, 1960).

6. Alexis de Tocqueville, *Democracy in America*, 1835, ed. Richard Hefner (New York: Penguin Books, 1956).

7. Elwell, Craig K.; Labonte, Marc; and Morrison, Wayne M. 2007. "Is China a Threat to the U.S. Economy?" *Congressional Research Service Report for Congress*, January 23. Available at www.fas.org/sgp/crs/row/RL33604.pdf.

8. Ruchir Sharma. 2012. "China Slows Down, and Grows Up." *The New York Times*, April 26.

CHAPTER 2

1. Fred Anderson, *The War That Made America: A Short History of the French-Indian War* (New York: Viking, 2005).

2. Robert Middlekauff, *The Glorious Cause* (New York: Oxford University Press, 1982).

3. *The Political Writings of Thomas Paine, Vol. 1* (Boston: J. P. Mendum Investigator Office, 1870).

4. David McCullough, *John Adams* (New York: Simon & Schuster, 2001), 119; Joseph Ellis, *Founding Brothers* (New York: Knopf, 2000), 212–213.

5. Pauline Maier, *American Scripture: Making the Declaration of Independence* (New York: Vintage, 1998).

6. Merrill Jensen, *The Articles of Confederation: An Interpretation of the Social-Constitutional History of the American Revolution, 1774–1781* (Madison: University of Wisconsin Press, 1959).

7. For an account of Massachusetts public policy during this period, see Van Beck Hall, *Politics Without Parties: Massachusetts 1780–1791* (Pittsburgh: University of Pittsburgh Press, 1972).

8. Robert Gross, ed., *In Debt to Shays* (Charlottesville: University of Virginia Press, 1993).

9. Christopher Collier, *Decision in Philadelphia: The Constitutional Convention of 1787* (New York: Ballantine Books, 2007).

10. For a discussion of the Founders' silence on slavery, see Joseph Ellis, *Founding Brothers* (New York: Knopf, 2000), 81–119.

11. Jacob E. Cooke, ed., *The Federalist* (Middletown, CT: Wesleyan University Press, 1961).

12. Saul Cornell, *The Other Founders: Anti-Federalism and the Dissenting Tradition in America 1788–1828* (Chapel Hill: University of North Carolina Press, 1999).

13. Henry Mayer, *A Son of Thunder: Patrick Henry and the American Republic* (Charlottesville: University of Virginia Press, 1992).

14. Paul Murphy, *The Historic Background of the Bill of Rights* (New York: Taylor & Francis, 1990).

15. See Jefferson–Madison correspondence republished in Philip Kurland, ed., *The Founders' Constitution* (Indianapolis: Liberty Fund, 2000).

16. There may be numerous legal problems implicated by the holding of such a convention, as noted in Russell Caplan, *Constitutional Brinksmanship: Amending the Constitution by National Convention* (New York: Oxford University Press, 1988). See also John R. Vile, *The Alternate Article V Mechanism for Proposing Amendments to the U.S. Constitution* (Athens: University of Georgia Press, 2016).

17. One of the better works on Marshall's tenure at the Court is R. Kent Newmyer, *John Marshall and the Heroic Age of the Supreme Court* (Baton Rouge: Louisiana State University Press, 2002).

18. 17 U.S. 316 (1819).

19. Robert Bork, *The Tempting of America* (New York: Simon & Schuster, 1990).

20. Justice Antonin Scalia, interview with 60 Minutes (episode aired April 27, 2008), www.cbsnews.com/news/justice-scalia-on-the-record/.

21. Lawrence Tribe, *Constitutional Choices* (Cambridge, MA: Harvard University Press, 2004).

22. John Hart Ely, *Democracy and Distrust* (Cambridge, MA: Harvard University Press, 1980).

23. 5 U.S. 137 (1803).

24. Obergefell v. Hodges, 576 U.S. _____ (2015).

Chapter 3

1. Stanley R. Sloan, *NATO, The European Union and the Atlantic Community: The Transatlantic Bargain Reconsidered* (New York: Rowman & Littlefield, 2002).

2. See McCulloch v. Maryland, 17 U.S. 316 (1819).

3. 14 U.S. 304 (1816).

4. 576 U.S. _____, 135 S. CT. 2584 (2015).

5. For example, in Supreme Court of New Hampshire v. Piper, 470 U.S. 274 (1985), the Supreme Court interpreted the privileges and immunities clause of Article IV to forbid states from excluding nonresidents from admission to the practice of law.

6. See New Jersey v. New York, 523 U.S. 767 (1998).

7. Stanley Elkins and Eric McKitrick, *The Age of Federalism: The Early American Republic 1788–1800* (New York: Oxford University Press, 1995).

8. 17 U.S. 316 (1819).

9. 22 U.S. 1 (1824).

10. Gideon v. Wainwright, 372 U.S. 335 (1963).

11. McDonald v. Chicago, 561 U.S. 742 (2010).

12. H. W. Brands, *Andrew Jackson: His Life and Times* (New York: Doubleday, 2005).

13. Railroad Retirement Board v. Alton Railroad Co., 295 U.S. 330 (1935); Carter v. Carter Coal Co., 298 U.S. 238 (1936).

14. William E. Leuchtenburg, *The Supreme Court Reborn: The Constitutional Revolution in the Age of Roosevelt* (New York: Oxford University Press, 1995).

15. Heart of Atlanta Motel v. United States, 379 U.S. 241 (1964); Katzenbach v. McClung, 379 U.S. 294 (1964).

16. 483 U.S. 203 (1987).

17. For an application of the term to welfare policy, see Pamela Winston, *Welfare Policymaking in the States: The Devil in Devolution* (Washington, DC: Georgetown University Press, 2002).

18. David Savage, *Turning Right: The Making of the Rehnquist Supreme Court* (New York: Wiley, 1993).

19. 514 U.S. 549 (1995).

20. 529 U.S. 598 (2000).

21. National Federation of Independent Business v. Sebelius, 567 U.S. _____, 132 S. CT. 2566 (2012).

22. John T. Noonan Jr., *Narrowing the Nation's Power: The Supreme Court Sides with the States* (Berkeley: University of California Press, 2003).

23. New State Ice Co. v. Liebmann, 285 U.S. 262, 311 (1932).

24. Gonzales v. Raich, 545 U.S. 1 (2005).

25. See www.census.gov/hhes/www/income/data/statemedian/.

Chapter 4

1. Antonin Scalia, "Law and the Winds of Change." Remarks made at the 24th Australian Legal Convention, Perth, West Australia, September 21, 1987.

2. Alexander Hamilton, James Madison, and John Jay, *The Federalist Papers*, ed. Clinton Rossiter (New York: New American Library, 1971).

3. Jefferson–Madison correspondence in Philip Kurland, ed., *The Founders' Constitution* (Indianapolis: Liberty Fund, 2000).

4. 32 U.S. 243 (1833).

5. Thomas Jefferson first coined that phrase in a letter he wrote as president to the Baptists of Danbury, Connecticut, in 1802. George Seldes, ed., *The Great Quotations* (Secaucus, NJ: Citadel Press, 1983), 369.

6. 319 U.S. 624 (1943).

7. 374 U.S. 398 (1963).

8. 406 U.S. 205 (1972).

9. 98 U.S. 145 (1878).

10. 494 U.S. 872 (1990).

11. Carolyn N. Long, *Religious Freedom and Indian Rights: The Case of Oregon v. Smith* (Lawrence: University Press of Kansas, 2000).

12. 482 U.S. 578 (1987).

13. Noah Feldman, *Divided by God* (New York: Farrar, Straus and Giroux, 2005).

14. 370 U.S. 421 (1962).

15. 374 U.S. 203 (1963).

16. 472 U.S. 38 (1985).

17. 536 U.S. 639 (2002).

18. 403 U.S. 602 (1971).

19. 505 U.S. 577 (1992).

20. 530 U.S. 290 (2000).

21. 249 U.S. 247 (1919).

22. 341 U.S. 494 (1951).

23. 304 U.S. 144 (1938).

24. 395 U.S. 444 (1969).

25. Harry Kalven, *A Worthy Tradition: Freedom of Speech in America* (New York: Harper & Row, 1988).

26. 376 U.S. 254 (1964).

27. Anthony Lewis, *Make No Law: The Sullivan Case and the First Amendment* (New York: Vintage Books, 1992).

28. 403 U.S. 713 (1971).

29. 413 U.S. 15 (1973).

30. 521 U.S. 844 (1997).

31. John W. Johnson, *The Struggle for Students' Rights: Tinker v. Des Moines and the 1960s* (Lawrence: University Press of Kansas, 1997).

32. Tinker v. Des Moines, 393 U.S. 503 (1969).

33. 391 U.S. 367 (1968).

34. 491 U.S. 397 (1989).

35. Robert Justin Goldstein, *Flag Burning and Free Speech: The Case of Texas v. Johnson* (Lawrence: University Press of Kansas, 2000).

36. Philippa Strum, *When the Nazis Came to Skokie: Freedom for Speech We Hate* (Lawrence: University Press of Kansas, 1999).

37. 528 U.S. 343 (2003).

38. Milton Heumann and Thomas W. Church, eds., *Hate Speech on Campus* (Boston: Northeastern University Press, 1997).

39. 554 U.S. 570 (2008).

40. 561 U.S. 742 (2010).

41. Lucas A. Powe Jr., *The Warren Court and American Politics* (Cambridge, MA: Belknap Press of Harvard University, 2002).

42. 389 U.S. 347 (1967).

43. 367 U.S. 643 (1961).

44. Kyllo v. United States, 533 U.S. 27 (2001).

45. It should be noted, however, that a majority of states have chosen to use grand juries, even without being compelled to do so by the U.S. Constitution.

46. 384 U.S. 436 (1966).

47. California v. Ciraolo, 476 U.S. 207 (1986).

48. U.S. v. Jones, 565 U.S. _____ 132 S. CT. 945 (2012).

49. Dickerson v. United States, 530 U.S. 428 (2000).

50. Gary Stuart, *Miranda: The Story of America's Right to Remain Silent* (Tucson: University of Arizona Press, 2004).

51. 372 U.S. 335 (1963).

52. Whole Woman's Health v. Hellerstedt, 579 U.S. _____ (2016).

53. 536 U.S. 304 (2002).

54. Austin Sarat, *When the State Kills* (Princeton, NJ: Princeton University Press, 2002).

55. 381 U.S. 479 (1965).

56. John W. Johnson, *Griswold v. Connecticut: Birth Control and the Constitutional Right of Privacy* (Lawrence: University Press of Kansas, 2005).

57. 410 U.S. 113 (1973).

58. N. E. H. Hull and Peter Charles Hoffer, *Roe v. Wade: The Abortion Rights Controversy in American History* (Lawrence: University Press of Kansas, 2001).

59. 505 U.S. 833 (1992).

60. 550 U.S. 124 (2007).

61. 539 U.S. 558 (2003).

CHAPTER 5

1. Such FBI arrest data are maintained by the Bureau of Justice Statistics (see www.ojjdp.gov/ojstatbb/ezaucr/asp/ucr_display.asp).

2. Louis R. Harlan, *Booker T. Washington: The Making of a Black Leader* (New York: Oxford University Press, 1975).

3. David Levering Lewis, *W. E. B. DuBois, 1868–1919: Biography of a Race* (New York: Owl Books, 1994).

4. 347 U.S. 483 (1954).

5. 60 U.S. 393 (1857).

6. Eric Foner, *Reconstruction: America's Unfinished Revolution* (New York: Harper, 2000).

7. 83 U.S. 36 (1873).

8. 109 U.S. 3 (1883).

9. 163 U.S. 537 (1896).

10. For a comprehensive account of the NAACP's strategy, see Richard Kluger, *Simple Justice* (New York: Vintage Books, 1975).

11. 161 F.2d 774 (9th Cir. 1947).

12. 358 U.S. 1 (1958).

13. Jennifer Hochschild, *The New American Dilemma: Liberal Democracy and School Desegregation* (New Haven, CT: Yale University Press, 1984).

14. 347 U.S. 475 (1954).

15. See Taylor Branch, *Pillar of Fire: America in the King Years, 1963–65* (New York: Simon & Schuster, 1999).

16. For two excellent accounts of the passage of the Civil Rights Act of 1964, see Todd Purdum, *An Idea Whose Time Has Come* (New York: Henry Holt & Co., 2014); Clay Risen, *The Bill of the Century: The Epic Battle for the Civil Rights Act* (New York: Bloomsbury, 2014).

17. www.ncsl.org/research/elections-and-campaigns/voter-id.aspx.

18. 208 U.S. 412 (1908).

19. 335 U.S. 464 (1948).

20. 368 U.S. 57, 61 (1961).

21. 404 U.S. 71 (1971).

22. 411 U.S. 677 (1973).

23. 429 U.S. 190 (1976).

24. www.businessweek.com/articles/2012-06-21/ equal-pay-plaintiffs-burden-of-proof.

25. Robert Jackson and Meredith Newman, "Sexual Harassment in the Federal Workplace Revisited: Influences on Sexual Harassment by Gender," *Public Administration Review* 64 (2004): 705–17.

26. 517 U.S. 620 (1996).

27. 539 U.S. 558 (2003).

28. 135 S. Ct. 2584 (2015).

29. 438 U.S. 265 (1978).

30. Howard Ball, *The Bakke Case: Race, Education and Affirmative Action* (Lawrence: University Press of Kansas, 2000).

31. 515 U.S. 200 (1995).

32. 539 U.S. 306 (2003).

33. 539 U.S. 244 (2003).

34. Michael Jones and Eileen Poe-Yamagata, *And Justice for Some* (Washington, DC: Building Blocks for Youth Press, 2000).

CHAPTER 6

1. Woodrow Wilson, *Congressional Government* (Baltimore: Johns Hopkins University Press, 1981; originally published in 1885).

2. www.WhoLeads.us.

3. For a good discussion of the Constitutional Convention and issues related to Congress, see Charles Stewart III, "Congress and the Constitutional System," in *Institutions of American Democracy: The Legislative Branch*, eds. Paul J. Quirk and Sarah A. Binder (New York: Oxford University Press, 2005).

4. Alexander Hamilton, James Madison, and John Jay, *The Federalist Papers* (Chicago: The New American Library of World Literature; reprinted in 1961).

5. Thomas Mann, *Unsafe at Any Margin: Interpreting Congressional Elections* (Washington, DC: Brookings Institution Press, 1978).

6. Paul Finkelman and Peter Wallenstein, *The Encyclopedia of American Political History* (Washington, DC: CQ Press, 2001), 55–56.

7. See, for example, *Baker v. Carr*, 369 U.S. 186 (1962); *Reynolds v. Sims*, 377 U.S. 533 (1964); *Wesberry v. Sanders*, 376 U.S. 1 (1964).

8. See James Madison, Federalist No. 63.

9. For a discussion of leadership in Congress, see Burdett A. Loomis, *The Contemporary Congress*, 3rd ed. (Boston: Bedford St. Martin's, 2000), chapter 6.

10. See Eric Schickler, "Institutional Development of Congress," in *Institutions of American Democracy: The Legislative Branch*, eds. Paul J. Quirk and Sarah A. Binder (New York: Oxford University Press, 2005), chapter 2.

11. A classic work on congressional committees is Richard F. Fenno Jr., *Congressmen in Committees* (Boston: Little, Brown, 1973).

12. See Stephen S. Smith and Christopher Deering, *Committees in Congress*, 2nd ed. (Washington, DC: CQ Press, 1990).

13. See Scott A. Frisch and Sean Q. Kelly, *Committee Assignment Politics in the U.S. House of Representatives* (Norman, OK: University of Oklahoma Press, 2006).

14. See John Manley, "Wilbur Mills: A Study of Congressional Influence," *American Political Science Review* 63 (1969): 442–64.

15. Chris Cillizza, "The Least Productive Congress Ever," *The Washington Post*, July 17, 2013.

16. Eric Redman, *The Dance of Legislation* (Seattle: University of Washington Press, 1974).

17. For a discussion of the motivations for senators to filibuster, see Sarah A. Binder and Stephen S. Smith, *Politics or Principles? Filibustering in the United States Senate* (Washington, DC: Brookings Institution Press, 1997).

18. Morris P. Fiorina, *Congress: Keystone of the Washington Establishment*, 2nd ed. (New Haven, CT: Yale University Press, 1989).

19. For an excellent discussion of the executive appointment process, see David E. Lewis, *The Politics of Presidential Appointments: Political Control and Bureaucratic Performance* (Princeton, NJ: Princeton University Press, 2008).

20. 462 U.S. 919 (1983).

21. Richard F. Fenno Jr., *Home Style: House Members in Their Districts* (Boston: Little, Brown, 1978).

CHAPTER 7

1. www.gallup.com/poll/183713/socialist-presidential-candidates-least-appealing.aspx?utm_source=Politics&utm_medium=newsfeed&utm_campaign=tiles.

2. Joseph Ellis, *His Excellency: George Washington* (New York: Knopf, 2004).

3. Dates provided after a president's name refer to year(s) of service as president of the United States.

4. H. W. Brands, *Andrew Jackson: His Life and Times* (New York: Random House, 2005).

5. John Seigenthaler, *James K. Polk, 1845–1849* (New York: Times Books, 2003).

6. See *Ex Parte Merryman*, 17 Fed. Cas. 144 (1961).

7. Edmund Morris, *Theodore Rex* (New York: Random House, 2001).

8. See Clinton Rossiter, *The American Presidency* (Baltimore: Johns Hopkins University Press, 1987).

9. See John Locke, *Two Treatises of Government and a Letter Concerning Toleration*, ed. Peter Laslett (Cambridge: Cambridge University Press, 1963).

10. Baron de Montesquieu, *The Spirit of the Laws*, eds. Anne M. Cohler et al. (Cambridge: Cambridge University Press, 1989).

11. Michael J. Gerhardt, *The Federal Appointments Process: A Constitutional and Historical Analysis* (Durham, NC: Duke University Press, 2003).

12. 272 U.S. 52 (1926).

13. Robert F. Kennedy Jr., *Thirteen Days: A Memoir of the Cuban Missile Crisis* (New York: W. W. Norton, 1999).

14. Mark Peterson, *Legislating Together: The White House and Capitol Hill from Eisenhower to Reagan* (Cambridge, MA: Harvard University Press, 1990).

15. Paul Light, *The President's Agenda: Domestic Policy Choice from Kennedy to Clinton* (Baltimore: Johns Hopkins University Press, 1999).

16. Lee Hamilton and Jordan Tama, *A Creative Tension: The Foreign Policy Roles of the President and Congress* (Washington, DC: Woodrow Wilson Press, 2003).

17. Kenneth Mayer, *With the Stroke of a Pen: Executive Orders and Presidential Power* (Princeton, NJ: Princeton University Press, 2001).

18. United States v. Texas, 579 U.S. _____ (2016).

19. The most recent version of this work is Richard Neustadt, *Presidential Power and the Modern Presidents: The Politics of Leadership from Roosevelt Through Reagan* (New York: Free Press, 1991).

20. Jules Witcover, *Crapshoot: Rolling the Dice on the Vice Presidency* (New York: Crown, 1991).

21. Bob Woodward, *Plan of Attack* (New York: Simon & Schuster, 2004).

22. For a comprehensive discussion of the various ways that modern presidents have organized the White House, see Stephen Hess, *Organizing the Presidency* (Washington, DC: Brookings Institution Press, 1988).

23. Bill Adler, *America's First Ladies* (New York: Taylor, 2002).

24. Samuel Kernell, *Going Public: New Strategies of Presidential Leadership* (Washington, DC: CQ Press, 1992).

25. Elizabeth Drew, *On the Edge: The Clinton Presidency* (New York: Touchstone, 1995).

26. See Kathleen Hall Jamieson and Paul Waldman, *The Press Effect: Politicians, Journalists, and the Stories That Shape the Political World* (New York: Oxford University Press, 2002).

27. John A. Maltese, *Spin Control: The White House Office of Communications and the Management of Presidential News* (Chapel Hill: University of North Carolina Press, 1992).

28. Ted Rueter, *The 267 Stupidest Things Republicans Ever Said/The 267 Stupidest Things Democrats Ever Said* (New York: Three Rivers Press, 2000).

Chapter 8

1. See *Washington Monthly*, a periodical that regularly reports on the excesses and waste in the federal bureaucracy.

2. For a comprehensive discussion of the virtues of modern bureaucracy, see Charles T. Goodsell, *The Case for Bureaucracy* (Chatham, NJ: Chatham House Publishers, 1994).

3. Max Weber, chapters 11 and 12 in *Economy and Society*, eds. Guenther Roth and Claus Wittich (New York: Bedminster Press, 1968).

4. For a good discussion of organizational issues in the federal bureaucracy, see James Q. Wilson, *Bureaucracy: What Government Agencies Do and Why They Do It* (New York: Basic Books, 1989).

5. See Joel Aberbach, *Keeping a Watchful Eye: The Politics of Congressional Oversight* (Washington, DC: Brookings Institution Press, 1990).

6. Beverly Cigler, "The Paradox of Professionalization," in *Democracy, Bureaucracy and the Study of Administration*, ed. Camilla Stivers (Boulder, CO: Westview Press, 2001).

7. For a good discussion of the growth of the federal bureaucracy during the New Deal era, see Brian J. Cook, "Serving the Liberal State," chapter 5 in *Bureaucracy and Self-Government: Reconsidering the Role of Public Administration in American Politics* (Baltimore: Johns Hopkins University Press, 1996).

8. David Osborne and Ted Gaebler, *Reinventing Government: How the Entrepreneurial Spirit Is Transforming the Public Sector* (New York: Penguin Books, 1993).

9. Harold S. Stanley and Richard G. Niemi, *Vital Statistics on American Politics, 2005–2006* (Washington, DC: CQ Press, 2006), 266.

10. Robert H. Wiebe, *The Search for Order: 1877–1920* (New York: Hill and Wang, 1967).

11. www.washingtonpost.com/politics/obama-ups-diversity-in-appointees/2015/09/20/5b042aac-5ffb-11e5-8e9e-dce8a2a2a679_graphic.html.

12. www.washingtonpost.com/politics/obama-has-vastly-changed-the-face-of-the-federal-bureau-cracy/2015/09/20/73ef803a-5631-11e5-abe9-27d53f250b11_story.html.

13. Data from the U.S. Bureau of Labor Statistics website, www.bls.gov/oco/cg/cgs041.htm.

14. www.ushistory.org/gov/8c.asp.

15. See Ari Hoogenboom, *Outlawing the Spoils: A History of the Civil Service Reform Movement, 1865–1883* (Champaign: University of Illinois Press, 1961).

CHAPTER 9

1. For an account of the ways in which the Supreme Court's methods contribute to its image and status as an institution, see John Brigham, *The Cult of the Court* (Philadelphia: Temple University Press, 1987).

2. John Merryman, *The Civil Law Tradition* (Palo Alto, CA: Stanford University Press, 1985).

3. G. Alan Tarr and Mary Cornelius Porter, *State Supreme Courts in State and Nation* (New Haven, CT: Yale University Press, 1988).

4. 5 U.S. 137 (1803).

5. Arthur Hellman, *Restructuring Justice: The Innovations of the Ninth Circuit and the Future of the Federal Courts* (Ithaca, NY: Cornell University Press, 1991).

6. One rare exception to the strict use of the adversarial approach in the American legal system comes in the form of "structural reform litigation," a term that describes certain types of lawsuits brought against bureaucracies such as prisons, school systems, or welfare systems. Judges in these types of cases often assume a more active managerial approach in the process, overseeing the implementation of remedies and occasionally taking a proactive role to ensure that the lawyers are properly representing their clients' interests. For comprehensive analysis of one example of structural reform litigation in action, see Malcolm Feeley and Edward Rubin, *Judicial Policymaking and the Modern State: How the Court Reformed America's Prisons* (Cambridge: Cambridge University Press, 2000). Of course, the more traditional adversarial system still tends to predominate in most other forms of civil litigation.

7. See George Fisher, *Plea Bargaining's Triumph: A History of Plea Bargaining in America* (Palo Alto, CA: Stanford University Press, 2003); Milton Heumann, *Plea Bargaining: The Experiences of Prosecutors, Judges, and Defense Attorneys* (Chicago: University of Chicago Press, 1981).

8. James Eisenstein, Roy Flemming, and Peter Nardulli, *The Contours of Justice* (New York: Addison-Wesley Publishing, 1988).

9. For an excellent analysis of the case, see R. Kent Newmyer, *The Supreme Court Under Marshall and Taney* (Arlington Heights, IL: Harlan Davison, 1968).

10. 17 U.S. 316 (1819).

11. 1 Wheat (14 U.S.) 304 (1816).

12. 358 U.S. 1 (1958).

13. 60 U.S. 393 (1857).

14. 347 U.S. 483 (1954).

15. 418 U.S. 683 (1974).

16. 506 U.S. 224 (1993).

17. 6 Pet. (31 U.S.) 515 (1832).

18. See Bob Woodward and Carl Bernstein, *The Final Days* (New York: Simon & Schuster, 1975).

19. Bradley Canon and Charles Johnson, *Judicial Policies: Implementation and Impact*, 2nd ed. (Washington, DC: CQ Press, 1999).

20. 347 U.S. 483 (1954).

21. 370 U.S. 421 (1962).

22. Robert Dahl, "Decision-Making in a Democracy: The Supreme Court as a National Policy-Maker," *Journal of Public Law* 6 (1957): 279–295.

23. Philip DuBois, *From Ballot to Bench: Judicial Elections and the Quest for Accountability* (Austin: University of Texas Press, 1980).

24. Sheldon Goldman, *Picking Federal Judges* (New Haven, CT: Yale University Press, 1997).

25. Barbara Perry, *A Representative Supreme Court* (Westport, CT: Greenwood Press, 1991).

26. www.americanbar.org/diversity.html.

27. www.brennancenter.org/publication/improving-judicial-diversity.

28. John Maltese, *The Selling of Supreme Court Nominees* (Baltimore: Johns Hopkins University Press, 1995).

29. Richard Davis, *Justices and Journalists: The U.S. Supreme Court and the Media* (Cambridge: Cambridge University Press, 2011), 100.

30. Ethan Bronner, *Battle for Justice: How the Bork Nomination Shook America* (New York: W. W. Norton, 1989).

31. 410 U.S. 113 (1973).

32. Richard Pacelle, *Between Law and Politics: The Solicitor General and the Structuring of Race, Gender, and Reproductive Rights Litigation* (College Station: Texas A & M University Press, 2003).

33. 376 U.S. 254 (1964).

34. 478 U.S. 186 (1986).

35. 539 U.S. 558 (2003).

36. 384 U.S. 436 (1966).

37. Jeffrey Segal and Harold Spaeth, *The Supreme Court and the Attitudinal Model* (Cambridge: Cambridge University Press, 1993), 246.

38. See, for example, Sheldon M. Novick, *Honorable Justice: The Life of Oliver Wendell Holmes, Jr.* (Boston: Little, Brown & Co., 1989).

39. 567 U.S. _____ (2012).

40. 558 U.S. 310 (2010).

41. 531 U.S. 98 (2000).

42. Justice Antonin Scalia, interview with CNBC, October 10, 2005.

Chapter 10

1. Vincent Price, *Public Opinion* (Newbury Park, CA: Sage Publications, 1992), 5–22.

2. E. E. Schattschneider, *The Semisovereign People: A Realist's View of Democracy in America* (New York: Holt, Rinehart and Winston, 1960).

3. V. O. Key Jr., *Public Opinion and American Democracy* (New York: Knopf, 1961).

4. Samuel P. Huntington, *American Politics: The Promise of Disharmony* (Cambridge, MA: Harvard University Press, 1981).

5. For a good discussion of the value of individualism in the American culture, see Herbert McCloskey and John Zaller, *The American Ethos* (Cambridge, MA: Harvard University Press, 1984).

6. The concept of partisanship and controversies surrounding it over the years are presented in Warren E. Miller and Merrill Shanks, *The New American Voter* (Cambridge, MA: Harvard University Press, 1996).

7. See M. Kent Jennings and Richard G. Niemi, *Generations and Politics: A Panel Study of Young Adults and Their Parents* (Princeton, NJ: Princeton University Press, 1981).

8. James Madison, Alexander Hamilton, and John Jay, Federalist No. 51, in *The Federalist Papers* (New York: Doubleday, 1966; originally published in 1788).

9. Walter Lippmann, *Public Opinion* (New York: Harcourt Brace Jovanovich, 1922).

10. Angus Campbell, Phillip E. Converse, Warren E. Miller, and Donald E. Stokes, *The American Voter* (New York: John Wiley and Sons, 1960).

11. This survey was commissioned by the Intercollegiate Studies Institute and included a national adult sample of 2,500 respondents, conducted by telephone.

12. V. O. Key Jr., *The Responsible Electorate* (Cambridge, MA: Belknap Harvard, 1966).

13. Benjamin I. Page and Robert Y. Shapiro, *The Rational Public: Fifty Years of Trends in Americans' Policy Preferences* (Chicago: University of Chicago Press, 1992).

14. Samuel Kernell, *Going Public: New Strategies of Presidential Leadership* (Washington, DC: CQ Press, 1997).

15. Jack Dennis, ed., *Socialization to Politics* (New York: John Wiley and Sons, 1973).

16. See, generally, David Easton, *A Systems Analysis of Political Life* (New York: John Wiley and Sons, 1965).

17. Michael X. Delli Carpini and Scott Keeter, *What Americans Know About Politics and Why It Matters* (New Haven, CT: Yale University Press, 1996).

18. Pew Global Attitudes Project, "Social Networking Popular Across the Globe," December 12, 2012, www.pewglobal.org/2012/12/12/social-networking-popular-across-globe/.

19. Herb Asher, *Polling and the Public*, 6th ed. (Washington, DC: CQ Press, 2004).

20. Charles W. Roll and Albert H. Cantril, *Polls: Their Use and Misuse in Politics* (New York: Basic Books, 1972).

21. www.latinodecisions.com/blog/2012/11/01/how-the-exit-polls-misrepresent-latino-voters-and-badly/.

22. An important book spelling out the variety of problems and issues with the wording of survey questions is Howard Schuman and Stanley Press, *Questions and Answers in Attitude Surveys* (New York: John Wiley and Sons, 1981).

23. For a more detailed discussion of these concepts, see W. Lance Bennett, *Public Opinion in American Politics* (New York: Harcourt Brace Jovanovich, 1980).

Chapter 11

1. James Madison, Federalist No. 10, in *The Federalist Papers* (reprinted by Mentor Books, 1961), 77.

2. Alexis de Tocqueville, *Democracy in America* (New York: Mentor Books, reprint edition, 1956).

3. Robert Dahl, *A Preface to Democratic Theory* (Cambridge: Cambridge University Press, 1956).

4. David B. Truman, *The Governmental Process* (New York: Alfred Knopf, 1951).

5. C. Wright Mills, *The Power Elite* (New York: Oxford University Press, 1956).

6. John P. Heinz, Edward O. Laumann, Robert L. Nelson, and Robert H. Salisbury, *The Hollow Core* (Cambridge, MA: Harvard University Press, 1993).

7. David Lowery and Holly Brasher, *Organized Interests and American Government* (New York: McGraw-Hill, 2004), 8.

8. See www.opensecrets.org/lobbyists/index.asp.

9. 558 U.S. 310 (2010).

10. See Theodore J. Lowi, *The End of Liberalism* (New York: W. W. Norton, 1979).

11. See William Gormley, "Regulatory Issue Networks in a Federal System," *Polity* 18 (1986): 595–620.

12. See www.uschamber.com.

13. Mancur Olson, *The Logic of Collective Action: Public Goods and the Theory of Groups* (Cambridge, MA: Harvard University Press, 1971), 22–35.

14. Robert Salisbury, "An Exchange Theory of Interest Groups," *Midwest Journal of Political Science* 13 (1969): 1–32.

15. Peter B. Clark and James Q. Wilson, "Incentives Systems: A Theory of Organization," *Administrative Science Quarterly* 6 (1961): 129–66.

16. For a good discussion of the influence of group member dedication to group effectiveness, see Olson, *The Logic of Collective Action: Public Goods and the Theory of Groups*, op. cit.

17. 410 U.S. 113 (1973).

18. Olson, *The Logic of Collective Action: Public Goods and the Theory of Groups*, op. cit.

19. See www.commoncause.org.

20. Ralph Nader, *Unsafe at Any Speed: The Designed-in Dangers of the American Automobile* (New York: Grossman Publishers, 1965).

21. Unitedwedream.org.

22. Blacklivesmatter.com.

23. David Lowery and Holly Brasher, *Organized Interests and American Government* (New York: McGraw-Hill, 2004), 247.

24. See www.uspirg.org/about-us.

CHAPTER 12

1. 250 U.S. 616 (1919).

2. 438 U.S. 726 (1978).

3. 484 U.S. 260 (1988).

4. See Philip Meyer, *Precision Journalism: A Reporter's Introduction to Social Science Methods* (Lanham, MD: Rowman & Littlefield, 2002).

5. The word *muckrakers* is derived from the idea that this group was "raking up the mud" from scandals and corruption of government and industry. For a descriptive history of the role the muckrakers played in progressive policymaking during the early nineteenth century, see Doris Kearns Goodwin, *The Bully Pulpit: Theodore Roosevelt, William Howard Taft and the Golden Age of Journalism* (New York: Simon & Schuster, 2013).

6. For a chronicle of the Watergate story, see Bob Woodward and Carl Bernstein, *All the President's Men* (New York: Simon & Schuster, 1974).

7. For a thorough review of the history of news, see Mitchell Stephens, *A History of News: From the Drum to the Satellite* (New York: Viking, 1989).

8. Kurt Lang and Gladys Lang, *Television and Politics* (Edison, NJ: Transaction Publishers, 2001).

9. Marshall McLuhan, *Understanding Media: The Extensions of Man* (New York: McGraw-Hill, 1964).

10. For a good review of the process and impact of presidential debates, see Alan Schroeder, *Presidential Debates* (New York: Columbia University Press, 2000).

11. www.womensmediacenter.com/pages/2015-wmc-divided-media-gender-gap.

12. See Doris Graber, *Processing Politics: Learning from Television in the Internet Age* (Chicago: University of Chicago Press, 2001).

13. Kenneth Dautrich, David Yalof, and Mark Hugo-Lopez, *The Future of the First Amendment* (New York: Rowman and Littlefield, 2008).

14. Robert Bond et al., "A 61-Million-Person Experiment in Social Influence and Political Mobilization," *Nature*, vol. 489 (September 13, 2012): 295–98.

15. Mass communications researcher Joseph Klapper was a pioneer of the minimal effects (or limited effects) theory. He introduced the theory in a book titled *The Effects of Mass Communication* (New York: Free Press, 1960).

16. For a good discussion of selection retention, see D. Sears and J. Freeman, "Selective Exposure to Information: A Critical Review," in *The Process and Effects of Mass Communication*, ed. Wilbur Lang Schramm (Chicago: University of Illinois Press, 1972).

17. To learn more about social learning theory, see Albert Bandura, *Social Foundations of Thought and Action* (Englewood Cliffs, NJ: Prentice-Hall, 1986).

18. See L. Berkowitz, "Some Effects of Thought on Anti- and Pro-Social Influences of Media Effects," *Psychological Bulletin* 95 (1984): 410–27.

19. A pioneer in developing cultivation theory was George Gerbner. See George Gerbner et al., "Growing Up with Television: The Cultivation Perspective," in *Media Effects: Advances in Theory and Research*, eds. Jennings Bryant and Dolf Zillman (Hillsdale, NJ: Lawrence Erlbaum, 1994), 17–41.

20. A number of studies have demonstrated the agenda-setting power of the media, including Maxwell E. McCombs, "The Agenda-Setting Approach," in *Handbook of Political Communication*, eds. Dan D. Nimmo and Keith Sanders (Thousand Oaks, CA: Sage, 1981), 121–140; and Shanto Iyengar and Donald R. Kinder, *News That Matters* (Chicago: University of Chicago Press, 1987).

21. Doris A. Graber, *Mass Media and American Politics* (Washington, DC: CQ Press, 2002), 207.

22. Kenneth Dautrich and Thomas H. Hartley, *How the News Media Fail American Voters* (New York: Columbia University Press, 1999), 92–95.

CHAPTER 13

1. "Toward a More Responsible Party System: A Report of the Committee on Political Parties, American Political Science Association," *American Political Science Review* 44, no. 3 (September 1950).

2. E. E. Schattschneider, *Party Government* (New York: Farrar and Rinehart, 1942).

3. See chapter 2 in John F. Bibby, *Politics, Parties and Elections in America*, 5th ed. (Belmont, CA: Wadsworth, 2002).

4. See Paul Finkelman and John Moore, "Political Parties," in *The Encyclopedia of American Political History*, eds. Peter Wallenstein and Paul Finkelman (Washington, DC: CQ Press, 2001).

5. See chapter 2 in Bibby, *Politics, Parties and Elections in America*, op. cit.

6. V. O. Key Jr., "A Theory of Critical Elections," *Journal of Politics* 16, no. 1 (1955): 13–18.

7. See Walter Dean Burnham, *Critical Elections and the Mainsprings of American Politics* (New York: W. W. Norton, 1970).

8. For a thorough analysis of how the American party system has changed since the New Deal, see Sidney M. Milkus, *The President and the Parties: The Transformation of the American Party System Since the New Deal* (New York: Oxford University Press, 1993).

9. Paul Allen Beck, "The Dealignment Era in America," in *Electoral Change in Advanced Industrial Democracies: Realignment or Dealignment*, eds. M. N. Dalton, T. T. Flanagan, and H. Beck (Princeton, NJ: Princeton University Press, 1984).

10. Angus Campbell, Philip E. Converse, Warren E. Miller, and Donald E. Stokes, *The American Voter* (New York: Wiley, 1960).

11. For a thorough discussion of the concept of party identification, see Warren E. Miller and J. Merrill Shanks, *The New American Voter* (Cambridge, MA: Harvard University Press, 1996).

12. Philip E. Converse, "The Concept of the Normal Vote," in *Elections and the Political Order*, eds. Angus Campbell, Philip E. Converse, Warren E. Miller, and Donald E. Stokes (New York: Wiley, 1966).

13. For a discussion of governance and the parties, see John H. Aldrich, *Why Parties? The Origin and Transformation of Political Parties in America* (Chicago: University of Chicago Press, 1995), chapter 7.

14. See Richard S. Conley, *The Presidency, Congress and Divided Government* (College Station: Texas A&M University Press, 2002).

15. For a good discussion of the rationale for America's two-party system, see Frank J. Sorauf, *Party Politics in America*, 5th ed. (Boston: Little, Brown, 1984).

16. To learn more about nineteenth- and twentieth-century third-party candidacies, see Steven J. Rosenstone, Roy L. Behr, and Edward H. Lazarus, *Third Parties in America*, 2nd ed. (Princeton, NJ: Princeton University Press, 1996).

17. Martin Wattenberg, *The Decline of American Political Parties* (Cambridge, MA: Harvard University Press, 1998).

18. See, for example, Jeff Cohen, Richard Fleisher, and Paul Kantor, eds., *American Political Parties: Decline or Resurgence?* (Washington, DC: CQ Press, 2001).

19. For a discussion of the struggle for suffrage, see William H. Flanigan and Nancy H. Zingale, *Political Behavior of the American Electorate* (Washington, DC: CQ Press, 1998), chapter 2.

20. 60 U.S. 393 (1857).

21. See Margaret M. Conway, *Political Participation in the United States* (Washington, DC: CQ Press, 2000), chapter 5.

22. Some southern states continued to use the poll tax in state elections after passage of the Twenty-fourth Amendment. In 1966, the U.S. Supreme Court in *Harper v. Virginia Board of Elections* [383 U.S. 663 (1966)] outlawed the use of the poll tax in state elections as well as federal elections.

23. See Nancy McGlen and Karen O'Connor, *Women, Politics and American Society*, 2nd ed. (Upper Saddle River, NJ: Prentice Hall, 1998).

24. A thorough discussion of the development of states' voter registration systems can be found in Joseph P. Harris, *Registration of Voters in the United States* (Washington, DC: Brookings Institution Press, 1929).

25. A federal statute requires that the waiting period from becoming a state resident to being eligible to vote may not exceed 30 days.

26. Michael D. Martinez and David B. Hill, "Did Motor Voter Work?," *American Politics Quarterly* 27 (1999): 296–315.

27. See Lee Sigelman et al., "Voting and Non-voting: A Multi-Election Perspective," *American Journal of Political Science* 29 (November 1985): 749–765.

28. See Raymond E. Wolfinger and Steven J. Rosenstone, *Who Votes?* (New Haven, CT: Yale University Press, 1980), 44–46.

29. Norman H. Nie, Jane Junn, and Kenneth Stehlik-Barry, *Education and Democratic Citizenship in America* (Chicago: University of Chicago Press, 1996).

30. Todd G. Shields and Robert K. Goidel, "Participation Rates, Socioeconomic Class Biases and Congressional Elections: A Cross Validation," *American Journal of Political Science* 41 (1997): 683–691.

31. Anthony Downs, *An Economic Theory of Democracy* (New York: Harper and Brothers, 1957).

32. Angus Campbell, Philip E. Converse, Warren E. Miller, and Donald E. Stokes, *Elections and the Political Order* (New York: Wiley, 1966).

33. For a comprehensive examination of the trends in voter turnout, see Thomas E. Patterson, *The Vanishing American Voter: Public Involvement in an Age of Uncertainty* (New York: Alfred A. Knopf, 2002).

34. See Ivor Crewe, "As the World Turns Out," *Public Opinion* 4 (February–March 1981).

35. For a discussion of trends in political efficacy, see also M. Margaret Conway, *Political Participation in the United States*, 3rd ed. (Washington, DC: CQ Press, 2000), 51–53.

36. 531 U.S. 98 (2000).

37. Robert Putnam, *Bowling Alone* (New York: Simon & Schuster, 2000).

38. www.politico.com/story/2012/11/study-youth-vote-was-decisive-083510

CHAPTER 14

1. See Lawrence D. Longley and Neal R. Pierce, *The Electoral College Primer* (New Haven, CT: Yale University Press, 1996).

2. For a good discussion of the development of parties in the early republic, see Stanley Elkins and Eric McKitrick, *The Age of Federalism: The Early American Republic 1788–1800* (New York: Oxford University Press, 1993).

3. See Paul Finkelman and John Moore, "The Democratic Party," in *The Encyclopedia of American Political History*, eds. Peter Wallenstein and Paul Finkelman (Washington, DC: CQ Press, 2001).

4. See Tadahisa Kuroda, *The Origins of the Twelfth Amendment: The Electoral College in the Early Republic 1787–1804* (Westport, CT: Greenwood Press, 1994).

5. A thorough discussion of the nomination process as well as other aspects of the presidential campaign can be found in Stephen Wayne, *The Road to the White House 2008*, 8th ed. (Boston: Wadsworth Press, 2008).

6. Larry M. Bartels, *Presidential Primaries and the Dynamics of Public Choice* (Princeton, NJ: Princeton University Press, 1988).

7. See John F. Bibby, *Politics, Parties and Elections in America* (Chicago: Nelson-Hall, 1992), chapter 6.

8. Ibid.

9. For a good discussion of the relevance of the New Hampshire primary, see Dante J. Scala, *Stormy Weather: The New Hampshire Primary and Presidential Politics* (New York: Palgrave Macmillan, 2003).

10. Nevada disrupted this traditional order in 2008 when it scheduled its Republican and Democratic caucuses for January 19, three days before the New Hampshire primary. New Hampshire then moved its primary to January 8.

11. See William G. Mayer and Andrew Busch, *The Frontloading Problem in Presidential Nominations* (Washington, DC: Brookings Institution Press, 2003).

12. For a history of party conventions, see CQ Press's *National Party Conventions 1831–2004* (2005).

13. See, for example, James Druckman, "The Power of Television Images: The First Kennedy-Nixon Debate Revisited," *Journal of Politics* 65, no. 2 (2003): 559–571.

14. See Alan Schroeder, *Presidential Debates: 50 Years of High Risk TV* (New York: Columbia University Press, 2008).

15. See Darrell M. West, *Television Advertising in Election Campaigns 1952–1996* (Washington, DC: CQ Press, 1997).

16. For an analysis of the effects of negative ads on voters, see Richard R. Lau and Gerald M. Pomper, *Negative Campaigning: An Analysis of U.S. Senate Elections* (Lanham, MD: Rowman and Littlefield, 2004).

17. For a discussion of why the electoral college was created and how it has changed, see Lawrence D. Longley and Neal R. Peirce, *The Electoral College Primer 2000* (New Haven, CT: Yale University Press, 1999), chapter 2.

18. Ibid., chapter 4.

19. 553 U.S. 181 (2008).

20. The psychological concept of party identification is developed in Angus Campbell, Philip E. Converse, Warren E. Miller, and Donald E. Stokes, *The American Voter* (New York: Wiley, 1960).

21. For discussion of the role of party identification in forming vote choices, see Warren E. Miller and J. Merrill Shanks, *The New American Voter* (Cambridge, MA: Harvard University Press, 1996); and William H. Flanagan and Nancy H. Zingale, *Political Behavior of the American Electorate*, 9th ed. (Washington, DC: CQ Press, 1998).

22. See Martin P. Wattenberg, *The Decline of Political Parties 1952–1996* (Cambridge, MA: Harvard University Press, 1998).

23. Miller and Shanks, *The New American Voter*, op. cit., chapter 12.

24. See Norman Nie, Sidney Verba, and John Petrocik, *The Changing American Voter* (Cambridge, MA: Harvard University Press, 1979).

25. Anthony Downs, *An Economic Theory of Democracy* (New York: Harper and Brothers, 1957).

26. Morris P. Fiorina, *Retrospective Voting in American National Elections* (New Haven, CT: Yale University Press, 1981).

27. See David B. Magleby and Candice J. Nelson, *The Money Chase* (Washington, DC: Brookings Institution Press, 1990).

28. 424 U.S. 1 (1976).

29. 540 U.S. 93 (2003).

30. 558 U.S. 310 (2010).

31. For a thorough discussion of congressional elections, see Paul S. Herrnson, *Congressional Elections: Campaigning at Home and in Washington* (Washington, DC: CQ Press, 2011).

32. For a complete discussion of the coattail effect, see Gary C. Jacobson, *Electoral Origins of Divided Government 1946–1988* (Boulder, CO: Westview Press, 1990).

33. See Gary C. Jacobson, *The Politics of Congressional Elections* (New York: Pearson, 2012), chapter 3.

34. Mary Beth Marklein. 2009. "Presidential Race Raised Student Political Involvement." *USA Today*. January 22.

CHAPTER 15

1. Charles Lindblom, "The Science of Muddling Through," *Public Administration Review* 19 (Spring 1959): 79–88.

2. Carl E. Van Horn, Donald Baumer, and William T. Gormley Jr., *Politics and Public Policy*, 3rd ed. (Washington, DC: CQ Press, 2001).

3. Ibid., 193–230.

4. William T. Gormley Jr., "Interest Group Interventions in the Administrative Process," in *The Interest Group Connection*, eds. Paul C. Herrnson, Ronald G. Shaiko, and Clyde Wilcox (Chatham, NJ: Chatham House, 1998), 213–223.

5. See Adam Smith, *The Wealth of Nations* (reprinted by New York: Modern Library, 1994).

6. John Maynard Keynes's most famous work is *The General Theory of Employment, Interest, and Money* (New York: Harcourt Brace Jovanovich, 1936).

7. See David Stockman, *The Triumph of Politics: How the Reagan Revolution Failed* (New York: Harper & Row, 1986).

8. John Steele Gordon, *Hamilton's Blessing: The Extraordinary Life and Times of Our National Debt* (New York: Penguin, 1998).

9. For a more detailed discussion of this argument, see the work of Michael Lewis-Beck, including *Economics and Elections: The Major Western Democracies* (Ann Arbor: University of Michigan Press, 1990).

10. Shelley Lynne Tomkin, *Inside OMB: Politics and Process in the President's Budget Office* (Armonk, NY: M. E. Sharpe, 1998).

11. See Allen Schick and Felix Lostracco, *The Federal Budget: Politics, Policy, Process* (Washington, DC: Brookings Institution Press, 2000).

12. Elizabeth Drew, *Showdown: The Struggle Between the Gingrich Congress and the Clinton White House* (New York: Touchstone, 1997).

13. Bowsher v. Synar, 478 U.S. 714 (1986).

14. Forbes's most recent proposal for a flat tax is discussed in Steve Forbes, *Flat Tax Revolution: Using a Postcard to Abolish the IRS* (Washington, DC: Regnery, 2005).

15. nces.ed.gov/programs/digest/d13/tables/dt13_203.60.asp?current=yes.

16. nces.ed.gov/fastfacts/display.asp?id=55.

17. William Greider, *Secrets of the Temple: How the Federal Reserve Runs the Country* (New York: Simon & Schuster, 1989).

18. This was especially true when Alan Greenspan headed the Federal Reserve. See Bob Woodward, *Greenspan's Fed and the American Boom* (New York: Simon & Schuster, 2001).

19. Herbert Packer, *The Limits of the Criminal Sanction* (Stanford, CA: Stanford University Press, 1968).

20. For a discussion of criminal justice in America more generally, see George Cole and Christopher Smith, *The American System of Criminal Justice* (Belmont, CA: Wadsworth, 2001).

21. Larry J. Siegel and Joseph J. Senna, *Introduction to Criminal Justice* (Boston: Wadsworth, 2005), 412.

22. David Baldus, George Woodworth, and Charles Pulaski, *Equal Justice and the Death Penalty: A Legal and Empirical Analysis* (Boston: Northeastern University Press, 1990).

23. Lawrence M. Friedman, *Crime and Punishment in American History* (New York: Basic Books, 1993), 264–265.

24. Jeffrey Rosen, "Dual Sovereigns," *The New Republic* (July 28, 1997): 16–19.

25. United States v. Lopez, 514 U.S. 549 (1995).

26. 135 S. Ct. 2480 (2015).

27. Hermann Beck, *The Origins of the Authoritarian Welfare State in Prussia* (Ann Arbor: University of Michigan Press, 1997).

28. William Leuchtenberg, *Franklin Roosevelt and the New Deal* (New York: HarperCollins, 1963).

29. Kristen Lindenmeyer, *A Right to Childhood: The U.S. Children's Bureau and Child Welfare* (Urbana: University of Illinois Press, 1997).

30. Jonathan Oberlander, *The Political Life of Medicare* (Chicago: University of Chicago Press, 2003).

31. Jeffrey Lehman and Sheldon Danziger, "Turning Our Back on the New Deal: The End of Welfare in 1996," in *Race, Poverty and Domestic Policy*, ed. C. Michael Henry (New Haven, CT: Yale University Press, 2004).

32. Robert Hudson, ed., *The New Politics of Old Age Policy* (Baltimore: Johns Hopkins University Press, 2005).

33. See Daniel Beland and Alex Waddan, *The Politics of Policy Change: Welfare, Medicare and Social Security Reform in the United States* (Washington, DC: Georgetown University Press, 2012); and Paul Light, *Still Artful Work: The Continuing Politics of Social Security Reform* (New York: McGraw Hill, 1994).

34. Jan Gregoire Coombs, *The Rise and Fall of HMOs: An American Health Care Revolution* (Madison: University of Wisconsin Press, 2005).

35. William Gesler and Thomas Ricketts, eds., *Health Care in Rural North America: The Geography of Health Care Services in North America* (Newark, NJ: Rutgers University Press, 1992).

CHAPTER 16

1. Aaron Wildavsky, "The Two Presidencies," *Transaction* 4, no. 2 (December 1966): 7–14.

2. Robert Dallek, *Franklin Delano Roosevelt and American Foreign Policy, 1932–1945* (New York: Oxford University Press, 1995).

3. A detailed (if uncritical) look at the events leading up to the Truman Doctrine and the Marshall Plan can be found in Joseph M. Jones, *The Fifteen Weeks* (New York: Harcourt, Brace, 1955).

4. D. F. Flemming, *The Cold War and Its Origins: 1917–1960* (New York: Doubleday, 1961).

5. David DiLeo, *George Ball, Vietnam and the Rethinking of Containment* (Chapel Hill: University of North Carolina Press, 1991).

6. Stanley Karnow, *Vietnam: A History* (New York: Penguin, 1997).

7. Frank Snepp, *Decent Interval: An Insider's Account on Saigon's Indecent End* (New York: Vintage Books, 1978).

8. Robert Litwak, *Détente and the Nixon Doctrine* (Cambridge: Cambridge University Press, 1986).

9. John Newhouse, "The Missile Defense Debate," *Foreign Affairs* 80, no. 4 (July/August 2001).

10. John Lewis Gaddis, *The Cold War: A New History* (New York: Penguin, 2005).

11. One of the key architects of this new understanding was Bush's secretary of state, James A. Baker III. See James A. Baker III, *The Politics of Diplomacy* (New York: Putnam, 1995).

12. Many of these criticisms are discussed in Samantha Power's award-winning book *A Problem from Hell: America and the Age of Genocide* (New York: Harper Perennial, 2003).

13. Perhaps the best book written to date about the problems in the military's 2003 intervention in Iraq is Michael Gordon and Bernard Trainor's *Cobra II: The Inside Story of the Invasion and Occupation of Iraq* (New York: Pantheon, 2006).

14. Niall Ferguson, *Colossus: The Rise and Fall of the American Empire* (New York: Penguin Books, 2005).

15. Joseph Nye, *Soft Power: The Means to Success in World Politics* (New York: Public Affairs, 2005).

16. Louis Fisher, "Without Restraint: Presidential Military Initiatives from Korea to Bosnia," in *Domestic Sources of American Foreign Policy*, 3rd ed., eds. Eugene Wittkopf and James McCormick (Lanham, MD: Rowman and Littlefield, 1999), 141–55.

17. www.huffingtonpost.com/ambassador-muhamed-sacirbey/defining-welcome-to-refugees_b_8511746.html.

18. Powell's shuttle diplomacy is described in great detail in Bob Woodward, *Plan of Attack* (New York: Simon & Schuster, 2004).

19. Geoffrey Kemp, "Presidential Management of the Executive Bureaucracy," in *United States Foreign Policy: The Search for a New Role*, eds. Robert J. Art

and Seyom Brown (Upper Saddle River, NJ: Prentice Hall, 1993).

20. See Bruce Berkowitz, "Information Age Intelligence," *Foreign Policy* 103 (Summer 1996): 35–50.

21. Jeremy D. Rosner, *The New Tug-of-War: Congress, the Executive Branch and National Security* (Washington, DC: Carnegie Endowment for International Peace, 1995).

22. George Crile, *Charlie Wilson's War* (New York: Grove Press, 2004).

23. Perot's daring rescue effort is described in dramatic fashion in Ken Follett, *On Wings of Eagles* (New York: William Morrow, 1983).

24. See William B. Quandt, "The Electoral Cycle and the Conduct of American Foreign Policy," *Political Science Quarterly* 101 (1986): 825–837.

25. John Mueller, "Public Opinion and Foreign Policy: The People's Common Sense," in *Domestic Sources of American Foreign Policy*, 3rd ed., eds. Eugene Wittkopf and James McCormick (Lanham, MD: Rowman and Littlefield, 1999), 51–60.

26. Peter Boone, "The Impact of Foreign Aid on Savings and Growth," Center for Economic Performance Working Paper No. 1265, London, October 1994, 25–26.

INDEX

NOTE: Terms in **boldface** type are key terms defined in the glossary. Page numbers in *italics* refer to tables, figures, and boxed features.

A

AARP, 291, *301,* 306

ABC, 325, 328, *329*

Abington School District v. Schempp (1963), 82–83

abortion

    constitutional right to, 99–100

    Partial Birth Abortion Act of 2003, 100

    pro-choice or pro-life groups, 302, 371

    Roe v. Wade (1973), 99–100, 250, 254, 255, 257, 299

Abramoff, Jack, *292*

Abrams v. United States (1919), 315

accountability, federalism and, 70

ActBlue, *306*

Adams, John

    ascension to presidency, 176

    Constitutional Convention and, 31

    court judges and justices of the peace appointed by, 239

    election of 1796, 342, 381

    election of 1800, 176, 342–343, 382

    federal workforce and, 222

    precedent of peaceful transition, 176

    as vice-president, 342

Adams, John Quincy

    ascension to presidency, 176

    election of 1824, 343, 381, *385*

    election of 1828, 343–344, *385*

    negative campaign, *385*

    as Secretary of State, 178

Adarand v. Peña (1995), 131

administrative discretion, 207

administrative law, 207–208, 231

affirmative action, 125–126, 130–132

Affordable Care Act. *See* Patient Protection and Affordable Care Act of 2010 (PPACA)

African Americans. *See also* civil rights movement; slavery

accommodation and, philosophy of, 109

affirmative action and, 125–126, 130–132

agitation and, philosophy of, 110

appointed to inner cabinet, 216, 218

Birmingham, Alabama race riots, 117–118

Black Lives Matter, *133, 303*

black nationalism and, 119, 120

Black Panther Party, 120

Brown v. Board of Education (1954), 110, 114, *115,* 131, *234,* 242, 243

bus boycott, Rosa Parks and, 116–115

Ferguson, Missouri race riots, 134

first American president, *187*

first appointed to cabinet, 216, 218

first appointed to Supreme Court, *234,* 247

first woman appointed to cabinet, 218

Ku Klux Klan, 86, 112–113, 118, 360–361

Los Angeles, California race riots, 95, 372

Malcolm X, 119

Million Man March, 120

NAACP, *7,* 110, 114, 118, 123, *234*

profiling, *108,* 132–134

racial discrimination, 111–113

racial segregation and, 113–116

Reconstruction era, 111–113

suffrage, 111, *129,* 359

voting rights, 359–360

Age Discrimination in Employment Act of 1967, 127

agenda-setting theory, 331

agents of political socialization, 271

Aid to Families with Dependent Children (AFDC), 432, 433

Albright, Madeleine, 216

Alito, Samuel, *246,* 247

Allen, George, 334, *334*

All Things Considered, 328, 329

Al Qaeda, 452, *455,* 458

Amazon, 414

C

C-SPAN, *181*, 249, *257*, 317, 325

Cuban missile crisis, 450

cultivation theory, 331

D

Dahl, Robert, 244, 292

"Daily Dish, The," *265*, 266

Daily Kos, The, 266

"Daisy Girl" commercial, 6, *6*

Dallas Morning News, 324

Dance of Legislation, The (Redman), 156

Dawes Severalty Act in 1887, 113

dealignment, 346

Dean, Howard, 403

Debs, Eugene V., *354*

"Decision-Making in a Democracy" (Dahl), 244

Declaration of Independence, 29

Declaratory Act of 1766, 27

defendant, 236, 237

Delaware v. Van Arsdall (1937), *78*

delegated congressional power, 207–208

democracy

  decline of, 17–21

  defined, 17

Democracy in America (de Tocqueville), 291–292

Democratic Party

  formation of, 343–347

  gender support of, 124, *351*

  party identification, *340*, 348–349

Democratic-Republicans, 342–343, 381

Dennis v. United States (1951), 85

Department of Commerce (DOC), *206, 211, 214, 215,* 415

Department of Commerce v. U.S. House of Representatives (1999), *275*

Department of Defense (DOD), *206*, 213, *214*, 216, 296, 304, 457

Department of Education (ED), *206*, 213, *215, 224*

Department of Energy (DOE), *206, 215,* 216

Department of Health and Human Services (HHS), *206, 215,* 436

Department of Homeland Security (DHS), 188, *192, 206,* 212, 213, *215,* 216, 218, 458

Department of Housing and Urban Development (HUD), *206, 215*

Department of Justice (DOJ), *206,* 209, 213, *214,* 414

Department of Labor (DOL), *206,* 211, *215,* 294

Department of State (DOS), *206,* 209, *214,* 445, 456

Department of the Interior (DOI), *206,* 209, *214*

Department of Transportation (DOT), *206,* 213, *215*

Department of Treasury, *206, 214,* 216

Department of Veterans Affairs (VA), *206, 215*

deregulation, 211–212

Detainee Treatment Act of 2005, 189

de Tocqueville, Alexis, 15, 291–292

devolution, 212

Dewey, Thomas, *276*

Dickerson v. United States (2000), 97

digital divide, *324,* 328

direct democracy, 12

direction (of public opinion), 283

direct primary election, 357

discount rate, 427–428

discovery, 236, 237–238

discretionary spending, 425–426

Disney Corporation, 328, *329*

dissenting opinion, 253

distributive tax policies, 423

District of Columbia v. Heller (2008), 91–92

diversity

  in American politics, 7–8

  of American soldiers in World War II, 16

  bureaucracy and, *219*

  changing racial categories in U.S. Census, *8*

  civil rights, contemporary movements for, *303*

  Congress and, *144*

  contemporary challenge to, *120*

  diverse presidential candidates, public support for, *175*

  diversity in classrooms, *427*

  federalism and, 68

N

presidency of, 183

presidential debates, 393

programs to boost diversity among executive branch appointees, *219*

public opinion polls, 196

same-sex marriage, 193, 196

secretary of health and human services choice, Tom Daschle, 185

signing statements, 189, *190*

spending policies, 426

Supreme Court nominations, 185, *234,* 245, *245, 246,* 247, 248–249, 257

Syrian refugees and, *456*

tax policy, 425

Tea Party protests, 370

Twitter and, 198, *198*

united government, 3

vetoes issued by, 188, *189*

voting youth for, *21, 373*

Obama, Michelle, 195

Obamacare. *See* Patient Protection and Affordable Care Act of 2010 (PPACA)

Obergefell v. Hodges (2015), *49,* 128, *129*

objectivity, 317

obscenity, *88,* 88–89

Occupational Safety and Health Act of 1970, 207

Occupational Safety and Health Administration (OSHA), 207, 208, 304

Occupy Wall Street, 371, *372*

O'Connor, Sandra Day, 66, 247, *257*

Office of Economic Opportunity, 191

Office of Management and Budget (OMB), 154, 194, 221, 420

Office of National Drug Control Policy, 221

Office of Personnel Management (OPM), 126, *206, 216,* 223

Office of Science and Technology, 221

Office of the U.S. Trade Representative, 194, 221

Old Age Pension Act of New York, *435*

older Americans, discrimination against, 127

oligarchy, 9

Olson, Mancur, 300

O'Malley, Martin, *386,* 387

open elections, 389

open market operations, 428

open primary, 384

open rule, 158

OpenSecrets.org, *290*

open shop, 300

O'Reilly, Bill, *318*

O'Reilly Factor, 318

original jurisdiction, 244

Orth, Franklin, *305*

Osborne, David, 212

Oslo accords, 452

outlays, 425

overriding, 160

P

Pacifica Foundation, 315

pacifism, 447

Packer, Herbert, 429

Page, Benjamin, 270–271

Palin, Sarah, 391

Panetta, Leon, *300*

paper trail, 204

pardon, 186

Parker, John J., *249*

Parker v. Gladden (1966), *78*

Parks, Rosa, 116–117

Partial Birth Abortion Act of 2003, 100

partisan press era, 319–320

partisanship, 267–268, *268*

party identification, *340,* 348–349

percentage viewing matters as "morally acceptable" by, *349*

in states, *350*

vote choice and, 397–398

party leader, president as, 191

party platform, 344

party ticket, 381

Patient Protection and Affordable Care Act of 2010 (PPACA), 3, 188, *241,* 242, *333,* 434–436